Communications in Computer and Information Science 1724

More information about this series at https://link.springer.com/bookseries/7899

Mufti Mahmud · Cosimo Ieracitano ·
M. Shamim Kaiser · Nadia Mammone ·
Francesco Carlo Morabito (Eds.)

Applied Intelligence and Informatics

Second International Conference, AII 2022
Reggio Calabria, Italy, September 1–3, 2022
Proceedings

 Springer

Editors
Mufti Mahmud (iD)
Nottingham Trent University
Nottingham, UK

M. Shamim Kaiser (iD)
Jahangirnagar University
Dhaka, Bangladesh

Francesco Carlo Morabito (iD)
University Mediterranea of Reggio Calabria
Reggio Calabria, Italy

Cosimo Ieracitano (iD)
University Mediterranea of Reggio Calabria
Reggio Calabria, Italy

Nadia Mammone (iD)
University Mediterranea of Reggio Calabria
Reggio Calabria, Italy

ISSN 1865-0929   ISSN 1865-0937 (electronic)
Communications in Computer and Information Science
ISBN 978-3-031-24800-9   ISBN 978-3-031-24801-6 (eBook)
https://doi.org/10.1007/978-3-031-24801-6

This Springer imprint is published by the registered company Springer Nature Switzerland AG
The registered company address is: Gewerbestrasse 11, 6330 Cham, Switzerland

Preface

The term 'Intelligence' refers to the capacity for acquiring and storing information and then converting the information into knowledge towards adaptive behaviours within an environment or context. Cognitive abilities include things like the ability to reason, understand, learn, understand one's emotions, plan, be creative, solve problems, and be self-aware. On the other hand, 'Informatics' is the study of both the natural and artificial worlds, including their structure, behaviour, and connections with one another. When intelligence and informatics are combined, the most challenging problems in the realms of research, engineering, practical manufacturing, military, management, government, and industry can be solved.

The 2nd International Conference on Applied Intelligence and Informatics (AII2022) provides a premier international forum to bring together researchers and practitioners from diverse domains for the sharing of cutting-edge research results obtained through the application of intelligence and/or informatics to solve problems that otherwise would not have been possible to solve. AII2022 also fosters the exchange and dissemination of innovative and practical development of methodologies and technologies with real-life applications.

The concept of the AII conference series was conceived in the year 2021 when the whole world was combating the various waves and variants of the Coronavirus disease (COVID-19). During that extremely challenging time, everyone, especially scientists and researchers from all disciplines wanted to contribute in their own ways to this war against COVID-19. When cities and countries were getting locked down, universities and research labs were evacuated to stop the aggressive spread of the disease, computational scientists and researchers contributed significantly by developing different methods of detecting and diagnosing the disease, building models to stop its spread and facilitating the development of the vaccine. However, most of these methods which were developed and published to fight the pandemic remained proprietary and had limited access for others to reproduce the results. Realising this, a set of committed academics felt the need for a dedicated avenue to discuss the 'Reproducibility of Research Results' through sharing the methods and the datasets. The AII conference series was born with a keen focus on the applications of 'Artificial Intelligence' and 'Informatics' not only in the field of healthcare but also in all walks of life.

After the first edition of AII which was planned to be held in Nottingham, UK but eventually took place virtually due to the COVID-19 restrictions, the second edition (AII2022) has been successfully held at Reggio Calabria, Italy. It has brought together around 100 academics, scientists, researchers, and industrialists from almost all continents. With the warm and generous hospitality of the Mediterranea University of Reggio Calabria (UNIRC), Reggio Calabria, Italy, the conference was supported by the UNIRC, the Applied Intelligence and Informatics (AII) laboratory, la SocietàItaliana Reti Neuroniche (SIREN), the Web Intelligence Consortium (WIC), the Nottingham Trent University (NTU), the International Neural Network Society (INNS), and the International Academic Communication Centre (IRNet).

As usual, the theme of AII2022 was "Fostering the Reproducibility of Research Results." The goal was to see how best we can promote open methodological contributions to reproduce the scientific results presented in the literature. The AII2022 addressed broad perspectives on applied research to facilitate the reproduction of results. These papers provide a good sample of state-of-the-art research advances on applications of artificial intelligence and informatics in diverse fields and disciplines. The selected papers cover four major tracks: (1) Track 1: Emerging Applications of AI and Informatics, (2) Track 2: Application of AI and Informatics in Healthcare, (3) Track 3: Application of AI and Informatics in Pattern Recognition, (4) Track 4: Application of AI and Informatics in Network, Security, and Analytics.

These four tracks of the AII2022 conference attracted 108 submissions from 20 countries. The submitted papers underwent a single-blind review process, soliciting expert opinions from at least three experts: at least two independent topic experts as reviewers and the handling track chair. After the rigorous review reports from the reviewers and the track chairs, the respective papers and, finally, 38 full papers with authors representing 17 countries, were accepted for presentation at the conference. Therefore, this volume of the AII2022 conference proceedings contains those 38 papers which were presented at the conference in Reggio Calabria, Italy.

We would like to express our gratitude to all AII2022 conference committee members for their instrumental and unwavering support. AII2022 had a very exciting program which would not have been possible without the generous dedication of the Program Committee members in reviewing the conference papers. AII2022 could not have taken place without the great team efforts and the generous support from our sponsors.

We would especially like to express our sincere appreciation to our kind sponsors, including Springer-Nature and Springer CCIS team. Our gratitude to UNIRC and AII lab for sponsoring 10 author registrations which were selected based on the quality of the submitted papers and their need for financial support.

We are grateful to the whole CCIS team from Springer-Nature for their continuous support in coordinating the publication of this volume.

Last but not the least, we thank all our contributors and volunteers for their support to make AII2022 a grand success.

October 2022

Mufti Mahmud
Cosimo Ieracitano
M. Shamim Kaiser
Nadia Mammone
Francesco Carlo Morabito

Organization

Conference Chairs

Cosimo Ieracitano   University Mediterranea of Reggio Calabria, Italy
Mufti Mahmud   Nottingham Trent University, UK

Honorary Chairs

Hojjat Adeli   Ohio State University, USA
Amir Hussain   Edinburgh Napier University, UK
Nikola Kasabov   Auckland University of Technology, New Zealand
Francesco C. Morabito   University Mediterranea of Reggio Calabria, Italy

Program Chairs

Anna Esposito   Universitàdella Campania "Luigi Vanvitelli", Italy
M. Shamim Kaiser   Jahangirnagar University, Bangladesh
Nadia Mammone   University Mediterranea of Reggio Calabria, Italy
Ning Zhong   Maebashi Institute of Technology, Japan

Track Chairs

Tingwen Huang   Texas A&M University, Qatar
Joarder Kamruzzaman   Federation University, Australia
Gianluca Lax   University Mediterranea of Reggio Calabria, Italy
M. Murugappan   Kuwait College of Science & Technology, Kuwait
Nelishia Pillay   University of Pretoria, South Africa
Guiseppe Maria Sarne   University Bicocca of Milan, Italy
Domenico Ursino   Universita Politecnica delle Marche, Italy
Salvatore Vitabile   University of Palermo, Italy

Competition Chairs

Noushath Shaffi   College of Applied Sciences, Oman
Gennaro Cordasco   Universitàdegli Studi della Campania "Luigi Vanvitelli", Italy
Stefano Marrone   Universitàdella Campania "Luigi Vanvitelli", Italy

Special Session, Tutorial and Workshop Chairs

Tianhua Chen	University of Huddersfield, UK
Massimiliano Ferrara	University Mediterranea of Reggio Calabria, Italy
Giancarlo Fortino	University of Calabria, Italy
Alessio Micheli	University of Pisa, Italy
Massimo Panella	University Sapienza of Rome, Italy
M. Arifur Rahman	Nottingham Trent University, UK
Domenico Rosaci	University Mediterranea of Reggio Calabria, Italy
Marta Savino	Aubay, Italy
Simone Scardapane	University Sapienza of Rome, Italy

Local Organising Chairs

Cosimo Ieracitano	University Mediterranea of Reggio Calabria, Italy
Nadia Mammone	University Mediterranea of Reggio Calabria, Italy
Francesco C. Morabito	University Mediterranea of Reggio Calabria, Italy
Mario Versaci	University Mediterranea of Reggio Calabria, Italy

Publicity Chairs

Abzetdin Adamov	ADA University, Azerbaijan
Manjunath Aradhya	JSS Science and Technology University, India
Nilanjan Dey	JSS University, India
Ramani Kannan	Universiti Teknologi PETRONAS, Malaysia
Juan P. Amezquita-Sanchez	Universidad Autonoma de Queretaro, Mexico
K. C. Santosh	University of South Dakota, USA
Stefano Squartini	UniversitàPolitecnica delle Marche, Italy

Conference Secretaries

Shamim Al Mamun	Jahangirnagar University, Bangladesh
Michele Lo Giudice	University Mediterranea of Reggio Calabria, Italy

Webmaster

Md Asif Ur Rahman	PropertyPro Plus, Australia

Technical Program Committee

Abzetdin Adamov	ADA University, Azerbaijan
Hojjat Adeli	The Ohio State University, USA
Tawfik Al-Hadhrami	Nottingham Trent University, UK

Shamim Al Mamun   Jahangirnagar University, Bangladesh
Michele Ambrosanio   Università di Napoli "Parthenope" Italy
Alessia Amelio   Universitàdegli Studi "G. d'Annunzio" Chieti –
                                   Pescara, Italy

Juan P. Amezquita-Sanchez   Universidad Autonoma de Queretaro, Mexico
Marco Appetito   Aubay, Italy
Manjunath Aradhya   JSS S&T University, India
Saiful Azad   Green University of Bangladesh, Bangladesh
Hamed Azami   University of Toronto Canada
Francesco Bardozzo   University of Salerno, Italy
Tiziana Ciano   University Mediterranea of Reggio Calabria, Italy
Tianhua Chen   University of Huddersfield, UK
Gennaro Cordasco   Universitàdegli studi della Campania Luigi
                                   Vanvitelli, Italy
M. Ali Akber Dewan   Athabasca University, Canada
Nilanjan Dey   JIS University, India
Khoo Bee Ee   Universiti Sains Malaysia, Malaysia
Anna Esposito   University of Campania, Luigi Vanvitell, Italy
Marcos Faundez-Zanuy   Escola Superior Politècnica Tecnocampus, Spain
Massimiliano Ferrara   University Mediterranea of Reggio Calabria, Italy
Giancarlo Fortino   University of Calabria, Italy
Fabio Frustaci   University of Calabria, Italy
Hamido Fujita   Iwate Prefectural University, Japan
Antonio Guerrieri   University of Calabria, Italy
Antonella Guzzo   University of Calabria, Italy
Marzia Hoque Tania   University of Oxford, UK
A. B. M. Aowlad Hossain   KUET, Bangladesh
Tingwen Huang   Texas A&M University, Qatar
Amir Hussain   Edinburgh Napier University, UK
Michele Ianni   University of Calabria, Italy
Cosimo Ieracitano   University Mediterranea of Reggio Calabria, Italy
Khan Iftekharuddin   Old Dominion University, USA
S. M. Riazul Islam   Sejong University, South Korea
Shariful Islam   Deakin University, Australia
M. Shamim Kaiser   Jahangirnagar University, Bangladesh
Omprakash Kaiwartya   Nottingham Trent University, UK
Joarder Kamruzzaman   Joarder Kamruzzaman, Australia
Ramani Kannan   Universiti Teknologi PETRONAS, Malaysia
Nikola Kasabov   Auckland University of Technology, New Zealand
Gianluca Lax   University Mediterranea of Reggio Calabria, Italy
Michele Lo Giudice   University Mediterranea of Reggio Calabria, Italy
Mufti Mahmud   Nottingham Trent University, UK

Nadia Mammone	University Mediterranea of Reggio Calabria, Italy
Stefano Marrone	Università degli studi della Campania Luigi Vanvitelli, Italy
Alessio Micheli	University of Pisa, Italy
Francesco C. Morabito	University Mediterranea of Reggio Calabria, Italy
M. Murugappan	College of Science and Technology, Kuwait
Massimo Panella	University Sapienza of Rome, Italy
Nelishia Pillay	University of Pretoria, South Africa
Emanuele Principi	UniversitàPolitecnica delle Marche, Italy
M. Arifur Rahman	University of Queensland, UK
A. K. M. Mahbubur Rahman	Independent University of Bangladesh, Bangladesh
Kanad Ray	Amity University, India
Antonello Rosato	University Sapienza of Rome, Italy
Oscar Russo	Aubay, Italy
K. C. Santosh	University of South Dakota, USA
Giuseppe Maria Sarné	University Bicocca of Milan, Italy
Suresh Chandra Satapathy	KIIT Deemed to be University, India
Claudio Savaglio	University of Calabria, Italy
Marta Savino	Aubay, Italy
Simone Scardapane	University Sapienza of Rome, Italy
Noushath Shaffi	College of Applied Sciences, Oman
Stefano Squartini	UniversitàPolitecnica delle Marche, Italy
Roberto Tagliaferri	University of Salerno, Italy
Anshul Tripathi	IIT Gandhinagar, India
Domenico Ursino	UniversitàPolitecnica delle Marche, Italy
Surapong Uttama	Mae Fah Luang University, Thailand
Marley Vellasco	Pontifícia Universidade Católica do Rio de Janeiro, Brazil
Mario Versaci	University Mediterranea of Reggio Calabria, Italy
Luca Virgili	UniversitàPolitecnica delle Marche, Italy
Salvatore Vitabile	University of Palermo, Italy
Yu-Dong Zhang	University of Leicester, UK
Ning Zhong	Maebashi Institute of Technology, Japan

Contents

Application of AI and Informatics in Healthcare

Application of AI and Informatics in Pattern Recognition

Application of AI and Informatics in Network, Security, and Analytics

Emerging Applications of AI and Informatics

A Hybrid Speed and Radial Distance Feature Descriptor Using Optical Flow Approach in HAR

Guanghui Hua[1]([✉])[iD], G. Hemantha Kumar[1][iD],
and V. N. Manjunath Aradhya[2][iD]

[1] Department of Studies in Computer Science, University of Mysore,
Mysuru 570006, Karnataka, India
glory_hua@yahoo.com
[2] Department of Computer Applications, JSS Science and Technology University,
Mysuru 570006, Karnataka, India
aradhya@sjce.ac.in

Abstract. Video surveillance is ubiquitous in the public area of the world now. Human activity recognition based on video surveillance automatically identifies and analyses the human activity of continuous frame or video sequence data from various sensors. Human activity such as walking, standing, running, sitting, jogging, interaction and so on is a good representation. The human activity contains such inter-class differences, intra-class similarities and so forth challenges to tackle. In this paper, recognizing human actions based on the Optical Flow approach in video sequences has been addressed. The descriptor with Optical Flow vector of boundaries of activity performance includes silhouette speed on several frames, different areas and the eight different angle's radial distance. The proposed descriptor with a multi-class Support Vector Machine classifier has achieved good accuracy for each action of the Weizmann datasets.

Keywords: Human action recognition · Action feature · Optical flow · Multi-class Support Vector Machine (SVM) · Video surveillance

1 Introduction

Human activity recognition based on video surveillance as the remote eyes automatically for analysis management and security forces applicated has become a prominent area of research in the domain of computer vision, such as public safety, event video surveillance, abnormal detecting, sporting competition and so on. A human activity recognition study identifies and predicts the movement of a person or several people precisely in a scene. Human activities recognition is categorised into the following parts: input information, image preprocessing, feature extraction and representation. Finally, put the feature into a classifier

Project website: http://github.com/Gary-HUA/Optical_Flow_HAR.git.

M. Mahmud et al. (Eds.): AII 2022, CCIS 1724, pp. 3–13, 2022.
https://doi.org/10.1007/978-3-031-24801-6_1

for identification. Figure 1 displays the human activity recognition system. Video be captured using some of the sensors, preprocessing (removing noise/resizing frame/images/information detection and segmentation of objects). Relevant features extraction and representation. Finally, classify the objects with different activities. An intelligent human activity recognition system is more helpful and efficient than an artificial one. In the research approach, traditional and neural networks are the main branches. In the past decade, most research has focused on traditional human activity recognition methods, such as the Optical Flow Method, Histogram of Oriented Gradients (HOG), feature description methods based on silhouette, Space-Time Interest Point (STIP), human joint point and trajectories and so on are the global or local features approach. In recent years, there has been an increasing amount of literature on the Neural Network architecture that the Convolutional Neural Network (CNN), two-stream network, hybrid network and so on applied widely in image or video segmentation, feature extraction and identification. Due to the higher compute complexity of video data and varietal activity scenes, the neural network architecture application of reality is unfavourable now. A traditional feature based on the Optical Flow method that Speeds information, the radial distance from the centroid to the edge point is classified by multi-class Support Vector Machine (SVM). The structure of this paper is as below: Sect. 2 gives the recent related work. Section 3 is the proposed methodology. In Sect. 4, an experiment results using Optical Flow-based features to classify human action in the Weizmann benchmark datasets. Moreover, Sect. 5 gives the conclusion.

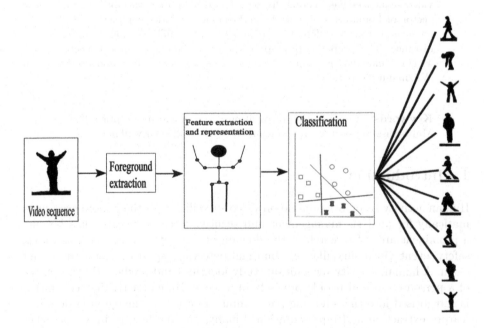

Fig. 1. Architecture of Human activity recognition

2   Related Work

For video-based human activity recognition. The traditional method that global or local features are considered the most popular approach. Vrigkas et al. [1], described a detailed review of the state of the art and recent research development in the human activity recognition domain. It proposed a categorization of the human activity recognition methodology and discussed the advantages and disadvantages of the human activity classification. Subetha et al. [4], collectively summarizes various methodology, challenges, and issues of the human activity recognition system. Human to object, human to human interaction and varied benchmark datasets are researched. Pareek et al. [29], Discussed the human activity recognition techniques in which machine learning and deep learning. It also discussed action representation, action analyses and applications of the benchmark datasets. Zhang et al. [7], emphasizes the advance of the recent activity identification approach, activities representation, classification method and available datasets are introduced. Tripathi et al. [9], presents suspicious human activity recognition with its issues and challenges. Ali et al. [10], introduces a detail of recent advances in presentation and feature extraction, presenting publicly available datasets, depth maps approach etc. Boualia et al. [13], provides a detailed review of the state-of-art research in the human activity recognition domain. It presents a category of human activity methods and discusses their advantage and limitations. Finally, it discusses the open challenges and possible solutions. Singh et al. [14], categorized datasets into two parts, two-dimensional (2D-RGB) datasets and three-dimensional (3D-RGB) datasets. Girdhar et al. [17], an extensive review of the state-of-the-art methods is given in this paper. The identification of challenging areas of the human activity recognition ecosystem. The datasets of training in the HAR system and the publicly available datasets are also discussed. Kolekar et al. [3], proposed Optical Flow and shape features are fused for human activity recognition. Hidden Markov Model generated for activities classification. Kumar et al. [2], proposed Optical Flow vectors along with the edges of the action performers with a Multi-class Support Vector Machine (SVM) classifier. Abdelhedi et al. [5], introduces a mid-level representation based on the Optical Flow approach. An Artificial Neural Network classifier (ANN) was used to test and evaluated KTH and Weizmann action datasets. Abdelhedi et al. [6], from a smart camera, a shape representation of the human through the use of silhouette. A real-time and fuzzy logical inference system was developed for fall detection. Boufama et al. [8], a feature extraction algorithm has been proposed. A mid-level features method based on trajectories for human activities and the Standard Bag of Word algorithm for activity identification. Hbali et al. [11], proposed a skeleton-based approach to describe the spatio-temporal aspects of the human activity sequence. Using the Extremely Randomised Trees algorithm to train and test on MSR 3D and MSR Daily Activity 3D action datasets. Ramirez et al. [30] proposed a fall detection and action recognition system by skeleton features of vision-based approaches. It is more comfortable and always feasible than wearable devices in the real environment. Weng et al. [12], obtains effectively and compactly action representation with

Length Variable Edge Trajectory (LV-ET) and Spatio-Temporal Motion Skeleton (STMS) descriptor. Kim et al. [15], proposed skeleton joint features based on depth video to recognize the daily activities of elderly people in indoor conditions. Tracking the human silhouettes and body joints information to classify the human activities by the Hidden Markov Model. Tanberk et al. [16], proposed a hybrid deep model which combines Dense Optical Flow and auxiliary movement information for human activity recognition. Khan et al. [31], hybrid deep learning models which CNN and LSTM to extract spatial features and temporal information for human activity recognition. Umar et al. [32], using the hybrid model in which I3D CNN, Optical Flow approach in the feature extraction step and LSTM softMax classifier to classify human activity recognition.

3   Proposed Methodology

Partial occlusion, inter-class variance and intra-class similarities are the main challenges for Human activity recognition based on global feature descriptors. The Optical Flow approach in video frames extracts the object's body shape information from the movement foreground. The features of global such as colour, context, silhouette or body shape represent the activities attribute. We proposed a fusion feature descriptor whose speed and radial distance are put into multi-class SVM to validate the inter-class variance and intra-class similarities problems.

3.1   Human Activity Recognition Framework

We detect the foreground (interest object) from the video sequences. The Gaussian Mixture Model (GMM) [18] and Optical Flow [19] techniques extract boundaries of human activity performance. We propose a novel feature vector based on the Optical Flow method to calculate the edge points from the object of the human action silhouette. The global speed information and radial distance of different parts of the human body from the centroid are feature vectors. Finally, a widely multi-class Support Vector Machine (SVM) [21] classifies human action.

3.2   Feature Descriptor

The video-based human activity recognition poses a lot of challenges. Thus, the main problem is to characterize the kinds of features of human activities for identification. In the HAR system, feature extraction and representation are signification steps. The fit information of features will present the essence of an activity pattern. An appropriate descriptor of features is helpful to classify for an expected result. In this paper, the Optical Flow-based method extracted features vector along with the boundaries of human action which is represented in Fig. 2. The Horn and Schunck algorithm [19] based Optical Flow extraction technique calculates the Optical Flow vectors along with the boundaries. At first, we detect the foreground (object) from the input information by the GMM method. The

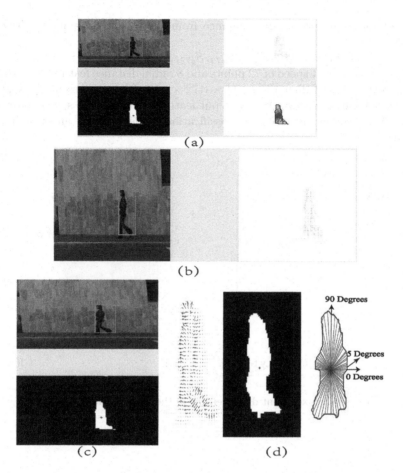

Fig. 2. (a) Collected video performance to feature extraction of HAR. (b) The Optical Flow detection from the video sequence. (c) Boundaries based on Optical Flow and foreground. (d) Features extraction and representation from an object.

current frame of the moving object was calculated with last frame. The moving dimension vector is called Optical Flow which contains the direction and values of the neighbour frame interest object in the same pixel point. Figure 3 display the pixel point procedure of Optical Flow displacement. In our paper, Optical Flow vector and foreground detection based on boundaries extract 72 boundary points around human action by 5°. It is the speed feature of displacement in parts of the human body in 5 frames. The technique can distinguish the variance of intra-class behaviour well in different human action speed. Such as the variance of walking, running and jumping in movement speed of x and y direction. Base inter-class similarity challenge, the distance that eight edge points by 45° (0, 45, 90, 135, 180, 225, 270, 315) to the centre of gravity are extracted and stored.

Figure 4 shows an eight radial distance from the centroid gravity to the edge points.

Feature vector = $\{S_{x1}, S_{y1}, ...S_{x72}, S_{y72}, D_1, D_2, D_3....D_8\}$;

The displacement speed of 72 points and 8 radial distance features are ordered into a row vector of dimensional $(1 \times ((72 \times 2) + 8))$ to represent the Optical Flow-based feature vector. And then put features that fuse the speed and radial distance of different parts into a classification model to train and test human activity.

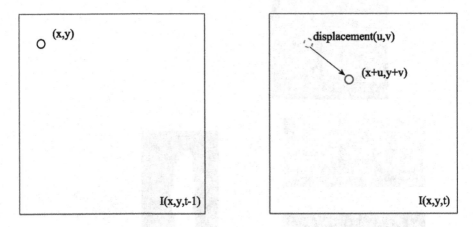

Fig. 3. A pixel point displacement in the Optical Flow method

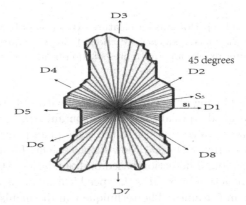

Fig. 4. 72 Different parts of human action speed and 8 key radial distance

3.3 Multi-class SVM

The Support Vector Machine (SVM) [22] was originally a binary classification method. The main idea follows: construct a hyperplane to separate two classes (Labelled $y = 1, -1$). The SVM aims to find the optimal classification plane in the case of linear separability, there given a training dataset of n points:

$(x_1, y_1), (x_2, y_2).....(x_n, y_n)$

where y_i is either 1 or -1, each indicating the class of points x_i belongs. Each x_i is a p-dimensional feature vector. And then, to find the hyperplane to separate the point x_i from the labels $y_i = 1$ or $y_i = -1$.

Any hyperplane can be written as:

$$\mathbf{w}^T \mathbf{x} - b = 0 \tag{1}$$

Although SVM originally developed binary classification. It can extend to multi-class SVM that consists of the One-against-Rest and One-against-One methods.

The One-against-Rest is also called the One-against-All method. It needs N classifiers for N-class classification problems. The sample of a certain class has a positive label while the remainders have a negative label. So suppose the class is N_1 and the residual is $N - N_1$.

The One-against-One method constructs an SVM model for samples of any two classes. It needs $N(N-1)/2$ classifiers for the N-class classification problem.

This paper proposed a Radial Basis Function (RBF) kernel-based multi-class SVM classification to validate the feature vector. The 'One-against-Rest' method has been used to train each classifier.

4 Experimental Result

4.1 Human Action Datasets

The Weizmann dataset [20] is an easily available dataset. It was captured with a stationary camera and uncomplicated background in 2005. It includes 90 video sequences (low-resolution 180 × 144, deinterlaced 50 fps). It involves a total of 5701 frames, each performing 10 natural actions by 9 different people. The actions are bend, jack, jump, p-jump (jump-in-place-on-two-legs), run, side (gallop sideways), skip, wave1 and wave2. The datasets only contain a single action in each clip. Figure 5 displays a frame for each activity from the dataset.

Fig. 5. Represent actions of the Weizmann datasets

4.2   Experiment Result and Comparison Analysis

The proposed method is validated on the Weizmann benchmark dataset. The Leave-one-Out approach has been used to test the efficiency of the proposed method. Table 1 gives a result of the proposed method in the Weizmann datasets. The result is 75% for Walk, 85% for Bend, 100% for Jack, 100% for P-jump, 86% for Run, 86% for Side, 91% and 80% for Wave1 and Wave2. Simple and more efficient features classified by multi-class SVM give a satisfying result in Bend, Jack, and Side. But 75% of walk action accuracy still is not ideal. Although speed can distinguish the intra-class action well in the Weizmann dataset, Walk is similar to side action in silhouette and speed. Table 2 displays the feature dimension comparison with the previous research. The comparison displays that our feature dimension is 152. It is better than earlier research based on the Optical Flow method in human activity recognition. Due to the low-dimension features, the proposed approach is simple and more efficient than the compared method. In the proposed method based on Optical Flow technology, a fused human action speed and radial distances vector are classified by multi-class SVM. Table 3 displays comparison accuracy with the previous research based on the Optical Flow method in Human Activity Recognition.

Table 1. The results of the proposed method on Weizmann datasets.

Method	Human action	Classification rate
Proposed method	Walk	75%
	Bend	85%
	Jack	100%
	Pjump	100%
	Run	86%
	Side	86%
	Wave1	91%
	Wave2	80%

Table 2. A comparison of feature dimension in the Optical Flow method

Methods	Feature dimension
Optical Flow Method [2]	72×9
Optical Flow Method [27]	120×120
Optical Flow+Action FlowNet [28]	512
Proposed method	$\mathbf{72 \times 2 + 8}$

Table 3. A comparison of HAR accuracy on Weizmann dataset

Method	Activity accuracy
Hong, et al. [23]	76.6%
Dorin, et al. [24]	81.9%
Gomathi, S. et al. [25]	82.0%
Nadeem, et al. [26]	89.4%
Proposed method	**87.8%**

5 Conclusion

In this paper, we have proposed a new descriptor of features. The feature extraction and representation descriptors are based on foreground detection and an Optical Flow approach. It includes GMM and a global technique (Optical Flow approach) that estimates Dense Optical Flow fields. Finally, a fused descriptor in which speed and radial distance feature vectors are used to classify action by multi-class SVM. The proposed method has considered accuracy and feature dimension space problems. Traditional descriptors as much as possible to extract activities information relevantly of a human. In the proposed method, a hybrid speed and radial distance feature descriptor is applied to Weizmann benchmark datasets for extracting lower-dimensional feature space which helped us in achieving better results at the time of classifying different human action recognition when compared to other existing approaches. In future work, we wish to open up with several new feature descriptor techniques for efficiently recognizing various human actions from different applications in the field of machine learning.

References

1. Vrigkas, M., Nikou, C., Kakadiaris, I.A.: A review of human activity recognition methods. Front. Robot. AI **2**, 28 (2015)
2. Kumar, S.S., John, M.: Human activity recognition using optical flow based feature set. In: 2016 IEEE International Carnahan Conference on Security Technology (ICCST), pp. 1–5. IEEE (2016)
3. Kolekar, M.H., Dash, D.P.: Hidden Markov model based human activity recognition using shape and optical flow based features. In: 2016 IEEE Region 10 Conference (TENCON), pp. 393–397. IEEE (2016)
4. Subetha, T., Chitrakala, S.: A survey on human activity recognition from videos. In: 2016 international Conference on Information Communication and Embedded Systems (ICICES), pp. 1–7. IEEE (2016)
5. Abdelhedi, S., Wali, A., Alimi, A.M.: Human activity recognition based on mid-level representations in video surveillance applications. In: 2016 International Joint Conference on Neural Networks (IJCNN), pp. 3984–3989. IEEE (2016)
6. Abdelhedi, S., Wali, A., Alimi, A.M.: Fuzzy logic based human activity recognition in video surveillance applications. In: Abraham, A., Wegrzyn-Wolska, K., Hassanien, A.E., Snasel, V., Alimi, A.M. (eds.) Proceedings of the Second International Afro-European Conference for Industrial Advancement AECIA 2015. AISC, vol. 427, pp. 227–235. Springer, Cham (2016). https://doi.org/10.1007/978-3-319-29504-6_23
7. Zhang, S., Wei, Z., Nie, J., Huang, L., Wang, S., Li, Z.: A review on human activity recognition using vision-based method. J. Healthcare Eng. (2017)
8. Boufama, B., Habashi, P., Ahmad, I.S.: Trajectory-based human activity recognition from videos. In: 2017 International Conference on Advanced Technologies for Signal and Image Processing (ATSIP), pp. 1–5. IEEE (2017)
9. Tripathi, R.K., Jalal, A.S., Agrawal, S.C.: Suspicious human activity recognition: a review. Artif. Intell. Rev. **50**(2), 283–339 (2018)
10. Ali, H.H., Moftah, H.M., Youssif, A.A.: Depth-based human activity recognition: a comparative perspective study on feature extraction. Future Comput. Inf. J. **3**(1), 51–67 (2018)
11. Hbali, Y., Hbali, S., Ballihi, L., Sadgal, M.: Skeleton-based human activity recognition for elderly monitoring systems. IET Comput. Vis. **12**(1), 16–26 (2018)
12. Weng, Z., Guan, Y.: Action recognition using length-variable edge trajectory and spatio-temporal motion skeleton descriptor. EURASIP J. Image Video Process. **2018**(1), 1–15 (2018). https://doi.org/10.1186/s13640-018-0250-5
13. Boualia, S.N., Amara, N.E.B.: Pose-based human activity recognition: a review. In: 2019 15th International Wireless Communications & Mobile Computing Conference (IWCMC), pp. 1468–1475. IEEE (2019)
14. Singh, T., Vishwakarma, D.K.: Human activity recognition in video benchmarks: a survey. In: Rawat, B.S., Trivedi, A., Manhas, S., Karwal, V. (eds.) Advances in Signal Processing and Communication. LNEE, vol. 526, pp. 247–259. Springer, Singapore (2019). https://doi.org/10.1007/978-981-13-2553-3_24

15. Kim, K., Jalal, A., Mahmood, M.: Vision-based human activity recognition system using depth silhouettes: a smart home system for monitoring the residents. J. Electr. Eng. Technol. **14**(6), 2567–2573 (2019)
16. Tanberk, S., Kilimci, Z.H., Tükel, D.B., Uysal, M., Akyokuş, S.: A hybrid deep model using deep learning and dense optical flow approaches for human activity recognition. IEEE Access **8**, 19799–19809 (2020)
17. Girdhar, P.: Vision based human activity recognition: a comprehensive review of methods & techniques. Turkish J. Comput. Math. Educ. (TURCOMAT) **12**(10), 7383–7394 (2021)
18. Li, H., Achim, A., Bull, D.R.: GMM-based efficient foreground detection with adaptive region update. In: 2009 16th IEEE International Conference on Image Processing (ICIP), pp. 3181–3184. IEEE (2009)
19. Horn, B.K., Schunck, B.G.: Determining optical flow. Artif. Intell. **17**(1–3), 185–203 (1981)
20. Gorelick, L., Blank, M., Shechtman, E., Irani, M., Basri, R.: Actions as space-time shapes. IEEE Trans. Pattern Anal. Mach. Intell. **29**(12), 2247–2253 (2007)
21. Schuldt, C., Laptev, I., Caputo, B.: Recognizing human actions: a local SVM approach. In: Proceedings of the 17th International Conference on Pattern Recognition, ICPR 2004, vol. 3, pp. 32–36. IEEE (2004)
22. Weston, J., Watkins, C.: Multi-class support vector machines, pp. 98–04. Technical Report CSD-TR-98-04, Department of Computer Science, Royal Holloway, University of London (1998)
23. Hong, S., Kim, M.: A framework for human body parts detection in RGB-D image. J. Korea Multimed. Soc. **19**(12), 1927–1935 (2016)
24. Dorin, C., Hurwitz, B.: Automatic body part measurement of dressed humans using single RGB-D camera. In: Proceedings of the 2016 CHI Conference Extended Abstracts on Human Factors in Computing Systems, pp. 3042–3048 (2016)
25. Gomathi, S., Santhanam, T.: Application of rectangular feature for detection of parts of human body. Adv. Comput. Sci. Technol **11**, 43–55 (2018)
26. Nadeem, A., Jalal, A., Kim, K.: Human actions tracking and recognition based on body parts detection via artificial neural network. In: 2020 3rd International Conference on Advancements in Computational Sciences (ICACS), pp. 1–6. IEEE (2020)
27. Zhang, N., Hu, Z., Lee, S., Lee, E.: Human action recognition based on global silhouette and local optical flow. In: International Symposium on Mechanical Engineering and Material Science (ISMEMS 2017), pp. 1–5. Atlantis Press (2017)
28. Ng, J.Y.H., Choi, J., Neumann, J., Davis, L.S.: ActionFlowNet: learning motion representation for action recognition. In: 2018 IEEE Winter Conference on Applications of Computer Vision (WACV), pp. 1616–1624. IEEE (2018)
29. Pareek, P., Thakkar, A.: A survey on video-based human action recognition: recent updates, datasets, challenges, and applications. Artif. Intell. Rev. **54**(3), 2259–2322 (2021)
30. Ramirez, H., Velastin, S.A., Meza, I., Fabregas, E., Makris, D., Farias, G.: Fall detection and activity recognition using human skeleton features. IEEE Access **9**, 33532–33542 (2021)
31. Khan, I.U., Afzal, S., Lee, J.W.: Human activity recognition via hybrid deep learning based model. Sensors **22**(1), 323 (2022)
32. Umar, I.M., Ibrahim, K.M., Gital, A.Y.U., Zambuk, F.U., Lawal, M.A., Yakubu, Z.I.: Hybrid model for human activity recognition using an inflated I3-D two stream convolutional-LSTM network with optical flow mechanism. In: 2022 IEEE Delhi Section Conference (DELCON), pp. 1–7. IEEE (2022)

Innovative Soft Computing Techniques for the Evaluation of the Mechanical Stress State of Steel Plates

Mario Versaci[1]([✉])[ID], Giovanni Angiulli[2][ID], Fabio La Foresta[1], Paolo Crucitti[3], Filippo Laganá[1][ID], Diego Pellicanó[3], and Annunziata Palumbo[4]

[1] DICEAM Department, "Mediterranea" University, Reggio Calabria, Italy
{fabio.laforesta,filippo.lagana,mario.versaci}@unirc.it
[2] DIIES Department, "Mediterranea" University, Reggio Calabria, Italy
giovanni.angiulli@unirc.it
[3] TEC Cooperative, Spin-in DICEAM Department, "Mediterranea" University, Reggio Calabria, Italy
diego.pellicano@unirc.it
[4] MIFT Department, University of Messina, Messina, Italy
apalumbo@unime.it

Abstract. Thin rectangular steel plates deform locally under biaxial symmetric loads (the specimen is subjected to the load through two orthogonal test axes) with respect to their center, causing extremely complex mechanical stress distributions which are not directly measurable in order to obtain $2D$ representations. Strengthened by the fact that suitably induced eddy currents in these plates are locally related to mechanical stresses, in this paper, we propose an innovative approach based on eddy currents to build $2D$ maps capable of reconstructing the distribution of the stress state of a plate and, consequently, facilitating the evaluation of its state of health. The proposed procedure, using techniques related to AI (in particular, soft computing and fuzzy similarities), evaluates the mechanical integrity of plates in terms of an equivalent classification problem. The results obtained (with a classification percentage close to 100%) are similar to those obtained using soft computing techniques characterized by a higher computational complexity.

Keywords: Artificial intelligence · Soft computing · Fuzzy similarities · Eddy currents

1 Introduction

At present, metal structures are in widespread use in the field of civil engineering, as they present good mechanical qualities with low seismic action, given the

Supported by both the NdT&E Lab, DICEAM Department "Mediterranea" University, Reggio Calabria, Italy and the Italian National Group of Mathematical Physics (GNFM-INdAM) and the University of Messina through FFO 2021.

The original version of this chapter was revised: The author affiliations have been rearranged in the correct way. The correction to this chapter is available at https://doi.org/10.1007/978-3-031-24801-6_39

reduced masses involved[1]. In steel buildings, the connecting plates are the structural elements which experience the most stress (i.e., external biaxial loads) [1], requiring periodic non-destructive integrity checks [1–4]. However, steels, due to repeated heat treatments used during their production process, could show problems due to inhomogeneity, especially during their operational lifetime, causing electrical run-outs with evident repercussions for any measurement campaigns, as well as marked alterations in electrical conductivity and magnetic permeability [5–7]. These phenomena have already been extensively studied in [8,11,12], especially in finite elasticity regimes, obtaining links (although, unfortunately, not explicit ones) between deformations and external biaxial loads (subjecting the specimen to loads oriented along two orthogonal axes), with great difficulty in obtaining deformations [12]. Therefore, the use of numerical approaches seems to be the obvious solution, even though these may provide ghost solutions[2] [13]. Obviously, it is possible to produce $2D$ maps of the mechanical stresses starting from $2D$ maps of the deformations by exploiting suitable constitutive laws. Unfortunately, modern technology does not offer adequate instrumentation to carry out in situ measurements of deformations, referring instead to computationally expensive analytical calculations that are not suitable for use in real-time applications or technological transfers [7]. It is imperative to observe that the operating regimes of steel structures refer to small deformations [1]; therefore, in the absence of high-precision instrumentation, any measurement campaign could provide unreliable results. Thus, it would be ideal to know the possible biaxial load that produces the acquired deformation scenario in order to highlight whether the steel plate has undergone significant stresses. On the basis of these assumptions, $2D$ maps of mechanical deformations[3] can be considered to be equivalent to the $2D$ maps reconstructed using Eddy Currents (ECs) measured by means of a mechanical procedure consisting of automatic scanning of the plate by taking the electric voltage signal; for example, using a FLUXSET probe (see Fig. 1a) [13]. However, it is experimentally observable that similar external biaxial loads (i.e., in terms of amplitude) produce equally similar deformation states. Therefore, they can be grouped into a single class of biaxial loads [1,4]: for each external biaxial load (similar to a fixed load ζ), the respective ECs maps can be evaluated in order to achieve a class of $2D$ images similar to each other. By setting $\widetilde{A}$ external biaxial loads, $\widetilde{A}$ biaxial load classes can automatically be considered (Class 1, Class 2, ..., Class ζ, ..., Class $\widetilde{A}$); note that care should be taken to construct an auxiliary class consisting of ECs $2D$ maps obtained from plates not subjected to biaxial loads (see Fig. 1b). Using a soft computing image fusion technique, each ECs $2D$ Image Class, starting from all the images it contains, can be represented by a single image. Therefore, a $2D$ ECs map obtained for a plate under analysis (and subjected to an unknown

---

[1] In reinforced concrete structures, the masses involved are considerable, with evident increases in seismic actions.

[2] That is, numerical solutions that do not satisfy any analytical conditions of existence and uniqueness.

[3] Under the same external biaxial load conditions.

biaxial load) can be compared with all images representative of the $\widetilde{A}+1$ classes using algebraic soft computing approaches based on fuzzy similarities (FSs)[4], thus obtaining $\widetilde{A}+1$ values of similarity, the highest value of which establishes the membership of the ECs map to the biaxial load class that determines the highest fuzzy similarity value [14,15]. Furthermore, it is worth noting that the fuzzy approach presented here is also necessary due to the fact that the signals sampled by the probe could be affected by further uncertainties (due, for example, to slight malfunctions of the probe itself).

The remainder of this paper is structured as follows. The analytical model [8] is detailed in Sect. 2, while the specifications of the measurement campaign—carried out at the NDT/NDE Lab of the Mediterranea University of Reggio Calabria—are detailed in Sect. 3. Section 4 describes the proposed approach based on FSs, while Sects. 5 and 6 detail the exploited fuzzy image fusion approach and the technique used to compare the results, respectively. A discussion of the obtained results is presented in Sect. 7, while our conclusions and future research perspectives are provided in Sect. 8.

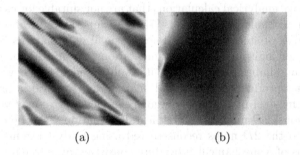

(a)   (b)

Fig. 1. A typical 2D ECs map when (a) an external bi-axial load is applied to the steel plate and (b) when no external bi-axial load is applied.

2   The Analytical Model

Let $\Omega \subset \mathbb{R}^2$ be a homogeneous and regular region (with boundary $\partial\Omega$) representing an elastic body consisting of a homogeneous, incompressible, and isotropic material. By applying a biaxial load to Ω, an isochoric deformation, $d_{is} \in C^1(\overline{\Omega}, \mathbb{R}^2)$, occurs[5]. Moreover, we denote by M the whole set of isochoric deformations, such that [8]:

$$d_{is} \in M = \{d_{is} \in C^1(\overline{\Omega}, \mathbb{R}^2) \ : \ \underline{\underline{H}} = \nabla d_{is}, \ |\underline{\underline{H}}| = 1\}. \tag{1}$$

---

[4] This is because the ECs 2D maps are characterized by poorly defined transition zones.

[5] By hypothesis, the volume does not change; in addition, this deformation must be a continuous function, together with its first derivatives, in order to ensure the absence of tears and/or the onset of further defects.

With defined $\underline{\underline{H}}$, the stretch tensor $\sqrt{\underline{\underline{H}}\,\underline{\underline{H}}^T}$ has to be considered, as its eigenvalues, λ_1 and λ_2, are the principal stretches of the deformation [8], which serve as main parameters for the definition of the strain-energy function of the material, $Y = Y(\lambda_1, \lambda_2) \in C^\infty(\Omega)$. When an external biaxial load is applied, Cauchy's tensorial relationship gives $\boldsymbol{t} = \underline{\underline{T}} \cdot \hat{n}$ where, as usual, $\underline{\underline{T}}$ represents the traction tensor and $\hat{n}$ is the unit outer normal to $\partial\Omega$, while $\boldsymbol{t}$ is the traction vector. We apply the first criterion of energy stability, according to which any isochoric deformation assumes stability if and only if it minimizes the following residual energy [8]:

$$\text{Energy} = \int_\Omega [Y(\lambda_1, \lambda_2) - \underline{\underline{T}} \cdot \nabla \boldsymbol{d}_{is}] d\Omega. \tag{2}$$

As $\underline{\underline{H}}$ is a local minumum for each point of discontinuity, it seems legitimate to indicate by $\underline{\underline{H}}^+, \underline{\underline{H}}^-$ the possible gap of $\underline{\underline{H}}$ on each point of discontinuity[6], such that $\boldsymbol{d}_{is}$ (corresponding to $\underline{\underline{H}}^+, \underline{\underline{H}}^-$) is a global minimum. However, as $Y = Y(\lambda_1, \lambda_2)$, it follows that Y depends on $\underline{\underline{H}}$, such that it makes sense to write:

$$Y(\underline{\underline{H}}^+) - Y(\underline{\underline{H}}^-) = \underline{\underline{S}}(\underline{\underline{H}}^\pm) \cdot (\underline{\underline{H}}^+ - \underline{\underline{H}}^-) = \underline{\underline{S}}(\underline{\underline{H}}^\pm) \cdot (\boldsymbol{a} \otimes \boldsymbol{n}), \tag{3}$$

with $\underline{\underline{S}}(\underline{\underline{H}}^\pm)$, the Piola–Kirchhoff tensor and $\boldsymbol{a} \in \mathbb{R}^2$, and $\boldsymbol{n} \in \mathbb{R}^2$. Thus, $\boldsymbol{d}_{is}$ is affine (and continues in pieces), consisting of a set of layers whose gradients are given by the sequence $\underline{\underline{H}}^+/\underline{\underline{H}}^-/\underline{\underline{H}}^+/\underline{\underline{H}}^-, \cdots$ on the side of an appropriately oriented interface, such that the average deformation gradient of these layers satisfies the conditions of compatibility. Energetically, these configurations are minimization sequences converging weakly to a deformation, $\boldsymbol{d}_{is}^*$, thus not minimizing the total free energy. It follows that $Y(\lambda_1, \lambda_2)$ is semi-continuous lower in the Sobolev functional space $W^{1,p\geq1}(\Omega, \mathbb{R}^2)$ (weak convergence), which fails in the presence of phase changes due to the non-ellipticity of the functional. Furthermore, the decay of the ellipticity property of the functional imposes that the integrals of the calculus of variations converge to a minimum in a particular functional space consisting of generalized curves, which represent the limits of minimizing sequences that fluctuate more and more finely; proving that, in $2D$ geometry, $\boldsymbol{d}_{is}^*$ admits global stability iff $Y(\boldsymbol{d}_{is}^*) \leq Y(\boldsymbol{d}_{is})$ minimizes $Y(\lambda_1, \lambda_2)$. Obviously, this analytical model, although interesting from a theoretical point of view, is unfortunately computationally impractical, due to the prohibitive computational load, making it unattractive both for in situ applications and for any technological transfers.

Remark 1. This analytical model may be addressed numerically through the use of modern approaches made available by numerical analysis. However, the impossibility of obtaining easily usable conditions of existence and uniqueness of

---

[6] It is worth noting that the analytical model is formulated in the framework of the finite elasticity of the material in which fields with discontinuity of their gradients are allowed, generating smooth deformations, except for particular areas in which the gradient gap takes place.

the solution make numerical reconstruction of the solution highly problematic, as it does not eliminate the problem of any ghost solutions (i.e., numerical solutions that do not satisfy the aforementioned conditions of existence and uniqueness), thus invoking the need to use alternative techniques (e.g., relating to AI and, in particular, to soft computing) to reconstruct the solution.

3   The Experimental Dataset

We analyzed 200 mm × 200 mm × 8 mm S235 hot-rolled steel plates for civil structures in our NDT/NDE Lab (whose characteristic physical parameters are given in Table 1), subjecting each of them to gradually increasing tensile external biaxial loads, followed by investigation with *ECs*. In particular, each plate was subjected to a biaxial tensile load starting from 180 kN up to 250 kN in steps of 10 kN. Each external biaxial load applied locally modifies the magnetic properties of the specimen as it locally modifies its microstructure, thus causing deformations. The FLUXSET® probe, designed by COMSOL Multiphysics® by means of an FEM approach and built in our Lab, was characterized by the geometric and electrical properties given in Table 2. The pick-up voltage sampled by the probe, as is well-known, is proportional to $|\mathbf{H}|$ (i.e., the amplitude of the magnetic field), which is parallel to the longitudinal axis of the sensor [9,10].

Table 1. Characteristic physical parameters of S235 hot-rolled steel plates.

Physical parameter	Value
γ (Specific weight)	$78.5\,\mathrm{kN/m^3}$
E (Young's modulus)	210,000 MPa
G (Shear modulus of elasticity)	80,769 MPa

Table 2. Characteristics of the FLUXSET® probe.

Parameter	Value
Length of the exciting coil	6 mm
Inner/outer diameter of the exciting coil	7 mm/11 mm
Length of the sensor/diameter of the sensor	7 mm/1.3 mm
Lift-off (exciting coil)/lift-off (sensor)	3 mm/0.7 mm
Frequency of AC sinusoidal exciting current	1 kHz
Electric current	120 mA
Driving signal frequency	100 kHz
Driving signal amplitude	2 Vpp

The probe, mounted on a mechanical automatic scanning device, investigated the central part of each specimen (the area where the greatest deformations are concentrated) after it had been subjected to biaxial loading. Figure 2 displays an image of the Lab, including the handling system on which the probe connected to the data acquisition system is mounted.

Fig. 2. *ECs* probe and mechanical automatic scanning device.

The probe provided four $2D$ signals (*ECs* images): The real part, imaginary part, amplitude, and phase of the pick-up voltage. Figure 1a displays a typical *ECs* image, representing the amplitude of the pick-up voltage of a specimen subjected to a biaxial load. Furthermore, observing that biaxial loads close to each other produce similar deformations, increasing biaxial loads were applied to each specimen. As such, we obtained eight classes of *ECs* images, taking care to create an additional class of *ECs* images built using specimens which had not been subjected to any load. The number of images in each class is specified in Table 3. Finally, a test database was created, consisting of 100×4 *ECs* images obtained without subjecting the specimen to any load.

Table 3. Details of *ECs* image data set.

Class	*ECs* images	Class	*ECs* images
C_{180kN}	100×4	C_{190kN}	105×4
C_{200kN}	111×4	C_{210kN}	110×4
C_{220kN}	107×4	C_{230kN}	104×4
C_{240kN}	102×4	C_{250kN}	103×4
C_{WL} (Without Loads)	100×4		

4   The Proposed Soft Computing Approach

4.1   Adaptive Fuzzification of the ECs Maps and Evaluation of Fuzziness

The first step of the proposed soft computing procedure consists of fuzzifying the $M \times N$ ECs images (each of them indicated as **EC**). If L quantifies the gray level, let us associate to each pixel of **EC**, denoted by (i, j), a related gray level a_{ij}. Furthermore, on **EC**, define a fuzzy membership function (FMF), $m_{\mathbf{EC}}(a_{ij})$: **EC** $\rightarrow [0, 1]$, which is used to formalize how fuzzily a_{ij} belongs to **EC**. Obviously, if $m_{\mathbf{EC}}(a_{ij}) = 1$, a_{ij} totally belongs to **EC**; while, if $m_{\mathbf{EC}}(a_{ij}) = 0$, then a_{ij} does not totally belong to **EC**. Thus, in the case where $m_{\mathbf{EC}}(a_{ij}) \in (0, 1)$, then a_{ij} partially belongs to **EC**. By $F(\mathbf{EC})$, we indicate the fuzzified image of **EC**, in which each pixel is represented by $m_{\mathbf{EC}}(a_{ij})$. In this paper, to build a suitable adaptive FMF, we use the fuzziness minimization and contrast maximization criterion exploiting two suitable fuzzifiers (both equal to 0.5) in order to check the amount of fuzziness contained in an **EC**. Therefore, if $\overline{a}_{ij}$ is the gray level of **EC** before the application of the procedure, the adaptive FMF can be formulated as [16]:

$$m'_{\mathbf{EC}}(\overline{a}_{ij}) = \left(\frac{1 + \left(\max(\overline{a}_{ij}) - \overline{a}_{ij} \right)}{0.5} \right)^{0.5}, \tag{4}$$

with the peculiarity that $m'_{\mathbf{EC}}(\overline{a}_{ij}) \rightarrow 1$ as $\overline{a}_{ij} \rightarrow \max(a_{ij})$, providing the maximum brightness phenomenon. From (4), it is easy to obtain $m_{\mathbf{EC}}(a_{ij})$. In fact, by stretching the contrast among that membership values [16], if $0 \leq m'_{\mathbf{EC}}(\overline{a}_{ij}) \leq 0.5$, one can write

$$m_{\mathbf{EC}}(a_{ij}) = \frac{(m'_{\mathbf{EC}}(\overline{a}_{ij}))^2}{0.5}; \tag{5}$$

otherwise, if $0.5 \leq m'_{\mathbf{EC}}(\overline{a}_{ij}) \leq 1$,

$$m_{\mathbf{EC}}(a_{ij}) = 1 - \frac{(1 - m'_{\mathbf{EC}}(\overline{a}_{ij}))^2}{0.5} \tag{6}$$

and a_{ij} is evaluable as:

$$a_{ij} = \max(a_{ij}) - 2\Big\{ (m_{\mathbf{EC}}(a_{ij}))^2 - 1 \Big\}. \tag{7}$$

To evaluate the fuzziness content of $F(\mathbf{EC})^7$, we use the following index of fuzziness presented in the previous literature [16]:

$$\text{Index of Fuzziness} = \frac{\text{distance}(m_{\mathbf{EC}}(a_{ij}), \widehat{m_{\mathbf{EC}}(a_{ij})})}{0.5(M \times N)^2}, \tag{8}$$

---

[7] Quantification of the fuzziness content of $F(\mathbf{EC})$ is essential, in order to justify the application of the soft computing procedure presented in this paper.

where distance$(m_{\mathbf{EC}}(a_{ij}), \widehat{m_{\mathbf{EC}}(a_{ij})})$ represents the distance between $m_{\mathbf{EC}}(a_{ij})$ and $\widehat{m_{\mathbf{EC}}(a_{ij})}$ (membership values of the nearest ordinary set); which is computed, here, in terms of fuzzy divergence, as this operator has been shown to be a distance function in the reference metric space $C^0[(0,1)]^8$.

4.2   Fuzzy *ECs* Maps and Fuzzy Similarities

If $F(\mathbf{EC}_x)$ and $F(\mathbf{EC}_y)$ are two fuzzy *ECs* maps, in which $m_{\mathbf{EC}_x}(a_{ij})$ and $m_{\mathbf{EC}_y}(b_{ij})$ are their respective pixels, they are considerable as two particular fuzzy sets (belonging to a certain universe of discourse, U) and $m_{\mathbf{EC}_x}(a_{ij})$ and $m_{\mathbf{EC}_y}(b_{ij})$ are their *FMFs*, respectively. Considering the fuzzy Cartesian product, $F(\mathbf{EC}_x) \times F(\mathbf{EC}_y)$, an *FSs* function can be defined such that

$$FS : F(\mathbf{EC}_x) \times F(\mathbf{EC}_y) \rightarrow [0,1]. \tag{9}$$

(9) must be formulated in such a way that it is reflexive, symmetric, and transitive [16]. Particularly, the reflexivity imposes that each image must be similar to itself (obviously, with fuzzy degree equal to unity). Therefore, $\forall F(\mathbf{EC}_x) \in U$, it follows that

$$FS(F(\mathbf{EC}_x), F(\mathbf{EC}_x)) = \sup_{F(\mathbf{EC}_x), F(\mathbf{EC}_y) \in U} FS(F(\mathbf{EC})_x, F(\mathbf{EC})_y) = 1. \tag{10}$$

It should be emphasized that FS must be symmetric, such that it does not depend on the order in which the images appear; in other words:

$$FS(F(\mathbf{EC}_x), F(\mathbf{EC}_y)) = FS(F(\mathbf{EC}_y), F(\mathbf{EC}_x)). \tag{11}$$

Moreover, $FS(F(\mathbf{EC}_x), \overline{F(\mathbf{EC}_x)}) = 0$, in which $\overline{F(\mathbf{EC}_x)}$ is the complementary fuzzy image of $F(\mathbf{EC}_x)^9$. Considering that we must impose transitivity for FS, for all $F(\mathbf{EC}_x)$, $F(\mathbf{EC}_y)$, $F(\mathbf{EC}_z)$, with $F(\mathbf{EC}_x) \subset F(\mathbf{EC}_y) \subset F(\mathbf{EC}_z)$, it follows that

$$m_{\mathbf{EC}_x}(a_{ij}) \leq m_{\mathbf{EC}_y}(b_{ij}) \leq m_{\mathbf{EC}_z}(c_{ij}), \tag{12}$$

in which a_{ij}, b_{ij}, and c_{ij} represent the gray levels for $\mathbf{EC}_x$, $\mathbf{EC}_y$, and $\mathbf{EC}_z$, respectively. Therefore

$$FS(F(\mathbf{EC}_x), F(\mathbf{EC}_y)) \geq FS(F(\mathbf{EC}_x), F(\mathbf{EC}_z)) \tag{13}$$

and

$$FS(F(\mathbf{EC}_y), F(\mathbf{EC}_z)) \geq FS(F(\mathbf{EC}_x), F(\mathbf{EC}_z)). \tag{14}$$

---

[8] As specified in the analytical model, $d_{is} \in C^1(\overline{\Omega}, \mathbb{R}^2) \subset C^0(\overline{\Omega}, \mathbb{R}^2)$. It follows that $m_{\mathbf{EC}(a_{ij})}$ (which represents the fuzzification of the equivalent *ECs* of the mechanical deformation, d_{is}) takes into account deformations whose origin is not necessarily mechanical, confirming that the *ECs* analysis is complete with regards to the strain mapping investigation.

[9] In other words, its FMF is $1 - m_{\mathbf{EC}_x}(a_{ij})$..

Keeping our aims in mind, we propose the use of FSs[10] as being able to satisfy the properties expressed in Subsect. 4.2. Particularly, four FS formulations—Hong-Kim [17], Liang-Shi [18], Ye [19], and Li [20]—are taken into account:

$$FS_1(F(\mathbf{EC}_x), F(\mathbf{EC}_y)) = 1 - \frac{\sum_{i=1}^M \sum_{j=1}^N |m_{\mathbf{EC}_x}(a_{ij}) - m_{\mathbf{EC}_y}(b_{ij})|}{M \times N}, \quad (15)$$

$$FS_2(F(\mathbf{EC}_x), F(\mathbf{EC}_y)) = 1 - \sqrt{\frac{\sum_{i=1}^M \sum_{j=1}^N |m_{\mathbf{EC}_x}(a_{ij}) - m_{\mathbf{EC}_y}(b_{ij})|}{M \times N}}, \quad (16)$$

$$FS_3(F(\mathbf{EC}_x), F(\mathbf{EC}_y)) = \frac{1}{M \times N} \sum_{i=1}^M \sum_{j=1}^N \frac{m_{\mathbf{EC}_x}(a_{ij}) \cdot m_{\mathbf{EC}_y}(b_{ij})}{\sqrt{(m_{\mathbf{EC}_x}(a_{ij}))^2 + (m_{\mathbf{EC}_y}(b_{ij}))^2}}, \quad (17)$$

$$FS_4(F(\mathbf{EC}_x), F(\mathbf{EC}_y)) = 1 - \sqrt{\sum_{i=1}^M \sum_{j=1}^N \frac{(m_{\mathbf{EC}_x}(a_{ij}) - m_{\mathbf{EC}_y}(b_{ij}))^2}{M \times N}}. \quad (18)$$

The following result yields.

Theorem 1.

$$1 - FS_s(F(\mathbf{EC}_x), F(\mathbf{EC}_y)), \quad s \in \{1, 2, 3, 4\}, \quad (19)$$

in $C^0([0,1])$ represent measurements of distances among fuzzified images. Therefore, it follows that the FSs, as defined in (15)–(18), quantify the similarity of two fuzzified images (or, in other words, how closely they approach each other).

Proof. The proof is as trivial as it is tedious (and quite extensive). Therefore, interested parties are invited to contact the authors for any details.

4.3 External Biaxial Loads and Class Constitutions

Definition 1. *If $\widetilde{A}$ is the number of external biaxial loads, to each we associate the ECs map $F(\mathbf{I}_k)$ of the ζth class, $\zeta = 1, \ldots, \widetilde{A}$.*

Definition 2. *If an unknown external load is applied, $F(\mathbf{I}_{unknown})$ indicates the corresponding ECs map.*

Definition 3. *If no external load is applied, $F(\mathbf{I}_{Without\ Load})$ represents the corresponding ECs map.*

---

[10] Obviously, with reduced computational load for any technological transfers and/or real-time applications.

Our primary goal is to associate an unknown load with one of the known classes. Therefore, $\forall \zeta = 1, \ldots, \widetilde{A}$, the following quantities (scalars) are evaluated:

$$Q_1 = \{FS_1(F(\mathbf{I}_{\text{unknown}}), F(\mathbf{I_1})), \ldots, FS_1(F(\mathbf{I}_{\text{unknown}}), \ldots F(\mathbf{I_n})), \ldots, \quad (20)$$
$$FS_1(F(\mathbf{I}_{\text{unknown}}), F(\mathbf{I}_{\widetilde{A}})), FS_1(F(\mathbf{I}_{\text{unknown}}), F(\mathbf{I}_{\text{Without Load}}))\},$$

$$Q_2 = \{FS_2(F(\mathbf{I}_{\text{unknown}}), F(\mathbf{I_1})), \ldots, FS_2(F(\mathbf{I}_{\text{unknown}}), \ldots F(\mathbf{I_n})), \ldots, \quad (21)$$
$$FS_2(F(\mathbf{I}_{\text{unknown}}), F(\mathbf{I}_{\widetilde{A}})), FS_2(F(\mathbf{I}_{\text{unknown}}), F(\mathbf{I}_{\text{Without Load}}))\},$$

$$Q_3 = \{FS_3(F(\mathbf{I}_{\text{unknown}}), F(\mathbf{I_1})), \ldots, FS_3(F(\mathbf{I}_{\text{unknown}}), \ldots F(\mathbf{I_n})), \cdots \quad (22)$$
$$, \ldots, FS_3(F(\mathbf{I}_{\text{unknown}}), F(\mathbf{I}_{\widetilde{A}})), FS_3(F(\mathbf{I}_{\text{unknown}}), F(\mathbf{I}_{\text{Without Load}}))\},$$

$$Q_4 = \{FS_4(F(\mathbf{I}_{\text{unknown}}), F(\mathbf{I_1})), \ldots, FS_4(F(\mathbf{I}_{\text{unknown}}), \ldots F(\mathbf{I_n})), \cdots \quad (23)$$
$$, \ldots, FS_4(F(\mathbf{I}_{\text{unknown}}), F(\mathbf{I}_{\widetilde{A}})), FS_4(F(\mathbf{I}_{\text{unknown}}), \ldots F(\mathbf{I}_{\text{Without Load}}))\}.$$

Then, $FS_s(F(\mathbf{I}_{\text{unknown}}), F(\mathbf{I}_{\overline{n}}))$, $s = 1, 2, 3, 4$ and $\overline{\zeta} \in \{1, \ldots, \widetilde{A}+1\}$ provide the following evaluation:

$$\max\left\{ \max\{Q_1\}, \max\{Q_2\}, \max\{Q_3\}, \max\{Q_4\}\right\}, \quad (24)$$

which establishes the link between the unknown load and the class $\overline{\zeta}$.

5 Soft Computing Approach for Construction of the $2D$ ECs Representative of Each Class of Biaxial Loads

To achieve $F(\mathbf{I_k})$, in this work, we propose a soft computing image fusion approach exploiting all FS_s values. Denoting by $F(\mathbf{I_k}^{z_1})$ and $F(\mathbf{I_k}^{z_1})$ two generic images belonging to the generic Class ζ, they are subdivided into R non-overlapping sub-images. Let these be $F(\mathbf{I_k}^{z_1})_{h_1}$ and $F(\mathbf{I_k}^{z_2})_{h_2}$, with $h_1, h_2 \in T = \{1, \ldots, R\}$. Therefore, with $s = 1, 2, 3, 4$, $FS_s(F(\mathbf{I_k}^{z_1})_1, F(\mathbf{I_k}^{z_2})_1)$ are evaluated. Moreover, let us consider $F(\mathbf{I_k}^{\overline{z_1}})_1$ and $F(\mathbf{I_k}^{\overline{z_2}})_1$ as the pair of sub-images such that
$$\max\left\{FS_s(F(\mathbf{I_k}^{\overline{z_1}})_1, F(\mathbf{I_k}^{\overline{z_2}})_1)\right\}. \quad (25)$$

If $F(\mathbf{I_k})_1$ is the portion of $F(\mathbf{I_k})$ in the sub-images $F(\mathbf{I_k}^{\overline{z_1}})_1$ and $F(\mathbf{I_k}^{\overline{z_2}})_1$, it is sufficient to set [16]:

$$(F(\mathbf{I_k})_1)_{i,j} = \cfrac{1}{1 + \cfrac{1}{e^{0.5\left(F(\mathbf{I_k}^{\overline{z_1}})_1)_{i,j} + (F(\mathbf{I_k}^{\overline{z_2}})_1)_{i,j}\right)}}}, \quad (26)$$

such that $\forall i, j \in F(\mathbf{I}_k)_1$ it is obtained, for example, by sigmoidal computation on the arithmetic average of the corresponding pixels of both $F(\mathbf{I}_k^{z_1})_1$ and $F(\mathbf{I}_k^{z_2})_1$. Obviously, the previous computations must be repeated $\forall h_1, h_2 \in T$, thus achieving $F(\mathbf{I}_k)$ (i.e., the fuzzy image associated to the kth class. Finally, the procedure must be repeated $\forall k = 1, \ldots, \widetilde{A} + 1$, in order to obtain the fuzzy images associated to each Class.

6   Comparison of the Results: Standard Soft Computing Approaches

The performance of the proposed procedure was evaluated through comparison with the classification performance obtained by Sugeno/Mamdani Fuzzy Inference Systems ($FISs$), as well as the use of technologies based on Fuzzy k-means clustering and Self-Organizing Map (SOM). As is well-known, any FIS is able to construct the mapping between inputs and outputs through a bank of linguistic rules $IF, \ldots, THEN$[11], in which the single variables take on linguistic values expressed in terms of $FMFs$ [16]. According to the Mamdani procedure, the output is evaluated starting with the fuzzification of the inputs (through appropriate $FMFs$), which are combined by means of a bank of fuzzy rules that are associated to a particular output fuzzy set, obtained by applying an operator that simulates the implication of the syllogism. This suitably defuzzified output fuzzy set provides the output value. On the other hand, Sugeno's approach, starting from the structure of the FIS according to Mamdani, considers a polynomial instead of the output of $FMFs$. Moreover, Sugeno's $FISs$ allows for automatic extraction of fuzzy rule banks and related inferences. In this work, using the MatLab® Fuzzy Toolbox R2019a, a Mamdani FIS with a bank comprised of 27 fuzzy rules was designed, in which the four antecendents were FS_s, while the Classes represent the outputs of the procedure. In parallel, using the same TookBox, a Sugeno FIS (consisting of 33 fuzzy rules) was created and the $FMFs$ tuning operator ANFIS was applied to it.

Furthermore, in this paper, we propose the use of a variant of an unsupervised clustering algorithm available in the MatLab® Fuzzy Clustering Toolbox. If the considered classes represent the clusters (i.e., outputs of the procedure), each FS_s (which represents a point in the space occupied by the clusters) is associated with the closest cluster. Updating of the positions of the clusters was carried out by minimizing an objective function on the quadratic error, which was constructed starting from the measurement of distances between data points and cluster centers.

Finally, for the comparison of performances, SOM maps (particular neural networks with unsupervised learning) were also used, which produced discretized $2D$ maps of the [16] input space. Through a competitive process, the input data participate in the formation of the $2D$ map, with the aim of automatic classification of the data. In this work, an SOM was used, in which FS_s represent the inputs, which was readily available in the MatLab® SOM Toolbox.

---

[11] That is, Aristotelian syllogisms.

7 Relevant Results and Discussion

The soft computing procedure proposed in this paper was implemented on a machine with an Intel Core 2 1.79 GHz CPU and using MatLab® R2019a. Preliminarily, for each Class of external biaxial loads applied, the index of fuzziness (IoF) intervals were evaluated as was formulated in [16], in order to both evaluate the fuzziness content of the data set and to evaluate the fuzziness of the representative image of each class. This computation showed, for each input of the data set, high values of IoF confirming the high content fuzziness of each ECs map (which justifies the use of the proposed procedure based on fuzzy computations). Table 4 shows such ranges, highlighting that the higher the biaxial load applied, the greater the fuzziness contained in the respective ECs maps. This was due to the fact that the increase in the applied biaxial load causes distortions in the plates, such that the ECs in the plate do not pass through preferential circuits but, instead, are channeled into unusual paths inside the plate.

Table 5 displays all the classification performances obtained by the techniques used, highlighting that the procedure proposed in this paper correctly classified more than 99.6% of the images under examination. However, fluctuations in

Table 4. IoF Ranges.

Class	Range IoF	IoF of $F(\mathbf{I_k})$	Class	Range IoF	IoF of $F(\mathbf{I_k})$
C_{180kN}	0.83–0.86	0.84	C_{190kN}	0.83–0.88	0.84
C_{200kN}	0.84–0.87	0.85	C_{210kN}	0.85–0.86	0.89
C_{220kN}	0.87–0.92	0.90	C_{230kN}	0.89–0.93	0.91
C_{240kN}	0.91–0.95	0.92	C_{250kN}	0.93–0.97	0.94
Without Loads	0.95–0.99	0.97			

Table 5. Proposed approach vs. standard soft computing approaches: performance classification.

Technique	CPU time	Pick-up voltage (Real Part)	Pick-up voltage (Imaginary Part)	Pick-up voltage (Amplitude)	Pick-up voltage (Phase)
FS_1	0.34	99.6%	99.7%	99.8%	99.7%
FS_2	0.32	99.9%	99.8%	99.9%	99.9%
FS_3	0.23	99.7%	99.7%	99.7%	99.6%
FS_4	0.14	99.6%	99.7%	99.6%	99.6%
Mamdani	0.34	99.4%	99.5%	99.3%	99.4%
Sugeno	0.96	99.8%	99.7%	99.8%	99.8%
Fuzzy K-Means	1.12	99.5%	99.6%	99.5%	99.5%
SOM	0.88	99.7%	99.5%	99.7%	99.8%

the percentages were highlighted, depending on whether the analyzed images represented the real part, imaginary part, amplitude, or phase of the pick-up voltage. These percentages significantly increased when FS_2 was applied, with obvious advantages both in terms of computational time and complexity, making FS_2 more attractive for real-time applications. By way of example, Fig. 3 depicts an example of classification carried out with the proposed procedure, which clearly highlights that the analyzed ECs image belonged to the C_{220kN} class. Finally, we observed that the classification obtained through all formulations of FS_s offered performances comparable to those obtained by techniques with higher computational complexity (considered in this paper for comparison).

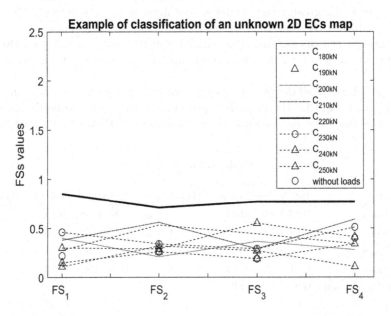

Fig. 3. A classification example related to an unknown 2D ECs image. FSs values obtained with the images representing C_{180kN}, C_{190kN}, C_{2000kN}, C_{210kN}, C_{220kN}, C_{230kN}, C_{240kN}, C_{250kN}, and No Load, respectively. The unknown 2D ECs image belongs to C_{210kN}.

8   Conclusions and Perspectives

In this work, evaluations of FSs were used to assess the integrity of steel plates subjected to biaxial loading. Through ECs of suitable frequency, 2D experimental maps (representing the amplitude, phase, and real and imaginary parts of the pick-up voltage probe) were obtained, which were similar to 2D experimental maps of the deformation distribution over the plate (which, through constitutive laws, provide maps of the distributions of mechanical stresses). These maps were collected in different axes, satisfying the principle according to which similar biaxial loads produce similar deformation distributions. Then, the $2D$ maps were fuzzified with appropriate $FMFs$ and, after evaluating the fuzziness content of each of them, for each class a map was obtained through a new approach based on fuzzy image fusion, giving a $2D$ representative. Subsequently, four different formulations of FSs were exploited to associate (i.e., classify) an unknown load (and, consequently, the distribution of its deformation state) to a class of externally applied biaxial loads. The proposed procedure, thus, translates the study of the distribution of deformations into an equivalent classification problem, confirming the equivalence between $2D$ maps of mechanical deformations with $2D$ maps based on ECs, which are easily obtainable through in situ measurement campaigns thanks to modern portable instruments. The results obtained encourage future research, as the classification performances obtained are completely comparable to the performances obtained with soft computing techniques previously presented in the literature which, computationally, turn out to be more onerous. We observed that the steel plates locally modified their morphology when subjected to dynamic biaxial loads, with consequent variation in the electrical conductivity and magnetic permeability, along with an increase in the uncertainties of the ECs signals sampled in the experimentation phase and/or during the in situ measurement campaigns. It follows that the FSs formulations used in this work could be unsuitable when the applied biaxial loads lose their static characteristic, leaving more refined FSs formulations to future research. Finally, it would be advisable to use step electrical voltages to excite the probe, such that a greater number of frequencies can be used for the excitation current, in order to ensure various depths of penetration into the material.

References

1. Landolfo, R., Mazzolani, F., Dubina, D., da Silva, L.S., D'Aniello, M.: Design of Steel Structures for Buildings in Seismic Areas: Eurocode 8: Design of Structures for Earthquake Resistance. Part 1-1 - General Rules, Seismic Actions and Rules for Buildings. Wiley Online Library (2017)
2. Burrascano, P., Callegari, S., Montisci, A., Ricci, M., Versaci, M.: Ultrasonic Nondestructive Evaluation Systems: Industrial Application Issues. Springer, Heidelberg (2015)
3. Paslar, N., et al.: Investigation of the infill plate boundary condition effects on the overall performance off the steel plate shear walls with circular openings. Structures **27**, 829–836 (2020)
4. Silva, L.C., et al.: Segmented analysis of time-of-flight diffraction ultrasound for flaw detection in welded steel plates using extreme learning machines. Ultrasonics **102**(106057) (2020)
5. Doomra, A., et al.: Effect of post weld heat treatment on metallurgical and mechanical properties of electron beam welded AISI 409 ferritic steel. Metall. Mater. Eng. **26**(3), 545–561 (2020)
6. Murkute, P., et al.: Metallurgical and electrochemical properties of super duplex stainless steel clads on low carbon steel substrate produced with laser powder bed fusion. Sci. Rep. **10**(10162) (2020)

7. Cacciola, M., La Foresta, F., Morabito, F.C., Versaci, M.: Advanced use of soft computing and eddy current test to evaluate mechanical integrity of metallic plates. NDT E Int. **40**(5), 357–362 (2007)
8. Tsukada, K., et al.: Detection of inner corrossion of steel construction using magnetic resistence sensor and magnetic spectroscopy analysis. IEEE Trans. Magn. **52**(7), 1–4 (2016)
9. Morabito, F.C.: Independent component analysis and feature extraction techniques for NdT data. Mater. Eval. **58**(1), 85–92 (2000)
10. Greco, A., et al.: A Morlet wavelet classification technique for ICA filtered sEMG experimental data. In: Proceedings of the International Joint Conference on Neural Networks, pp. 166–171 (2003)
11. Bachmann, M., et al.: Finite element modeling of an alternating current electromagnetic weld pool support in full penetration laser beam welding of thick duplex stainless steel plates. J. Laser Appl. **28**(022404) (2016)
12. Lu, M., et al.: Determination of the magnetic permeability, electrical conductivity, and tickness of ferrite metallic plates using a multifrequency electromagnetic sensing system. IEEE Trans. Ind. Inf. **15**(7), 4111–4119 (2019)
13. Angiulli, G., et al.: Reconstructing the membrane detection of a $1D$ electrostatic-driven mems device by the shooting method: convergence analysis and ghost solutions identification. Comput. Appl. Math. **37**(4), 4484–4498 (2018)
14. Versaci, M., Calcagno, S., Cacciola, M., Morabito, F.C., Palamara, I., Pellicanò, D.: Innovative fuzzy techniques for characterizing defects in ultrasonic nondestructive evaluation. In: Burrascano, P., Callegari, S., Montisci, A., Ricci, M., Versaci, M. (eds.) Ultrasonic Nondestructive Evaluation Systems, pp. 201–232. Springer, Cham (2015). https://doi.org/10.1007/978-3-319-10566-6_7
15. Postorino, M.N., Versaci, M.: A neuro-fuzzy approach to simulate the user mode choice behaviour in a travel decision framework. Int. J. Model. Simul. **28**(1), 64–71 (2008)
16. Chaira, T., Ray, A.K.: Fuzzy Image Processing and Applications with MATLAB. CRC Press, Taylor & Francis Group (2015)
17. Hong, D.H., Kim, C.: A note on similarity measures between vague sets and between elements. Inf. Sci. **12**, 922–927 (2016)
18. Liang, Z.Z., Shi, P.F.: Similarity measures on intuitionistic fuzzy sets. Pattern Recogn. Lett. **24**, 2687–2693 (2003)
19. Ye, J.: Cosine similarity measure for intuitionistic fuzzy sets and their applications. Math. Comput. Model. **53**, 91–97 (2011)
20. Li, Y., et al.: Similarity measures between vague sets and vague entropy. J. Comput. Sci. **29**, 129–132 (2012)

An Indirect Approach to Forecast Produced Power on Photovoltaic Plants Under Uneven Shading Conditions

Valentina Lucaferri[1], Martina Radicioni[1], Francesco De Lia[2],
Antonino Laudani[5], Roberto Lo Presti[2], Gabriele Maria Lozito[3],
Francesco Riganti Fulginei[5(✉)], Massimo Panella[4], and Riccardo Schioppo[2]

[1] Department of Engineering, University of Roma Tre,
Via Vito Volterra 62, 00146 Rome, Italy
[2] Casaccia Research Center, ENEA, via Anguillarese 301, 00060 Rome, Italy
[3] Department of Information Engineering, University of Florence, Via S.Marta 3,
50139 Firenze, Italy
[4] Department of Information Engineering, Electronics and Telecommunications,
Sapienza University of Rome, via Eudossiana 18, 00184 Rome, Italy
[5] Department of Industrial, Electronic and Mechanical Engineering - DIIEM,
University of Roma Tre, Via Vito Volterra 62, 00146 Rome, Italy
riganti@uniroma3.it

Abstract. In this paper a forecasting method is proposed for the prediction of the generated power in photovoltaic systems. The approach exploits the combination of a virtual irradiance sensing methodology and a neural network forecasting system. The strength of this approach resides in its capability to support forecasting in presence of distributed shading patterns along the PV plant, without the necessity of external pyranometers or a complex data acquisition system. The technique was validated experimentally by forecasting the produced power on a PV array mounted on the building roof at the ENEA research center of Casaccia (Rome, Italy), and shows very good results in the forecasting of One Day- Ahead PV generated power. The results obtained validate this approach as a competitive option to pyranometer-based monitoring in PV installations.

Keywords: Photovoltaic · Power forecasting · Irradiance estimation · Neural networks

1 Introduction

The last two decades have experienced a deep penetration of renewable energy sources in the world energy market driven by both economic and environmental factors. Among renewable energies, photovoltaics (PV) deserve a prominent place. When dealing with PV, the main concern is the intermittent nature of the supplied power. The great variability of PV produced power, strongly dependent on environmental conditions, creates problems for the PV energy management,

© The Author(s), under exclusive license to Springer Nature Switzerland AG 2022
M. Mahmud et al. (Eds.): AII 2022, CCIS 1724, pp. 29–43, 2022.
https://doi.org/10.1007/978-3-031-24801-6_3

especially if enclosed in a Smart Grid where the control of power flows is fundamental [3], or in a Renewable Energy Community, where the daily profiles of generated power are key assets in managing energy exchange [17]. Indeed, a strategy commonly adopted to overcome production variability in smart grids is to couple the PV system with a storage system. In this case it is important to estimate accurately the amount of energy produced in order to optimize its distribution among load(s) and battery banks [15].

In a broader perspective, management decisions should be implemented to inject/withdraw energy in/from the electricity grid as required (i.e., according to excess or lack of energy with respect to the load demand). Lastly, but not less important, energy production estimation is relevant for trading tin the energy market, also in view of energy community. Hence, effective power prediction methods are needed for an optimal management of the electricity grid and to preserve energy quality. However, the development of a prediction methodology for energy production is far from simple, due to the non-linear nature of the current-voltage (I-V) characteristic of PV devices and their remarkable variability with environmental conditions, above all temperature and irradiance. The resulting challenge is the necessity of installing several dedicated sensors for these quantities. Although, theoretically, the environmental information could be acquired from the closest meteorological station, the spatial variability of the quantities often makes these measurements useless for energy production assessment. Consequently, expensive irradiance sensors, known as pyranometers, are used to address the problem by acquiring locally the irradiance. In this case, the problem of the number (and therefore the cost) and displacement of these irradiance sensors for large PV arrays, where the shading pattern has to be detected all along the plant, represents a serious drawback that influences the performance of any energy forecasting approach. For this reason, this issue is widely treated in scientific and technical literature. In particular, PV power forecasting methods are often divided in three groups. Statistical methods are based on the use of past information, trying to establish relations between historical data and output, see [20]; physical methods do not require large sets of data and are based on mathematical models for PV power forecasting [2]; finally, approaches based on Artificial Intelligence (AI) are gaining the greatest interest in the scientific community. Most of them belong to the Machine Learning (ML) and Deep Learning (DL) families, and in particular, with the use of Artificial Neural Networks (ANN). Several recent works can be found using ANNs for power forecasting, analyzing the problem with different methodologies and points of view. In the following, some of the most interesting approaches will be briefly introduced. In [23], a hybrid model based on deep learning is proposed, which makes use of sky image opportunely pre-processed and clustered, and the results are compared with those of other ANN-based techniques, such as Convolutional Neural Networks (CNN) and Long-Short Term Memory Neural Networks (LSTM). In [11] a method based on the preprocessing through Wavelet Packet Decomposition (WPD) and a Long-Short-Term Memory (LSTM) neural network from is implemented to provide PV power forecasting and the results are compared with other architectures such as stand-alone LSTM, Recurrent

Neural Networks (RNN), Multi-Layer Perceptrons (MLP) and Gate-Recurrent Units (GRU) presented in literature.

In [18] a tool is proposed to provide an hourly-averaged day-ahead photovoltaic power forecast, based on data-driven machine learning approaches and on a statistical post-processing stage. In particular, the system consists of an ANN, a weather clustering for classifying daily irradiance profiles and a post-processing optimizing stage. In [12] different types on ANNs are developed and compared for different time horizons and tested on a microgrid installed at University of Trieste, achieving very good accuracy results. In [22] a day-ahead PV power forecasting approach is presented, based on two novel CNN, involving historical PV power series, numerical weather predictions and meteorological elements. In many cases, different AI approaches are mixed together to constitute powerful prediction tools, see for example [13]. [19] presents three PV power prediction models based on deep learning neural network (CNN, LSTM and hybrid models based on CNN and LSTM); the three solutions are compared and the results confirm the robustness and stability of the proposed models. Lastly, in [10], once again, two different types of neural networks are mixed to achieve accurate results. The heterogeneous nature of these works, and the heavy use of hybrid architectures, underline that the main attention was given to creating complex strategies to overcome the limitations of data availability and accuracy. Thus, implementing a reliable strategy to acquire data can create opportunities to enhance all the machine learning techniques. In this work a simple and general approach is proposed for power generation forecasting. The approach exploits the synergy between a virtual irradiance sensor, able monitor locally any partial shadowing, and a well-established neural network approach [14] for power forecasting. The combination of the two approaches allows the forecasting even in the non-uniform shading conditions that are present in the specific PV plant chosen for this study. The proposed strategy is modular, and the virtual irradiance sensing part can be combined with more complex ML or DL approaches to manage larger problem or create forecasting for longer time horizons. By itself, the strategy manages to achieve excellent accuracy through a lean ANN structure, creating a simple and economic solution that does not need any commercial pyranometer or dedicated irradiance sensor.

The paper is structured as follows: Sect. 2 introduces the problem of the power estimation on a generic PV plant and the methods developed in this paper to effectively produce an accurate power prediction; then, the forecasting strategy is presented and the case of study is illustrated. In Sect. 3 the results are reported for both the accuracy of the virtual sensing strategy and the power forecasting, and comparisons are made with other works present in literature such as LSTM and CNN neural networks. Conclusions and final remarks close this paper.

2   Materials and Methods

This section presents the challenge of locally assessing solar irradiance on a generic PV plant, and the methods developed in this work to provide the ANN with reliable data to create an accurate forecasting. In particular, the proposed approach is compared with a traditional one using pyranometers for irradiance estimation. Concerning the ANN model, the architecture developed in [14] is herein adapted for the present case and it is briefly presented. Lastly, the case of study is presented and details are given on the PV plant.

2.1   Power Estimation from Irradiance Data on a PV Plant

Power production from a PV source is subject to an efficiency that is influenced by several factors. Among these, the irradiance and its spatial distribution play a central role. For instance, in a PV plant that is not uniformly irradiated some shaded cells or modules have lower power production and if precautions are not taken, can act as bottlenecks for the whole string. These conditions determines, in general, power losses. For this reason, the accuracy of irradiance data fed to any ML model (including the ANN proposed in this work) deeply influences the precision of predicted power. Moreover, the training data set is built upon measurements, and the ones related to solar radiation levels must be as correlated as possible with effective normal irradiance on the PV plant/string/module. For this reason, an approach able to overcome the use of specific irradiance sensors, by substituting them with virtual ones, is proposed. In order to show the features and the characteristics of this novel strategy, a comparison against a traditional approach, using a physical sensor, is proposed. The following methods will be denominated as "*Method 1*" for the use of a real physical irradiance sensor, and "*Method 2*" for the use of a virtual irradiance sensor.

Method 1 (Real Sensor). The traditional way to determine irradiance is based on data acquired through dedicated sensors. Such devices are known as pyranometers and have to be rigidly secured to the PV device whose irradiance value is needed. If the irradiance pattern of a large PV plant has to be known, several sensors should be placed along the plant in order to detect any possible shadow. If the individual modules are not equipped with a pyranometer, local shadowing could pass undetected. For instance, in Fig. 1, the installed pyranometer would only be able to sense the irradiance value of the left module, but the cloudiness affecting the right module would not be detected. The most obvious solution to this problem might seem to be increasing the number of sensors throughout on the plant. However, the mounting procedure on the PV device is not trivial, since the pyranometer should be fixed to obtain the same tilt and angle of the module, which requires a specific rigid structure perfectly parallel to the PV device. Moreover, a pyranometer is not an economic equipment; beyond the cost of the sensor itself, a pyranometer needs periodic calibrations to be carried out in specific testing laboratories to keep its accuracy high - such as prescribed in the IEC 61724-1: 2017 standards.

Method 2 (Virtual Sensor). A valid alternative to a real sensor is to use the PV device as a sensor itself. If the PV device performs the sensing, it is possible detect any shading pattern affecting PV plants, see for example Fig. 2. At the core of the virtual sensor approach is a closed form formula developed in [1], based on the well-known One Diode equivalent circuit model for PV devices. The approach is so accurate that offers the possibility of completely replacing the pyranometers with virtual sensors. The closed-form for the calculation of irradiance derives from algebraic manipulations of the photogenerated current formula as explained in [1,6]:

$$i_{pv} = I_{Irr} - I_0\left[exp\left(\frac{v_{pv} + R_s i_{pv}}{nqkT}\right) - 1\right] - \frac{v_{pv} + R_s i_{pv}}{R_p} \tag{1}$$

In the Eq. (1) it is possible to recognize some important parameters such as the series resistance, R_S, the shunt resistance, R_P, the ideality factor of the diode, n, the irradiation current, I_{Irr}, and the saturation current of the diode, I_0: the knowledge of these 5 parameters is fundamental for the calculation of the irradiance (see [9]); finally, T is the operating temperature of the device, $k = 1.38 \times 10^{-23} \frac{J}{K}$ the Boltzmann constant and $q = 1.602 \times 10^{19} C$ is the electron charge. In Eq. (1), the dependencies of the parameters from atmospheric conditions, i.e., irradiance and temperature, have to be considered [16]; the subscript ref refers to quantities measured at Standard Reference Conditions of temperature and irradiance, i.e., $T_{ref} = 25\ C^\circ$ and $G_{ref} = 1000\ \frac{W}{m^2}$:

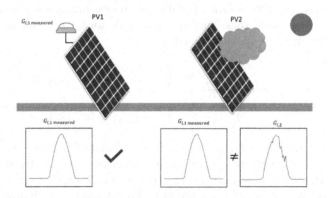

Fig. 1. Method 1 for assessing solar irradiance on a PV module.

$$R_s = R_{s,ref} \tag{2}$$

$$R_p = R_{p,ref} \cdot \frac{G_{ref}}{G} \tag{3}$$

$$I_{irr} = I_{irr,ref} \cdot \frac{G}{G_{ref}} \cdot (1 + \alpha_T(T - T_{ref})) \tag{4}$$

$$I_0 = I_{0,ref} \cdot \left[\frac{T}{T_{ref}}\right]^3 e^{\frac{E_{g,ref}}{k \cdot T_{ref}} - \frac{E_g(T)}{k \cdot T}} \tag{5}$$

$$n = n_{ref} \tag{6}$$

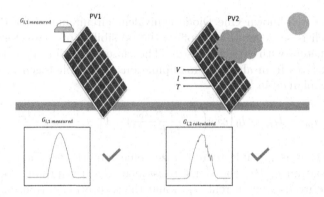

Fig. 2. Method 2 for calculating solar irradiance on a PV module.

where α_T the short circuit temperature coefficient and $Eg(T)$ the bandgap energy of silicon in eV expressed as a function of T ($E_{g,ref} = E_g(T_{ref})$).

The other information necessary to use the formula are the cell temperature and the operating point of the photovoltaic device, i.e., operating current and voltage, see Fig. 2. Having entered this data and injected equations from 2 to 6 in Eq. (1), it is possible to trace a daily irradiance profile on any module or photovoltaic array. After some algebraic manipulations, the resulting analytical formula for irradiance G_{cal} is obtained:

$$G_{cal} = G_{ref} \frac{i_{pv} + I_{0,ref}\left[\frac{T}{T_{ref}}\right]^3 [e^{\left(\frac{v_{pv}+i_{pv}R_{s,ref}}{nqkT}\right)} - 1]e^{\left(\frac{E_{g,ref}}{kT_{ref}} - \frac{E_g}{kT}\right)}}{I_{irr,ref} + \alpha_T(T - T_{ref}) - \frac{v_{pv}+i_{pv}R_{s,ref}}{R_{p,ref}}} \quad (7)$$

The previous formula is effective and able to calculate irradiance with an error around 5% with respect to the measured quantities, see [1] for details. The accuracy of the approach can be estimated with precision through a sensitivity analysis, as shown in [6]. In our approach the calculated irradiance is used to define a term, $S(t)$, to take into account the shading affecting the PV string or group of strings. Such a term is the ratio between the afore-mentioned calculated irradiance, G_{cal}, and the forecasting of irradiance from meteorological station, $G_{forecast}$

$$S(t) = \frac{G_{cal}(t)}{G_{forecast}(t)} \quad (8)$$

This term will be used to feed ANN, as will be explained in the following Sect. 3.2.

2.2   ANN Structure

The scientific literature underlines the wide use of ANN in forecasting applications thanks to their ability to adapt and generalize to very difficult functional relationships. The well-known Feed-Forward (FF) architecture, thanks to its simple structure, it is able to achieve good performance with low computational costs. At the same time, the presence of a single hyperparameter (the number of neurons in the hidden layer) simplifies the process of optimal sizing of the ANN. The FF networks can also be used to process time-series for the purpose of forecasting. Management of time-series is in general obtained by considering a delay line at the input of the network (thus spreading the same quantity, at different times, on different inputs). However, a more advanced approach involves the use of ANNs that are inherently dynamic. These network, often addressed as Recurrent Neural Networks (RNN) reuse past inputs and/or outputs that are re-injected into the network through feedback loops. A network of this type is generally more efficient in determining time dependent models. Therefore, in the present case, the architecture of the FF network has been modified by adding dynamic feedback: each neuron of the hidden layer has the ability to process previous values together with new input signals. The network profile is shown in Fig. 3. In particular, the proposed neural network provides a daily forecast of the power produced and has the following input: t, a variable representing the time mapping, having a sinuosidal shape with a period of 24 h; T, ambient temperature; $G(t)_{forecast} S(t)$, actual irradiance (further details will be given in the following section) and $P(t - \Delta t)$, former prediction of power for the previous quarter of hour. In particular, at each computing step, the last forecasted power value, $P(t - \Delta t)$, is brought back as an input of the network in a closed loop feedback. The ANN is trained to give in output the next power value, $P(t)$. As far as the network layers is concerned, as will be demonstrated in the final Sections, a single hidden layer is sufficient to achieve accurate prediction results: hence, it was not necessary to include additional layers that would only make the architecture of the ANN more complex and the forecasting stage computationally demanding. The activation function used are sigmoidal for the hidden layer and linear for the output layer. The number of neurons, instead, was determined in a range from 5 to 10, which guarantees a good trade-off between accuracy and simplicity, allowing its implementation also in low cost microcontroller and embedded system [7, 8].

Finally, in order to provide the ANN with a reasonable training set, it has been chosen to use input data relative to 20 days before the forecasting. For the forecast of each day, the ANN must be trained with the previous 20 days of data. The training of the ANN is performed using the Levenberg-Marquardt algorithm, running under Matlab2021 environment, also used for the setup and simulation. The measurement of the accuracy of any forecast model is performed by means of standardized performance errors: Root Mean Square Error (RMSE), Weighted Mean Absolute Percentage Error (WMAPE) and Mean Absolute Error (MAE) are evaluated in order to simplify the comparison with other neural models present in the literature.

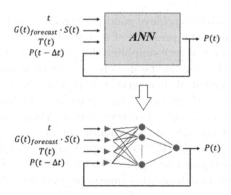

Fig. 3. Input data of the ANN for the forecasting stage.

2.3 Case Study

ENEA F40 Smart Building and Installed PV System. Data used for this study is acquired from the Demonstrator of the F40 building of ENEA research center of Casaccia (Rome, Italy). The F40 is a *"second generation"* Smart Building, that includes energy production and storage systems, as well as control and management devices for the energy flow. All the monitoring and control equipment can be remotely managed.

The photovoltaic system, installed on the roof of the F40 building, has a peak power of approximately 18 kW, and is equipped with a 12 kWh lithium storage system. The plant is equipped with an intelligent monitoring system that allows the acquisition of the physical and electrical quantities relating to its operation. The system consists of 56 mono c-Si photovoltaic modules installed on the roof of the building. The 18.2 kWp photovoltaic generator consists of 6 independent strings (4 of them consist of 9 modules and 2 of 10 modules) connected according to the series configuration (S). The strings of 9 and 10 modules have, respectively, nominal power of 3.25 kW and 2.925 kW; each of the modules has a nominal power of 325 W.

The PV system is also equipped with special sensors to allow the acquisition of environmental quantities. Air temperature, backside modules temperature, relative humidity and irradiance (both horizontal and normal to the modules) are measured with a time step of 15 s, and recorded every 24 h on a daily file saved on the plant NAS (Network Attached Storage). Each file is composed by 5760 samples. The plant has been in operation since December 2019. For this application, it was chosen to carry out quarter-hour averages of the data collected, obtaining daily files of 96 samples. As far as the operating point of the PV device is concerned, a code has been developed in Matlab capable of acquiring the working point of the string at one minute step. The code makes it possible to read the operating voltage and current values of the string with a preset time step. The Matlab work environment allowed the implementation of a Modbus-TCP type communication with the plant inverters and direct access to the Modbus registers of interest.

The Issue of the Shading Pattern of the PV Field. Figure 4 shows the photovoltaic system installed on the roof of the F40 building, described above. For clarity, it is necessary to say that the 6 strings that make up the system are divided into groups of 2 strings each, forming 3 independent arrays. The 3 groups of strings will be indicated as React1, React2 and React3, to distinguish them from each other. Irradiance sensors are mounted only on React1. Since React1 has different daily shading patterns from the ones of React2 and React3, the daily irradiance vector acquired by the irradiance sensors takes into account shadows that fall on React1, and does not consider those present on React2 and React3. The shadows on the strings are determined by some structures placed on the roof of the building and adjacent to the system, see Figs. 5 and 6. The shadings that these structures determine are not constant throughout the year, but are concentrated in winter, approximately in the months between November and February. In particular, the shadows are distributed as explained below:

- React 1: shading is present during the morning (approximately between 10 a.m. and 11 a.m.);
- React 2: the shadows are concentrated in the middle of the day, and then again in the early afternoon;
- React 3: shading occurs only in the afternoon.

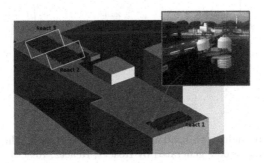

Fig. 4. The photovoltaic system installed on the roof of the F40 building: the irradiance sensor is mounted on React1.

Since the shadings are different among the 3 Reacts, their power production profile will be different as well. However, only the profile from React1 will be coherent with the irradiance profile. This can be clearly seen in Fig. 7.

Fig. 5. The shadows that fall on React1 at 10am and 11am on 11 March 2021.

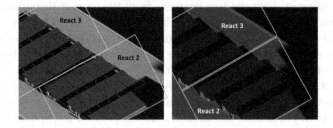

Fig. 6. The shadows that fall on React2 and React3 at 1pm and 3pm on 11 March 2021.

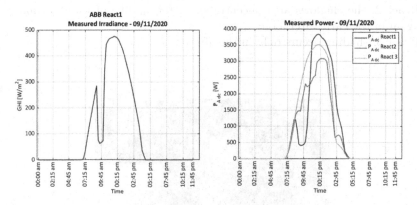

Fig. 7. From left to right: the irradiance profile measured by the pyranometer on React1; the PV power profile generated by React1, React2, React3.

3   Results

This section is dedicated to the presentation of obtained results. The first test presented in Sect. 3.1, and regards the accuracy of the virtual sensor. The sensor accuracy is validated on the PV system under exam against the measurements achieved by the pyranometer of React1; test are performed on different days with various degrees on cloudiness. The second test, presented in Sect. 3.2, assess the capabilities of PV power production forecasting by using the neural system described in Sect. 2.2.

3.1 Effectiveness of Closed-Form Irradiance

As a first step, the validity of the analytical formula introduced in the previous section is demonstrated for the present application. Hence, irradiance profiles of React1 related to different days are compared against the irradiance calculated through the virtual irradiance sensor. The calculated irradiance profiles of React 1 are compared with the measurements of the installed pyranometer. The results presents a percentage error that is always lower than 7%, in particular, it is equal to 5.9% for 17/02, 5.6% for 26/02, 4.2% for 07/03 and 5.5% for 11/03, see Fig. 9. From the results obtained it is evident that the calculation of irradiance in closed form is able to approximate the measured irradiance profile with a very low percentage error with respect to the measured quantity, both in the case of perfectly sunny days and in days with partial cloud cover. The excellent results justify the use of this indirect approach to estimate irradiance for PV modules and string for which irradiance sensors are not available.

3.2 Forecast

The second validation test regards the power forecast for all the available sub-plants. In order to better analyze the gain in performance of the implemented strategy, two different configurations are compared. For each configuration, the results shows the sum of the predicted power of the three React.

Each configuration comes from the application of one method instead of another, Method 1 of Method 2 as explained in Sect. 2.1, see Fig. 8. In particular:

– Configuration 1: Irradiance is obtained by Method 1 from the sensors on React 1. The same irradiance is considered for React2 and React3, thus introducing the errors related to the uneven shading of the PV plant.
– Configuration 2: Irradiance is obtained on the three Reacts individually by means of Method 2. Individual shadings of the Reacts are detected.

In order to calculate irradiance values, as can be seen from Eq. (7), the operating point of the PV plant has to be acquired. This is managed periodically by a specific routine that acquires the operating voltages and currents for the three React. Using this data, the irradiance profiles were calculated and used to create the training datasets for the ANN. Once the training is completed, some additional data is needed for the forecasting stage. The prediction for the following day makes use of weather predictions, but irradiance prediction, in particular, is not able to take into account the systematic shadows affecting the plant. In other words, a shading profile representing the effect of the geometric structures present on the roof of F40 building must be included. For this purpose, to perform the power forecasting, the actual irradiance input of the ANN consists of a shading term multiplied by the forecasted irradiance for the next day:

$$G_{input}(t) = G_{forecast}(t) \cdot S(t) \tag{9}$$

where G_{input} is the input to be fed to the ANN (previously shown in Fig. 3) and $G_{forecast}$ the irradiance prediction for the following day. A comparison between

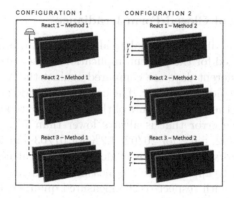

Fig. 8. Explanation of the two implemented Configurations.

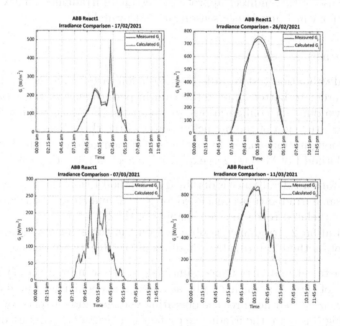

Fig. 9. Comparisons between measured and calculated irradiance for 4 different days.

the PV power forecasted through each of the 2 configurations and the measured power was made on different days and their results obtained are summarized in Table 1. It can be concluded that Configuration 2 is the more effective: for all days, errors are lower in this case. Lastly, the presented method is compared with other forecasting strategies proposed in literature, see Table 2. In [4] an LSTM (long-short term memory) neural network is used; in this work minimum WMAPE is reported to be around 20 % while in our case it is always less than 6 %. In [21] another ANN-based PV power prediction method is shown in which the ANN is trained through satellite images. The paper reports a minimum WMAPE that is 22.5 %, similar to that reported for the previous work. Paper [12] instead, analizes some of the most promising deep-learning techniques present in literature such as LSTM, recurrent networks with GRU (Gated Recurrent Units) and Convolutional Neural Networks (CNN); the minimum error reached, reported as MAPE, is 8 %, slightly above our results. Finally in [5] a probabilistic approach is presented based on a CNN that reports errors around 20 %; definitively, our approach can be considered effective and suitable for providing good PV power predictions.

Table 1. Errors (RMSE, WMAPE and MAE) on power predictions of the whole system obtained using 3 Configurations of methods and referred to different days.

	11/03/2021		
	RMSE [W]	WMAPE [%]	MAE [W]
Configuration 1 - React1 + React2 + React3	566.15	5.45	195.37
Configuration 2 - React1 + React2 + React3	187.29	2.60	94.99
	26/05/2021		
	RMSE [W]	WMAPE [%]	MAE [W]
Configuration 1 - React1 + React2 + React3	1615.00	19.12	1011.00
Configuration 2 - React1 + React2 + React3	237.83	2.92	154.46
	27/05/2021		
	RMSE [W]	WMAPE [%]	MAE [W]
Configuration 1 - React1 + React2 + React3	591.50	6.17	328.33
Configuration 2 - React1 + React2 + React3	167.25	1.82	96.82
	06/06/2021		
	RMSE [W]	WMAPE [%]	MAE [W]
Configuration 1 - React1 + React2 + React3	623.92	12.78	386.16
Configuration 2 - React1 + React2 + React3	359.35	6.17	186.63
	07/06/2021		
	RMSE [W]	WMAPE [%]	MAE [W]
Configuration 1 - React1 + React2 + React3	1371.00	17.59	836.44
Configuration 2 - React1 + React2 + React3	411.91	3.92	186.45

Table 2. Error comparison with state of the art: WMAPE in our application is always below 6 %.

	WMAPE [%]
LSTM, [4]	20
Hybrid LSTM, [21]	22.5
GRU, [12]	8
Hybrid CNN, [5]	20

4 Conclusions

This paper addresses the issue of One Day-Ahead forecasting of PV generated power. The developed method is based on an analytical formulation for virtual irradiance estimation and a lean neural model. The method differs from complex ML and DL strategies since it is based on a shallow neural architecture, which allows simpler training with lower computational costs. Since the strategy uses virtual sensors, the problems associated to the classic use of pyranometers are not present, resulting in technical and economical advantages. The strategy of simple implementation since all the quantities required for the virtual sensing are the PV module operating conditions and the five parameters characterizing the equivalent One Diode model. The irradiance values calculated through this method yields predictions as accurate as those obtained using the physical pyranometer. This evidence further supports the possibility to substitute physical pyranometers with the developed innovative virtual sensing approach. The method was tested on real case study featuring a PV plant where the problem of recurrent shading is significant. The strategy outperformed the classic approaches showing excellent forecasting results. Finally, in order to overcome the actual limits when you face with more complex systems, in the next works the authors will try to use deep neural networks.

References

1. Carrasco, M., Laudani, A., Lozito, G., Mancilla-David, F., Fulginei, F.R., Salvini, A.: Low-cost solar irradiance sensing for PV systems. Energies **10**, 998 (2017). https://doi.org/10.3390/en10070998
2. Dolara, A., Leva, S., Manzolini, G.: Comparison of different physical models for PV power output prediction. Sol. Energy **119**, 83–99 (2015). https://doi.org/10.1016/j.solener.2015.06.017
3. Hasankhani, A., Hakimi, S.M.: Stochastic energy management of smart microgrid with intermittent renewable energy resources in electricity market. Energy **219**, 119668 (2021)
4. Hossain, M.S., Mahmood, H.: Short-term photovoltaic power forecasting using an LSTM neural network and synthetic weather forecast. IEEE Access **8**, 172524–172533 (2020). https://doi.org/10.1109/ACCESS.2020.3024901
5. Huang, Q., Wei, S.: Improved quantile convolutional neural network with two-stage training for daily-ahead probabilistic forecasting of photovoltaic power. Energy Convers. Manag. **220**, 113085 (2020). https://doi.org/10.1016/j.enconman.2020.113085
6. Laudani, A., Lozito, G.M., Fulginei, F.R.: Irradiance sensing through PV devices: a sensitivity analysis. Sensors **21**(13), 4264 (2021). https://doi.org/10.3390/s21134264
7. Laudani, A., Lozito, G.M., Fulginei, F.R., Salvini, A.: An efficient architecture for floating point based miso neural networks on FPGA. In: 2014 UKSim-AMSS 16th International Conference on Computer Modelling and Simulation, pp. 12–17. IEEE (2014)

8. Laudani, A., Lozito, G.M., Riganti Fulginei, F., Salvini, A.: On training efficiency and computational costs of a feed forward neural network: a review. Comput. Intell. Neurosci. **2015** (2015)
9. Laudani, A., Riganti-Fulginei, F., Salvini, A.: Identification of the one-diode model for photovoltaic modules from datasheet values. Solar Energy **108** (2014)
10. Li, G., Xie, S., Wang, B., Xin, J., Li, Y., Du, S.: Photovoltaic power forecasting with a hybrid deep learning approach. IEEE Access **8**, 175871–175880 (2020). https://doi.org/10.1109/access.2020.3025860
11. Li, P., Zhou, K., Lu, X., Yang, S.: A hybrid deep learning model for short-term PV power forecasting. Appl. Energy **259**, 114216 (2020). https://doi.org/10.1016/j.apenergy.2019.114216
12. Mellit, A., Pavan, A.M., Lughi, V.: Deep learning neural networks for short-term photovoltaic power forecasting. Renew. Energy **172**, 276–288 (2021). https://doi.org/10.1016/j.renene.2021.02.166
13. Niccolai, A., Dolara, A., Ogliari, E.: Hybrid PV power forecasting methods: a comparison of different approaches. Energies **14**, 451 (2021). https://doi.org/10.3390/en14020451
14. Radicioni, M., et al.: Power forecasting of a photovoltaic plant located in ENEA Casaccia research center. Energies **14**(3), 707 (2021). https://doi.org/10.3390/en14030707
15. Ruiz-Abellón, M.C., Fernández-Jiménez, L.A., Guillamón, A., Falces, A., García-Garre, A., Gabaldón, A.: Integration of demand response and short-term forecasting for the management of prosumers' demand and generation. Energies **13**(1), 11 (2020)
16. Soto, W.D., Klein, S., Beckman, W.: Improvement and validation of a model for photovoltaic array performance. Solar Energy **80**(1), 78–88 (2006). https://doi.org/10.1016/j.solener.2005.06.010
17. Talluri, G., Lozito, G.M., Grasso, F., Iturrino Garcia, C., Luchetta, A.: Optimal battery energy storage system scheduling within renewable energy communities. Energies **14**(24), 8480 (2021)
18. Theocharides, S., Makrides, G., Livera, A., Theristis, M., Kaimakis, P., Georghiou, G.E.: Day-ahead photovoltaic power production forecasting methodology based on machine learning and statistical post-processing. Appl. Energy **268**, 115023 (2020). https://doi.org/10.1016/j.apenergy.2020.115023
19. Wang, K., Qi, X., Liu, H.: A comparison of day-ahead photovoltaic power forecasting models based on deep learning neural network. Appl. Energy **251**, 113315 (2019). https://doi.org/10.1016/j.apenergy.2019.113315
20. Wang, Y., Feng, B., Hua, Q.S., Sun, L.: Short-term solar power forecasting: a combined long short-term memory and gaussian process regression method. IEEE Trans. Ind. Electron. **13**, 3665 (2020). https://doi.org/10.3390/su13073665
21. Yu, D., Lee, S., Lee, S., Choi, W., Liu, L.: Forecasting photovoltaic power generation using satellite images. Energies **13**(24), 6603 (2020)
22. Zang, H., Cheng, L., Ding, T., Cheung, K.W., Wei, Z., Sun, G.: Day-ahead photovoltaic power forecasting approach based on deep convolutional neural networks and meta learning. Int. J. Electr. Power Energy Syst. **118**, 105790 (2020). https://doi.org/10.1016/j.ijepes.2019.105790
23. Zhen, Z., et al.: Deep learning based surface irradiance mapping model for solar PV power forecasting using sky image. IEEE Trans. Ind. Appl. **56**, 3385–3396 (2020). https://doi.org/10.1109/tia.2020.2984617

An FPGA-Based Hardware Accelerator for the k-Nearest Neighbor Algorithm Implementation in Wearable Embedded Systems

Antonio Borelli[1], Fanny Spagnolo[2], Raffaele Gravina[2],
and Fabio Frustaci[2(✉)]

[1] Capgemini Engineering Italy, Milano, Italy
antonio.borelli@capgemini.com
[2] Department of Computer Science, Modelling, Electronics and Systems, DIMES,
University of Calabria, Rende, CS, Italy
{f.spagnolo,r.gravina,f.frustaci}@dimes.unical.it

Abstract. The k-Nearest Neighbor (k-NN) is one of the most used Machine-Learning based algorithm performing the classification task. The latter is very used in many application fields, especially in the context of Body Sensor Networks (BSNs) where features of interest have to be extracted from the data collected by wearable sensors. In the last few years, the ever increasing size of the collected data, as well as low-power and high-speed constraints, have brought out the need for hardware-based implementations of the k-NN algorithm. This paper describes an effective approach to design k-NN FPGA-based hardware accelerators. Low-power and high-speed are achieved by exploiting the dedicated Digital Signal Processing (DSP) slices and their fast interconnections typically available in commercial FPGA devices. Moreover, an effective hardware-friendly strategy is proposed in order to avoid the computational bottleneck shown by the sorting step of the algorithm when implemented in software. The new design has been implemented within a complete embedded system on the FPGA platform hosted on the Xilinx Zynq XC7Z020-1CLG400C heterogeneous System on Chip (SoC), and it has been tested for a real wearable application. Compared to the pure software implementation, the new design has shown an execution speed-up of several orders of magnitude, with a total power dissipation of only 198 mW.

Keywords: FPGA · Embedded systems · Machine Learning · HW/SW co–design · k-NN algorithm

1 Introduction

The rapid growth of the wireless sensor technology has enabled a broad range of applications specifically in the context of Body Sensor Networks (BSNs). A

M. Mahmud et al. (Eds.): AII 2022, CCIS 1724, pp. 44–56, 2022.
https://doi.org/10.1007/978-3-031-24801-6_4

BSN is a network of sensors allowing the continuous monitoring of physiological parameters of a user, such as the body temperature, the sleep phase, the heart rate, the EGG and EMG signals, the oxygen saturation, the posture and many others [1]. In a BSN, the sensors may be worn by the user, or implanted in his/her body or also located within his/her proximity. The data gathered by the sensors are typically sent via a wireless communication to a centralized computing platform to be processed and/or sent to the cloud for further computation and feature extraction [2]. The application context where BSNs can be employed is very wide, ranging from health monitoring to entertainment, wellness, work and emergency. Depending on the application scenario, complex computational routines have to be performed on the data acquired by the sensors. Indeed, this is the case when Artificial Intelligence- (AI) and Machine Learning- (ML) based models need to be applied. As an example, a typical computation in the context of a wearable BSN-based application is the extraction of the features of interest from the gathered data in order to perform a classification [3]. The latter is computed by means of ML-based classifiers such as Decision Tree (DT), Support Vector Machine (SVM) and k-Nearest Neighbor algorithm (kNN) [4–6]. Demanding the execution of these computational-intensive ML algorithms to the cloud is a feasible and versatile solution to cope with the hardware resource limitation of embedded sensor systems [2]. Nevertheless, cloud-based approaches need to face relevant issues regarding power consumption of data transmission, data ownership and security and unpredictable latency [7]. For these reasons, moving the computation towards the edge of the BSN has become crucial [8,9]. The edge computing paradigm enables the processing of data directly in the same system where they are gathered, hence assuring a reduced communication delay, higher responsiveness, data protection and lower power dissipation. However, the edge system must be able to locally process the incoming data without failing to meet the latency constraints dictated by the application. Embedded systems based on general purpose processors may not be able to satisfy the constraints imposed by the edge computing design paradigm due to their intrinsic serial execution of the instructions [10].

Field Programmable Gate Arrays (FPGAs) are a promising technology to implement embedded edge systems that can solve the aforementioned issues. Indeed, FPGAs allow to design hardware accelerators of ML-based classifiers by efficiently mapping the task onto a parallel architecture. In the last few years, several research works have proposed FPGA-based hardware architectures for ML-based classifiers [11–17]. In particular, the works [15–17] deal with hardware architectures for the acceleration of the k-NN algorithm. The latter is one of the most used supervised algorithm for the classification of an unknown input instance [18]. The classification process consists in attaching to the instance a label that is typical of a class within a known set. The algorithm has two time consuming computational step: a) the distance calculation phase of the input instance with respect to all of the instances of the training set; and b) the sorting phase. In order to simplify the design time, the works [15–17] make use of High Level Synthesis (HLS) descriptions of the hardware accelerator. An HLS-based tool allows the designer to describe the hardware architecture by means of a high level language such as C/C++. The tool is then able to generate a Hardware Description Language (HDL) version of the architecture that is the actual source to synthesize and implement the intended digital circuit onto the FPGA. Despite its easiness of utilization, the HLS flow requires a fine control over the design and synthesis process, which can be obtained only if directives are used in conjunction with proper hardware-oriented codification. This is especially true for common sorting algorithms such as the bubble sort and bitonic approaches employed in k-NN [15–17], whose straightforward HLS description may fail to use the hardware primitives of the FPGA in the most effective way, thus resulting in inefficient architectures.

This paper deals with a low-power high-speed FPGA-based hardware architecture to accelerate the k-NN algorithm to be employed in embedded edge computing systems for wearable BSN. The proposed design has been described in HDL and the optimized hardware resources of the FPGA, such as the Digital Signal Processing (DSP) slices and their dedicated fast routing, have been instantiated into the code at a low level in order to use them efficiently. For the purpose of a high computational speed, the architecture exploits parallelism for the distance calculation phase and a two stages reduced sorting circuit for the sorting phase. A complete embedded system has been implemented into the Xilinx Zynq XC7Z020-1CLG400C heterogeneous System on Chip (SoC), consisting of a FPGA-based programmable logic (PL) and an ARM-based general purpose processing system (PS), hosted on the Xilinx PynQ-Z1 development board. The designed hardware accelerator has been implemented in the PL, whereas the PS has been used to run the software code (in bare metal mode) needed to orchestrate the data flow from/to the external dynamic memory (DDR). The functionality of the system has been demonstrated on an actual wearable application, coping with the human activity recognition, based on real acquired data. Compared with a pure software solution running on a personal computer (PC), the proposed architecture has shown a speed-up of several orders of magnitude, thus demonstrating its capability to be used in edge computing embedded systems.

2   The k-NN Algorithm

The k-NN algorithm is a classifier that is particularly used in pattern recognition. Its purpose is to classify an unknown input instance $X = (X_n, X_{n-1}, \cdots, X_1)$ by attaching to it a label L, i.e. a reference that identifies the class the instance may belong to. The instance is an $n-$dimensional vector, whose components are named *attributes*. The label can assume a value that is typically an integer number within a finite range, i.e. $L \in [1, \cdots, N]$. The algorithm makes use of a so-called *training set* that is a set of m $n-$dimensional instances Y_i, with $i \in [1, \cdots, m]$, whose labels are known a priori. The first step of the algorithm is the distance calculation d_i between X and each Y_i of the training set. After that, all the m distances are sorted in ascending order and the first k distances, associated to k instances of the training set, are taken into consideration. Eventually, the label for X is chosen as the one with the most of the occurrences within the labels associated to the first k instances of the training set, found by the sorting procedure. The parameter k is an odd positive integer, whose value is typically 3 or 5. The distance calculation can be different according to the chosen metrics. The most used one is the euclidean distance, as reported in Eq. (1):

$$d_i = |X - Y_i| = \sqrt{\sum_{j=1}^{n}(X_j - Y_{ij})^2} \tag{1}$$

The computational complexity of the distance calculation phase is $O(n \cdot m)$. From the above analysis, it is clear that the computational time of the k-NN algorithm mainly depends on n and m. When the training set is composed by a huge number of instances and the number of attributes per instance is large, the latency of a software-based execution of the algorithm may be intolerable for the running application. In the following Sections, a FPGA-based hardware architecture, that is able to speed-up the execution of Eq. (1), will be described and tested for a real-life case study.

3   The FPGA-Based Hardware Accelerator

Figure 1 depicts the scheme of the proposed architecture based on the computational steps of the k-NN algorithm above described. It is composed of four main blocks: the training set memory, the euclidean distance engine, the sorter and the voter. In the following, the hardware implementation of each block will be detailed.

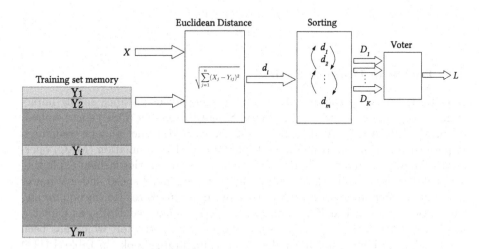

Fig. 1. Scheme of the proposed architecture

3.1   Training Set Memory

The k-NN algorithm requires the distance calculation between the unknown instance X and each instances of the training set Y_i, with $i \in [1, \cdots, m]$. It is therefore important to store the entire training set in order to retrieve the generic instance Y_i when it is needed. In the proposed architecture, the training set is stored into a Block RAM memory (BRAM) within the FPGA chip. FPGA devices, indeed, are equipped with plenty of such hardware primitives. They can be configured as single port and dual port memory. In the proposed design, the memory is supposed to be initialized with the training set data at the beginning of all the operations. The initialization phase, that needs a data flow from the external DDR into the BRAM, will be explained in the following Section. Each attribute of the generic instance Y_i is supposed to be a number expressed in the fixed point format. The number of bits for the integer and decimal part are chosen at design time depending on the possible excursion range of each attribute and the required precision. The attributes are concatenated together so that each instances is composed by $\sum_{j=1}^{n} n\_bit_j$ bits, where n_bit_j is the number of bits required to represent the j-th attribute. After the initialization phase, the memory can be accessed to retrieve the instances of the training set. Single port BRAMs have been used in the proposed design. In a single port BRAM, one single read operation can be performed for each clock cycle. It follows that the subsequent block, i.e. the euclidean distance engine, receives a new data with the same frequency of the clock. It is worth noting that the number of training instances (i.e. m) has an impact on the number of required BRAMs. As an example, in the Xilinx FPGA devices, the available BRAM memories are quantized in 36Kbit blocks. It follows that the number of the required BRAM blocks is:

$$\frac{\sum_{j=1}^{n} n\_bit_j \times m}{36K}$$

3.2   Euclidean Distance Engine

In order to speed-up the execution time, the euclidean distance engine implementing Eq. (1) makes use of the Digital Signal Processing (DSP) slices embedded in the FPGA chip. As depicted in Fig. 2a, each DSP slice may be configured to perform addition, subtraction, multiplication and accumulation (MAC) operations. Moreover, multiple DSPs can be connected in a series fashion exploiting a fast dedicated routing that enables high computational speed and low power dissipation. Such an architecture is particularly useful to realize the square and summation described in Eq. (1) through n series-connected DSPs, as depicted in Fig. 2b. Each term $(X_j - Y_{ij})$ is calculated by a subtractor, which has been described in HDL and implemented with the configurable Look-Up Table (LUTs) of the FPGA. Then, the j-th DSP (DSP_j) performs the squaring operation of the term $(X_j - Y_{ij})$, which is sent to the embedded multiplier through both the input A and B, and accumulates the result with the output $P_{cout,j-1}$ of the previous $(j-1)$-th DSP (DSP_{j-1}). It is worth noting that the output of each DSP slice is registered in order to enable a pipelined computation process and to further increase the system performance. As a consequence, some series-connected registers need to be added on the A and B inputs of the DSP slices with the purpose of synchronizing the latency of each data path. The number of required DSP slices is equal to the number of the attributes n, whereas the number of required FFs is depending both on the number of attributes and their bit length as it follows: $\sum_{j=1}^{n} n\_bit_j \times j$.

After that, it is required to calculate the square root of the final output of the DSP chain. Towards this goal, the proposed architecture exploits a hardware block implementing the COordinate Rotational DIgital Computer (CORDIC) algorithm. The latter is a well-known algorithm typically adopted to implement several non linear mathematical operations such as trigonometric functions and square root. For the sake of design easiness, the available hardware IP logic core, developed by the ARM Xilinx, has been used in the proposed architecture [19]. The IP core has been configured in the parallel operation mode that guarantees the maximum data throughput (one new output each clock cycle) at the expense of a higher number of used hardware resources. In order to alleviate the latter drawback, a numerical approximation has been adopted on the term $\sum_{j=1}^{n}(X_j - Y_{ij})^2$, i.e. the input to the CORDIC block: its decimal part has been truncated so that the square root is applied only to the integer part. Such an approximation allows to have a CORDIC hardware module that has a latency of only 27 clock cycles. In the following, it will be shown that the adopted approximation does not have any impact on the accuracy of the classification for the chosen wearable application. Moreover, the hardware implementation of the CORDIC module

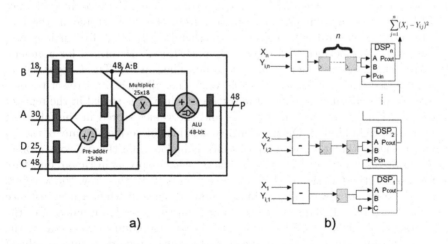

a)   b)

Fig. 2. a) The simplified internal architecture of the DSP48E1 slice and b) the proposed hardware implementation of $\sum_{j=1}^{n}(X_j - Y_{ij})^2$.

onto the Xilinx XC7Z020-1CLG400C SoC will require only 188 LUTs (0.36% of the total) and 256 Flip-Flops (FFs) (0.25% of the total).

3.3 Sorting Module and Voter

In the k-NN algorithm, the computed distances need to be sorted to find the k smallest ones. The key idea is to store only k distances at a time. Once a new distance is produced by the euclidean distance engine, it is compared with the previously stored k values and, if its value is the largest one, it is discarded. On the contrary, if the new distance is lower than at least one of the k distances, the new distance is stored and the highest distance among the previous k ones is discarded. For the described strategy to correctly work, it is important to have the information about which of the k distances is the largest one. Toward this aim, the sorting module has been designed according to the architecture depicted in Fig. 3. It is composed of k registers whose values $Q_1, Q_2, ...Q_k$ are stored in ascending order, i.e. $Q_i \leq Q_{i+1} \forall i \in [1, k-1]$. The activity of each register can be idled by setting its clock enable (CE) input to logic 0. The same CE signal acts as the selector of a following multiplexer. All the CE signals (Sel) are produced by a combinatorial logic described in HDL according to the following Eq. (2):

$$Sel_j = 1 \Leftrightarrow d_i \leq Q_j \quad \forall j \in [1, \ldots, k] \tag{2}$$

From Eq. (2), the following conditions (3) can be inferred:

$$\begin{cases} Sel_j = 0 \Rightarrow Sel_{j-1} = 0 & \forall j \in [2, \ldots, k], \\ Sel_j = 1 \Rightarrow Sel_{j+1} = 1 & \forall j \in [1, \ldots, k-1]. \end{cases} \tag{3}$$

The control logic produces the Sel_i signals by comparing the incoming distance d_i with the Q_i signals in parallel. Starting from the value stored in the first register Q_1, the control logic monitors whether Eq. (2) is verified: if it is not, the same check is performed for $Q_2 \cdots Q_k$ until Eq. (2) is verified for a generic Q_j. After that, the Sel_j signals are set as described in (3). The k registers are first initialized with the highest possible value (i.e. all their bits are set to logic 1). Once a new distance d_i enters the sorting module, it is stored in the register whose position j is individuated by (2) and the values stored in the following positions are right shifted. On the contrary, if (2) is not verified for any of the Q_j values, it means that the incoming distance is higher than the previous k ones, so it can be discarded. Indeed, this is exactly what happens in the architecture of Fig. 3 since the CE signal of all the registers is 0. In this way, the k values in the registers are always stored in ascending order and when a new distance needs to be stored, the largest one goes out form the pipe. Eventually, after the computation of the last euclidean distance, the sorting module stores exactly the k lowest distances. It is worth noting that the sorting module is fully pipelined so that it does not reduce the throughput of the system.

The final k distances, together with their associated label, go into the voter. As stated in the introduction, the typical value of k is 3 or 5. For such low values

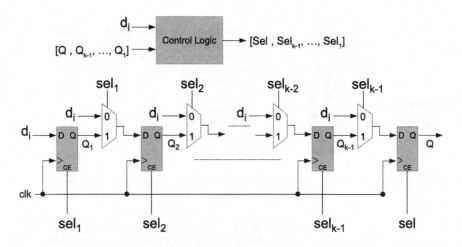

Fig. 3. The hardware architecture of the sorting module.

```
if (Q1.label==Q2.label or Q1.label==Q3.label) then
        label_out <= Q1.label;
elsif (Q2.label ==Q3.label) then
        label_out <= Q2.label;
else
        label_out <= Q1.label;
end if;
```

Fig. 4. Excerpt of the pseudo code describing the voter for $k = 3$.

of k, it is quite easy to describe the voter in HDL by counting the number of instances with the same label. As an example, Fig. 4 reports an excerpt of the pseudocode describing the voter for $k = 3$. It is worth noting that, when all the k labels are different, the first label (i.e. Q1.label in Fig. 4) is selected by default.

4   Case Study

The architecture described in the previous Section is general and it can be adopted regardless of the applications. In this paper, it has been customized for a real wearable computing application performing the user's posture classification. Figure 5 depicts the application scenario. The application requires two inertial sensors about the x, y and z acceleration: the first sensor is located on the user's waist whereas the second one can be put either on his/her shoe or on his/her ankle. The training set features have been selected by means of the Sequential Floating Forward Selection (SFFS) algorithm within a larger set of possible features [20]. The table in Fig. 5 shows the nine attributes for each instance (i.e. $n = 9$) and the required number of bits to code each attribute into a two-complement number. The latter have been dictated by the used 12-bit

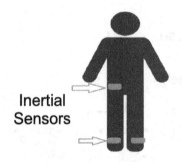

Attribute	MIN	MAX	# of bit
AccXMeanWaist	-1056	280	12
AccYMeanWaist	-1035	1027	12
AccZMeanWaist	-994	1027	12
AccZMaxWaist	-970	1314	12
AccStDevWaist	2	609	11
AccXMeanLeg	-1087	245	12
AccYMeanLeg	-1021	1005	11
AccZMeanLeg	-1001	1031	12
AccZStDevLeg	0	562	11

Inertial
Sensors

Fig. 5. The case study adopted to test the proposed hardware accelerator.

ADCs, which are typically employed in the BSNs. However, our analysis showed that just eleven bits are enough to code the standard deviation measurements. As stated in Sect. 3.1, all the attributes are concatenated to form a single word that results to have 105 bits. The number of possible labels is four, namely *Stand*, *Walk*, *Sit* and *Lye*. Each label has been coded with two bits and concatenated to each instance of the training set. It follows that the word size of the BRAM storing the training set is 107 bits.

Real life experiments have been conducted to gather 1200 instances with a known associated label. After that, the data set has been divided into two sets: the training set, composed of 80% of the collected instances (i.e. 960), and a testing set, composed of 20% of the collected instances (i.e. 240). The latter has been used to test the proposed hardware accelerator.

5   The Complete Embedded System

The proposed hardware accelerator has been integrated as an IP into an embedded system implemented onto the Xilinx Zynq XC7Z020-1CLG400C heterogeneous System on Chip (SoC), hosted on the PynQ-Z1 development board. The complete embedded system architecture is depicted in Fig. 6. The developed accelerator has been implemented on the PL part of the SoC. A Direct Memory Access (DMA) module is used to transfer data from/to the external DDR memory to/from the hardware accelerator via the AXI-Stream interface [21]. The Dual Core ARM-based processor is exploited to program the DMA via an AXI-Lite transaction. Moreover, the processor communicates with the hardware accelerator, through an AXI-Lite interface, in order to configure the latter into two possible operating configuration: initialization and inference. During the initialization phase, the training set is transferred form the DRR into the BRAM of the accelerator via the DMA. The 960 instances of the training set, completed with their associated labels, are transferred via an AXI-Stream interface that allows a parallel transfer of 32-bit for each clock cycle. A purposely designed Finite State Machine (FSM) opportunely concatenates the incoming bits to form 107-bit words. Moreover, it automatically manages the control signals of the BRAM to properly store the assembled words into the right location

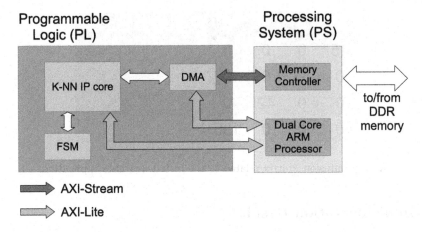

Fig. 6. The case study adopted to test the proposed hardware accelerator.

of the memory. To further increase the computational speed, the proposed accelerator has been parallelized with a factor of 3. That means that the embedded system is provided with 3 copies of the system depicted in Fig. 1 working in parallel. As a consequence, the embedded system employs three BRAMs, each containing $960/3 = 320$ 107-bit locations, where the training set is stored during the initialization phase. It is worth noting that, in this case, the BRAMs requirement is well below the number of resources available on-chip (i.e. 140 BRAMs), which suggests larger training set can be easily mapped within the proposed system. As the training set instances are continuously retrieved from the DDR, the FSM automatically diverts the incoming data towards the following empty BRAM once the previous one has been completely filled.

During the inference phase, the FSM sets the BRAMs into the read mode and three instances of the training set are read in parallel from the three BRAMs at the same clock cycle. Via the DMA, the unknown instance to be classified is transferred from the DDR into the accelerator. Thanks to the adopted parallelism, the euclidean distance calculation is performed in parallel over the three subset the training sets has been divided into: this allows to speed-up the computational time by a factor of about $3\times$. Once the last euclidean distance instance has been computed, each of the three copies of the accelerator eventually stores the k lowest distances (and their associated labels) that refer to a single subset of the training set. After that, a multiplexer sends the $3 \times k$ instances, one for each clock cycle, to a global sorting module, whose design is the same than the one discussed in the previous subsection. After $3 \times k$ clock cycles, the latter module selects the k lowest distances that are finally elaborated by a subsequent voter. In the proposed implementation, the K-NN IP core can be configured to handle two different values of k: 3 and 5. The configuration is selected by the PS that sends the information about the value of k to the IP by an AXI-Lite transaction.

a	b	c	d	← classified as
45	0	0	0	a=0 (stand)
0	53	0	0	b=1 (walk)
0	0	42	0	c=2 (sit)
0	0	0	100	d=4 (lye)

Fig. 7. Confusion Matrix related to the tested wearable application.

6   Implementation Results

The proposed embedded system has been tested for the case study described in Sect. 4. Figure 7 depicts the confusion matrix related to the tested wearable application showing that all the test instances are correctly classified. Table 1 shows the implementation results of the proposed hardware accelerator. It is worth noting that the hardware footprint is particularly limited: indeed, the design occupies just 1827 LUTs (3.4% of the total), 2500 FFs (2.3% of the total) and 27 DSPs (12.3% of the total). The hardware accelerator has a maximum operating frequency of 208 MHz dissipating just 92 mW of dynamic power.

The embedded systems depicted in Fig. 6 has been tested with a frequency of 100 MHz, limited by the DMA module. Experimental tests showed that the time needed to store the training set into the three BRAMs is about 59.6 μs. This time, however, is only required once during the initialization of the system, and it does not affect the classification time. The latter, indeed, has been found to be about 7.3 μs for each input instance. The performance of the proposed embedded system has been compared with the one of a software-based implementation of the k-NN algorithm. The latter has been written in Python and C++ and it has been run on the ARM Cortex A9 dual core CPU (650 MHz clock frequency), hosted in the PS of the used heterogeneous SoC, and on an Intel i7-6500U personal computer (2.5 GHz clock frequency), respectively. Table 2 collects the classification time of each of the implementations. Most notably, it is interesting to underline that the proposed hardware accelerator achieves a speed-up of the classification operation that is more than 5 orders of magnitude faster than the one shown by the software-based implementation of the k-NN algorithm. Such a result clearly demonstrates that FPGAs are ideal platform where implementing ML-based hardware accelerators, such as the proposed k-NN engine. This

Table 1. Implementation features of the proposed k-NN accelerator.

LUTs	FFs	DSP	Tot Power (mW)	Dyn. power (mW)	Frequency (MHz)
1827	2500	27	198	92	208

Table 2. Comparison of the proposed design with a software-based implementation.

Platform	Impl. type	Classification time
ARM A9	Software	46 s
Intel i7-6500U	Software	2.8 s
Proposed Xilinx Zynq XC7Z020	Hardware	7.3 μs

is mostly remarkable for wearable computing applications, where a low power consumption and a reduced hardware footprint are strongly required.

7 Conclusions and Future Works

This paper has described an FPGA-based hardware accelerator of the k-NN algorithm to be applied in the context of Body Sensor Networks (BSNs). The proposed design achieves a low power consumption and a fast classification time by exploiting the DSP slices, to realize the squaring and accumulation operations required by the algorithm, and the dedicated fast interconnects among consecutive DSP slices. Moreover, the design makes use of a smart sorting methodology to take care about the least minimum k distances. When compared with software-based k-NN implementations, the proposed hardware accelerator is able to speed-up the classification phase by more than 5 orders of magnitude, dissipating only 92 mW of dynamic power. The obtained results confirm the effectiveness of the proposed approach to be applied in the context of wearable application, where high performances, low power consumption and a reduced hardware footprint are strongly required. Motivated by the obtained results, we plan to extend the proposed design methodology exploring the possibility to use different FPGA devices. Indeed, more advanced Xilinx FPGA platforms, such as the those based on the Ultrascale architectures, are equipped with more advanced DSP slices that are able to perform not only the accumulation but also the quadratic operation.

Acknowledgement. This work was supported in part by PON Ricerca & Innovazione - MUR (grant 062_R24_INNOVAZIONE), Ministero dell'Università e della Ricerca, Italian Government.

References

1. Gravina, R., Fortino, G.: Wearable body sensor networks: state-of-the-art and research directions. IEEE Sens. J. **21**(11), 12511–12522 (2021)
2. Rofouei, M., Pedram, M., Fraternali, F., Ashari, Z.E., Ghasemzadeh, H.: Resource-efficient computing in wearable systems. In: 2019 IEEE International Conference on Smart Computing (SMARTCOMP), Washington D.C. (US), pp. 150–155 (2019)
3. Baraka, A., Shaban, H., Abou El-Nasr, M., Attallah, O.: Wearable accelerometer and sEMG-based upper limb BSN for tele-rehabilitation. Appl. Sci. **9**(14), 1–22 (2019)

4. Balkhi, P., Moallem, M.: A multipurpose wearable sensor-based system for weight training. Automation **3**(1), 132–152 (2022)
5. Raj, S., Ray, K.C., Shankar, O.: Cardiac arrhythmia beat classification using DOST and PSO tuned SVM. Comput. Methods Programs Biomed. **136**, 163–177 (2016)
6. Ferreira, P.J.S., Cardoso, J.M.P., Mendes-Moreira, J.: kNN prototyping schemes for embedded human activity recognition with online learning. Computers **9**(4), 1–20 (2020)
7. Sun, F., Zang, W., Gravina, R., Fortino, G., Li, Y.: Gait-based identification for elderly users in wearable healthcare systems. Inf. Fusion **53**, 134–144 (2020)
8. Shi, W., Cao, J., Zhang, Q., Li, Y., Xu, L.: Edge computing: vision and challenges. IEEE Internet Things J. **3**(5), 637–646 (2016)
9. Savaglio, C., Gerace, P., Di Fatta, G., Fortino, G.: Data mining at the IoT edge. In: 28th International Conference on Computer Communication and Networks, ICCCN 2019, Valencia, Spain, 29 July–1 August, pp. 1–6 (2019)
10. Liu, X., Zhiqiang, W.: Distributed computing system based on microprocessor cluster for wearable devices. In: 2017 International Conference on Computer Network, Electronic and Automation (ICCNEA), Xi'an, China, pp. 66–71 (2017)
11. Buschjäger, S., Morik, K.: Decision tree and random forest implementations for fast filtering of sensor data. IEEE Trans. Circuits Syst. I Regul. Pap. **65**(1), 209–222 (2018)
12. Kyrkou, C., Bouganis, C.-S., Theocharides, T., Polycarpou, M.M.: Embedded hardware-efficient real-time classification with cascade support vector machines. IEEE Trans. Neural Netw. Learn. Syst. **27**(1), 99–112 (2016)
13. Saqib, F., Dutta, A., Plusquellic, J., Ortiz, P., Pattichis, M.S.: Pipelined decision tree classification accelerator implementation in FPGA (DT-CAIF). IEEE Trans. Comput. **64**(1), 280–285 (2015)
14. Fernandez, D., Gonzalez, C., Mozos, D., Lopez, S.: FPGA implementation of the principal component analysis algorithm for dimensionality reduction of hyperspectral images. J. Real-Time Image Proc. **16**(5), 1395–1406 (2019)
15. Liu, L., Khalid, M.A.S.: Acceleration of k-nearest neighbor algorithm on FPGA using Intel SDK for OpenCL. In: IEEE 61st International Midwest Symposium on Circuits and Systems (MWSCAS), Windsor, ON, Canada, pp. 1070–1073 (2018)
16. Li, Z.-H., Jin, J.-F., Zhou, X.-G., Feng, Z.-H.: K-nearest neighbor algorithm implementation on FPGA using high level synthesis. In: IEEE International Conference on Solid-State and Integrated Circuit Technology (ICSICT), Hangzhou, China, pp. 1–4 (2016)
17. Pu, Y., Peng, J., Huang, L., Chen, J.: An efficient KNN algorithm implemented on FPGA based heterogeneous computing system using OpenCL. In: IEEE 23rd Annual International Symposium on Field-Programmable Custom Computing Machines, Vancouver, BC, Canada, pp. 167–170 (2015)
18. Zhang, S., Li, X., Zong, M., Zhu, X., Wang, R.: Efficient kNN classification with different numbers of nearest neighbors. IEEE Trans. Neural Netw. Learn. Syst. **49**(5), 1774–1785 (2018)
19. AMD Xilinx, CORDIC v6.0 - LogiCORE IP Product Guide, PG105 6 August 2021. https://docs.xilinx.com/v/u/en-US/pg105-cordic. Accessed 15 Apr 2022
20. Saeys, Y., Inza, I., Larrañaga, P.: A review of feature selection techniques in bioinformatics. Bioinformatics **23**(19), 2507–2517 (2007)
21. AMD Xilinx, AXI Reference Guide, UG1037 15 July 2017. https://docs.xilinx.com/v/u/en-US/ug1037-vivado-axi-reference-guide. Accessed 15 Apr 2022

Designing Low-Power and High-Speed FPGA-Based Binary Decision Tree Hardware Accelerators

Roman Huzyuk[1], Fanny Spagnolo[2], and Fabio Frustaci[2]

[1] Akka Italia s.r.l., Milan, Italy
roman.huzyuk@akka.eu

[2] Department of Computer Science, Modelling, Electronics and Systems, DIMES, University of Calabria, Rende, CS, Italy
{f.spagnolo,f.frustaci}@dimes.unical.it

Abstract. With the rapid development of Internet-of-Things (IoT) technologies and edge computing, identifying efficient solutions for data mining tasks such as classification is becoming crucial. Binary Decision Trees (DT) are one of the most used classifiers, due to their ability to handle a large amount of data with a high accuracy. More important, inference of DTs is well suited to be accelerated through custom hardware designs that allow enabling parallel and power-efficient computations with respect to the software-based counterpart. This is very important especially in the context of edge computing, where the computation is performed locally to the data acquisition with a reduced hardware-power budget. This paper describes a novel approach to design low-power and high-speed FPGA-based hardware accelerators of DTs. It is based on the idea of a novel hardware processing element, the so-called *Super PE*, that can be configured to execute in parallel the operation of three nodes belonging to two consecutive levels of the tree: a parent and its two children nodes. When implemented on the FPGA platform hosted on the Xilinx Zynq XC7Z020-1CLG400C heterogeneous System on Chip (SoC), the new design has shown a dynamic power reduction of up to 41%, in comparison with previously published designs based on the conventional PE. Moreover, compared to a pure software-based DT implementation, the proposed hardware accelerator, integrated into a complete embedded system, has shown an execution speed-up of about 21×.

Keywords: FPGA · Embedded systems · Machine Learning · HW/SW co-design · Binary decision trees

1 Introduction

In the last few years, the importance of data mining has rapidly grown in a number of different applications, such as security, multimedia, marketing, medical diagnoses, wearable computing and many others [1]. Data mining is a computational process aiming at extracting useful information from a set of raw data. The latter can have a different nature and they can be analyzed offline, i.e. to support marketing/financial strategies, and/or in real-time, i.e. in wearable medical smart devices in order to monitor the user's condition simultaneously with the data acquisition by sensors. With the growing complexity of the applications, the amount of data to be processed has grown as well and, as a result, data mining algorithms have become more complex and sophisticated. Generally, such algorithms are based on Artificial Intelligence (AI) or Machine Learning (ML) approaches. Despite their proven accuracy and robustness, such techniques demand a huge computational effort that requires powerful and efficient computing platforms to be accomplished. In portable applications, such as wearable devices, the computation can not be realized locally (i.e. close to the acquiring sensors) due to the limited hardware resources and power budget. A typically employed solution is gathering the data by sensors and sending them via a wireless communication to a centralized computing platform. Very often data are sent to the cloud to dedicated servers where the complex software routines, aiming at extracting the features of interest, can be efficiently accomplished [2]. However, cloud-based approaches entail further issues such as power consumption of data transmission, data ownership and security and unpredictable latency [3]. For these reasons, moving the algorithm executions locally has become crucial [4].

A typical data mining task is classification [5]. It consists in assigning a label to a set of measured data (*instance*) identifying the class or the category the monitored scenario belongs to. Classification is typically accomplished by means of ML-based models that are built during a training phase based on a so-called *data set*, i.e. a set of acquired data records. In supervised approaches, the label of the records of the data set are known. The training of a ML model can be executed offline by software routine. Once trained, the model can be deployed onto the intended computing platform for the execution of the inference process. The latter aims at classifying an incoming instance whose label is unknown and its execution is critical for the whole application in terms of power dissipation and latency.

Binary Decision Tree (DT), Support Vector Machine (SVM) and k-Nearest Neighbor algorithm (k-NN) are among the most commonly used ML-based classifiers [6–8]. Embedded systems based on microcontrollers or general purpose processors are typical computing platforms where software-based ML classifiers are locally implemented. Unfortunately, such platforms may not be able to satisfy the power and latency constraints imposed by the local processing paradigm due to the intrinsic serial execution nature of the software instructions [9]. This issue has been exacerbated also by the ever increasing complexity of the classifiers, which are demanded to perform the inference in increasingly complex scenarios. For such a reason, in the last few years, there has been a growing research interest devoted to develop hardware accelerators for ML-based classifiers in order to cope with their high execution times and their demand to handle larger and more complex data sets [10–20]. Field Programmable Gate Arrays (FPGAs) are suitable platforms where implementing hardware accelerators that can solve the aforementioned issues. Indeed, a FPGA-based implementation of a ML classifier can efficiently exploit the power and latency benefits coming from the available parallel hardware resources typically embedded onto a FPGA device.

In particular, the works [10–14] deal with FPGA-based hardware architectures for the acceleration of the binary Decision Tree algorithm. The latter infers the label of the input instance by performing several consecutive comparisons. The comparisons are nested in a tree fashion, where each node of the tree represents a single comparison. The tree is traversed from the root node to one of the leaf nodes, and the particular followed path is based on the results of the comparison operations. The hardware architectures described in previous works [10–14] are based on a replica of a number of so-called *Processing Element* (PE), i.e. a hardware module that can be configured to map the operation of a single layer of the intended decision tree. The hardware design of the previously proposed PEs has been done by means of either High Level Synthesis (HLS) or Hardware Description Language (HDL) descriptions. Previous works demonstrated the effectiveness of a hardware implementation of a DT over its software-based counterpart, both in terms of power dissipation and latency. However, they did not explore the feasibility offered by FPGA devices to achieve further possible improvements.

This paper proposes a novel approach that can be useful to implement low-power and high-speed inference of bynary DT-based classifiers on FPGA devices. The proposed design is still based on the concept of using several PEs. However, differently from the previous works where a single PE maps a single layer of the tree, the proposed PE, named *Super-PE* (DPE), aims at exploiting dependencies between DT nodes to parallelize computations and reduce the amount of resources by mapping two consecutive layers through the same hardware component. The proposed approach is inspired by the working principle of the well-known *Carry Select Adder* topology [21] and it exploits the capability of FPGA-based designs to perform parallel operations. The DT hardware accelerator has been included in a complete embedded system implemented into the Xilinx Zynq XC7Z020-1CLG400C heterogeneous System on Chip (SoC), consisting of a FPGA-based programmable logic (PL) and an ARM-based general purpose processing system (PS), hosted on the PynQ-Z1 development board. The hardware implementation of the DT has been hosted into the PL, whereas the PS has been used to run the software code (in bare metal mode) needed to orchestrate the data flow from/to the external dynamic memory (DDR). The functionality of the system has been demonstrated for actual classification tasks, each of them based of its own DT model. Experimental results showed that the proposed DPE approach is able to reduce the power dissipation by up to 41% compared to the simple PE design methodology. Moreover, the proposed design entails a lower hardware footprint since it needs up to 35.8%, 42.3% and 50% fewer Look-Up Tables (LUTs), Flip-Flops (FFs) and Block RAMs (BRAMs), respectively. Finally, the proposed designed embedded system effectively speeds up the classification task that results to be up to 21× faster than a software-based implementation. All in all, we believe that the presented work is a step forward about efficiently implementing ML-based techniques in the context of edge computing, where hardware resources and power consumption are severely constrained. The rest of the manuscript is organized as follows: Sects. 2 and 3 provide, respectively, a background on DTs and a review of related works; the new *Super-PE* design is described in Sect. 4; implementation results are presented in Sects. 5 and 6, which also show the integration of the proposed *Super-PE* within a complete embedded system; finally, conclusions are drawn in Sect. 7.

2   Working Principle of a Binary Decision Tree

A binary DT classifies an input instance $X = (X_n, X_{n-1}, \cdots, X_1)$ by finding for it a label ω indicating the class the instance may belong to. Generally, the instance can be represented as an n−dimensional vector, whose components are named *attributes*, whereas the label can assume a value that is typically represented by an integer number within a finite range, i.e. $\omega \in [1, \cdots, \Omega]$. A binary DT can be visualized as a tree-fashion structure evolving through several layers, as depicted in Fig. 1. The tree has a *root node* (RN) and several *internal* (IN) and *leaf nodes* (LN). The nodes are organized into k levels $L_1, L_2, \cdots, L_k$ and each internal node has a parent node and two children nodes (left and right). The aim of each INs is to divide the data set into two or more classes. Each node of the binary tree (except the leaf nodes) performs a comparison between an attribute of the input instance X and a fixed value (threshold). The result of the comparison detects a path along the left or right child. The input instance X is inputted to the RN and traverses the tree following a path to a LN depending on the results of the comparison operations. The final LN dictates the label ω of the identified class for X. As an example, Fig. 2 depicts the inference operation of a binary DT where $n = 2$, $\Omega = 3$ and $k = 4$. The tree topology, the attribute and the threshold for the RN and each IN, and the label for each LN define the DT model that is built offline during the training phase. A software-based implementation of a DT model is generally realized with nested *if-then-else* statements. However, as the DT complexity grows up, i.e. for large values of Ω and k, such a strategy is not straightforward, leading to inefficient execution of

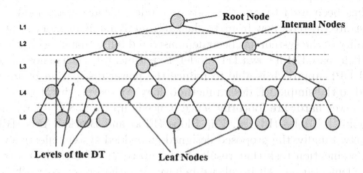

Fig. 1. A general scheme of a Decision Tree

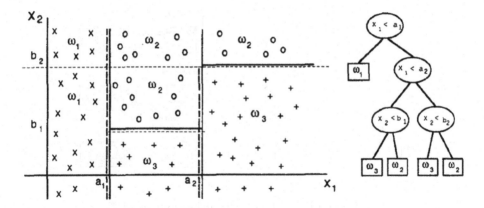

Fig. 2. The inference phase of a binary DT

the resulting software code. In such a case, hardware accelerators of binary DT are highly required.

3 Related Works

The most popular architectural strategy to design a FPGA-based hardware accelerator of a DT, such as the one used in the previous works [10–14], is depicted in Fig. 3. It is based on the fact that a generic input instance X follows a path starting from the RN to a final LN. It follows that, during the inference phase for X, only a subset of the INs are traversed. More importantly, for each level of the DT, only one IN is activated each time. Such a property allows using one hardware module for each level, i.e. one PE that is able to perform the operation of each node belonging to the level. For this purpose, each level is assisted by a Block RAM (BRAM). i.e. a memory storing all the information needed to configure the PE according to which node of the level is active each time. More specifically, each BRAM stores the following information for each of the nodes belonging to the corresponded level: *attribute index* and *threshold*. *Attribute index* is a natural number $i \in [1, \cdots, n]$ identifying the index of the attribute of X that the node needs to compare with the threshold; *threshold* is the number X_i should be compared with. It is worth noting that the generic $BRAM_j$ needs to store such information for all the possible nodes of the level j. For this reason, the information related to each node is concatenated into a single binary word and all the words correspondent to all the nodes of the level are stored in the $BRAM_j$ into consecutive memory locations. Previous works, such as [12], propose the design of two kinds of PE: one emulating an IN and one emulating a LN. Their architecture is very similar with the only exception that the former manages the comparison operation and the latter produces the final classification label. Figure 4 depicts the hardware architecture of the PE for an IN described in [12] with the related BRAM. The PE receives as inputs

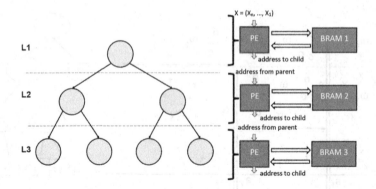

Fig. 3. The PE-based hardware architecture of a DT

the instance to classify (X) and the address (*address_in*) both coming from the previous PE: *address_in* is the memory address (computed by the previous PE) where the PE needs to retrieve the information of the node it has to emulate. The outputs of the PE, going into the subsequent PE, are: *address_out* and X. *Address_out* is computed by the *Next Address Calculation* module. Moreover, the PE is furnished with a pipeline: that means that the DT implemented as in Fig. 3 can accept a stream of instances to be classified and the throughput of the inference phase is one clock cycle, i.e. a new classification each clock period.

The *Next Address Calculation* module is the main core of the PE. It is responsible to perform the comparison operation and to send to the following PE the memory address where the latter can retrieve the needed configuration information based on the result.

In order to make the module able to calculate the memory address needed by its child, it is important that the data in the BRAM of each PE is organized according to a predefined way. One possible addressing strategy is the one depicted in Fig. 5. The starting point is assigning an address to the RN, i.e. the address 1. The address associated to the left (right) child is then obtained by concatenating a 0 (1) bit to the address of the parent node. This procedure is iterated until the last level of the tree. In this way, the *Next Address Calculation* module can easily produce an output address (to one of its child) based on the result of the comparison operation. Figure 5b shows how the data of the nodes belonging to the third level of the tree are organized within the correspondent BRAM. As an example, if the PE in the third level has to behave as the node D, the memory address calculated by its parent node is *100*.

The described strategy can be applied to design any DT, regardless of its model and tree topology, as long as the tree is balanced, i.e. all the LNs belong to the same (last) level. Once a DT model is selected, it can be easily designed in hardware by serially connecting a number of PEs equal to the number of the tree levels. The topology of the tree, as well as the information about which attribute X_i and threshold need to be compared at each node, can be set by properly initialize the content of the BRAMs.

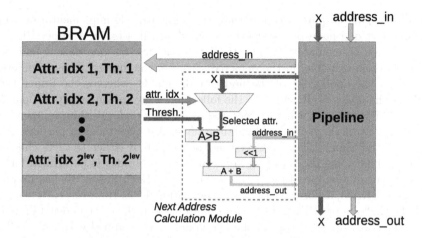

Fig. 4. A typical PE hardware architecture

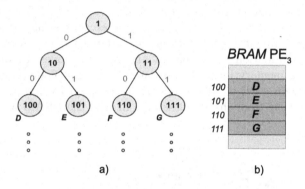

Fig. 5. a) addressing strategy of the DT nodes; b) example of the BRAM content.

4   The Proposed PE Hardware Design

This Section describes the proposed novel PE design with the aim of optimizing a FPGA-based DT hardware accelerator. The idea behind the new design is inspired by the working principle of the adder architecture named *Carry Select Adder* (CSA) [21], depicted in Fig. 6a. In a CSA, the addition operation of the input operands is divided into different blocks (in Fig. 6a, a 8-bit adder is divided into two blocks). The block performing the addition on the input bits $A_{[7:4]}$ and $B_{[7:4]}$ is designed with two sub-adders working in parallel, each of them receiving a constant carry input bit, *0* and *1*, respectively. The outputs of the block is then selected by a multiplexer based on the actual carry out result of the sub-adder working on the $A_{[3:0]}$ and $B_{[3:0]}$ inputs.

Figure 6b depicts the proposed strategy to design the PE, hereafter named the *Super PE*. Inspired by the CSA working principle, the proposed Super PE aims at emulating the activity of three nodes belonging to two consecutive levels of the DT. This is quite different than the standard PE implementation that emulates just one node in a single level. As shown in Fig. 6b, a Super PE can be configured to emulate the activity of three nodes, i.e. one parent and two children. As an example, in the depicted scenario, the Super PE1 is configured to perform the operations of the nodes A, B and C, whereas the Super PE2 emulates the nodes D, H and I. In the following, a group consisting of a parent and two children nodes will be referenced as a *super node*. Within a Super PE, the operations of the parent and children nodes are performed in parallel. The output of the Super PE is obtained as the output of either the left child or the right child node: the selection between the two options is performed based on the result of the operation of the parent node. Each Super PE has its own associated BRAM, as for the case of the conventional PE. However, each word of the BRAM of a Super PE stores the information about the three nodes. Figure 7a shows the addressing strategy of the DT nodes when mapped with Super PEs. The root super node (S_A) has the address 1. The addresses of the four super node children (S_B, S_C, S_D and S_E) are calculated by concatenating the address of the super node parent with *00*, *01*, *10* and *11*, starting from the left and moving to the right. Each memory location, whose address has been defined by the above procedure, stores the information related to one super node of the level, i.e. the information of the parent and children nodes. Figure 7b depicts the content of a memory location associated to a super node. It can be noted that proposed Super PE is able to operate as both an IN and a LN. For such a reason, differently from the PE described in [12], the BRAM associated to a

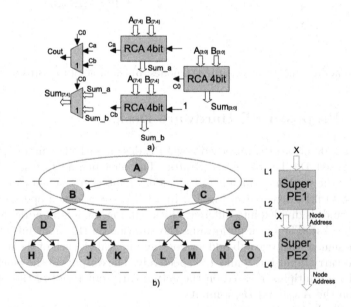

Fig. 6. a) The CSA working principle; b) the design of a binary DT based on the proposed *Super PE* concept.

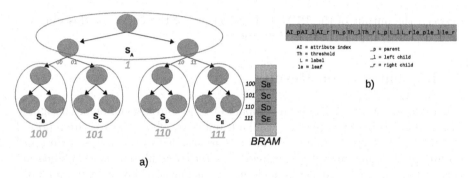

Fig. 7. a) The addressing strategy in a DT with Super PE; b) information stored in each word of the BRAM.

Super PE should contain *all* the information of the three nodes i.e. the *attribute index*, the *threshold*, the *label* and the *leaf bit*. Label is a binary word coding the classification label of the node in case it acts as a LN. The latter scenario is identified by the *leaf bit*, whose value is 1 (0) if the node inside the Super PE is a LN (IN). The information the three nodes are concatenated to form a single binary word. The number of levels of a binary DT organized into super nodes is halved with respect to the case with conventional nodes. The number of super nodes within the k-th level in a binary DT results to be $2^{2 \cdot (k-1)}$.

Figure 8 depicts the hardware architecture of the proposed Super PE. The Pipeline module is composed of series connected registers, as for the case of the conventional design based on simple nodes. However, differently from the latter, the pipeline latency of the new design is halved since each Super PE implements two levels of the DT. A Super PE makes use of three comparator modules, one for each internal node (i.e. the parent and the two children nodes). The three modules operate in parallel performing a comparison between an attribute of the input instance X and the correspondent threshold, as depicted in Fig. 9a. The attribute index and the threshold for each comparator are read from the BRAM location whose address is furnished as an input by the previous Super PE. Figure 9b shows the shifting and concatenation operations of the Shift & Concatenate module: the next node address is obtained by left-shifting the input node address and by concatenating the results of the parent and the selected child comparison modules. Finally, Fig. 10 depicts the Label Management module. It is based on four multiplexers: the Parent Label mux (PLM), the Child Label mux (CLM), the Leaf mux (LeM) and the Label mux (LaM). The PLM selects one between the label_in (to be propagated to the next Super PE) and the parent label (if the parent is a leaf node). The CLM selects the label from the left child or the right child node, based on the results of the parent comparator module. With the same control signal, the LeM selects the leaf information from the selected child node. This information is useful if one of the two children is a leaf node. Indeed, in such a case, the label of the selected child node should be the label_out of the Super PE. Finally, the LaM selects the final label_out as one between the output of the PLM and the output of the CLM. To this aim, the LaM uses the output of the LeM as selector.

5 Implementation Results

The proposed approach has been compared to the conventional one in designing five DT models based on publicly available datasets, whose features are reported in Table 1 [22–25]. The DT models have been obtained by training software procedures implemented in Python, using the *Scikit-learn* library. The classification accuracy of the analyzed DT models has been found to be the same for both their software and hardware implementations: *Breast Cancer* → 93.4%, *Obesity* → 93.85%, *Post Operative* → 72.2%, *Dishonest* → 80.0%, *Glass* → 72.1%. All the designs have been described in VHDL and implemented for the Xilinx Zynq XC7Z020-1CLG400C FPGA chip by means of the Xilinx 2019 Vivado Tool. For the sake of a fair comparison, all the designs have been implemented for the same target clock frequency (166 MHz). Table 2 summarizes the obtained hardware results. It is worth noting that the DTs implemented with the proposed Super PE methodology show a power dissipation that is on average 16.6% lower than the conventional design. In particular, for deep DT models, such as the ones based on the *Obesity* and *Glass* datasets, the proposed design shows a power dissipation improvement of about 18%. For small DT models, such as the one trained for the *Dishonest* dataset, the power consumption improvement is even larger (about 42%). Only for the DT based on the *Breast Cancer* dataset, the

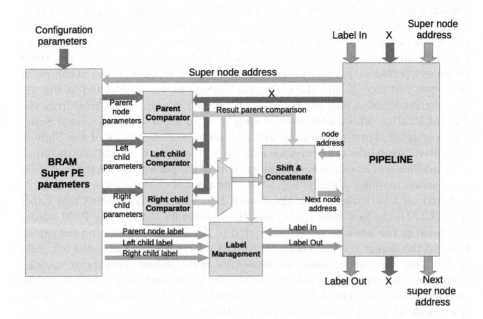

Fig. 8. The architecture of the proposed Super PE.

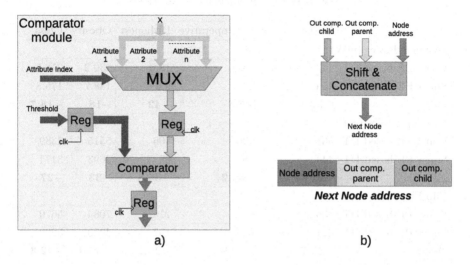

Fig. 9. a) The Comparator module; b) the Shift & Concatenate module.

Table 1. The used datasets features.

Parameters	Breast cancer	Post operative	Dishonest	Obesity	Glass
Attribute number	9	8	4	16	9
Bits per Th./Attr.	4	3	2	15	24
Bits per instance	36	24	8	240	216
Bits/BRAM word	10	9	6	23	32
# of Labels	2	3	2	7	7
# of Levels	9	12	6	14	12
# of simple nodes	51	73	17	215	79

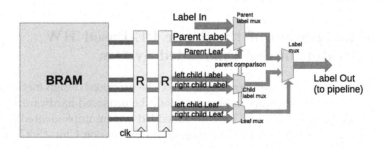

Fig. 10. The Label Management module.

Table 2. Hardware implementation results.

	Breast cancer	Post operative	Dishonest	Obesity	Glass
Dynamic Power (mW)					
Conv. PE-based DT	44.2	48.1	16.6	230.2	216.5
Super PE-based DT	45.0	45.5	9.6	188.7	175.8
$\Delta(\%)$	+1.9	−5.3	−42	−18	−18.7
Look-up Tables (#)					
Conv. PE-based DT	568	596	106	5515	4389
Super PE-based DT	444	386	68	3693	3174
$\Delta(\%)$	−21.8	−35.2	−35.8	−33	−27
Flip-Flops (#)					
Conv. PE-based DT	836	938	210	7084	5670
Super PE-based DT	621	620	157	4220	3269
$\Delta(\%)$	−25.7	−33.9	−25.2	−40.4	−42.3
36 Kbits BRAM (#)					
Conv. PE-based DT	4.5	6.5	3	18	8.5
Super PE-based DT	2.5	4	1.5	18.5	11
$\Delta(\%)$	−44.4	−38.4	−50	+2.7	+29.4

proposed design shows a negligible power consumption increase (lower than 2%): this is attributable to the fact that the such a DT model has an odd number of levels, so that the mapping of the tree with Super PEs is not optimal in the last level. Interestingly, the proposed design methodology entails a significant reduction of the hardware utilization: on average, the number of used Look-up Tables, Flip-Flops and BRAMs is 30.7%, 33.5% and 20.1% lower than the conventional design. As a final remark, the BRAM utilization of the Super PE-based design is higher than the design with the conventional PE in two cases: *Obesity* and *Glass*. This is due to the fact that for such two datasets, the number of bits for the attributes is pretty large. Nevertheless, this does not prevent the proposed design reaching a lower power dissipation.

6 The Integration of the Super PE-Based HW Accelerator into an Embedded System

In order to compare the timing performance of the proposed design methodology with respect to a pure software implementation, the proposed hardware accelerator has been integrated as an IP into an embedded system implemented onto the Xilinx Zynq XC7Z020-1CLG400C heterogeneous System on Chip (SoC), hosted on the ARM Xilinx PynQ-Z1 development board. The SoC consists of a FPGA-based programmable logic (PL) and an 650 MHz ARM-based general purpose processing system (PS). The hardware accelerator has been implemented into

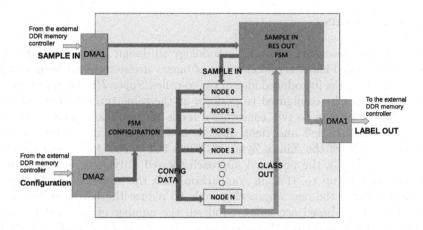

Fig. 11. The complete embedded system architecture.

Table 3. Comparison of the hardware- and software-based implementations on the Xilinx Zynq XC7Z020-1CLG400C heterogeneous SoC.

Platform	Impl. type	Classification time
ARM A9 (PS)	Software	13.1 ms
ARM A9 (PS) + Xilinx Artix^{TM}-7 (PL)	Hardware/Software	0.62 ms

the PL, whereas the PS has been exploited to manage the data flow from/to the off-chip DDR memory located on the board by activating the required Direct Memory Access (DMA) modules. The complete embedded system architecture is depicted in Fig. 11. The DMA1 module is used to transfer the input instances from the external DDR memory and to send to the memory the classification results (Label_out) via the AXI-Stream interface [26]. A second DMA module, DMA2, is used in the initialization phase of the system to initialize the content of the BRAMs according to the DT model and topology. Two Finite State Machine (FSMs) are employed to orchestrate the activity of the hardware accelerator and to allow the IP to communicate with the AXI-stream interface of the DMAs. The embedded systems depicted in Fig. 11 has been configured with the DT model and topology related to the *Breast Cancer* dataset and tested with a clock frequency of 100MHz, limited by the DMA modules. Table 3 summarizes the obtained timing results for the classification of 137 input instances. The computational time of the embedded system includes also the data flow latency from/to the off-chip DDR memory. It is worth noting that, compared to a pure software implementation of the DT model running on the ARM-based PS, the proposed hardware accelerator, integrated into a complete embedded system, entails a speed-up of about 21×.

7 Conclusions

This paper has described a novel methodology to design low-power and high-speed FPGA-based hardware accelerators of binary decision trees. The new approach is based on the introduced idea of the so-called *Super PE*, i.e. a processing element that can be configured to perform at the same time the operation of three nodes belonging to two consecutive levels of the binary decision tree: a parent node and its left and right children nodes. When implemented on the FPGA-based PL of the Xilinx Zynq XC7Z020-1CLG400C heterogeneous System on Chip (SoC), the proposed approach showed a dynamic power dissipation reduction of up to 41%, in comparison with the conventional PE-based design. Moreover, the new approach is able to reduce the hardware footprint of the DT FPGA-based accelerator. Indeed, the number of required Look-up Tables, Flip-Flops and BRAMs is, on average, 30.7%, 33.5% and 20.1% lower in comparison with the traditional technique, respectively. Finally, a complete DT hardware accelerator, designed according to the proposed methodology, has been integrated into an embedded system implemented on the Xilinx Zynq XC7Z020-1CLG400C heterogeneous System on Chip (SoC). When compared with a pure software-based implementation, the proposed embedded system showed a classification speed-up of about 21×.

Acknowledgement. This work was supported in part by PON Ricerca & Innovazione - MUR (grant 062_R24_INNOVAZIONE), Ministero dell'Università e della Ricerca, Italian Government.

References

1. Wu, X., Zhu, X., Wu, G.-Q., Ding, W.: Data mining with big data. IEEE Trans. Knowl. Data Eng. **26**(11), 97–107 (2014)
2. Rofouei, M., Pedram, M., Fraternali, F., Ashari, Z.E., Ghasemzadeh, H.: Resource-efficient computing in wearable systems. In: 2019 IEEE International Conference on Smart Computing (SMARTCOMP), Washington D.C. (US), pp. 150–155 (2019)
3. Sun, F., Zang, W., Gravina, R., Fortino, G., Li, Y.: Gait-based identification for elderly users in wearable healthcare systems. Inf. Fusion **53**, 134–144 (2020)
4. Shi, W., Cao, J., Zhang, Q., Li, Y., Xu, L.: Edge computing: vision and challenges. IEEE Internet Things J. **3**(5), 637–646 (2016)
5. Baraka, A., Shaban, H., Abou El-Nasr, M., Attallah, O.: Wearable accelerometer and sEMG-based upper limb BSN for tele-rehabilitation. Appl. Sci. **9**(14), 1–22 (2019)
6. Balkhi, P., Moallem, M.: A multipurpose wearable sensor-based system for weight training. Automation **3**(1), 132–152 (2022)
7. Raj, S., Ray, K.C., Shankar, O.: Cardiac arrhythmia beat classification using DOST and PSO tuned SVM. Comput. Methods Programs Biomed. **136**, 163–177 (2016)
8. Ferreira, P.J.S., Cardoso, J.M.P., Mendes-Moreira, J.: kNN prototyping schemes for embedded human activity recognition with online learning. Computers **9**(4), 1–20 (2020)

9. Liu, X., Zhiqiang, W.: Distributed computing system based on microprocessor cluster for wearable devices. In: 2017 International Conference on Computer Network, Electronic and Automation (ICCNEA), Xi'an, China, pp. 66–71 (2017)
10. Buschjäger, S., Morik, K.: Decision tree and random forest implementations for fast filtering of sensor data. IEEE Trans. Circuits Syst. I Regul. Pap. **65**(1), 209–222 (2018)
11. Saqib, F., Dutta, A., Plusquellic, J., Ortiz, P., Pattichis, M.S.: Pipelined decision tree classification accelerator implementation in FPGA (DT-CAIF). IEEE Trans. Comput. **64**(1), 280–285 (2015)
12. Van Essen, B., Macaraeg, C., Gokhale, M., Prenger, R.: Accelerating a random forest classifier: Multi-core, GP-GPU, or FPGA? In: The IEEE 20th International Symposium on Field-Programmable Custom Computing Machines, pp. 232–239 (2012)
13. Narayanan, R., Honbo, D., Memik, G., Choudhary, A., Zambreno, J.: An FPGA implementation of decision tree classification. In: 2007 Design, Automation & Test in Europe Conference & Exhibition, pp. 1–6 (2007)
14. Owaida, M., Alonso, G., Fogliarini, L., Hock-Koon, A., Melet, P.-E.: Lowering the latency of data processing pipelines through FPGA based hardware acceleration. Proc. VLDB Endow. **13**(1), 71–85 (2019)
15. Kyrkou, C., Bouganis, C.-S., Theocharides, T., Polycarpou, M.M.: Embedded hardware-efficient real-time classification with cascade support vector machines. IEEE Trans. Neural Netw. Learn. Syst. **27**(1), 99–112 (2016)
16. Fernandez, D., Gonzalez, C., Mozos, D., Lopez, S.: FPGA implementation of the principal component analysis algorithm for dimensionality reduction of hyperspectral images. J. Real-Time Image Proc. **16**(5), 1395–1406 (2019)
17. Liu, L., Khalid, M.A.S.: Acceleration of k-nearest neighbor algorithm on FPGA using Intel SDK for OpenCL. In: IEEE 61st International Midwest Symposium on Circuits and Systems (MWSCAS), Windsor, ON, Canada, pp. 1070–1073 (2018)
18. Li, Z.-H., Jin, J.-F., Zhou, X.-G., Feng, Z.-H.: K-nearest neighbor algorithm implementation on FPGA using high level synthesis. In: IEEE International Conference on Solid-State and Integrated Circuit Technology (ICSICT), Hangzhou, China, pp. 1–4 (2016)
19. Pu, Y., Peng, J., Huang, L., Chen, J.: An efficient KNN algorithm implemented on FPGA based heterogeneous computing system using OpenCL. In: IEEE 23rd Annual International Symposium on Field-Programmable Custom Computing Machines, Vancouver, BC, Canada, pp. 167–170 (2015)
20. Zhang, S., Li, X., Zong, M., Zhu, X., Wang, R.: Efficient kNN classification with different numbers of nearest neighbors. IEEE Trans. Neural Netw. Learn. Syst. **49**(5), 1774–1785 (2018)
21. Ramkumar, B., Kittur, H.M.: Low-power and area-efficient carry select adder. IEEE Trans. Very Large Scale Integr. (VLSI) Syst. **20**(2), 371–375 (2012)
22. Dua, D., Graff, C.: UCI Machine Learning Repository. https://archive.ics.uci.edu/ml. Accessed Mar 2022
23. D'Angelo, G., Rampone, S., Palmieri, F.: Developing a trust model for pervasive computing based on Apriori association rules learning and Bayesian classification. Soft. Comput. **21**, 6297–6315 (2017)
24. D'Angelo, G., Rampone, S., Palmieri, F.: An artificial intelligence-based trust model for pervasive computing. In: International Conference on P2P, Parallel, Grid, Cloud and Internet Computing (3PGCIC), Krakow, Poland, pp. 701–706 (2015)

25. Palechor, F.M., de la Hoz Manotas, A.: Dataset for estimation of obesity levels based on eating habits and physical condition in individuals from Colombia, Peru and Mexico. Data Brief **25**, 1–5 (2019)
26. AMD Xilinx, AXI Reference Guide, UG1037 15 July 2017. https://docs.xilinx.com/v/u/en-US/ug1037-vivado-axi-reference-guide. Accessed 15 Apr 2022

MEMS and AI for the Recognition of Human Activities on IoT Platforms

Luigi Bibbo'[1]([✉]) [iD], Massimo Merenda[3], Riccardo Carotenuto[1],
Vincenzo Francesco Romeo[1], and Francesco Della Corte[2]

[1] DIIES Department, University Mediterranea of Reggio Calabria, 89126 Reggio Calabria, Italy
luigi.bibbo@unirc.it
[2] DIETI Department, University Federico II, 80125 Napoli, Italy
[3] Center for Digital Safety & Security, Austrian Institute of Technology, 1210 Vienna, Austria

Abstract. The increase in the elderly population has led to the need for new medical, social, and care services, resulting in a significant rise in health costs and the number of health workers involved. For example, IoT (Internet of Things) and wearable technologies can help contain healthcare spending and enable better living conditions of elderly. Moreover, nanotechnologies such as MEMS (micro-electromechanical system) that offer the advantage of small size, negligible need for power and motion acquisition are of considerable benefit. These technologies are able to detect and signal dangerous situations in order to ensure immediate action. In this article, we present an implementation of an IoT application on a latest-generation microcontroller. Kinematics and environmental data are transferred to a CNN (Convolutional Neural Network) to recognize the daily activities of the elderly in their homes or nursing homes. Finally, to determine the position of subjects, we associate the prototype with a positioning system on the ultrasonic platform. Finally, applying the Edge Machine Learning technique, we developed an application on the STM32L475VG microprocessor on which motion acquisition and activity recognition functions are activated.

Keyword: Internet of things · Healthcare · Wireless sensor networks · Human activity recognition · Convolutional neural network · Indoor positioning · Ambient assisted living · Edge machine learning

1 Preface

In the last few years, the number of older adults has grown considerably, becoming a phenomenon of global importance. The increase in lifespan has been achieved mainly thanks to medical and technological advances. However, this improvement has led to an increasing people needing assistance. It is long-lasting and involves numerous services: medical, rehabilitation, nursing and social assistance which increase public health costs. To contain these costs, an efficient home assistance service based on information technology can be used. [1]. It also allows you to improve the quality of life of the elderly and maintain their home habits [2]. In this context, Ambient Assisted Living (**AAL**) arises. It is a new area that uses an **IoT** platform governed by artificial intelligence

M. Mahmud et al. (Eds.): AII 2022, CCIS 1724, pp. 73–89, 2022.
https://doi.org/10.1007/978-3-031-24801-6_6

algorithms to provide supports that can transparently assist the daily lives of people in need of assistance [3]. In fact, by increasing life expectancy, it is essential to extend the period in which people can live independently or with home care and perform daily tasks in their preferred environment. Ambient Assisted Living, making our home as active, intelligent, and helpful as possible to those who live there to carry out all daily activities in the best possible way and complete autonomy helps to guarantee the health and functional abilities of those who are elderly. In light of the considerations, using wireless networks and artificial intelligence, the IoT can help improve remote patient monitoring while reducing healthcare expenses and workload. Finally, the IoT is closely connected to ubiquitous computing, which represents the technique of computer management of embedded and interconnected devices that are part of everyday objects and activities.

Ubiquitous computing (Ubicomp). Offers significant benefits by combining sensors, wireless networks, and artificial intelligence for data analysis to monitor and detect anomalies allowing early interventions or preventing more considerable damages. For example, IoT refers to devices, sensing, and wearable technologies. It is a technology that groups different components such as communications, connectivity, information technology, intelligence, security, and data collection to connect people and objects anytime and anywhere through communication networks [4].

IoT in the healthcare field can provide the following services:

- Automatic collection of patient physiological data through sensors worn by the patient and connected to medical instruments
- Patient's localization
- Send the acquired data to the medical center for storing and processing.
- Continuous monitoring of patients' health status.
- Collaboration between teams of internal staff and external specialists, and medical data sharing.

IoT devices, generally, don't have large processing and memory capacity so they cannot handle large volumes of data so they need a connection with cloud systems. But the delays associated with data transfer are incompatible with the need for quick decisions to be taken in cases of necessity, as can happen in the care of the elderly. Today, having devices equipped with local intelligence, it is possible to limit cloud traffic. With the advent of **edge computing**, IoT devices will analyze and process the incoming data at the origin and determine what needs to be processed by more powerful cloud algorithms than locally. Edge ML (Machine Learning) solves security problems related to storing users' personal information in the cloud and reduces the strain on cloud networks by processing data locally and in real-time. In edge computing, the data processing is done on the same device connected to the sensors.

These characteristics can improve the homecare service of older adults or those needing assistance by monitoring the activities carried out and the subject's physiological data. The monitoring of habitual activities carried out by the elderly helps to notice any behavioral changes. For example, the technology can help detect and alert healthcare professionals or family members about older people's behavioral changes, preventing serious problems. With the help of these technologies, the system is able to detect the patient's status in according with his e specific pathology, tracking, and the exact location.

2 State of the Art

For a complete analysis, we report technologies and related works in the localization and HAR classification to focus our work better. Nowadays, wearable devices like smartwatches, smart shoes, etc., can be combined with smartphones to measure and capture personal bio-metrics like blood pressure, heart rate, respiratory rate, and blood oxygen concentration [5]. There are two technologies that allow to detect human activities: one based on vision [6] and other on sensors [7]. Video-based systems require the installation of cameras and microphones in all rooms of a house to record the movements of a body. In addition to being expensive, the recognition accuracy depends on the brightness of the environment and the inevitable visual disturbances. MEMS sensors are preferred because they are miniaturized, economical, and have low-power consumption [8]. Moreover they can monitor activities such as standing, sitting, walking, climbing, and descending stairs. These data are important to be able to understand if there are behaviours different from the usual ones such as not getting out of bed, not having lunch, not washing [9]. The physiological state of the subject can also be determined through the heartbeat which normally varies from 60 to 100 beats per minute. Rate variability (HRV) indicates heart rate diseases such as arrhythmia, ischemia, and long QT syndrome. The variation from the range could also depend on the type of activity carried out by the elderly [10]. Activity recognition is a classification method based on feature extraction as all other classification systems. The feature extraction algorithm aims to find a subset of features where the information relevant to recognition is contained in a minimum number of functions. Traditional methods are based on extraction features from kinetic signals chosen mainly on a heuristic basis [11]. **Deep Learning** technology, through the **Machine Learning** model, has made the process of selecting the representative characteristics of the collected data. The structure of the DL (Deep Learning) models, in several layers, gives them a high ability to learn descriptive features from complex data, favoring the ability to analyze multisensory data, which translates into a greater degree of accuracy in the recognition phase. Convolutional neural networks (**CNNs**), which represent a branch of the Deep Neural Network (**DNN**), has proved to be very effective in object recognition [12]. An important information in the home assistance system is represented by the exact knowledge of the position of the subject inside the home in order to be able to intervene promptly in the event of sudden malaise or accidents. The location must provide information on the older adult's place [13]. We also associate the elderly persons' paths within their homes (tracking). Different systems determine the coordinates of a subject moving in an indoor environment; they differ in the technological platform and the type of algorithm used [14, 15]. Numerous IoT applications differ in the technology used and the field of application. Below is a summary of several attractive solutions adopted. For example, **Awadalla** et al. [16] proposed a platform to manage and provide comprehensive services for the elderly. Through wearable sensors, they acquired real-time information on the physical activities carried out by the subjects and transferred them to a served cloud via smartphone.

Doctors can access the web-based database to acquire useful information on the state of health of patients. An exciting experience is proposed by **Žaric** et al. [17], in which a monitoring system for specific cooking activities and a decision-making system, that can recognize unwanted and possibly critical conditions, are designed. The suggest plan falls within the Ambient Assisted Living (AAL) area to meet the needs of the elderly. The monitoring system is based on ultrasonic sensors, temperature, and humidity. The data collected are then transferred to the decision-making system, which generates, if necessary, warning signs for caregivers or family members. Still, **Misra** et al. [18] have drawn an application in which the fundamental parameters of patients' health, such as heart rate, blood pressure, respiratory rate, body temperature, and body movements, are acquired by various sensors and stored in the Internet of Things. The data are displayed through the website, which can access remote monitoring. **Iranpak** et al. [19] used a prioritization system to prioritize sensitive information in IoT and cloud computing. They also applied a deep neural network LSTM (long short-term memory) to remotely classify and monitor patients' conditions. The sensors used include heart rate, body temperature, blood pressure, blood sugar, stress, consciousness, pulse counter, and accelerometer. The acquired data are transferred to a microcontroller according to the priority criterion established by the IoT interface. The priority of sensitive and non-sensitive information, determines aqueue that is transferred to the microcontroller at prefixed time intervals. If LSTM detects the patient's abnormal condition based on the information received, it alerts all health professionals and family members. **Jara** et al. [20] developed an IoT-based Intelligent Pharmaceutical Information System (PIIS) to examine dangerous effects of drugs, renal absorption reactions, side effects during pregnancy or lactation, and certain diseases such as tuberculosis. Drug compliance and Adverse Drug Reactions (ADRs) are two important factors in patient safety across the global healthcare industry. For this purpose, the authors designed an innovative system based on the Internet of Things (IoT) to examine drugs to detect harmful side effects. After identifying the drug, the Pharmaceutical Intelligent Information System (PIIS) verifies compatibility with the patient's profile. This system verifies the suitability of the drug based on the allergy profile and anamnesis of the patient through the personal medical record (PHR) or personal health cards also based on RFID. Within the HAR, **Aruban** et al. [21] have made a studio collecting human activity data from 60 participants across two different days for six activities. The process is enabled by capturing the raw activity signals from gyroscope and accelerometer sensors in a modern smartphone, using an Android application, "AndroSensor". After data collection, the tri-axial raw accelerometer and gyroscope signals were subdivided into 10-s segments trough sliding window approach with no overlapping to compute the feature set. Researchers have developed analyses to verify which features based on the time and frequency domain better identify individuals' types of motor activity. This process generated 304 unique characteristics of the two domains. They used Machine learning algorithms for the classification phase, achieving 98% accuracy. Still, **Sikder** et al. [22] designed a system on a two-channel Convolutional Neural Network (CNN) based on the frequency and power features of the collected signals. The frequency and power information obtained from the raw time-domain accelerometer signals are then sent as two sets of samples to two-channel CNN.

Finally, the authors used the datasets hosted by the University of California Irvine (UCI) to classify their Machine Learning Repository signals.

3 Methodology

We designed a system to Recognize Human Activities (HAR) to create an innovative home care system for the elderly or per-need assistance. The prototype differs from other applications for having an architecture on a single IoT platform capable of:

- collect inertial and environmental data through a multisensory system;
- acquire location data through different Wireless connective systems;
- recognize the activities carried out by the subjects through a neural network.

Through this solution, we realized the application of HAR in **Edge Machine Learning** technology [23]. The data relating to the activities carried out by the subjects are sent to the neural network, installed directly on the device, which processes the data locally and classifies, after the calculation of the inference, the activities of Stationary, Walking, Jogging, Stairs without necessarily connecting to the cloud, as schematically shown in Fig. 1.

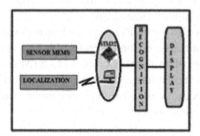

Fig. 1. HAR Functional scheme

3.1 Hardware

The main components of the architecture used are described below: microprocessor, sensors, and WIFI module.

The core of the entire system is the board B-L475E-IOT01A Discovery kit for IoT node (STML32L475VG) (Fig. 2), produced by STMicroelectronics, which has a number of components useful to realize the project of IoT. It can handle different low-power communication protocols and is provided with multiple environmental and inertial sensors and a microcontroller of the low-power STM32L4 series based on the Arm Cortex-M4 core. The microcontroller mounted on the board is the STM32L475VG, a 32-bit microcontroller with a maximum frequency of 80 MHz; it has a Flash memory of 1Mbyte while the SRAM (Static Random Memory) memory is 128 KByte. It has numerous features such as ADCs (Analog to Digital Converter), timers, communication interfaces, and multiple channels (Fig. 2).

Fig. 2. STML32L475VG layout

As for power, the STM32L475VG Discovery kit for IoT node, is devised to be supplied from a 5V DC (Direct Current) power. The board integrates different components, among which the following sensors are highlighted: two omnidirectional digital microphones (MP34DT01), a capacitive sensor for temperature and humidity measurement (HTS2211), a 3-axis magnetometer (LIS3MDL), a digital barometer (LPS22HB), a TOF (Time OF Flight) proximity sensor (VL53L0X), a 3D Accelerometer and Gyroscope (LSM6DSL) with and an I2C (Inter-Integrated Circuit)/SPI (Serial Peripheral Interface) for output communication. In addition, it has an integrated FIFO (First Input First Output) buffer of up to 4 Kbytes in size that allows dynamic batching of significant data (external sensors, pedometer, timestamps, etc.).

On the board, there is also the WiFi (Wireless Fidelity) module (ISM43362-M3G-L44) used for TCP/IP (Transmission Control Protocol/Internet Protocol) communication with the Server. It consists of an Arm® Cortex®-M3 STM32 processor, an integrated antenna (or possibly an external antenna), and a Broadcom device. It only needs AT commands to work correctly to establish the WiFi connection minimizing host CPU (Central Processing Unit) requirements (Fig. 3).

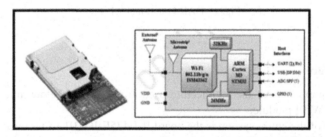

Fig. 3. View of WiFi module and its architecture (ST Microelectronics)

For the implementation of the prototype, we used an Integrated Development Environment (IDE) software suite for helping to implement applications. The first step of the project is the activation of the components on the chosen board. This phase is developed with the STM32CubeMX FP (extension of STM32Cube), a graphical tool that guides the entire process of initializing the project. It is represented by the selection, within the list of processors from ST Microelectronics, the board used with the relative sensors for data acquisition. It was also necessary to set the Clock to a frequency of 80 MHz. With the X-Cube MEMS software have been downloaded the drivers of the various sensors: LSM6DL (Accelerometer and Gyroscope) for their configuration and setting. For the next initialization phase, with the function MEMS_Init (), the parameters for proper functioning have been declared. In the end, it was necessary to configure in the "connectivity" window the I2C protocol to activate the data acquisition function from sensors. The data collected by the sensors are fused by applying an algorithm based on the Kalman filter and then sent to CNN to classify activities.

3.2 CNN

We used A CNN to recognize the daily activities of the elderly in their homes. A convolutional neural network (CNN) is a deep learning method that falls into the artificial neural networks (ANNs) category. It is a sequential structure multi-layered feedforward, mainly used to analyze images. It comprises an input layer, hidden layers, and an output layer. The first layers analyze the images by extracting their characteristic features while the fully connected layers perform the classification. Each processing step consists of a convolutional filter (CONV), followed by an activation function (ReLU), a pooling function, and finally, a fully connected layer (FC) [24]. The convolutional levels task is to extract the initial image's specific features that will constitute the feature map of the next layer. Through this cascade process, the network converts the original input representation level to a higher and more abstract representation level. The output is the creation of the reference feature maps that the researchers will use to compare with the output feature maps. At the end of the sequence of convolutional layers, we finally find the fully connected level that allows us to identify the classes obtained in the previous levels in accord with defined probabilities. To be used, the network must be previously trained and tested. Finally, datasets are available on the market and designed to facilitate network development. Finally, it is common practice to use 80% of the data for training and 20% for testing. Ultimately, the errors between the real and the above values are determined and marked with the same accuracy.

In this section, we illustrate the main software functions used to create a neural network capable of classifying human activities through the signals collected by sensors. The choice of the STM32L475VG board allowed us to use a comprehensive embedded-software platform of functions for the implementation of project. To implement the neural network in the project, we used the X-CUBE-AI tool, Expansion Package of the STM32Cube. It is a software configuration tool for the Artificial Intelligence (AI) project development from conception to the realization. It includes STM32CubeMx, a graphical software configuration tool that allows the automatic generation of C initialization code, and STM32CubeProg, a programming tool. X-CUBE-AI has an automatic neural network library generator that allows to convert pre-trained Neural Networks from most used DL frameworks into a library automatically integrated into the user's project. Therefore, through this tool we extracted from the Keras Library a pre-trained CNN for HAR to be converted into C code.

Moreover, it generates the files related to the model (weights, layers, etc.), and the necessary libraries, for the use of the model, which is integrated into the IDE. For example, memory usage RAM (Random Access Memory) and ROM (Read Only Memory) is optimized during the C code generation process, considering inference calculation time and power consumption. A layer merging operation is carried out to optimize the process. Some layers are entirely removed, while others are fused. As a result, the *'converted'* network has fewer layers than the original one. Finally, as far as RAM is concerned, this is optimized by defining an *'activation'* buffer, exploited during inference, and reused by several layers. Once these processes are completed, the specific C files are generated depending on the chosen DL model (type of network, weights/bias). These files' names are the same as those assigned to the network on CubeMX. These files are implemented with the Application Program Interface (API) of the static library network_runtime.a. The entire process of importing the pre-trained network and converting it into C code and its optimization is graphically shown in (Fig. 4).

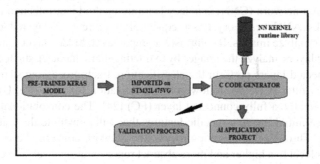

Fig. 4. The flow of X-CUBE-AI to import and convert a pre-trained Keras model into C code.

The X-CUBE-AI Tool and converting the neural network model into C code validate the model on both the host and the target. For this purpose, we have used the following features:

- System Performance: provides a measure of CPU load during inference and memory usage.
- Validation Project: the neural network is tested on both the host and the target.
- Application Template: a set of basic libraries is generated to develop the AI project. To display the parameters produced by the first two functions, we have configured the serial terminal (TERA Term) on the host for communication with the board, through the UART (Universal Asynchronous Receiver-Transmitter) of the ST-Link, with the parameters required.

System Performance
It is an on-target application that provides parameters for integrating the system/board and the generated neural network. It estimates the number of CPU cycles performed by inference, the duration in ms, the RAM and ROM memory commitment, and the MACC (Multiply-and-Accumulate complexity). This unit indicates the complexity of a DL model from the point of view of processing. It also provides the device's information, such as the ID, the Clock, and the toolchain/IDE used. Some of the values obtained from our application were:

- Complexity: 68928 MACC
- C-model nodes: 4
- Activations (RAM): 6976 bytes
- Weights (Flash): 5908 bytes
- Average inference duration: 12,705 ms

Validation Project

It is an application that compares the accuracy of the generated C model with that of the original model. The benchmark is the relative error L2 (least-squares method), only close to the output layer. If this is less than 0.01, then the model is considered valid. It is obtained from the formula [25]:

$$L_2 = \frac{\|F_j - f_j\|}{\|F_j\|} \tag{1}$$

Fj is the output relative to the layers of the c model, while fj are those close to the original model.

The validation methods are:

- Validation on the desktop directly compares the DL model with the generated C model on the host.
- Validation on target makes the comparison on the target device.

The validation performed on desktop and target showed that the C-model is valid because the errors are infinitesimal: L2Error $1.56 \times 10^{(-7)}$, accuracy ~ 100%.

After the generation of the neural network, we implemented the network's initialization functions on the chosen IDE and execution of the inference. Next, we allocated three buffers: the input, output, and network activation buffers; the latter is a memory space used during inference execution to store intermediate results. Next, we preprocessed the data acquired by the sensors to remove, through a high pass filter (4th order, cut-off frequency around 1 Hz), the gravitational component from the dynamic part (oscillating) of the acceleration. The active element of gravity is always oriented in the same direction and is independent of the orientation of the sensor. Rodrigues's rotation formula is used to turn the active part:

$$\text{Vrot} = v \cos\theta + (k \times v)\sin\theta + k(k \cdot v)(1 - \cos\theta) \tag{2}$$

where v is a three-dimensional vector and k is the unit vector that describes the axis of rotation around which we want to rotate v by an angle θ [26].

The entire preprocessing phase is performed through the gravity_suppress_rotate function, which accepts raw data as input and returns filtered. The HAR function is significant for monitoring the health of the elderly to ensure their well-being. Many actions are carried out daily at home, but our study focuses on those that are the most common and essential to understanding the patient's condition. Since these are activities related to body movements that can be recorded through accelerometric measurements and also characterized by repetitive patterns, their recognition is easier. For data collection, several people are involved in the experiments who are asked to carry out the actions under investigation. The activity data collected for each person are accelerometer values according to the x.y-z axes. The data constitute the asset classes under consideration that, after a preprocessing phase, are transferred to the model that activates a function known as SOFTMAX that creates the output values between 0 and 1 for each activity examined. For example, we used a pre-trained KERAS model as a neural network in our work for recognizing walking, jogging, standing, climbing upstairs, and going downstairs activities. The data used for the training are those of Wireless Sensor Data Mining (WISDM), widely used by multiple researchers. The data were acquired through activities carried out by 36 participants equipped with Android phones placed in the front pocket of their pants; it was asked to carry out the actions previously mentioned for a specific time.

The network created is shown in the architectural graph with the characteristics of each layer. (Fig. 5). It is a. h5 model generated with the Keras library, HAR_IGN_WISDM, trained on the public Wireless Sensor Data mining (WISDM) dataset [27]. The network consists of two convolutional layers, three Relu layers, two pooling layers, and two fully connected layers. Downstream of the Max pooling, a Dropout layer is placed to regularize and avoid the fitting, followed by a flatten layer. Softmax is enabled for classification. The convolutional layers have 16 filters and Kernel size = 3,3; pooling window size = 2,2, which implies that the height and width of the window are 2 and 2; dropout = 0,5.

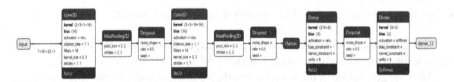

Fig. 5. CNN architecture

With the smartphone connected to the STM32L475VG via BLE applyinghe STBLE Sensor application, the data transmitted by the sensors are displayed. In addition to the inertial data through which the CNN identifies the classes of activity under examination, environmental data of temperature, pressure, and humidity are also transmitted, allowing the patient's well-being to be assessed. From plotting the acceleration diagrams, we observe multiple peaks in walking and jogging activities compared to the almost stationary standing, confirming the movement actions connected with the activities carried out. Between walking and jogging, while presenting the same track type, the frequency of peaks is higher in the second case.

3.3 Localization

To integrate the application with the localization determination, we chose a dedicated solution despite having the board a proximity sensor, as this performance does not satisfy a system (HAR). Proximity estimation is an approximate technique for a localization system for the elderly. It allows one to estimate the subject's position when it is close to a fixed reference but does not calculate the exact position coordinates of the subject

For this reason, an internal localization system has been applied exclusively to obtain an accurate measurement [28–30]. In implementing such systems, it is necessary to comply with specific conditions: the data must be reliable and continuous, and the calculation time must reduce delays in calculating the position. Among the different technologies available, we have chosen an ultrasonic network. This technology allows you to create low-cost solutions while ensuring higher accuracy than other systems. The low speed of ultrasonic waves in the air results in high time-of-flight accuracy and, consequently, high positioning accuracy. The system used is based on the presence of four ultrasonic beacons and one or more mobile receivers [31]. Beacons transmit a periodic ultrasonic sequence. Positioning calculations are performed onboard each mobile receiver. The system does not use a trigger signal between beacons and mobile units, so the absence of RF communication reduces the complexity of the system and the power consumption between the beacon and the mobile receiver. The calculation process is divided into two phases. In the first phase, the distances between fixed points and mobile units are determined. In the second phase these allow to obtain geometrically the position of the moving mobile units within the reference system defined by the positioning of the anchors. Distances are measured by ultrasonic signals and are based on time-of-flight (TOF) calculation. The time is calculated as the difference between the moment of reception of the signal and that of transmission. The accuracy in measuring distance depends on the accuracy in measuring time; therefore, it is necessary to ensure perfect synchronization between the times of the transmitters and those of the receivers. A synchronization difference of 1 μs results in an unknown distance of about 0.43 mm. The calculation is carried out with the multilateration technique which uses the intersection of the spheres drawn with a radius equal to the distance between the mobile unit and the beacons and centered in the points of the beacons. The network uses four beacons that can communicate wirelessly and be placed at different points within the area to be monitored. They are placed at the corners of a square on the room's ceiling of dimension $4 \times 4 \times 3$ m^3. The ANT platform (designed and marketed by ANT Wireless) is a communication protocol. This adaptive transmission allows many devices to communicate concurrently without interfering and establishes standard rules of coexistence. It is suitable for low-power, low-throughput network sensors with the same modes as Bluetooth networks. It differs from Bluetooth, which is applicable instead with relatively high transmission.

The signal detection is activated by the the master unit that, using the Broadcast Reference Synchronization technique, sends a broadcast message to all the receivers that synchronize while receiving this signal simultaneously. The control unit emits ultrasonic chirp signals sequentially through the four beacons enabled to transmit to mobile units. Each mobile unit receives the ultrasonic signal and can so calculates its position.

The PC receives, in serial mode, from the master unit the positioning data and subsequently transfers these coordinates, in the form of a string, to the HAR system via TCP/IP. To implement the transmission of location data to the STM32L475VG board, we configured the TCP connection, both on the Client (Board) and Server (PC) side, with both devices connected on the same WIFI network. For the transfer of the positioning data we have created a Matlab script with which we configure and start the server to communicate with the client. The hw components are the Master Unit, consisting of an N5 module (Dynastream Innovations, Cochrane, Alberta, Canada) connected to a PC via UART/USB (Universal Serial Bus) interface. Mobile Unit equipped with a D52 module (Dynastream Innovations, Cochrane, Alberta, Canada) built around the nRF52832 chip (Nordic Semiconductor ASA, Oslo, Norway). It includes a 12-bit ADC set at 200 kSamples/s and features a 64 MHz ARM Cortex M4 powered by a rechargeable lithium-ion battery. Central Unit comprises an N5 module and a microcontroller PIC16F1704 (MicrochipTechnology Inc., Chandler, AZ, USA) for the ultrasonic chirp storage and output through the built-in 8-bit DAC. A linear up-chirp in the bandwidth of 30–50 kHz is employed. The ultrasonic transducers are Series 7000 Electrostatic Transducer (SensComp Inc., Livonia, MI, USA).

4   Results

We connected a smartphone (ALCATEL mod. 5024DEEA) to the STM32L475VG board via BLE, and we used the Android STBLE Sensor application with which we configure the device and view the data transmitted by the sensors. The acquired data are both environmental and inertial. Environmental data, such as temperature, pressure, and humidity, are transmitted every 500 ms and are shown on the mobile device's display. The inertial data sent every 50 ms are used to recognize the activities carried out. The recognized activities are shown on the mobile device's display with a stylized graphic representation (Fig. 6). In it is displayed one of the following recognized activities: stationary, walking, jogging, or stairs. They usually appear grey and then turn blue once recognition begins.

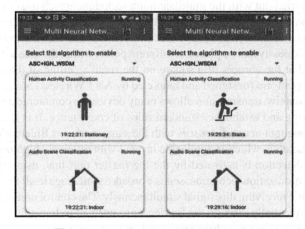

Fig. 6. Screenshot of recognized activities

We have chosen ten subjects to whom we have asked to carry out, at their choice, 100 activities as part of those to be monitored. For example, in the 1000 samples of activities carried out, we found 37.2% for walking, 29.2% for jogging, 22.2% for the stairs, and 11.4% for standing, as shown in the following distribution (Fig. 7).

The CNN network's recognition of these activities is implemented on the same sensor board. The identification is based on the analysis of the acceleration values. The activities related to the movements of the legs are characterized by periodic behaviors

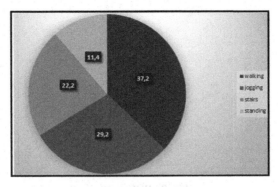

Fig. 7. Activities distribution

with acceleration peaks that facilitate their identification. On the other hand, activities of the standing type are characterized by almost constant acceleration values. The activities related to go upstairs and down stairs are difficult to identify as the two movements can be confused. To simplify the classification, we have combined the two activities by calling it stairs and using the location to interpret the movement correctly. The following figure (Fig. 8) shows the values obtained with the prediction and the accuracy values found in the right column. We got the best result on the walking activity.

PREDICTED VALUES

	Walking	Jogging	Stairs	Standing	Accuracy %
Walking	370	1	0	1	99,4
Jogging	2	289	1	0	98,9
Stairs	1	1	220	0	99
Standing	1	0	0	113	99,1

ACTUAL VALUES

Fig. 8. Confusion matrix

Figure 9 shows the Roc Curve (Receiver Operating Characteristic) which represents the performance of the classification model in which they are reported on the x-axis "*False Positive Rate*" (FPR) and on the y-axis "True Positive Rate" (TPR) where:

$TRP = \frac{TP}{TP+FN}$ and $FPR = \frac{FP}{FP+TN}$ with TP = True Positive, FP = False Positive, TN = True negative, FN = false Negative.

The area below the curve represents the AUC (Area Under the Curve). Its value indicates how much the model is able to distinguish between the various asset classes examined.

Integrating the internal localization model with the recognition system makes it possible to identify potentially dangerous situations.

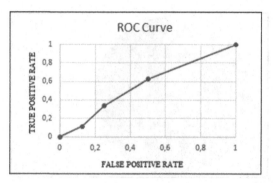

Fig. 9. ROC curve

5 Discussion

In this work, we have shown how, with an IoT platform (STML475VG) and a smartphone, it is possible to detect and recognize the daily activities carried out by older adults. We verified the validity of the methodological approach applied: the transformation of accelerometer data into classes transferred to the convolutional neural network for HAR classification, the use of commonly used smartphones, the absence of highly complex algorithms to obtain acceptable data, and verification of the model. From the results obtained, we can consider that the CNN model has proven to be valid for recognizing daily activities with greater accuracy for walking. The average accuracy was 99.1%, a value comparable to other asset classification models. However, there are few solutions like ours in microprocessors and sensors installed on a single small device. However, it has an advantage over other accelerometer-based systems that do not require additional data collection equipment and accurate recognition. Many solutions use multiple accelerometers or a combination of accelerometers and other sensors that can identify a wide field of activities but are impractical. There are also other experiences in which different combinations of sensors (GPS, accelerometers, and cameras) available on numerous commercial smartphones have been explored to recognize the usual activities. Although the prototype has been tested in the laboratory, its characteristics make it a potential home care solution. It can support caregivers and reduce health care costs by avoiding hospitalization and helping people maintain independent lifestyles. Therefore, IoT applications integrated into remote care services can support healthcare services and extend their use to a larger number of patients living in remote areas.

6 Conclusions

In this article, we have proposed an IoT application for the recognition of activities through the actions carried out by elderly This identification can be obtained using different sensors: we preferred a smartphone that connects to the STM32L475VG microcontroller via BLE and uses an Android STBLE Sensor application. The solution adopted represents an Edge Machine Learning solution because it integrates on the same IoT board both the collection of data for identifying activities and the CNN network for the classification of the same. This solution has many advantages. First, the opportunity to equip the patient with a device economically accessible and easy to use avoids wearing additional sensors that can annoy during the performance of the activities. Another important aspect is represented by choice of the microprocessor mentioned above, which is equipped with an internal STM32Programmer development environment that supports the entire development cycle of a project through the STM32CubeIDE environment, greatly facilitating the activity of researchers. It also benefits from a localization system based on an ultrasonic network for precisely defining the patient's position inside the house. The results showed an accuracy greater than 99% for the reconnaissance of walking, stairs, and standing activities comparable with other similar applications and precision in the localization of the order of cm. This is a low-cost and low power (3.8 μW) solution. In the literature, there are not numerous applications that combine localization with the activities carried out by patients, a determining factor to improve the accuracy of the position and facilitate interventions in cases of emergency. Our work is also characterized by having addressed this issue. Finding technological, low-cost, and low-complex solutions can be a stimulus. Further investigations may include other analysis models and test the algorithm in different areas and with various participants. Finally, we believe it can be integrated into a telemedicine architecture with the Cloud solution.

Acknowledgments. This work is supported by the Italian MIUR Project under GRANT PON Research and Innovation 2014–2020 Project Code C35E19000020001, AIM 1839112–1: Technologies for the living environment.

Conflicts of Interest. The authors declare no conflict of interest.

References

1. L'assistenza Agli Anziani non Autosufficienti in Italia 7 Rapporto 2020/2021
2. Pal, D., Triyason, T., Funikul, S.: Smart homes and quality of life for the elderly: a systematic view. IEEE Int. Symp. Multimed. (ISM) **11**(1), 413–419 (2017). https://doi.org/10.1109/ISM.2017.83
3. Cicirelli, G., Marani, R., Petitti, A., Milella, A., D'Orazio, T.: Ambient assisted living: a review of technologies, methodologies and future perspectives for healthy aging of population. Sensors **21**, 3549 (2021). https://doi.org/10.3390/s21103549
4. Nguyen, H.H., Mirza, F., Naeem, M.A., et al.: A review on IoT healthcare monitoring applications and a vision for transforming sensor data into real-time clinical feedback. In: IEEE 21st International Conference on Computer Supported Cooperative Work in Design (CSCWD), pp. 257–262 (2017). https://doi.org/10.1109/CSCWD.2017.8066704
5. Castillejo, P., Martinez, J., Rodriguez-Molina, J., Cuerva, A.: Integration of wearable devices in a wireless sensor network for an E-health application. IEEE Wirel. Commun. **20**(4), 38–49 (2013). https://doi.org/10.1109/MWC.2013.6590049
6. Shi, L., Wang, Y., Li, J.: A real time vision-based hand gestures recognition system. In: Cai, Z., Hu, C., Kang, Z., Liu, Y. (eds.) ISICA 2010. LNCS, vol. 6382, pp. 349–358. Springer, Heidelberg (2010). https://doi.org/10.1007/978-3-642-16493-4_36
7. Guan, D., Yuan, W., Jihad Sarkar, A., Ma, T.: Review of sensor-based activity recognition systems. IETE Tech. Rev. **28**(5), 418–433 (2011). https://doi.org/10.4103/0256-4602.85975

8. Zebin, T., Scully, P.J., Ozanyan, K.B.: Human activity recognition with inertial sensors using a deep learning approach. IEEE Sens. **66**, 1–3 (2016). https://doi.org/10.1109/ICSENS.2016. 7808590

9. Chander, H., et al.: Wearable stretch sensors for human movement monitoring and fall detection in ergonomics. Int. J. Environ. Res. Public Health **17**(10), 3554 (2020). https://doi.org/ 10.3390/ijerph17103554

10. Porta, A., Girardengo, G., Bari, V., George, A.L., Brink, P.A., Goosen, A., et al.: Autonomic control of heart rate and QT interval variability influences arrhythmic risk in long QT syndrome type 1. J. Am. Coll. Cardiol. **65**(4), 367–374 (2015). https://doi.org/10.1016/j.jacc. 2014.11.015

11. Antonic, D., Zagar, M.: Heuristic algorithms for extracting relevant features in signal analysis. Automatika **43**(1–2), 39–46 (2002)

12. Bibbo, L., Morabito, F.C.: Neural network design using a virtual reality platform. Glob. J. Comput. Sci. Technol. D Neural Artif. Intel. **22**(1), 45–61 (2022). https://doi.org/10.34257/ GJCSTDVOL22IS1PG45

13. Njima, W., Ariz, L., Zayani, R., Terre, M., Bouallegue, R.: Deep CNN for indoor localization in IoT-sensor systems. Sensors **19**(14), 3127 (2019). https://doi.org/10.3390/s19143127

14. Wang, J., Ghosh, R., Das, S.: A survey on sensor localization. J. Control Theory Appl. **8**, 2–11 (2010). https://doi.org/10.1007/s11768-010-9187-7

15. Liu, H., Darabi, H., Banerjee, P., Liu, J.: Survey of wireless indoor positioning techniques and systems. Systems Man Cybern. **37**, 1067–1080 (2007). https://doi.org/10.1109/TSMCC. 2007.905750

16. Awadalla, M., Kausar, F., Ahsan, R.: Developing an IoT platform for the elderly health care. Int. J. Adv. Comput. Sci. Appl. (IJACSA) **12**(4), 1–8 (2021). https://doi.org/10.14569/IJA CSA.2021.0120453

17. Žaric, N., Radonjic, M., Pavlicevic, N., Paunovic Žaric, S.: Design of a kitchen-monitoring and decision-making system to support AAL applications. Sensors **21**, 4449 (2021). https:// doi.org/10.3390/s21134449

18. Misra, A., Agnihotri, P., Dwivedi, J.K.: Advanced IoT based combined remote health monitoring and alarm system. Int. J. Adv. Res. Dev. **3**(4), 6–11 (2018)

19. Iranpak, S., Shahbahrami, A., Shakeri, H.: Remote patient monitoring and classifying using the internet of things platform combined with cloud computing. J. Big Data **8**(1), 1–22 (2021). https://doi.org/10.1186/s40537-021-00507-w

20. Jara, A.J., Zamora, M.A., Skarmeta, A.F.: Drug identification and interaction checker based on IoT to minimize adverse drug reactions and improve drug compliance. Pers. Ubiquit. Comput. **18**(1), 5–17 (2012). https://doi.org/10.1007/s00779-012-0622-2

21. Aruban, A., Alobaid, H., Clarke, N., Li, F.: Physical activity recognition by utilising smartphone sensor signals. In: The International Conference on Pattern Recognition Applications and Methods at: Prague, Czech Republic Conference Paper (2019). https://doi.org/10.5220/ 0007271903420351

22. Sikder, N., Chowdhury, M.S., Arif, A.S.M., Nahid, A.A.: Human activity recognition using multichannel convolutional neural network. In: 5th International Conference on Advances in Electrical Engineering (ICAEE), pp. 560–565 (2019). https://doi.org/10.1109/ICAEE48663. 2019.8975649

23. Merenda, M., Porcaro, C., Iero, D.: Edge machine learning for AI-enabled IoT devices: a review. Sensors **20**(9), 2533 (2020). https://doi.org/10.3390/s20092533

24. India, S., Goswami, A.K., Mishra, S.P., Pooja Asopa, P.: Conceptual understanding of convolutional neural network- a deep learning approach. Procedia Comput. Sci. **132**, 679–688 (2018). https://doi.org/10.1016/j.procs.2018.05.069

25. UM2526 User Manual – Getting started with X-CUBE-AI Expansion Package for Artificial Intelligence (AI) (2022)

26. https://en.formulasearchengine.com/wiki/Rodrigues%27_rotation_formula
27. Kwapisz, J.R., Weiss, G.M., Moore, S.A.: Activity recognition using cell phone accelerometers. ACM SIGKDD Explor. **12**(2), 74–82 (2011). https://doi.org/10.1145/1964897.196 4918
28. Obeidat, H., Shuaieb, W., Obeidat, O., Abd-Alhameed, R.: A review of indoor localization techniques and wireless technologies. Wirel. Pers. Commun. **119**(1), 289–327 (2021). https://doi.org/10.1007/s11277-021-08209-5
29. Din, M.M., Jamil, N., Maniam, J., Mohamed, M.A.: Review of indoor localization techniques. Int. J. Eng. Technol. **7**(2), 201–204 (2018)
30. Carotenuto, R., Merenda, M., Iero, D., Della Corte, F.G.: Indoor object positioning using smartphone and RFID or QRcode. In: 5th International Conference on Smart and Sustainable Technologies (SpliTech), pp. 1–6 (2020). https://doi.org/10.23919/SpliTech49282.2020.924 3703
31. Carotenuto, R., Merenda, M., Iero, D., Della Corte, F.G.: Mobile synchronization recovery for ultrasonic indoor positioning. Sensors **20**(3), 702 (2020). https://doi.org/10.3390/s20030702. The proposed method and the dataset analysed during the current study are available in the Git-Hub repository at the following link: https://github.com/Luigi2020357/MEMS-AI-HAR

Tackling the Linear Sum Assignment Problem with Graph Neural Networks

Carlo Aironi[(✉)], Samuele Cornell, and Stefano Squartini

Department of Information Engineering, Universitá Politecnica delle Marche,
Ancona, Italy
{c.aironi,s.cornell}@pm.univpm.it, s.squartini@univpm.it

Abstract. Linear Assignment Problems are fundamental combinatorial optimization problems that appear throughout domains such as logistics, robotics and telecommunications. In general, solving assignment problems to optimality is computationally infeasible even for contexts of small dimensionality, and so heuristic algorithms are often employed to find near-optimal solutions. The handcrafting of a heuristic usually requires expert-knowledge to exploit the problem structure to be addressed, however if the problem description changes slightly, a previously derived heuristic may no longer be appropriate.

This work explores a more general-purpose learning approach, based on the description of the problem through a bipartite graph, and the use of a Message Passing Graph Neural Network model, to attain the correct assignment permutation.

The simulation results indicate that the proposed structure allows for a significant increase in classification accuracy if compared with two different DNN approaches based on Dense Networks and Convolutional Neural Networks, furthermore, the GNN has proved to be very efficient with regard to the processing time and memory requirements, thanks to intrinsic parameter-sharing capability.

Keywords: Linear assignment problem · Graph neural networks · Deep neural networks

1 Introduction

Linear assignment [2] is a fundamental problem of combinatorial optimization; it aims to assign the elements of some finite set to the elements of another set. This is done under one-to-one matching constraints such that the resulting assignment satisfies some optimality conditions, like a minimum cost, or, in a dual way, a maximum profit. Let the sum of the costs be the objective to be minimized, it is called Linear Sum Assignment Problem (LSAP).

This kind of problem is found in many computer vision applications such as point matching [13], handwritten characters and mathematical expressions recognition [8], multi-object tracking (MOT) [18] and object segmentation [7].

© The Author(s), under exclusive license to Springer Nature Switzerland AG 2022
M. Mahmud et al. (Eds.): AII 2022, CCIS 1724, pp. 90–101, 2022.
https://doi.org/10.1007/978-3-031-24801-6_7

On wireless communication systems it plays an important role in tasks such as mode selection for device-to-device communications [23], joint resource allocation in MIMO systems [14], and unlicensed channel management for LTE systems [19]. On audio processing field, the permutation ambiguity problem of multiple source separation [22] is closely related to LSAP, as well as the end-to-end neural diarization [5].

A well-established method for linear assignment is the Hungarian algorithm, developed in 1955 by H. Kuhn [11] and reviewed in 1957 by J. Munkres [15], which can obtain the optimal solution without a greedy search. However, its computational complexity is $\mathcal{O}(N^3)$ thus it is extremely sensitive to the size of the problem. Since then, several approximate algorithms have been proposed to seek acceptable sub-optimal solutions with time and resource constraints: deep greedy switching [16], interior point algorithms [9] and auction algorithm [1] to name a few. Some of these have polynomial complexity and can solve the problem very efficiently, however, it is difficult to formulate the gradients of these heuristic linear assignment solvers, which prevents them from being directly embedded into learning frameworks.

Recently, deep neural networks (DNNs) have achieved interesting results on mathematical optimization problems, such as wireless resource management allocation [21], link scheduling optimization [10] or interference management [20].

In this work we build upon the framework proposed by Lee et al. [12] where LSAP of different dimensionality N are decomposed into N sub-assignment problems, and two types of DNNs, a feed-forward neural network (FNN) and a convolutional neural network (CNN) are applied to address the sub-assignments as independent classification tasks.

In this work, a graph-based description of the problem is proposed, and a GNN learning technique is applied to solve the assignment task; we aim to show that the proposed graph representation of the cost matrix allows for an efficient information spread, exploiting relations between all agent-job pairs even for GNNs with limited depth. Conversely, in the CNN approach the convolutional kernels cover a narrow receptive field, requiring the stacking of several layers to cover the whole cost matrix as the size of the problem increases.

This paper is organized as follows: in Sect. 2 the LSAP problem is formalized, while in Sect. 3 GNNs and graphs are briefly introduced. Following, in Sect. 4 we explain in detail the proposed approach, the loss function, the evaluation metric criterion and the neural architectures employed in the experiments. We present and discuss the dataset generation policy and the experimental results in Sect. 5, and finally in Sect. 6 we draw conclusions and outline possible future works. Code is made available at: github.com/aircarlo/GNN_LSAP.

2   LSAP Problem Formulation

Assignment problems are generally described as dealing with the question of how to assign N items (e.g. *jobs*) to N different *workers* or *agents*. Given a finite set of agents: $I = \{1, 2, ..., N\}$ and a finite set of jobs $J = \{1, 2, ..., N\}$, both with the same cardinality, let assume that the assignment of job i to agent j incurs a cost $c_{i,j}$. The problem can be expressed as an integer binary programming problem, where the decision variable $x_{i,j}$ is set to 1 if job j is assigned to agent i, and is set to 0 otherwise. Therefore, the linear assignment problem can be expressed as the minimization of the following objective function:

$$\sum_{i=1}^{N}\sum_{j=1}^{N} c_{i,j} x_{i,j} \tag{1}$$

subject to the constraints:

$$\sum_{i=1}^{N} x_{i,j} = 1 \qquad j = 1..N \tag{2}$$

$$\sum_{j=1}^{N} x_{i,j} = 1 \qquad i = 1..N \tag{3}$$

$$x_{i,j} \in \{0,1\} \qquad i,j = 1..N \tag{4}$$

Mathematically, assignments can be modeled and visualized in different ways, such as a *permutation* ϕ of the elements inside set I or set J, or with a *permutation matrix* X_ϕ, whose elements $x_{i,j} = 1$ if $j = \phi(i)$, and $x_{i,j} = 0$ if $j \neq \phi(i)$. This square binary matrix can also be viewed as the *Adjacency matrix* of a *bipartite assignment graph* (Fig. 1).

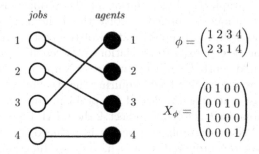

Fig. 1. Different representations for the same assignment permutation.

3   Graph Neural Networks

In many real-world applications, such as social networks, chemistry, physics and, broadly, semantic knowledge representation, data can be naturally modeled with a graph structure [24]. However, due to the absence of an Euclidean structure, machine learning over graph data is challenging to process using DNNs in a conventional way. For this reason, Graph Neural Networks (GNNs) have been developed, historically with the aim to provide a powerful tool for graph representation learning.

A Graph is represented as $G = (V, E)$, where V is the set of *vertices* or *nodes*, and E is the set of *edges*; let $v_i \in V$ to denote a node, and $e_{ij} = (v_i, v_j) \in E$ to denote a directed edge from node i to node j. The overall topology is provided by the *Adjacency matrix* $A \in \{0,1\}^{|V| \times |V|}$, where $A_{ij} = 1$ if $e_{ij} \in E$ and $A_{ij} = 0$ otherwise. A node may have numerical attributes, $\mathbf{x} \in \mathbb{R}^D$, as can edges, $\mathbf{e_{i,j}} \in \mathbb{R}^F$.

The notion of graph neural networks was initially outlined in Gori et al. [6] and further elaborated in Scarselli et al. [17]. These early models implicitly define the *Spatial Convolution* operator, first coining the concept of *Message Passing* (MP) mechanism, which tries to capture information from the graph structure as well as from the nodes and edges feature vectors, by aggregating informative "messages" gathered from neighboring nodes. ConvGNNs generalize the operation of convolution, which is a widely popular concept on image processing field, from grid data to non-Euclidean graph data. A general framework is described by Eq. 5, it expresses the updating rule of node v_i's representation at network layer k: the node feature vector is computed by aggregating its own previous features $\mathbf{x}_i^{(k-1)}$, neighbors' features $\mathbf{x}_j^{(k-1)}$ and their edge features $\mathbf{e}_{j,i}$:

$$\mathbf{x}_i^{(k)} = \gamma^{(k)} \left(\mathbf{x}_i^{(k-1)}, M_{j \in \mathcal{N}(i)} \left(\phi^{(k)} \left(\mathbf{x}_i^{(k-1)}, \mathbf{x}_j^{(k-1)}, \mathbf{e}_{j,i} \right) \right) \right) \tag{5}$$

where M represents a differentiable, permutation invariant function (tipically, *sum*, *mean* or *max*), γ and ϕ denote differentiable functions such as MLPs (Multi Layer Perceptrons).

An intresting strenght point of ConvGNNs, compared with other architectures such as *dense networks* or CNNs, is their scalability towards large graphs, this is due to the localized action of the MP mechanism, which results in an efficient parameter sharing and consequent memory savings.

4   Proposed Method

In the following, given the assignment problem, the cost overview has been modeled with a fully connected bipartite graph, a structure where the set of vertices can be divided into two disjoint sets or classes, and the only edges connect vertices from one class to those of the other class. Let N be the problem dimensionality, the associated graph has $2N$ nodes; N of which represent agents while the rest represent jobs.

The input raw feature vectors of the nodes, $\mathbf{x}_{i,j}$, are initialized with the cost values between source agents and receive jobs, according to the cost matrix $C \in \mathbb{R}^{N \times N}$:

$$\mathbf{x}_i = [C_{i,1} \ldots C_{i,N}] \qquad i = 1..N \quad agents$$

$$\mathbf{x}_j = [C_{1,j} \ldots C_{N,j}] \qquad j = 1..N \quad jobs$$

Conversely, all the raw attributes of the edges $\mathbf{e}_{ij}$ in the constructed graph are initialized with zero-valued vectors, hence they are not taken into account by the convolution operator (Fig. 2).

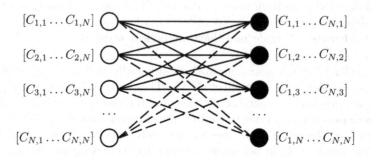

$[C_{1,1}\ldots C_{1,N}]$ $[C_{1,1}\ldots C_{N,1}]$

$[C_{2,1}\ldots C_{2,N}]$ $[C_{1,2}\ldots C_{N,2}]$

$[C_{3,1}\ldots C_{3,N}]$ $[C_{1,3}\ldots C_{N,3}]$

$[C_{N,1}\ldots C_{N,N}]$ $[C_{1,N}\ldots C_{N,N}]$

Fig. 2. Illustration of the nodes and edges definition, from the cost matrix to the corresponding bipartite graph.

The GNN structure is composed of K layers, through which graph preserves its bipartite layout, while node feature vectors are updated according to the message passing operator expressed by the following equation:

$$\mathbf{x}_i^{(k)} = \frac{1}{|\mathcal{N}(i)|} \sum_{j\in\mathcal{N}(i)} MLP\left(\mathbf{x}_i^{(k-1)}|\mathbf{x}_j^{(k-1)}\right) \tag{6}$$

On Eq. 6 MLP is a dense network with a single hidden layer, and its input vector is obtained by concatenating the attribute vector of node i with that of each of its neighbours.

Finally, the feature map at last layer, $X^{(K)} = [\mathbf{x}_1^{(K)}\ldots\mathbf{x}_{2N}^{(K)}]^\top$ is transformed to the actual output $Y \in \mathbb{R}^{N\times N}$ through a linear projection with learnable parameters $\Theta \in \mathbb{R}^{N\times 2N}$, to obtain the estimated assignment matrix:

$$Y = \Theta X^{(K)} \tag{7}$$

4.1   Loss Function and Evaluation Metric

The proposed model solves the assignment task as $2N$ separate classifiers to jointly comply both constraints of the assignment problem formulation (Eq. 2–3); at train stage, the predicted scores are obtained from the output logits Y by applying softmax operations, in both row-wise and column-wise directions:

$$\mathbf{r}_i = softmax\left(\mathbf{y}_{i,1}\ldots\mathbf{y}_{i,N}\right) \tag{8}$$

$$\mathbf{c}_j = softmax\left(\mathbf{y}_{1,j}\ldots\mathbf{y}_{N,j}\right) \tag{9}$$

then, given the ground truth binary assignment matrix $\hat{Y} \in \mathbb{R}^{N \times N}$, the cross-entropy loss is computed for each of the $2N$ separate classifiers, in the form of *negative-log likelihood*:

$$\mathcal{L}_r = -\frac{1}{N} \sum_{i=1}^{N} \sum_{j=1}^{N} \mathbf{r}_{ij} \cdot \log\left(\hat{\mathbf{y}}_{i,j}\right) \tag{10}$$

$$\mathcal{L}_c = -\frac{1}{N} \sum_{i=1}^{N} \sum_{j=1}^{N} \mathbf{c}_{ij} \cdot \log\left(\hat{\mathbf{y}}_{i,j}\right) \tag{11}$$

finally, the total loss $\mathcal{L} = \mathcal{L}_r + \mathcal{L}_c$ is backpropagated to update the network weights.

At inference stage, the output prediction matrix Y passes through a threshold criterion, to obtain a binary assignment map, whose rows and columns are one-hot encoded vectors: to avoid "collisions" (e.g. multiple jobs assigned to the same agent or multiple agents assigned to the same job) the N highest values are detected from the prediction matrix, requiring that each row and each column have exactly one of them.

To benchmark our proposed approach we use Accuracy as defined in [12], that is, the amount of jobs correctly matching their optimal agents, divided by N. This also lets us to compare directly with methods proposed in [12].

4.2 Network Architecture

The Graph Neural Network consisted of $K = 2$ layers, which has been proven to be the optimal depth for each of the problem dimensionality (N) evaluated. A higher number of layers showed the same performance with the drawback of parameters, memory and time consumption increase.

The MLP network used for message propagation has one input layer of size $2N$, an hidden layer with 128 neurons, a ReLU activation and an output layer of size N. This configuration was applied identically for all investigated values: $N = \{2, 4, 8, 12, 16\}$.

4.3 Dataset

The policy we adopted to generate data samples follows those implemented in the reference paper, although we investigated some minor variations. First we generated 100.000 synthetic cost matrices, drawing samples from a continuous uniform distribution: $c_{i,j} \sim U[0,1)$, then, 20% of such matrices were reserved for the validation process, while the remaining 80% were used for training.

Running experiments, several times with identical settings, we ensured that the chosen amount of data is sufficiently large to avoid the model to overfit. With the same criterion we generated 20.000 samples which are used for testing.

In order to further reduce the dependence of the results to a specific data distribution, we tried to run train and validation phases generating different samples at every epoch, but did not obtain a noticeable improvement.

The ground truth decision matrix $\hat{Y}$ is obtained at runtime for each sample, using the Hungarian algorithm; specifically we used the *munkres* Python package [3] which implements the original algorithm.

4.4   Compared Approaches

The FNN and CNN approaches we took as comparison [12] face LSAP by first decomposing it into N separate sub-assignment problems on how to assign one of N jobs to agent j. Only constraints of Eq. 2 and Eq. 4 are strictly guaranteed, while the constraint of Eq. 3 is not taken in consideration at train time, hence there may exist some collisions such that one job may be assigned to different agents simultaneously. To prevent this issue, a greedy collision-avoidance rule is applied to finally state the actual assignment.

The FNN and CNN architectures consisted of N models in parallel; the former has four layers with 32, 64, 256, and N hidden neurons, and ReLU nonlinearity, while the latter (CNN) includes five convolutional layers, each containing 32, 32, 32, 32, and N kernels of size 1×1, and an output projection map. In both cases, cross-entropy is taken as objective criterion, while Adam is used as optimization algorithm.

5   Experiments and Results

Models were trained up to 50 epochs; the learning rate was initially set to the value of $6 \cdot 10^{-3}$, and then halved if validation loss is not improved within a patience interval of 5 epochs. Empirically, it has been found that the learning rate is halved only once within the entire training stage; an extension of the training interval does not lead to further improvements. Sthochastic Gradient Descent (SGD) was used as optimization algorithm, with L_2 weight decay of $5 \cdot 10^{-4}$.

We investigated the role of batch size during training, finding that large values decelerate the convergence in terms of total required epochs, thus nullifying the advantage given by parallel computation. On the other hand, contrary to what reported in [12], a low batch size did not lead to unstable convergence behavior, in fact we were able to achieve the optimal results in the least number of epochs, using the batch value of 1.

Once the training is over, the model checkpoint with best validation accuracy is selected and evaluated on the test set.

5.1   Results

We report in Table 1 the results obtained in terms of accuracy, in conjuction with the bar plot of Fig. 3, where we compared the proposed graph approach with the other solutions described on Sect. 4.4: FNN and CNN.

Table 1. Accuracy performance comparison for the proposed GNN architecture and reference learning approaches, for different problem size N.

Model	$N = 2$	$N = 4$	$N = 8$	$N = 12$	$N = 16$
FNN [12]	0.9849	0.9763	0.7019	0.5918	0.5614
CNN [12]	0.9974	**0.9829**	0.8295	0.6605	0.6274
GNN	**0.9997**	0.9660	**0.8477**	**0.7856**	**0.7361**

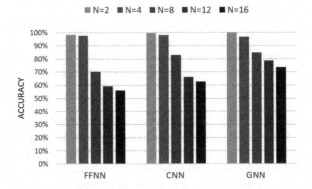

Fig. 3. Accuracy comparison bar chart between the proposed GNN architecture and reference learning approaches.

The proposed GNN model exhibited performance improvements of 0,2% ($N = 2$), 2,2% ($N = 8$), 18,9% ($N = 12$) and 17,3% ($N = 16$) if compared with the conventional CNN, while the improvements have risen to 1,5% ($N = 2$), 20,8% ($N = 8$), 32,7% ($N = 12$) and 31,1% ($N = 16$) if compared with the conventional FNN. Conversely, a slight worsening of accuracy has been observed for $N = 4$, however, the significant improvement achieved as N increases suggests that large LSAP problems may benefit more from the GNN approach than the CNN or FNN ones; this is one of the aspects we are planning to investigate as future developement.

An interesting aspect which characterizes the GNN framework is the limited amount of memory required. Since the FNN and the CNN approached the LSAP problem as N different classifiers, the parameters are shared to a limited extent within each of these classifiers; moreover, each of them needs the entire cost matrix as input, which causes a noticeable overhead. On the other hand, the message passing operator (Eq. 6) allows for efficient reuse of the internal MLP, since it operates at node-level. Table 2 reports the exact count of learnable params and MAC, Multiply and Accumulate operations involved for each of the considered architectures; the values has been estimated feeding the networks in forward mode, with a single-batch input sample.

Figure 4 helps to better visualize the trends of required parameters (Fig. 4, top) and MAC (Fig. 4, bottom) as N increases.

Table 2. Resource requirements and MAC operations for different models.

Size N	Learnable parameters					MACs				
	2	4	8	12	16	2	4	8	12	16
FNN [12]	38.8k	81.3k	183.1k	317.7k	497.4k	38.1k	79.8k	180.2k	313.3k	491.5k
CNN [12]	9.7k	13.7k	32.1k	64.4k	125.9k	26.4k	215.5k	1.79M	6.29M	15.46M
GNN	2.5k	4.9k	9.6k	14.4k	19.2k	18.4k	147.5k	1.18M	3.98M	9.44M

Finally, on Table 3 and Fig. 5 we report an estimation of mean execution time, obtained over 10.000 runs, between the proposed approach, the comparison ones, and the Hungarian algorithm implemented in plain Python language [3].

We can note the explosion in time burden, which makes the Hungarian algorithm impracticable to apply, even for small dimensions.

All experiments were conducted on an Ubuntu 16.04 machine, with six Intel(R) Core(TM) i7-6850K CPUs @ 3.60 GHz and 32 GB RAM; network models were developed in Python language with PyTorch and PyTorch geometric [4] framework libraries.

Table 3. Measurement of CPU payload mean time when processing a single-batch LSAP instance, for different architectures. Times are expressed in microseconds.

Model	$N = 2$	$N = 4$	$N = 8$	$N = 12$	$N = 16$
FNN [12]	177,2	340,8	639,2	1023,6	1314,4
CNN [12]	221,5	454,0	934,0	1731,0	2324,4
GNN	331,1	353,8	446,7	583,5	813,3
Hungarian [3]	28,7	88,2	518,6	1719,2	4197,5

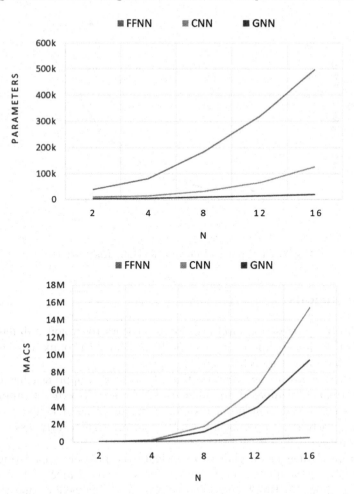

Fig. 4. Trend in demand for memory parameters requirements (top) and MAC operations (bottom) as N increases.

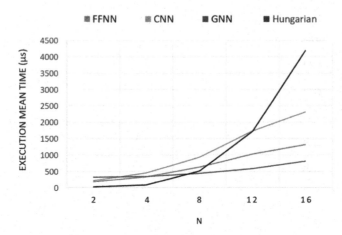

Fig. 5. CPU payload mean time comparison chart.

6   Conclusions

In this work we proposed a novel learning framework to exploit a differentiable approach of the linear sum assignment problem, and then compared the performances with two existing NN-based strategies.

We demonstrated experimentally that the proposed approach has competitive performance, compared to previous FNN and CNN based approaches, regarding small assignment problems. For larger problems it is able to outperform significantly these approaches, while requiring significantly less computational resources.

As future challenge, we plan to investigate the possible application of the proposed GNN assignment solver, in the aforementioned area of Permutation Invariant Training for Blind Audio Source Separation; we believe that the information learned from the assignment task can be integrated with profit in the signal separation model, in order to obtain better performance or speed up training time, as number of concurrent speakers scales up.

References

1. Bertsekas, D.P.: The auction algorithm: a distributed relaxation method for the assignment problem. Ann. Oper. Res. **14**(1), 105–123 (1988)
2. Burkard, R., Dragoti-Cela, E.: Linear assignment problems and extensions. Supplement Volume A, 1 edn., pp. 75–149. Kluwer Academic Publishers, Netherlands (1999)
3. Clapper, B.M.: Munkres implementation for python. https://github.com/bmc/munkres. Accessed 10 May 2022
4. Fey, M., Lenssen, J.E.: Fast graph representation learning with PyTorch geometric. In: ICLR Workshop on Representation Learning on Graphs and Manifolds (2019)
5. Fujita, Y., Kanda, N., Horiguchi, S., Xue, Y., Nagamatsu, K., Watanabe, S.: End-to-end neural speaker diarization with self-attention. In: 2019 IEEE Automatic

Speech Recognition and Understanding Workshop (ASRU), pp. 296–303. IEEE (2019)

6. Gori, M., Monfardini, G., Scarselli, F.: A new model for learning in graph domains. In: International Joint Conference on Neural Networks, vol. 2, pp. 729–734. IEEE (2005)

7. Haralick, R.M., Shapiro, L.G.: Image segmentation techniques. Comput. Vision Graph. Image Process. **29**(1), 100–132 (1985)

8. Hirata, N.S., Julca-Aguilar, F.D.: Matching based ground-truth annotation for online handwritten mathematical expressions. Pattern Recogn. **48**(3), 837–848 (2015)

9. Karmarkar, N., Ramakrishnan, K.: Computational results of an interior point algorithm for large scale linear programming. Math. Program. **52**(1), 555–586 (1991)

10. de Kerret, P., Gesbert, D., Filippone, M.: Decentralized deep scheduling for interference channels. arXiv preprint arXiv:1711.00625 (2017)

11. Kuhn, H.W.: The Hungarian method for the assignment problem. Naval Res. Logist. Q. **2**(1–2), 83–97 (1955)

12. Lee, M., Xiong, Y., Yu, G., Li, G.Y.: Deep neural networks for linear sum assignment problems. IEEE Wirel. Commun. Lett. **7**(6), 962–965 (2018)

13. Lian, W., Zhang, L.: A concave optimization algorithm for matching partially overlapping point sets. Pattern Recogn. **103**, 107322 (2020)

14. Lu, X., Ni, Q., Li, W., Zhang, H.: Dynamic user grouping and joint resource allocation with multi-cell cooperation for uplink virtual MIMO systems. IEEE Trans. Wireless Commun. **16**(6), 3854–3869 (2017)

15. Munkres, J.: Algorithms for the assignment and transportation problems. J. Soc. Ind. Appl. Math. **5**(1), 32–38 (1957)

16. Naiem, A., El-Beltagy, M., Ab, P.: Deep greedy switching: a fast and simple approach for linear assignment problems. In: 7th International Conference of Numerical Analysis and Applied Mathematics, p. 9999 (2009)

17. Scarselli, F., Gori, M., Tsoi, A.C., Hagenbuchner, M., Monfardini, G.: The graph neural network model. IEEE Trans. Neural Netw. **20**(1), 61–80 (2008)

18. Smith, K., Gatica-Perez, D., Odobez, J.M., Ba, S.: Evaluating multi-object tracking. In: 2005 IEEE Computer Society Conference on Computer Vision and Pattern Recognition (CVPR 2005)-Workshops, p. 36. IEEE (2005)

19. Song, H., Fang, X., Fang, Y.: Unlicensed spectra fusion and interference coordination for LTE systems. IEEE Trans. Mob. Comput. **15**(12), 3171–3184 (2016)

20. Sun, H., Chen, X., Shi, Q., Hong, M., Fu, X., Sidiropoulos, N.D.: Learning to optimize: training deep neural networks for interference management. IEEE Trans. Signal Process. **66**(20), 5438–5453 (2018)

21. Sun, H., Chen, X., Shi, Q., Hong, M., Fu, X., Sidiropoulos, N.D.: Learning to optimize: training deep neural networks for wireless resource management. In: 2017 IEEE 18th International Workshop on Signal Processing Advances in Wireless Communications (SPAWC), pp. 1–6. IEEE (2017)

22. Yu, D., Kolbæk, M., Tan, Z.H., Jensen, J.: Permutation invariant training of deep models for speaker-independent multi-talker speech separation. In: 2017 IEEE International Conference on Acoustics, Speech and Signal Processing (ICASSP), pp. 241–245. IEEE (2017)

23. Yu, G., Xu, L., Feng, D., Yin, R., Li, G.Y., Jiang, Y.: Joint mode selection and resource allocation for device-to-device communications. IEEE Trans. Commun. **62**(11), 3814–3824 (2014)

24. Zhou, J., et al.: Graph neural networks: a review of methods and applications. AI Open **1**, 57–81 (2020)

A Nonparametric Model for Forecasting Life Expectancy at Birth Using Gaussian Process

Pranta Biswas[1], Fahmida Islam Ireen[1], Fairooz Ahsan Nawar[1],
Maisha Tabassum[1], Muhammad Arifur Rahman[2(✉)], Mufti Mahmud[2,3],
M. Shamim Kaiser[4], and David J. Brown[2,3]

[1] Department of ICT, Bangladesh University of Professionals, Dhaka, Bangladesh
[2] Department of Computer Science, Nottingham Trent University,
Nottingham NG11 8NS, UK
muhammad.rahman02@ntu.ac.uk
[3] CIRC and MTIF, Nottingham Trent University, Nottingham NG11 8NS, UK
[4] IIT, Jahangirnagar University, Dhaka, Bangladesh
arif@juniv.edu

Abstract. Gaussian Process Regression (GPR), a Bayesian nonparametric machine learning modelling technique, is gaining interest in recent times in many fields as a practical and powerful approach. To plan for economic services for any nation, projections of future Life Expectancy (LE) are required. In our research, we have proposed a model to forecast LE using GPR up to 2040. Initially, we sub-categorized countries into four sections based on income level. Then we treated LE at birth for different countries as a time series to create our model. Among the data of 165 countries we have, we used 27 countries' 60 years of LE data (1960–2019) to optimize and visualize the performance of our model. In our model, we used to maximize log-marginal-likelihood (LML) for each prediction while optimizing the hyper-parameters of our models. We further verified our model using cross-validation, fitting the model into 40 years of data and validating the other 20 available. Our prediction model's results demonstrated the subtle increase of LE over the years, which varied depending on the income groups. We have made the data processing and model development code publicly available via GitHub to carry forward this research.

Keywords: Life expectancy · Gaussian process · Prediction · Income level

1 Introduction

Life Expectancy (LE) [11,13,32] at birth is one of the key indicators of how prosperous and civilized a society is. LE reflects not only medical advancements that lead to a longer lifespan over time, but also various factors such as economics, education, geographical and environmental conditions. Thus, predicting

M. Mahmud et al. (Eds.): AII 2022, CCIS 1724, pp. 102–116, 2022.
https://doi.org/10.1007/978-3-031-24801-6_8

the future human lifespan will give us a brief idea of these parameters. It will also be valuable for a country to plan for the future in terms of resource management. LE at birth has been treated as a time series and assumes that it follows Gaussian Process (GP) [23,27]. Gaussian Process Regression (GPR) has long been proven to be an effective and powerful Bayesian non-parametric technique, with applications in a variety of domains. We have treated LE as a time series and used GPR to forecast future values of the different countries' LE.

Over the last decade machine learning (ML), Deep Learning (DL) and explainable AI (XAI) has been successfully applied to a diverse range of applications. i.e. Engagement Analysis, Autism Spectrum Disorder (ASD) detection and prediction [5,16,24,30], classification [6,9], recommendation system [10,18], trust management [15], spoof detection [7], healthcare [26] and many more domains. For LE prediction, so far the approaches that have been used are mostly based on parametric statistics [13,32]. There has been little to no use of a non-parametric approach in this field of prediction. While LE at birth is counted only on a yearly basis for a country, the recent year's LE contributes more to the future year's LE so it is wise to create a regression model with only the last few years' data. Thus, it further limits the dataset. GP has been proven to be an extremely powerful Bayesian non-parametric approach for regression problems [23,25,27]. It requires only a few data points to show excellent performance. So, using GPR can become a really viable method for forecasting LE at birth. In the proposed work, we analyzed and provided a verdict on the outcome of our model for different income groups, where we made comments about similarities within the same income group and dissimilarities between different groups, finding exceptions in our outcomes and providing valid reasons for these. The following research concentrates on 3 points and contributes to them: i). Prediction of LE up to year 2040, ii). Finding similarity in LE between same income groups, iii). Analysis of LE trend to identify progress for different countries.

2   Literature Review

The majority of the work that had been done on LE prediction is based on parametric approaches. While GPR is a viable non-parametric approach to prediction, when there is only a small amount of data is available for usage. The following subsections verify our claims.

2.1   Life Expectancy

The most popular method of forecasting life expectancy was the Lee-Carter method [13]. The model used the life table of US to forecast LE for different years up to 2065. Standard statistical methods have been used for the purpose of prediction. Death rates based on age-specific phenomena is the strongest part of this model rather than traditional models of that era. Kontis et al. proposed a probabilistic Bayesian Model Averaging approach to forecast mortality and LE of 35 industrialized countries until 2030 [11]. Their approach used 21 models, and ensembles of those models contributed to the final projections. Torri et al. proposed a model that predicts the future values of the LE by using Brownian motion which uses discrete geometry and a mean-reverting process model [32]. Here, the LE of all countries is modeled by an Autoregressive Integrated Moving Average model. Raftery et al. proposed a model based on Bayesian Hierarchy which makes probabilistic forecasts about the LE of a male at birth for all countries to 2100 [21]. Data from 1950 to 1995 has been fitted to their model, and they are using that data to forecast for the next ten years for verification purposes. Later they extended their work by projecting the female LE. They proceeded to project the LE gap between males and females using the frequentist model to project the LE of both genders [22]. Pascariu et al. used the double-gap LE method involving three steps [19]. Initially, a linear model has been used to predict female LE which is called the best-practice trend. The discrepancy between the gathered data from the initial model and country-specific female LE is then forecast using an ARIMA model. Finally, by projecting the discrepancy between male and female LE into a linear model, a final result is produced. Bennett et al. developed a Bayesian Spatiotemporal model to forecast age-specific LE and mortality at a small-area level [4]. They developed five forecasting models to integrate the characteristics of mortality rates in relation to birth cohort and age, as well as throughout place and time, to predict both sexes' LE. It was a unique approach to calculate LE but the feasibility of this method at large scale is yet to be proven. Wolf et al. investigated continuous patterns in expectancy at childbirth and death rates (deaths per 100,000) in the US, focusing on midlife, which is classified as people aged 25–60 [33]. The result showed that for the majority of the previous six decades, LE in the US has increased, but the pace of increase has reduced with time, while LE began to decline after 2014.

2.2   Gaussian Process

Rasumussen et al. first introduced GP for regression [27]. They initially discussed the Bayesian approach to Neural Networks and its complex prior distribution over functions. They applied GP priors over functions, which allowed predictive Bayesian analysis for fixed valued hyperparameters. A new design of the GPR model has been proposed by Lam et al. by using the spectral mixture covariance function and the natural cubic spline mean function as an advanced proposal for fertility and mortality modeling and forecasting [12]. It showcased the GPR model in a discrete yet intensive manner by using two empirical data. Although this Gaussian process regression model accurately captures the patterns in historical demographic data, it is unable to incorporate and model other relevant data. Wu et al. proposed a model to forecast mortality rates using GPR [34]. Initially, four conventional GPR models were used to forecast the mortality rates at different age-specific ranges. Then, to increase the forecasting accuracy, the spectral mixture covariance function and weighted mean function have been used in the GPR model. Sheng et al. presented a strategy that uses a weighted GPR technique to give data samples with higher outlier potential a low weight [29]. This method provides a simple way to obtain information from large amounts of data. Feature extraction technologies might be integrated for systems with greater real-time requirements in order to improve operational efficiency. Ahmed et al. performed a comparison of ML models for time series forecasting and regression by challenging them on a massive scale [2]. Multilayer perceptron and then Gaussian processes proved to be the best approach. Makridakis et al. compared statistical and ML forecasting in terms of error rate and computational resources [17]. Even though their tests demonstrated that statistical models outperformed ML models, GPR emerged as the best performing ML model.

3   Methodology

3.1   Gaussian Process Regression

A probability distribution over all possible values has been inferred by the Bayesian approach for GPR [27]. Let's consider a noisy non-linear regression model

$$y = f(z) + \varepsilon \tag{1}$$

The Bayesian approach works by providing a prior distribution, $f(t)$, on the parameter, t, and relocating probability depending on observed data using Bayes' Rule

$$p(z|y, X) = \frac{p(y|X, z)p(z))}{p(y|X)} \tag{2}$$

where $p(z)$ is a GP prior, $(y|X, z)$ is likelihood, $p(y|X)$ is marginal likelihood and $p(z|y, X)$ is posterior process. The predictive distribution can be determined by weighing all possible predictions by their calculated posterior distribution to produce predictions at unseen points of interest, x^*

$$p(f^*|x^*, y, X) = \int_z (f^*|x^*, t)p(z|y, X)dt \tag{3}$$

The likelihood and prior are considered to be Gaussian. We use this assumption to generate a Gaussian distribution and solve for the predictive distribution, from which we may extract a point prediction using the mean and quantify uncertainty using the variance.

In GP, it is assumed that f has a GP prior with a covariance function k and thought to be a random function. The covariance function connects two points and is defined as:

$$k(z, z'; \theta) = Cov(f(z), f(z')) \tag{4}$$

Here hyper-parameters which need to be tuned are denoted by the set of θ. Let be our noisy dataset $D = (z_1, y_1), (z_2, y_2), ..., (z_n, y_n)$, thus we have

$$y = f(z_i) + \varepsilon_i \tag{5}$$

3.2   Covariance Function

In our LE data, two common features can be noted among different countries. Initially, we noted a long-term smooth rising trend. To model this feature, squared exponential covariance function is used

$$k_1(x, x') = \theta_1^2 exp\left(-\frac{(x - x')^2}{2\theta_2^2}\right)$$ (6)

In Eq. 6, θ_1 controls the amplitude and θ_2 controls the length-scale. And the second feature we noted is medium term irregularities and to deal with this a rational quadratic covariance function is used

$$k_2(x, x') = \theta_3^2 exp\left(1 + \frac{(x - x')^2}{2\theta_4\theta_5^2}\right)^{-\theta_4}$$ (7)

Here, the magnitude is the shape parameter that determines the diffuseness of the length scale in this case, and the length scale is controlled by respectively θ_3 θ_4 and θ_5. Lastly, a noisy model has been suggested as the sum of a RBF kernel and an independent component, which defines the noise in our data

$$k_3(x_m, x_n) = \theta_6^2 exp\left(-\frac{(x - x')^2}{2\theta_7^2}\right) + \theta_8^2 \delta_{mn}.$$ (8)

Here, the magnitude, length-scale, and the magnitude of noise component are controlled by θ_6 θ_7 and θ_8. So, we get our final covariance function as follows,

$$k(x, x') = k_1(x, x') + k_2(x, x') + k_3(x, x')$$ (9)

To ensure best fitting of the data in our model, we maximized the log-marginal-likelihood by optimizing the prior value of hyperparameters. As we fed more data into the model, the functional distribution of the covariance function changed. To best visualize such an event, we took the squared exponential covariance function and fed data points gradually as shown in Fig. 1. We can clearly understand how the data provides shapes to the function distribution and more data we give, the better the model is being fitted. Here, the mean of the distribution will give our actual prediction value at any point.

Cross-Validation: We used the cross-validation method to evaluate our model's performance in terms of predicting LE for a given country's data. The primary concept is to divide the training set into two separate sets, one for training and the other for performance monitoring. The validation set's performance is utilized as a proxy for the generalization error, and evaluation is carried out using the outcome.

4   Data Set

The data for this study was gathered from the World Digital Indicator (WDI) [31]. WDI is a collection of development indicators from officially recognized international sources gathered by the World Bank. It contained data of 266 countries from 1960 to 2021 along with 1,442 features.

We focused our research on a subset of this data that included the calendar years 1960 to 2019 and the 27 countries and regions and only life expectancy at birth (unisex) and Gross National Income (GNI) of those countries has been extracted. Based on GNI per capita in 2019 at nominal values, we further divided the data into four income groups (Low, Lower-Middle, Upper-Middle and High) using the Atlas Method, a World Bank-developed indicator of income distribution, where,

$$GNI = Gross\ Domestic\ Product$$
$$+ (Money\ Flowing\ from\ Foreign\ Countries$$
$$- Money\ flowing to\ Foreign\ Countries)$$

and

$$GNI\ per\ Captia = \frac{GNI}{Total\ Population}.$$

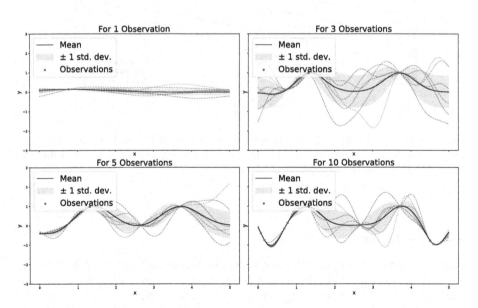

Fig. 1. Functional distribution of covariance function based on how many observations points are fed into the process. More data points shaping the distribution for better fitting and the standard deviation region getting narrowed.

To conduct our research, we used Python 3.10 environment as our platform. We prepared our own code with the assistance of publicly available packages/library i.e. Scikit-learn 1.1.1 [20]. We have made the data processing and model development code open to public via GitHub[1] to carry forward this research.

5   Result Analysis

Initially, the prediction of aggregated income group's LE has been carried out to show the trend in LE change over the years in Fig. 2. It can be seen that the higher the GNI-per-capita, the higher the LE at birth, which is to be expected. Also, an interesting observation is that the lower-Middle income group's LE congruence with Upper-Middle near 2040 demonstrates developing countries (Lower-Middle) progress in comparison developed countries (Upper-Middle). For high-income countries, a smooth rising trend can be observed, which indicates a lesser impact of economic factors from a certain time point and more about the progress of other factors.

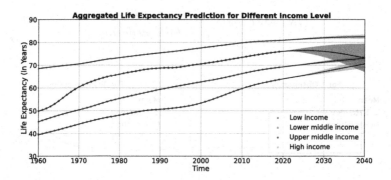

Fig. 2. Predicted LE for Different Income Group up to 2040 based on the average of LE for countries of respective groups. Increase of life expectancy is more visible for lower income group than higher.

5.1   Low-Income

Countries having GNI per capita of $1,045 or less in 2020 are classified having low-income economies. Table 1 shows the predicted LE of low-income countries and their 95% PI at 2040 along with their respective GNI.

Figure 3(a) shows combination of predicted LE for the selected low-income countries along with aggregated low-income countries' LE, where the solid line indicates the prediction and the shaded area indicates the 95% PI. Here it can be

---

[1] https://github.com/brai-acslab/life-expectancy-GP.

Table 1. Predicted LE and 95% PI at 2040 for Low-Income Group

Country	GNI per capita	Predicted LE at 2040	95% PI
Afghanistan	530	69.62	71.05-68.18
Ethiopia	850	71.28	76.06-66.51
Niger	600	64.35	66.71-62.00
Sierra Leone	540	60.42	64.40-56.45
Sudan	820	70.00	71.55-68.46
Yemen, Rep.	852	61.38	69.47-53.29

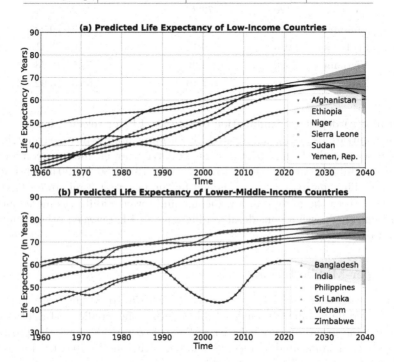

Fig. 3. Combined LE Prediction of (a) Low-Income Countries (b) Lower-Middle-Income Countries up to year 2040. For these groups, even though they are from geographically different places, clear similarity of LE are visible.

seen that almost all the countries are trending towards the 60 to 72 year range in 2040. Among the selected countries, the trend of Sierra Leone was slightly different. It's worth mentioning that its GNI per capita was one of the lowest among the selected countries, indicating an economic influence on LE.

5.2   Lower-Middle-Income

Lower-middle-income economies are defined as those with a 2020 GNI per capita of $1,046 to $4,095. Table 2 shows the predicted LE of Lower-Middle income group and its 95% PI at 2040 along with their respective GNI.

Table 2. Predicted LE and 95% PI at 2040 for the Lower-Middle-Income Group

Country	GNI per capita	Predicted LE at 2040	95% PI
Bangladesh	1,940	75.84	80.07-71.62
India	2,120	73.32	74.84-71.79
Philippines	3,850	73.15	75.37-70.94
Sri Lanka	4,010	80.13	83.04-77.21
Vietnam	2,590	74.92	79.55-70.28
Zimbabwe	1,200	57.16	63.39-50.92

Figure 3(b) depicts a combination of forecast LE for selected lower-middle-income countries, as well as aggregated LE for lower-middle-income countries. In a similar way to the trend of low-income countries, lower-middle-income countries also exhibit a similar trend towards ages 73 to 80 by 2040, except for Zimbabwe. This finding can be explained by the fact that Zimbabwe's GNI per capita is close to the margin of low-income and lower-middle-income countries. As a result, there was a considerable difference in LE between other countries and Zimbabwe.

5.3   Upper-Middle-Income

Countries with a 2020 GNI per capita of $4,096 to $12,695 are classified as upper-middle-income economies. Table 3 shows the predicted LE of upper-middle-income group and its 95% PI at 2040. Figure 4(a) shows the projected LE for selected upper-middle-income countries with aggregated LE for upper-middle-income countries. Except for South Africa, all the selected countries showed a similar rising trend towards ages 73 to 80 in the prediction. South

Table 3. Predicted LE and 95% PI at 2040 for Upper-Middle-Income Group

Country	GNI per capita	Predicted LE at 2040	95% PI
Brazil	9,270	79.43	82.23-78.63
China	10,390	76.02	83.47-68.57
Jordan	4,410	77.38	78.89-75.87
Malaysia	11,230	79.50	80.59-78.49
South Africa	6,040	61.08	66.68-55.47
Thailand	7,260	79.04	81.82-76.26

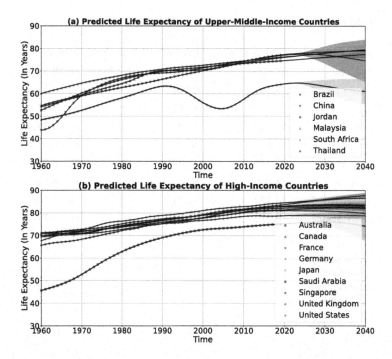

Fig. 4. Combined LE Prediction of (a) Upper-Middle-Income Countries (b) High-Income Countries. Higher the income range, the LE looks more subtle than lower income range.

Africa has experienced a long history of adversity, which may have been a factor in it having a diverse LE, with resultant influence on our model [14].

5.4 High-Income

Countries with a GNI per capita of $12,696 or more in 2020 are considered high-income economies. Table 4 shows the predicted LE of high-income group and their 95% PI at 2040. The forecast LE for selected high-income nations is shown collectively in Fig. 4(b), along with the aggregated LE for high-income countries. Each country showed similar LE at 2040 (ranging in between 78 to 89) over the years with little deviation, except for Saudi Arabia. During the 1970s and 1980s, Saudi Arabia's economy grew rapidly, fueled by huge earnings from oil exports [8]. This is reflected in the rapid growth in LE, thus affecting our model.

Gathering all of the LE data (Kept to only six countries from high-income countries for symmetry) at 2040 into single plane, we can see the subtle increase of LE from one income class to another in Fig. 5. A perhaps surprising outcome is that even lower-income countries are set to hit a LE of around 70 years in 2040. Currently, however, upper-middle-income or high-income countries have this high level of LE. This result indicates that a higher level of life quality can be expected, even in underdeveloped or developing countries. Additionally, it can

Table 4. Predicted LE and 95% PI at 2040 for high-income group

Country	GNI per capita	Predicted LE at 2040	95% PI
Australia	55,100	83.52	85.36-81.69
Canada	46,460	82.60	83.80-81.40
France	42,270	83.17	84.53-81.82
Germany	48,550	79.91	81.25-78.56
Japan	41,570	86.58	89.09-84.07
Saudi Arabia	22,840	75.30	78.56-72.04
Singapore	58,390	87.57	88.81-86.70
United Kingdom	42,130	82.14	83.41-80.87
United States	65,910	78.80	80.35-77.24

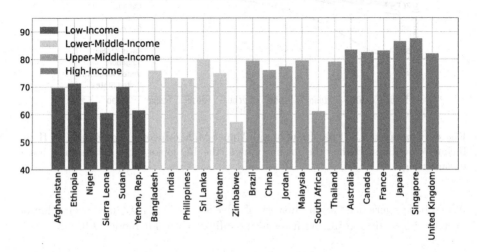

Fig. 5. Direct Comparison of LE at Year 2040 Between All Income Classes. The rising trend of LE from one group to higher group is clearly visible. Also, the variation among the same group's countries is less visible than the previous lower income group, indicating the clear impact of the economy on LE in future.

be noted that sub 90 years of life can be expected from high-income countries. However, it is important to remember that our world's resources are limited, and higher LE will lead to lower mortality, thus to an increase in population. So, limited resources need to be allocated properly and fairly, otherwise higher LE may become another strain on these already scarce resources.

5.5 Validation

To cross-validate our prediction model we split our dataset into two parts. As we have 60 years of LE data from each country, we used the first 40 years of data (1960–1999) to fit our prediction model and predicted the LE of the next

20 years (2000–2019). We call this in-sample life expectancy prediction. Then we cross-referenced with the actual value to evaluate our model's performance.

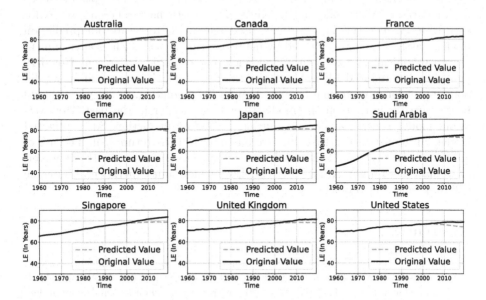

Fig. 6. In-sample LE Prediction of (a) Low-income countries (b) High-Income Countries. Close alignment of predicted LE and actual LE shows the effectiveness of the proposed model.

In Fig. 6 the cross-validation of low-income countries and high-income countries predictions are made. We can see in most cases the predicted values are close to the actual values. Also, GPR works better as more data is fed into the model. So in our actual model, in theory, predictions should be more accurate as it contains 60 years of data per country. Thus, it verifies our model's excellent performance.

6   Conclusion

Gaussian Process, is a non-parametric Bayesian approach for regression analysis and we used this to predict the LE of multiple countries up to 2040. Even though it has cubic complexity, GPR has the power to work exceptionally well with few data points compared to other regression models. We combined multiple co-variance functions and created a complex kernel for the best fitting of our data. We found distinct patterns between each income group despite being geographically in different places in the world. This indicates economic effects without considering social and geographical aspects, although exceptions can be found in these groups and a rationale was forwarded for these. For each country, a distinct rise in LE can be seen, which indicates that above 90 years of LE might be possible in the near future. Despite the excellent performance of our model, there is room for improvement via future work. We used a unified model for all countries, even though there are countries with various types of trends in our dataset. Also, male and female's LE at birth have different trends for each country, however, here we have used unisex LE to create our prediction model. Lastly, LE can be affected by many external factors such as environmental, geographical, and on-going pandemics. For example, the recent Covid-19 pandemic has reduced LE in the United States [3,28]. In our research, we did not account for any external factors. Also, in LE prediction, recent years should have a greater impact on the model than years deeper in the past. However, in our model, every year has an equivalent effect on prediction. So, a weighted model can be used to further improve our model in the future [34]. The use of a different data set might have different outcome as suggested by [1]. However, as we have used a non-parametric model, we believe our experimental outcome will overcome that problem.

References

1. Adiba, F.I., Islam, T., Kaiser, M.S., Mahmud, M., Rahman, M.A.: Effect of corpora on classification of fake news using naive bayes classifier. Int. J. Autom. Artif. Intell. Mach. Learn. **1**(1), 80–92 (2020). https://researchlakejournals.com/index. php/AAIML/article/view/45
2. Ahmed, N.K., Atiya, A.F., Gayar, N.E., El-Shishiny, H.: An empirical comparison of machine learning models for time series forecasting. Economet. Rev. **29**(5–6), 594–621 (2010)
3. Andrasfay, T., Goldman, N.: Reductions in 2020 us life expectancy due to covid-19 and the disproportionate impact on the black and latino populations. Proc. Natl. Acad. Sci. **118**(5), e2014746118 (2021)
4. Bennett, J.E., et al.: The future of life expectancy and life expectancy inequalities in England and wales: Bayesian spatiotemporal forecasting. Lancet **386**(9989), 163-170 (2015). https://doi.org/10.1016/S0140-6736(15)60296-3, https://www. sciencedirect.com/science/article/pii/S0140673615602963
5. Biswas, M., Kaiser, M.S., Mahmud, M., Al Mamun, S., Hossain, M.S., Rahman, M.A.: An XAI based autism detection: the context behind the detection. In: Mahmud, M., Kaiser, M.S., Vassanelli, S., Dai, Q., Zhong, N. (eds.) BI 2021. LNCS (LNAI), vol. 12960, pp. 448–459. Springer, Cham (2021). https://doi.org/10.1007/978-3-030-86993-9_40
6. Das, S., Yasmin, M.R., Arefin, M., Taher, K.A., Uddin, M.N., Rahman, M.A.: Mixed Bangla-English spoken digit classification using convolutional neural network. In: Mahmud, M., Kaiser, M.S., Kasabov, N., Iftekharuddin, K., Zhong, N. (eds.) AII 2021. CCIS, vol. 1435, pp. 371–383. Springer, Cham (2021). https://doi. org/10.1007/978-3-030-82269-9_29
7. Das, T.R., Hasan, S., Sarwar, S.M., Das, J.K., Rahman, M.A.: Facial spoof detection using support vector machine. In: Kaiser, M.S., Bandyopadhyay, A., Mahmud, M., Ray, K. (eds.) Proceedings of International Conference on Trends in Computational and Cognitive Engineering. AISC, vol. 1309, pp. 615–625. Springer, Singapore (2021). https://doi.org/10.1007/978-981-33-4673-4_50

8. Economy of Saudi Arabia. https://www.britannica.com/place/Saudi-Arabia/ Economy#ref259141. Accessed 15 Nov 2021
9. Ferdous, H., Siraj, T., Setu, S.J., Anwar, M.M., Rahman, M.A.: Machine learning approach towards satellite image classification. In: Kaiser, M.S., Bandyopadhyay, A., Mahmud, M., Ray, K. (eds.) Proceedings of International Conference on Trends in Computational and Cognitive Engineering. AISC, vol. 1309, pp. 627–637. Springer, Singapore (2021). https://doi.org/10.1007/978-981-33-4673-4_51
10. Hossain, A.B.M.K., Tasnim, Z., Hoque, S., Rahman, M.A.: A Recommender system for adaptive examination preparation using pearson correlation collaborative filtering. Int. J. Autom. Artif. Intell. Mach. Learn. 2(1), 30–43 (2021). https://researchlakejournals.com/index.php/AAIML/article/view/55
11. Kontis, V., Bennett, J.E., Mathers, C.D., Li, G., Foreman, K., Ezzati, M.: Future life expectancy in 35 industrialised countries: projections with a Bayesian model ensemble. Lancet 389(10076), 1323-1335 (2017). https://doi.org/10.1016/S0140-6736(16)32381-9, https://www.sciencedirect.com/science/article/pii/S0140673616323819
12. Lam, K.K., Wang, B.: Robust non-parametric mortality and fertility modelling and forecasting: Gaussian process regression approaches. Forecasting 3(1), 207-227 (2021). https://doi.org/10.3390/forecast3010013, https://www.mdpi.com/2571-9394/3/1/13
13. Lee, R.D., Carter, L.R.: Modeling and forecasting us mortality. J. Am. Stat. Assoc. 87(419), 659–671 (1992)
14. Lockhat, R., Van Niekerk, A.: South African children: a history of adversity, violence and trauma. Ethnicity Health 5(3–4), 291–302 (2000)
15. Mahmud, M., et al.: A brain-inspired trust management model to assure security in a cloud based IoT framework for neuroscience applications. Cogn. Comput. 10(5), 864–873 (2018). https://doi.org/10.1007/s12559-018-9543-3
16. Mahmud, M., Kaiser, M.S., Rahman, M.A.: Towards explainable and privacy-preserving artificial intelligence for personalisation in autism spectrum disorder. In: Antona, M., Stephanidis, C. (eds.) HCII 2022. LNCS, vol. 13309, pp. 356–370. Springer, Cham (2022). https://doi.org/10.1007/978-3-031-05039-8_26
17. Makridakis, S., Spiliotis, E., Assimakopoulos, V.: Statistical and machine learning forecasting methods: concerns and ways forward. PLoS One 13(3), e0194889 (2018)
18. Nawar, A., Toma, N.T., Al Mamun, S., Kaiser, M.S., Mahmud, M., Rahman, M.A.: Cross-content recommendation between movie and book using machine learning. In: 2021 IEEE 15th International Conference on Application of Information and Communication Technologies (AICT), pp. 1–6 (2021). https://doi.org/10.1109/AICT52784.2021.9620432
19. Pascariu, M.D., Canudas-Romo, V., Vaupel, J.W.: The double-gap life expectancy forecasting model. Insur. Math. Econom. 78, 339–350 (2018)
20. Pedregosa, F.: Scikit-learn: machine learning in Python. J. Mach. Learn. Res. 12, 2825–2830 (2011)
21. Raftery, A.E., Chunn, J.L., Gerland, P., Ševčíková, H.: Bayesian probabilistic projections of life expectancy for all countries. Demography 50(3), 777–801 (2013). https://doi.org/10.1007/s13524-012-0193-x
22. Raftery, A.E., Lalic, N., Gerland, P.: Joint probabilistic projection of female and male life expectancy. Demogr. Res. 30, 795 (2014)
23. Rahman, M.A.: Gaussian process in computational biology: covariance functions for transcriptomics. Ph.D., University of Sheffield (2018). https://etheses.whiterose.ac.uk/19460/

24. Rahman, M.A., Brown, D.J., Shopland, N., Burton, A., Mahmud, M.: Explainable multimodal machine learning for engagement analysis by continuous performance test. In: Antona, M., Stephanidis, C. (eds.) HCII 2022. LNCS, vol. 13309, pp. 386–399. Springer, Cham (2022). https://doi.org/10.1007/978-3-031-05039-8_28

25. Rahman, M.A., Lawrence, N.D.: A Gaussian process model for inferring the dynamic transcription factor activity. In: Proceedings of the 7th ACM International Conference on Bioinformatics, Computational Biology, and Health Informatics, BCB 2016, pp. 495–496. Association for Computing Machinery, New York (2016). https://doi.org/10.1145/2975167.2985651

26. Rakib, A.B., Rumky, E.A., Ashraf, A.J., Hillas, M.M., Rahman, M.A.: Mental healthcare chatbot using sequence-to-sequence learning and BiLSTM. In: Mahmud, M., Kaiser, M.S., Vassanelli, S., Dai, Q., Zhong, N. (eds.) BI 2021. LNCS (LNAI), vol. 12960, pp. 378–387. Springer, Cham (2021). https://doi.org/10.1007/978-3-030-86993-9_34

27. Rasmussen, C.E.I., Williams, C.K.I.: Gaussian Processes for Machine Learning. MIT Press, Cambridge (2008)

28. Sadik, R., Reza, M.L., Noman, A.A., Mamun, S.A., Kaiser, M.S., Rahman, M.A.: COVID-19 pandemic: a comparative prediction using machine learning. Int. J. Autom. Artif. Intell. Mach. Learn. 1(1), 1–16 (2020). https://www.researchlakejournals.com/index.php/AAIML/article/view/44

29. Sheng, H., Xiao, J., Cheng, Y., Ni, Q., Wang, S.: Short-term solar power forecasting based on weighted gaussian process regression. IEEE Trans. Industr. Electron. 65(1), 300–308 (2018). https://doi.org/10.1109/TIE.2017.2714127

30. Shopland, N., et al.: Improving accessibility and personalisation for HE students with disabilities in two countries in the Indian subcontinent - initial findings. In: Antona, M., Stephanidis, C. (eds.) HCII 2022. LNCS, vol. 13309, pp. 110–122. Springer, Cham (2022). https://doi.org/10.1007/978-3-031-05039-8_8

31. World bank. Life expectancy at birth, total (years) (2021). https://data.worldbank.org/indicator/SP.DYN.LE00.IN. Accessed 16 Nov 2021

32. Torri, T., Vaupel, J.W.: Forecasting life expectancy in an international context. Int. J. Forecast. 28(2), 519–531 (2012). https://doi.org/10.1016/j.ijforecast.2011.01.009, https://www.sciencedirect.com/science/article/pii/S0169207011000586

33. Woolf, S.H., Schoomaker, H.: Life expectancy and mortality rates in the United States, 1959–2017. JAMA 322(20), 1996–2016 (2019). https://doi.org/10.1001/jama.2019.16932

34. Wu, R., Wang, B.: Gaussian process regression method for fore-casting of mortality rates. Neurocomputing 316, 232-239 (2018). https://doi.org/10.1016/j.neucom.2018.08.001, https://www.sciencedirect.com/science/article/pii/S092523121830907X

Optimized Layout: A Genetic Algorithm for Industrial and Business Application

Pasquale Fotia[1] (✉) [iD] and Massimiliano Ferrara[1,2] [iD]

[1] Department of Law, Economics and Human Sciences and Decisions Lab, University Mediterranea of Reggio Calabria, 89125 Reggio Calabria, Italy
{pasquale.fotia.digies,massimiliano.ferrara}@unirc.it
[2] ICRIOS - The Invernizzi Centre for Research in Innovation, Organization, Strategy and Entrepreneurship, Department of Management and Technology, Bocconi University, Via Sarfatti, 25, 20136 Milan, MI, Italy

Abstract. Covid-19 epidemic has harmed the global economy. Particularly, the restaurant sector has been severely impacted by the rapid spread of the virus. The use of digital technology (DT) has been utilized to execute risk-reduction methods as service innovation tools. In this work, a genetic algorithm optimization is used to cope with the problems caused by the restrictions due to Covid-19 to optimize the management of the spaces in commercial and industrial structures. The approach through the GA involves the selection of the best members of a population that change genome based on the epochs. The digitization of a commercial or industrial environment becomes an optimal methodology for carrying out virtual design of work environments. Digitization thus becomes a strategy for the reduction of both monetary and time cost. Focusing on the case study, satisfactory results emerge supported by tests that reveal an appreciable robustness and open new scenarios for different applications of the methodology developed in this work, always in the context of optimal management of industrial and commercial spaces.

Keywords: COVID-19 · Genetic algorithm optimization · Bidimensional space management

1 Introduction

1.1 COVID-19 Global Impact

Current global pandemic, Covid-19, has posed a threat to the global community since its emergence. COVID-19, also known as the novel coronavirus, is a variation of the corona virus family that causes SARS in humans. The virus is transmitted primarily through coughing and sneezing. Due to the lack of a good vaccine, the majority of countries have instituted lockdowns to prevent the spread of the virus. Based on the experiences of countries that faced the initial attacks of this zoonotic fierce-full virus, some nations have established aggressive health policies and adapted their resources to the reality of this global health disaster. However, many developing nations with sluggish economic growth and new emerging economies are unable to take similar actions as industrialized or wealthy developing nations. This event is growing more challenging due to the fragile global economy, which is projected to decrease by 2.8% in 2020. Such a global depression would result in a decline of −12.5% during the third quarter. One of the effects of this global economic recession will be an increase in pricing pressure, which will subside by mid-2022. According to predictions, the global unemployment rate would grow to more than 10% by the end of 2020, up from 5.2% in 2019. Consequently, regardless of its socioeconomic status, every nation must take steps that strike a balance between the demand for health safety and the demands of its people. Sumner et al. [23] affirmed in the UN study that, for the first time since 1990, worldwide poverty could increase. This indicates that COVID poses a significant danger to the 2030 Sustainable Development Goals (SDGs) of the United Nations. Despite their advanced healthcare system, Europeans view the COVID-19 pandemic as an unanticipated health emergency that had a significant impact on the healthcare system and economies in several European regions. Additionally, household incomes, employment, and welfare benefits were affected (European Commission, 2020). The high number of COVID-19-positive cases in Europe had a detrimental impact on production networks, causing a major decrease in agricultural operations, tourism, and commerce. Compared to the middle of February, European stock markets have declined almost 30%. According to figures from the European Trade Union Confederation (ETUC), at least one million people lost their jobs within two weeks; this number is likely to be significantly higher given the large number of freelancers and contract employees in Europe. Therefore, all European nations are exploring methods to mitigate the current economic crisis. EU leaders have discussed phasing out measures and the economic recovery strategy following the COVID 19-induced economic crisis. The European Council identified four priorities: the internal market's functioning, a huge investment strategy, the EU's external operations, and the EU's resilience and governance. In addition to the European Commission, numerous non-profit groups are assisting the most vulnerable individuals during the pandemic. The European Union responded to the crisis precipitated by COVID 19 by implementing a variety of measures to support the citizens, businesses, and economy of its member states, therefore mitigating its negative effects (European Commission, 2020) [2]. In Italy, following the spread of the coronavirus, restrictive measures have been put in place to contain the transmission of the disease. The development of the pandemic caused a strong economic and social impact. One measure in particular had a major impact on the catering sector. This measure provides for a reduction in the exploitation of the surface of the restaurant, as a minimum distance to be respected was established between each table. A problem of this kind involves the intervention of continuous measurements and manual adjustments in order to optimize the space available with a consequent reduction in loss of revenues.

1.2 Service Innovation in the Restaurant Sector During COVID-19: Digital Technologies

Recent Covid-19 pandemic epidemic has harmed the global economy. Particularly, the restaurant sector (RS), which is regarded a high-risk industry [22], has been severely impacted by Covid-19, which has necessitated the development of novel strategies to combat it. The rapid spread of the virus led to limits on restaurants, resulting in a decline in revenue, job losses, and, in some cases, the permanent shutdown of commercial activity [16]. In addition, a substantial shift in consumers' intentions to remain at home has emerged [19]. Due to the concern of being exposed to the potential Covid-19 hazards, customers' willingness to dine in restaurants has decreased dramatically [5, 8]. Similarly, it has been established that restaurant employees are susceptible to getting the virus, and their willingness to report to work has decreased significantly. The restaurants have been ordered to restructure their operations in order to continue operating in an environment characterized by the necessity to protect health safety, decrease the perception of risk, and comply with government survival measures. Despite the World Health Organization's declaration that food is not a means of Covid-19 transmission, the restaurant supply chain (SC) operations have been deemed hazardous because to the frequent interactions between the actors involved [16]. As a result, restricting measures, such as limiting operation hours and reducing seating capacities, have been imposed on a global scale. In the most recent month, however, following the introduction of the vaccination campaign, the intensity of such measures has been lowered because society needs to assist enterprises' economic and social recovery. From this vantage point, Service Innovation (SI) to improve existing restaurant offerings and generate new service options has emerged as the sole means of addressing these key concerns. Although SI has always been viewed as a strategic factor for competitiveness and at the discretion of managers [7, 11, 13], the pandemic has created an imperative to innovate in the RS in order to ensure the survival and resilience of the organization [4, 10]. This "forced service innovation" was predicted to lessen negative repercussions by stimulating a paradigm shift and unanticipated business prospects [1, 18]. The use of digital technology (DT), such as contactless digital payment, sophisticated cleaning systems, digital menus accessible through QR code, service robots, touchless elevators, food delivery applications, etc., has been utilized to execute risk-reduction methods as service innovation tools. Through these capabilities, it is anticipated that DT will reduce interactions between guests and employees and enhance restaurant cleanliness [21]. In this context, scholars have demonstrated that, during the post-pandemic era, customers' risk perception should be viewed as one of the most significant barriers to the resumption of food service activities, as it influences the purchase decision-making process [3, 15]. Esposito et al. [6] conducted a quantitative analysis on a sample of Italian customers and found that the implementation of DT prompts restaurants to adopt measures that strike a balance between the need to maintain health safety and the desire to reduce customers' risk perception in order to increase their willingness to dine out. In this work, in line with the needs caused by the restrictions, a genetic algorithm is developed that optimizes the available spaces in such a way as to comply with the regulations and at the same time reduce losses from lost earnings. This wants to be a further tool belonging to the DT that allows the digitization of space, of industrial and commercial activities, for the automated design of its use.

2 Methodology

2.1 Genetic Algorithm

Since its inception, computer science has attempted to create systems capable of simulating the human brain's function (neural networks), its learning mechanisms (machine learning), and biological evolution (evolutionary calculus). The concept underlying evolutionary calculus, of which genetic algorithms are just one example, is to evolve a population of candidate solutions for a given problem using genetic operators and natural selection. Using a model of the problem to be solved, GAs enable the identification of a solution from a vast number of potential options [12]. In the evolution of biological species, it is well recognized that the "best appropriate" individuals are chosen for survival and reproduction. Thus, their genetic material is transmitted to subsequent generations. The appropriateness of a biological organism is determined by its capacity to survive the environmental features and to compete or cooperate with other organisms. In genetic algorithms, it is assumed, based on biological similarity, that a possible solution to a problem can be represented as a set of parameters (called genes), which, when combined, generate a string of values known as a "chromosome". Holland initially shown, and many still agree, that the optimal encoding is the string's representation in the binary alphabet. In order to express a three-parameter function F (x, y, z), for instance, you can encode each variable with a 10-bit binary number. The chromosome corresponding to the answer will include three genes and thirty digital digits. The essential genetic algorithm operators are coding, evaluation, selection, crossover, and mutation. In coding, each human is assigned a chromosome based on the collection of characteristics that define it. Using a model of the problem to be solved, the assessment operator determines the suitability of each participant. In the process of selection, the chromosomes destined for reproduction are picked; the greater the fitness of the individual, the more frequently his chromosome will be chosen for reproduction. Reproduction is accomplished by crossing the chromosomes of the "parent" individuals to produce children; the crossing can be accomplished in a variety of methods, the simplest of which is to randomly select a location in the string and swap the two portions into which the parents' chromosome is divided. Once the "child" individuals have been formed, the mutation operator is applied with a very low probability to alter each bit of each chromosome; the objective of this operator is to inject genetic variety into the population during evolution. To increase the effectiveness of research, it may be determined to preserve the best individual of the previous generation in the new generation, a process known as elitism. Several expedients, such as non-binary encodings, different crossover modes, elitism approaches, repeated mapping, etc., were invented during the development of genetic algorithms to increase the algorithm's convergence towards the absolute optimum. See specialized literature [9, 17] for a thorough overview of these methodologies. In order to maximize the effectiveness of the genetic algorithm in discovering the absolute optimum, it is required to increase the population's variability. Using a very high number of individuals in the population and the mutation operator to explore new possibilities is one technique to accomplish this. Alternately, micro-GA [9], which was established by Krishakumar [14] and consists of employing a very small number of individuals (e.g. five) and validating the convergence of the micro population, can be employed. If the difference in bits between all members of a generation is smaller than a predefined threshold (for example, 5%), it is assumed that the population has reached convergence. When this occurs, the algorithm generates a new population in which the best individual from the population that has reached convergence is kept and the remaining individuals are generated at random.

2.2 GA Application in Python: Allocation of Restaurant Tables for Surface Optimization

The algorithm implemented in Python can be used in many sectors and for different application purposes. Being a work in the development phase, the structure of the code provides for the resolution of a problem related to the correct allocation of circular tables in a floor plan in which there are structural constraints, such as pillars and recesses, and operational constraints, such as paths used for the passage of personnel. The structure of the code in order to function requires, as input data in peg format, the polygons of the areas of interest, both as regards the surface of the table allocation and as regards the areas that cannot be used (structural and operational constraint). The following figures show the images of the plan of a structure that is part of a location for weddings and receptions, and the polygons used as input for the algorithm given by a graphic processing phase.

Fig. 1. Plan of the room used for the use of the genetic algorithm for space optimization.

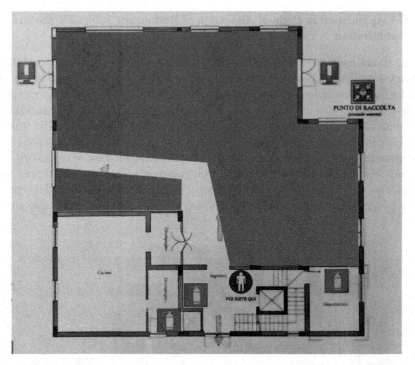

Fig. 2. Polygons of the surfaces on which it is possible to insert the tables.

In addition to Fig. 2, six additional figures representing the six pillars of the structure seen in Fig. 1 are imported into the code. Once the polygon files have been loaded, it is possible to identify the Cartesian coordinates of the points that comprise the various polygons from the jpeg photos using the CV2 library. The structural and operational limitations are handled via the Shapely library, which enables you to work with polygons and execute operations such as defining a distance buffer between polygons and belonging to one polygon within another. These operations are used to filter the GA's constituent functions. Continuing with the code, the functions needed to initiate the search for the optimal location of the item to be allocated are constructed according to the GA pillars described in Sect. 2.1. The fit-ness function is the one that permits the best selection among the generated tables, both during the research phase on the full floor plan and during the local search among the finest feasible options. In reality, owing to the Shapely functions, a function is generated that enables the development of a machine-executable number of objects (in our case, circular tables) that cover and belong to the complete surface. In its place, the second function generates a sequence of tables in the space specified by the first function. All of this follows the logic of the fitness function, which states that the further apart two tables are, the higher the score for the genetically superior table.

3   Results

To test the validity of the algorithm, a square-shaped plan was created in which if you try to optimally allocate the positions of nine tables, the optimal solution turns out to be only one. Using the algorithm developed in Python, the only optimal solution is identified, thus proving the accuracy of the method. Before the execution of the code for the application of the algorithm, a practical case relating to the filling of a wedding hall was examined, in which the tables used refer to measures actually used for events ranging between 150 and 200 people.

The parameters used are the following:

1. Table diameter: small tables of 150 cm, large tables of 160 cm;
2. Distance between tables: 200 cm [20];
3. Distance of the tables from the wall: 10 cm;
4. Starting table coordinates: [12.44199134199134, 10.152813852813853];
5. Sitting space around table: 36 cm;
6. Sequence of tables for optimization: 11 large tables (including starting tables) and 10 small tables.

The parameter number 2 depends of the minimum distance applied for Covid-19 [20]. Using a random table as a starting point, the parameter number 4 is obtain with the application of the algorithm. The parameter number 6 is a discretionary variable that depends on the operational needs of the structure based on the event to be hosted. The other parameters indicated above depend on measurements made inside the room used for receptions. By executing the code, one at a time, the 160 cm tables are inserted first and then the 150 cm ones. The ranking of the best table choice is based on adding the distances between the table to be inserted and those already inserted. The following figures show the procedure indicated above (Fig. 3).

The process then ends when the entire surface is filled and it is no longer possible to insert additional tables. The expected results of executing the code are the optimal placement of 11 large and 4 small tables (Fig. 4).

4   Discussion and Further Development

The work presented is intended to be a further support to cope with the restrictions applied due to Covid-19. The algorithm thus composed has not been tested with different orders of insertion of the objects to be placed as it is still a work under development. The digitization of a commercial or industrial environment, however, becomes an optimal methodology for carrying out virtual design of work environments integrated with genetic algorithms that make everything automated. A further advantage from the application of this methodology becomes that of being able to satisfy various needs, both of a purely operational nature and of a regulatory nature. Digitization thus becomes a strategy for the reduction of both monetary and time resources. The work is open to further developments both in terms of the efficiency of the code itself, and for the optimization of three-dimensional spaces. In fact, the code used is mainly valid for flat surfaces. Future developments will concern different applications of the same algorithm.

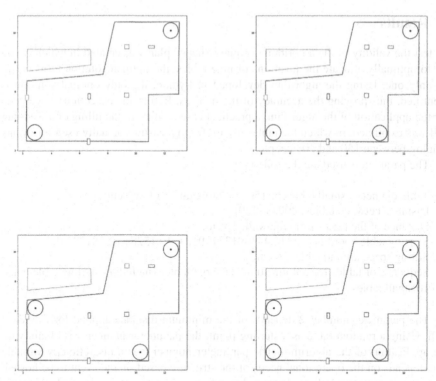

Fig. 3. Display of optimization results: position estimate of the second, third, fourth and fifth table.

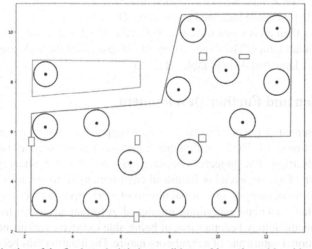

Fig. 4. Visualization of the final result: it is impossible to add another table without violating the imposed constraints.

References

1. Batat, W.: How Michelin-starred chefs are being transformed into social bricoleurs? An online qualitative study of luxury foodservice during the pandemic crisis (2020)
2. Buheji, M., et al.: The extent of covid-19 pandemic socio-economic impact on global poverty. A global integrative multidisciplinary review. Am. J. Econ. **10**(4), 213–224 (2020). Author, F.: Contribution title. In: 9th International Proceedings on Proceedings, pp. 1–2. Publisher, Location (2010)
3. Dedeoğlu, B.B., Boğan, E.: The motivations of visiting upscale restaurants during the COVID-19 pandemic: the role of risk perception and trust in government. Int. J. Hosp. Manag. **95**, 102905 (2021)
4. Edvardsson, B., et al.: Examining how context change foster service innovation. J. Serv. Manag. (2018)
5. Esposito, B., Sessa, M.R., Sica, D., Malandrino, O.: Exploring the link between customers' safety perception and the use of information technology in the restaurant sector during the Covid-19. In: Visvizi, A., Troisi, O., Saeedi, K. (eds.) RIIFORUM 2021. SPC, pp. 403–415. Springer, Cham (2021). https://doi.org/10.1007/978-3-030-84311-3_37
6. Esposito, B., Sessa, M.R., Sica, D., Malandrino, O.: Service innovation in the restaurant sector during COVID-19: digital technologies to reduce customers' risk perception. TQM J. (ahead-of-print) (2022)
7. Feng, C., Ma, R., Jiang, L.: The impact of service innovation on firm performance: a meta-analysis. J. Serv. Manag. **32**(3), 289–314 (2020)
8. Galanakis, C.M.: The food systems in the era of the coronavirus (COVID-19) pandemic crisis. Foods **9**(4), 523 (2020)
9. Goldberg, D.E.: Genetic Algorithms in Search, Optimization & Machine Learning. Addison-Wesley (1989)
10. Heinonen, K., Strandvik, T.: Reframing service innovation: COVID-19 as a catalyst for imposed service innovation. J. Serv. Manag. (2020)
11. Helkkula, A., Kowalkowski, C., Tronvoll, B.: Archetypes of service innovation: implications for value cocreation. J. Serv. Res. **21**(3), 284–301 (2018)
12. Holland, J.: Adaptation in Natural and Artificial Systems, vol. 7, pp. 390–401. University of Michigan Press, Ann Arbor (1975)
13. Kowalkowski, C., Witell, L.: Typologies and frameworks in service innovation. In: The Routledge Handbook of Service Research Insights and Ideas, pp. 109–130. Routledge (2020)
14. Krishnakumar, K.: Micro-genetic algorithms for stationary and non-stationary function optimization. In: Intelligent Control and Adaptive Systems, vol. 1196, pp. 289–296. SPIE (1990)
15. Leung, X.Y., Cai, R.: How pandemic severity moderates digital food ordering risks during COVID-19: an application of prospect theory and risk perception framework. J. Hospit. Tour. Manag. **47**, 497–505 (2021)
16. Min, J., Yang, K., Kim, J.: The role of perceived vulnerability in restaurant customers' co-creation behavior and repatronage intention during the COVID-19 pandemic. J. Vacat. Mark. **28**(1), 38–51 (2022)
17. Mitchell, M.: Introduzione agli algoritmi genetici. Apogeo (1998)
18. Nenonen, S., Storbacka, K.: Don't adapt, shape! Use the crisis to shape your minimum viable system–and the wider market. Ind. Mark. Manage. **88**, 265–271 (2020)
19. Rizou, M., Galanakis, I.M., Aldawoud, T.M., Galanakis, C.M.: Safety of foods, food supply chain and environment within the COVID-19 pandemic. Trends Food Sci. Technol. **102**, 293–299 (2020)

20. Setti, L., et al.: Airborne transmission route of COVID-19: why 2 meters/6 feet of interpersonal distance could not be enough. Int. J. Environ. Res. Public Health **17**(8), 2932 (2020)
21. Shin, H., Kang, J.: Reducing perceived health risk to attract hotel customers in the COVID-19 pandemic era: focused on technology innovation for social distancing and cleanliness. Int. J. Hospit. Manag. **91**, 102664 (2020)
22. Song, H.J., Yeon, J., Lee, S.: Impact of the COVID-19 pandemic: evidence from the US restaurant industry. Int. J. Hosp. Manag. **92**, 102702 (2021)
23. Sumner, A., Hoy, C., Ortiz-Juarez, E.: Estimates of the impact of COVID-19 on global poverty (No. 2020/43). WIDER working paper (2020). Author, F., Author, S.: Title of a proceedings paper. In: Editor, F., Editor, S. (eds.) CONFERENCE 2016, LNCS, vol. 9999, pp. 1–13. Springer, Heidelberg (2016)

Application of AI and Informatics in Healthcare

Explainable Deep Learning for Alzheimer Disease Classification and Localisation

Marcello Di Giammarco[1], Giacomo Iadarola[1], Fabio Martinelli[1],
Francesco Mercaldo[1,2(✉)], Fabrizio Ravelli[2], and Antonella Santone[2]

[1] Institute for Informatics and Telematics, National Research Council of Italy
(CNR), Pisa, Italy
{marcello.digiammarco,giacomo.iadarola,fabio.martinelli,
francesco.mercaldo}@iit.cnr.it
[2] Department of Medicine and Health Sciences "Vincenzo Tiberio", University of
Molise, Campobasso, Italy
{francesco.mercaldo,antonella.santone}@unimol.it,
f.ravelli@studenti.unimol.it

Abstract. Alzheimer's disease is an irreversible neurological brain disorder that causes nuero-degenerative cognitive function like memory loss and thinking abilities. The accurate diagnosis of Alzheimer's disease at an early stage is very crucial for patient care and conducting future treatment. Deep learning can help to reach the diagnosis: for this reason we propose a method aimed to distinguish and properly classify four Alzheimer disease's stages. Two different deep learning models are exploited: Alex_Net and a model designed by authors, obtaining an average accuracy equal to 0.97 with the deep learning network developed by authors applying a colormap to brain magnetic resonance images. Our method provides also the localization areas used by the model to perform the classification (by adopting the heatmap overlapping provided by Gradient-weighted Class Activation Mapping algorithm) in order to ensures the explainability of the method.

Keywords: Alzheimer · Neural network · Machine learning · Deep learning · Explainability · Classification

1 Introduction

Alzheimer's disease (AD), the most common cause of dementia in the elderly, is a progressive neuro-degenerative disease that gradually robs patients of cognitive function and ultimately leads to death We review the epidemiology, clinical features, patho-physiology, and treatment of Alzheimer's disease [3]. AD accounts for 50–80% of dementia cases and it does not represent a normal element of aging, even if the highest known risk factor is represented by increasing age, and most people with Alzheimer's disease are 65 and over. However, Alzheimer's is not just a disease of old age. Up to 5% of people suffering from this disease have an early onset of Alzheimer's disease (also known as "early onset"), which

M. Mahmud et al. (Eds.): AII 2022, CCIS 1724, pp. 129–143, 2022.
https://doi.org/10.1007/978-3-031-24801-6_10

often appears when a person is between the ages of forty and fifty, or between the ages of fifty and sixty years. This is the reason why the correct diagnosis of AD assumes relevant importance in terms of collective well-being. To this aim in this paper we design and evaluate a method for automatic AD classification and localisation. The proposed method, by analysing a brain Magnetic Resonance Imaging (MRI), is able to detect the presence of moderate, mild and very mild dementia. Furthermore, our approach is able to highlight the areas of the brain MRI symptomatic of the AD and for this reason the proposed approach is devoted to localise the disease areas, thus providing explainability [14,19] behind the classifier decision. As a matter of fact, by exploiting the proposed method in the real-world the doctor not only is able to obtain in an automatic way the prediction of the degree of disease but he/she is able to visualize the areas that have been responsible for that particular decision by the model. We think this aspect can also provide confidence on the part of medical personnel in the real-world adoption of automatic techniques for disease classification and localisation. The proposed method is based on machine learning models, in particular we resort to deep learning (DL) and, more in detail, we adopt Convolutional Neural Network (CNN) i.e., artificial networks that in the proposed context are able to learn and subsequently manage to classify healthy patients from AD affected ones. To properly train a DL model data are needed, in our case we analyse brain MRI of patients suffering or not from the pathology. Once obtained the MRI brain, we proceed with a series of pre-processing steps with the aim of reducing artifacts or noises and more generally improving the features of the images (for instance, quality, contrast and resizing). At this point, different DL models with different parameters are built to get the best results in terms of classification and localization. Prints information about individual classes, such as: B. Accuracy and Precision. An important aspect certainly has to do with explainability. H. The algorithm's ability to classify according to patterns matching regions of an image in order to provide confidence in the predictions of deep learning models. The paper proceeds as follows: in next section preliminary notions are provided about the techniques involved by the proposed method and the Alzheimer disease, Sect. 3 presents the proposed method for Alzheimer disease classification and localisation, the experimental analysis is conducted in Sect. 4, current state-of-the-art literature is discussed in Sect. 5 and, finally, conclusion and future research directions are drawn in the last section.

2   Background

This section provides preliminary ideas about widely used concepts considered by the proposed method, with the aim of making the paper self-contained.

2.1   CNN and Grad-CAM

The classical image classification problem is one of the most common tasks for deep learning models It consists of classifying images containing objects or common shapes (such as letters written on a typewriter) as accurately as possible A DL model uses information from an input sample data set to complete a task. During the training phase, the DL model extracts and stores features and patterns specific to a particular output class, thereby learning to distinguish between different input samples One of the most commonly used DL models for image classification is the Convolutional Neural Network (CNN). It extracts features using a mathematical convolution operator on the input image. The input image undergoes multiple layers of convolution to combine pixels with neighboring pixels and undersampling to reduce the size of the two-dimensional matrix while preserving the most relevant information Finally, the final part of a CNN usually consists of dense layers formed by varying numbers of *perceptrons*). This last part of the model performs classification and can be trained with standard backpropagation algorithms. For more information on CNN, please refer to the literature [8,12]. Many complex CNN variants have been proposed in the literature. They differ mainly in the size of the architecture and the number of layers of convolution. For example, AlexNet used his ReLU as the enablement function instead of the Tanh function and introduced optimizations for multiple GPUs It also corrects overfitting using data augmentation techniques and dropout layers. In this article, we try this architecture and another CNN designed by the author. For architectural details, please refer to the original work [10,21]. Gradient-weighted Class Activation Mapping (Grad-CAM) is a technique that extracts the gradients of convolutional layers of a DL model and uses them to provide graphical information about the inference steps. In other words, gradients capture high-level visual patterns and can explain which areas of the input image had the most influence on model output decisions. Convolutional layers also hold spatial information, so Grad CAM uses this data to provide a heat map of the input image This heatmap highlights the input image space that the DL model uses to classify a given input. Provides a visual 'explanation' of a particular decision Grad-CAM adopted in this work is an implementation of the one presented in this work [20].

2.2 Alzheimer Disease

Alzheimer's disease (AD) is biologically defined by the presence of β amyloid-containing plaques and τ-containing neuro-fibrillary tangles Alzheimer's disease is a hereditary and sporadic neuro-degenerative disorder whose typical form causes amnestic cognitive impairment and less common variants cause non-amnestic cognitive impairment [9]. Alzheimer's disease (AD) is a innovative sickness wherein dementia signs steadily get worse over years In the early stages, amnesia is mild. However, as Alzheimer's sickness progresses, human beings lose the cappotential to talk and react to their surroundings. Alzheimer's sickness is the 6th main motive of dying withinside the United States AD sufferers stay a mean of eight years after signs end up obvious to others. However, life expectancy varies from 4 to 20 years, depending on age and other health conditions AD is currently incurable, but as research progresses, treatments for the symptoms will become available. Current treatments for Alzheimer's disease cannot stop the progression of the disease, but they can temporarily slow the deterioration of dementia symptoms and improve the quality of life for patients and their caregivers Efforts are being made around the world to find better ways to treat, delay, and prevent disease onset[1]. MRI-based structural imaging is an important part of the clinical evaluation of patients with suspected Alzheimer's dementia Brain atrophy detected by high-resolution MRI correlates with both tau deposition and neurobehavioral deficits and is a valid marker of AD and its progression The degree of atrophy of medial temporal structures such as the hippocampus is a diagnostic marker for mild cognitive impairment stage AD [4].

3   The Method

In this section, we present a proposed method for the classification and localization of explainable Alzheimer's disease utilizing deep learning techniques
Figure 1 shows the overall picture related to the proposed approach.

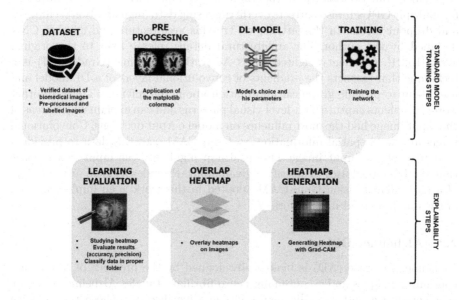

Fig. 1. The main picture of the proposed approach aimed to explainable AD classification and localisation.

As shown from Fig. 1 the seven distinct steps compose our method. The first is the choice of the dataset: as is well known, in the machine learning of any model based on it is necessary to have a large set of carefully labeled samples available. It is important that the set of samples is as general as possible: In fact, different medical specialists can use different imaging techniques with different machine

---

[1] https://www.nia.nih.gov/health/what-alzheimers-disease.

settings to extract images. Therefore, a correctly labeled dataset with a good degree of variability is essential to have a classifier capable of producing a model that is as generalizable as possible. The second step is to preprocess the dataset. The preprocessing carried out consists in the application of a colormap to the images of the dataset. Once you have chosen a dataset, the next step is to test the various DL models. The goal is to find the models that best respond to that given dataset, i.e. the models that classify images with better metrics (accuracy, accuracy and recall). This is a quantitative analysis, but qualitative feedback is also needed. In this article, we considered the following neural networks i) the first is developed by the authors and is called *STANDARD_CNN* and (ii) that *ALEX_NET*. Having already introduced the ALEX_NET model in the previous section, the structure of the STANDARD_CNN model is a combination of 14 layers, as shown in Fig. 2.

Layer (type)	Output Shape	Param #
conv2d (Conv2D)	(None, 248, 248, 32)	320
max_pooling2d (MaxPooling2D)	(None, 124, 124, 32)	0
conv2d_1 (Conv2D)	(None, 122, 122, 64)	18496
max_pooling2d_1 (MaxPooling2	(None, 61, 61, 64)	0
conv2d_2 (Conv2D)	(None, 59, 59, 128)	73856
max_pooling2d_2 (MaxPooling2	(None, 29, 29, 128)	0
flatten (Flatten)	(None, 107648)	0
dropout (Dropout)	(None, 107648)	0
dense (Dense)	(None, 512)	55116288
dropout_1 (Dropout)	(None, 512)	0
dense_1 (Dense)	(None, 256)	131328
dropout_2 (Dropout)	(None, 256)	0
dense_2 (Dense)	(None, 2)	514

Total params: 55,340,802
Trainable params: 55,340,802
Non-trainable params: 0

Fig. 2. The STANDARD_CNN architecture.

A brief description of the layers used is given:

- *Conv2D*: this layer performs the two-dimensional (2D) convolution used mainly on images. More technically, the purpose is to generate an output tensor as a result of the convolution between a kernel and the input layer;
- *MaxPooling2D*: consists of a maximum pooling operation for 2D spatial data. It aims to obtain, for each input channel, the maximum value of an input window with a set pool size, downsampling the input to its spatial dimensions (length and height).

– *Flatten*: this layer has the task of making the input multidimensional, and is normally used between two layers: in the convolutional one to the completely connected one.
– *Dropout*: this layer is intended to avoid overfitting, by randomly setting the input units to a zero value with a change in the rate at each epoch during training. Inputs that have not been set to a null value are set to a value of $1/(1 - \text{rate})$, making sure that the sum on all inputs is unchanged;
– *Dense*: This is a very common layer in DL models that have as their purpose the classification of objects. This layer has each node connected to all nodes of the previous layer, which act as input. The purpose is to perform a matrix-vector multiplication with values representing parameters that can be trained and updated through error backpropagation.

To foster reproducibility of research results the developed code is available for research purposes[2]. Figure 2 shows in detail the deep learning model designed by authors: as a matter fact for each layer involved there is the detail about the shape of the output and number of parameters. Moreover in Fig. 2 the number of total trainable parameters is shown. Once the DL models and the dataset are defined in the next phase, the various models are trained using an 80/10/10 splitting between training, validation and testing respectively. Several metrics are calculated at the output to evaluate the effectiveness of the models to classify and then generate predictions about classes. The metrics that have been implemented are: accuracy, precision, recall, F-measurement, and area under the curve (AUC). We propose an experiment aimed to distinguish between the different AD stages: in particular the method that we propose must be able to distinguish between non demented, very mild demented, mild demented, moderated demented patients by analysing brain MRIs. After testing the models, in the next step, we generate heat maps for retinal images using the Grad-CAM algorithm [20]. What the Grad-CAM algorithm does is to give visual explainability to the output classified images. Thus, we are interested not only in the quantitative aspects provided by the metrics, but also and above all in the qualitative aspects responsible for a certain classification. The qualitative aspect is given, in fact, by the explainability of a prediction concerning its localization in the image, which must correspond to a certain area of interest in the biomedical image. It is thus possible to see if the model is classifying correctly, based on highlighted area. These regions of interest must represent physiological and pathological studies concerning AD. In the traditional approach using Grad-CAM, the correct target pattern is known and Grad-CAM is a powerful tool for debugging the DL model training phase For classification tasks such as object detection, no expertise is required to check if the heatmap correctly highlights the target object. On the other hand, for classification tasks involving clinical and medical images, the DL developer may not have the necessary knowledge to understand whether the DL model has learned the correct patterns. This is an important point. DL models can achieve high accuracy in training tests, but

---

[2] https://github.com/Djack1010/tami.

they can learn the wrong patterns and make mistakes in real-world scenarios, resulting in detrimental outcomes.

4 Experimental Analysis

In this section we present the experiments we performed in order to assess the effectiveness of the proposed method for AD classification and localisation. The database used was taken from the Kaggle website[3]. The dataset is made up of a total of 6400 MRI images (an image is considered for each patient thus we considered 6400 different patients), divided into the following categories:

1. Non demented (896 images);
2. Very mild demented (2240 images);
3. Mild demented (896 images);
4. Moderate demented (64 images).

The images come from a preprocessed MRI set resized to 128 × 128 pixels. The images gathered from the Kaggle repository are obtained from various websites and certified public repositories. Figure 3 shows a selection of 4 images from the dataset, one image for each class.

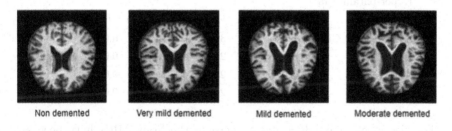

Non demented   Very mild demented   Mild demented   Moderate demented

Fig. 3. A selection of images belonging to the 4 classes of the dataset.

We perform a preprocessing consisting in the application of a colormap, in particular the "magma" colormap provided by the Matplotlib library[4]. The preprocessing script was developed by authors using the Python programming language and at the end of this step the images are saved with a size of 369 × 369 pixels. The colormap application was designed for trying to improve the classification of the images when their are analysed in RGB mode. The Fig. 4 shows the same MRIs in Fig. 3 after the colormaps application.

The deep learning models adopted in this study are STANDARD_CNN and ALEX_NET network. For each network different hyper-parameter combinations were tested such as the epochs number, the batch size and the learning rate.

---

[3] https://www.kaggle.com/datasets/tourist55/alzheimers-dataset-4-class-of-image.
[4] https://matplotlib.org/stable/tutorials/colors/colormaps.html.

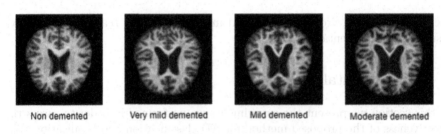

Non demented   Very mild demented   Mild demented   Moderate demented

Fig. 4. Application of "Magma" colormap to brain MRIs. (Color figure online)

In particular, the STANDARD_CNN network was calibrated using 30 epochs, a 0.001 learning rate and a batch size equals to 16, for the original dataset. The images dimensions were not changed. Regarding the dataset to which the colormap was applied, called AD_COLOR, all parameters remained unvaried with the exception of the epochs number which was brought to 25. Whereas, for ALEX_NET network, for both datasets, were used 25 epochs, 0.001 learning rate and a batch size equals to 16. For experiment replicability, in Table 1 the hyper-parameters we considered are shown.

Table 1. Hyperparameters used for model tuning.

Hyper-parameters				
Model	Preprocessing	Epochs	Batch size	Learning rate
STANDARD_CNN	No	30	16	0.001
	Yes	25	16	0.001
ALEX_NET	No	25	16	0.0001
	Yes	25	16	0.0001

For classification building and evaluation, the brain MRIs have been split into two groups, training and testing groups (i.e., 80:20 splitting) as follows:

- 5120 images for the training phase;
- 1280 images for the testing phase.

The obtained results reveal that the STANDARD_CNN neural network generally achieves better results for the AD stage classification. In Table 2 we show the metrics obtained in the testing phase. Even though the STANDARD_CNN results obtained with AD_COLOR dataset are slightly lower to the ones obtained with the original dataset, applying the Grad-CAM a clear enhancement of the localisation can be noticed. Figure 5 shows the confusion matrix obtained from the STANDARD_CNN model on the original dataset and on the AD_COLOR dataset.

In Figs. 7 and 8 we observe the results of applying Grad-CAM on the same brain MRI, before and after applying the colormap. The model used is the STANDARD_CNN and the images belong to the Mild_Demented class. We can see how

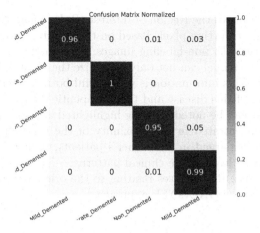

Fig. 5. Confusion matrix on the original and preprocessed dataset

Table 2. Metrics obtained during the testing phase

Results of multiclass classification - NonDemented/VeryMildDemented/MildDemented/ModerateDemented												
Model	Preprocessing	Output	Accuracy		Precision		Recall		F-Measure		AUC	
STANDARD_CNN	No	Non	0.97862	0.97404	0.96686	0.97400	0.99074	0.97251	0.97865	0.97326	0.97875	0.99768
		VeryMild	0.97404		0.97309		0.95175		0.96230		0.96885	
		Mild	0.99541		1.0000		0.96875		0.98412		0.98437	
		Moderate	1.00000		1.00000		1.00000		1.00000		1.00000	
	Yes	Non	0.97251	0.96641	0.99038	.96932	0.95370	0.96488	0.97169	0.96710	0.97232	0.99836
		VeryMild	0.96793		0.92592		0.98684		0.95541		0.97234	
		Mild	0.99236		0.98924		0.95833		0.97354		0.97827	
		Moderate	1.00000		1.00000		1.00000		1.00000		1.00000	
ALEX_NET	No	Non	0.89618	0.87328	0.96043	0.87981	0.82407	0.87175	0.88704	0.87576	0.89542	0.98099
		VeryMild	0.92977		0.89565		0.90350		0.89956		0.92365	
		Mild	0.92213		0.65957		0.96875		0.78481		0.94144	
		Moderate	0.99847		1.0000		0.85714		0.92307		0.92857	
	Yes	Non	0.89465	0.85343	0.99610	0.86448	0.79012	0.84732	0.88123	0.85582	0.89355	0.95511
		VeryMild	0.90992		0.85062		0.89912		0.87420		0.90740	
		Mild	0.91603		0.64539		0.94791		0.76793		0.92923	
		Moderate	0.98625		0.43750		1.00000		0.60869		0.99305	

the regions that were classified as of interest but belonging to the background are considerably reduced following the application of the colormap. This allows us, at the expense of a slight reduction in performance metrics, a greater explainability of the model. In Fig. 8, the combination of the preprocessing colormaps and the heatmaps ensures the most accurate localization of the patterns through which the model categorizes. This means that the Grad-CAM, combined with the obtained excellent results, identify areas that could escape the human eye, greatly helping the medical staff to a correct diagnosis. The importance of explainability, expressed by Grad-CAM, is subtle to grasp but extremely relevant for the IT and medical context. Heat maps that overlap images provide location information, that is, highlight anatomical areas that show recurring patterns on which the model classifies. Unlike images that show clearly visible tumor masses, here the presence or absence of the disease could escape even doctors. The overlapping of the heat maps guarantees the Region of Interest (RoI), where the algorithm recognizes a pattern of recurring pixels based on the training received. The results of the testing phase with non-labeling images, confirm that in the presence of unknown inputs, the model can not only recognize the disease, but also find the areas of the latter. This information is very useful both from a point of view of research and study of this disease and the therapeutic one.

In particular, it can be noted that the highlighted areas in the heatmaps are almost entirely concentrated in the proximity of the cerebral ventricles, thus, since the latter are enlarged in Alzheimer's patients, it may indicate that the network has correctly learned the clinical patterns.

Figure 6 shows the ROC curves relating to the original dataset. The ROCs were obtained using the ONEvsALL approach.

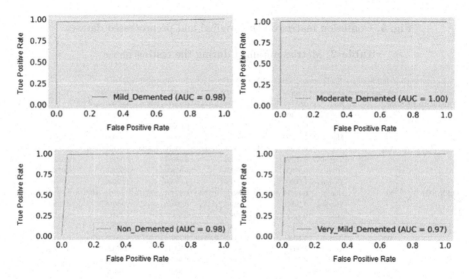

Fig. 6. ROCs on original dataset.

5   Related Work

In this section, we review the current state of the art in applying deep learning to AD detection These papers are described below. AD in the work of [11] is classified by using a deep convolutional neural network (DCNN). The DCNN was trained on the ADNI dataset. This dataset contains a total of 17773 images obtained by magnetic resonance imaging (MRI). The work focuses on the classification between subjects with Alzheimer's disease (AD), subjects with mild cognitive impairment (MCI) and healthy control subjects (CN). 9540 of the images was used for the training phase wherease the remaining part of the images was used for the testing phase. The work carried out by Salehi et al.

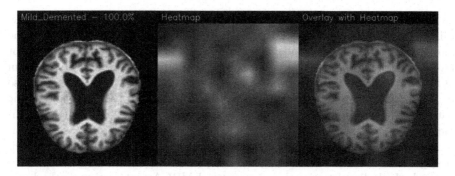

Fig. 7. Grad-CAM overlay on the original dataset. (Color figure online)

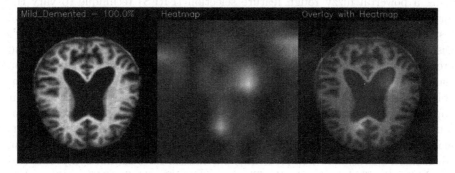

Fig. 8. Grad-CAM overlay on the preprocessed dataset. (Color figure online)

[18] focuses on the classification between three classes of subjects (AD, MCI, CN) using a dataset of 6225 images obtained from MRI. A CNN is used for the training-testing phase and the results show 99% accuracy. Researchers in [6] used a dataset with 4 classes of subjects representing the stages of the disease starting from the very mild condition up to the moderate condition. The authors of [16] have proposed a hybrid approach based on the ResNet18 and Densenet121 networks. This approach has led to the achievement of a weighted average precision of 99.61%. In [13], the use of a methodology based on trasfer learning was proposed. The network uses the freeze features extracted from the ImageNet dataset for binary or ternary classification. Thanks to the use of a VGG architecture the results obtained are significantly better than those obtained with ResNet and InceptionV3 architectures. A further approach that exploits transfer learning is the one proposed by [5]. Reseachers used a modified AlexNet network pre-trained on the ImageNet dataset. The model obtained reaches an accuracy of 0.917 and a miss rate of 0.083. In the work presented by Al-Adhaileh et al. [1], researchers used pre-trained ResNet50 and AlexNet CNNs using transfer learning. The AlexNet network achieved good performances based on the evaluation of five metrics: accuracy, precision, specificity, sensitivity and F1 score. Ruiz et al. [17] proposes his four-way classification of 3D MRI images using

an ensemble implementation of 3D Densely Connected Convolutional Networks (3D DenseNets) models. The author uses tight his linking which improves the movement of data in the model because each layer is linked to all subsequent layers in a block configuration, followed by three fully connected layers. The aim of their work is to distinguish between AD subjects and CN subjects but also to analyze the impact of the preprocessing used, the data partitioning and the dataset's dimension. Taj Noor et al. [15] used existing deep learning (DL) techniques to detect neurological disorders, focusing on Alzheimer's disease, Parkinson's disease, and schizophrenia, from MRI data acquired with different modalities) promoted a review examining and comparing the performance of the based methods. Including functional and structural MRI An interesting method was proposed in the paper of Chen et al. [2]. Their work supports such analysis by using a powerful fuzzy rough feature selection (FRFS) technique to vary the underlying similarity function and search strategy used in FRFS Experimental results were evaluated against the benchmarks of the well-known Alzheimer's Disease Neuroimaging Initiative repository, demonstrating the importance and predictive power of different cognitive assessments when using different common classifiers. In 2022, Janan et al. [7] in their study proposes a novel and explainable predictive model for Alzheimer's disease using multimodal datasets. Their approach performs data-level fusion with clinical data, Freesurfer MRI segmentation data, and psychological data For Alzheimer's disease and cognitively normal predictions, the random forest classifier provides 100% accuracy. In addition, Alzheimer's disease and non-Alzheimer's dementia have similar symptoms and should be classified appropriately. They presented for the first time a three-class classification of Alzheimer's disease, cognitively normal, and non-Alzheimer's dementia, and achieved an accuracy of 99.86 using an ensemble model Table 3 shows a comparison between the works presented in this section and the one proposed in this paper. The main results obtained are reported, the purpose of the work, the dataset exploited by authors and whether the explainability in terms of automatic disease localisation is considered by authors.

As emerged from the state-of-the-art comparison shown in Table 3 the main contribution provided by the proposed method is the localisation of the Alzheimer disease.

Table 3. Comparison between the proposed method and the state of the art

Authors	Focus	Localisation	Dataset	Results
Kundaram et al.	Classification between AD, MCI and CN	No	ADNI dataset 9540 images for training 4193 images for testing	Training accuracy: 0.9857 Validation accuracy: 0.8772
Salehi et al.	Classification between AD, MCI and CN	No	ADNI-3 dataset 6625 images	Accuracy: 0.99
Islam et al.	Classification between different stages of AD	No	OASIS dataset	Accuracy: 0.7375
Odusami et al.	Multiclass classification	No	MRI images	Weighted average macro precision: 0.9961 Loss: 0.003
Naz et al.	Classification between AD/MCI, AD/CN and MCI/CN with VGG architecture	No	3925 images from ADNI dataset	AD/MCI accuracy: 99.27% AD/CN accuracy: 98.89% MCI/CN accuracy: 97.06%
Backstrom et al.	Classification between AD and CN	No	340 subjects and 1128 MRI from ADNI dataset	Test accurcy of 98.74% 100% AD detection rate 2.4% false alarm
Ghazal et al.	Classification between different stages of AD	No	Dataset from Kaggle with 4 classes of MRI images	Accuracy: 91.7% Miss rate: 8.3%
Ruiz et al.	4-way classification of 3D MRI images	No	3the ADNI dataset	Good performances
Al-Adhaileh et al.	Classification and recognition of AD	No	Dataset from Kaggle website	Accuracy: 94.53% Specificity: 98.21% F1 score: 98.21% Sensitivity: 100%
Taj Noor et al.	Review of detecting neurological disorder	No	MRI and fMRI datasets	Accuracy: from 85% to 98%
Janan et al.	Classification of AD	No	Multimodal MRI dataset	Accuracy: 99.86%
Chen et al.	Fuzzy-Rough Feature Selection (FRFS) technique	No	Unknown	Good performance%
Our method	Classification between different stages of AD and localisation of ROIs	Yes	6400 images from Kaggle dataset 5745 images for training 655 images for testing	Non-Preprocessed dataset accuracy: 97.4% Preprocessed dataset accuracy: 96.64%

6 Conclusion and Future Work

Considering that the AD is nowadays diagnosed through neurologist visits and imaging techniques, with different degrees of uncertainty, in this paper we proposed a method aimed to automatically detect and localise the AD with the two different deep learning models. The approach we designed concentrates on evaluating deep learning models in terms of a set of modified predictions (taking into account the quantitative perspective), but fails to correctly identify disease in medical images. From the point of view of the ability to do so (considered from a qualitative point of view). Use class activation cards. Experimental analysis shows that the STANDARD_CNN model yields interesting results from a quantitative and qualitative point of view. The pre-processing is needed to ensure better results and to provide heatmaps more reliable, which can be used by doctors for diagnosis and subsequent therapy, and by researchers to study and deepen the unknown aspects of this disease. Future research plans include experiments with an equal samples for each analysed class (also exploiting data augmentation) but also on other brain diseases. Furthermore, we will evaluate the effectiveness of other widespread deep learning architecture in AD detection (for instance, VGG16).

Acknowledgment. This work has been partially supported by MIUR - SecureOpen-Nets, EU SPARTA, CyberSANE, E-CORRIDOR and MIUR - REASONING.

References

1. Al-Adhaileh, M.H.: Diagnosis and classification of Alzheimer's disease by using a convolution neural network algorithm. Soft Comput. 1–12 (2022)
2. Chen, T., et al.: Assessing significance of cognitive assessments for diagnosing Alzheimer's disease with fuzzy-rough feature selection. In: Jansen, T., Jensen, R., Mac Parthaláin, N., Lin, C.-M. (eds.) UKCI 2021. AISC, vol. 1409, pp. 450–462. Springer, Cham (2022). https://doi.org/10.1007/978-3-030-87094-2_40
3. Cummings, J.L., Cole, G.: Alzheimer disease. Jama **287**(18), 2335–2338 (2002)
4. Frisoni, G.B., Fox, N.C., Jack, C.R., Scheltens, P., Thompson, P.M.: The clinical use of structural MRI in Alzheimer disease. Nat. Rev. Neurol. **6**(2), 67–77 (2010)
5. Ghazal, T.M., et al.: Alzheimer disease detection empowered with transfer learning (2022)
6. Islam, J., Zhang, Y.: A novel deep learning based multi-class classification method for Alzheimer's disease detection using brain MRI data. In: Zeng, Y., et al. (eds.) BI 2017. LNCS (LNAI), vol. 10654, pp. 213–222. Springer, Cham (2017). https://doi.org/10.1007/978-3-319-70772-3_20
7. Jahan, S., et al.: Explainable AI-based Alzheimer's prediction and management using multimodal data (2022)
8. Khan, S., Rahmani, H., Shah, S.A.A., Bennamoun, M.: A guide to convolutional neural networks for computer vision. Synthesis Lect. Comput. Vision **8**(1), 1–207 (2018)
9. Knopman, D.S., et al.: Alzheimer disease. Nat. Rev. Dis. Primers **7**(1), 1–21 (2021)
10. Krizhevsky, A., Sutskever, I., Hinton, G.E.: ImageNet classification with deep convolutional neural networks. Adv. Neural. Inf. Process. Syst. **25**, 1097–1105 (2012)
11. Kundaram, S.S., Pathak, K.C.: Deep learning-based Alzheimer disease detection. In: Nath, V., Mandal, J.K. (eds.) Proceedings of the Fourth International Conference on Microelectronics, Computing and Communication Systems. LNEE, vol. 673, pp. 587–597. Springer, Singapore (2021). https://doi.org/10.1007/978-981-15-5546-6_50
12. LeCun, Y., Bottou, L., Bengio, Y., Haffner, P.: Gradient-based learning applied to document recognition. Proc. IEEE **86**(11), 2278–2324 (1998)
13. Naz, S., Ashraf, A., Zaib, A.: Transfer learning using freeze features for Alzheimer neurological disorder detection using ADNI dataset. Multimed. Syst. **28**(1), 85–94 (2022)
14. Nigri, E., Ziviani, N., Cappabianco, F., Antunes, A., Veloso, A.: Explainable deep CNNs for MRI-based diagnosis of Alzheimer's disease. In: 2020 International Joint Conference on Neural Networks (IJCNN), pp. 1–8. IEEE (2020)
15. Noor, M.B.T., Zenia, N.Z., Kaiser, M.S., Mamun, S.A., Mahmud, M.: Application of deep learning in detecting neurological disorders from magnetic resonance images: a survey on the detection of Alzheimer's disease, Parkinson's disease and schizophrenia. Brain Inform. **7**(1), 1–21 (2020)

16. Odusami, M., Maskeliūnas, R., Damaševičius, R., Misra, S.: ResD hybrid model based on resnet18 and densenet121 for early Alzheimer disease classification. In: Abraham, A., Gandhi, N., Hanne, T., Hong, T.-P., Nogueira Rios, T., Ding, W. (eds.) ISDA 2021. LNNS, vol. 418, pp. 296–305. Springer, Cham (2022). https://doi.org/10.1007/978-3-030-96308-8_27

17. Ruiz, J., Mahmud, M., Modasshir, Md., Shamim Kaiser, M., Alzheimer's Disease Neuroimaging Initiative: 3D DenseNet ensemble in 4-way classification of Alzheimer's disease. In: Mahmud, M., Vassanelli, S., Kaiser, M.S., Zhong, N. (eds.) BI 2020. LNCS (LNAI), vol. 12241, pp. 85–96. Springer, Cham (2020). https://doi.org/10.1007/978-3-030-59277-6_8

18. Salehi, A.W., Baglat, P., Sharma, B.B., Gupta, G., Upadhya, A.: A CNN model: earlier diagnosis and classification of Alzheimer disease using MRI. In: 2020 International Conference on Smart Electronics and Communication (ICOSEC), pp. 156–161. IEEE (2020)

19. Sarica, A., Quattrone, A., Quattrone, A.: Explainable boosting machine for predicting Alzheimer's disease from MRI hippocampal subfields. In: Mahmud, M., Kaiser, M.S., Vassanelli, S., Dai, Q., Zhong, N. (eds.) BI 2021. LNCS (LNAI), vol. 12960, pp. 341–350. Springer, Cham (2021). https://doi.org/10.1007/978-3-030-86993-9_31

20. Selvaraju, R.R., Cogswell, M., Das, A., Vedantam, R., Parikh, D., Batra, D.: Gradcam: Visual explanations from deep networks via gradient-based localization. In: Proceedings of the IEEE International Conference on Computer Vision, pp. 618–626 (2017)

21. Simonyan, K., Zisserman, A.: Very deep convolutional networks for large-scale image recognition. arXiv preprint arXiv:1409.1556 (2014)

ML-Based Radiomics Analysis for Breast Cancer Classification in DCE-MRI

Francesco Prinzi[1]([envelope])[ORCID], Alessia Orlando[2][ORCID], Salvatore Gaglio[3,4][ORCID], Massimo Midiri[1][ORCID], and Salvatore Vitabile[1][ORCID]

[1] Department of Biomedicine, Neuroscience and Advanced Diagnostics (BiND), University of Palermo, Palermo, Italy
{francesco.prinzi,massimo.midiri,salvatore.vitabile}@unipa.it
[2] Section of Radiology - Department of Biomedicine, Neuroscience and Advanced Diagnostics (BiND), University Hospital "Paolo Giaccone", Palermo, Italy
orlandoalessiamed@hotmail.it
[3] Department of Engineering, University of Palermo, Palermo, Italy
salvatore.gaglio@unipa.it
[4] ICAR-CNR, Palermo, Italy

Abstract. Breast cancer is the most common malignancy that threatening women's health. Although Dynamic Contrast-Enhanced Magnetic Resonance Imaging (DCE-MRI) for breast lesions characterization is widely used in the clinical practice, physician grading performance is still not optimal, showing a specificity of about 72%. In this work Radiomics was used to analyze a dataset acquired with two different protocols in order to train Machine-Learning algorithms for breast cancer classification. Original radiomic features were expanded considering Laplacian of Gaussian filtering and Wavelet Transform images to evaluate whether they can improve predictive performance. A Multi-Instant features selection involving the seven instants of the DCE-MRI sequence was proposed to select the set of most descriptive features. Features were harmonized using the ComBat algorithm to handle the multi-protocol dataset. Random Forest, XGBoost and Support Vector Machine algorithms were compared to find the best DCE-MRI instant for breast cancer classification: the pre-contrast and the third post-contrast instants resulted as the most informative items. Random Forest can be considered the optimal algorithm showing an Accuracy of 0.823, AUC-ROC of 0.877, Specificity of 0.882, Sensitivity of 0.764, PPV of 0.866, and NPV of 0.789 on the third post-contrast instant using an independent test set. Finally, Shapley values were used as Explainable AI algorithm to prove an high contribution of Original and Wavelet features in the final prediction.

Keywords: Radiomics · Machine learning · Image processing · Explainable AI

1 Introduction

Breast cancer is the most common malignancy that threatens the health of women. According with [17] more than two million cases were diagnosed in 2020

M. Mahmud et al. (Eds.): AII 2022, CCIS 1724, pp. 144–158, 2022.
https://doi.org/10.1007/978-3-031-24801-6_11

representing the most common cancer worldwide. Through the ability to provide both morphologic and hemodynamic features, Dynamic Contrast-Enhanced Magnetic Resonance Imaging (DCE-MRI) play a pivotal role in the diagnosis of breast lesion. The DCE-MRI consists in the acquisition of the same image in consecutive instants of time after the emission of a contrast medium, composing a sequence of MRI. This acquisition method is particularly useful thanks to the different absorption of the contrast medium between malignant and benign lesions: it appears that malignant lesions immediately show an increase in the intensity of the contrast medium and a very fast excretion, while the benign lesions show a slow increase followed by a persistent increase. However, despite DCE-MRI has shown very high performance for the diagnosis with sensitivity over 90%, specificity for lesion characterization is still suboptimal (72%) [12].

Artificial Intelligence (AI) algorithms have shown impressive results in medical image analysis and have the potential to aid the breast cancer diagnosis process. Through an appropriate extraction of imaging features computed from the medical volume, it is possible to retrieve a salient and informative representation of the Region of Interest (ROI) to be analyzed from a quantitative point of view. Deep Learning architectures such as Convolutional Neural Networks, Deep Belief Network, Autoencoder, etc., are state-of-the-art methods for deep features extraction and currently represent the first choice for solving classification, localization, detection, segmentation and registration problems [8]. However, these architectures require the training of millions of parameters and this demands a large amount of well-annotated data. In addition, to the best of our knowledge, Deep Learning for breast cancer classification task is mainly performed on mammography with medium/large available public dataset, while only few publications deal with breast cancer classification on Magnetic Resonance public data. In the last case, publications deal with proprietary data or very small public dataset, so that effective training methods, such as Transfer Learning, are not suitable. Also, the segmented 3D breast cancer volumes could be composed by few voxels in MRI, making a very difficult classification task when Convolutional Architectures are used.

In recent years, in medical imaging filed, the feature extraction task is addressed through Radiomics. Radiomics is a new multidisciplinary approach, which includes data acquisition, ROIs segmentation, features extraction, features selection and training of AI algorithms, with the aim of converting routine clinical images into meaningful data and information, with high selectivity and sensitivity and high productivity [4]. An accurate and precise feature extraction does not require a large amount of data, as in the case of Deep Learning, and for this reason it is particularly relevant in medical applications. The radiomics workflow is a complex process because an effective and robust extraction requires the setting of many parameters: there are the parameters for the discretization of the image, the distance to pixel-neighbour and the angles to consider, and the transformations to be applied to the original images. Furthermore, considering the high dimensionality that can be achieved through extraction, there is a high risk of training overfitting models with no appropriate feature processing and selection.

In this work, Radiomics and Machine Learning algorithms were used to propose a model to classify malignant and benign breast lesions in DCE-MRI. A multi-protocol dataset coming from the real clinical practice of the Radiology section of the University Hospital "Paolo Giaccone" (Palermo, Italy) was used. In this regard, the extraction of radiomic features is performed at all seven instants of the DCE-MRI sequence (one pre-contrast image and six post-cotrast images), considering the original images, filtered with Laplacian of Gaussian filter and Wavelet Transformed, to evaluate if their use can increase classification performance. The features of the seven instants of the sequence were used to select the most descriptive features for the phenomenon and to find out the most appropriate temporal instant of the sequence for the classification. Random Forest, XGBoost and Support Vector Machine were compared for classification and tested on an independent test dataset. An Explanation of the best achieved results was also provided through the Shapley values [9] in order to show the global importance of each feature in the final prediction process. The use of multiple protocols increases the difficulty of the task but moves the work toward a real clinical scenario.

The article is organized as follow: Sect. 2 describes the related works for the classification of breast cancer in DCE-MRI. Section 3 explains data preparation, features extraction, data harmonization and features selection step to train and validate the Machine Learning algorithms. Section 4 exposes the results obtained after features selection, training/validation and test phase. Finally, in Sect. 5, discussion and conclusion are provided.

2   Related Works

Several works have been proposed for the classification of breast lesions in DCE-MRI using radiomics. Gibbs et al. [3] analyzed a court of 165 lesions, classified as BI-RADS 4 or 5 and containing sub 1-cm Breast Lesion. Four distinct heuristic parameter maps have been calculated for radiomic features extraction: Initial Enhancement, Overall Enhancement, Washout and AUC. For each parameter maps, first order, two-dimensional Gray Level Co-Occurrence Matrix (GLCM), Gray Level Run Length Matrix (GLRLM), Gray Level Size Zone Matrix (GLSZM) and Neighbouring Gray Tone Difference Matrix (NGTDM) radiomic features were extracted. A Support Vector Machine binary linear classifier was trained for the four parameter maps independently using the most discriminant features, getting for the best model Initial Enhancement features map, respectively with 0.75–0.81, 67% and 100% for AUC, Sensitivity and Specificity. A court of 133 patients was analyzed by Zhou et al. [19] through radiomics and deep learning. Focusing on radiomics, as in the previous case, radiomic features was performed on parametric maps: Washin Signal Enhancement, Maximum Signal Enhancement and Washout Slope Map. On each parametric map, 20 GLCM and 13 first order features have been calculated for a total of 99 features. A logistic regression model was trained using 15 more discriminating features and 5 ROI features, obtaining respectively 85%, 65%, 78% for sensitivity, specificity and accuracy. Parekh et al. [15] have extracted radiomic features from multiparametric breast MR imaging, including DCE-MRI, aggregated and classified with the isoSVM algorithm. Considering a court of 124 patients, they obtained sensitivity and specificity of 93% and 85%, respectively, with an AUC of 0.91. Zhang et al. [18] extract a total of 862 features (shape features, first-order, GLCM, GLDM, GLRLM, GLSZM and NGTDM) from five different imaging sequences, including DCE-MRI. An SVM was trained for the classification task, demonstrating that considering the performance of each acquisition method separately, pharmacokinetic parameters maps has greater discriminative power, with AUC and accuracy of 0.83 and 0.75 respectively. In addition, performance increases significantly when considering different acquisition methods. Nagarajan et al. [11] focused on the evaluating of features extracted by small lesion (mean lesion diameter of 1.1 cm). They extracted GLCM features in the five post-tagged images and a support vector regression and a fuzzy k-nearest neighbor classifier were trained, yielding an AUC of 0.82. Militello et al. [10] analyzed a court of 111 patients using the original features extracted with Pyradiomics toolkit. They explored different selection algorithms to find the best radiomic signature for classification and to train an SVM. Using the strongest enhancement phase of the DCE-MRI sequence they obtained 0.725 ± 0.091 of AUC-ROC, 0.709 ± 0.176 of sensitivity, 0.741 ± 0.114 of specificity, 0.72 ± 0.093 of PPV, and 0.75 ± 0.114 of NPV.

In this work, the original radiomic features were expanded by considering Wavelet Transforms and Laplacian of Gaussian filtering to evaluate possible improvement of models prediction. Moreover, all seven instants of the DCE-MRI sequence were considered to find the simultaneously significant features in multiple instants and to evaluate the most informative instant for classification. Finally, an interpretation of the best achieved results was carried out to show the most relevant features.

3   Materials and Methods

3.1   Data Preparation

Patient Population. In our study we included 166 breast mass enhancement (Mean Size $\pm$ Standard Deviation (SD) in millimeters: 15,3 $\pm$ 10,5; size range: 3–75;) revealed at dynamic contrast-enhanced MRI (DCE-MRI) in 104 patients (103 woman and 1 man; Mean Age $\pm$ SD: 51 $\pm$ 11 years; Age Range: 31–79 years) underwent Breast MRI examination at our Institute from April 2018 to March 2020. These 166 breast mass enhancements were classified by two experienced breast radiologists in consensus, respectively 73 in BI-RADS category 2–3 and 93 in BI-RADS category 4–5. Among mass enhancements found in breast MR exams acquired in the same period 48 were excluded from this study due to inconsistent follow-up (less than 24 months) for BI-RADS 3 masses and to the lack of a pathological diagnosis (patient refusal to undergo biopsy or withdrawn by our

Institute) for BI-RADS 4 or 5 masses. 12 Breast MR exams were excluded due to the presence of technical or motion artifacts. Breast non mass-enhancement were excluded from our study.

Breast MRI Protocols. In our Institute breast MR exams were performed with a 1,5T MR Scanner (GE Signa HDxt, General Electric Healthcare, United States) by using a 4-channels breast coil, by two different breast radiologists, with 12 and 10 years of experience in breast MR imaging, respectively. Breast MRI protocols performed consisted of axial T2w FSE, STIR and DWI sequences, and a dynamic contrast-enhanced (DCE) sequence, in detail a 3D GRE T1w with fat saturation sequence (called Vibrant), with an acquisition before and 6 acquisitions after contrast media administration, and with a temporal resolution of 70–90 s. The contrast agent, 0.1 mmol/kg Gd-DO3A-butrol, was intravenously injected after the pre-contrast images were acquired, at a rate of 2 ml/s, followed by a 20-ml saline flush at the same rate. For the purpose of this study only DCE sequence was analyzed. Table 1 resumes DCE sequence parameters of the two different breast MRI protocols, each one performed by one of the two breast radiologists.

Table 1. Breast MRI protocols.

	1st	2nd
Number of slices	342	402
Matrix size	452×452	352×352
In-plane resolution (mm)	0.8×0.8	1×1
Slice thickness (mm)	0.8	1
Bandwidth	62.5	83.33
Field of view	35×35	35×35
Time repetition	4.7	3.5
Echo time	2.2	1.6
Flip angle	10	15
Number of lesions	81	85

ROI Segmentation. The same 166 breast mass enhancements underwent manual segmentation, by using 3D-Slicer software, by three independent operators, three senior radiologist residents with 4 years of experience in breast MR imaging. Each reviewer chose the post-contrast phase better demonstrating lesions contours, and included few millimeters of perilesional fat in each image segmentation, by using the minimum width of a circular ROI. A third independent breast radiologist (with 10 years of experience in breast MR imaging) checked all the 166 breast masses segmentation, expressing its consent in all the 166 cases.

Training/Validation and Test Split. The whole dataset consisting of 166 lesions was divided into two groups useful for training/validation (80%) and test (20%) respectively. In a completely random fashion, data was split in a stratified manner, using the class labels to ensure a balance of malignant and benign lesions in the two groups. At the end, the training/validation dataset counted 132 lesions of which 67 malignant and 65 benign, while the test dataset counted 34 examples perfectly divided between the two classes.

3.2 Radiomic Features Extraction

In this work, radiomic features were extracted with pyradiomics toolkit [5,20]. The Table 2 summarizes the number of extracted features per class. Figure 1 shows an example of how the use of Wavelet Transforms and Laplacian of Gaussian filtering provides a complementary representation to the original image.

Table 2. Summary of all extracted features. LLH, LHL, etc., identify a decomposition direction of the wavelet, where L and H represent Low-Pass Filter and High-Pass Filter. σ identifies the smooth size of the LoG filter.

Features	N	Description
Original	107	93 no-shape features + 14 shape 3D features
Wavelet	744	93×8, where 93 are the Total Classic no-shape features and 8 are the image considering LLH, LHL, LHH, HLL, HLH, HHL, HHH and LLL filters
LoG	186	93×2, where 93 are the Total Classic no-shape features and 3 are $\sigma = [2,3]$
Total	**1037**	

Original Features. Features extracted on the original images are briefly described. The same features, except for those of shape, were then extracted from the LoG and Wavelet images.

- *Shape 3D*: only 3D shape features has been extracted because we considered a 3D ROI. These features are in no way related to the intensities of the voxels but from three-dimensional size and shape of the mask.
- *First Order*: the features of the first order define the intensity distribution of the voxels in a specified ROI.
- *Gray Level Co-occurrence Matrix (GLCM)*: the GLCM was defined to capture the distribution of co-occurrence pixel values at a given distance d and angle θ. The distances d between the center voxel and the neighbor was considered 1. No weighted distance was used and the symmetrical GLCM was calculated. The value of GLCM features was calculated for each angle θ separately and the mean of these was return.

- *Gray Level Run Length Matrix (GLRLM)*: the GLRLM gives the size of homogeneous runs for each grey level, where the runs are consecutive pixels with the same gray level value. The same considerations of GLCM were made for the choice of angles.
- *Neighboring Gray Tone Difference Matrix (NGTDM)*: the NGTDM has been used to extract features capable of highlighting changes in the intensity of the voxels. The difference between a gray value and the average gray value of its neighbours was considered using distances 1.
- *Gray Level Size Zone Matrix (GLSZM)*: GLSZM was introduced to take into account that homogeneous texture is composed of large areas of the same intensity and not small groups of pixels or segments in a certain direction.
- *Gray Level Dependence Matrix (GLDM)*: a GLDM quantifies gray level dependencies in an image, where a gray level dependency is defined as a the number of connected voxels within some distance that are dependent on the center voxel.

Wavelet Transform. The Discrete Wavelet Transform (DWT) provides a multi-resolution representation of the image, allowing for image compression and resulting in noise reduction. DWT can be formulated through the high-pass h_ψ and low-pass h_ϕ filtering operation, representing a dilated and translated version of a particular signal. Using a single layer of DTW, 8 decompositions are obtained applying the two filters in the 3 axes of the image. Only the first level was considered to avoid inaccurate extraction in case of too small lesions. Haar was used as type of wavelet decomposition. All original features, except shape features, were then computed for each of the 8 decompositions obtained.

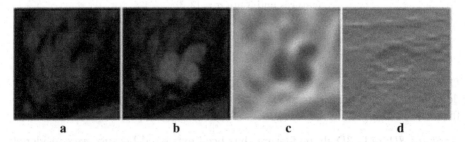

Fig. 1. An example of the same Breast Lesion represented in different setting at the same slice volume. a) Is the pre-contrast image. b) Is the third post-contrast image. c) Laplacian of Gaussian filtered image with $\sigma = 2$. d) Wavelet Transform using LHL decomposition.

Laplacian of Gaussian Filtering. The Laplacian of Gaussian filter (LoG) is used to highlights regions of rapid intensity change. It is defined as a second order derivative operators that detect the edge at the zero-crossing of the second derivative, resulting less sensitive to noise then first order derivative operator. The filter required the setting of σ to manage the smoothing: large values means pronounced smoothing (better denoising but less precision in edge localization) and small values means soft smoothing (lower noise reduction but better boundary preservation). The σ value was set to 2 and 3, then the features discussed, except shape features, were extracted for all the specified values of σ.

3.3   Data Harmonization

The extraction of radiomic features is strongly dependent on the acquisition protocol of medical images: the acquisition protocol varies depending on the center, the scanner and also to consider some specific aspects of the lesion. In real scenarios it is not reasonable that all images are acquired in the same way and consequently the distribution of extracted radiomic features could differ depending on the acquisition protocols. For this reason, when multi-centric or in general multi-protocol data are processed, it is necessary to consider data harmonization. In this work, the ComBat harmonization method was used for data harmonization [1,6]. ComBat directly applies to the features already extracted from the images, without the need for retrieving the images, to align the distributions of the protocols. In this case no covariate terms were used because the number of benign and malignant lesions were similar at both sites (protocol 0: 43% benign and 57% malignant; protocol 1: 55% benign and 45% malignant) and the use of covariate does not affect the transformation [13].

3.4   Radiomic Features Selection

Baseline Features Selection. The steps described in this phase were performed at all instants of the DCE-MRI sequence separately. A first skimming of the features was carried out by removing those with constant or near-constant values and therefore have no predictive value. For this purpose, all features with variance < 0.01 were discarded. The Spearman's rank correlation coefficient was used to remove correlated features, considering $|\rho| < 0.9$ as threshold. Finally, the Mann-Whitney U test was used to test the difference between malignant and benign distributions considering $p < 0.05$.

Multi-instant Features Selection. This selection step simultaneously involved all 7 instants of the DCE-MRI sequence. In particular, it was assumed that a feature must be significant at multiple instances to be descriptive of the phenomenon. For this reason, the features were additionally reduced by selecting those that in at least 5 of the 7 instants of the sequence were considered robust in the baseline step. At the end of this step, we ensure that the features selected at each instant are descriptive for lesion classification in general and not for a particular instant in the sequence.

Tuning Features Selection. Given the still high-dimensionality of the radiomic features and the small size of the dataset considered, a further selection step was performed on the remaining features after the first two reduction steps, to find the best radiomic signature. For this task the Sequential Forward Floating Selection (SFFS) algorithm was used [16]. SFFS is greedy search algorithm used to select a subset of features that is most relevant to the problem. Using the floating variant, a larger number of feature subset combinations can be sampled because an additional exclusion step is computed to remove features once they were included.

In this step we chose to select a number of features proportionate to the size of the dataset. Considering the training dataset composed of 133 samples and exploiting the proportion proposed in [14], we decided to select the number of features for each instant in a range 8–13. The algorithm, applied for each instant of the sequence, was used by setting the three classifiers used (Random Forest, XGBoost and Support Vector Machine), evaluated using a stratified 10 fold CV and using accuracy as score.

3.5   Model Training

In this work 3 different classifiers were used. Specifically Random Forest (RF) and XGBoost (XGB) which are two of the most common Tree Ensemble algorithms. In XGB the objective is to minimize the loss function of the model by adding weak learners using gradient descent (Boosting Ensemble Method). RF uses the bagging technique to build several weak learner considering random subset of features and bootstrap sample data, to aggregate the decision of each learner (Bagging Ensemble Method). Tree ensemble algorithms have proven effective for classification in small dataset [2,7] and are the most used along with Support Vector Machines (SVM): for this reason RF, XGB and SVM were considered. RF was trained with default parameters using 100 estimators, gini criterion and bootsrtap technique. XGB was trained also with default parameters using 100 estimators, 0.3 as learning rate and gane as importance type. For SVM training, the features were standardized and the RBF was used as kernel. Due to the reduced dataset size, the 10-repeated 10-fold cross-validation was used to get a better estimation of the model generalization performance. The 100 simulations were performed to minimize model performance dependencies when assessing differences in classifications using different test set. Considering the 100 models, the best model was selected in terms of accuracy and used for the testing phase on a independent test set.

4   Results

To evaluate model performance, Accuracy, Area Under the Receiver Operating Characteristic (AUC-ROC), Specificity, Sensitivity, Positive Predictive Value (PPV) and Negative Predictive Value (NPV) were considered. To ensure accurate comparison between different algorithms and sequence instants, the same seed was set for all probabilistic terms in the algorithms and for the splits generation for the stratified cross validation.

Features Selected. Figure 2 shows the number of the features selected in each instant of the DCE-MRI sequence after Baseline features selection. In the pre-contrast instant more features were selected than the others. It can be seen that the number of Wavelet features was much higher than Original and LoG features in each instant. However this effect is due to the fact that the starting Wavelet features were 744 per instant, 4 times more than LoG and about 8 times more than Original features. Proportionally the Original features are the most selected, followed by LoG and finally Wavelet. This trend was confirmed for all 7 instants.

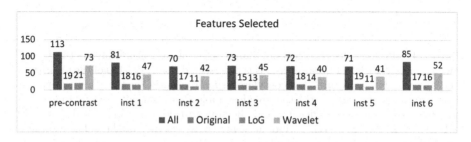

Fig. 2. Number of selected features for each instant of the DCE-MRI sequence after Baseline features selection.

Figure 3 shows the application of SFFS in the third post-contrast instant of the sequence, considering the three used algorithms RF, XGB and SVM. It can be deduced that in general the inclusion of too many features or too few beyond the established range threshold $8 - 13$, does not allow to make the model generalize better, on the contrary it makes the performances less robust (lower accuracy and/or higher standard deviation). Same trend was confirmed in the other time instant.

Model Training/validation. Table 3 shows the result for the three algorithms RF, XGB and SVM using the cross validation procedure. It can be seen from the table that there was no significantly better instant for classification. The first post-contrast instant and the fourth were the worst in terms of accuracy and AUC-ROC compared to the other instants. The pre-contrast instant instead would seem to be one of the best in terms of AUC-ROC and Accuracy especially for Tree Ensembles. All 3 models have overlapping performances in the third post-contrast instant. Comparing the Tree Ensemble algorithms, RF would seem more reliable. In terms of accuracy it beats in all instants XGBoost, except for the pre-contrast one; moreover it generally provides a better balance between sensitivity and specificity, thus allowing a balanced classification between the

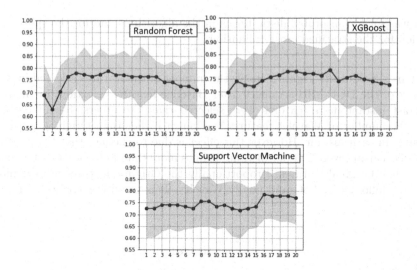

Fig. 3. The three graphs were generated after selecting 20 features on the third post-contrast instant with SFFS. In the x-axis is represented the $n-th$ step of the algorithm, then at each step n features are considered simultaneously; in the y-axis is instead shown the value of accuracy. For the Tree Ensemble algorithms after about 15 features the performance drops significantly and the standard deviation of the calculated 10 folds increases. For SVM the performance increases but the standard deviation also raises, making the model less unstable.

two classes. Therefore, RF and SVM were found the best models, and their generalization performance was evaluated on the independent test set.

Model Testing. The results presented in the training/validation phase were reflected on the performances in the test set. As shown in Table 4, it was confirmed that in the pre-contrast phase and in the third post-contrast instant, RF and SVM generalize almost in the same way. In particular, the pre-contrast instant can be considered one of the best for classification. However, the third post-contrast phase is the one that absolutely highlights the differences between the two classes, obtaining excellent values for all the metrics considered. The result was interesting because there is a contrast of meaning between the two instants of the sequence. The pre-contrast instant is the one that absolutely maintains the original characteristics of the lesion, in terms of gray levels and texture. The third post-contrast instant, on the other hand, is the one in which both benign and malignant lesions have absorbed the contrast agent. It is important to emphasize that SVM in the second and fourth post-contrast instants obtains questionable performances, with a very high specificity and a very low sensitivity. RF instead, in all cases, maintains a good balance and an AUC-ROC always higher than SVM (except pre-contrast phase). It can be concluded that RF was the algorithm that guarantees the best and reliable performance.

Table 3. Validation performance for each time instant and for each algorithm. Instant 0 is the pre-contrast, the others are post-contrast. For each metric, mean ± standard deviation is provided.

Inst	Model	Accuracy	AUC-ROC	Specificity	Sensitivity	PPV	NPV
0	RF	.737 ± .121	.809 ± .125	.737 ± .181	.740 ± .170	.757 ± .150	.749 ± .144
	XGB	.749 ± .104	.812 ± .113	.715 ± .180	.785 ± .149	.758 ± .133	.777 ± .141
	SVM	.703 ± .131	.745 ± .156	.732 ± .177	.677 ± .187	.737 ± .157	.701 ± .160
1	RF	.686 ± .126	.736 ± .141	.692 ± .200	.682 ± .190	.713 ± .155	.693 ± .161
	XGB	.645 ± .114	.698 ± .129	.645 ± .175	.643 ± .190	.659 ± .145	.657 ± .147
	SVM	.690 ± .116	.725 ± .146	.751 ± .182	.636 ± .171	.745 ± .153	.673 ± .133
2	RF	.717 ± .130	.748 ± .140	.715 ± .193	.721 ± .170	.740 ± .150	.721 ± .154
	XGB	.705 ± .122	.752 ± .120	.671 ± .183	.741 ± .159	.711 ± .139	.728 ± .157
	SVM	.696 ± .124	.738 ± .143	.732 ± .173	.662 ± .184	.730 ± .154	.692 ± .145
3	**RF**	**.710 ± .130**	**.741 ± .135**	**.738 ± .177**	**.683 ± .178**	**.743 ± .153**	**.703 ± .145**
	XGB	.703 ± .129	.742 ± .143	.692 ± .194	.713 ± .190	.720 ± .152	.717 ± .152
	SVM	.717 ± .126	.757 ± .141	.752 ± .174	.681 ± .183	.754 ± .150	.710 ± .143
4	RF	.691 ± .121	.719 ± .144	.689 ± .182	.692 ± .174	.710 ± .144	.699 ± .148
	XGB	.689 ± .127	.728 ± .143	.682 ± .205	.696 ± .158	.713 ± .157	.688 ± .147
	SVM	.723 ± .128	.756 ± .131	.775 ± .167	.672 ± .185	.764 ± .153	.708 ± .140
5	RF	.717 ± .130	.765 ± .136	.744 ± .193	.693 ± .183	.753 ± .159	.712 ± .146
	XGB	.688 ± .123	.736 ± .148	.681 ± .204	.696 ± .162	.713 ± .155	.695 ± .149
	SVM	.731 ± .123	.761 ± .138	.721 ± .190	.740 ± .181	.747 ± .154	.747 ± .143
6	RF	.709 ± .114	.726 ± .141	.694 ± .168	.724 ± .168	.718 ± .126	.722 ± .145
	XGB	.687 ± .133	.752 ± .148	.653 ± .196	.720 ± .158	.695 ± .146	.698 ± .158
	SVM	.744 ± .118	.798 ± .118	.741 ± .165	.747 ± .174	.760 ± .136	.756 ± .143

Table 4. Performance on the independent test set for each time instant and for RF and SVM algorithms. Instant 0 is the pre-contrast, the others are post-contrast.

Inst	Model	Accuracy	AUC-ROC	Specificity	Sensitivity	PPV	NPV
0	RF	.794	.813	.882	.705	.857	.750
	SVM	.794	.858	.882	.705	.857	.750
1	RF	.705	.787	.764	.647	.733	.684
	SVM	.794	.750	.823	.764	.812	.777
2	RF	.794	.816	.882	.705	.857	.750
	SVM	.735	.757	.882	.588	.833	.681
3	**RF**	**.823**	**.877**	**.882**	**.764**	**.866**	**.789**
	SVM	.823	.837	.882	.764	.866	.789
4	RF	.764	.809	.823	.705	.800	.736
	SVM	.764	.809	.941	.588	.909	.695
5	RF	.794	.842	.882	.705	.857	.750
	SVM	.823	.840	.823	.823	.823	.823
6	RF	.794	.821	.882	.705	.857	.750
	SVM	.764	.820	.764	.764	.764	.764

Features Importance. Another interesting result concerns the best features selected with SFFS for RF and SVM. In order to understand which features were the most important for classification and to which category they belong, Shapley values [9] were used as Explainable AI algorithm to provide a post-hoc explanation and to compute the global features importance of the trained model. Figure 4 shows the two signatures used to train the algorithms in order of importance. Wavelet features were the ones that most affect the prediction of the models. In both cases, the Major Axis Length shape feature was the most important, which represents the major axis of the ellipsoid enclosing the region of interest. No LoG features were selected for SVM. The radiomic signature selected depends mainly on the used classification algorithms, however it can be concluded that Wavelet Transforms affect more than the other feature classes.

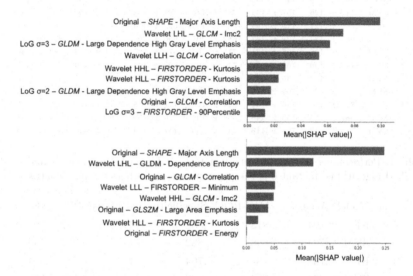

Fig. 4. Global explanation for RF (upper) and SVM (down). Using the Shapley values, the graphs show feature importance on independent test set.

5   Discussion and Conclusion

This work aims to analyze the entire DCE-MRI sequence for breast cancer classification. The dataset coming from real clinical practice perfectly reflects the heterogeneity of a real scenario: images were acquired with different protocols, and different types and size of lesions have been considered, increasing the validity of the work conducted. Data harmonization was performed to align distributions from the two protocols. A strict feature selection and the Multi-Instant selection have made possible the selection of the descriptive features for the classification of lesions, independently from the instant of the sequence considered: in this case we can affirm that the selected features are descriptive of the phenomenon considered. A comparison between 3 common Machine Learning algorithms (RF, XGB, SVM) was performed to evaluate the most significant DCE-MRI sequence instant for breast lesion classification. The ML choice derives from the certainty that Deep Learning models reliability is closely related to dataset size and it is well-known that a dataset with less than 200 samples is unsuitable for successful deep training. As result, the works cited in the Related Works section are focused on radiomic signatures and use ML algorithms (mainly SVM) with similar small dataset. For this reason, our paper was focused on the role of radiomic features, discarding the deep features (usually extracted with convolutional networks). Although all three algorithms on average show similar performance at all instants of the sequence, it can be concluded that RF is the most robust and consistent. In particular, the pre-contrast and third post-contrast instants were the most significant for classification. In the first case this can be attributed to the fact that the contrast agent has not altered the pixel values of the ROI and therefore all the original information is retained. On the other hand, in the second case, the contrast medium has been absorbed in both malignant and benign lesions, highlighting the peculiarities that each type of lesion brings with it. Although the ratio of extracted and selected features for Original, LoG, and Wavelet features is similar, the explanation of the results was important to understand that Original and Wavelet features were more discriminating than LoG features. Despite the use of a multi-protocol dataset, which certainly increases the difficulty of classification, the performances obtained are higher or in line with the state of the art. Compared with Parekh [15], in which other images over DCE-MRI were used, a slightly higher specificity and a lower sensitivity was calculated. Compared to the other works the performances in terms of Accuracy and AUC-ROC are significantly higher [3,10,11,18,19]. These results lay a solid foundation for a prospective study validated in real clinical practice.

Acknowledgements. The authors would like to thank Laura Alonzo, Clara Cumbo, Francesca Pandolfo, Lidia Rabiolo and Calogero Zarcaro for their substantial contribution to the dataset preparation phase.

References

1. Fortin, J.P., Cullen, N., Sheline, Y.I., et al.: Harmonization of cortical thickness measurements across scanners and sites. Neuroimage **167**, 104–120 (2018)
2. Ghiasi, M.M., Zendehboudi, S.: Application of decision tree-based ensemble learning in the classification of breast cancer. Comput. Biol. Med. **128**, 104089 (2021). https://doi.org/10.1016/j.compbiomed.2020.104089
3. Gibbs, P., et al.: Characterization of sub-1 cm breast lesions using radiomics analysis. J. Magn. Reson. Imaging **50**(5), 1468–1477 (2019). https://doi.org/10.1002/jmri.26732
4. Gillies, R.J., Kinahan, P.E., Hricak, H.: Radiomics: images are more than pictures, they are data. Radiology **278**(2), 563–577 (2016). https://doi.org/10.1148/radiol.2015151169

5. van Griethuysen, J.J., Fedorov, A., Parmar, C., et al.: Computational radiomics system to decode the radiographic phenotype. Cancer Res. **77**(21), e104–e107 (2017). https://doi.org/10.1158/0008-5472.CAN-17-0339

6. Johnson, W.E., Li, C., Rabinovic, A.: Adjusting batch effects in microarray expression data using empirical Bayes methods. Biostatistics **8**(1), 118–127 (2006)

7. Kabiraj, S., Raihan, M., Alvi, N., et al.: Breast cancer risk prediction using XGBoost and random forest algorithm. In: 2020 11th International Conference on Computing, Communication and Networking Technologies (ICCCNT), pp. 1–4. IEEE (2020)

8. Litjens, G., et al.: A survey on deep learning in medical image analysis. Med. Image Anal. **42**, 60–88 (2017). https://doi.org/10.1016/j.media.2017.07.005

9. Lundberg, S.M., Lee, S.I.: A unified approach to interpreting model predictions. In: Guyon, I., et al. (eds.) Advances in Neural Information Processing Systems, vol. 30, pp. 4765–4774. Curran Associates, Inc. (2017)

10. Militello, C., et al.: 3D DCE-MRI radiomic analysis for malignant lesion prediction in breast cancer patients. Acad. Radiol. **29**(6), 830–840 (2022). https://doi.org/10.1016/j.acra.2021.08.024

11. Nagarajan, M.B., Huber, M.B., Schlossbauer, T., Leinsinger, G., Krol, A., Wismüller, A.: Classification of small lesions in breast MRI: evaluating the role of dynamically extracted texture features through feature selection. J. Med. Biol. Eng. **33**(1) (2013). https://doi.org/10.1002/jmri.27098

12. Orlando, A., Dimarco, M., Cannella, R., Bartolotta, T.V.: Breast dynamic contrast-enhanced-magnetic resonance imaging and radiomics: state of art. Artif. Intell. Med. Imaging **1**, 6–18 (2020)

13. Orlhac, F., et al.: A guide to combat harmonization of imaging biomarkers in multicenter studies. J. Nucl. Med. **63**(2), 172–179 (2022)

14. Papanikolaou, N., Matos, C., Koh, D.M.: How to develop a meaningful radiomic signature for clinical use in oncologic patients. Cancer Imaging **20**(1), 1–10 (2020). https://doi.org/10.1186/s40644-020-00311-4

15. Parekh, V.S., Jacobs, M.A.: Integrated radiomic framework for breast cancer and tumor biology using advanced machine learning and multiparametric mri. NPJ Breast Cancer **3**(1), 1–9 (2017). https://doi.org/10.1038/s41523-017-0045-3

16. Raschka, S.: MLxtend: providing machine learning and data science utilities and extensions to python's scientific computing stack. J. Open Sour. Softw. **3**(24), 638 (2018). https://doi.org/10.21105/joss.00638

17. Sung, H., et al.: Global cancer statistics 2020: GLOBOCAN estimates of incidence and mortality worldwide for 36 cancers in 185 countries. CA Cancer J. Clin. **71**(3), 209–249 (2021)

18. Zhang, Q., et al.: Radiomics based on multimodal MRI for the differential diagnosis of benign and malignant breast lesions. J. Magn. Reson. Imaging **52**(2), 596–607 (2020). https://doi.org/10.1002/jmri.27098

19. Zhou, J., et al.: Diagnosis of benign and malignant breast lesions on DCE-MRI by using radiomics and deep learning with consideration of peritumor tissue. J. Magn. Reson. Imaging **51**(3), 798–809 (2020). https://doi.org/10.1002/jmri.26981

20. Zwanenburg, A., Vallières, M., Abdalah, M.A., Aerts, H.J., et al.: The image biomarker standardization initiative: standardized quantitative radiomics for high-throughput image-based phenotyping. Radiology **295**(2), 328 (2020). https://doi.org/10.1148/radiol.2020191145

Decoding Motor Preparation Through a Deep Learning Approach Based on EEG Time-Frequency Maps

Nadia Mammone[1]([✉]) [iD], Cosimo Ieracitano[1] [iD], Rossella Spataro[2,3] [iD],
Christoph Guger[4] [iD], Woosang Cho[4] [iD], and Francesco C. Morabito[1] [iD]

[1] DICEAM Department, University Mediterranea of Reggio Calabria,
Via Graziella, Feo di Vito, 89122 Reggio Calabria, Italy
nadia.mammone@unirc.it
[2] IRCCS Centro Neurolesi Bonino Pulejo, Palermo, Italy
[3] ALS Clinical Research Center, University of Palermo, Palermo, Italy
[4] g.tec Medical Engineering GmbH, 4521 Schiedlberg, Austria

Abstract. In this paper, a novel Electroepncephalography (EEG)-based
Brain Computer Interface (BCI) approach is proposed to decode motion
intention from EEG signals collected at the scalp of subjects performing
motor execution tasks. The impact of such systems, generally based on
the ability to discriminate between the imagination of right/left hand
movements, would greatly benefit from the ability to decode the intention to perform sub-movements of the same limb like opening or closing
the same hand. In this research, a system meant for decoding the intention to open or close the same hand is proposed. To this end, a dataset
of EEG segments preceding hand open/close movement initiation as well
as segments with no movement preparation (resting) was created from
a public database of EEG signals recorded during upper limb motor
execution experiments. Time-frequency maps were constructed for every
EEG signal and used to build channel × frequency × time volumes. A
system based on a custom deep Convolutional Neural Network (CNN),
named *EEGframeNNET* was designed and developed to discriminate
between pre-hand-opening, pre-hand-closing and resting. The proposed
system outperformed a comparable method in the literature (TTF-NET)
achieving an average accuracy of 86.5% against the 76.3% of TTF-NET.
The proposed system offers a novel perspective on EEG signals evolution by projecting EEGs into a sequence of channel × frequency frames
constructed by means of time-frequency analysis.

Keywords: Deep learning · Brain Computer Interface · Convolutional
Neural Networks · Electroencephalography

1 Introduction

Brain Computer Interface (BCI) systems based on decoding movement imagination from electroencephalographic (EEG) signals have been proven able to

M. Mahmud et al. (Eds.): AII 2022, CCIS 1724, pp. 159–173, 2022.
https://doi.org/10.1007/978-3-031-24801-6_12

solicit neural plasticity and help the brain to recover after inter-neural connection damages caused, for example, by stroke [6]. Such systems consist in recording the EEG signals of the subject during movement imagination and processing them with the aim of decoding what type of movement the subject is imagining. The decoded intention is then translated into a proper command to an external device (a computer, a prosthesis, etc.) in order to produce the desired control and to give a feedback to the user at the same time. When the subject receives a feedback endorsing that the imagined movement has been correctly decoded, the mechanism of neural plasticity is solicited. Systems of this kind have been successfully applied in clinical practice so far [7,8], they are generally based on the ability to discriminate between the imagination of the movement of the right hand, of the left hand, sometimes also of both feet. The same cortical areas in the brain are activated both in case of imagination and of actual execution of the aforementioned movements. The execution/imagination of the movement of right hand, left hand and feet can be discriminated with a fair reliability as the cortical areas activated by such movements are localized and relatively far apart [1]. In particular, the imagination/execution of the right or left hand movement mainly involve the areas of the primary motor cortex in the contralateral hemisphere, whereas the imagination/execution of feet movement mainly involves the central part in the primary motor cortex [20]. By relying on spatial filtering, differences can be emphasized in the EEGs and the imagined/executed movement can be decode with good accuracy [12,13]. In this work, the attention will be focused on executed movements, specifically on their motor preparation phase. In particular, the ability to decode the preparation of sub-movements of the same limb will be explored. Being able to decode different sub-movements of the same limb (like opening/closing the same hand) would indeed significantly extend the potential of motor BCI systems as the subject would be able to issue a wider number of control signals that naturally match with the user intention. Since the same cortical areas are involved, decoding the sub-movements of the same limb is inherently more challenging than decoding the movements of different limbs [15]. Some studies have explored the possibility of discriminating sub-movements of the same limb from EEG signals with encouraging results [18,19]. The goal becomes even more challenging if the aim is to discriminate the preparatory phases of the sub-movements execution, thus to decode the subject's intention from EEG preceding motion onset. Such ability would offer the advantage of being able to detect the intention to perform movements also in those subjects who are not actually able to implement them, allowing for the control of an external device on the basis of the motor preparation phases [14]. Some studies have investigated the possibility of discriminating motor preparation phases of sub-movements of the same limb from EEG signals and achieved promising results [4,5,14]. The present work focuses on decoding of the preparatory phases of sub-movements of the same limb, in particular, the goal is to develop a system that is able to decode the intention to open or close the same hand by discriminating between no movement preparation (resting: RE), preparation of hand opening (HO) and preparation of hand closing (HC). To this end, a public set of data collected from subjects who participated in motor execution experiments, made available in 2017 [18], was employed. EEG data were co-registered with motion data, which allows for the detection of motion onset [18]. Despite being released recently, the aforementioned database has been investigated by many research groups. Cho et al. [2] proposed a method based on common spatial patterns (CSP) and regularized linear discriminant analysis (RLDA) to classify motor execution (ME) EEGs, achieving an average accuracy of 56.83%. Namazi et al. [17] investigated changes in the complexity of EEG signals during the execution or the imagination of different upper limb movements. EEGs exhibited high complexity levels in elbow flexion and hand-close movements in ME and the low complexity levels in hand-open and rest condition in ME. Jeong et al. [9] designed a method to decode Movement-Related Cortical Potentials (MRCP) by introducing a subject-dependent and a section-wise spectral filtering (SSSF) approach. A binary motor execution classification was performed, achieving an average accuracy of 0.72 ± 0.09 in hand closing vs resting and of 0.76 ± 0.06 in hand opening vs resting classification. Jeong et al. [10] proposed a Hierarchical Flow CNN to perform a 3-way classification between right forearm supination vs right forearm pronation vs resting, achieving an average accuracy of 0.52 ± 0.03. Ofner et al. [18] evaluated the performance that their classifier for varying length of the input EEG segments. The maximum accuracy they achieved in sub-movement execution vs resting EEG classification was 80% whereas the largest accuracy in sub-movement execution vs sub-movement execution was 40%. The aim of the aforementioned works was to discriminate which movement was under execution, by taking into account its whole evolution from preparation to initiation. In this paper, a method is proposed to decode motor preparation phases from EEGs and predict whether the subject is planning to open or close his/her hand or planning no movement. The present work is motivated by encouraging results achieved by the authors in the recent years along the direction of motion planning investigation [4,5,14]. In particular, the purpose of the present work is to design and train a deep learning system to learn to discriminate between EEG signals preceding HC/HO/RE. The proposed method aims at performing a 3-way classification (HC vs HO vs RE) so that the presence of motion planning can be detected (by discriminating HC/HO it from RE) and, at the same time, HC vs HO sub-movement planning can be decoded. To this end, a dataset of EEG signals preceding hand open/close movements as well as resting EEG signals was necessary for training and testing. A publicly available collection of EEG signals and motion data was adopted and a dataset of EEG signals preceding the onset of hand opening, hand closing, and preceding no movement, was constructed. In order to provide a comparison with the literature, the performance of the proposed technique was compared to those achieved by methods applied to the same public database, even though most of them were focused on the classification of motor execution (preparation + implementation) rather than motor preparation only. The main novelty of the present research lays in introducing a novel view of EEG behaviour by projecting EEG segments (channels × time maps) into the time-frequency domain and then considering the resulting channel × frequency × time volumes as a sequence of channels × frequency frames. In this way, the temporal evolution of the spatial and spectral characteristics of EEG signals can be analysed globally. The developed system is based on a stage of time frequency analysis to be carried out on EEG segments of 1 s, on a stage of channel × frequency × time volumes construction, and on a custom CNN (named *EEGframeNNET*) meant to process the channels × frequency frames and classify them as HC/HO/RE. The original EEG segment will be classified accordingly. The proposed method achieved an average accuracy of $86.5 \pm 18.2\%$ in the 3-way HO vs HC vs RE discrimination, improving the performance of $76.21 \pm 3.77\%$ achieved by a recent comparable method introduced by the authors in the literature [5]. The paper is organized as follows: Sect. 2.1 will describe the adopted database (Sect. 2.1), how it was processed to construct the dataset of EEG segments necessary to train the proposed system (Sect. 2.1), how the time-frequency analysis was conducted (Sect. 2.1) and how the channel × frequency frames were derived from the time-frequency maps (Sect. 2.1). Section 2.2 will briefly introduce basic concepts about CNN and describe the proposed network, named EEGframeNNET. Section 3 will report the achieved results, Sect. 4 will discuss strengths and limitations of the present work and Sect. 5 will draw some conclusions.

2   Methodology

The framework of the procedure designed to train the proposed system to discriminate EEG segments preceding HC/HO/RE phases is concisely depicted in Fig. 1 and will be illustrated block by block in the subsequent sections. Further information on the proposed method and dataset analysed during the current study are available from the corresponding author (nadia.mammone@unirc.it) upon request.

2.1   Extraction and Preprocessing of Pre-motor EEG Segments

EEG Data Description. In order to train and validate the proposed system, the public collection of EEG and motion data [18] acquired during experiments of motor imagery/execution, available at http://bnci-horizon-2020.eu/database/data-sets (dataset n. 25), was adopted. In the present work, we will focus on the data collected during motor execution experiments. EEG signals were collected by means of 59 active EEG electrodes and four 16-channel amplifiers (g.tec medical engineering GmbH, Austria). Right mastoid channel was set as the reference and the electrode AFz was set as the ground channel. More information about channel montage can be found in [18]. Motion data were collected by means of motion sensors embedded in a glove. EEG signals were band-pass filtered between 0.01 Hz 200 Hz, through a 8-th Chebyshev filter, were notch filtered 50 Hz and sampled 512 Hz. Participants were asked to remain seated on a comfortable chair. The chair was equipped with an anti-gravity exoskeleton (Hocoma, Switzerland) supporting the participant's right arm to prevent fatigue

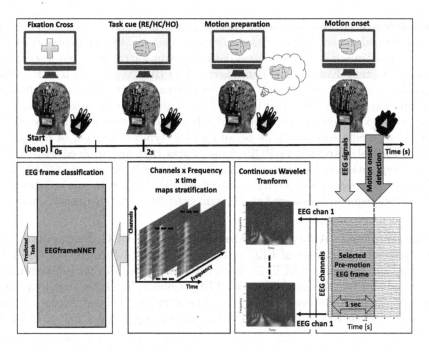

Fig. 1. Framework of the proposed system. The top part of the figure illustrates the paradigm of data acquisition described in detail in Sect. 2.1. The participant sits comfortably in front of a screen in a resting condition with his/her hand in a neutral start position. The trial starts at 0 s, a beep sound is produced and a fixation cross is displayed. After 2 s, the task cue is displayed (i.e., hand open or close). The subject performs the required cued movement and then moves his/her hand back to the starting neutral position. EEGs are co-registered with motion data by means of motion sensors embedded in a glove. The onset of motion is detected and marked by processing motion data. The EEG segments of 1 s preceding the onset of motion (i.e., pre-motion EEG epoch) are selected, labelled (HC/HO/RE) and stored in a dataset as channels × time matrices.

while performing the motor execution experiments. Every participant performed cue-based movements of the right upper limb starting from a neutral position with his/her lower arm in a neutral rotation and extended to 120°C with the hand half open) [18]. Each experiment consisted in the execution of 60 HC, 60 HO and 60 RE trials. The paradigm is structured as follows: at second 0, a fixation cross is displayed on the screen to draw the participant's attention on the upcoming cue. After two seconds, the cue (HC/HO/RE) is displayed so that the participant is instructed about the movement to be performed. At a certain undefined time depending on the subject's responsiveness, the subject starts performing the movement and then brings his/her hand back to the starting neutral position. The data collected by means of the glove motion sensors allows for the detection of the movement onset.

Extraction of EEG Segments Preceding Motion. EEG signals and motion data described in Sect. 2.1 were used to extract a set of EEG segments preceding motion onset in order to construct a dataset meant for training and testing the proposed system. Every participant executed 60 HC, 60 HO and 60 RE motor execution trials. For every trial, the timing of movement onset was estimated from motion data as described in [18]. EEG segments of 1 s preceding motion onset were extracted, properly labelled (HC/HO/RE) and stored. The width of EEG segments was set at 1 s because of the typical duration of movement related cortical potentials (MRCP), brain waves that are involved with movements preparation and initiation [14,22,23]. In this way, a dataset of 2520 (=14 subjects × 3 classes (HC/HO/RE) × 60 trials) EEG segments was constructed. Every EEG segment was stored as a matrix sized 59 × 512 (channels × samples).

Time-Frequency Analysis of Motor Planning EEG Segments. The time-frequency behaviour of EEG signals was analyzed through the Continuous Wavelet Transform (CWT) [3]. Each EEG time series was projected into the 2D time-frequency domain. Given an EEG segment EEG_s, a time-frequency map was extracted for every EEG channel resulting in 59 time-frequency maps. Given the $c - th$ EEG channel and the corresponding signal $EEG_{s,c}$, CWT is defined as:

$$CWT_{s,c}(\sigma,\tau) = \frac{1}{\sqrt{\sigma}} \int EEG_{s,c}(t)\psi^*(\frac{t-\tau}{\sigma})dt \qquad (1)$$

where $CWT_{s,c}(\sigma,\tau)$ is the wavelet coefficient calculated for a scale σ and a shift τ [3]. The complex conjugate operator is denoted by the symbol *, ψ represents the wavelet mother function. The parameters σ and τ control the dilation and shift of the *wavelet mother* [3], respectively. The selected mother wavelet is *db4* [3]. The frequency band of interest was 0.5 Hz and 45 Hz, which allowed to cover the bands typically related to motor planning and initiation, namely: MRCP (<5 Hz) [23], sensory motor rhythms (13–15 Hz) and the beta band (nearly 13–40 Hz). With *db4*, considering the frequency band of interest (0.5–45 Hz), and the sampling rate 512 Hz, a set of scales was determined so that the corresponding pseudo-frequencies (the pseudo-frequency is equal to the central frequency of the mother wavelet divided by the scale) uniformly represent the band of interest. By means of the *Matlab* function *scal2freq* a set of 82 frequencies was produced.

In summary, for every EEG segment s and every EEG channel c, a scalogram $|CWT_{s,c}(\sigma,\tau)|^2$ is determined and herein denoted as "time-frequency map". In the end, for every EEG segment, 59 time-frequency maps are generated (one for each EEG channel).

Construction of the Dataset of Channels × Frequency Frames. Given a subject and an EEG segment, the 59 two-dimensional time-frequency maps are arranged as a channel × frequency × time volume sized 59 × 82 × 512. The volume is then partitioned into 512 two-dimensional channel × frequency maps (each one sized 59 × 82) which represent the temporal evolution of the channel-frequency characteristics of EEG signals. In this way, every EEG segment preceding motion onset is described by 512 channel × frequency maps that represent the frames of a sequence beginning one second before motion onset and ending with the motion onset itself. The sequence represents successive frames of the same motor preparation process. Considering, for example, the frames of a sequence preceding hand opening (HO), every frame will be labelled as "HO" as belonging to the HO motor preparation process. This represents a novel view of the time-frequency behaviour of EEG signals. So far in literature, time-frequency maps of different EEG channels were taken into account independently, although they actually represent the time-frequency behaviour of different spatially filtered versions of the same set of cortical sources [14]. Since every subject carried out 60 trials per class (60 HC, 60 HO, 60 RE), in the end, the final dataset of channel × frequency frames included, for every subject, of 92160 (=3 classes (HC/HO/RE) × 60 trials × 512) frames.

2.2 EEGframeNNET

Section 2.1 described how channel × frequency frames derived from EEG segments preceding hand open/close motion onset were constructed and how a dataset of frames labelled as HC/HO/RE was created. In the present section, *EEGframeNNET*, a CNN developed on purpose to learn how to classify such frames, hence how to decode motor preparation from the original EEG segments, will be described. First of all, some basic concepts about CNN will be summarized.

Brief Introduction to Convolutional Neural Networks. A CNN is a deep learning neural architecture generally based on two main stages: features extraction and classification. The first stage consists in a sequence of convolution (*conv*), activation (*act*) and pooling (*pool*) layers. The convolution layer includes a number N_f of learnable filters (each one sized $b_f \times h_f$) and calculates the dot product between the filter and the input X (sized $b_x \times h_x$). Each filter scans every single part of the input (receptive field) with a stride s_f and produces a number of N_f *features maps* (*FM*, or *activation maps*) with size $b_m \times h_m$, where:

$$b_m = \frac{b_x - b_f + 2p}{s_f} + 1 \tag{2}$$

and

$$h_m = \frac{h_x - h_f + 2p}{s_f} + 1 \tag{3}$$

where p denotes the zero padding parameter. In the present work, p is set at zero and the *Rectified Linear Unit* (ReLU) activation function is adopted [16]. After convolution and activation, a max pooling operation is performed with a pooler of dimension $b_p \times h_p$ and a stride of s_p scanning the feature map FM, resulting in a downsampled map sized $\bar{bm}_1 \times \bar{hm}_2$, with:

$$\bar{b}_{m1} = \frac{b_m - b_p}{s_p} + 1 \tag{4}$$

and

$$\bar{h}_{m1} = \frac{h_m - h_p}{s_p} + 1 \tag{5}$$

The classification stage of the CNN architecture includes a multi layer perceptron neural network with softmax output layer.

The Proposed CNN Architecture. The proposed CNN, named *EEGframeNNET*, was trained and tested over the dataset described in Sect. 2.1, hence the network receives as input the channel × frequency frames, that are matrices sized 59×82. After several trial-and-error test, the architecture was set as follows (as consisely depicted in Fig. 2): a first convolutional layer with $N_{f1} = 4$ filters sized 4×3, stride $s_1 = 1$, padding $p_1 = 0$, ReLU activation function and followed by a max pooling layer with a pooler sized 4×3 and stride $s_p1 = 2$. At the end of the first convolution-activation-pooling block, 4 feature maps sized 28×38 are produced. The size of the feature maps can be derived from Eq. 2–5. A second convolutional layer is introduced with $N_{f2} = 4$ filters sized 3×3, stride $s_2 = 1$, padding $p_2 = 0$, ReLU activation function and followed by a max pooling layer with a pooler sized 4×3 with a stride $s_{p2} = 2$. At the end of the second convolution-activation-pooling block, 4 feature maps sized 13×17 are produced. After the second max pooling stage, a randomized dropout based regularization approach with a dropout rate of 0.5 was applied in order to improve the generalization ability of the network. In the end, the four extracted features maps are flattened in a feature vector sized $1 \times (4 \times 13 \times 17) = 1 \times 884$ and used as input to the multi-layer perceptron made of 2 layers with 150 and 3 neurons, respectively. The last block of the network is a softmax output layer for the final 3-way classification (HC vs HO vs RE). *EEGframeNNET* was designed and implemented in MATLAB R2021b. The CNN was trained by a workstation equipped with a GeForce GTX 660 GPU and 16 GB RAM installed. The network was trained over the dataset described in Sect. 2.1, which included 92160 input samples per subject. The network was trained and tested subject by subject, and a k-fold cross-validation approach was adopted with k = 10. The Adaptive Moment optimization algorithm [11] was used for training with a learning rate $\eta = 0.01$, first and second moment decay parameters set at 0.9 and at 0.999, respectively. The training lasted about 1 h for every fold of every subject.

The performance of *EEGframeNNET* was quantified by computing the accuracy:

$$Accuracy = \frac{TP + TN}{TP + TN + FP + FN} \tag{6}$$

TP and FP account for the number the true positive and false positive, respectively, whereas TN and FN represent the true negative and false negative,

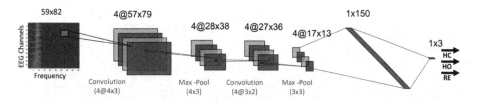

Fig. 2. Architecture of the proposed convolutional neural network (*EEGframeNNET*). It consists in a custom CNN with two convolution + activation layers, two max pooling layers and multi layer perceptron with two layers with 150 and 3 neurons, respectively, and a final softmax layer.

respectively [21]. Since the classification is 3-way (HC vs HO vs RE), a TP, FP, TN and FN set of values must be calculated for every class (HC, HO, RE) where the "positive" class represents a given class under consideration and the "negative" class represent the remaining two classes. For example, considering "HC" as positive class, the negative one will be "not HC" (hence HO or RE). Overall, the accuracy will provide an estimation of the rate of correctly labelled input samples. Since a k-fold cross-validation approach was adopted, therefore, for every subject, the network was trained and tested 10 times, independently, the accuracy is reported in terms of average accuracy ± standard deviation.

3   Results

The results of the application of the proposed method to the dataset discussed in Sect. 2.1 will be reported in the present section and compared to the results achieved by TTF-NET, a comparable method introduced in the literature by the authors [5]. First of all, an example of the EEG signals that belong to the database is shown in Fig. 3. Figure 3 (top) reports an example of EEG signals preceding the onset of hand closing. Signals have been averaged over the 59 channels and are displayed as mean ± std. The profile of the mean EEG is depicted in red. In Fig. 3 (bottom), an example of the channel × frequency maps extracted from the channel × freq × time volume constructed from EEG by means of CWT is displayed. This figure explains, visually, how the 59 EEG signals are represented in the channel × frequency × time domain and how they can be viewed as a temporal sequence of channel × frequency map.

Figure 4 shows the average accuracy achieved over the test set, subject by subject. The average accuracy is represented as vertical bars, the blue bars account for the proposed method whereas the red ones account for TTF-NET.

It is worth to note that the proposed method outperformed TTF-NET in 9 out of 14 subjects and that the mean gap between the two accuracies within this group of 9 subjects was remarkable (+23.95) whereas, in the remaining 5 subjects, the average accuracy was higher with TTF-NET but with a smaller mean gap (+14.71).

In order to provide a further insight into performance comparison, Fig. 5 shows, for every subject, the average accuracy achieved by the two approaches

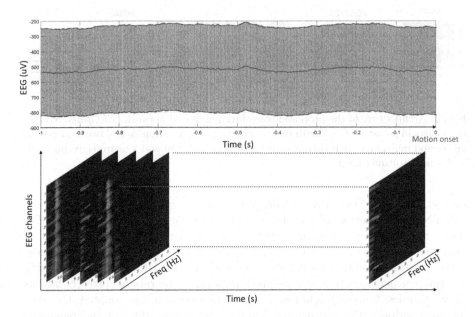

Fig. 3. (Top) An example of EEG signals preceding the onset of hand closing. Signals have been averaged over the 59 channels and are displayed as mean ± std. The profile of the mean EEG is depicted in red. Motion onset occurs at time "t = 0". Every EEG signal undergoes time-frequency analysis (based on CWT) and a time-frequency map is generated. Time-frequency maps are arranged as channel × freq × time volumes. (Bottom), an example of the channel × frequency maps extracted from the channel × freq × time volume. This figure explains, visually, how the 59 EEG signals are represented in the channel × frequency × time domain and how they can be viewed as a temporal sequence of channel × frequency maps. (Color figure online)

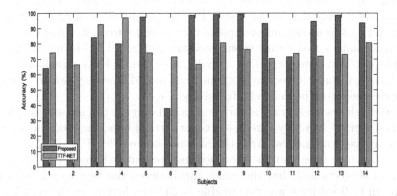

Fig. 4. Average accuracy achieved over the test set, subject by subject. The average accuracy is represented as vertical bars, the blue bars account for the proposed method whereas the red ones account for TTF-NET (Color figure online)

alongside with the error bar of standard deviation. The overall average mean accuracy is displayed as an horizontal dashed line. The proposed method, based on *EEGframeNNET*, provided a higher average accuracy, $86.5 \pm 18\%$, against the $76.3 \pm 8.9\%$ achieved by TTF-NET. The higher standard deviation is due to subject 1, 6 and 11. By inspecting the performance of the single subject, it is worth to note that, except subjects 6 and 11, all the participants exhibited a lower standard deviation with the proposed method rather than with TTF-NET. Another key point is that all the subjects, except 1, 6 and 11, exhibited an accuracy higher than 80%, which is a result of key importance towards the future prospect of practical online applicability. Figure 6 allows to make some considerations about the potential of the proposed method to extend the cohort of subjects that might succeed in controlling a BCI, in this case based on decoding motor planning phases from EEGs, which plays a key role in the possible practical applicability of the method. Figure 6 shows the boxplots of the average accuracies achieved by the proposed method vs TTF-NET. Each single boxplot represents the data distribution according to five parameters: the minimum, the first quartile (Q1, 25th percentile), the median, the third quartile (Q3, the 75th percentile), and the maximum. It is worth noting that, by means of the proposed method, the median increased from 75% to 96%; Q3 increased from 80 to 98, which means that an increased number of subjects achieved a high classification performance; Q1 increased from 73 to 80, which means that an increased number of subjects succeeded in achieving a good performance.

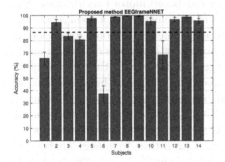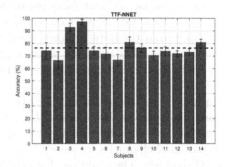

Fig. 5. Average accuracy achieved by the two methods (the proposed one, based on *EEGframe NNET* and TTF-NET) alongside with the error bar of standard deviation. The overall average mean accuracy is displayed as an horizontal dashed line.

4 Discussion

In the present paper, the importance of EEG-based Brain Computer Interfaces has been emphasized, focusing on motor BCI, i.e. systems that aim at decoding the subjects' intention to perform a movement by processing his/her brain waves and then converting it into a command control. Motivated by the interest

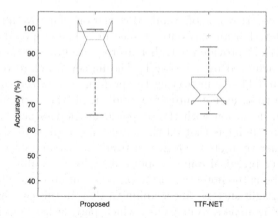

Fig. 6. Boxplot of the average accuracies achieved by the proposed method vs TTF-NET. Data distribution is represented according to five parameters: the minimum, the first quartile (Q1, 25th percentile), the median, the third quartile (Q3, the 75th percentile), and the maximum. Red crosses represent the outliers. (Color figure online)

in motor planning [15], the analyses presented in this work were carried on a public a database made available by the Graz University of Technology [18] that was suitable for the study. The adopted public data collection is made of EEG signals co-registered with motion data during cue-based motor execution experiments. Motion data allows to detect the onset of movement with a good precision. Starting from the data acquired during the experiments of motor execution, a dataset of 1 s EEG segments preceding the movement onset was created in order to study the EEG waves in this specific stage and investigate the possibility to distinguish between resting and motor preparation phases of hand opening or closing. In this paper, a novel EEG signal processing system was introduced, based on a custom CNN named *EEGframeNNET*. From the theoretical point of view, the method offers a novel view of EEG signals' behaviour as the temporal evolution of channel × frequency frames derived from time-frequency analysis of EEG channels. The resulting channel × frequency × time volumes offer an overall view of the evolution over time and over space (i.e. the channels) of EEG characteristics in the frequency domain. All the frames preceding a certain motion onset (hand open or close), can be considered part of the evolution of the same motor planning process. In the present work, EEG channel × frequency frames have been analysed frame by frame. The developed system based on *EEGframeN-NET* outperformed a comparable method proposed in the literature, TTF-NET [5], in 9 out of 14 subjects. *EEGframeNNET*, provided a higher average accuracy, $86.5 \pm 18\%$, against the $76.3 \pm 8.9\%$ achieved by TTF-NET. All the subjects, except 1, 6 and 11, exhibited an accuracy higher than 80%, which offers interesting perspectives about the possible practical application of the proposed approach. However, this study presents some drawbacks and limitations that deserve to be discussed to improve the methodology in the future. First of all, the number of available EEG segments was limited, only 60 input EEG segments were available per class (HC, HO, RE), per subject. Furthermore, the movement onset was detected and marked by processing the motion signals co-registered with the EEGs. Motion signals change smoothly across the initiation of motion thus the onset cannot be determined with a very high temporal precision. As a result, the selected EEG segments may account not only for motor preparation but also for the early part of motor initiation stage, in this way, similar characteristics might emerge in HC and HO EEG segments and undermine the discrimination ability of the system. In the future, the authors aim at recruiting a large cohort of subjects, at carrying out a large number of trials per subject and co-registering EEGs with motion data that can allow for a sharp motion onset detection.

5   Conclusion

In the present work, the importance of EEG-based Brain Computer Interfaces designed to decode the preparation phases of movements was addressed. A public collection of EEG signals co-registered with motion data was analysed to construct a dataset of EEG segments preceding hand open/close movement onset. EEG segments collected during resting (no motion planning) experiments were also included in the database. An EEG signal processing system is introduced, based on the construction of a sequence of channel $\times$ frequency frames derived from the projection of EEG signals into the time-frequency domain. A custom CNN, *EEGframeNNET*, was proposed to process such frames and was trained and tested over the available dataset. The system outperformed a previous and more complex system named TTF-NNET, achieving an average accuracy of $86.5 \pm 18\%$ against the $76.3 \pm 8.9\%$ of TTF-NET. Except 2 subjects out of 14, all the participants exhibited an accuracy with a lower standard deviation when the proposed method rather than with TTF-NET was applied. Furthermore, 11 out 14 subjects exhibited an accuracy higher than 80%, which offers a promising perspective on the future practical application of the approach here presented.

Acknowledgment. This work was supported in part by PON 2014–2020, COGITO project - Grant Ref. ARS01_00836; by "iCARE" project (CUP J39J14001400007) - action 10.5.12 - funded within POR FESR FSE 2014/2020 of Calabria Region with the participation of European Community Resources of FESR and FSE, of Italy and of Calabria and by the Programma Operativo Nazionale (PON) "Ricerca e Innovazione" 2014–2020 CCI2014IT16M2OP005 (CUP C35F21001220009 code: I05).

References

1. Catani, M.: A little man of some importance. Brain **140**(11), 3055–3061 (2017)
2. Cho, J.H., Jeong, J.H., Shim, K.H., Kim, D.J., Lee, S.W.: Classification of hand motions within EEG signals for non-invasive BCI-based robot hand control. In: 2018 IEEE International Conference on Systems, Man, and Cybernetics (SMC), pp. 515–518. IEEE (2018)

3. Daubechies, I.: Ten lectures on wavelets. In: Society for Industrial and Applied Mathematics (1992)
4. Ieracitano, C., Mammone, N., Hussain, A., Morabito, F.C.: A novel explainable machine learning approach for EEG-based brain-computer interface systems. Neural Comput. Appl. **34**(14), 11347–11360 (2021). https://doi.org/10.1007/s00521-020-05624-w
5. Ieracitano, C., Morabito, F.C., Hussain, A., Mammone, N.: A hybrid-domain deep learning-based BCI for discriminating hand motion planning from EEG sources. Int. J. Neural Syst. **31**(09), 2150038 (2021)
6. Irimia, D., et al.: recoveriX: a new BCI-based technology for persons with stroke. In: 2016 38th Annual International Conference of the IEEE Engineering in Medicine and Biology Society (EMBC), pp. 1504–1507. IEEE (2016)
7. Irimia, D.C., et al.: Brain-computer interfaces with multi-sensory feedback for stroke rehabilitation: a case study. Artif. Organs **41**(11), E178–E184 (2017)
8. Irimia, D.C., Ortner, R., Poboroniuc, M.S., Ignat, B.E., Guger, C.: High classification accuracy of a motor imagery based brain-computer interface for stroke rehabilitation training. Front. Robot. AI **5**, 130 (2018)
9. Jeong, J.H., Kwak, N.S., Guan, C., Lee, S.W.: Decoding movement-related cortical potentials based on subject-dependent and section-wise spectral filtering. IEEE Trans. Neural Syst. Rehabil. Eng. **28**(3), 687–698 (2020)
10. Jeong, J.H., Lee, B.H., Lee, D.H., Yun, Y.D., Lee, S.W.: EEG classification of forearm movement imagery using a hierarchical flow convolutional neural network. IEEE Access **8**, 66941–66950 (2020)
11. Kingma, D.P., Ba, J.: Adam: a method for stochastic optimization. arXiv preprint arXiv:1412.6980 (2014)
12. Lotte, F., et al.: A review of classification algorithms for EEG-based brain-computer interfaces: a 10 year update. J. Neural Eng. **15**(3), 031005 (2018)
13. Lotte, F., Jeunet, C.: Online classification accuracy is a poor metric to study mental imagery-based BCI user learning: an experimental demonstration and new metrics. In: 7th International BCI Conference, pp. hal-01519478 (2017)
14. Mammone, N., Ieracitano, C., Morabito, F.C.: A deep CNN approach to decode motor preparation of upper limbs from time-frequency maps of EEG signals at source level. Neural Netw. **124**, 357–372 (2020)
15. Müller-Putz, G.R., Schwarz, A., Pereira, J., Ofner, P.: From classic motor imagery to complex movement intention decoding: the noninvasive Graz-BCI approach. Prog. Brain Res. **228**, 39–70 (2016)
16. Nair, V., Hinton, G.E.: Rectified linear units improve restricted Boltzmann machines. In: Proceedings of the 27th International Conference on Machine Learning (ICML 2010), pp. 807–814 (2010)
17. Namazi, H., Ala, T.S., Kulish, V.: Decoding of upper limb movement by fractal analysis of electroencephalogram (EEG) signal. Fractals **26**(05), 1850081 (2018)
18. Ofner, P., Schwarz, A., Pereira, J., Müller-Putz, G.R.: Upper limb movements can be decoded from the time-domain of low-frequency EEG. PLoS ONE **12**(8), e0182578 (2017)
19. Ofner, P., Schwarz, A., Pereira, J., Wyss, D., Wildburger, R., Müller-Putz, G.R.: Attempted arm and hand movements can be decoded from low-frequency EEG from persons with spinal cord injury. Sci. Rep. **9**(1), 7134 (2019)
20. Pereira, J., Ofner, P., Schwarz, A., Sburlea, A.I., Müller-Putz, G.R.: EEG neural correlates of goal-directed movement intention. Neuroimage **149**, 129–140 (2017)

21. Powers, D.M.W.: Evaluation: from precision, recall and F-measure to ROC, informedness, markedness and correlation. J. Mach. Learn. Technol. **2**(1), 37–63 (2011)
22. Shakeel, A., Navid, M.S., Anwar, M.N., Mazhar, S., Jochumsen, M., Niazi, I.K.: A review of techniques for detection of movement intention using movement-related cortical potentials. Comput. Math. Methods Med. **2015**, 346217 (2015)
23. Spring, J.N., Place, N., Borrani, F., Kayser, B., Barral, J.: Movement-related cortical potential amplitude reduction after cycling exercise relates to the extent of neuromuscular fatigue. Front. Hum. Neurosci. **10**, 257 (2016)

A Novel Fuzzy Semi-supervised Learning Approach for the Classification of Colorectal Cancer (FSSL-CRCC)

Sara Karim[1], Muhammed J. A. Patwary[1(✉)],
Mohammad Shahadat Hossain[2(✉)], and Karl Andersson[3(✉)]

[1] Department of Computer Science and Engineering,
International Islamic University Chittagong, Chittagong, Bangladesh
mjap@iiuc.ac.bd
[2] Department of Computer Science and Engineering,
University of Chittagong, Chittagong, Bangladesh
hossain_ms@cu.ac.bd
[3] Department of Computer Science, Electrical and Space Engineering,
Lulea University of Technology, Skelleftea, Sweden
karl.andersson@ltu.se

Abstract. Colorectal Cancer (CRC) is a form of cancer that develops in the colon or rectum. It is also referred as bowel cancer, colon cancer, or rectal cancer. CRC has become the second most prevailing sort of cancer in the human race. But CRC until now remains linked to a poor diagnosis in patients with severe illness. The concern for early detection drew researchers' consciousness to a variety of machine learning-based methods. Semi-Supervised Learning (SSL) clear up this challenge in an enhanced way than every alternative Machine learning approaches through incorporating vast quantities of labeled and unlabeled data to generate superior analysis method. The paper presents a novice fuzziness-based semi-supervised learning technique within colorectal cancer diagnosis in which it uses mislabeled data alongside training classified data to improve the model's dependability. In accustomed to other classification models such as Support Vector Machine, Random tree, Linear Regression and others, the prediction performance using this strategy on the dataset exhibited remarkable breakthroughs in enhancing the classifier's results.

Keywords: Fuzziness · Semi-supervised learning · Colorectal cancer (CRC) · Neural Network with Random Weight (NNRW)

1 Introduction

In modern populations, colorectal cancer is a serious area of concern. According to current statistics, the average life expectancy odds ratio of colorectal cancer for male population is 46.5 per 100,000 community annually, while for females it is 33.2 per 100,000 inhabitants per year [1]. In medical science, this topic is a

M. Mahmud et al. (Eds.): AII 2022, CCIS 1724, pp. 174–185, 2022.
https://doi.org/10.1007/978-3-031-24801-6_13

now a frequent hot issue including a lofty rates of death and depression. Between all kinds of tumors, it has the third highest fatality rate [2]. The necessity for early identification of diverse diseases motivated researchers to look into different machine learning-based concepts [3]. Analyzing breakdowns of every challenges in the field of medical healthcare [4,5] at an early stage remains a challenging task; however, it has a positive impact since it encourages the public to recognize and not be scared of the impairment. Our research will examine the approach of SSL, conveying researchers to figure out and clarifying the subsequent investigation prevailing the subject of Colorectal cancer detection, in order to bring greater attention to these serious and dangerous concerns.

Although semi-supervised learning strategies have performed admirably in machine learning tasks, the challenge into how to appropriately utilize the process in both labelled and unlabeled data stay behind unsolved. Meanwhile, no semi-supervised learning methods for detecting Colorectal cancer has been demonstrated in details. In this paper, we will provide a novice approach of a of SSL derived dependent on fuzzy logic (FSSL), to solve the issue of Colorectal cancer breakdown. Collecting labelled data for figuring Colorectal cancer is somehow pricey and difficult because to a lack of medical and professional resources. On the other hand, public picture repositories have a variety of unlabeled images and videos available and accessible. In small sample size situations, supervised learning loses its effectiveness since there is limited unlabeled data and cannot be used efficiently. In order to properly exploit unlabeled samples, semi-supervised learning can been widely explored in this field.

The principal intention of this research study is to find novel approaches to:

– Propose a competent SSL algorithm that can be used to forecast Colorectal cancer and work as a link between supervised and unsupervised learning.

Moreover, we anticipate that by emphasizing the novel techniques in this study far more than possible, researchers in the future will be capable to reveal different territory for treating diseases utilizing assorted machine learning [6,7] and data mining [8–12] methodologies.

The remaining subsections are as follows:

We covered relevant studies in Sect. 2. Section 3 illustrates the methodology of our experiment, and Sect. 4 presents the findings and a discussion. Section 5 summarizes and concludes the study and offers suggestions for future exploration.

2   Literature Review

Although great progress has been made in the sphere of machine learning and data mining as a result of this alarming situation, several challenges remain, notably in SSL, fuzzy logic, and diverse learning objectives.

In relation to the research objectives, Patwary et al. [13] investigated a divide-and-conquer scheme, a novel outlook of SSL approach, to upgrade model efficiency. It has also been noticed that the change was highly relying on the efficiency of the basic classifier, with the best results obtained when the accuracy was within 70% and 80%.

Patwary et al. [14] outlined a advanced way through integrating low-fuzziness sequences. As per the outcomes of the entire study's trials, the fuzziness processes of the pattern employed to figure out the fuzziness of particular model maintained a notable mark on the enhancement of SSL efficiency.

Ending with shaping up the efficiency of the classifier for IDSs, Ashfaq et al. [15] proposed a SSL technique that combines data amidst a supervised learning algorithm. The experimental results obtained after employing this strategy greatly improve the performance of the classifier.

For physically incapacitated patient detection and tracking, a novel FSS multimodal learning technique termed FSSL-PAR was introduced by Patwary MJ. et al. [16]. For the first period in SSL environment, they applied a synergic effect to test the influence of optical multimodality. Analysis were carried out on a dataset created by simulating Acute Brain Injury (ABI) patients from a specialized care center. The outcomes demonstrated the projected algorithm's supremacy above established supervised learning methods.

Yucan et al. [17] explored the workability of adopting machine learning technology to forecast physical recurrence hazard surrounded by phase-IV colorectal cancer patients. Furthermore, the study also indicated that input-specialized algorithms are moreover effective than fundamental algorithms.

Dmitrii et al. [18] combined convolutional and recurrent architectures to train a deep network to predict colorectal cancer outcome based on images of tumour tissue samples. The study's result suggested that state-of-the-art deep learning techniques can extract more prognostic information from the tissue morphology of colorectal cancer than an experienced human observer.

Athanasia et al. [19] explored the aspect of current progress in Artificial intelligence scheme regarding medicinal analysis and remedy, accompanying a lot of hopeful outcome. The findings highlight the need of fully grasping the problems and opportunities displayed through AI-based modeling techniques inside the areas of CRC diagnosis, treatment, and healthcare.

3   Methodology

The proposed scheme in our paper is the fundamental SSL method designed with colorectal cancer diagnosis, and it significantly achieves aspiring outcomes, resulting in a significant feedback loop between labeled sample discrimination and assuming defined samples in distinction to undefined samples.

3.1   Semi-supervised Learning

Semi-Supervised Learning combines supervised and unsupervised learning techniques. Collecting information that has been classified in label data is both costly and tedious, and it necessitates the assistance of experts in the field. Aside from this difficulty, unlabeled data is widely available for a variety of useful applications. And this is the reason, SSL method [20] probability learns to cope with related tactics using both labeled and unlabeled data. SSL bears upon classifications by changing both unlabeled and labeled cases before developing an improved classification prototype. Researchers have been quite interested in various semi-supervised learning systems.

Since its initial conception, SSL has been successfully employed to cover a ample category of real-world issues. Various SSL strategies have been proposed by many scholars during the previous few decades.

3.2 Fuzziness

The membership function of fuzzy sets underpins the phrase "fuzziness," which points out to the ambiguous intersection of double grammatical meanings. Zadeh [21] was the arch to illustrate it in 1965. The study of [22] identified fuzziness as a stereotype of ambiguity and provided a quantitative fuzziness statistic placed on non-feasible decay, which came out to be similar to Shannon's propaganda disorder. They also proposed three characteristics for fuzziness:

Theorem 1. *The scope of fuzziness is greatest during all elements of a fuzzy set have the equal value.*

Theorem 2. *The scope of fuzziness is at its lowest during all elements of a fuzzy set are equal to 0 or 1.*

Theorem 3. *The scope of fuzziness exist between maximum and lowest values during the elements of a fuzzy set have values that are neither 0 nor 1 and even do not have equal values.*

The following characteristics show that the degree of fuzziness should be largest when the degree of membership of all elements is similar, and least when practically all elements seemingly link to or is not equated to the fuzzy property.

Y's fuzziness can be expressed as:

$$F(Y) = -\tfrac{1}{n} \sum_{i=1}^{n} (\mu_i \log \mu_i + (1 - \mu_i) \log(1 - \mu_i)) \qquad (1)$$

3.3 Neural Network with Random Weight (NNRW)

Schmidt et al. [23] did not really gave an identity about it's proposed method, therefore we experimented with NNRW to recognize their accomplishments. Because there is no substantial association in the midst of the nodes layers, this paper focused on evaluating the biases in the NNRW given in our research.

The combined result of hidden layer nodes looks like this:

$$f(\mathbf{s}) = \sum_{i=1}^{N} \tilde{\alpha}_i f(\mathbf{w}_i, b_i, \mathbf{s}), \mathbf{s} \epsilon \mathbb{R}^n \qquad (2)$$

Here, w_i and b_i represent input values as well as distortions in Eq. (2). In accordance with this, $\alpha\,\tilde{}_i \in \mathbb{R}^m$ represents the value products and services. The potency of the hidden factor(i) accompanying s is given by $\alpha\tilde{}_i\, f(w_i, b_i, s)$.

In context of this, using a specific dataset,

$$\sum_{i=1} \alpha\tilde{}_i f(w_i, b_i, \boldsymbol{x}) = \mathbf{t}_j \qquad (3)$$

As a logical consequence, the Eq. (3) is frequently written as:

$$\mathbf{F}\alpha\tilde{} = \mathbf{S} \qquad (4)$$

As a conclusion, Eq. (4), which consists of a series of algebraic model, may almost always be transformed into a standard system of algebraic statements.

$$\mathbf{F}^S\mathbf{F}\alpha\tilde{} = \mathbf{F}^S S \qquad (5)$$

Eq. (5)'s overall hypothesis is therefore expressed as follows:

$$\alpha\tilde{} = (\mathbf{F}^S\mathbf{F})^{-1}F^S S \qquad (6)$$

3.4   Fuzziness Based Divide-and-Conquer Strategy

Wang et al. [24] has designed a revolutionary method established on a divide-and-conquer strategy. Their approach is described as one in which the training phase includes certain samples with ambiguous class and low fuzziness. The essential phases of Wang et al's [24] suggested technique are discussed below.

Algorithm 1 : Divide-and-conquer strategy with fuzziness.

---

1. Figure out the fuzzy unit vector of every classifier C.
2. Determine the training accuracy (T_r), and testing accuracy (T_s) of each output vector.
3. The fuzziness of T_s output samples should be separated into two categories: medium fuzziness and low fuzziness. G_low, G_mid, and G_high are the three levels of fuzziness.
4. Acquire $T_{r'}$ by associating the highest level of accuracy with groupings (a new training set)
5. Retrieve $T_{r'}$ and Ts by retraining the classifier C on the training set (the testing accuracy).
6. Compare the results of steps 3 and 5 to evaluate how precise they were.

3.5 Proposed Algorithm:

We incorporated the algorithm and predicted a unique way in support of screening colorectal cancer named Fuzzy Semi-supervised Learning for Colorectal Cancer Classification (FSSL-CRCC) based on early studies of [24].

First of all we pre-processed our training and testing data. At the next step, different classifiers were used and then the fuzziness was calculated with the help of Eq. 1. Later the samples were added with fuzziness to the Tr. Furthermore the classifiers were retrained along with new $T_{r'}$. Finally we evaluated our results. Within the specified dataset, our approach collaborates with T_r to train hidden layers. The unit vector of each unique data collected using above mentioned procedure is further used ending with obtaining the fuzziness F(Y) by applying Eq. (1).

Algorithm 2. Proposed Algorithm : (FSSL-CRCC)

Require: T_s Accuracy: Testing accuracy
Ensure: Compute fuzziness F(Y)

Input:
- Tr : Labeled dataset $(xi, yi \mid 1 \leq i \leq N)x$
- U : Unlabeled dataset $(ui, \mid 1 \leq i \leq U)$
- Ts : Test dataset $(ti, yi \mid 1 \leq i \leq K)$
- Classifier: CNNRw
- L : Number of hidden nodes

Output:
- T_sAccuracy: Testing accuracy

Process:
- F' = NNRw (T_r).
- Generate F' (Y)
- Obtain membership vector V of every unlabeled example from F' (Y)
- Compute fuzziness F(Y) of every sample in U
- Sample categorization F_Glow, F_Gmid, and F_Ghigh
- $T_{r'}$new = T_r + (F_Glow + F_Ghigh)
- F' = NNRW $(T_{r'}$)
- Generate F'(T_S)

---

4 Result and Discussion

4.1 Dataset

The dataset "Real Colorectal Cancer Datasets" was obtained from the kaggle and used in this study. This dataset (Colorectal Cancer Patient Data.csv) consists of the group of colorectal cancer patient information.

The patient dataset consists of the following variables:

- Age: at Diagnosis (in Years)
- Dukes Stage: A to D (development/progression of disease)
- Sex: Male or Female
- Position: Left, Right, Colon or Rectum
- DFS: Disease-free survival, months (survival without the disease returning)
- DFS event: 0 or 1 (with 1 = event)
- AdjRadio: Whether the participant was additionally treated with radiotherapy
- AdjChem: Whether the participant was additionally treated with chemotherapy

4.2 Data Pre-processing

The data was separated in a way that all samples from the same variables would be in either the train or the test, but never both. This allows for more precise training and testing of the model's performance while also preventing data leaks. To establish a training and testing set, we employed a 8:2 ratio with 80% T_r and the leftover 20% with T_s.

Features with the same frequency for over 99 % of the participants are deleted. The survival criteria are chosen so that roughly half of the labeled data are in the positive category and the remaining are in the negative category.

4.3 Experimental Results

After executing the essential steps, we carried out the experiment to see if the provided methodology was enough and checked the Correlations with the features (Fig. 1a), Distributions between DFS and Age (Fig. 1b), Dukes Stage (Fig. 1c), Histogram of DFS event (Fig. 1d), Locations of cancer (Fig. 1e), Distributions of Sex (Fig. 1f), Adj Radio (Fig. 1g), Adj Chem (Fig. 1h). As shown in Tables 1 and 2, we examined how different initialization time frames impacted NNRW's efficiency level during the simulation.

According to the data in Table 3, the total accuracy acquired by our suggested approach is convenient, with an accuracy of 93.47% when compared to other classifiers, which used different classification strategies to obtain the results on the same dataset. Table 3 compares the accuracy of previous algorithms to our proposed method. The leading contribution of this exploration is to straighten out evaluation's efficiency by verifying entire types of fuzzily bound relationships. Because of its ability to successfully extract and test data, machine learning within Semi-supervised learning can be a hope that can be used to identify colorectal cancer (CRC).

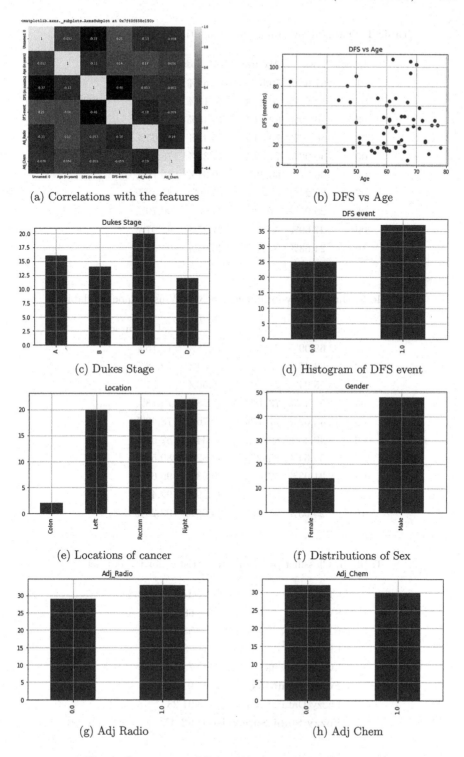

(a) Correlations with the features

(b) DFS vs Age

(c) Dukes Stage

(d) Histogram of DFS event

(e) Locations of cancer

(f) Distributions of Sex

(g) Adj Radio

(h) Adj Chem

Fig. 1. Statistics on different features in CRC prediction

Table 1. Outlining by formulating a multi layer perceptron Model

Epoch	Loss	Accuracy	val_loss	val_accuracy
01	61.68%	70.57%	53.67%	70.45%
02	53.89%	70.41%	48.15%	70.39%
03	46.59%	69.54%	45.43%	69.34%
04	46.06%	70.54%	40.43%	70.65%
05	40.92%	74.33%	36.32%	75.54%
06	36.71%	80.43%	30.91%	80.76%
07	33.24%	83.37%	25.89%	85.68%
08	29.95%	87.94%	24.04%	90.79%
09	27.69%	90.32%	21.25%	92.07%
10	24.63%	90.86%	20.97%	94.37%

Table 2. Outlining by formulating a NNRW using labelled data

Epoch	Loss	Accuracy	val_loss	val_accuracy
01	65.09%	70.36%	64.38%	72.15%
02	63.47%	70.64%	60.64%	72.58%
03	55.94%	71.78%	56.50%	73.81%
04	51.45%	73.43%	45.26%	75.78%
05	45.62%	77.67%	40.76%	78.49%
06	40.45%	80.81%	37.34%	82.58%
07	35.54%	85.69%	33.82%	89.56%
08	31.03%	87.71%	30.53%	90.67%
09	28.65%	89.67%	27.29%	92.45%
10	25.63%	91.34%	24.65%	93.29%

Table 3. Classifier performance statistics for the dataset

Classifier	Test_acc(%)
SVM	68.698
RF	53.38
LR	73.42
LGBMClassifier	72.16
Fuzzy MinMax	**91.57**
Fuzzy Data Mining	91.28
Fuzzy Semi-Supervised	**93.47**

4.4 Discussion

The break rate among patients with CRC was as acute as 93.47% in our research. In modern decades, colorectal cancer is now on the expansion all across the globe. Several people have serious phases of disease by the time they are admitted to the hospital because to the ignoring of initial symptoms. This greatly raises the probability of death. CRC is found to be the third highest prevalent cancer in males and the second much popular in women. Throughout this research, sex was reported to be a factor in the recurrence of colorectal cancer patient.

To summarize, this study has a superior influence on the classification of experimental data when compared to study results from other researchers, minimizing diverse experiment contexts.

5 Conclusion and Future Work

Our study suggested the new Fuzzy SSL mechanism in consideration of improving efficiency in colorectal cancer (CRC) prediction and discovered that the FSSL outperforms in terminology of authentic colorectal cancer (CRC) diagnosis. The goal of this research is to boost adaptability through working out with interaction in the middle of fuzziness. We intend to enlarge and build up the dataset and extend unique DL-supported procedure to tumble into anomalies in colorectal cancer (CRC) in the future. We also plan to create a DL system adequate of efficiently analyzing and segregating data related to colorectal cancer (CRC). Machine learning's capacity to dispatch with SSL offers a myriad of opportunities: it might be acclimated to bounce off potential colorectal cancer categorization(CRC).

In the case of colorectal cancer (CRC) predictions, we are optimistic that the FSSL method described in our study will assist scholars in the future in building creative and advantageous schema, and that additional work in the area of finding colorectal cancer (CRC) breakdowns will be welcomed.

References

1. Sprangers, M., Taal, B., Aaronson, N., Te Velde, A.: Quality of life in colorectal cancer. Dis. Colon Rectum **38**(4), 361–369 (1995)
2. Toft, N.J., Arends, M.J.: DNA mismatch repair and colorectal cancer. J. Pathol. J. Pathol. Soc. Great Br. Irel. **185**(2), 123–129 (1998)
3. Karim, S., Akter, N., Patwary, M.J., Islam, M.R.: A review on predicting autism spectrum disorder (asd) meltdown using machine learning algorithms. In: 2021 5th International Conference on Electrical Engineering and Information & Communication Technology, pp. 1–6 (ICEEICT). IEEE (2021)
4. Alam, M.S.B., Patwary, M.J., Hassan, M.: Birth mode prediction using bagging ensemble classifier: a case study of bangladesh. In: 2021 International Conference on Information and Communication Technology for Sustainable Development (ICICT4SD), pp. 95–99 IEEE (2021)

5. Hossain, S., Zahid Hasan, M., Patwary, M.J.A., Uddin, M.S.: An expert system to determine systemic lupus erythematosus under uncertainty. In: Uddin, M.S., Bansal, J.C. (eds.) Proceedings of International Joint Conference on Advances in Computational Intelligence. AIS, pp. 117–130. Springer, Singapore (2021). https://doi.org/10.1007/978-981-16-0586-4_10

6. Osman, A.B., et al.: Examining mental disorder/psychological chaos through various ML and DL techniques: a critical review. Ann. Emerg. Technol. Comput. (AETiC) **6**, 61–71 (2022)

7. Neloy, M.A.I., Nahar, N., Hossain, M.S., Andersson, K.: A weighted average ensemble technique to predict heart disease. In: Kaiser, M.S., Ray, K., Bandyopadhyay, A., Jacob, K., Long, K.S. (eds.) Proceedings of the Third International Conference on Trends in Computational and Cognitive Engineering. LNNS, vol. 348, pp. 17–29. Springer, Singapore (2022). https://doi.org/10.1007/978-981-16-7597-3_2

8. Cao, W., Patwary, M.J., Yang, P., Wang, X., Ming, Z.: An initial study on the relationship between meta features of dataset and the initialization of NNRW. In: 2019 International Joint Conference on Neural Networks (IJCNN), pp. 1–8. IEEE (2019)

9. Ahmed, T.U., Jamil, M.N., Hossain, M.S., Islam, R.U., Andersson, K.: An integrated deep learning and belief rule base intelligent system to predict survival of COVID-19 patient under uncertainty. Cogn. Comput. **14**(2), 660–676 (2022)

10. Sumi, T.A., Hossain, M.S., Andersson, K.: Automated acute lymphocytic leukemia (ALL) detection using microscopic images: an efficient CAD approach. In: Kaiser, M.S., Bandyopadhyay, A., Ray, K., Singh, R., Nagar, V. (eds.) Proceedings of Trends in Electronics and Health Informatics. LNNS, vol. 376, pp. 363–376. Springer, Singapore (2022). https://doi.org/10.1007/978-981-16-8826-3_31

11. Rezoana, N., Hossain, M.S., Andersson, K.: Face mask detection in the era of COVID-19: a CNN-based approach. In: Kaiser, M.S., Ray, K., Bandyopadhyay, A., Jacob, K., Long, K.S. (eds.) Proceedings of the Third International Conference on Trends in Computational and Cognitive Engineering. LNNS, vol. 348, pp. 3–15. Springer, Singapore (2022). https://doi.org/10.1007/978-981-16-7597-3_1

12. Basnin, N., Sumi, T.A., Hossain, M.S., Andersson, K.: Early detection of Parkinson's disease from micrographic static hand drawings. In: Mahmud, M., Kaiser, M.S., Vassanelli, S., Dai, Q., Zhong, N. (eds.) BI 2021. LNCS (LNAI), vol. 12960, pp. 433–447. Springer, Cham (2021). https://doi.org/10.1007/978-3-030-86993-9_39

13. Patwary, M.J., Wang, X.-Z.: Sensitivity analysis on initial classifier accuracy in fuzziness based semi-supervised learning. Inf. Sci. **490**, 93–112 (2019)

14. Patwary, M.J., Wang, X.-Z., Yan, D.: Impact of fuzziness measures on the performance of semi-supervised learning. Int. J. Fuzzy Syst. **21**(5), 1430–1442 (2019)

15. Ashfaq, R.A.R., Wang, X.-Z., Huang, J.Z., Abbas, H., He, Y.-L.: Fuzziness based semi-supervised learning approach for intrusion detection system. Inf. Sci. **378**, 484–497 (2017)

16. Patwary, M.J., Cao, W., Wang, X.-Z., Haque, M.A.: Fuzziness based semi-supervised multimodal learning for patient's activity recognition using RGBDT videos. Appl. Soft Comput. **120**, 108655 (2022)

17. Xu, Y., Ju, L., Tong, J., Zhou, C.-M., Yang, J.-J.: Machine learning algorithms for predicting the recurrence of stage IV colorectal cancer after tumor resection. Sci. Rep. **10**(1), 1–9 (2020)

18. Bychkov, D., et al.: Deep learning based tissue analysis predicts outcome in colorectal cancer. Sci. Rep. **8**(1), 1–11 (2018)

19. Mitsala, A., Tsalikidis, C., Pitiakoudis, M., Simopoulos, C., Tsaroucha, A.K.: Artificial intelligence in colorectal cancer screening, diagnosis and treatment. a new era. Curr. Oncol. **28**(3), 1581–1607 (2021)
20. Scudder, H.: Probability of error of some adaptive pattern-recognition machines. IEEE Trans. Inf. Theory **11**(3), 363–371 (1965)
21. Zadeh, L.A.: Probability measures of fuzzy events. J. Math. Anal. Appl. **23**(2), 421–427 (1968)
22. De Luca, A., Termini, S.: A definition of a nonprobabilistic entropy in the setting of fuzzy sets theory. Inf. Control **20**(4), 301–312 (1972)
23. Schmidt, W.F., Kraaijveld, M.A., Duin, R.P.: Feed forward neural networks with random weights. In: International Conference on Pattern Recognition. IEEE Computer Society Press, pp. 1–1 (1992)
24. Wang, X.-Z., Ashfaq, R.A.R., Fu, A.-M.: Fuzziness based sample categorization for classifier performance improvement. J. Intell. Fuzzy Syst. **29**(3), 1185–1196 (2015)

Machine Learning Models to Analyze the Effect of Drugs on Neonatal-ICU Length of Stay

Farzana Islam Adiba$^{(\boxtimes)}$ (iD) and Mohammad Zahidur Rahman

Department of Computer Science and Engineering, Jahangirnagar University,
Dhaka, Bangladesh
fadiba@ufl.edu, rmzahid@juniv.edu

Abstract. The Neonatal intensive care unit (NICU) is a specialized
section for newborn babies. The neonates are in vulnerable conditions in
the ICU, so the predictive models will help to indicate the seriousness
of the patients and assist the doctors in taking immediate actions. The
Medical Information Mart for Intensive Care III (MIMIC-III) dataset
is used in this research. The medicines medicated in critical newborn
children were detected, and how the drugs and the doses of drugs can
affect the Length of Stay (LOS) in NICU is analyzed. The predictive
result of ICU Length of Stay (LOS) for the patients admitted to NICU
for seven days is analyzed. Different Machine Learning algorithms were
implemented for developing the classification model, and Logistic Regression Algorithm performed well and showed an F1 score of about 85%,
which was better than the F1 score of the deep learning model long Short-
Term Memory (LSTM). The automated Machine Learning (AutoML)
tool, AutoNLP was also implemented for classifying LOS. But traditional
methods demonstrated better performance in comparison to AutoML.

Keywords: Machine Learning · Deep learning · AutoML · NICU ·
LOS · Classification

1 Introduction

A neonate can be defined as a child aged less than 28 days. The babies who
are suffering from any critical conditions after birth like premature baby, lack
of oxygen, heart problem, etc. are admitted into NICU [26]. The death rate of
newborns is very alarming all over the world. According to World Health Organization (WHO), in 2019 about 2.4 million children had breathed their last within
their first month after being born all over the world. And the egregious matter
is that about 700 newborns lose their lives each day. From the statistics from
WHO, among the top ten countries with high newborn death rates, Bangladesh
is placed in 8th position [58]. Particularly during the Covid-19, The government
of Bangladesh was struggling to cope with the pandemic. Especially the scarcity
of ICUs impacted directly, as a result, many newborn children lost their lives

© The Author(s), under exclusive license to Springer Nature Switzerland AG 2022
M. Mahmud et al. (Eds.): AII 2022, CCIS 1724, pp. 186–204, 2022.
https://doi.org/10.1007/978-3-031-24801-6_14

in this situation [46]. Neonatal patients are mostly affected with low weights, sepsis, etc. If it is possible to arrange their admission to the NICU at the right time many death of newborns could be prevented [55]. The classification analysis of the patient's ICU length of stay can show a study for predicting when the beds can be available. It can help many healthcare providers to understand when they can arrange new beds in the incentive cares.

There are some drugs are used for vital patients in the NICU, for example, Gentamicin, Heparin, Sodium Acetate, Beractant, Ampicillin Sodium, D10W, etc. Here Gentamicin is used as antibacterial medicine, D10W is a Dextrose injection used to keep blood glucose levels in normal condition, and Heparin is used for preventing blood clotting [20]. So various medicines can influence the health of the babies, thus it will have an impact on the total length of the ICU stays. In this work how LOS can be predicted from the different drugs is discussed. It might be helpful for the doctors' to analyze the effects of drugs used in very serious conditions and also assist them in taking decisions on the Length of Stay (LOS) of the neonates.

In recent years artificial intelligence (AI), in particular machine learning (ML), has attracted many researchers to contribute in diverse fields and challenging research assignments such as: anomaly detection [33,59,60], neurodevelopmental disorder assessment and classification focusing on autism [3,5,6,14,25,39,53,56,57], neurological disorder detection and management [4, 7,15,28,52], supporting the detection and management of the COVID-19 pandemic [11,27,32,37,47,48,51], elderly monitoring and care [45], various disease diagnosis [17,19,31,40,43,44,61], smart healthcare service delivery [16,22,30], etc. Machine Learning (ML) is a part of Artificial Intelligence (AI). It implies a combination of various disciplines such as Mathematics, Statistics, Bioinformatics, etc. There are some popular ML methods such as Linear Regression(LR), Naive Bayes classifier(NB), Decision tree(DT), Support Vector Machines (SVM), Random Forests(RF), K Nearest Neighbors (KNN), etc. But sufficient knowledge and time are required for developing models to predict or classify data. So an automation technique for generating Machine Learning Models is developed known as Automated Machine Learning or AutoML [38].

AutoML is a very newly invented tool. It has a set of important packages that can generate Machine Learning models automatically. It can employ various libraries like Auto-sklearn, AutoNLP, H2OAutoML [10,36]. Using these tools data can be processed for classification, prediction, etc. Data preprocessing, model selection, etc. are the important steps to predicting datasets. AutoML can implement all the techniques automatically. As handling categorical features, text features are very complex tasks in traditional Machine Learning methods, this automated method prepares features and selects appropriate methods also. So we want to explore whether the AutoML method outperforms the traditional methods or not. For analyzing how drugs can affect the LOS of the NICU traditional ML methods, the Deep learning method Long Short-Term Memory (LSTM), and AutoNLP will be implemented. Then a comparative analysis will be shown which performs better for this work.

In this research, we extracted the NICU data from the famous MIMIC III dataset. We especially focus on the relationship between ICU LOS and the parameters related to the medication of the neonates such as drugs, drug type, and their dosages. The main objective of this work is to show classification studies for NICU LOS for 7 days applying traditional and automated machine learning methods.

This paper is organized as follows. Section 2 covers the related works, Sect. 3 introduces the methodology which was followed in this work. In Sect. 4 the analysis of the results is described and in the last portion, the conclusion is drawn in Sect. 5.

2   Related Works

Some significant research has been conducted for analyzing the Length of Stay in the ICU and other factors which have an important impact on LOS. Mansouri et al. proposed data mining techniques for predicting NICU LOS with the MIMIC III dataset. They implemented 24 h data for evaluating the results with machine learning algorithms. For LOS prediction, two variables, Ethnicity and Insurance Type were considered. Ensemble methods with some machine learning methods were used. Among them, the Random forests classifier showed better results in this research [41].

Toptas et al. analyzed some factors statistically which affect the LOS of the patients in the ICU. They used Haseki ICU data containing information about 3925 ICU patients. The statistical correlation with the LOS and other features age, sex, alive or not, urea, creatinine, sodium rate, etc. were measured using SPSS software. The statistical significance value or p-value was measured and a p-value less than .005 was accepted. Patients with cardiovascular diseases showed a long stay in the ICU according to this paper [54].

Alsinglawi et al. proposed methods for predicting LOS for long-term Heart Failure (HF) patients [9]. The prediction was performance based on the data of patients admitted to the coronary care unit (CCU). For univariate analysis LOS < 7 and LOS > 7 in CCU patients were selected from the MIMIC III dataset. Ensemble regressors and Deep Learning Regressors were implemented. In this analysis, 10 features were considered, for example, temperature, age, weight, gender, etc. Among them, Deep Learning Regressor (DNN) did not show better performance in comparison to the other regressor models.

Another work on ICU LOS prediction was done by Ma et al. [35]. They proposed a method by categorizing patients according to their age and setting a mortality risk score for each age group according to their LOS. A combination of just-in-time learning (JITL) and one-class extreme learning machine (one-class ELM) which is called JITL-ELM was implemented for LOS prediction. SVM and ELM were compared with this combined system and showed improved performance in this research work.

Gentimis et al. [24] developed a prediction model showing results for two categories of lengths of stay one was a short stay and the other was a long stay.

The categories were counted as either less than 5 days or more than 5 days and more than 20 days were removed. For LOS prediction neural network was trained using WEKA software and the code was written in R language. Ensemble method as Random Forest Method was also applied for LOS prediction. For the neural network, the attribute diagnosis ICD9 code was implemented and the neural network showed good results as the final output. For evaluating LOS prediction various methods were applied and input attributes were chosen from various perspectives which contribute to the changes in ICU LOS. Although various features have been used for ICU LOS prediction or classification, the drug, which is essential for ICU patients, has not received significant attention to this important feature.

3 Methodology

The workflow of the overall system has been shown with Fig. 1 which is describing below.

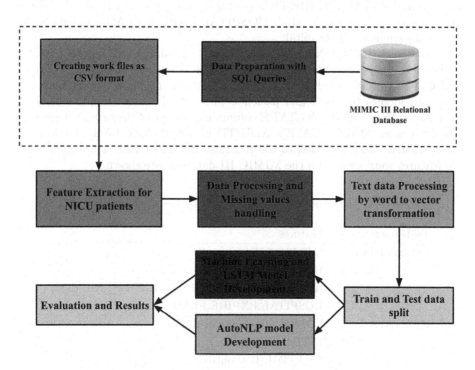

Fig. 1. System design for the development of the NICU Length of Stay classification analysis.

3.1 MIMIC-III Data Collection

MIMIC-III is a large clinical database also known as Medical Information Mart for Intensive Care III. In MIMIC-III Database there are 26 tables or attributes and there are data about a total of 53,423 patients. Among them 7863 data for the admissions of neonates. The data were collected from the intensive care units at Beth Israel Deaconess Medical Center from 2001 to 2002 and then maintained by the Massachusetts Institute of Technology (MIT) [8]. As MIMIC-III is a relational database, In the PATIENTS table there is a unique ID named SUBJECT_ID for every single patient. In the ADMISSIONS table, the information of the patients with the same SUBJECT_ID was collected. The columns collected from this table are HOSPITAL_EXPIRE_FLAG, ADMISSION_TYPE. Here for the NICU patients, the admission type is newborn. From the ICUS-TAYS table, the rows with the same SUBJECT_ID were extracted and the selected columns are LOS, INTIME, OUTTIME and the ICU length of stay can also be measured from the difference between OUTTIME and INTIME. HOSPITAL_EXPIRE_FLAG is for the patient who died or did not die in the hospital. HOSPITAL_EXPIRE_FLAG = 0 is for the patients who did not die in the hospital. On the other hand, HOSPITAL_EXPIRE_FLAG = 1 depicts the deceased patient in the hospital.

The PRESCRIPTIONS table stores data containing different entries for medication purposes. The columns collected from this table are DRUG, DRUG_TYPE, and DOSE_VAL_RX which contain the information about the drugs provided to the particular patients. The DRUG column simply stands for the name of the drug. DRUG_TYPE column is the type of the drugs categorized into 3 types as 'MAIN', 'BASE', 'ADDITIVE'. DOSE_VAL_RX is the doses of the particular drugs provided to the patients [29, 42]. In Table 1 the tables and the features were used from the MIMIC III database are shown.

Table 1. Table showing the tables and features used in this work

Table name	Features
ADMISSIONS	SUBJECT_ID(unique ID)
	HADM_ID(patient admission ID)
	ADMISSION_TYPE("NEWBORN" for NICU data)
	HOSPITAL_EXPIRE_FLAG
ICUSTAYS	LOS(Length of stay in ICU)
	INTIME(ICU intime)
	OUTTIME(ICU outtime)
PRESCRIPTIONS	DRUG
	DRUG_TYPE
	DOSE_VAL_RX

3.2 Feature Extraction

Some features were extracted for critical patients in NICU. The drugs for the patients in critical conditions were taken into consideration. Features are extracted according to some conditions. The conditions are-

- age of the patients less than 28 days.
- ADMISSION_TYPE is "NEWBORN" and CAREUNIT is "NICU"
- HOSPITAL_EXPIRE_FLAG = 0 which indicates the patients are not dead.
- LOS ≤ 20 days is considered

From the conditions above 2634 unique patients data were extracted.

Handling Missing Values: There were 20 missing values in the DOSE_VAL_RX columns. In the column, empty values were replaced with null values. There were some values of dose as range 1–2, these values were replaced with the mean values of the range.

Creating Labels for LOS Column: A new column is created for the classification of the length of stays such as LOS is less than 7 days or LOS is more than 7 days.

- If LOS > 7 then label is 'Yes'
- If LOS < 7 then label is 'No'

The number of labels 'Yes' is 14321 and the total number of labels 'No' is 11331. The drugs for each patient or for the same SUBJECT_ID of each patient the multiple drugs along with the dosages were considered.

TFIDF Vectorization for 'DRUG' Column: TFIDF stands for "Term Frequency times Inverse Document Frequency". It is a tokenization technique for transforming text into numerical values. It converts the words by multiplying the term frequency of a word by the inverse document frequency [12]. The Eq. 1 can be written as follows:

$$W(d,t) = TF(d,t) \times log\frac{N}{df(t)} \tag{1}$$

From the equation N is the number of texts, $df(t)$ represents number of texts for t terms. The parameters used in converting text to vector is explaining below [34]:

- **sublinear_tf:** It is a boolean parameter that is generally expressed as true or False. It is used to modify the IDF values by adding 1 so that it can prevent the equation to become infinity if the denominator turns zero.

- **min_df:** It is a cut-off value. Using it the document frequency can be avoided which has values less than the cut-off value.
- **norm:** It is used to normalize the term frequency. Generally, norm = l2 is used by default.
- **encoding:** It is normally used to decode the files.
- **ngram_range:** It is the range of minimum and maximum values of n-gram. In this work, the lower limit is 1 and the upper limit is 3. So the sentences can be converted into corpus from the range of 1 to 3.
- **stop_words:** In the text corpus there are some less important elements that are included. In the "DRUG" column there were some elements as Syringe (Neonatal) *D5W*. Stop words can remove them.

The "DRUG" column was in text format. To transform the drug name into the vector, first, we converted the text data into a TF-IDF vector which ranges from unigram to 3-grams (1,3). The 20 most features for the drugs are shown in the Table 2 for unigram to the trigram. After completing all the feature engineering data was split into train and test datasets.

Table 2. Table showing N-gram representation for top 20 features using TF-IDF vectorizer where we extracted 3-gram value

Number of N	Value
N = 1	'neo', 'iv', 'sodium', 'syringe', 'neonatal', 'd5w', 'gentamicin', 'ampicillin'
N = 2	'neo iv', 'syringe neonatal', 'neonatal d5w', 'ampicillin sodium'
N = 3	'syringe neonatal d5w'

Train Test Split: After extracting the values and removing the duplicates there were 2257 rows of data. Then for train and test split the dataset is split into 70–30% train-test data. After splitting, there were 1579 values for training data and the rest 678 values for testing purposes.

3.3 Machine Learning Models Development

Logistic Regression: Logistic Regression(LR) works very well for binary classification. As it uses a sigmoid function, it generates outcomes in the range of 0 to 1 [21]. As it is very easy to develop, it is a popular method to create a classification model.

Naive Bayes: Naive Bayes (NB) classifier is a very simple approach. From some independent features, it can create assumptions and then classify or predict labels [13].

K Nearest Neighbors: K Nearest Neighbors (KNN) Regression is a clustering method. It is also used to show the association of the independent variables with the output variables. This method can minimize the mean-squared error by averaging the observation of the closest neighbors [13].

Support Vector Machines: Support Vector Machines (SVM) is another Supervised algorithm. But it is different from the LR method. The main task of the SVM is to determine the hyperplane area for classifying the data points. Support vectors are created which are nearest to the hyperplane space. Thus it can classify the outcome [18,21].

Decision Trees: A Decision Tree (DT) is a method that can create decision rules from training data. It can also be represented into a tree alike representation for developing prediction [21]. For classification, a set of values are taken as target variables in this algorithm. Each node or leaf of the tree is used to represent the class label which is actually the probability of distribution [23].

Random Forest: Random Forest (RF) is an ensemble method. For the implementation of the RF model, the data do not need to be correlated or data with missing values can also be used to classify the dataset [21,49].

Long Short-Term Memory (LSTM): LSTM is a deep learning method that is used in this classification. It is a modified version of the Recurrent Neural Network (RNN) [50]. It may perform better as it overcomes the long-term dependencies which are typically faced in the RNN method. It has a forget cell which helps to reduce the vanishing gradient problem causes for long-term dependencies [2].

Word tokenizer is downloaded from the Keras library. It is used to convert the text corpus into vectors. In this method, the tokenizer places a numeric number opposite to a unique word. Then sort by number in descending order, as the word most frequently comes will be at 1st position, then the next word which comes after the 1st highest frequent word and so on. Figure 2 shown below is used to describe which drugs were applied most.

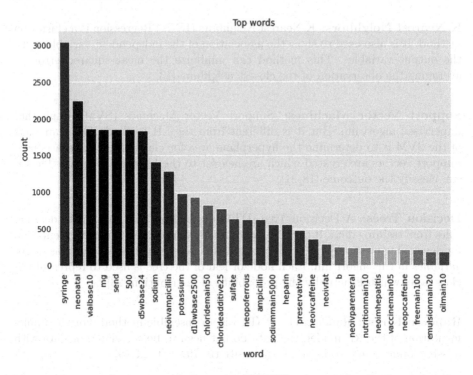

Fig. 2. The most frequent words from the "DRUG" column after implementing the word-tokenizer method where the y-axis represents the total number of frequencies of the words.

4   Result Analysis

4.1   Evaluation Metrics

Evaluation metrics are the measurement of the performance of the machine learning models which indicates which model is showing better performance. The evaluation metrics are used in this work are Accuracy, Precision, Recall, and F1-score.

Precision: Precision is the measurement of the labeled positive values which are actually positive [21].

$$Precision = \frac{TP}{TP + FP} \tag{2}$$

Recall: Recall is the measurement that how many of the real positive cases were labeled correctly [21].

$$Recall = \frac{TP}{TP + FN} \tag{3}$$

Accuracy: The accuracy is the measure of the total correct predictions from all of the predictions [21].

$$Accuracy = \frac{TP + TN}{TP + TN + FP + FN} \tag{4}$$

F1-Score: It is the total accuracy generated from the overall predictions [21].

$$F1 - score = \frac{2 \times Recall \times Precision}{Recall + Precision} \tag{5}$$

From the Eq. 2, 3, 4, TP and TN represents True Positive and True Negative values respectively. FP and FN represents False Positive and False Negative values respectively.

4.2 Results for Machine Learning and LSTM Approaches

In Fig. 3 the comparison of the results for Logistic Regression (LR), Support Vector Machines (SVM), Decision Trees (DT), Random Forest (RF), Naive Bayes (NB), and K-Nearest Neighbor (KNN) is represented.

When only the "DRUG" feature was used the Logistic Regression (LR) showed 0.723 or about 72% accuracy which is a good result among the other machine learning models. But the F1 score is about 69% for both Logistic Regression (LR) and Random Forest (RF). Although the accuracy of RF is lower than LR which is 69%. After LR and RF, Support Vector Machines (SVM) show a better performance of about 68%, and the F1 score is 64%. If we observe other performance metrics, such as precision, the highest score is achieved by the Naive Bayes(NB) classifier. As it is the measure of the correctly predicted positive values. But the highest F1 score is achieved by the LSTM model which is 0.7212, even though it is more than the F1 score achieved by LR. The accuracy of LSTM is 0.7194 which is almost similar to LR.

In the second scenario, two features, "DOSE_VAL_RX" and "DRUG" were taken into consideration. The good performance is shown by the LSTM model which is 0.8095 or about 81%. LR also performs well among the other ML methods. But for LR, the F1 score is 83% which is the highest among all other methods. F1 score generally bears more significance than accuracy where the data is imbalanced. Although LSTM showed good accuracy the F1 score is 73% only. SVM and RF also improved their accuracy and F1 score than the previous scenario. The F1 score of the K-Nearest Neighbor(KNN) method also improved and it is 0.8163.

Finally, three features ("DRUG", "DOSE_VAL_RX", and "DRUG_TYPE") were used to generate the classification result. The highest accuracy is achieved by LSTM which is about 82%. Then among the ML methods, LR performs really well. It acquired the accuracy of 81% and the F1 score is 0.8456 which is about 85%. But LSTM could not achieve that much score, it only scored about 79% for the F1 score. After training the data with the RF method we achieved an 84% F1 score. SVM and KNN achieved the F1 score of 83.3% and 82.3% respectively. Among all

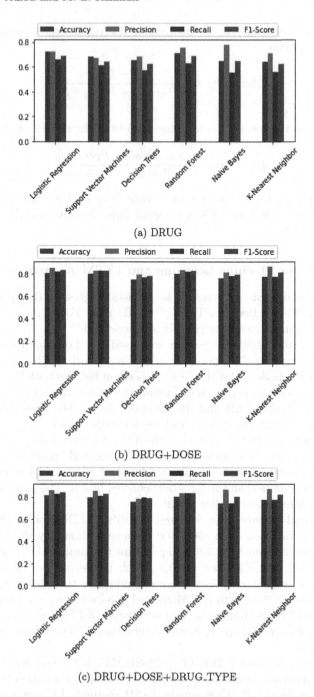

(a) DRUG

(b) DRUG+DOSE

(c) DRUG+DOSE+DRUG_TYPE

Fig. 3. NICU LOS classification results comparison of performance metrics for various machine learning methods Fig (a) when only "DRUG" feature is used. Figure (b) when "DRUG+DOSE" features are used and Fig (c) when "DRUG+DOSE+DRUG_TYPE" features are used.

the methods Decision Tree(DT) showed poor performance. It showed only 72.8% accuracy with 79.1% of the F1 score. For each algorithm, it is observable that the accuracy eventually increased with the increment of the features. With the rapid number of text corpus, the accuracy of the methods increases [1].

For LSTM the train test split was the same as the previous methods. First using the word embedding layer, the word vectors are converted into matrix dimensions and in this work, the embedded_dim is used as 100. For training data, 35 epochs were used. After running the LSTM model, the accuracy achieved for the data using the "DRUG" column was 0.7194 or 72%. Next, we used drugs along with doses for classification, then the accuracy was increased by 0.8095 or 81% and when the drugs were used along with the doses and drug types then the accuracy was 0.8245 or 82% and the F1-score is 78%. Figure 4 is shown for comparing the train and test accuracy for the drugs and doses. In each graph of Fig. 4 x-axis represents the number of epochs and y-axis represents the accuracy. So as the features have increased the performance is also increased. It can be understood that not only drug names, but also the doses of drugs have an important impact on LOS. For different methods, the accuracy was improved after implementing three features drugs, drug doses, and drug types.

The results of different traditional machine learning algorithms and LSTM are showed in the following Table 3.

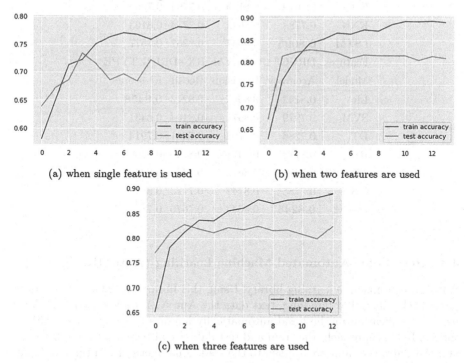

(a) when single feature is used   (b) when two features are used

(c) when three features are used

Fig. 4. Training and test accuracy comparison for three cases using LSTM model for NICU LOS classification (a) when drug name feature was used (b) when drug name and drug doses were used (c) when drug name, doses and drug types all three features were used.

Table 3. Performance Evaluation for different ML Models with LSTM model showing the classification results for NICU LOS for 7 days

Feature	DRUG			
Model	Accuracy	Precision	Recall	F1-score
LR	**0.723**	0.72	0.657	0.6874
SVM	0.684	0.67	0.6146	0.6411
DT	0.6435	0.67	0.5654	0.6224
RF	0.6919	0.70	0.6195	0.6878
NB	0.6456	0.78	0.5571	0.6500
KNN	0.6435	0.71	0.5613	0.6269
LSTM	0.7194	0.6590	0.7963	**0.7212**
Features	DRUG+DOSE_VAL_RX			
Model	Accuracy	Precision	Recall	F1-score
LR	0.8065	0.8512	0.8170	**0.8338**
SVM	0.8036	0.8277	0.8277	0.8276
DT	0.7559	0.7989	0.7786	0.7825
RF	0.8051	0.8381	0.8231	0.8279
NB	0.7619	0.8120	0.7794	0.7954
KNN	0.7783	0.8642	0.7734	0.8163
LSTM	**0.8095**	0.6667	0.8257	0.7377
Features	DRUG+DOSE_VAL_RX+DRUG_TYPE			
Model	Accuracy	Precision	Recall	F1-score
LR	0.8142	0.8647	0.8273	**0.8456**
SVM	0.7979	0.8571	0.8104	0.8331
DT	0.7286	0.7794	0.7641	0.7914
RF	0.8112	0.8471	0.8346	0.8360
NB	0.7478	0.8672	0.7457	0.8018
KNN	0.7788	0.8747	0.7773	0.8231
LSTM	**0.8245**	0.8044	0.7676	0.7855

4.3   Results for Automated Machine Learning (AutoML)

AutoML is a machine learning library. Using this library the LOS for 7 days or not was classified. For handling, text data the AutoNLP tool is used. AutoNLP uses a classification method and automatically handles the data with TfidfVectorizer. In this approach, the train and test data are also split into 70–30% train and test data, the same we applied to the traditional methods. In three different cases, the performance was measured. For the DRUG column, the accuracy is 68% and the run time is 0.5 min and the F1 score is 71%. Then with two features, "DRUG" and "DOSE_VAL_RX", the accuracy is 73% and the run time

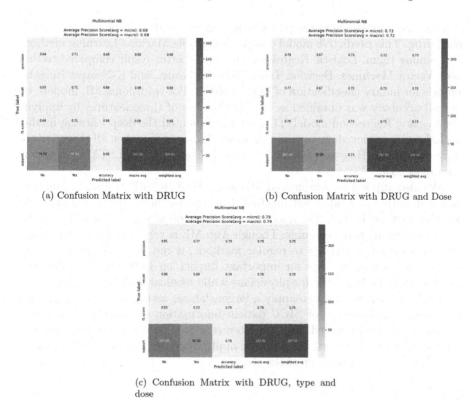

(a) Confusion Matrix with DRUG   (b) Confusion Matrix with DRUG and Dose

(c) Confusion Matrix with DRUG, type and dose

Fig. 5. Confusion Matrix generated for AutoNLP method for NICU LOS classification where Fig (a) only "DRUG" feature is used, Fig (b) when "DRUG+DOSE" features are used, Fig (c) "DRUG+DOSE+DRUG_TYPE" features are used.

was 0.7 min. Finally, the accuracy was increased by 79% with the combination of all three columns "DRUG", "DOSE_VAL_RX", and "DRUG_TYPE" and the time required was 0.9 min. For these features, the F1 score also increased eventually and it became 73%. Figure 5 shows the classification report for the AutoNLP method for the three different scenarios.

5   Conclusion

The neonates admitted to the NICU are in a very vital condition. It requires emergency medications considering various crucial signs. In this work, we identified the drugs or medicines applied to critical patients, then developed a predictive model showing how drugs can be responsible for the patients' Length of Stay (LOS) in the NICU for 7 days. Along with drug names, drug types and doses of the drugs were also considered to classify the length of stay. When we only used drugs then the accuracy was not that much but gradually it increased after implementing the other two features. In addition to just the drug, the dosage of the drug is also important, as the performance improves after including the doses of each drug. This predictive model compares multiple Machine Learning methods. But among them, Logistic Regression showed a better result compared to Support Vector Machines, Decision Trees, Random Forest, and K-Nearest Neighbor models for binary classification of LOS in NICU. For traditional ML models, the overall accuracy was obtained as 81% in the case of three features by applying the Logistic Regression model. Then we implemented the deep learning method LSTM and it achieved an accuracy of about 0.824 or 82% when all three features were considered. However, for the F1 score, LR outperforms LSTM by achieving a score of 85%.

We also applied an Automated ML tool, the AutoNLP approach, and compared it with the traditional machine learning methods and a popular deep learning method LSTM. The maximum accuracy obtained by AutoML was 79% by implementing three columns. Though AutoML is very easy to develop a classification model, compared to regular methods, it did not perform well. Since drugs and drug doses have an important impact on LOS, these classification results might be beneficial for physicians while medicating ICU patients.

In the future, we want to apply a larger dataset as the MIMIC dataset only contains a small number of NICU patient information so that the classification accuracy can be improved. We are interested to examine the effects of drugs on various larger datasets. We will also apply more deep learning and ensemble models for the improvement of the study.

References

1. Adiba, F.I., Islam, T., Kaiser, M.S., Mahmud, M., Rahman, M.A.: Effect of corpora on classification of fake news using Naive Bayes classifier. Int. J. Autom. AI Mach. Learn. (IJAAIML) 1(1) (2020). https://researchlakejournals.com/index.php/AAIML/article/view/45/32
2. Adiba, F.I., Sharwardy, S.N., Rahman, M.Z.: Multivariate time series prediction of pediatric ICU data using deep learning. In: 2021 International Conference on Innovative Trends in Information Technology (ICITIIT), pp. 1–6 (2021). https://doi.org/10.1109/ICITIIT51526.2021.9399593
3. Ahmed, S., Hossain, M.F., Nur, S.B., Shamim Kaiser, M., Mahmud, M.: Toward machine learning-based psychological assessment of autism spectrum disorders in school and community. In: Kaiser, M.S., Bandyopadhyay, A., Ray, K., Singh, R., Nagar, V. (eds.) Proceedings of Trends in Electronics and Health Informatics. LNNS, vol. 376, pp. 139–149. Springer, Singapore (2022). https://doi.org/10.1007/978-981-16-8826-3_13
4. Niamat Ullah Akhund, T.M., Mahi, M.J.N., Hasnat Tanvir, A.N.M., Mahmud, M., Kaiser, M.S.: ADEPTNESS: Alzheimer's disease patient management system using pervasive sensors - early prototype and preliminary results. In: Wang, S., et al. (eds.) BI 2018. LNCS (LNAI), vol. 11309, pp. 413–422. Springer, Cham (2018). https://doi.org/10.1007/978-3-030-05587-5_39
5. Akter, T., Ali, M.H., Satu, M.S., Khan, M.I., Mahmud, M.: Towards autism subtype detection through identification of discriminatory factors using machine learning. In: Mahmud, M., Kaiser, M.S., Vassanelli, S., Dai, Q., Zhong, N. (eds.) BI 2021.

LNCS (LNAI), vol. 12960, pp. 401–410. Springer, Cham (2021). https://doi.org/10.1007/978-3-030-86993-9_36

6. Al Banna, M.H., Ghosh, T., Taher, K.A., Kaiser, M.S., Mahmud, M.: A monitoring system for patients of autism spectrum disorder using artificial intelligence. In: Mahmud, M., Vassanelli, S., Kaiser, M.S., Zhong, N. (eds.) BI 2020. LNCS (LNAI), vol. 12241, pp. 251–262. Springer, Cham (2020). https://doi.org/10.1007/978-3-030-59277-6_23

7. Al Mamun, S., Kaiser, M.S., Mahmud, M.: An artificial intelligence based approach towards inclusive healthcare provisioning in society 5.0: a perspective on brain disorder. In: Mahmud, M., Kaiser, M.S., Vassanelli, S., Dai, Q., Zhong, N. (eds.) BI 2021. LNCS (LNAI), vol. 12960, pp. 157–169. Springer, Cham (2021). https://doi.org/10.1007/978-3-030-86993-9_15

8. Johnson, A., Pollard, T., Mark, R.: MIMIC-III clinical database demo (version 1.4) (2019). https://doi.org/10.13026/C2HM2Q

9. Alsinglawi, B., et al.: Predicting length of stay for cardiovascular hospitalizations in the intensive care unit: machine learning approach. In: 2020 42nd Annual International Conference of the IEEE Engineering in Medicine Biology Society (EMBC), pp. 5442–5445 (2020). https://doi.org/10.1109/EMBC44109.2020.9175889

10. AutoML.org: What is AutoML? https://www.automl.org/automl/. Accessed 31 Mar 2022

11. Bhapkar, H.R., Mahalle, P.N., Shinde, G.R., Mahmud, M.: Rough sets in COVID-19 to predict symptomatic cases. In: Santosh, K.C., Joshi, A. (eds.) COVID-19: Prediction, Decision-Making, and its Impacts. LNDECT, vol. 60, pp. 57–68. Springer, Singapore (2021). https://doi.org/10.1007/978-981-15-9682-7_7

12. Bird, S., Klein, E., Loper, E.: Natural Language Processing with Python: Analyzing Text with the Natural Language Toolkit. O'Reilly Media (2009). https://books.google.com.bd/books?id=KGIbfiiP1i4C

13. Bishop, C.M.: Pattern Recognition and Machine Learning (Information Science and Statistics). Springer, Heidelberg (2006)

14. Biswas, M., Kaiser, M.S., Mahmud, M., Al Mamun, S., Hossain, M.S., Rahman, M.A.: An XAI based autism detection: the context behind the detection. In: Mahmud, M., Kaiser, M.S., Vassanelli, S., Dai, Q., Zhong, N. (eds.) BI 2021. LNCS (LNAI), vol. 12960, pp. 448–459. Springer, Cham (2021). https://doi.org/10.1007/978-3-030-86993-9_40

15. Biswas, M., et al.: Indoor navigation support system for patients with neurodegenerative diseases. In: Mahmud, M., Kaiser, M.S., Vassanelli, S., Dai, Q., Zhong, N. (eds.) BI 2021. LNCS (LNAI), vol. 12960, pp. 411–422. Springer, Cham (2021). https://doi.org/10.1007/978-3-030-86993-9_37

16. Biswas, M., et al.: ACCU^{3}RATE: a mobile health application rating scale based on user reviews. PLoS ONE **16**(12), e0258050 (2021)

17. Chen, T., et al.: A dominant set-informed interpretable fuzzy system for automated diagnosis of dementia. Front. Neurosci. **16**, Article ID 867664 (2022)

18. Das, T.R., Hasan, S., Sarwar, S.M., Das, J.K., Rahman, M.A.: Facial spoof detection using support vector machine. In: Kaiser, M.S., Bandyopadhyay, A., Mahmud, M., Ray, K. (eds.) Proceedings of International Conference on Trends in Computational and Cognitive Engineering. AISC, vol. 1309, pp. 615–625. Springer, Singapore (2021). https://doi.org/10.1007/978-981-33-4673-4_50

19. Deepa, B., Murugappan, M., Sumithra, M., Mahmud, M., Al-Rakhami, M.S.: Pattern descriptors orientation and map firefly algorithm based brain pathology classification using hybridized machine learning algorithm. IEEE Access **10**, 3848–3863 (2021)

20. Drugs.com.   https://www.drugs.com/search.php?searchterm=heparin&a=1. Accessed 25 Mar 2022

21. Elaziz, M., Al-qaness, M., Ewees, A., Dahou, A.: Recent Advances in NLP: The Case of Arabic Language. Studies in Computational Intelligence. Springer, Cham (2019). https://books.google.com.bd/books?id=HQ3BDwAAQBAJ

22. Farhin, F., Kaiser, M.S., Mahmud, M.: Secured smart healthcare system: blockchain and Bayesian inference based approach. In: Kaiser, M.S., Bandyopadhyay, A., Mahmud, M., Ray, K. (eds.) Proceedings of International Conference on Trends in Computational and Cognitive Engineering. AISC, vol. 1309, pp. 455–465. Springer, Singapore (2021). https://doi.org/10.1007/978-981-33-4673-4_36

23. Ferdous, H., Siraj, T., Setu, S.J., Anwar, M.M., Rahman, M.A.: Machine learning approach towards satellite image classification. In: Kaiser, M.S., Bandyopadhyay, A., Mahmud, M., Ray, K. (eds.) Proceedings of International Conference on Trends in Computational and Cognitive Engineering. AISC, vol. 1309, pp. 627–637. Springer, Singapore (2021). https://doi.org/10.1007/978-981-33-4673-4_51

24. Gentimis, T., Alnaser, A.J., Durante, A., Cook, K., Steele, R.: Predicting hospital length of stay using neural networks on MIMIC III data. In: 2017 IEEE 15th International Conference on Dependable, Autonomic and Secure Computing, 15th International Conference on Pervasive Intelligence and Computing, 3rd International Conference on Big Data Intelligence and Computing and Cyber Science and Technology Congress (DASC/PiCom/DataCom/CyberSciTech), pp. 1194–1201 (2017). https://doi.org/10.1109/DASC-PICom-DataCom-CyberSciTec.2017.191

25. Ghosh, T., et al.: Artificial intelligence and internet of things in screening and management of autism spectrum disorder. Sustain. Cities Soc. **74**, 103189 (2021)

26. Health Science Center: The Neonatal Intensive Care Unit (NICU). https://www.stanfordchildrens.org/en/topic/default?id=the-neonatal-intensive-care-unit-nicu-90-P02389. Accessed 24 Mar 2022

27. Jesmin, S., Kaiser, M.S., Mahmud, M.: Artificial and internet of healthcare things based Alzheimer care during COVID 19. In: Mahmud, M., Vassanelli, S., Kaiser, M.S., Zhong, N. (eds.) BI 2020. LNCS (LNAI), vol. 12241, pp. 263–274. Springer, Cham (2020). https://doi.org/10.1007/978-3-030-59277-6_24

28. Jesmin, S., Kaiser, M.S., Mahmud, M.: Towards artificial intelligence driven stress monitoring for mental wellbeing tracking during Covid-19. In: Proceedings of the WI-IAT, pp. 845–851 (2020)

29. Johnson, A.E., et al.: MIMIC-III, a freely accessible critical care database. Sci. Data **3**, 160035 (2016). https://doi.org/10.1038/sdata.2016.35

30. Kaiser, M.S., et al.: 6G access network for intelligent internet of healthcare things: opportunity, challenges, and research directions. In: Kaiser, M.S., Bandyopadhyay, A., Mahmud, M., Ray, K. (eds.) Proceedings of International Conference on Trends in Computational and Cognitive Engineering. AISC, vol. 1309, pp. 317–328. Springer, Singapore (2021). https://doi.org/10.1007/978-981-33-4673-4_25

31. Kumar, I., et al.: Dense tissue pattern characterization using deep neural network. Cogn. Comput. **14**, 1–24 (2022). https://doi.org/10.1007/s12559-021-09970-2

32. Kumar, S., et al.: Forecasting major impacts of Covid-19 pandemic on country-driven sectors: challenges, lessons, and future roadmap. Pers. Ubiquitous Comput. 1–24 (2021)

33. Lalotra, G.S., Kumar, V., Bhatt, A., Chen, T., Mahmud, M.: iReTADS: an intelligent real-time anomaly detection system for cloud communications using temporal data summarization and neural network. Secur. Commun. Netw. **2022**, 1–15, Article ID 9149164 (2022)

34. Scikit learn: sklearn.feature_extraction.text.tfidfvectorizer. https://scikit-learn. org/stable/modules/generated/sklearn.feature_extraction.text.TfidfVectorizer. html. Accessed 5 Jan 2022

35. Ma, X., Si, Y., Wang, Z., Wang, Y.: Length of stay prediction for ICU patients using individualized single classification algorithm. Comput. Methods Programs Biomed. **186**, 105224 (2020). https://doi.org/10.1016/j.cmpb.2019.105224. https://www. sciencedirect.com/science/article/pii/S0169260719316529

36. Mahima, K.T.Y., Ginige, T.N.D.S., De Zoysa, K.: Evaluation of sentiment analysis based on AutoML and traditional approaches. Int. J. Adv. Comput. Sci. Appl. **12**(2) (2021). https://doi.org/10.14569/IJACSA.2021.0120277

37. Mahmud, M., Kaiser, M.S.: Machine learning in fighting pandemics: a COVID-19 case study. In: Santosh, K.C., Joshi, A. (eds.) COVID-19: Prediction, Decision-Making, and its Impacts. LNDECT, vol. 60, pp. 77–81. Springer, Singapore (2021). https://doi.org/10.1007/978-981-15-9682-7_9

38. Mahmud, M., Kaiser, M.S., Hussain, A., Vassanelli, S.: Applications of deep learning and reinforcement learning to biological data. IEEE Trans. Neural Netw. Learn. Syst. **29**(6), 2063–2079 (2018)

39. Mahmud, M., et al.: Towards explainable and privacy-preserving artificial intelligence for personalisation in autism spectrum disorder. In: Antona, M., Stephanidis, C. (eds.) HCII 2022. LNCS, pp. 356–370. Springer, Cham (2022). https://doi.org/ 10.1007/978-3-031-05039-8_26

40. Mammoottil, M.J., Kulangara, L.J., Cherian, A.S., Mohandas, P., Hasikin, K., Mahmud, M.: Detection of breast cancer from five-view thermal images using convolutional neural networks. J. Healthcare Eng. **2022**, Article ID 4295221 (2022)

41. Mansouri, A., Noei, M., Abadeh, M.S.: Predicting hospital length of stay of neonates admitted to the NICU using data mining techniques. In: 2020 10th International Conference on Computer and Knowledge Engineering (ICCKE), pp. 629–635 (2020). https://doi.org/10.1109/ICCKE50421.2020.9303666

42. MIT-LCP: MIMIC-III documentation. https://mimic.mit.edu/docs/iii/. Accessed 2 Jan 2022

43. Mukherjee, H., et al.: Automatic lung health screening using respiratory sounds. J. Med. Syst. **45**(2), 1–9 (2021)

44. Mukherjee, P., Bhattacharyya, I., Mullick, M., Kumar, R., Roy, N.D., Mahmud, M.: *i*ConDet: an intelligent portable healthcare app for the detection of conjunctivitis. In: Mahmud, M., Kaiser, M.S., Kasabov, N., Iftekharuddin, K., Zhong, N. (eds.) AII 2021. CCIS, vol. 1435, pp. 29–42. Springer, Cham (2021). https://doi.org/10. 1007/978-3-030-82269-9_3

45. Nahiduzzaman, M., Tasnim, M., Newaz, N.T., Kaiser, M.S., Mahmud, M.: Machine learning based early fall detection for elderly people with neurological disorder using multimodal data fusion. In: Mahmud, M., Vassanelli, S., Kaiser, M.S., Zhong, N. (eds.) BI 2020. LNCS (LNAI), vol. 12241, pp. 204–214. Springer, Cham (2020). https://doi.org/10.1007/978-3-030-59277-6_19

46. UAPR Office: Counting what matters - MPDSR report maternal and perinatal death surveillance and response systems in Asia-pacific during the Covid-19 pandemic. https://asiapacific.unfpa.org/en/counting-what-matters-MPDSR-report. Accessed 2 Feb 2022

47. Paul, A., Basu, A., Mahmud, M., Kaiser, M.S., Sarkar, R.: Inverted bell-curve-based ensemble of deep learning models for detection of Covid-19 from chest X-rays. Neural Comput. Appl. 1–15 (2022)

48. Prakash, N., Murugappan, M., Hemalakshmi, G., Jayalakshmi, M., Mahmud, M.: Deep transfer learning for Covid-19 detection and infection localization with super-pixel based segmentation. Sustain. Cities Soc. **75**, 103252 (2021)

49. Rahman, M.A., Brown, D.J., Shopland, N., Burton, A., Mahmud, M.: Explainable multimodal machine learning for engagement analysis by continuous performance test. In: Antona, M., Stephanidis, C. (eds.) HCII 2022. LNCS, vol. 13309, pp. 386–399. Springer, Cham (2022). https://doi.org/10.1007/978-3-031-05039-8_28

50. Rakib, A.B., Rumky, E.A., Ashraf, A.J., Hillas, M.M., Rahman, M.A.: Mental healthcare chatbot using sequence-to-sequence learning and BiLSTM. In: Mahmud, M., Kaiser, M.S., Vassanelli, S., Dai, Q., Zhong, N. (eds.) BI 2021. LNCS (LNAI), vol. 12960, pp. 378–387. Springer, Cham (2021). https://doi.org/10.1007/978-3-030-86993-9_34

51. Satu, M.S., et al.: Short-term prediction of Covid-19 cases using machine learning models. Appl. Sci. **11**(9), 4266 (2021)

52. Shaffi, N., et al.: Triplet-loss based Siamese convolutional neural network for 4-way classification of Alzheimer's disease. In: Mahmud, M., He, J., Vassanelli, S., van Zundert, A., Zhong, N. (eds.) BI 2022. LNCS, vol. 13406, pp. 277–287. Springer, Cham (2022). https://doi.org/10.1007/978-3-031-15037-1_23

53. Sumi, A.I., Zohora, M.F., Mahjabeen, M., Faria, T.J., Mahmud, M., Kaiser, M.S.: ƒASSERT: a fuzzy assistive system for children with autism using internet of things. In: Wang, S., et al. (eds.) BI 2018. LNCS (LNAI), vol. 11309, pp. 403–412. Springer, Cham (2018). https://doi.org/10.1007/978-3-030-05587-5_38

54. Toptas, M., Samanci, N.S., et al.: Factors affecting the length of stay in the intensive care unit: our clinical experience. Biomed. Res. Int. **2018**, 1–4 (2018)

55. UNICEF: Pregnant mothers and babies born during Covid-19 pandemic threatened by strained health systems and disruptions in services. https://www.unicef.org/bangladesh/en/press-releases/pregnant-mothers-and-babies-born-during-covid-19-pandemic-threatened-strained-health. Accessed 2 Feb 2022

56. Wadhera, T., Mahmud, M.: Brain networks in autism spectrum disorder, epilepsy and their relationship: a machine learning approach. In: Chen, T., Carter, J., Mahmud, M., Khuman, A.S. (eds.) Artificial Intelligence in Healthcare. BIH, pp. 125–142. Springer, Cham (2022). https://doi.org/10.1007/978-981-19-5272-2_6

57. Wadhera, T., Mahmud, M.: Influences of social learning in individual perception and decision making in people with autism: a computational approach. In: Mahmud, M., He, J., Vassanelli, S., van Zundert, A., Zhong, N. (eds.) BI 2022. LNCS, vol. 13406, pp. 50–61. Springer, Cham (2022). https://doi.org/10.1007/978-3-031-15037-1_5

58. WHO: Newborns: improving survival and well-being. https://www.who.int/news-room/fact-sheets/detail/newborns-reducing-mortality. Accessed 24 Mar 2022

59. Yahaya, S.W., Lotfi, A., Mahmud, M.: Towards the development of an adaptive system for detecting anomaly in human activities. In: Proceedings of the SSCI, pp. 534–541 (2020)

60. Yahaya, S.W., Lotfi, A., Mahmud, M.: Towards a data-driven adaptive anomaly detection system for human activity. Pattern Recogn. Lett. **145**, 200–207 (2021)

61. Zohora, M.F., Tania, M.H., Kaiser, M.S., Mahmud, M.: Forecasting the risk of type II diabetes using reinforcement learning. In: Proceedings of the ICIEV icIVPR, pp. 1–6 (2020)

iConDet2: An Improved Conjunctivitis Detection Portable Healthcare App Powered by Artificial Intelligence

Mainak Adak[1], Aayushman Chatterjee[1], Nilanjana Dutta Roy[1(✉)],
and Mufti Mahmud[2,3,4(✉)]

[1] Department of Computer Science and Engineering, Institute of Engineering
and Management, Kolkata, India
`nilanjana.duttaroy@iemcal.com`
[2] Department of Computer Science, Nottingham Trent University, Clifton,
Nottingham NG11 8NS, UK
[3] Computing and Informatics Research Centre, Nottingham Trent University,
Clifton, Nottingham NG11 8NS, UK
[4] Medical Technologies Innovation Facility, Nottingham Trent University, Clifton,
Nottingham NG11 8NS, UK
`mufti.mahmud@ntu.ac.uk, muftimahmud@gmail.com`

Abstract. Conjunctivitis is one of the common and contagious ocular diseases which affects the conjunctiva of the human eye. Both the bacterial and viral types of it can be treated with eye drops and other medicines. It is important to diagnose the disease at its early stage to realise the connection between it and other diseases, especially COVID-19. Mobile applications like iConDet is such a solution that performs well for the initial screening of Conjunctivitis. In this work, we present with iConDet2 which provides an advanced solution than the earlier version of it. It is faster with a higher accuracy level (95%) than the previously released iConDet.

Keywords: Conjunctivitis · iConDet · Resnet · Transfer learning · Mobile application

1 Introduction

Conjunctivitis, which is mostly a contagious and seasonal ocular disease, can also be seen throughout the year. It affects the Conjunctiva which is a clear and thin outer layer of the human eye. Any discomfort in Conjunctiva caused by bacteria or virus is commonly termed pink eye disease or Conjunctivitis. There are a few symptoms like inflammation, irritation, swelling, itching, and red eyes occur by which it can be characterised. Virus and bacteria are the major causes of Conjunctivitis. However, there are some other factors like chemical and allergic

---

M. Adak and A. Chatterjee—Contributed equally.

M. Mahmud et al. (Eds.): AII 2022, CCIS 1724, pp. 205–218, 2022.
https://doi.org/10.1007/978-3-031-24801-6_15

infections which may trigger the level of discomfort. Viral type Conjunctivitis which transmits through tears and droplets is treated with steroid-based eye drops [4]. The use of antibiotics is a common practice to treat the bacterial type of it [9]. In some cases of allergic and chemical Conjunctivitis, cool compress and flushing with saline water may also give relief to the discomfort [2].

Interestingly, in some of the Covid-19 positive patients, the occurrence of the pink eye has been noticed [15]. A few studies claim that "Covid-19 may be detected in the tears and conjunctival secretions in novel coronavirus pneumonia patients with conjunctivitis" [13,23]. In a few asymptomatic cases, severe Covid-19 infections have been detected with only irritations in the eye, swollen and red eyes, and photophobia. A series of cases are reported where Conjunctivitis followed by transparent serous secretions were the only symptoms of coronavirus infection [13]. So during the coronavirus outbreak, ophthalmologists may play a vital role in indicating the Covid-19 infections if they work closely in proper clinical settings [7]. In some cases, Reverse Transcriptase Polymerase Chain Reaction (RT-PCR) testing on tears witnessed the presence of the novel coronavirus. Although the coronavirus infected patients generally show respiratory distress, a typical manifestation like Conjunctivitis may also be observed [11]. Another case history witnessed the presence of coronavirus in ocular fluids even after two weeks of the nasopharyngeal RT-PCR results were negative [5]. However, the virus transmission through ocular fluids remains unknown and more research needs to be carried out to confirm its ability to spread the disease through ocular fluids. Therefore, transmission through contact with conjunctiva is an important issue for consideration that needs to be explored [11,14].

Looking into the present scenario, preparing an AI based-user-friendly mobile or web application for initial screening is desirable. So, based on the facts gathered, we focused on developing an AI-based android application to detect Conjunctivitis in the human eye. The first version of the model named iConDet was released in 2021, where the presence of Conjunctivitis was detected through a mobile application [10]. iConDet was designed specifically as a useful solution to detect Conjunctivitis. It was done as a preliminary screening and preventive measure for the coronavirus disease. It was capable enough to perform necessary pre-processing on eye images captured through a mobile camera. The Efficient-Net was used as a background deep learning model for the purpose of binary classifications, which could only segregate healthy eyes from the infected eyes. Nevertheless, it could not detect the severity level of Conjunctivitis on a small dataset prepared by us. However, to improve the model's performance and face other relevant challenges, we release the new version of it as iConDet-V2. This new version comes with improved performance on a comparatively bigger dataset prepared by us. Here, the best suitable deep learning model, ResNet has been implemented for this purpose, among many other models. We gathered conjunctival images from different hospitals and prepared a dataset that consisted of 310 conjunctival images, out of which 280 images have been used for training and 30 for testing.

The following points describe the major contribution of the work:

– Creation and labelling a comparatively bigger dataset with healthy and infected eye images.
– Comparative study done among all best deep learning models and chosen the best suitable one with improved performance.
– Release of the new and improved version of the mobile application suitable for Andriod devices, *i*ConDet-V2.

The rest of the paper is organised as follows: the literature review is reported in Sect. 2. The methodology is defined in Sect. 3. Section 4 covers the results and discussions and Sect. 5 draws the final conclusion.

2   Related Work

Artificial intelligence has significant applications in facial and retinal recognition. Recently, an open-source computer vision library, OpenCV, has been widely used in this domain which has pre-trained classifiers that help in facial and eye recognition. Another classifier, named Haar Feature-based Cascading Classifier, is used to detect faces in a rectangular frame and extract eyes. For the use of the application, they have cropped the image using an open-source tool on Android known as Freehand Image Cropper. As the dataset was limited, deep learning models were not efficient enough to feed the classification models [21].

For the detection of the sclera region, Zhou et al. proposed a comprehensive sclera image quality measure that can detect if the eye image is valid [24]. Another group of researchers proposed a new method for vessel detection in the sclera by implementing the concept of frangi filter and wavelet transform [3]. They detected the sclera region based on the Otsus threshold method. A pattern stabilization method was presented by Kaya et al. that can be applied in laser eye surgery [6]. They extracted the features from the eye vessels of the sclera region, and an image processing algorithm was used to track the pattern in the patient's eye. During feature extraction, they applied SIFT algorithm to the whole image and selected the images' ROI. Authors Wu and Harada [22] presented algorithms that detect the blood vessels in the sclera part of the conjunctival eye. They used Otsu's method to build a pseudo vessel removal technique to remove the noise from the images. An automatic image processing method was designed to distinguish the conjunctival eye from the normal eye and classify it as either allergic, bacterial, or viral [17]. The system also analyses and classifies seven ocular diseases like trachoma, conjunctivitis, corneal ulcer, etc. [1]. The method automatically recognises the eye region from the facial components, and these features were applied in DCNN and SVM models. They have used the PCA and t-SNE for feature selection and is classified using the SVM model. Using the Computer-Aided System (CAD), some researchers applied deep learning algorithms for image processing, segmentation, and classification. In some cases, the fuzzy technique was also used for the image segmentation [16].

3   Methodology

3.1   Proposed Pipeline

This section covers the overall description of the system. The architecture is structured as follows:

- The user selects an eye image either using the camera feature or from the local storage (e.g., gallery) in the mobile application.
- The image is processed using the hand-eraser tool and the rectangular cropper to segment the irrelevant part of the eye image.
- The cropped image gets saved in the local storage, and the saved image is further selected to feed to the machine learning model that was trained on cropped eye images dataset.
- The model calculates the classification scores and displays the predicted eye label on the mobile application. Finally, all the previously saved images are automatically deleted from the local storage (Fig. 1).

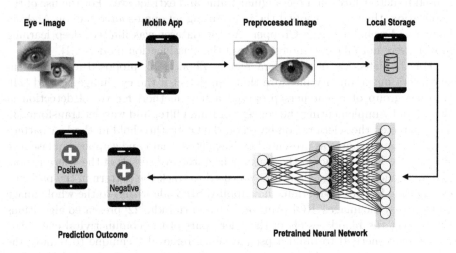

Fig. 1. The execution pipeline diagram for *i*ConDet - V2.

3.2   Image Pre-processing

Image pre-processing is an essential work here as the raw dataset carries a variety of eye images. Since the images were collected from different sources, there exists a non-uniformity in the raw image dataset. There is variety observed in the overall eye structures, iris structures and iris colours, etc. The size and resolution of the images significantly differ due to the non-uniform image capturing techniques. This is important at this stage to remove noise and convert the images to a uniform format using image processing techniques. The dataset size has increased in this version compared to the first release. Here, both the training and testing datasets have been prepared with the infected and healthy eye images. Here, an open-source cropping tool named "Freehand image cropper" is used to crop the training and testing dataset. This helps to remove the unwanted noise related to regions outside the eye (sclera) region. It doesn't carry many contributions to the decision-making process of the proposed model. The hand-cropper thus acts as a manual segmentation tool and helps to extract the relevant features from the eye images. Whereas, after deploying the model into the mobile application, the same task of manual segmentation is done together with a free-hand eraser and a rectangular cropper. The application's free-hand eraser feature helps draw the boundary around the eye (sclera). As the background outside the drawn boundary is cleared, the rectangular cropper is used to crop the former image and remove the cleared-background region. Finally, the images are converted into a fixed size of 224 × 224 to maintain uniformity in model training and testing. During model training, data augmentation is also used to increase the diversity of data, preventing the model from learning unnecessary features and helping to reduce overfitting. We use the following transformations in data augmentation:

- Random horizontal flip
- Random vertical flip
- Random rotation $[-360°, +360°]$

3.3 Machine Learning Model

Our approach includes both the transfer learning [3] and end-to-end training of deep learning models. In case of the end-to-end learning, we train a network on the data from scratch. On the other hand, transfer learning is the method where a model trained for one task can be re-used for other [18]. It can effectively perform in limited-data domains and save the computational overhead needed for training end-to-end. Generally, transfer learning can be used in 2 ways:

1. Feature Extraction: The base model's learned representation is used to extract features in the new target data. We generally remove the final layer and can add trainable layers on top of the base model. The base model's layers are frozen (no backpropagation), and only the top added layers are trained as per the new target data.
2. Fine Tuning: In fine-tuning, instead of freezing all the base model's layers, we train both the last few layers of the base model and the added top layers. This allows the model to capture the higher-order representations in that task.

The best suitable model used in our experimentation is described below:

ResNet. ResNet, also known as Residual Network, is a Convolutional Neural Network. The network was devised to solve the problem of any deep neural network vanishing or exploding gradients. ResNet counter this issue by providing skip connections. The model was trained on the ImageNet dataset. We have used ResNet18, ResNet34 and ResNet50, which are named after the number of layers or depth of the model. Irrespective of the base ResNet model variant, the final layer is modified by plugging four linear layers of sizes 256, 128, 64 and 3, respectively. The base ResNet model helps extract the information from the image and generalise using its previously acquired knowledge. The last 4 linear layers guide the model to make proper decisions regarding classification. The ultimate differentiator of ResNet is the residual block. The skip connection skips a few training layers and connects to the output layer.

The two types of residual blocks are as follows:

1. Identical residual block: The output and shortcut input sizes have the same dimension.
2. Convolutional residual block: The output and shortcut input sizes have different dimensions, and the shortcut layer applies different filter sizes and strides to match the output dimension.

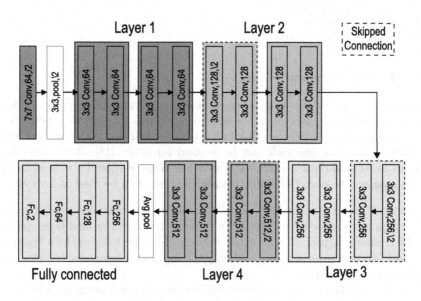

Fig. 2. The modified ResNet18 Architecture (Modified from [12]).

Table 1. ResNet model architecture with different depths 18, 34, 50

Layer	ResNet-18	ResNet-34	ResNet-50
Conv1	7×7, 64, stride 2		
Conv2_x	3×3 MaxPool, stride 2		
	$[3 \times 3, 64]$	$[3 \times 3, 64]$	$[1 \times 1, 64]$
	$\times 2$	$\times 3$	$[3 \times 3, 64] \times$ 3
	$[3 \times 3, 64]$	$[3 \times 3, 64]$	$[1 \times 1, 256]$
Conv3_x	$[3 \times 3, 128]$	$[3 \times 3, 128]$	$[1 \times 1, 128]$
	$\times 2$	$\times 4$	$[3 \times 3, 128] \times$ 4
	$[3 \times 3, 128]$	$[3 \times 3, 128]$	$[1 \times 1, 512]$
Conv4_x	$[3 \times 3, 256]$	$[3 \times 3, 256]$	$[1 \times 1, 256]$
	$\times 2$	$\times 6$	$[3 \times 3, 256] \times$ 6
	$[3 \times 3, 256]$	$[3 \times 3, 256]$	$[1 \times 1, 1024]$
Conv5_x	$[3 \times 3, 512]$	$[3 \times 3, 512]$	$[1 \times 1, 512]$
	$\times 2$	$\times 3$	$[3 \times 3, 512] \times$ 3
	$[3 \times 3, 512]$	$[3 \times 3, 512]$	$[1 \times 1, 2048]$
FC1	AveragePool, 256 - FC		
FC2	128 - FC		
FC3	64 - FC		
FC4	2 - FC		

3.4 Evaluation Metrics

We have chosen cross-entropy as the loss function for our classification task. The loss function works as follows:

$$l(x, y) = L = l_1, .. l_N^T$$

$$l_n = -log \frac{exp(x_n, y_n)}{\sum_{c=1}^{C} exp(x_n, c)}$$

$$l(x, y) = \frac{\sum_{n=1}^{N} l_n}{N}$$

where x is the input, y is the target, C is the number of classes, and N spans the batch dimension. The experiment uses Accuracy as a metric to track the performance of our models. Formally Accuracy is defined as,

$$Accuracy = \frac{Number\ of\ correct\ predictions}{Total\ number\ of\ predictions}$$

In the case of binary classification, this reduces as follows:

$$Accuracy = \frac{TP + TN}{TP + TN + FP + FN}$$

where TP = True Positives, TN = True Negatives, FP = False Positives, and FN = False Negatives.

The experiment uses the F1 score, also referred to as the balanced score or F-measure [8]. F1 score is defined as the harmonic mean of precision and recall. Its value ranges from 0 for the worst value to 1 for the best value.

$$F1 = 2 * \frac{(precision \ * \ recall)}{(precision \ + \ recall)}$$

Precision [8] is defined as the count of true positives over the sum of the count of true positives and false positives.

$$precision = \frac{TP}{(TP \ + \ FP)}$$

Recall [8] is defined as the count of true positives over the sum of true positives and false negatives.

$$recall = \frac{TP}{(TP \ + \ FN)}$$

where TP = True Positives, FP = False Positives, and FN = False Negatives.

4   Results and Discussion

4.1   Dataset Creation

Due to the lack of any open-source conjunctivitis dataset, we have built our own suitable one with some of the available images. Scarcity of segregation between healthy and infected eye images is observed on the internet. We have collected 310 healthy and infected eye images from different sources altogether. We have focused on keeping the right balance on the total number of images in each category (105 images for healthy and infected eye images). Most images of conjunctivitis-infected human eyes (both bacterial and viral) are collected from the internet. The rest of the images are collected from some known eye clinics. The collected images have to go through pre-processing at this stage as all of them are not uniform in nature. As the images are of different shapes and sizes, we removed the unnecessary portions outside the effective eye region. It is done to increase the performance of the model. We used a hand-cropper before assorting the cropped images into their respective healthy and infected folders. The data is further divided into training and testing data, containing 280 (140 infected-140 healthy split) and 30 (15 infected-15 healthy) images, respectively.

4.2   Experimentation

We have conducted our experiments on the local machine with the following configuration: Windows 10 Operating System, Intel(R) Core(TM) i7-9750H CPU @ 2.60 GHz, 2592 MHz, 6 Cores, 12 Processors, and Nvidia GPU @ 1660Ti. All the scripts for model development, data pre-processing, training, and testing are developed using Python (Version-3.8) language and the PyTorch framework. First, the raw datasets are pre-processed using a free-hand cropper tool to prepare the data for the model learning phase. The transformations mentioned in Sect. 3.3 are then applied to the eye images. Figure 3 shows the original eye images and transformed eye images for both of the categories: healthy and infected.

After pre-processing of the raw datasets, it is tested for the breadth of models and learning rate. We have used Adam optimiser for this task. The learning algorithm used the Stratified K-Fold cross-validation technique, providing approximately the same percentage of data for each of the target categories [20]. We used 10 folds cross-validation, and the training was done over 50 epochs. The loss and accuracy scores are tracked throughout the training phase. The curves (loss curve, accuracy curve) are plotted by averaging the scores in a particular epoch over all folds. The curves are saved for different models at different learning rates for better understanding and further comparisons. Finally, the mobile application is built on Android Studio. The development relied on XML for the front-end UI and Java for the backend.

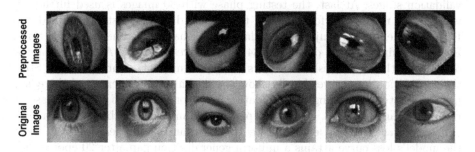

Fig. 3. The first row depicts the pre-processed images, and the second row depicts the original images. Labels 0 and 1 represent infected and healthy eyes, respectively.

Table 2. Optimiser parameters

Parameter	Value
Learning rate	0.01, 0.001, 0.0001
Momentum parameter	0.9
Propagation	0.99

4.3 Validation and Testing

The different models are trained for 50 epochs with 10 folds cross-validation learning. The loss and accuracy scores are collected throughout the learning

Table 3. A comparative study of Accuracy and Execution time among different experimented models.

Model	LR	Training			Validation			Testing			Ex. time (min)
		Acc	F1-S	ROC	Acc	F1-S	ROC	Acc	F1-S	ROC	
ResNet 18	1e–2	96.70	0.9669	0.9663	95.00	0.9523	0.9428	96.66	0.9677	0.99	112.99
ResNet 18	1e–3	96.58	0.9558	0.9943	95.00	0.9526	0.9801	100	1.00	1.00	103.46
ResNet 18	1e–4	94.76	0.9478	0.9863	94.28	0.9439	0.9918	96.66	0.9677	0.99	122.93
ResNet 34	1e–2	96.58	0.9658	0.9650	96.07	0.9596	0.9571	96.66	.9655	0.99	126.42
ResNet 34	1e–3	96.34	0.9634	0.9603	96.58	0.9606	0.9714	93.33	.9285	0.94	144.54
ResNet 34	1e–4	96.63	0.9664	0.9771	95.36	0.9550	0.9838	100	1.00	1.00	127.94
ResNet 50	1e–2	96.66	0.9667	0.9654	95.35	0.9537	0.9642	96.42	0.9677	0.99	143.27
ResNet 50	1e–3	96.58	0.9656	0.9634	96.07	0.9602	0.9642	93.33	0.9333	0.96	160.76
ResNet 50	1e–4	95.71	0.9573	0.9531	94.28	0.9423	0.9464	96.66	0.9677	0.99	134.35

Legend–LR: Learning Rate, Acc: Accuracy, F1-S: F1-Score, ROC: AUC-ROC, Ex. time (min): Execution time (min).

process. Graphs are plotted for each model tracking the loss and accuracy values for the 50 epochs averaged over the epochs in the respective training and validation stages. At last, the testing phase with 30 images is used further to validate the models' performance on the unseen dataset. First, we trained our ResNet model on the conjunctivitis dataset. We have experimented using three ResNet architectures of depth 18, 34, and 50, respectively. At learning rates of 1e–2, all the three ResNet variants display significant accuracy scores. Still, their validation loss curves hardly show any declining movement, and there is a huge gap between training and validation loss scores at epoch 1. In the case of training using ResNet18, the model performs comparatively better in training and testing accuracy at learning rate 1e-4 than at 1e-3. At learning rate 1e-4, the model's loss curve attains a uniform generalisation gap after 20 epochs and approximately 94% in both training and validation accuracy beyond 15 epochs. Moreover, the model curves (loss and accuracy) are comparatively more stable in this configuration than in the other learning rate settings. Secondly, in the case of ResNet34, the model performs better at a learning rate of 1e-4 than 1e-3. At 1e-4, the curve is more stable, whereas, at 1e-3, the model has more frequent perturbations in its curve. Lastly, in ResNet50, the model has better accuracy scores at learning rate 1e-3 but has more frequent perturbations. At 1e-4, the model curve looks more stable, and the generalisation gap is almost the same for both configurations. All of these three models do not have a stark difference in their accuracy scores or the curve pattern in a specific learning rate configuration.

Figure 4 depicts the training loss and accuracy curve of the ResNet 34 model in the 3 different learning rates. Figures (a) and (c) show that the model performs similarly in terms of accuracy in the 3 respective learning rates of 1e-2, 1e-3, and 1e-4. In the validation phase, the models seemed to show greater variance in the mean accuracy scores than in the training phase. Figure (b) depicts the training loss curve in the different learning rates. The model with a learning rate of 1e-2 has the lowest loss scores and lowest variance. And 1e-4 configuration has comparatively higher loss scores, and the 1e-3 configuration fits in-between the rest-two configurations. Figure (d) depicts the validation loss curve - the 1e-4 configuration has higher loss scores, and the other 2 configurations have comparatively lower and almost similar loss scores and curves.

Figure 5 depicts the accuracy and loss curves of the training and validation phase of the ResNet18 model variant. In Figure (a), we can see that both the training and validation phase has a similar curve and mean accuracy scores. However, the validation mean accuracy scores carry more variance than the training scores. In Figure (b), the validation loss scores are comparatively greater than training loss scores, and both the curves attain a generalisation gap after 20 epochs of learning.

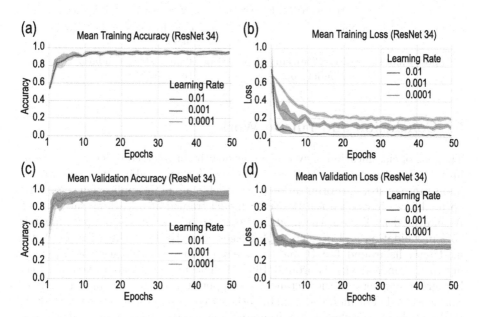

Fig. 4. The mean accuracy and loss for training and validation for the ResNet34 model. The shaded areas show the standard deviations of the values obtained during the 10-fold cross-validation.

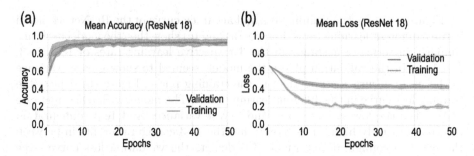

Fig. 5. The training and validation loss and accuracy curve for ResNet18 for a learning rate of 1e-4.

Table 4. A comparative study of the accuracy scores of models of existing works

Existing work	Model or concept used	Accuracy
[10]	EfficientNet	84%
[3]	Digital image processing	93%
[16]	DLCNN	Train - 95%, Test - 93%
[17]	Multiclass SVM, KCNN	SVM - 95%, KCNN - 85%
[19]	CNN	Healthy eye - 94.17%, Red-eye - 99.99%
Proposed model	ResNet-18 variant (deployed in the icondet app)	Train - 96%, Validation - 95%, Test - 97%

5 Conclusion and Future Work

The task of classification of eye images as healthy or infected is achieved successfully by our 3 experimental ResNet models. However, taking into account the importance of storage optimisation of a model in a mobile application to perform optimally, we have used the ResNet18 model trained at a learning rate of 1e-4. As indicated in Table 2, the model attains the best accuracy of approximately 95% in validation and predicts 97% images correctly in testing. The ResNet18 model weighs around 44 MB, and the size of the mobile application after deploying to a mobile device is around 165 MB. The integrated tool combining the background eraser and the rectangular cropper and the mobile application itself can be extended or modified in many other use-cases in future research work. In future work, we can devise an automated image segmentation algorithm to segment the eye from the rest of the background. Also, building a massive dataset might also help experiment with the deep-learning segmentation models that can successfully achieve this task. In addition, we would also like to explore the performance of a range of different models to build and present a more broad comparative study of the performance of these models in this specific problem.

The GitHub link for the repository is available at: https://github.com/braiacslab/incondet-v2.

References

1. Akram, A., Debnath, R.: An automated eye disease recognition system from visual content of facial images using machine learning techniques. Turk. J. Electr. Eng. Comput. Sci. **28**(2), 917–932 (2020)
2. Chen, X., Xu, Y., Wong, D.W.K., Wong, T.Y., Liu, J.: Glaucoma detection based on deep convolutional neural network. In: 2015 37th Annual International Conference of the IEEE Engineering in Medicine and Biology Society (EMBC), pp. 715–718. IEEE (2015)
3. Gunay, M., Goceri, E., Danisman, T.: Automated detection of adenoviral conjunctivitis disease from facial images using machine learning. In: 2015 IEEE 14th International Conference on Machine Learning and Applications (ICMLA), pp. 1204–1209. IEEE (2015)
4. Holland, E.J., Fingeret, M., Mah, F.S.: Use of topical steroids in conjunctivitis: a review of the evidence. Cornea **38**(8), 1062–1067 (2019)
5. Hu, Y., et al.: Positive detection of SARS-CoV-2 combined HSV1 and HHV6B virus nucleic acid in tear and conjunctival secretions of a non-conjunctivitis COVID-19 patient with obstruction of common lacrimal duct. Acta Ophthalmol. **98**(8), 859–863 (2020)
6. Kaya, A., Can, A.B., Çakmak, H.B.: Designing a pattern stabilization method using scleral blood vessels for laser eye surgery. In: 2010 20th International Conference on Pattern Recognition, pp. 698–701. IEEE (2010)
7. Lai, T.H.T., Tang, E.W.H., Chau, S.K.Y., Fung, K.S.C., Li, K.K.W.: Stepping up infection control measures in ophthalmology during the novel coronavirus outbreak: an experience from Hong Kong. Graefes Arch. Clin. Exp. Ophthalmol. **258**(5), 1049–1055 (2020). https://doi.org/10.1007/s00417-020-04641-8
8. Scikit learn: precision-recall (2022). https://scikit-learn.org/stable/auto_examples/model_selection/plot_precision_recall.html. Accessed 15 May 2022
9. Leung, A.K., Hon, K.L., Wong, A.H., Wong, A.S.: Bacterial conjunctivitis in childhood: etiology, clinical manifestations, diagnosis, and management. Recent Pat. Inflamm. Allergy Drug Discov. **12**(2), 120–127 (2018)
10. Mukherjee, P., Bhattacharyya, I., Mullick, M., Kumar, R., Roy, N.D., Mahmud, M.: *i*ConDet: an intelligent portable healthcare app for the detection of conjunctivitis. In: Mahmud, M., Kaiser, M.S., Kasabov, N., Iftekharuddin, K., Zhong, N. (eds.) AII 2021. CCIS, vol. 1435, pp. 29–42. Springer, Cham (2021). https://doi.org/10.1007/978-3-030-82269-9_3
11. Ozturker, Z.K.: Conjunctivitis as sole symptom of COVID-19: a case report and review of literature. Eur. J. Ophthalmol. **31**(2), NP145–NP150 (2021)
12. He, K., Zhang, X., Ren, S., Sun, J.: Deep residual learning for image recognition. In: Proceedings of the IEEE Conference on Computer Vision and Pattern Recognition, pp. 770–778 (2016)
13. Salducci, M., La Torre, G.: COVID-19 emergency in the cruise's ship: a case report of conjunctivitis. Clin. Ter. **171**(3), e189–e191 (2020)
14. Seah, I., Agrawal, R.: Can the coronavirus disease 2019 (COVID-19) affect the eyes? A review of coronaviruses and ocular implications in humans and animals. Ocul. Immunol. Inflamm. **28**(3), 391–395 (2020)
15. Soysa, A., De Silva, D.: A mobile base application for cataract and conjunctivitis detection. In: Proceedings of ICACT, pp. 76–78 (2020)
16. Sundararajan, S.K., et al.: Detection of conjunctivitis with deep learning algorithm in medical image processing. In: 2019 Third International Conference on I-SMAC (IoT in Social, Mobile, Analytics and Cloud) (I-SMAC), pp. 714–717. IEEE (2019)

17. Tamuli, J., Jain, A., Dhan, A.V., Bhan, A., Dutta, M.K.: An image processing based method to identify and grade conjunctivitis infected eye according to its types and intensity. In: 2015 Eighth International Conference on Contemporary Computing (IC3), pp. 88–92. IEEE (2015)

18. Torrey, L., et al. (eds.): Handbook of Research on Machine Learning Applications and Trends: Algorithms, Methods, and Techniques: Algorithms, Methods, and Techniques. IGI Global, Hershey, PA (2009)

19. Verma, S., Singh, L., Chaudhry, M.: Classifying red and healthy eyes using deep learning. Int. J. Adv. Comput. Sci. Appl. **10**(7), 525–531 (2019)

20. Versloot, C.: Machine learning articles (2022). https://github.com/christianverslo ot/machine-learning-articles/blob/3995782892d6f34b70c139265acdfa1c7b9ee07e/how-to-use-k-fold-cross-validation-with-pytorch.md

21. Viola, P., Jones, M.J.: Robust real-time face detection. Int. J. Comput. Vis. **57**(2), 137–154 (2004). https://doi.org/10.1023/B:VISI.0000013087.49260.fb

22. Wu, C., Harada, K., et al.: Study on digitization of TCM diagnosis applied extraction method of blood vessel. J. Signal Process. Syst. **2**(04), 301 (2011)

23. Xia, J., Tong, J., Liu, M., Shen, Y., Guo, D.: Evaluation of coronavirus in tears and conjunctival secretions of patients with SARS-CoV-2 infection. J. Med. Virol. **92**(6), 589–594 (2020)

24. Zhou, Z., Du, E.Y., Thomas, N.L., Delp, E.J.: A comprehensive approach for sclera image quality measure. Int. J. Biom. **5**(2), 181–198 (2013)

Ensemble Classifiers for a 4-Way Classification of Alzheimer's Disease

Noushath Shaffi[1]([✉])[iD], Faizal Hajamohideen[1][iD], Abdelhamid Abdesselam[2][iD], Mufti Mahmud[3,4][iD], and Karthikeyan Subramanian[1]

[1] Department of Information Technology, University of Technology
and Applied Sciences-Sohar, Sohar 311, Oman
{noushath.soh,faizalh.soh,karthikeyan.soh}@cas.edu.om
[2] Department of Computer Science, Sultan Qaboos University, Muscat 123, Oman
ahamid@squ.edu.om
[3] Department of Computer Science, Nottingham Trent University,
Nottingham NG11 8NS, UK
[4] CIRC and MTIF, Nottingham Trent University, Nottingham NG11 8NS, UK

Abstract. Machine Learning (ML) techniques remain a massively influential tool in the Computer-Aided Diagnosis (CAD) of several health applications. Mainly due to its ability to rapid learning of end-to-end models accurately using compound data. Recent years have seen an extensive application of Deep Learning (DL) models in solving the 4-way classification of Alzheimer's Disease (AD) and achieved good results too. However, traditional machine learning classifiers such as KNN, XGBoost, SVM, etc perform either the same or better than the DL models and usually require less data for training. This property is very useful when it comes to medical applications which is characterized by unavailability of large labelled datasets. In this paper, we demonstrate the application of state-of-the-art ML classifiers in the 4-way classification of AD using the OASIS dataset. Furthermore, an ensemble classifier model is proposed based on ML models. The proposed ensemble classifier achieved an accuracy of 94.92% which is approximately 5% accuracy increase compared to individual classifier approach. The source code used in this work are publicly available at: https://github.com/snoushath/AII2022.git

Keywords: Alzheimer's Disease · Machine Learning · Ensemble Classifier · XGBoost · K-Nearest Neighbor · Support Vector Machine · Random Forest

1 Introduction

Alzheimer's Disease (AD) is an incurable, life-altering, and progressive neuro-degenerative disease. AD is characterised by the gradual degradation of protein

This work is funded by the Ministry of Higher Education, Research and Innovation (MoHERI) of the sultanate of Oman under the Block Funding Program (Grant number-MoHERI/BFP/UoTAS/01/2021).

M. Mahmud et al. (Eds.): AII 2022, CCIS 1724, pp. 219–230, 2022.
https://doi.org/10.1007/978-3-031-24801-6_16

components in the brain cells known as plaques and tangles. Such disruption in the protein component communication will lead to a significant decline in cognitive abilities which in turn can severely impair an individual's personal and social life [7,22]. Mild Cognitive Impairment (MCI) is a phase where patients will be in a transition from a Cognitively Normal (CN) state to a dementia state (also known as major neuro-cognitive disorder [7]) that has a 10% conversion rate to AD. According to the latest World Alzheimer's report [7], 55 million people worldwide are diagnosed with this deadly disease with innumerable cases unaccounted for due to a lack of awareness about AD. The report also quotes that AD is the seventh leading cause of death worldwide.

An array of discomforts will afflict the individuals wherein patients will have memory discomposure, behavioural disorderliness, and various other physical issues causing vision and mobility complications. The main roadblock to the early detection of AD is that the general public is not knowledgeable about this disease. As a consequence, progressive cognitive decline and associated behavioural changes are often thought of as phenomena associated with the normal ageing process or mistaken for other psychiatric disorders. Furthermore, factors such as remote locations, shortage of trained caregivers, inaccessibility to specialists, and non-availability of expert diagnostic tools will add more to the suffering of patients [7]. These will manifest into compound suffering to the extent of interfering with an individual's autonomy in daily and social life activities. Hence it is imperative to detect AD at an early stage so that the suffering of the patient and care-giving family can be curtailed to a greater extent.

AD is diagnosed mainly by observation of patients' symptoms and sometimes it usually takes years to perceive the existence of the disease. However, advancements in diagnostic research have led to the discovery of several biomarkers (MRI, PET, CT, blood tests, etc.) that assist in the early prediction of AD. These biomarkers when coupled with AI technologies can assist doctors in the accurate diagnosis and subsequent patient care. Machine learning (ML) classifiers have encompassed many healthcare sectors and have been found to be very effective in AD classification [3,20,27]. In the recent past, there has been a propensity of applying deep learning (DL) algorithms for every single application and they have performed well too [19]. However, for the data-scarce situation such as the classification of AD, the DL algorithms may not yield satisfactory results and simple ML algorithms may outperform the DL models.

In this paper, we investigate the use of state-of-the-art (SOTA) ML classifiers for the classification of AD and provide substantiating result analysis. We use MRI as a biomarker from the Open Access Series of Imaging Studies (OASIS) dataset [17]. Furthermore, an ensemble classifier model is proposed using the max voting and probability based fusion approach which resulted in a best accuracy of 94.92% on the OASIS dataset.

The remainder of this paper is organised as follows. Section 2 provides the review of related literature, Sect. 3 provides the proposed methodology, and Sect. 4 presents the experimental results followed by conclusion and future work in Sect. 5.

2   Related Literature

The ML techniques have been widely used in medical applications and have shown significant success in the detection and diagnosis of different diseases. The AD studies are mostly conducted as a classification task to identify the disease status: MCI, stable MCI (sMCI), progress to AD (pMCI), and Vascular Dementia (VD) or distinguish CN from AD cases. This type of techniques requires labelled datasets. The most commonly-used neuroimaging datasets in AD studies are Alzheimer Disease Neuroimaging Initiative (ADNI, https://adni.loni.usc.edu/) that includes MRI and PET images along with several other biomarkers. Two other datasets have also been used for AD studies, these are the Open Access Series of Imaging Studies (OASIS) (www.oasis-brains.org), developed by Marcus et al. [17], and the Australian Imaging Biomarkers and Lifestyle Flagship Study of Imaging (AIBL. https://aibl.csiro.au/) developed by Ellis et al. [6]. Recent methods for classifying AD images can be categorised into three main groups, Artificial Neural Network (ANN) models, DL methods, and traditional ML techniques. In this paper we focus on five traditional ML techniques that have been extensively used for the detection and classification of AD; these are K-Nearest Neighbours (KNN), Support Vector Machine (SVM), Random Forest (RF), XGBoost and some other ensemble methods. An exhaustive list of methods are described in the following surveys [3,20,27].

KNN. Several works on AD classification using kNN have been reported in the literature. Acharya et al. [1] developed a Computer-Aided-Brain-Diagnosis system that can determine if a brain scan shows signs of AD using the k-NN classifier. They tested various feature extraction techniques on 66 2D MRI images collected from University Malaya, and the Harvard Brain Atlas. They found that the Shearlet Transform (ST) feature extraction technique offers better performance for AD and reported an average accuracy of 94.54%, and a precision, sensitivity and specificity of 88.33%, 96.30% and 93.64% respectively. Kamathe RS and Joshi KR [11] developed Computer Aided Diagnosis tool for Alzheimer's disease detection and classification into MCI and AD. A set of Gray Level Co-occurrence Matrix (GLCM) features are extracted and underwent a feature selection process combining forward selection and/or backward elimination method. Selected features are fed to kNN model to perform the classification. They tested their model on the OASIS dataset and reported the following accuracies 92.31%, 92.75%, and 83.33% for AD vs. MCI, AD vs. CN, and MCI vs. CN respectively. Kruthika et al. [16] proposed a multistage classifier consisting of Naive Bayes classifier, SVM, and kNN using MRI images of three classes obtained from ADNI (AD = 178, MCI = 160, and CN = 137). The images were processed and normalized by FreeSurfer software and particle swarm optimization (PSO) was used as a feature selection method. The Gaussian Naive Bayes Classifier was trained as a binary classifier (for detection of AD, MCI and CN), the SVM classifier was trained as a binary classifier (for classification of MCI or CN), while the kNN classifier was trained as a multiclass classifier (AD, MCI and CN). The authors reported the following performance results 96.31 ± 1.22, 91.27 ± 1.44, 89.90 ± 1.14, and 96.05 ± 1.21 for accuracy, sensitivity, specificity and precision, respectively.

SVM. SVM is probably the most used method for AD classification, Khedher et al. [12] applied independent component analysis (ICA) on 818 MRI images (CN = 229, MCI = 401, AD = 188) extracted from the ADNI dataset (to extract the most discriminant features from MRI brain images and used SVM to perform three types of binary classification. They reported the following classification accuracies of 89% (CN vs AD), 79% (CN vs MCI), and 85% (MCI vs AD). Lin et al. [18] used a dictionary learning-based technique and SVM to predict the progression of MCI to AD in ADNI MRI images (pMCI = 40 and sMCI = 124). Dictionary bases were learned for pMCI and sMCI categories. Then, each patch in the training set was classified as a severe atrophy patch (SAP) or a common atrophy patch (CAP) by solving an objective function using DL-COPAR method [14]. The, features are then calculated as the proportion of the patches classified as SAP in the training set for each patient and are fed into the SVM for the final classification. The authors reported an accuracy of 97.3%. Zeng et al. [30] proposed a technique that optimizes the parameters of SVM for several binary classifications using ADNI MRI images (CN = 92, AD = 92, sMCI = 82, pMCI = 95). The optimization technique is based on switching delayed particle swarm optimization (SDPSO). The authors reported the following accuracies 69% (sMCI vs. pMCI), 81% (CN vs. AD), 76% (CN vs. sMCI), 85% (CN vs. pMCI), 71% (sMCI vs. AD) and 0.57 (pMCI vs. AD).

Random Forest. Alickovic and Subasi [2] used a histogram to represent useful features extracted from ADNI brain images (CN = 195, AD = 72). Several classifiers (SVM, MLP, KNN, RF, Naïve Bayes, Logistic regression, and Decision Tree) were applied to the produced histogram; the authors reported that RF provided the highest classification accuracy rate (85%). Bloch and Friedrich [4] combined MRI images from ADNI (513 subjects: sMCI = 340, pMCI = 173) and AIBL (22 subjects). They studied the use of volumetric measurements extracted from MRI scans to predict the future conversion of patients with MCI to patients with AD. They used RF with 25-fold bootsrapping for classification and applied minority over-sampling technique to compensate class imbalances. Their results show that RF classification achieves a better performance when a combined dataset is used compared with using a single dataset. The reported results for the best scenario are as follows 75.49, 80.52%, and 60%, for accuracy, specificity and sensitivity respectively. Gray et al. [8] proposed a multi-modality classification framework in which manifolds are constructed based on pairwise similarity measures derived from RF classifiers. Similarities from multiple modalities (MRI, PET, CSF and categorical genetic information) extracted from ADNI dataset are combined to generate an embedding that simultaneously encodes information about all the available features. A total of 147 images (AD = 37, pMCI = 34, sMCI, = 41 and CN = 35) were used. Classification based on the joint embedding constructed from all four modalities out-performs the classification based on any individual modality. The authors reported the following accuracy, sensitivity and specificity results: for CN vs AD classification, 89%, 87.9% and 90%. For CN vs. MCI classification, 75%, 77.5%, and 67.9%, and for pMCI vs. sMCI, 58%, 57.1%, and 58.7%.

XGBoost. The work done by Rye et al. [23] is among the few works using XGBoost for AD classification. The proposed method applies gradient boosting to evaluate variable importance from the independent variables and then generates derived variables. The top-N groups (for various values of N) resulting from an importance variable analysis are identified. For each group, a hyperparameter tuning is conducted leading to optimized groups. The performance of the XGBoost model based classifier on each group is recorded. The authors reported that Top-20 model showed the best performance with an accuracy of 85.61%, and an F1-score of 79.28%. Harsimran Guram and Ashok Sharma [9] proposed a method that combines an attention-based transfer learning for feature extraction and XGBoost model for classification and applied it to fMRI data obtained from the ADNI database. Their experiments showed, that the proposed method outperformed a 4-layer hand-crafted CNN model, the hand-crafted CNN with attention layer and the pre-trained ResNet50 in four metrics (accuracy, precision, recall and F-score). The model achieved 94.6% recall rate and was better than the closest method (pre-trained ResNet) by about 4% in all performance metrics.

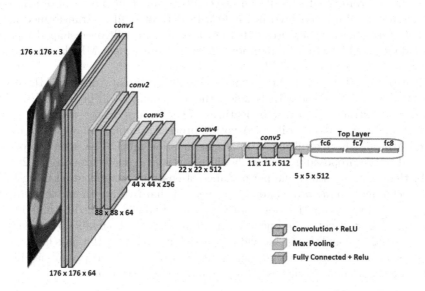

Fig. 1. The VGG16 architecture used as feature extractor (without the top layer)

3   Proposed Methodology

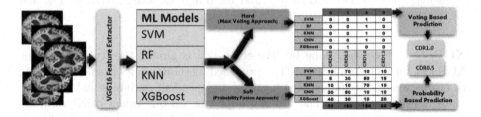

Fig. 2. The ensemble of machine learning classifiers

3.1   ML Based Ensemble Classifier

The VGG16 model [26] has been successfully applied in solving health-sector problems [25]. Motivated by its demonstrated success, we have used it as a feature extractor. This will help to remove linear dependency in the input and keep only features that are not correlated which eventually helps to enhance the subsequent classifier's performance. The architecture of the VGG16 model is as shown in Fig. 1. The top layer constituting 3 fully connected layers will be removed. From this figure, it can be seen that the input image of dimension $176 \times 176 \times 3$ (dimension used in the OASIS dataset) will be transformed into a $5 \times 5 \times 512$ block of features. This block of feature will be reshaped into a single dimensional vector of dimension 12800. All subsequent ML classifiers will receive feature vectors in $\mathbb{R}^{12800}$.

The proposed approach of ensemble classifiers employs distinct ML algorithms. Prior to using the ML classifiers the MRI images will be fed to VGG16 network to extract 1D vector of features. This feature vector will then pass through individual ML classifiers. A voting process is applied to output of individual ML classifiers resulting in final classification label. The overall process involved in the proposed ensemble classification is explained through Fig. 2.

In this work, we study the performance of ensemble classification using two basic techniques: *hard-voting* and *soft-voting*. The hard-voting ensemble predicts the final label by taking the mode of the predicted labels obtained by individual classifiers. The soft-voting on the other hand predicts the final label by summing the predicted probabilities by individual classifiers and taking the class label with largest sum of probability value. Let K be the number of individual classifiers and C be the number of classes ($C = 4$ in our AD classification).

Hard-Voting or Max Voting Approach. Let $e^j = (e_1^j, e_2^j, \cdots, e_k^j)$ be a vector consisting classification labels from each of the K classifiers for the jth

test sample. Here, e_k^j represents the label obtained by k^{th} classifier. The final classification label l^j is determined as follows:

$$l^j = mode(e_1^j, e_2^j, \cdots, e_k^j) \tag{1}$$

Soft-Voting or Probability Based Approach. Let the probabilities of individual classifiers assigned to C classes for a jth sample are:

$$\Omega^{kj} = (\beta_1^{kj}, \beta_2^{kj}, \cdots, \beta_C^{kj}) \tag{2}$$

Here, β_i^{kj} indicates the probability of class i (where $i = 1, 2, \cdots, C$) by the classifier k (where $k = 1, 2, \cdots, K$) for the jth sample.

When the probability output for C classes by K classifiers have been calculated for the jth sample, the final prediction label l^j is determined by probability based fusion method as follows:

$$l^j = argmax(\sum_{k=1}^{K} \beta_1^{kj}, \sum_{k=1}^{K} \beta_2^{kj}, \cdots, \sum_{k=1}^{K} \beta_C^{kj}) \tag{3}$$

3.2 Experimentation

MRI Data. We present here a series of experiments with appropriate analysis to corroborate the efficacy of SOTA ML algorithms and in specific our proposed ML based ensemble classifier approach. We used the widely-preferred OASIS dataset [17] for our experimentation. The dataset is divided into 4 classes based on the Clinical Dementia Rating (CDR) score. The CDR score of 0 indicates *No Dementia*, 0.5 indicates *Very Mild Dementia*, 1.0 indicates *Mild-Dementia*, and 2.0 indicates *Moderate AD*. The number of samples in CDR-0, CDR-0.5, CDR-1.0, and CDR-2.0 are respectively, 3200, 2240, 896, and 64 images. The dimension of each sample is 176×176 and it was converted to 3D space for compatibility with VGG16 feature extractor. Images from each class are augmented and number of samples in train and test samples are respectively 8192 and 2560.

Performance Metrics. We used 3 different performance metrics useful in the medical test analysis [10]: *Accuracy*, *Sensitivity*, and *Specificity*. Accuracy refers to the fraction of correctly classified samples over all samples. Sensitivity (or recall) counts how often a test rightly predicts a positive result for people who have the condition that's being tested for. This is also known as the *true positive rate (TPR)*. This measure also helps to discover the *false negative rate (FNR)* as 1-sensitivity. Specificity counts a test's ability to rightly generate a negative result for people who don't have the condition that's being tested for (also known as the *true negative rate (TNR)*). This measure also helps to discover the *false positive rate (FPR)* as 1-specificity. All reported values are average obtained with the one vs. all strategy.

Implementation. The implementation of ML models was done using the *Scikit-learn* open source package [21] in Python 3.7. The overall performance evalaluation was done on a standalone local machine equipped with Intel's i7 1.6 GHz CPU with 16 GB RAM. This was further complemented with a NVidia GeForceMX330 GPU.

4   Results and Discussion

4.1   Individual Classifier Performance

Firstly, we report the performance of SOTA ML classifiers on the OASIS dataset. The results of which are tabulated in Table 1.

Table 1. Performance evaluation of various methods.

Methods	Sensitivity (TPR)	Specificity (TNR)	1-Sensitivity (FNR)	1-Specificity (FPR)	Accuracy	Time (in mins)
KNN	0.913	0.970	0.086	0.029	0.912	3.051
Random Forest	0.950	0.853	0.146	0.049	0.853	3.142
SVM	0.963	0.891	0.108	0.039	0.890	3.215
XGBoost	0.917	0.972	0.082	0.021	0.916	8.461

Some important observation from this experiment are:

1. The KNN is a better-performing algorithm in terms of both time and accuracy. This is because the KNN algorithm is known to perform well when the number of training samples and dimension of the feature is on par with each other [13]. However, the value of K and distance metric should be wisely selected which has consequential effect on the overall performance. In addition, KNN is computationally intensive when sample size become sufficiently large [29].
2. Although the XGBoost performance metrics are marginally better than KNN, this algorithm is very slow. This is because XGboost uses regression trees which will be equal to number of classes. So it builds as many trees as number of classes in our problem per every iteration. Hence, the running time of this algorithm scales quadratically with number of classes.
3. The performance of the Random Forest algorithms is not as expected. This may be due to high-sparseness in the image data which will lead to formation of highly correlated decision trees in the bootstrap data aggregation step of this algorithm [15].
4. Although SVM is known to perform robustly even for problems that has non-linear decision boundaries, it resulted in a below-par performance in our study. For SVM to perform well, one must be well versed in selection of kernel functionalities and do optimal parameter selection [5]. Furthermore, SVM is not a good choice of algorithm in real time as it will have large number of training samples [28].

4.2   Ensemble Classifier Performance

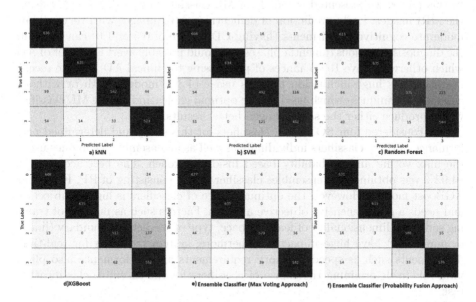

Fig. 3. Confusion Matrices: a) KNN (accuracy = 91.25% b) SVM (accuracy = 89.02% c) Random Forest (accuracy = 85.31%) d) XGBoost (accuracy = 91.67%) e) Max-Voting Ensemble (accuracy = 92.22%) f) Probability Fusion Ensemble (accuracy = 94.92%)

In this section, we present the results of ML based ensemble classifier approach. We considered the top two performing models (KNN and XGBoost) from the previous experiments to determine the efficacy of the ensemble approach. The accuracy and classification performance of individual models as well as ensemble classifiers are shown in Fig. 3. Two main things can be observed from this experiment:

1. The hard ensemble classifier based on majority voting approach produced only incremental performance than the individual classifiers. This approach uses labels that appeared most among the classifiers and disregards completely the magnitude of corresponding class probability. That means if two incertitude classifiers wrongly votes for a class, that will be considered instead of one strong classifier that indeed rightly votes.
2. As can be seen that, the performance of the ensemble approach based on probability values (soft voting) performed superior when compared with rest of the models. Since this approach combines the class probability values from different classifiers, the margin of error will be less even in the presence of incertitude classifiers.

5   Conclusion and Future Work

In this paper, we presented ensemble of ML classifiers to predict the AD using the MRI images. Early prediction of dementia in MRI images with very mild or moderate cognitive impairments (having CDR score of 0.5 or 1.0) can assist in the diagnosis of various dimentia phases and could possibly avert the onset of AD which otherwize have 10% chances of progressing to clinical AD [7]. The recent literature has huge inclination towards usage of DL models (with or without ensemble techniques) which need not be optimal choice and simple ML classifier would produce either the same or even better results.

We considered four SOTA ML classifiers for this study and determined performance of these classifiers individually as well as an ensemble techniques using the max voting and probability based fusion approach. The best accuracy of 94.92% was obtained for ensembles classifier model consisting of RF, KNN and XGBoost models. However, the optimal choice of classifiers is highly subjective and needs a comprehensive objective analysis. Factors such as number of training samples, dimensionality of feature space, type of prediction boundary (linear or non-linear) have huge impact. Furthermore, system requisites for real-time deployments such as speed, memory requirements and performance also plays vital role in determining the choice of classifiers for the ensemble classification task.

This leads to below mentioned avenues which deserve a meticulous independent study:

1. It would be interesting to see the performance of XGBoost with reduced feature dimension (through the application transformations such as subspace methods, DCT, etc.) which would remove correlated or rank correlated features. This will improve not only the training time but also enhance the model performance.
2. After this work, a natural extension would be to observe ensemble performance using advanced ensemble techniques such as Weighted Average Ensemble (blending), Stacked Generalization (stacking), etc. [24].
3. The ADNI dataset could be utilised and MRI images from different planes (sagittal or axial) could be considered to see the applicability of the proposed model.

Our goal of figuring out a simple yet robust model for AD classification task resulted in an accuracy that is on par or better than the DL models reported in the literature. Hence we can conclude that the ML classifier using ensemble model is relatively a simple approach yet yields robust solutions.

References

1. Acharya, U.R., et al.: Automated detection of Alzheimer's disease using brain MRI images–a study with various feature extraction techniques. J. Med. Syst. **43**(9), 1–14 (2019). https://doi.org/10.1007/s10916-019-1428-9

2. Alickovic, E., Subasi, A.: Automatic detection of Alzheimer disease based on histogram and random forest. In: Badnjevic, A., Škrbić, R., Gurbeta Pokvić, L. (eds.) CMBEBIH 2019. IP, vol. 73, pp. 91–96. Springer, Cham (2020). https://doi.org/10.1007/978-3-030-17971-7_14

3. Bhatele, K.R., Bhadauria, S.S.: Brain structural disorders detection and classification approaches: a review. Artif. Intell. Rev. **53**(5), 3349–3401 (2019). https://doi.org/10.1007/s10462-019-09766-9

4. Bloch, L., Friedrich, C.M.: Classification of Alzheimer's disease using volumetric features of multiple MRI scans. In: 2019 41st Annual International Conference of the IEEE Engineering in Medicine and Biology Society (EMBC), pp. 2396–2401. IEEE (2019)

5. Chandra, M.A., Bedi, S.S.: Survey on SVM and their application in image classification. Int. J. Inf. Technol. **13**(5), 1–11 (2018). https://doi.org/10.1007/s41870-017-0080-1

6. Ellis, K.A., et al.: The Australian Imaging, Biomarkers and Lifestyle (AIBL) study of aging: methodology and baseline characteristics of 1112 individuals recruited for a longitudinal study of Alzheimer's disease. Int. Psychogeriatr. **21**(4), 672–687 (2009)

7. Gauthier, S., Webster, C., Sarvaes, S., Morais, J.A., Rosa-Neto, P.: World Alzheimer report 2022: life after diagnosis - navigating treatment, care and support. Alzheimer's Dis. Int. (2022)

8. Gray, K.R., et al.: Random forest-based similarity measures for multi-modal classification of Alzheimer's disease. Neuroimage **65**, 167–175 (2013)

9. Guram, M.H., et al.: Improved demntia images detection and classification using transfer learning base convulation mapping with attention layer and XGBOOST classifier. Turk. J. Comput. Math. Educ. **12**(6), 217–224 (2021)

10. Hicks, S.A., et al.: On evaluation metrics for medical applications of artificial intelligence. Sci. Rep. **12**(1), 1–9 (2022)

11. Kamathe, R.S., Joshi, K.R.: A robust optimized feature set based automatic classification of Alzheimer's disease from brain MR images using K-NN and AdaBoost. ICTACT J. Image Video Process. **8**(3), 1665–1672 (2018)

12. Khedher, L., Illán, I.A., Górriz, J.M., Ramírez, J., Brahim, A., Meyer-Baese, A.: Independent component analysis-support vector machine-based computer-aided diagnosis system for Alzheimer's with visual support. Int. J. Neural Syst. **27**(03), 1650050 (2017)

13. Kim, J., Kim, B., Savarese, S.: Comparing image classification methods: K-nearest-neighbor and support-vector-machines. In: Proceedings of the 6th WSEAS International Conference on Computer Engineering and Applications, and Proceedings of the 2012 American Conference on Applied Mathematics, vol. 1001, pp. 48109–2122 (2012)

14. Kong, S., Wang, D.: A dictionary learning approach for classification: separating the particularity and the commonality. In: Fitzgibbon, A., Lazebnik, S., Perona, P., Sato, Y., Schmid, C. (eds.) ECCV 2012. LNCS, vol. 7572, pp. 186–199. Springer, Heidelberg (2012). https://doi.org/10.1007/978-3-642-33718-5_14

15. Konukoglu, E., Glocker, B.: Random forests in medical image computing. In: Handbook of Medical Image Computing and Computer Assisted Intervention, pp. 457–480. Elsevier (2020)

16. Kruthika, K., Maheshappa, H., Initiative, A.D.N., et al.: Multistage classifier-based approach for Alzheimer's disease prediction and retrieval. Inform. Med. Unlocked **14**, 34–42 (2019)

17. LaMontagne, P.J., et al.: OASIS-3: longitudinal neuroimaging, clinical, and cognitive dataset for normal aging and Alzheimer disease. medRxiv (2019). https://doi.org/10.1101/2019.12.13.19014902

18. Lin, Y., et al.: Predicting the progression of mild cognitive impairment to Alzheimer's disease by longitudinal magnetic resonance imaging-based dictionary learning. Clin. Neurophysiol. **131**(10), 2429–2439 (2020)

19. Loddo, A., Buttau, S., Di Ruberto, C.: Deep learning based pipelines for Alzheimer's disease diagnosis: a comparative study and a novel deep-ensemble method. Comput. Biol. Med. **141**, 105032 (2022)

20. Mirzaei, G., Adeli, H.: Machine learning techniques for diagnosis of Alzheimer disease, mild cognitive disorder, and other types of dementia. Biomed. Signal Process. Control **72**, 103293 (2022)

21. Pedregosa, F., et al.: Scikit-learn: machine learning in python. J. Mach. Learn. Res. **12**(85), 2825–2830 (2011). http://jmlr.org/papers/v12/pedregosa11a.html

22. Rizzi, L., Rosset, I., Roriz-Cruz, M.: Global epidemiology of dementia: Alzheimer's and vascular types. Biomed. Res. Int. **2014**, 908915 (2014)

23. Ryu, S.E., Shin, D.H., Chung, K.: Prediction model of dementia risk based on XGBoost using derived variable extraction and hyper parameter optimization. IEEE Access **8**, 177708–177720 (2020)

24. Sewell, M.: Ensemble learning. RN **11**(02), 1–34 (2008)

25. Shorfuzzaman, M., Hossain, M.S.: MetaCOVID: a Siamese neural network framework with contrastive loss for n-shot diagnosis of COVID-19 patients. Pattern Recogn. **113**, 107700 (2021)

26. Simonyan, K., Zisserman, A.: Very deep convolutional networks for large-scale image recognition. arXiv preprint arXiv:1409.1556 (2014)

27. Tanveer, M., et al.: Machine learning techniques for the diagnosis of Alzheimer's disease: a review. ACM Trans. Multimed. Comput. Commun. Appl. **16**(1s), 1–35 (2020)

28. Tomar, D., Agarwal, S.: A comparison on multi-class classification methods based on least squares twin support vector machine. Knowl.-Based Syst. **81**, 131–147 (2015)

29. Uddin, S., Haque, I., Lu, H., Moni, M.A., Gide, E.: Comparative performance analysis of K-nearest neighbour (KNN) algorithm and its different variants for disease prediction. Sci. Rep. **12**(1), 1–11 (2022)

30. Zeng, N., Qiu, H., Wang, Z., Liu, W., Zhang, H., Li, Y.: A new switching-delayed-PSO-based optimized SVM algorithm for diagnosis of Alzheimer's disease. Neurocomputing **320**, 195–202 (2018)

Identification of Crown and Rump in First-Trimester Ultrasound Images Using Deep Convolutional Neural Network

Samuel Sutton[1], Mufti Mahmud[1,2,3](✉), Rishi Singh[4], and Luis Yovera[5]

[1] Department of Computer Science, Nottingham Trent University, Clifton, Nottingham NG11 8NS, UK
mufti.mahmud@ntu.ac.uk, muftimahmud@gmail.com
[2] Medical Technologies Innovation Facility, Nottingham Trent University, Clifton, Nottingham NG11 8NS, UK
[3] Computing and Informatics Research Center, Nottingham Trent University, Clifton, Nottingham NG11 8NS, UK
[4] Stevens Institute of Technology, Hoboken, NJ 07030, USA
[5] Kypros Nicholaides Fetal Medicine Centre, Southend University Hospital, Westcliff-on-Sea, Essex SS0 0RY, UK

Abstract. First-Trimester Ultrasound scans provide invaluable insight into early pregnancies. The scan is used to estimate the gestational age by providing a measurement of the Crown to Rump Length (CRL), it is a crucial scan as it informs obstetric practitioners of the optimal timing for any necessary interventions at the earliest point. Inter-observer variation creates problems for Obstetric Practitioners as any variation in the measurement of the CRL can carry complications to the fetus' health. Existing machine learning systems to solve this problem are limited; this work details the creation of a machine learning pipeline that implements three Convolutional Neural Networks models (CNNs) to help identify the Crown and Rump regions in First-Trimester Ultrasound Images. The system segments the fetus in the image using a U-Net Model. The segmented image is then subject to an image classification model that implements a pre-trained CNN model, namely, VGG-16. This model is used to classify the segmented images into 'Good' and 'Bad'. Finally, the segmented images are entered into a pre-trained ResNet34 model that identifies the Crown and Rump regions. This can be used by obstetric practitioners to provide an accurate CRL of the fetus and to comment on the actual development of the fetus from the First-trimester Ultrasound images. The system will mitigate issues with the estimation of the gestational age and reduce the inter-observer variations.

Keywords: Convolutional neural network · Machine learning · Fetal ultrasound imaging · Image segmentation · Crown to rump length · Medical imaging · Transfer learning

M. Mahmud et al. (Eds.): AII 2022, CCIS 1724, pp. 231–247, 2022.
https://doi.org/10.1007/978-3-031-24801-6_17

1   Introduction

Machine Learning (ML) has been utilised to create effective solutions across many disciplines and problems. The capability that Machine Learning, particularly Deep Learning, holds is crucial to the future of the medical industry. A Convolutional Neural Network (CNN) is a Deep Learning method that has been implemented successfully in various medical imaging as it automatically detects features in an image without human supervision [8]. Successful CNN Models used for image segmentation and disease classification have been achieved in MRI and CT Scans of the Brain, Lung and Liver [10,15,30,40,44]. CNNs have been applied successfully for ultrasound images to inform better decisions, an example of this is in the classification of thyroid and breast diseases in ultrasound images [45]. Despite this, the use of Machine Learning in Fetal Ultrasound Imaging is limited.

The First-Trimester Ultrasound Scan, which is offered during the 11 − 13 + 6 week period, is the earliest and most appropriate time to assign a gestational age of the fetus and to confirm the validity of the pregnancy. Correct assignment of the gestational age ensures that practitioners can choose the optimal timing of any necessary interventions [13]. The Crown-to-Rump (CRL) Length is used as it is the most reliable metric to measure the gestational age during early pregnancy [37]. Additionally in a study, the Crown-to-Rump Length is the 'best fetal parameter' to estimate the gestational age of a fetus during the First-Trimester (11 − 13 + 6-week) Ultrasound Scan [26] when compared with other metrics. The Crown-to-Rump length requires the Crown and Rump of the fetus to be identified, an issue that arises whilst taking these measurements is inter-observer variation. Variations in the measurement of the CRL can risk serious complications of the pregnancy, including miscarriage, as the detection of major aneuploidies can only be achieved if the gestational age is accurate [2].

A study conducted in 2012 showed that 95% of cases had within 5mm or 2.5 days of gestation between two CRL measurements [25]. This demonstrates that a small under or over-estimation in the CRL measurement can impact the associated risks of a fetus by under or over-estimating potential risks. This study highlights the challenge that Obstetric Practitioners face and the importance of a reliable and accurate Machine Learning System to complete measurements of the CRL.

This investigation aims to develop an ML system to reduce the effects of inter-observer variation during First-Trimester Ultrasound scans. The system implements three ML models into an ML pipeline to successfully identify the Crown and Rump regions in First-Trimester Ultrasound scans. These models include an image segmentation model and a transfer learning approach using VGG-16 and ResNet34 architectures.

The main contributions of the work includes:

1. Creation of a machine learning pipeline existing of three models.
2. Utilisation of a U-Net image segmentation model adapted for first-trimester fetal ultrasound images.

3. Creation of an image classification model to classify fetal ultrasound images into Good or Bad categories for Crown and Rump identification.
4. Comparison and evaluation into transfer learning architectures for image classification.
5. Creation of a Crown and Rump identification model using ResNet34.
6. Comparison and evaluation into transfer learning architectures in identifying the Crown and Rump in fetal ultrasounds.

In the following article, Sect. 2 details relevant literature, Sect. 3 describes the method used, Sect. 4 evaluates the performance of the model, Sect. 5 discusses the obtain results and Sect. 6 concludes the paper whilst discussing potential future work.

2   Related Works

Artificial Intelligence (AI) and machine learning (ML)-based techniques have been applied to diverse domains to solve a wide range of problems including anomaly detection [6, 7, 16–18, 29], disease detection [11, 14, 20, 28, 35, 38, 39], management of patients with neural disorders [1, 3, 4, 11, 20, 34, 47–49] and smart data analytics [5, 12, 19, 21, 22, 36, 42, 43, 50]. Among these, medical image analysis has been one of the main domains where ML-based tools have excelled [32]. These methods have been developed for various imaging modalities including brain imaging, radiography, ultrasound, etc. Though these methods primarily use CNN, there have been other ML architectures in use as well [33].

CNNs have been applied previously by Singh et al. in fetal ultrasound imaging [46]. They have focused on different areas, and there is only one related study about first-trimester ultrasound scans published. They discussed the classification of fetal ultrasound images into 'Correct' and 'Incorrect' categories for the measurement of the CRL, this ML solution employs a pre-trained ResNet50 model to perform the classification. The dataset of fetal ultrasound images used in the study is shared with this investigation owing to the connection to Southend University Hospital. The study illustrates that the ResNet50 model performs at a higher accuracy when using Segmented images than compared against non-segmented images, however, the study does not implement an automatic segmentation model as it is implemented manually using MATLAB Tools. This model helps to train sonographers to take accurate first-trimester fetal ultrasound scans and informs the practitioner if an accurate CRL measurement can be taken from the image.

The use of image segmentation in medical imaging has been conducted by various investigations, popular image segmentation models include U-Net and Mask R-CNN, and automatic image segmentation in first-trimester fetal ultrasounds is a novel concept to investigate. A Mask R-CNN and InceptionV3 model is used in an investigation to segment the lesion of an organ to aid in the diagnosis of prostate cancer [31]. The model uses ground truth masks to segment the lesion from the ultrasound image, this investigation compared the accuracy of the model with and without image segmentation, and the model achieved

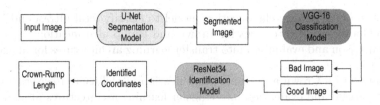

Fig. 1. Block diagram of the proposed analysis pipeline.

a higher accuracy of 80% using segmented data. The U-Net Model is derived from an initial paper by Ronneberger et al. [41], which details the structure and implementation of the model, the paper concludes by stating that the model can be used throughout the medical domain. Since the publication, several different studies have been published successfully implementing the U-Net model for various medical imaging [9,23,27,51], including ultrasounds.

Image segmentation is implemented with the use of a U-Net model to automatically segment the abdominal region in CT scans in a study by Weston et al. [51]. The U-Net model significantly outperforms other existing methods, such as thresholding, due to the complex image data in abdominal scans. Ground Truth masks were used for the segmentation, the model trains to identify regions, then predicts and generates masks for new images. Furthermore, the U-Net model is used to segment the fetal head in ultrasound images in the work of Kim et al. [27], the U-Net model segments the fetal abdominal region using Ground Truth masks. The segmented image is then inputted into CNN models to identify key points of reference to estimate the fetal abdominal circumference, the segmentation is accurate but the model 'lacks reliability' to measure the circumference. A paper [52], documents the challenge of applying deep learning methods in ultrasounds due to the 'low signal-to-noise ratio' that makes edge detection difficult.

Research into the use of CNNs in Medical Imaging has revealed Transfer Learning as a viable solution for classification problems. Papers from Deepak and Ameer [15], Serte and Demirel [44] and Singh et al. [46], show successful implementation of pre-trained architectures. Serte and Demirel evaluate the performance of pre-trained architectures, including DenseNet121, ResNet50 and ResNet18 to classify 3D CT Scans, both ResNet models display high performance once fine-tuned for their hyperparameters. The work of Singh et al. evaluates the performance of 4 pre-trained architectures to classify the first-trimester fetal ultrasound images into 'Correct' and 'Incorrect' categories, the models discussed are DenseNet121, InceptionNetV3, ResNet50, and VGG-16 [46].

3   Proposed Method

Background research revealed the importance of using different ML methods to accurately identify the Crown and Rump in First-Trimester Ultrasound Images. The importance of image segmentation for higher accuracy within medical imaging [27,46,51] and in particular, the strength of the U-Net model is well known.

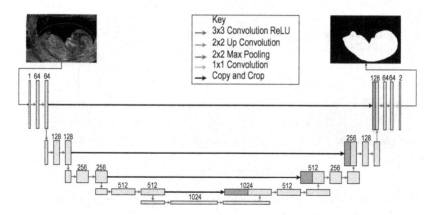

Fig. 2. The U-Net model architecture used for image segmentation of the fetal ultrasound images.

This identifies a U-Net model to be used in the ML pipeline. Additionally, Transfer Learning (TL) was identified as a viable solution for a classification model to be developed [15, 44, 46], this work compares pre-trained models such as ResNet50, InceptionV3, VGG-16 and Xception. The model classifies the results of the segmented image, returned from the U-Net model, into 'Good' and 'Bad' segmentation categories to inform Obstetric Practitioners if the fetus has been identified accurately and inform sonographers if the inputted image is correct for the measurement of the CRL. Finally, TL will be used in the identification model to identify the coordinates of the Crown and the Rump on the segmented fetus. The flow of data between each model is shown in Fig. 1. Due to the lack of scaling data present in the dataset, the ML system will be unable to estimate the Crown-to-Rump length that is used to predict the gestational age. Instead, the final model will identify the Crown and Rump regions on the segmented fetus that will allow for the CRL length to be calculated once scaling data is available, this highlights a future work to be considered. The code and the associated dataset are available for download from the link: https://github.com/braiacslab/CRL-UlS.

3.1   U-Net Architecture

The structure of a U-Net model consists of an Encoder and Decoder path, the Encoder is on the left side of the U-Net and consists of the repeated application of two 3 × 3 convolutions, followed by a ReLU and a 2 × 2 max pooling operation. At each downsampling step, the feature channels are doubled, and the spatial dimensions are halved. The decoder path (right-side of Fig. 2) consists of upsampling the feature map which is followed by a 2 × 2 convolution that reverses the steps carried out on the Encoder path and halves the number of feature channels. This is followed by a concatenation with the cropped feature map from the contracting path and two 3 × 3 convolutions followed by a ReLU

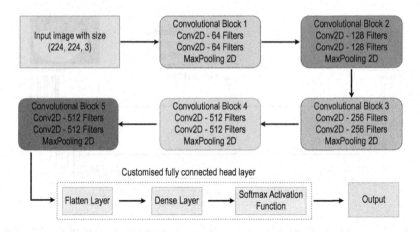

Fig. 3. The network architecture of the VGG-16 model.

function, the final layer consists of a 1×1 convolution to map the channels to the classes [41]. The complete structure of the model is shown in Fig. 2.

Figure 2 shows the layers implemented in the model and demonstrates its working process using input/output images. The code used in the ML pipeline was adapted from a GitHub repository [24] that used the U-Net model to segment other medical imaging. The dataset obtained from the Southend University Hospital was split into training, validation and testing sets. This dataset contained a total of 900 images, 450 of which were suitable to be used in the U-Net model. The training and validation set were sized to 256×256 and were in a TIF format as it is a prerequisite for training a U-Net model. Ground truth masks were created manually by experts for all 450 suitable fetal ultrasound images in the dataset to identify the fetus. Data augmentation was used to increase the overall size of the dataset to increase the model's performance and to allow the model to be trained on different variations of data that it may encounter. As shown in Fig. 2, the model generated a predicted mask which was outputted as a binary image, showing where the fetus was located. The original image was then applied to the predicted mask using an AND function to return the segmented image. The testing data was in a JPEG format as per the model's requirement.

3.2   Image Classification

In the pipeline, the image classification model classifies the segmented images from the U-Net model into 'Good' and 'Bad'. This classification acts as a data pre-processing stage to ensure that the segmentation is accurate and the regions of interest can be identified. The performance of pre-trained architectures such as ResNet50, InceptionV3, VGG-16 and Xception were evaluated, with the best-suited model selected. Figure 3 depicts the design of the best suited pre-trained model VGG-16 that is used for the binary classification model.

The model includes 5 convolutional (CONV) blocks; each block consists of two CONV layers and a Max Pooling layer. After the CONV blocks, the default output layers are set to be untrained so that the pre-trained model can be adapted to suit the dataset. In Fig. 3, the output layers are displayed in orange and use a Flatten layer to create a 1-D array of values. A dense layer is then applied to convert the array into a vector prediction for the Softmax activation function, which is the final layer in the VGG-16 model and converts the vector into a probability distribution for both categories.

Prior to entry into the pre-trained architectures, the images will be pre-processed specifically for each architecture. Data is augmented during the training process to build a robust classification model. The images are in a JPEG format, and 200 segmented images are split into 80% Training data, 10% Validation data and 10% Testing Data. Upon selection as the best-suited model, the pre-trained VGG-16 model was hyper-tuned to ensure optimal performance over 50 epochs, additionally, in-built TensorFlow callbacks such as Learning Rate Reducer and Model Checkpoint were used during the tuning process. The adaptive learning rate used in the Learning Rate Reducer callback attempts to increase the accuracy of the model once it starts to plateau. Model Checkpoint is used in all 3 models developed and is used to store the most accurate model based on the Validation Loss metric.

Classification Evaluation Metrics. Evaluation metrics are pivotal to ensuring that an ML model is optimised for the task. The following metrics were used to analyse the performance of the VGG-16 model that is used to classify the segmented images into 'Bad' and 'Good' segmentations of the fetus.

Accuracy. The Accuracy metric is used to create a percentage score based on the number of correct predictions divided by the total number of predictions.

Precision. The Precision metric is the ratio of true positive values to the combined total of true positives and false positives.

Recall. The Recall metric is the ratio of true positive values to the combined total of true positives and false negatives.

F1-score. The F1 Score metric is the mean of the Precision and Recall values, with the highest value being 1.

Confusion Matrix. The Confusion matrix visualises True Positives, False Positives, False Negatives and True Negatives.

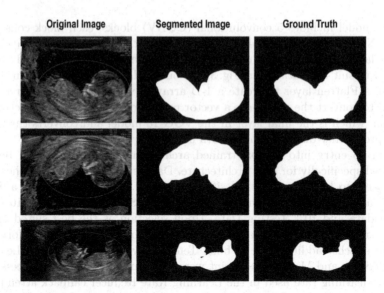

Fig. 4. Examples of segmented images using the U-Net model (middle column) along with the original images (left column) and the ground truth (right column).

3.3   Identifying the Crown and Rump

Existing solutions for a model that identifies two points in an image are limited. The identification model aims to plot the coordinates of the Crown and the Rump in the first-trimester ultrasound image. The identification model receives the segmented image from the U-Net model due to segmented images providing increased accuracy due to less background noise in several papers [27, 46, 51]. The identification model was challenging to develop due to the lack of existing solutions and how best to create label data to identify the coordinates. The python library Fast.Ai was identified as a solution to this problem due to its use of a function to map coordinates to images for training data and the capability to deploy pre-trained architecture.

Labelled data was generated via software called LabelMe, which saved the identified Crown and Rump regions in JSON files to be parsed during the training process, the dataset contained a total of 450 images. The library used allowed for pre-trained architectures to be deployed on the dataset, the models evaluated were DenseNet121, ResNet34 and ResNet50, each model was trained across 50 epochs with performance metrics of Training Loss and Validation Loss. The final model was an adaptation of the ResNet34 model due to its high performance compared to other available architectures. The prediction of the coordinates was returned as a tensor of coordinates, outputted in a range between −1 and 1. The scaling of the prediction is required to convert the values into a scale between 0 and 1 before multiplying by the image height or width. The Eq. 1 was used to convert the scale. The scaled coordinates are plotted on the segmented image and displayed to the user to aid in the CRL measurement process.

$$f(x) = \frac{x+1}{2} \tag{1}$$

4   Results

4.1   Segmentation Model Performance

The ML system created uses a U-Net model to increase the accuracy of the identification model, which, when concatenated with the classification model, informs the Obstetric Practitioners if the inputted image is acceptable to identify the Crown and Rump regions. The U-Net model utilises TensorFlow callbacks discussed previously to ensure a high-performance model, the model is accurate for the segmentation of first-trimester ultrasound images and illustrates the adaptability of the U-Net architecture. Figure 4 shows the results of the U-Net model and shows high performance across different rotations of the fetus.

4.2   Comparison of Classification Models

The pre-trained architectures identified in the previous section were analysed against each other over 25 epochs with the performance metrics of Training Accuracy, Training Loss, Validation Accuracy and Validation Loss. Learning curve graphs were plotted for deeper analysis and showed overfitting of the dataset for the ResNet50 and InceptionV3 models. In addition to Table 1, the analysis showed that the VGG-16 model should be selected due to consistent high performances. The Table 1 shows Training Accuracy (TA), Training Loss (TL) Validation Accuracy (VA) and Validation Loss (VL) for the various models.

Table 1. Performance comparison of different CNN models.

Model	TA	TL	VA	VL
ResNet 50	0.8750	0.2824	0.7	0.6653
InceptionV3	0.8295	0.4341	0.75	0.8611
VGG-16	0.89	0.2736	0.95	0.2123
Xception	0.9	0.7376	0.9	0.73763

4.3   Classification Model Performance

The VGG-16 Model was fine-tuned across 50 epochs, leading to an increase in Training Accuracy to '0.9062', Training Loss to '0.2428', Validation Accuracy

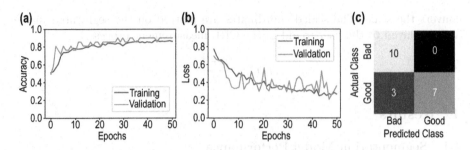

Fig. 5. Performance of the hypertuned VGG-16 model in terms of accuracy (a), loss (b), and confusion matrix (c).

to '0.95', Validation Loss to '0.1767' and Testing Accuracy to '0.85'. The learning curve shown in Fig. 5, displays a more consistent learning rate despite the fluctuating validation loss.

The classification model is used as a pre-processing tool before identifying the Crown and Rump. Performance metrics indicated earlier are used to ensure that the classification model is to an appropriate standard. Table 2 shows the model's high performance by the Macro and Weighted Average score achieving '85%'. Figure 5(c) shows that despite a limited dataset of 200 images, the model correctly classifies 17 out of 20 images and misclassifies 3 images. Both performance metrics highlight the model's strength in identifying 'Bad' segmented images but struggles in comparison with the classification of 'Good' segmented images.

Table 2. Classification performance for image classification model.

Class	Precision	Recall	F1 score	Accuracy
Bad	0.77	1.0	0.87	0.85
Good	1.0	0.70	0.82	

4.4   Comparison with the State-of-the-Art Methods

Due to the limited amount of research on the topic, only one paper [46] details the use of State-of-the-Art architectures in image classification of first-trimester ultrasound images. As shown in Fig. 6, the method proposed in this work achieves similar performance in comparison to those used in [46]. It should be noted that the proposed method achieves greater accuracy across a range of performance metrics.

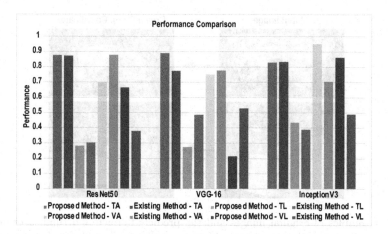

Fig. 6. Comparison of the proposed method's classification accuracy with the State-of-the-Art methods as in [46].

4.5 Identifying the Crown and Rump

The proposed model ResNet34 is compared with two other pre-trained architectures, ResNet50 and DenseNet121. Due to the nature of plotting coordinates, the model can only be evaluated using loss metrics, Table 3 highlights that ResNet34 is the best-suited model across 50 epochs.

Table 3. Comparison of different models in detecting Crown and Rump points.

Model	Training loss	Validation loss
ResNet 50	0.456535	0.301995
ResNet 34	**0.433047**	**0.256483**
DenseNet121	0.454696	0.273414

The results of the model used to identify the Crown and Rump in first-trimester ultrasound imaging are shown in Fig. 7, the predicted coordinates of the crown and rump are plotted in blue onto the segmented image. The model performs inconsistently with different images inputted. The ResNet34 model works well for most ultrasound images but coordinates are often plotted a small margin away from where they should be. Unfortunately, this would impact Obstetric Practitioners in their use of the system, to see the full benefit of the proposed system further work would have to be performed to improve the performance of the ResNet34 model.

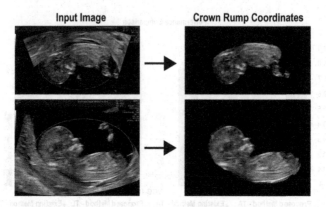

Fig. 7. Examples of original images and the predicted crown and rump coordinates. This figure illustrates the model's capability to predict the coordinates for images with different orientations.

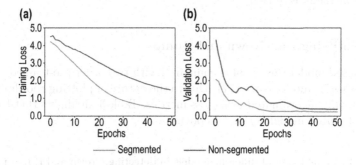

Fig. 8. Performance of the model in segmented and non-segmented images in terms of training loss (a) and validation loss (b).

4.6   Comparison of Segmented Versus Non-Segmented Data

The literature review identified the importance of image segmentation in the classification of medical imaging [10, 30, 41]. Comparison of performance between segmented and non-segmented data is vital to prove the importance of the proposed U-Net model. This comparison was performed with training both segmented and non-segmented data on the ResNet34 model developed with the Fast.Ai library. The results illustrated that segmented data performed better in successfully identifying the crown and the rump and Fig. 8 highlights this with both learning curves over 50 epochs. Despite marginal improvement in validation loss for segmented data at '0.256483' to '0.400736' for non-segmented data, the key difference exists in the training loss where segmented data has significantly greater performance. Figure 8 depicts the learning curve for Training Loss and Validation Loss on Segmented versus non-segmented data.

Both the curves plateau significantly for the Validation Loss metric, this highlights that further analysis of the selected model will be required to further improve the results of an inconsistent identification model. Furthermore, a study on the fetal abdominal circumference [27], documents that ultrasound imaging contains a 'low signal-to-noise ratio' during edge detection means ML models can struggle to pick out the regions of interest.

5 Discussion

This investigation contributes to solve the issue with inter-observer variation within CRL measurement as it details a machine learning pipeline that will allow Obstetric Practitioners to input a fetal ultrasound image to be analysed. The pipeline produces an accurate segmented fetus from the images and classifies the image depending on if the segmentation is correct for the identification of the Crown and the Rump. The performance of the identification of the Crown and Rump regions varies depending on the augmentation of the fetus and for use in medical imaging this would need to be more reliable.

Segmentation of the fetus is pivotal to increasing the accuracy of the model as discussed in the Results section above. Segmentation has been performed in medical imaging [27,41,51] but the segmented images provides insight into how image segmentation can be performed on a range of different medical imaging, including fetal ultrasounds, which shows how machine learning can be applied across medicine.

6 Conclusion and Future Work

This investigation aimed to reduce the effects of inter-observer variation for Obstetric Practitioners when calculating the gestational age on First-Trimester Ultrasounds. The proposed system is a novel concept, it makes use of three machine learning methods to successfully identify the Crown and Rump regions of the fetus. This will help Obstetric Practitioners in their day-to-day jobs in measuring the Crown Rump Length to better predict the gestational age of the fetus.

The developed concept of an automatic image segmentation model for first-trimester ultrasound imaging is novel, this will allow for future work to create accurate models due to the reduction of background noise. The pipeline also implements the classification of the segmented fetuses into 'Good' or 'Bad' segmentations to a Validation Accuracy of '0.95', this will inform the practitioner if the scan is appropriate for the measurement of the Crown and Rump. The lack of scaling data available does not allow for the system to provide a measurement for the CRL, a dataset in DICOM format would allow for scaling data to be inputted into the model. Despite the lack of scaling data, the Crown and Rump are identified, however, the model is inconsistent and would require further work to fulfil the potential of the system.

In the future, different tasks can be carried out to ensure higher-performing models. An increased dataset of first-trimester ultrasound images would aid increased performance. Additionally, labels created by medical professionals would significantly improve the model's ability to segment the fetus and identify the Crown and Rump regions, due to accurate labels based on years of experience and training.

Acknowledgments. Data used in this study was obtained from the Fetal Medicine Centre at Southend University Hospital.

References

1. Ahmed, S., Hossain, M.F., Nur, S.B., Shamim Kaiser, M., Mahmud, M.: Toward machine learning-based psychological assessment of autism spectrum disorders in school and community. In: Kaiser, M.S., Bandyopadhyay, A., Ray, K., Singh, R., Nagar, V. (eds.) Proceedings of Trends in Electronics and Health Informatics. LNNS, vol. 376, pp. 139–149. Springer, Singapore (2022). https://doi.org/10.1007/978-981-16-8826-3_13
2. Aksoy, H., et al.: A prospective study to assess the clinical impact of interobserver reliability of sonographic measurements of fetal nuchal translucency and crown-rump length on combined first-trimester screening. North. Clin. Istanb. **2**(2), 92 (2015)
3. Akter, T., Ali, M.H., Satu, M.S., Khan, M.I., Mahmud, M.: Towards autism sub-type detection through identification of discriminatory factors using machine learning. In: Mahmud, M., Kaiser, M.S., Vassanelli, S., Dai, Q., Zhong, N. (eds.) BI 2021. LNCS (LNAI), vol. 12960, pp. 401–410. Springer, Cham (2021). https://doi.org/10.1007/978-3-030-86993-9_36
4. Al Banna, M.H., Ghosh, T., Taher, K.A., Kaiser, M.S., Mahmud, M.: A monitoring system for patients of autism spectrum disorder using artificial intelligence. In: Mahmud, M., Vassanelli, S., Kaiser, M.S., Zhong, N. (eds.) BI 2020. LNCS (LNAI), vol. 12241, pp. 251–262. Springer, Cham (2020). https://doi.org/10.1007/978-3-030-59277-6_23
5. Al Banna, M.H., et al.: Attention-based bi-directional long-short term memory network for earthquake prediction. IEEE Access **9**, 56589–56603 (2021)
6. Al Nahian, M.J., Ghosh, T., Uddin, M.N., Islam, M.M., Mahmud, M., Kaiser, M.S.: Towards artificial intelligence driven emotion aware fall monitoring framework suitable for elderly people with neurological disorder. In: Mahmud, M., Vassanelli, S., Kaiser, M.S., Zhong, N. (eds.) BI 2020. LNCS (LNAI), vol. 12241, pp. 275–286. Springer, Cham (2020). https://doi.org/10.1007/978-3-030-59277-6_25
7. Al Nahian, M.J., et al.: Towards an accelerometer-based elderly fall detection system using cross-disciplinary time series features. IEEE Access **9**, 39413–31 (2021)
8. Alzubaidi, L., et al.: Review of deep learning: concepts, CNN architectures, challenges, applications, future directions. J. Big Data **8**(1), 1–74 (2021)
9. Amiri, M., Brooks, R., Behboodi, B., Rivaz, H.: Two-stage ultrasound image segmentation using u-net and test time augmentation. Int. J. Comput. Assist. Radiol. Surg. **15**(6), 981–988 (2020)
10. Balafar, M.A., et al.: Review of brain MRI image segmentation methods. Artif. Intell. Rev. **33**(3), 261–274 (2010)
11. Biswas, M., Kaiser, M.S., Mahmud, M., Al Mamun, S., Hossain, M.S., Rahman, M.A.: An XAI based autism detection: the context behind the detection. In: Mahmud, M., Kaiser, M.S., Vassanelli, S., Dai, Q., Zhong, N. (eds.) BI 2021. LNCS (LNAI), vol. 12960, pp. 448–459. Springer, Cham (2021). https://doi.org/10.1007/978-3-030-86993-9_40

12. Biswas, M., Tania, M.H., Kaiser, M.S., et al.: ACCU3RATE: a mobile health application rating scale based on user reviews. PLoS One **16**(12), e0258050 (2021)
13. Butt, K., et al.: Determination of gestational age by ultrasound. J. Obstet. Gynaecol. Can. **36**(2), 171–181 (2014)
14. Deepa, B., et al.: Pattern descriptors orientation and map firefly algorithm based brain pathology classification using hybridized machine learning algorithm. IEEE Access **10**, 3848–3863 (2022)
15. Deepak, S., Ameer, P.: Brain tumor classification using deep cnn features via transfer learning. Comput. Biol. Med. **111**, 103345 (2019)
16. Fabietti, M., Mahmud, M., Lotfi, A.: Anomaly detection in invasively recorded neuronal signals using deep neural network: effect of sampling frequency. In: Mahmud, M., Kaiser, M.S., Kasabov, N., Iftekharuddin, K., Zhong, N. (eds.) AII 2021. CCIS, vol. 1435, pp. 79–91. Springer, Cham (2021). https://doi.org/10.1007/978-3-030-82269-9_7
17. Fabietti, M., Mahmud, M., Lotfi, A.: Channel-independent recreation of artefactual signals in chronically recorded local field potentials using machine learning. Brain Inform. **9**(1), 1–17 (2022). https://doi.org/10.1186/s40708-021-00149-x
18. Fabietti, M., et al.: Artifact detection in chronically recorded local field potentials using long-short term memory neural network. In: Proceedings of AICT, pp. 1–6 (2020)
19. Faria, T.H., Shamim Kaiser, M., Hossian, C.A., Mahmud, M., Al Mamun, S., Chakraborty, C.: Smart city technologies for next generation healthcare. In: Chakraborty, C., Lin, J.C.-W., Alazab, M. (eds.) Data-Driven Mining, Learning and Analytics for Secured Smart Cities. ASTSA, pp. 253–274. Springer, Cham (2021). https://doi.org/10.1007/978-3-030-72139-8_12
20. Ghosh, T., et al.: Artificial intelligence and internet of things in screening and management of autism spectrum disorder. Sustain. Cities Soc. **74**, 103189 (2021)
21. Ghosh, T., et al.: An attention-based mood controlling framework for social media users. In: Mahmud, M., Kaiser, M.S., Vassanelli, S., Dai, Q., Zhong, N. (eds.) BI 2021. LNCS (LNAI), vol. 12960, pp. 245–256. Springer, Cham (2021). https://doi.org/10.1007/978-3-030-86993-9_23
22. Ghosh, T., et al.: A hybrid deep learning model to predict the impact of COVID-19 on mental health form social media big data. Preprints **2021**(2021060654) (2021)
23. Guo, Y., Duan, X., Wang, C., Guo, H.: Segmentation and recognition of breast ultrasound images based on an expanded u-net. PLoS One **16**(6), e0253202 (2021)
24. Huang, Y.J.: Hands-on Medical image segmentation using U-net architecture implemented by deep learning framework Keras (2021). https://github.com/Huangyuren/unet_SCM
25. Kagan, K.O., Hoopmann, M., Baker, A., Huebner, M., Abele, H., Wright, D.: Impact of bias in crown-rump length measurement at first-trimester screening for trisomy 21. Ultrasound Obstetr. Gynecol. **40**(2), 135–139 (2012)
26. Karki, D., Sharmqa, U., Rauniyar, R.: Study of accuracy of commonly used fetal parameters for estimation of gestational age. JNMA J. Nepal Med. Assoc. **45**(162), 233–237 (2006)
27. Kim, B., et al.: Machine-learning-based automatic identification of fetal abdominal circumference from ultrasound images. Physiol. Meas. **39**(10), 105007 (2018)
28. Kumar, I., et al.: Dense tissue pattern characterization using deep neural network. Cogn. Comput. 1–24 (2022). [ePub ahead of print]
29. Lalotra, G.S., Kumar, V., Bhatt, A., Chen, T., Mahmud, M.: iReTADS: an intelligent real-time anomaly detection system for cloud communications using temporal

data summarization and neural network. Secur. Commun. Netw. **2022**, 9149164 (2022)

30. Liu, X., et al.: Automatic organ segmentation for CT scans based on super-pixel and convolutional neural networks. J. Digit. Imaging **31**(5), 748–760 (2018)

31. Liu, Z., Yang, C., Huang, J., Liu, S., Zhuo, Y., Lu, X.: Deep learning framework based on integration of S-mask R-CNN and inception-v3 for ultrasound image-aided diagnosis of prostate cancer. Future Gener. Comput. Syst. **114**, 358–367 (2021)

32. Mahmud, M., Kaiser, M.S., McGinnity, T.M., Hussain, A.: Deep learning in mining biological data. Cogn. Comput. **13**(1), 1–33 (2021)

33. Mahmud, M., et al.: Applications of deep learning and reinforcement learning to biological data. IEEE Trans. Neural Netw. Learn. Syst. **29**(6), 2063–2079 (2018)

34. Mahmud, M., et al.: Towards explainable and privacy-preserving artificial intelligence for personalisation in autism spectrum disorder. In: Antona, M., Stephanidis, C. (eds.) HCII 2022. LNCS, vol. 13309, pp. 356–370. Springer, Cham (2022). https://doi.org/10.1007/978-3-031-05039-8_26

35. Mammoottil, M.J., Kulangara, L.J., Cherian, A.S., Mohandas, P., Hasikin, K., Mahmud, M.: Detection of breast cancer from five-view thermal images using convolutional neural networks. J. Healthc. Eng. **2022**, 4295221 (2022)

36. Nawar, A., Toma, N.T., Al Mamun, S., et al.: Cross-content recommendation between movie and book using machine learning. In: Proceedings AICT, pp. 1–6 (2021)

37. Ohuma, E.O., Papageorghiou, A.T., Villar, J., Altman, D.G.: Estimation of gestational age in early pregnancy from crown-rump length when gestational age range is truncated: the case study of the intergrowth-21stproject. BMC Med. Res. Methodol. **13**(1), 1–14 (2013)

38. Paul, A., et al.: Inverted bell-curve-based ensemble of deep learning models for detection of COVID-19 from chest X-rays. Neural Comput. Appl. 1–15 (2022)

39. Prakash, N., et al.: Deep transfer learning COVID-19 detection and infection localization with superpixel based segmentation. Sustain. Cities Soc. **75**, 103252 (2021)

40. Riquelme, D., Akhloufi, M.A.: Deep learning for lung cancer nodules detection and classification in CT scans. AI **1**(1), 28–67 (2020)

41. Ronneberger, O., Fischer, P., Brox, T.: U-net: convolutional networks for biomedical image segmentation. In: Navab, N., Hornegger, J., Wells, W.M., Frangi, A.F. (eds.) MICCAI 2015. LNCS, vol. 9351, pp. 234–241. Springer, Cham (2015). https://doi.org/10.1007/978-3-319-24574-4_28

42. Satu, M.S., Rahman, S., Khan, M.I., Abedin, M.Z., Kaiser, M.S., Mahmud, M.: Towards improved detection of cognitive performance using bidirectional multilayer long-short term memory neural network. In: Mahmud, M., Vassanelli, S., Kaiser, M.S., Zhong, N. (eds.) BI 2020. LNCS (LNAI), vol. 12241, pp. 297–306. Springer, Cham (2020). https://doi.org/10.1007/978-3-030-59277-6_27

43. Satu, M.S., et al.: TClustVID: a novel machine learning classification model to investigate topics and sentiment in COVID-19 tweets. Knowl. Based Syst. **226**, 107126 (2021)

44. Serte, S., Demirel, H.: Deep learning for diagnosis of COVID-19 using 3D CT scans. Comput. Biol. Med. **132**, 104306 (2021)

45. Shen, Y.T., Chen, L., Yue, W.W., Xu, H.X.: Artificial intelligence in ultrasound. Eur. J. Radiol. **139**, 109717 (2021)

46. Singh, R., Mahmud, M., Yovera, L.: Classification of first trimester ultrasound images using deep convolutional neural network. In: Mahmud, M., Kaiser, M.S.,

Kasabov, N., Iftekharuddin, K., Zhong, N. (eds.) AII 2021. CCIS, vol. 1435, pp. 92–105. Springer, Cham (2021). https://doi.org/10.1007/978-3-030-82269-9_8

47. Sumi, A.I., Zohora, M.F., Mahjabeen, M., Faria, T.J., Mahmud, M., Kaiser, M.S.: ƒASSERT: a fuzzy assistive system for children with autism using internet of things. In: BI 2018. LNCS (LNAI), vol. 11309, pp. 403–412. Springer, Cham (2018). https://doi.org/10.1007/978-3-030-05587-5_38

48. Wadhera, T., Mahmud, M.: Brain networks in autism spectrum disorder, epilepsy and their relationship: a machine learning approach. In: Chen, T., Carter, J., Mahmud, M., Khuman, A.S. (eds.) Artificial Intelligence in Healthcare. Brain Informatics and Health, pp. 125–142. Springer, Singapore (2022). https://doi.org/10.1007/978-981-19-5272-2_6

49. Wadhera, T., Mahmud, M.: Influences of social learning in individual perception and decision making in people with autism: a computational approach. In: Mahmud, M., He, J., Vassanelli, S., van Zundert, A., Zhong, N. (eds.) BI 2022. LNCS, vol. 13406, pp. 50–61. Springer, Cham (2022). https://doi.org/10.1007/978-3-031-15037-1_5

50. Watkins, J., Fabietti, M., Mahmud, M.: SENSE: a student performance quantifier using sentiment analysis. In: Proceedings of IJCNN, pp. 1–6 (2020)

51. Weston, A.D., et al.: Automated abdominal segmentation of CT scans for body composition analysis using deep learning. Radiology **290**(3), 669–679 (2019)

52. Zhang, J., Petitjean, C., Lopez, P., Ainouz, S.: Direct estimation of fetal head circumference from ultrasound images based on regression CNN. In: Medical Imaging with Deep Learning, pp. 914–922 (2020)

A Pyramidal Approach for Emotion Recognition from EEG Signals

M. S. Thejaswini[1]([envelope]) [iD], G. Hemantha Kumar[1] [iD],
and V. N. Manjunath Aradhya[2] [iD]

[1] Department of Studies in Computer Science, University of Mysore, Mysuru 570006,
Karnataka, India
thejaswini@compsci.uni-mysore.ac.in
[2] Department of Computer Applications, JSS Science and Technology University,
Mysuru 570006, Karnataka, India
aradhya@sjce.ac.in

Abstract. Brain Computer Interfaces (BCI) is one of the key technology gaining intense mode of interest in various fields of research in artificial intelligence. In recent years, physiological signals with advanced BCI applications, successively concerned in the direction of recognizing various human emotional states. In this paper, a new feature representation technique based on pyramidal approach is determined. The proposed approach uses the Interpolation Forward Difference signal computations in different levels of iterations, which leads to reduction of dimensions in an effective way for recognizing emotions. Then application of General Regression Neural Network (GRNN) is presented for efficient classification of signals into four different emotional states from EEG based GAMEEMO Dataset. The experimental results are promising and performed well, compared to other state of art techniques.

Keywords: BCI · EEG signals · Emotion recognition · Pyramidal approach · Classification-GRNN

1 Introduction

Emotion is essential part of every human beings in framing their rapport interactions with external environment. With growing body of literature in BCI has recognized, analysis of emotions are empathetic aspect in developing various applications of entertainment, marketing, medical diagnosis, education system and smart environments. Typically facial expression [1,22], body gestures [2] and speech [3] are proficiently used in discrimination of human emotional states ranging from basic emotions to complex ones. However these representations analysis will introduce probability of counterfeit responses for the reason, emotions evoked from physical experiences can be purposely controlled and transformed according to individual personality traits. In this regard to overthrow this drawback, developing a system of automatically recognizing emotions from physiological signals is a significant task. Recent evidence propounds that Electroencephalogram (EEG) [4] signals is widely used noninvasive technique of BCI,

M. Mahmud et al. (Eds.): AII 2022, CCIS 1724, pp. 248–259, 2022.
https://doi.org/10.1007/978-3-031-24801-6_18

which is well known for developing automatic emotion recognition models and also its efficiency is increasing in the study of human emotion recognition [5]. Generally activities in the brain is directly reflecting central nervous system from where EEG signals are received, and they more adequate in delivering emotional states of individuals. Enlighten properties from EEG signals for intently recognizing emotions are firmly entrenched to date. The most renowned EEG based emotion datasets is DEAP [9], SEED [36], MANHOBHCI [10], DREAMER [11], ASCERTAIN [12], AMIGOS [13] and GAMEEMO [14] and Exhaustive knowledge and related works on these familiar databases can be found in [6–8,15–17]. Recognition of emotions based on EEG signals are split into the sequence of steps:(1) inducing emotions (2) recording EEG signals (3) prepossessing of signals (4) feature extraction (5) EEG feature dimensional reduction from feature selection or feature transformation techniques and (6) study of emotional patterns and classifications. In above all mentioned phases, each one is bottom-line factors in analysing emotional states [25,33]. Good deal of efforts from researchers for all phases have been accomplished in adaptive EEG based BCI systems. This paper centred attention on an mapping high dimension data into new reduced low dimensions one, for making the classification stage much easier in predicting emotional states.

2   Related Work

Dimensional Reduction (DR) [18,19,23,27] approach has paid increasing attention in many growing research fields of application like signal processing, speech processing, neuroinformatic [20], bioinformatics [21], to effectively examine huge amount of data, dealing with transformation of data from massive dimensional space into small dimensional space. It has been stimulated to scale down the gigantic volume of data by retaining relevant properties of original data. Function with high dimension spaces can be unattractive by the reason of raw data are generally sparse as consequence of the curse of dimensionality at the time of analysing data which is usually computationally stubborn. DR mainly utilized in operations of noise reduction, number of feature reduction, data visualization, cluster analysis. Essential benefits can be earned by processing dimensionality reduction methods (i) reduction of data storage (ii) minimum computation time (iii) redundant, extraneous data can be removed (iv) reducing noise can lead to good data quality (v) It simplifies classification process resulting best accuracy (vi) data visualising can be boosted. Typically, dimensional reduction methods are grouped into two categories as feature extraction: reduction takes place by extracting relevant features from data with losing much feature information. Whereas in feature selection subset of features are selected from original data to improve performance of model. Many researchers in literature worked on dimensional reduction techniques on trying to reduce enormous amount of data into subset of data by the means of different techniques like (PCA, ICA, GA, LDA etc). In the year 2020 emotion classification from EEG signals based on PCA approach by fusing power spectrum and wavelet energy entropy features was proposed by Gao et al. [24], Relating to supervised and unsupervised DR techniques known as maximum relevance and minimum redundancy approaches, Liu et. [28], was able to develop emotion recognition model, performing extraction of 14 types of features from time, frequency and time-frequency domains, adding SVM (support vector machines) and Random Forest (RF) as classifier with better outcomes. In order to enhance the efficiency of classifier Taherisadr et al. [26], proposed tensor based framework for reducing dimensions of time-frequency input data of CNN model in contributing great results. Naga et al. [29], utilized PCA in dimensional reduction of extracted Fourier transform and power spectral density feature vectors which is given as input to ANN for classifying emotional states. Dongkooshan et al. [30], effectively analysed stress from DEAP dataset using genetic algorithm for selecting subset of features to enhance the performance of KNN classifier.

From the above mentioned literature states that reducing higher dimensions into lower sets are Paramount task in analysis of EEG signals for emotion recognition due to recorded EEG data, contains enormous amount of samples for each individual at different instances of time, these larger sample features may lead to complex systems effecting on prediction accuracy. The primary desire of any machine learning algorithms is to have lesser number of features as input for adequately producing prominent results for all type of data domains. In this context we started our proposed study in bringing about enhanced classification rates for emotion recognition from EEG signals followed by developing feature selection algorithm in pyramidal structure for reducing dimensions of features and trained the new optimized set of features based on neural networks, finally the proposed algorithm has been tested on GAMEEMO dataset on four emotional class: Boring, Funny, Calm and Horror. The presented work performed well in achieving promising results when compared to other state of art techniques. This paper has followed by different sections. Next section explains proposed methodology and related theory to the proposed work. Section 4 explains about the data set and experimental results. The Sect. 5 gives discussion and conclusion of proposed study.

3   Proposed Methodology

Our proposed research study is carried-out for designing the classification model in recognizing four different emotions. One of the most essential and necessary factor that influence the classification performance is to have set of smaller input features selected from high dimensional database of different classes. Unquestionably the original set of features contains more information, which can be treated as input to classifier in achieving results [24]. However considering this enormous set of input features, decreases the performance efficiency of the positive impact at the stage of classification. In this scenario dimensional reduction plays a prominent role as feature selector in gathering relevant features as input for better classification results. The main purpose of this research study is to develop feature selection algorithm in reducing dimension of data for recognizing emotions. In accomplishing this task a new method of pyramidal structured dimensional reduction algorithm is developed as feature generator in performing forward difference interpolation technique. This difference approach of dimensional reduction was inspired from one of the most important process derived in numerical analysis which is known as Newton Interpolation Forward Differences.

3.1 Interpolation

Assuming that $f(x)$ is single valued and continuous function, then the values of $f(x)$ corresponding to certain values of X, say $X_0, X_1 \ldots \ldots X_n$ can be easily computed and tabulated satisfying some conditions in each level of iterations, where the previous output of each iteration will be treated as input to next level of iteration such a process is called interpolation.

3.2 Newton Interpolation Forward Differences

It is a process of differencing (interpolating value's) finite set of values continuously for a given function $f(x)$ applying forward interpolation procedure in various iterations in order to find the unique root for a given function. Considering the finite set of values as (x_i, y_i), where $i = 0, 1, 2 \ldots n$ of any given functions $y = f(x)$ to recover the values of $f(x)$ for some intermediate values of X or to obtain derivative of $f(x)$ for ranging from $X_0 \leq X_n$. This operation in numerical analysis take place, in finding solution for the problems based on differencing set of values. Forward differences particularly useful for interpolating the values in function $f(x)$. If $y_0, y_1, y_2, \ldots .y_n$ is a set of finite values of Y, then $(y_0 - y_1), (y_2 - y_3) \ldots (y_n - y_{n-1})$ these representation are called differencing factors of Y, which is Denoted by $\Delta y_0, \Delta y_1 \ldots \Delta y_{n-1}$ and $\Delta y_0 = y_0 - y_1, \Delta y_1 = y_2 - y_1, \Delta y_{n-1} = \Delta y_n - \Delta y_{n-1}$. Where Δ: Forward Difference Operations Δy_0 :First Forward Differences Δy_1: Second Forward Differences Δy_{n-1} : Final Forward Differences. From all the above discussion related to newton interpolation forward difference. In our proposed study for recognition of emotions we adopted forward difference interpolation technique in the direction of performing new form of feature representation from where high dimensional data is reduced to lower dimension the obtained features experimentally worked better in classifying four different emotions.

3.3 Pyramidal Structured Dimension Reduction

Pyramidal structured forward interpolation technique is employed for selection of relevant features from high dimensional time domain EEG signals. This study is considered in differencing discrete samples of given database discontinuously (samples varies from one another) in the closed loop of intervals (consecutive samples of even and odd terms) in different levels of iterations, for reducing the high dimensional data into half of its samples, successively in each level of iterations. Since our input set of samples are discrete in nature the obtained results are also discrete. In general the notation of our proposed work in each level of interpolation is given by $\Delta(x) : \Delta(n) - \Delta(n+1)$. Where $n = 1, 2, 3 \ldots n$ (38000 samples of each subject from four different classes). $\Delta(x)$: Different levels of forward Difference operations. $\Delta(n)$ and $\Delta(n+1)$: Values in each samples.

5 Different level of forward difference interpolation iterations for dimensional reduction is as follows

$\Delta^1(x) = x_n - x_{n+1}$: First level of forward difference.
$\Delta^2(x) = \Delta^1 n(x) - \Delta^1_{n+1}(x)$: Second level of forward difference.
$\Delta^3(x) = \Delta^2 n(x) - \Delta^2_{n+1}(x)$: Third level of forward difference.
$\Delta^4(x) = \Delta^3 n(x) - \Delta^3_{n+1}(x)$: Fourth level of forward difference.
$\Delta^5(x) = \Delta^4 n(x) - \Delta^4_{n+1}(x)$: Fifth level of forward difference.

Following Figs. 1 and 2 explains the proposed pyramidal structure forward interpolation procedure we followed in reduction of dimension.

3.4   GRNN for Classification

In this proposed study we exploited GRNN as classifiers in order to enhance the authenticity of the results and to improve evaluation performance in classifying the EEG signals into four different emotion classes with dimensional reduction approach. Artificial Neural Network (ANN), explicitly influenced by biological neural network from virtue of its properties which mimic human brain through set of algorithms, are considered to be one of important exposure of AI with various applications. In recent past Generalized Regression Neural Network (GRNN) called as memory based neural network have shown extensive performance in solving real world problems with wide range of applications. It is supervised learning model involved inherent abilities which is good at classifications and time series prediction tasks when compared to other classifiers. GRNN are variants of radial basis function, where analytically weights of these networks are estimated and the hidden layers of these networks make use of Gaussian activation function. Some of the principle advantages of GRNN: It is a single pass and quick learning network as they don't require iterative training procedure as other neural networks and also with given enough data it performs well in noisy environments. The topology of GRNN consists of three layers: Input layer, Hidden Layer (pattern layer and summation layer) and Output layer. Total number of observed attributes are treated as input units i.e. input vector I (Feature matrix) and these input layers are connected to pattern layers which contains neurons in providing training patterns and its outcomes to the summation layer to implement normalization of the resultant output set. All of pattern layers is connected to the neurons in summation layer [34, 35, 39–41] and for calculating weight vector the following Eq. 1 is used.

$$F(I) = \frac{\sum_{i=1}^{n} T_i W_i}{\sum_{i=1}^{n} W_i}, \quad W_i = e^{[\frac{||I - I_t||^2}{2h^2}]} \tag{1}$$

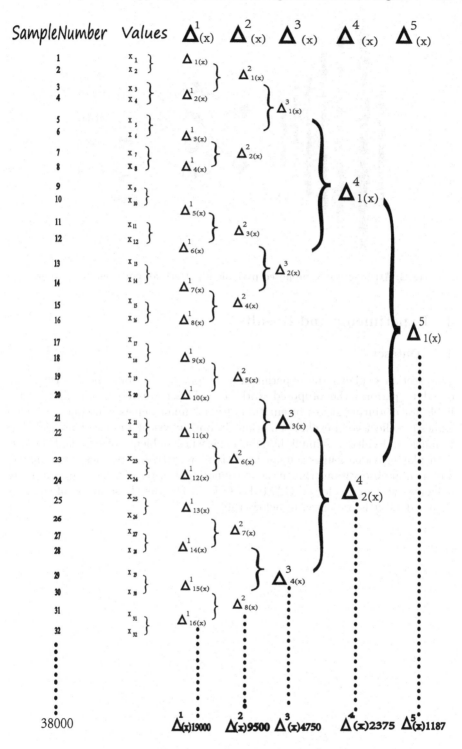

Fig. 1. Pyramidal structured forward difference.

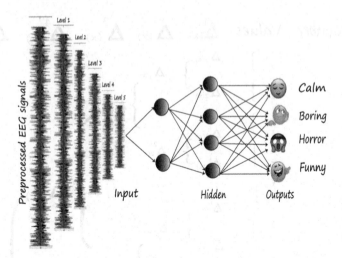

Fig. 2. Architecture of proposed pyramidal pattern for emotion recognition.

4   Experiments and Results

4.1   Dataset

This section explains the experimental design, results and about dataset we opted to perform the proposed work. In substance external stimuli is much liable for conjuring states of emotions from human beings subsequently video games are effective in evoking emotions in both physical and psychological way. In music and video as stimuli, humans experience ambience of sounds. However, with playing video games human brain is more active in physical experiments and mental observations this influences emotional states of the subjects in more enhanced way so we elected GAMEEMO EEG Dataset. Description of the particular dataset is presented in below Table 1.

Table 1. Description of GAMEEMO dataset

Description	Values
Type of signal recorded	EEG
Device Name	EMOTIVE EPOCH + MOBILE DEVICE
No of channels	14 (AF3, F7, F3, FC5, T7, O1, O2, P8, T8,FC6, F4, F8, AF4)
Sampling rate	Signals are down sampled 128 Hz
Signal bandwidth	0.16 HZ and 43 HZ
Sample length	38252 samples for each subject in every classes
Number of classes	4 (Boring, Calm, Funny, Horror)
Participants	28 (ranging from 20–27 ages)
Recording time duration	5 min for each game

4.2   Results

Matlab programming has been used in conducting experiments to stimulate our current study. In the empirical studies publicly available video game based GAMEEMO dataset was used. As we quoted in the earlier section the dataset contains EEG signals recorded from 14 channel emotive epoch device from 28 healthy participants while they are playing video games. Earlier sections illustrated the proposed work in how large number of EEG features is reduced into smaller set of data using new approach of dimensional reduction without disturbing original dimension of the dataset.

To start with the implementation phase, the prepossessed EEG features in time domain of all subjects in each class of emotion with length of 38000 are selected in order to diminished the large set of features (38000) into 1187 features followed by five different level of iterations. As we observed in the proposed architectures the large number of features from high dimension is reduced to half of its size with forward difference interpolation technique in 5 different levels of iterations in pyramidal pattern, obtained input EEG features are divided into training and testing sets in the ratio of 80–20 for classification purpose, the same procedure was carried out for all 14 channels of EEG signals collected from 28 subjects in all four classes of emotions. Finally GRNN classifiers was preferred due to its high performance in wide range of applications and also it is good at prediction task for classifying four different emotions. The results obtained for all 14 channels in proposed method is given in the below Table 2 and 3. It is noticeable from tabulated results comparing the proposed study, that is combination of dimensional reduction and GRNN outperforms with other existing methods.

Table 2. Comparison table of different dimensional reduction methods

Study	Methods	Data-set	Accuracy
Yu Chen [31]	Linear Discriminant Analysis+Ada-boost	DEAP	88.70
Qiang GAO [30]	Principal Component Analysis+SVM	Own data-set	89.17
DongKoo [32]	Genetic Algorithm	DEAP	71.76
Proposed method	**Pyramidal Approach**	**GAMEEMO**	100

Table 3. Comparison table on accuracy (percentage) using GAMEEMO dataset for all 14 channel EEG signals

Method	AF3	AF4	F3	F4	F7	F8	FC5	FC6	O1	O2	P7	P8	T7	T8
Alakus et al., method +KNN [14]	61	75	59	67	67	75	64	68	65	65	61	73	61	64
Alakus et al., method +SVM [14]	81	88	63	72	84	80	66	68	57	70	59	81	65	81
Alakus et al., method +MLPN [14]	86	87	79	83	84	84	79	85	79	83	79	77	75	79
Tuncer et al., method +LEDPatNet19 [32]	98.75	98.57	99.11	98.39	98.21	98.75	98.57	99,29	99.11	98.39	98.57	98.57	98.04	98.57
Tuncer et al., method +SVM [37]	99.33	99.55	98.66	98.21	98.66	99.78	99.88	98.66	97.32	99.33	99.78	98.88	98.88	100
Toramanl et al., method +Capsule Networks [38]	–	90.37	–	–	–	–	–	–	–	–	–	–	–	–
Our Proposed Method+GRNN	100	100	100	100	100	100	100	100	100	100	100	100	100	100

5   Discussion and Conclusion

This research study presents a new emotion classification model based on EEG signals. The prime objective was to reduce the higher dimension data into lower dimension for better classification results. The presented model is defined as pyramidal structured forward interpolation dimension reduction pattern. Empathetically, the proposed study has considerably positive impact when compared to existing dimension reduction methods. Because traditional dimension reduction methods performs data transformation approach where one dimensional EEG data is transformed into two dimensional data, in order to reduce the high dimension data to lower dimension, certainly our proposed work concentrated in dimension reduction procedure without disturbing the original dimension of dataset (only time domain features are considered) interpolation operations is executed for reducing dimensions and our model has Superiorly performed well without data transformation procedure. Conventional networks such as GRNN have generalization and convergence properties, in this direction we used GRNN for classifying four different emotions. This developed model was tested on GAMEEMO dataset in generating most efficient features in five different levels of iteration, which are utilized as input to GRNN classifier. It has been experimentally observed that proposed model achieved promising results for all 14 channel EEG signals in the particular dataset over contemporary studies. As per our knowledge base this concept of pyramidal structured dimension reduction is being first kind in literature. As future work we wish to open-up with several new dimension reduction approaches which is required for various emotion recognition applications in the field of machine learning.

Significant Contributions of this Study are as Follows:

- Pyramidal Approach, a new feature extraction method was used instead of conventional feature extraction methods.

- In the proposed study, feature extraction was carried out with Interpolation Technique which reduced the higher dimension data into lower dimension without losing the original information for all 14 channel prepossessed EEG signals of 28 subjects from GAMEEMO dataset.
- The proposed method achieved a higher-accuracy emotion recognition results for all 14 channel EEG signals. Which was better than the classification performance achieved in other studies in the literature.
- The limitation of the study was that it examined a single dataset and classifier. Further studies may examine other EEG based emotion dataset along with different classifiers for Proposed pyramidal model.

Notes

Source Code: https://github.com/thejushrinivas/Pyramidal.git.

References

1. Saxena, A., Khanna, A., Gupta, D.: Emotion recognition and detection methods: a comprehensive survey. J. Artif. Intell. Syst. **2**(1), 53–79 (2020)
2. Piana, S., Stagliano, A., Odone, F., Verri, A., Camurri, A.:Real-time automatic emotion recognition from body gestures. arXiv preprint arXiv:1402.5047 (2014)
3. Jolad, B., Khanai, R.: ANNs for automatic speech recognition—a survey. In: Jeena Jacob, I., Gonzalez-Longatt, F.M., Kolandapalayam Shanmugam, S., Izonin, I. (eds.) Expert Clouds and Applications. LNNS, vol. 209, pp. 35–48. Springer, Singapore (2022). https://doi.org/10.1007/978-981-16-2126-0_4
4. Jiang, X., Bian, G.-B., Tian, Z.: Removal of artifacts from EEG signals: a review. Sensors **19**(5), 987 (2019)
5. Kharche, S., Varanasi, B., Uberoi, N., Vallabhan, V., Yadav, S.:Brain Activity Detection and Analysis using EEG (2017)
6. Ekman, P.: Are there basic emotions? p. 550 (1992)
7. The Nature of Emotions: Human emotions have deep evolutionary roots, a fact that may explain their complexity and provide tools for clinical practice
8. Izard, C.E.: Basic emotions, relations among emotions, and emotion-cognition relations, p. 561 (1992)
9. Koelstra, S., et al.: DEAP: a database for emotion analysis; using physiological signals. IEEE Trans. Affect. Comput. **3**(1), 18–31 (2011)
10. Liu, W., Qiu, J.-L., Zheng W.-L., Lu, B.-L.: Comparing recognition performance and robustness of multimodal deep learning models for multimodal emotion recognition. IEEE Trans. Cogn. Dev. Syst. **14**(2), 715–729 (2021)
11. Maeng, J.H., Kang, D.H., Kim, D.H.: Deep learning method for selecting effective models and feature groups in emotion recognition using an asian multimodal database. Electronics **9**, 1988 (2020)
12. Katsigiannis, S., Ramzan, N.: DREAMER: a database for emotion recognition through EEG and ECG signals from wireless low-cost off-the-shelf devices. IEEE J. Biomed. Health Inform. **22**(1), 98–107 (2018). https://doi.org/10.1109/JBHI. 2017.2688239
13. Miranda-Correa, J.A., Abadi, M.K., Sebe, N., Patras, I.: Amigos: a dataset for affect, personality and mood research on individuals and groups. IEEE Trans. Affect. Comput. **12**(2), 479–493 (2018)

14. Alakus, T.B., Gonen, M., Turkoglu, I.: Database for an emotion recognition system based on EEG signals and various computer games - GAMEEMO. Biomed. Signal Process. Control **60**, 101951 (2020). https://doi.org/10.1016/j.bspc.2020.101951
15. Santamaria-Granados, L., Munoz-Organero, M., Ramirez-Gonzalez, G., Abdulhay, E., Arunkumar, N.J.I.A.: Using deep convolutional neural network for emotion detection on a physiological signals dataset (AMIGOS). IEEE Access **7**, 57–67 (2018)
16. Maithri, M., et al.: Automated emotion recognition: current trends and future perspectives. Comput. Methods Program. Biomed. **215**, 106646 (2022)
17. Zhang, L., Wang, S., Liu, B.: Deep learning for sentiment analysis: a survey. Wiley Interdisc. Rev. Data Min. Knowl. Discov. **8**(4), e 1253(2018)
18. Sarveniazi, A.: An actual survey of dimensionality reduction. Am. J. Comput. Math. **4**(2), 18, 43977 (2014)
19. Su, B., et al.: Discriminative dimensionality reduction for multi-dimensional sequences. IEEE Trans. Pattern Anal. Mach. Intell. **40**(1), 77–91 (2017)
20. Kording, K., Blohm, G., Schrater, P., Kay, K.: Appreciating diversity of goals in computational neuroscience (2018)
21. Filipović, V.: Optimization, classification and dimensionality reduction in biomedicine and bioinformatics. Biol. Serbica **39**(1) (2017)
22. Arora, M., Kumar, M., Garg, N.K.: Facial emotion recognition system based on PCA and gradient features. Natl. Acad. Sci. Lett. **41**(6), 365–368 (2018)
23. Harikumar, R., Sunil Kumar, P.: Dimensionality reduction techniques for processing epileptic encephalographic signals. Biomed. Pharmacol. J. **8**(1), 103106 (2015)
24. Gao, Q., Wang, C.H., Wang, Z., Song, X.L., Dong, E.Z., Song, Y.: EEG based emotion recognition using fusion feature extraction method. Multimed. Tools Appl. **79**(37), 27057–27074 (2020)
25. Wang, S.-H., Li, H.-T., Chang, E.-J., Wu, A.-Y.A.: Entropy-assisted emotion recognition of valence and arousal using XGBoost classifier. In: Iliadis, L., Maglogiannis, I., Plagianakos, V. (eds.) AIAI 2018. IAICT, vol. 519, pp. 249–260. Springer, Cham (2018). https://doi.org/10.1007/978-3-319-92007-8_22
26. Taherisadr, M., Joneidi, M., Rahnavard, N.: EEG signal dimensionality reduction and classification using tensor decomposition and deep convolutional neural networks. In: 2019 IEEE 29th International Workshop on Machine Learning for Signal Processing (MLSP). IEEE (2019)
27. García-Laencina, P.J., Rodríguez-Bermudez, G., Roca-Dorda, J.: Exploring dimensionality reduction of EEG features in motor imagery task classification. Expert Syst. Appl. **41**(11), 5285–5295 (2014)
28. Li, M., Xu, H., Liu, X., Lu, S.: Emotion recognition from multichannel EEG signals using K-nearest neighbor classification. Technol. Health Care **26**, 1–11 (2018). https://doi.org/10.3233/THC-174836
29. Kanuboyina, S., Venkata Penmetsa, R.R.: Electroencephalograph based human emotion recognition using artificial neural network and principal component analysis. IETE J. Res. 1–10 (2021)
30. Shon, D., et al.: Emotional stress state detection using genetic algorithm-based feature selection on EEG signals. Int. J. Environ. Res. Public Health **15**(11), 2461 (2018)
31. Chen, Y., Chang, R., Guo, J.: Emotion recognition of EEG signals based on the ensemble learning method: AdaBoost. Math. Probl. Eng. **2021**, 12, 8896062 (2021)
32. Tuncer, T., Dogan, S., Subasi, A.: A new fractal pattern feature generation function based emotion recognition method using EEG. Chaos Solitons Fractals **144**, 110671 (2021)

33. Liu, J., Meng, H., Li, M., Zhang, F., Qin, R., Nandi, A.K.: Emotion detection from EEG recordings based on supervised and unsupervised dimension reduction. Concurr. Comput. Pract. Exp. **30**(23), e4446 (2018)
34. Prakash, B.V.A., Ashoka, D.V., Manjunath Aradhya, V.N.: An exploration of PNN and GRNN models for efficient software development effort estimation (2015)
35. Aradhya, V.N.M., et al.: Learning through one shot: a phase by phase approach for COVID-19 chest X-ray classification. In: 2020 IEEE-EMBS Conference on Biomedical Engineering and Sciences (IECBES). IEEE (2021)
36. Duan, R.-N., Zhu, J.-Y., Lu, B.-L.: Differential entropy feature for EEG-based emotion classification. In: 2013 6th International IEEE/EMBS Conference on Neural Engineering (NER). IEEE (2013)
37. Tuncer, T., Dogan, S., Baygin, M., Acharya, U.R.: Tetromino pattern based accurate EEG emotion classification model. Artif. Intell. Med. **123**, 102210 (2022)
38. Toraman, S., Dursun, Ö.O.: GameEmo-CapsNet: emotion recognition from single-channel EEG signals using the 1D capsule networks. Traitement Signal **38**(6), 1689–1698 (2021)
39. Aradhya, V.N.M., Niranjan, S.K., Hemantha Kumar, G.: Probabilistic neural network based approach for handwritten character recognition. Spec. Issue IJCCT **1**(2), 3 (2010)
40. Aradhya, V.N.M., Pavithra, M.S., Naveena, C.: A robust multilingual text detection approach based on transforms and wavelet entropy. Proc. Technol. **4**, 232–237 (2012)
41. Aradhya, V.N., Mahmud, M., Guru, D.S., Agarwal, B., Kaiser, M.S.: One-shot cluster-based approach for the detection of COVID-19 from chest X-ray images. Cogn. Comput. **13**(4), 873–881 (2021)

Evaluation of Galvanic Skin Response (GSR) Signals Features for Emotion Recognition

Kuryati Kipli[1]([⊠])[iD], Aisya Amelia Abdul Latip[1], Kasumawati Lias[1][iD], Norazlina Bateni[1][iD], Salmah Mohamad Yusoff[2][iD], Jamaah Suud[3], M. A. Jalil[4], Kanad Ray[5], M. Shamim Kaiser[6], and Mufti Mahmud[7]

[1] Faculty of Engineering, Universiti Malaysia Sarawak, 94300 Kota Samarahan, Malaysia
kkuryati@unimas.my
[2] Faculty of Cognitive Sciences and Human Development, Universiti Malaysia Sarawak, 94300 Kota Samarahan, Malaysia
[3] Polytechnic Kuching Sarawak, 93050 Kuching, Sarawak, Malaysia
[4] Department of Physics, Faculty of Science, Universiti Teknologi Malaysia, 81310 Skudai, Johor, Malaysia
[5] Amity School of Applied Sciences, Amity University, Rajasthan 303001, India
[6] Institute of Information Technology, Jahangirnagar University, Savar, Dhaka 1342, Bangladesh
[7] Nottingham Trent University, Clifton Lane, Nottingham NG11 8NS, UK

Abstract. Over the years, physiological signals have shown its efficiency in emotion recognition. Galvanic skin response (GSR) is a quantifiable physiological signal generated from the change of skin conductance in response to emotional stimulation. Understanding human emotions through GSR signals can be a challenging task because of the characteristic's complexity. The current performance on the analysis of GSR signals has yet to be satisfactory due to a lack of detailed evaluation on the performance of features extracted from GSR signals. Previous studies have compared the recognition rates between different physiological signals between electroencephalogram (EEG), electrocardiogram (ECG), and GSR as a group or focused on the performance of emotion recognition using a fusion of signals. This paper presents an evaluation of extracted features specifically from GSR signals from a public dataset named as AMIGOS database. The MATLAB software was used for the simulation. In the study, feature extraction techniques were performed to extract features in time domain and frequency domain features. These features are ranked using the one-way ANOVA method in MATLAB. Several subsets of different number of features based on the type of feature and significance level were formed for optimum selection. The state of art classification algorithm for GSR which is Support Vector Machine (SVM) was employed to evaluate the classification performance using the ranked features. The methodology proposed by this study was able to achieve high accuracy rates that are comparable with existing studies that had employed the same AMIGOS database. The frequency domain features achieved the highest accuracy for all four emotion classes.

Keywords: GSR signal · Emotion recognition · Classifier · Feature extraction

M. Mahmud et al. (Eds.): AII 2022, CCIS 1724, pp. 260–274, 2022.
https://doi.org/10.1007/978-3-031-24801-6_19

1 Introduction

Emotion recognition has been applied in various fields especially in the medical field for disease identification. For instance, studies such as [1–3] have shown that emotion could be a key feature in determining autism spectrum disorder (ASD) to name a few. In the early years, research conducted on emotion recognition had focused on analysing body language, facial expressions, and speeches [4]. However, emotion recognition based on mentioned factors may be inefficient as these factors can be controlled externally [5] which indicates that an individual can mask their true emotions. Hence, the use of bio-signals such as the galvanic skin response (GSR) are more effective for emotion recognition as it involves responses in the autonomic nervous system (ANS). ANS refers to the control system of the body that primarily executes unconscious bodily functions which utilizes the interaction between psychosocial and biological factors [6]. GSR is defined as the electrical changes measured in the skin's surface in response to changes in the ANS [5]. Sweat formed on the skin surface triggered by emotional stimulation results in the changes in skin conductance level, hence producing measurable variation in the GSR [7].

GSR can be further grouped into two main components which are skin conductance level (SCL) and skin conductance response (SCR). SCL is referred as the tonic level which represents the skin conductance baseline meanwhile SCR is referred as the phasic level which represents the reactive rapid changes which is mostly event-related [7, 8]. Emotions are commonly represented using the valence-arousal bipolar model [9]. Valence represents the quality of an emotion, whether the emotions are positive such as happy and excited or negative emotions such as sad and angry. Meanwhile, arousal represents the intensity or the quantitative activation level of an emotion.

In general, there are four main steps involved in GSR-based emotion recognition starting with signal acquisition, followed by pre-processing, feature extraction, and classification. Pre-processing is the process that involves the removal of any noises or unwanted information from the raw data signal. Feature extraction itself is a complex step as it involves the transformation of raw data signals into measurable features [10]. Features can be extracted in time domain, frequency domain, and time-frequency domain. The classification step comprises of predicting a class based on given data points involving machine learning techniques [11] such as Support Vector Machine (SVM), Decision Tree (DT), K-Nearest Neighbour (kNN), Quadratic Discriminant Analysis (QDA), Random Forest (RF), and Naïve Bayes (NB). Labelling the samples is important for classifiers to detect the class of each signal.

In this paper, emotion recognition was conducted using GSR signals from AMIGOS dataset, which is a publicly available multimodal dataset that contains measures of electroencephalogram (EEG), electrocardiogram (ECG) and GSR. The focus of this paper is on the evaluation of features extracted from the GSR signals. The four emotional classes investigated are high valence low arousal (HVLA), high valence high arousal (HVHA), low valence low arousal (LVLA), and low valence high arousal (LVHA). Furthermore, this paper critically discussed the obtained results.

2 Methodology

2.1 Materials

For this research, a personal computer with the specifications of Intel(R) Core™ i5-8300H microprocessor for CPU, 8 GB for Random Access Memory (RAM) and 64-bit operating system powered by Windows 10 was utilized.

MATLAB (R2019b) has been selected to perform this research because of its diverse choice of utility and easy interface. The software provides toolboxes and interactive apps that allow user to work with data using different algorithms which is useful for emotion recognition purposes. The toolbox and application selected for the proposed methodology are Signal Analyzer application from Signal Processing Toolbox, Classification Learner application from Statistics and Machine Learning Toolbox, and Diagnostic Feature Designer application.

2.2 Dataset

For this study, the AMIGOS dataset will be used to evaluate selected feature extraction method on GSR signals. AMIGOS dataset is a publicly available multimodal dataset that contains measures of EEG, ECG and GSR [12]. This study will be using the GSR data provided. Due to the fact that the long videos are more likely to elicit various emotional states from the participants instead of a specific category in valence and arousal level, this research specifically focuses on the dataset from short video experiment (16 short videos).

2.3 Proposed Methodology

Figure 1 describes the process of emotion recognition using GSR signals. For this research, an existing dataset will be used which is the AMIGOS Dataset which is discussed in Sect. 2.2. Then, a suitable software is selected to conduct the signal processing along with the relevant toolbox and apps to proceed with the pre-processing, data organizing and labelling, feature extraction, and classification of the GSR signals. Then, the collection of data is conducted and proceed with simulation and data analysis. Specifically, this study focuses on the feature extraction of GSR.

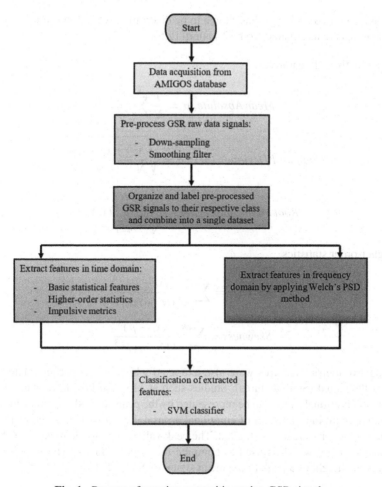

Fig. 1. Process of emotion recognition using GSR signals

2.4 Feature Extraction of GSR Signal

For this method, features of the processed signal are extracted using basic statistical value method for time domain, and Welch's power spectral density (PSD) method for frequency domain. Feature extraction is defined as the process of transforming raw data signal into a list of measurable features [13]. Diagnostic Feature Designer application was used to perform the extraction.

Feature Extraction in Time Domain. For the extraction of features in time domain, the Diagnostic Feature Designer application is used. The features extracted are basic statistical values [5] which are the standard deviation (SD), root mean square (RMS), and mean, followed by higher-order statistics which are skewness, and kurtosis as studies in [5, 8, 14] have shown that these statistical features are efficient. Hence, these features were selected based on how it has shown to be discriminative for emotion recognition. These features are as equated from (2.1) until (2.5).

Basic Statistical Features,

$$Mean\,Absolute, \mu = \frac{1}{N} \sum_{n=1}^{N} |x_n| \tag{2.1}$$

$$Standard\,Deviation\,(SD), \sigma = \sqrt{\frac{1}{N} \frac{\sum (x_i - \mu)^2}{N}} \tag{2.2}$$

$$Root\,Mean\,Square\,(RMS), \sqrt{\frac{1}{N} \sum_{n=1}^{N} (x_n)^2} \tag{2.3}$$

Higher-order statistics,

$$Kurtosis = \sum_{i=1}^{N} \frac{(x_i - \mu)^4}{(N-1)\sigma^4} \tag{2.4}$$

$$Skewness = \sum_{i=1}^{N} \frac{(x_i - \mu)^3}{(N-1)\sigma^3} \tag{2.5}$$

Impulsive metrics features were also extracted which are properties related to the peaks of the signal (SCR features). Studies such as [15] and [16] have stated that the intensity of emotional states can be represented by the peaks of GSR signals which gives quantitative input into the level of emotional arousal. Features such as the peak values and impulse factor were also extracted. The peak value refers to the maximum absolute value of the signal which is used to compute the impulse factor. The impulse factor compares the height of a peak to the mean signal of each GSR signal.

Feature Extraction in Frequency Domain. Next, features in frequency domain were extracted by using the same application which is the Diagnostic Feature Designer. For feature extraction in the frequency domain, the Welch's PSD method was selected as it has shown satisfactory accuracy in studies such as [5]. The Welch's PSD method is commonly referred as the weighted overlapped segment averaging method or periodogram averaging method [17]. This method returns the estimation of PSD of the input signal by using the averaging estimator of Welch's overlapping segment. The Welch's PDS method smooths over non-systematic noise and robust to some non-stationaries. For the extraction of frequency domain features, spectral estimation is required. According to [17], the main objective of spectral processing is to decompose data into a sum of weighted sinusoids. The frequency content of the phenomenon can be assessed from this decomposition. Welch's PSD spectral estimation analyses how the signal varies with frequency [17].

After the estimation, the frequency domain features extracted were the spectral peaks, which are the peak amplitude and peak frequency for four number of peaks, and band power. These extracted features were then saved together with the time domain features in a single table for selection and inserted to the Classification Learner application provided by the Statistic and Machine Learning Toolbox. After the extraction of all features, the Diagnostic Feature Designer have a ranking features tool which ranks the extracted features using the one-way ANOVA method and is further discussed in Sect. 2.6.

2.5 Feature Selection

The ranking tool provided by the application applies the one-way ANOVA method in sorting the features by importance. A bar graph and a table are generated based on the ranking. The bar chart legend was normalized to 1 for visual comparison purposes meanwhile the table displays unnormalized ranking scores. ANOVA is a popular method used for emotion recognition [8, 18–20] hence it was selected. According to [21], ANOVA is the analysis of variance which primarily involves the comparison of mean values of groups that are mutually independent groups. It studies the significance level differences of two or more group in a dataset. The significance level, $\propto$ is defined as the maximum acceptable error range that can reject the null hypothesis, H_0. It is also known as the measure of strength of evidence needed to be in a sample before the null hypothesis can be rejected. This helps in concluding the statistical significance of the variables for the study [21]. In this study, it involves 4 groups, HVLA, HVHA, LVLA, and LVHA. Hence, the null hypothesis is "the population means of these 4 groups are the same" and the alternative hypothesis, H_1 is "at least one of the populations mean among these 4 groups is different". In a mathematical term, the H_0 and H_1 are represented as follows:

$$H_0 : \mu_1 = \mu_2 = \mu_3 = \mu_4 \tag{2.6}$$

$$H_1 : \mu_1 \neq \mu_2 \text{ or } \mu_1 \neq \mu_3 \text{ or } \mu_1 \neq \mu_4 \text{ or } \mu_2 \neq \mu_3 \text{ or } \mu_2 \neq \mu_4 \text{ or } \mu_3 \neq \mu_4 \tag{2.7}$$

Hence, when the mean values of any two groups among the four groups are different from each other, the null hypothesis is rejected.

2.6 Classification

Classes are evaluated from four class which are HVLA, HVHA, LVLA, and LVHA [22]. For the classification, an application named the Classification Learner under the toolbox Statistic and Machine Learning is used. All features that have been extracted were presented in the workspace which allows the Classification Learner to identify the predictors and responses for classification. On training the dataset, the appropriate parameters of the classifiers are selected through a 5-fold cross-validation method which 80% of the data are trained while the remaining 20% is for the test [23].

In this study, the classifier used to analyse the accuracy of the features extracted is Support Vector Machine (SVM). SVM was observed to be the most common and best classifier for the classification of GSR signals [5, 13, 24–27]. The parameters of each classifier were selected based on trial-and-error method where different set of parameters were adjusted and tested accordingly. The set of parameters that provided optimum performance were selected. The type of SVM classifier selected is the Quadratic SVM classifier which uses the quadratic kernel function.

2.7 Performance Evaluation

To compare the performance results, the results obtained from the classification were compared with the prediction of affective states that was originally obtained by the authors of the AMIGOS database. The performance results are measured in terms of accuracy [22]. The accuracy was calculated using the values of true positive (TP), true negative (TN), false positive (FP), and false negative (FN) from the confusion matrix computed by the Classification Learner tool using the Eq. 2.8.

$$Accuracy = \frac{TP + TN}{TP + TN + FP + FN} \tag{2.8}$$

3 Result and Discussion

The AMIGOS database consist of 40 participants and the experiments were conducted in two settings. This research focused on the first setting only which only involved the 16 short videos because the long videos have the possibility to elicit various emotional states from the participants instead of a specific category in the bipolar model. The pre-processing methods selected for the proposed methodology are re-sampling and applying smoothing filters. As for feature extraction, the techniques selected are extracting statistical features for time-domain, and Welch's PSD for frequency domain. For classification, classifier trained is SVM. During the classification, classes were grouped into four; HVLA, HVHA, LVLA, and LVHA.

The following sections described the obtained results from feature extraction and classification of the GSR signals. The accuracy was computed and compared with existing studies including studies that had also used the GSR signals from the AMIGOS database.

3.1 Feature Extraction

A total of 16 features were extracted using the Diagnostic Feature Designer application. For time domain, three types of features were extracted which are the common statistical features, high order statistics and event related SCR features. For frequency domain, Table 1 shows the summary of the extracted features. For comparison purpose, the performance of the features is compared based on the domain type and importance.

3.2 Evaluation of Extracted Features (Feature Selection)

Figure 2 shows a chart computed using the simulation in MATLAB that has ranked the extracted feature by importance using the ANOVA method. From the top it represents the most significant feature meanwhile the bottom represents the feature that has the lowest significancy. The bar chart has been normalized for visual purposes and the table located at the right is the chart legend that represents the actual value of the significance level of each feature. In Fig. 2, it is shown that the most significant features are the frequency domain features based on the one-way ANOVA ranking method. The peak amplitude

Table 1. Summary of extracted features and the parameters

Domain	Features	Total number of features	Parameters
Time-domain	Statistical features	7	Mean absolute, standard deviation, and root mean square
	High order statistics		Skewness and kurtosis
	SCR features		Peak values and impulse factor
Frequency domain	Spectral peaks (number of peaks = 4)	9	Peak amplitude, and peak frequency
	Band power		Band power

and peak frequency of the first peak of each signal has shown the highest significance level, 61.5243 and 60.2998 respectively which indicates that the evidence needed to reject the null hypothesis is small. This shows that frequency domain features are able to sort the features according to their respective class more efficiently compared to the time domain features. The most significant time domain features based on the significance level are the kurtosis and skewness which is 13.6915 and 3.904, respectively.

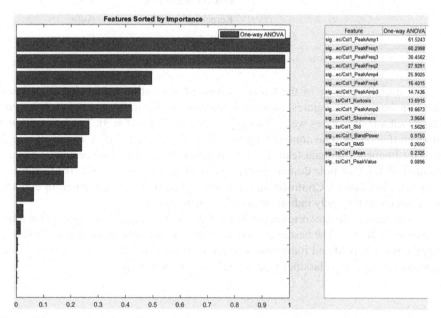

Fig. 2. Chart representation of extracted features sorted by importance using one-way ANOVA method

Despite most of the frequency domain features are shown to be the most significant compared to the time domain features, a few of the features show low significance level such as the band power and peak values which significance levels are 0.9750 and 0.0896 respectively. Meanwhile, most of the time domain features are less than 3. The performance evaluation of features through the box plots were further justified using this tool. Based on this variance analysis, features selection for the classification are conducted to observe the influence of the number of features inserted in the classifier and the importance of each feature towards the accuracy for emotion recognition.

3.3 Classification

Classifier employed was Support Vector Machine (SVM). Classification is not the main contribution of this research; thus, existing classifier was adopted to obtain the best recognition rates. Since it is important to select optimum parameters, different configurations for each classifier were applied and compared. The optimum parameters setting for the SVM classifier are summarized in Table 2.

Table 2. Classifier parameters selected for classification that had shown optimum performance

Classifier	Type	Parameters	
SVM	Quadratic SVM	Kernel function	Quadratic
		Box constraint level	1
		Kernel scale mode	Auto
		Multiclass	One-vs-one

The overall accuracy of the features extracted in emotion recognition is analysed based on the types of features, number of features and the importance of each feature. Several subsets of features were formed by taking the Top 3 (f = 3), Top 5 (f = 5), and all seven (f = 7) for time domain features, Top 5 (f = 5), Top 7 (f = 7) and all nine (f = 9) for frequency domain features, a combination of the Top 3 of frequency domain feature and Top 2 of time domain features (f = 5), and all sixteen (f = 16) features as summarized in Table 3. Confusion matrixes were generated for each subset for efficient visualization and to study individual accuracy performance.

The overall results are sorted according to the classifier type, feature type and number of features in Table 3. The best and worst accuracy for each type of features (by column) is highlighted in bold and italic letters respectively and the best overall accuracy over all feature subsets and classifier type is marked with an asterisk.

Table 3. Classification average accuracy (%) based on type of classifier, number of features, and features importance.

Classifier	Feature type, and number of features, f							
	Time domain only			Frequency domain only			Time and frequency domain	
	f = 3	f = 5	f = 7 (all)	f = 5	f = 7	f = 9 (all)	f = 5	f = 16 (all)
SVM	60.2	**63.3**	62.0	72.7	**83.0***	79.8	77.0	**79.5**

Based on Table 3, the highest accuracy is achieved by the subset of the Top 7 of only frequency domain features with the accuracy of 83.0% using the SVM classifier. Subsets that consist of only frequency domain features overall shows significantly better accuracy compared to time domain features. The lowest accuracy rate achieved by using only frequency domain features is 72.7% which is significantly higher when compared to the lowest accuracy achieved by using only time domain features which is 60.2% which is also the lowest accuracy achieved overall. Moreover, increasing the number of features from five to seven for the frequency domain features results in an increase in the accuracy. Furthermore, it is observed that increasing the features from seven to nine lowers the accuracy rate by a small rate, but higher overall when compared to when only the Top 5 features were used. A slight decrease in the accuracy is observed when all seven time-domain features were selected using SVM (from 63.3% to 62.0%).

To analyse the accuracy performance when both time and frequency domain features are selected, two subsets were created. The first subset consists of the Top 3 of frequency domain features and the Top 2 of time-domain features and the second subset consist of all 16 features. Statistically, the first subset of the time and frequency domain features shows better accuracy performance which is 77.0%. Increasing the number of features from f = 5 to f = 16 has shown an increase in accuracy to 79.5%.

3.4 Discussion

In this study, each results obtain were analysed and explained from the feature extraction to the classification. The ranking tool is used to highlight the importance of each feature using the one-way ANOVA ranking method. Several subsets were formed to compare the recognition rates score based on the type of features, the number of features, and significance. The calculation was based on the parameters true positive (TP), false positive (FP), true negative (TN), and false negative (FN) from the confusion matrices generated. The relation between the type, number, and significance of the features were discussed. Critical findings from the results have been discussed.

From the results, it can be observed that greater number of features used for emotion recognition does not guarantee higher accuracy. This is based on two observations. Firstly, when the number of features were increased, most of the subsets had their recognition rates decreased. However, it was also observed that too small of a number also yields a low recognition rate. The subset that contains only five frequency domain features yields a recognition rate of 72.7%. When increased the number to seven, the recognition rate increased to 83.0%. However, when all nine frequency domain features were used, the recognition rate decreased to 79.8%. This shows two opposite trends of the relation between the number of features and recognition rates. From this observation, it is first concluded that optimum number of features must be selected to achieve high recognition rate. This then leads to another observation which is the significancy of each feature has a bigger effect on the recognition rate. Based on Fig. 2, it is shown that frequency domain features dominate the top spots in terms of importance meanwhile most of the time domain features are observed to be in the lower spots. Hence, referring to the example used earlier, the subset that consist of only five frequency domain features are the Top 5 frequency domain features meanwhile the subset that consist of only seven frequency domain features are the Top 7, and the subset that uses all nine frequency domain features shows that in that subset, included a feature that is less significance, in other words, inefficient. From these observations, it is concluded that using features which are more significant yields higher recognition rate. Moreover, it was observed that using only frequency domain features overall give higher and more consistent rate of recognition rates compared to when only time domain features or both types of features were used. This shows that the significancy of each feature and type of feature have bigger influence on the recognition rates. It is noted that existing studies such as [16] have shown that statistical features are considered to be efficient for the detection of emotion. However, this research has found that frequency domain features are more efficient for the emotion recognition for GSR signals. The study by [5] have also shown frequency achieved higher recognition rates compared to time domain features.

Table 4 summarizes the comparison between the highest average accuracy rate achieved by this study and existing that had used the GSR signals from the AMIGOS database. The method applied by [8] is similar to this study where features in time domain and frequency domain were extracted, except, [8] had also extracted features in the time-frequency domain specifically Mel-frequency cepstral coefficients, DWT coefficients, and SWT features which totals up to 621 features altogether. The study was able to achieve a high accuracy rate of 85.75% and 83.90% for arousal and valence respectively. In the recent years, more studies had conducted emotion recognition using convolutional neural network. For instance, [22] had applied the deep learning approach using Deep Learning Convolutional Neural Network (DCNN) on the AMIGOS database which results in an accuracy rate of 75% and 71% for valence and arousal respectively. A study by [28] had proposed a Long Short-Term Memory (LSTM) and 1-Dimensional Convolutional Neural Network (1D-CNN) architecture for the emotion recognition using the GSR signals from the AMIGOS database which achieved an accuracy rate of 63.67%. Another study [29] had proposed a multimodal model for emotion recognition that applied a 3-Dimensional Convolutional Neural Network (3D-CNN) as well as 1D-CNN which results in an accuracy rate of 84.69%. In this project, the highest classification average accuracy achieved was when only the Top 7 frequency domain features were used using the SVM which was 83.0%. This shows that the study was able to achieve high accuracy that is comparable with existing studies that have used the same GSR signals from the AMIGOS database. This study was able to achieve higher accuracy compared to studies by [22] and [28] without using the complex convolutional technique. Besides this, study by [8] focused more on applying different feature selection techniques such as Joint Mutual Information (JMI) and Conditional Mutual Information Maximization (CMIM) and further involved the extraction of Mel-Frequency Cepstral Coefficients (MFCC) that enabled the study to achieved higher accuracy rates.

Table 4. Accuracy comparison between existing studies that had used AMIGOS database

Research	Year	Methodology/Features Extracted	Emotion classes	Accuracy rates
[8]	2019	Time-frequency domain, time domain, and frequency domain	Arousal and valence	85.75% (A) 83.90% (V)
[28]	2020	LSTM and 1D-CNN	HVLA, HVHA, LVLA, and LVHA	63.67%
[22]	2018	DCNN	Arousal and valence	71% (A) 75% (V)
[29]	2019	3D-CNN and 1D-CNN	HVLA, HVHA, LVLA, and LVHA	84.69%
This study	2021	Time domain, and frequency domain features	HVLA, HVHA, LVLA, and LVHA	83.0%

4 Conclusion and Recommendation

This paper presented feature extraction on GSR signals from the AMIGOS database. A total of 640 GSR signals were pre-processed using the toolbox and applications provided in MATLAB. Data organizing and labelling of the pre-processed signals were done carefully to correctly label each signal according to their respective emotion class. Using the variety of features selection provided by the Diagnostic Feature Designer application, for the time domain feature extraction, a total of seven time domain features were extracted which were mean, root mean square, kurtosis, standard deviation, skewness, peak values, and impulse factor. For frequency domain features, a total of nine features were extracted which were band power, peak frequency, and peak amplitude for all four number of peaks. For classification, for validation, 5-folds cross validation was applied, and the classifier used was SVM. The best configuration was selected based on optimum performance achieved.

The main contribution of the paper is the evaluation on the features extracted from the GSR signals. The one-way ANOVA method was used to rank the features according to feature importance. Eight subsets were created to compare the recognition rate based on the type of features, the number of features, and significance. It was observed that frequency domain features were able to yield the highest recognition rate overall with the highest being 83.0% achieved by the subset consists of the Top 7 frequency domain features. The time domain features performed the least efficient overall ($< 63.3\%$). Using both time and frequency domain were also able to achieve a high recognition rate with the highest being 79.5%. However, it was still lower compared to frequency domain features only. It was also observed that greater number of features used does not guarantee higher accuracy. It was found that the significancy of each feature type had a bigger effect on the recognition rate. Hence, the performance of the extracted features was successfully evaluated based on features importance and significancy from the average accuracy.

A limitation of this research is the accuracy performance achieved may not be as optimum as presented due to several factors such as the applied pre-processing and feature extraction techniques may have not been conducted optimally and because of the selection of classifier. Thus, further exploration on the performance of extracted features from GSR signals should be conducted to validate more efficiently. Furthermore, different classifications method such as kNN and Decision Tree classifiers can be applied to investigate the efficiency of extracted features on the recognition rate of emotion recognition using GSR signals. In addition, more types of features should also be explored such as the MFCC.

References

1. Rahman, M.A., Brown, D.J., Shopland, N., Burton, A., Mahmud, M.: Explainable multimodal machine learning for engagement analysis by continuous performance test (2022)
2. Mahmud, M., et al.: Towards explainable and privacy-preserving artificial intelligence for personalisation in autism spectrum disorder. Presented at the (2022)
3. Biswas, M., Kaiser, M.S., Mahmud, M., Al Mamun, S., Hossain, M.S., Rahman, M.A.: An XAI based autism detection: the context behind the detection. In: Mahmud, M., Kaiser, M.S., Vassanelli, S., Dai, Q., Zhong, N. (eds.) BI 2021. LNCS (LNAI), vol. 12960, pp. 448–459. Springer, Cham (2021). https://doi.org/10.1007/978-3-030-86993-9_40
4. Ménard, M., Richard, P., Hamdi, H., Daucé, B., Yamaguchi, T.: Emotion recognition based on heart rate and skin conductance. In: PhyCS 2015 - 2nd International Conference on Physiological Computing Systems, Proceedings, pp. 26–32 (2015). https://doi.org/10.5220/000524 1100260032
5. Das, P., Khasnobish, A., Tibarewala, D.N.: Emotion recognition employing ECG and GSR signals as markers of ANS. Conf. Adv. Signal Process. CASP **2016**, 37–42 (2016). https://doi.org/10.1109/CASP.2016.7746134
6. Sarchiapone, M., et al.: The association between electrodermal activity (EDA), depression and suicidal behaviour: a systematic review and narrative synthesis. BMC Psychiatry **18**, 1–27 (2018). https://doi.org/10.1186/s12888-017-1551-4
7. Gautam, A., Simões-Capela, N., Schiavone, G., Acharyya, A., de Raedt, W., van Hoof, C.: A data driven empirical iterative algorithm for GSR signal pre-processing. In: European Signal Processing Conference, vol. 2018, pp. 1162–1166 (2018). https://doi.org/10.23919/EUSIPCO.2018.8553191
8. Shukla, J., Barreda-Angeles, M., Oliver, J., Nandi, G.C., Puig, D.: Feature Extraction and Selection for Emotion Recognition from Electrodermal Activity. IEEE Trans. Affect. Comput. **12**, 857–869 (2019). https://doi.org/10.1109/TAFFC.2019.2901673
9. Goshvarpour, A., Abbasi, A., Goshvarpour, A.: Science direct an accurate emotion recognition system using ECG and GSR signals and matching pursuit method. Biomed. J. **40**, 355–368 (2018). https://doi.org/10.1016/j.bj.2017.11.001
10. Domínguez-Jiménez, J.A., Campo-Landines, K.C., Martínez-Santos, J.C., Delahoz, E.J., Contreras-Ortiz, S.H.: A machine learning model for emotion recognition from physiological signals. Biomed. Signal Process. Control **55**, 101646 (2020). https://doi.org/10.1016/j.bspc.2019.101646

11. Sohaib, A.T., Qureshi, S., Hagelbäck, J., Hilborn, O., Jerčić, P.: Evaluating classifiers for emotion recognition using EEG. In: Schmorrow, D.D., Fidopiastis, C.M. (eds.) AC 2013. LNCS (LNAI), vol. 8027, pp. 492–501. Springer, Heidelberg (2013). https://doi.org/10.1007/978-3-642-39454-6_53

12. Miranda-correa, J.A., Member, S., Abadi, M.K., Member, S.: AMIGOS : a dataset for affect. Pers. Mood Res. Individuals Groups. **3045**, 1–14 (2018). https://doi.org/10.1109/TAFFC.2018.2884461

13. Das, T.R., Hasan, S., Sarwar, S.M., Das, J.K., Rahman, M.A.: Facial spoof detection using support vector machine. Adv. Intell. Syst. Comput. **1309**, 615–625 (2021). https://doi.org/10.1007/978-981-33-4673-4_50/COVER/

14. Ayata, D., Yaslan, Y., Kamasak, M.: Emotion recognition via galvanic skin response: comparison of machine learning algorithms and feature extraction methods. Istanbul Univ. J. Electr. Electron. Eng. **17**, 3129–3136 (2017)

15. Bakker, J., Pechenizkiy, M., Sidorova, N.: What's your current stress level? detection of stress patterns from GSR sensor data. In: Proceedings - IEEE International Conference on Data Mining, (ICDM), pp. 573–580 (2011). https://doi.org/10.1109/ICDMW.2011.178

16. Hossein Aqajari, S.A., Labbaf, S., Rahmani, A.M., Dutt, N., Naeini, E.K., Mehrabadi, M.A.: GSR analysis for stress: development and validation of an open source tool for noisy naturalistic GSR data. arXiv (2020)

17. Solomon, M.O.: PSD Computations Using Welch's Method. Sandia National Laboratories, vol. 64 (1991)

18. Setyohadi, D.B., Kusrohmaniah, S., Gunawan, S.B., Pranowo, P.A.S.: Galvanic skin response data classification for emotion detection. Int. J. Electr. Comput. Eng. **8**, 4004–4014 (2018). https://doi.org/10.11591/ijece.v8i5.pp4004-4014

19. Gravenhorst, F., Muaremi, A., Tröster, G., Arnrich, B., Gruenerbl, A.: Towards a mobile galvanic skin response measurement system for mentally disordered patients. In: BODYNETS 2013 - 8th International Conference on Body Area Networks, vol. 1, pp. 432–435 (2013). https://doi.org/10.4108/icst.bodynets.2013.253684

20. Jang, E.H., Park, B.J., Kim, S.H., Chung, M.A., Park, M.S., Sohn, J.H.: Emotion classification based on bio-signals emotion recognition using machine learning algorithms. In: Proceedings - 2014 International Conference on Information Science, Electronics and Electrical Engineering, ISEEE, pp. 1373–1376 (2014)

21. Kim, T.K.: Understanding one-way anova using conceptual figures. Korean J. Anesthesiol. **70**, 22–26 (2017). https://doi.org/10.4097/kjae.2017.70.1.22

22. Santamaria-Granados, L., Munoz-Organero, M., Ramirez-Gonzalez, G., Abdulhay, E., Arunkumar, N.: using deep convolutional neural network for emotion detection on a physiological signals dataset (AMIGOS). IEEE Access **7**, 57–67 (2019). https://doi.org/10.1109/ACCESS.2018.2883213

23. Yadav, S., Shukla, S.: Analysis of k-fold cross-validation over hold-out validation on colossal datasets for quality classification. In: 2016 Proceedings of the 6th International Advanced Computing Conference (IACC), pp. 78–83 (2016). https://doi.org/10.1109/IACC.2016.25

24. Perez-Rosero, M.S., Rezaei, B., Akcakaya, M., Ostadabbas, S.: Decoding emotional experiences through physiological signal processing. In: IEEE International Conference on Acoustics, Speech and Signal Processing – Proceedings (ICASSP), pp. 881–885 (2017). https://doi.org/10.1109/ICASSP.2017.7952282

25. Wei, W., Jia, Q., Feng, Y., Chen, G.: Emotion recognition based on weighted fusion strategy of multichannel physiological signals. Comput. Intell. Neurosci. **2018**, 1–10 (2018). https://doi.org/10.1155/2018/5296523

26. Šalkevicius, J., Damaševičius, R., Maskeliunas, R., Laukienė, I.: Anxiety level recognition for virtual reality therapy system using physiological signals. Electronics **8**, 1039 (2019). https://doi.org/10.3390/electronics8091039

27. Wiem, M.B.H., Lachiri, Z.: Emotion assessing using valence-arousal evaluation based on peripheral physiological signals and support vector machine. In: 2016 4th International Conference on Control Engineering and Information Technology, CEIT (2017). https://doi.org/10.1109/CEIT.2016.7929117

28. Dar, M.N., Akram, M.U., Khawaja, S.G., Pujari, A.N.: CNN and LSTM-based emotion charting using physiological signals. Sensors **20**, 1–26 (2020). https://doi.org/10.3390/s20164551

29. Zhao, Y., Cao, X., Lin, J., Yu, D., Cao, X.: Multimodal emotion recognition model using physiological signals (2019)

Application of AI and Informatics in Pattern Recognition

A Privacy-Preserving Federated-MobileNet for Facial Expression Detection from Images

Tapotosh Ghosh[1]([✉]) [iD], Md. Hasan Al Banna[2] [iD], Md. Jaber Al Nahian[2] [iD],
M. Shamim Kaiser[3] [iD], Mufti Mahmud[4,5] [iD], Shaobao Li[6], and Nelishia Pillay[7]

[1] United International University, Dhaka, Bangladesh
tapotoshghosh@gmail.com
[2] Bangladesh University of Professionals, Dhaka, Bangladesh
{hasan.banna,jaber.nahian}@bup.edu.bd
[3] Jahangirnagar University, Savar, Dhaka, Bangladesh
mskaiser@juniv.edu
[4] Department of Computer Science, Nottingham Trent University, Clifton Campus, Nottingham NG11 8NS, UK
mufti.mahmud@ntu.ac.uk
[5] MTIF and CIRC, Nottingham Trent University, Clifton Campus, Nottingham NG11 8NS, UK
[6] School of Electrical Engineering, Yanshan University, Qinhuangdao 066004, China
shl@ysu.edu.cn
[7] Department of Computer Science, University of Pretoria, Hillcrest, Pretoria, South Africa
nelishia.pillay@up.ac.za

Abstract. Facial expression recognition is an intriguing research area that has been explored and utilized in a wide range of applications such as health, security, and human-computer interactions. The ability to recognize facial expressions accurately is crucial for human-computer interactions. However, most of the facial expression analysis techniques have so far paid little or no concern to users' data privacy. To overcome this concern, in this paper, we incorporated Federated Learning (FL) as a privacy-preserving machine learning approach in the field of facial expression recognition to develop a shared model without exposing personal information. The individual models are trained on the different client devices where the data is stored. In this work, a lightweight Convolutional Neural Network (CNN) model called the MobileNet architecture is utilised to detect expressions from facial images. To evaluate the model, two publicly available datasets are used and several experiments are conducted. The result shows that the proposed privacy-preserving Federated-MobileNet approach could recognize facial expressions with considerable accuracy compared to the general approaches.

Keywords: Emotion recognition · Facial expressions · Federated learning · Privacy-preserving

M. Mahmud et al. (Eds.): AII 2022, CCIS 1724, pp. 277–292, 2022.
https://doi.org/10.1007/978-3-031-24801-6_20

1   Introduction

Human emotions such as happiness, sadness, fear, disgust, anger, or surprise can be a great asset to detecting the mental state of a person, and based on that emotion-aware systems can be designed [4]. Emotion-aware systems are used for depression detection [17], distress prediction [32], on-call customer service [9,23], mode monitoring and control [13,16], sports highlight generation from excitement features [29], automated tiredness detection for drivers [38], elderly fall monitoring [30], action recognition [12], and many other day to day applications. Emotions can be detected from images, speech, or text [8]. For image-based emotion detection models, facial features are used to classify the images into one of the emotion categories. For image-based classification tasks, the amount of data for the machine learning model training is huge, which demands high computational power. Moreover, many people are not comfortable sharing their personal images for emotion-aware applications. Since the images in datasets are stored in the cloud for malicious activities. Therefore, a new secured approach is needed where confidentiality of the user data can be ensured with a limited increase of required resources.

The application of artificial intelligence (AI) based methods have been applied in various application domains [1–7,14,19,34,36,39,40]. However, most of these methods don't ensure the privacy of the data. To ensure the privacy of user data, the concept of federated learning was introduced in the year 2017 [26,27,35]. It is a decentralized training approach of machine learning models, where the privacy of the data is ensured. Since user data are trained in local models, and only the parameters of the model are sent to the global server, users can feel safe about their privacy. As image-based emotion-aware systems demand secure processing of user images, federated learning can be used for this kind of application. Yurochkin et al. [42] proposed to use federated learning with neural networks with a Bayesian non-parametric approach. Tsouvalas et al. [37] proposed a federated learning-based semi-supervised learning approach for speech emotion recognition where both labelled and unlabeled data are used. Chhikara et al. [10] proposed an emotion monitoring system to enhance the productivity of the office environment using a federated learning approach. They used both image and speech signals for this task. Yang et al. [41] proposed a privacy protection model using federated learning for human images. They used ensemble models for achieving this goal. In this paper, a federated learning-based approach has been approached for expression detection with a transfer learning approach.

Since MobileNet [15] is both lightweight and provides good detection accuracy, this paper used this model for expression recognition with federated learning. For testing the robustness of the proposed model 4 different testing experiments were done, where the proposed model was tested with only the FER2013 dataset, CK+ dataset, the combination of both, and an equal combination of the two datasets. In the federated learning approach, the two datasets were not merged or collected. The models were trained separately and after each iteration, only model parameters were passed to central. Hence, the central server did not have the data, but the model contained parameters that were obtained while training on different datasets, and this approach provided better robustness compared to other approaches. As the data was not needed to share in this approach, privacy of the owner of the data is preserved. The federated learning approach also provided better performance than the normal case. To the best of the authors' knowledge, the combination of federated learning and transfer learning for facial expression recognition has not been performed earlier.

This paper is organized in the following manner: Sect. 2 describes the existing research works in this field, Sect. 3 and Sect. 4 discuss the methodology and obtained result of the proposed approach. The paper is concluded with some recommendations in Sect. 5.

2 Literature Review

Several research works have been carried out already in emotion and expression recognition. Mustaqeem and Kwon [22] proposed to use self-attention with multi-layer perceptron and deep learning models for emotion detection. They used speech signals and tested their model with three datasets. Schoneveld et al. [33] proposed to use a recurrent neural network for classifying emotion for audio-visual data. Khaireddin and Chen [20] proposed to use a VGGNet architecture with tuned hyper-parameters. They used this model on the FER2013 dataset, which is used for this article as well. Kulkarni et al. [21] proposed a mood recognizing framework, where they extracted several parameters from facial images which were used to train several neural networks. Then, they tested some of the images with this initially trained neural networks, and found out the best performing ones. Then, they used the selected neural networks collectively to evaluate the data which were not used in previously training and testing set. Jain et al. [18] proposed a deep Convolutional Neural Network (CNN) model with residual blocks for emotion recognition on the Japanese Female Facial Expression dataset and CK+ dataset. They focused on real-time applications. Lee et al. [24] proposed an image processing based approach to detect facial expression where they at first marked the face portion from the image, and then, they extracted several features such as eyes, eyebrow, and mouth position from the face. These features were used to create a feature vector that was used to train a neural network that detected facial expression from an image of an user. [28] proposed to use CNN for facial emotion recognition but combined two models: one for background removal, and the other for extracting facial features. Through this model, he managed to achieve high accuracy. For lightweight applications of emotion recognition, Nan et al. [31] proposed the MobileNetV1 with an attention mechanism. This model achieved better results without the expansion of model parameters. Zhang et al. [43] also used a MobileNet model for expression recognition in robots.

3   Methodology

To detect expression from the facial images, the Facial Expression Recognition 2013 (FER2013) [11] and the Extended Cohn-Kanade (CK+) [25] datasets were used. Different training and testing sets were created from these two datasets to train and evaluate the proposed and related architectures. After that, the images of the training and testing sets were resized to feed into the MobileNet model. In this paper, a federated learning approach is proposed to train the MobileNet, a pretrained CNN model. In this method, the central server did not collect the data to train models which ensures confidentiality. This approach also increased the robustness of the proposed model by a large margin. After retraining the pretrained MobileNet model, the model was evaluated in four different testing scenarios and also compared with the performance of the generally trained MobileNet models.

3.1   Dataset Preparation and Preprocessing

In this work, two publicly available datasets, FER2013 and CK+ datasets were used. There were around 35887 images of 48×48 resolution in FER2013 dataset. These images were annotated into 7 different expressions: anger, disgust, fear, neutral, happy, sad, and surprise. Images of this dataset was collected using Google Search API. There were a lot of variations in the images of this dataset, including occlusions, eyeglasses, low contrast, partial faces, etc. CK+ is a public dataset used to recognize action units and emotions. Both posed and un-posed actions are included in this dataset. It contained 593 sequences of 123 subjects which were annotated into 7 different classes: anger, contempt, disgust, fear, happy, sad, and surprise. The last frame of the sequences was used for facial expression recognition. In order to match the expressions of the datasets, neutral images from the FER2013 dataset and contempt images from the CK+ dataset were deleted. Some sample images of the FER2013 dataset and CK+ dataset are illustrated in Fig. 1. Four different training-testing combinations were created from these datasets: FER2013 training-testing set, CK+ training-testing set, Merged training-testing set, and Equal testing set. Table 1 provides the number of images in all the training-testing sets. All the images were converted to $224 \times 224 \times 3$ before feeding to MobileNet model.

FER2013 Training-Testing Set. The FER2013 training set contained 21479 images, whereas the testing set had 5850 testing images. These sets were taken only from the FER2013 dataset. The highest number of images were in the happy class (6454 training, 1825 testing), whereas the disgust class had the lowest number of images (407 training, 111 testing). The sad and happy class also contained more than 3000 training and 1000 testing images. The training set was used to train client 1 of the proposed federated-MobileNet architecture, and another MobileNet model, where the testing set was used to evaluate all the trained models. All the images of the testing set were different from the training set.

Anger Disgust Fear Happy Sad Surprise

(a)

Anger Disgust Fear Happy Sad Surprise

(b)

Fig. 1. Sample images of (a) FER2013 dataset (b) CK+ dataset

CK+ Training-Testing Set. CK+ training set had 683 images, whereas the testing set contained 159 testing images. All the images of the testing set were different from the training set. These different sets were taken only from the CK+ dataset. The highest number of images was in the surprise class (208 training, 28 testing), whereas the fear class had the lowest number of images (52 training, 16 testing). The training set was used to train client 1 of the proposed federated-MobileNet architecture, and another MobileNet model, where the testing set was used to evaluate all the trained models.

Merged Training-Testing Set. In the merged set, we merged the FER dataset and CK+ dataset. All the images of training sets of CK+ and FER were in the training set of the merged training set, where the testing set was comprised of the images of the testing sets of the CK+ dataset and FER dataset. In total, there were 22162 images in training and 6009 in the testing set.

Equal Testing Set. CK+ dataset contained around 700 images, whereas the FER dataset had more than 27000 images. Therefore, the testing set of these datasets was also not balanced. In order to mitigate this issue, a small testing set containing the same number of images from the FER and CK+ dataset was created. These images were not used in any training-testing set of CK+, FER, or merged datasets. In total, 150 images were kept in this set, where 75 images were taken from each of the FER and CK+ datasets. All the classes contained between 20 and 32 images. Therefore, a balance in the number of images among the classes was kept in this testing set.

Table 1. Dataset properties

Attributes	FER		CK+		Merged		Equal
	Training	Testing	Training	Testing	Training	Testing	Testing
Total number of images	21479	5850	683	159	22162	6009	150
Number of images in anger class	3597	960	96	26	3693	986	26
Number of images in disgust class	407	111	116	34	523	145	26
Number of images in fear class	3693	1018	52	16	3745	1034	20
Number of images in happy class	6454	1825	151	40	6605	1865	32
Number of images in sad class	4445	1139	60	15	4505	1154	20
Number of images in surprise class	2883	797	208	28	3091	825	26

3.2 Proposed Federated-MobileNet Framework

In this work, a federated learning approach was taken to train MobileNet which is a lightweight CNN model and generally provides great performance in the recognition of images. We kept the base weights of the MobileNet which were acquired during training with the ImageNet dataset. Only the last layer of the model was changed to the Dense layer with 6 neurons and softmax activation functions, where 6 neurons denote the 6 facial expressions. Figure 2 shows the working of the proposed model.

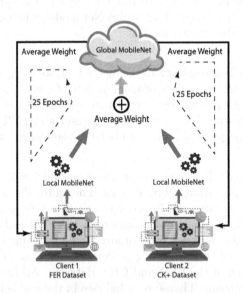

Fig. 2. Proposed federated learning approach. Here, client 1 was trained with the FER training set and client 2 were trained with the CK+ training set. The weights of the global model was updated using the average weights of the client models, and at each epoch client model's weights were initialised to the updated global model's weights. This whole process was repeated for 25 epochs.

In the federated learning approach, as a proof of concept, two clients were considered. Here one client trained the model with the FER2013 training set, and another client trained the model with the CK+ dataset. In this case, the central server, client1 and client2, all have the same MobileNet architecture which was initialized with imageNet weights. In each training epoch, client 1 and client 2 trained the model simultaneously with their own training set, and at the end of the epoch at their local end, they validated the model with their own validation set and transferred the weights of the local client models to the central server, where a global MobileNet model was considered. Then, an average of the weights of client1 MobileNet and client2 MobileNet were taken and set as the weights of the global MobileNet model. After that, the weight of the global MobileNet model was transferred to each client, which was validated using the local validation set of the clients. The whole process was repeated 25 times, and the epoch was set to 25. At the end of the training, the global model was evaluated using the 4 testing sets. Here, no data was available to the global server, which ensured data confidentiality and security as the facial data is very sensitive, and can easily be used as bio-metric evidence.

3.3   Training and Testing

The local MobileNet models were trained using the local training sets on the local client's end, and the global model was updated using the weights of the local models. The models were trained for 25 epochs, the optimizer was Adam, the learning rate was 0.001, and the loss function was set to categorical cross-entropy. Figure 3 shows the validation accuracy of the proposed federated learning approach during the training phase. The validation accuracy of the global model was initially quite low compared to client models, but as more epoch was completed, the global model converged. After 7 epochs, the global model provided similar validation accuracy as the local client models. To compare the impact of federated learning, another 3 MobileNet models were trained using FER, CK+, and merged training sets using the same hyper-parameters as used in the federated approach.

In the testing phase, the global model was tested using four testing sets: FER testing set, CK+ testing set, merged testing set, and equal testing set. Detailed result is discussed in the result analysis section.

4   Result Analysis and Discussion

In this section, results will be compared among the trained MobileNet models in a federated way, CK+ dataset, FER dataset, and merged dataset. Also, the robustness of the models will be considered in the case of selecting the best performing way of training. Figure 4 illustrates the confusion matrix obtained during testing with FER, CK+, merged, and equal testing sets.

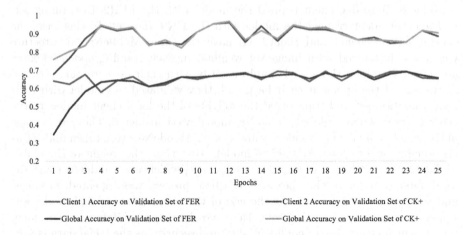

Fig. 3. Validation accuracy of local models and global model after each epoch completed. The global model caught up with local client after 7 epochs, and after 20 epoch, both local and global models converged.

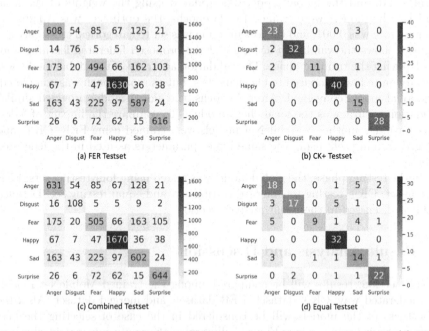

Fig. 4. Confusion matrix of Federated learning approach during testing with (a) FER testing set (b) CK+ testing set (c) merged testing set (d) equal testing set.

Result Analysis on FER Testing Set. The proposed federated MobileNet approach achieved 68.56% accuracy, whereas the same model trained with only the FER dataset in a classical way achieved 67.29% accuracy, and the MobileNet model trained with a merged training set achieved 67.74% accuracy. The MobileNet model which was trained using the CK+ dataset, could not perform good enough (38.44% accuracy, 38% precision, 34% recall), which proved that this model was not robust enough. In the case of class-wise accuracy, the federated approach performed the best in all the classes except the anger and sad classes. From Fig. 4(a), it can be noticed that the proposed approach misclassified 125 anger images as of fear class, and 225 sad images as of fear class. Figure 5 illustrates the performance comparison between the considered approaches, where it is clear that the proposed approach outperformed all the other approaches in most of the evaluation criteria.

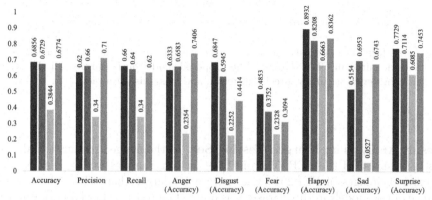

Fig. 5. Performance comparison between the considered models based on the obtained recognition performance in FER testing set. The proposed federated MobileNet approach outperformed all the other approaches in case of accuracy, recall, and the class-wise performance of disgust, sad, happy, and surprise.

Result Analysis on CK+ Testing Set. In the CK+ testing set, the proposed architecture achieved 93.71% accuracy, whereas models trained with the FER dataset and merged dataset achieved 69.81% and 78.61% accuracy respectively. Figure 6 depicts the comparison of the performance of the trained models in the CK+ testing set. The trained model on the CK+ training set performed better than the other two models, but could not achieve better accuracy, precision, or recall than the proposed federated MobileNet model. In terms of class-wise accuracy, the proposed model performed similar to or better than the other architectures except in the fear class. The proposed model misclassified around 11 out of 16 testing images of the fear class of CK+ testing set (from Fig. 4(b)).

Considering all the evaluation metrics, it can be said that, the proposed model outperformed all the other trained models in terms of CK+ dataset.

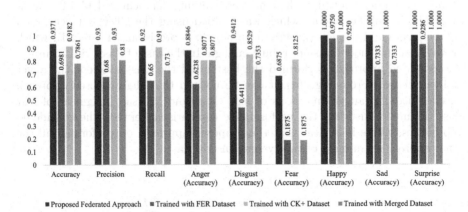

Fig. 6. Performance comparison between the considered models based on the performance acquired in CK+ dataset. The proposed model outperformed all the other models considering accuracy, precision, recall, and class-wise accuracy.

Result Analysis on Merged Testing Set. In the merged testing set, all the testing samples of the FER2013 and CK+ testing samples were taken. As the number of images of FER2013 was quite a bit larger than CK+, the performance of the models in this dataset was quite close to the achieved performance in the FER2013 testing set. In this testing set, the proposed federated MobileNet achieved 69.23% accuracy, 64% precision, and 68% recall. In terms of accuracy and recall, the proposed model outperformed all the other models. The trained model on the merged dataset achieved better precision than the proposed model. The proposed model performed the best in classifying the images of disgust, fear, happy, and surprise classes. The merged dataset performed better than the proposed architecture in sad and anger classes. The proposed model misclassified 128 anger images as sad images (from Fig. 4(c)). Considering the overall performance, the proposed model outperformed all the other models which are clearly depicted in Fig. 7.

Result Analysis on Equal Testing Set. To mitigate the imbalance of the number of images in the FER2013 and CK+ testing sets, a new testing set was created taking an equal number of images from the FER2013 and CK+ testing sets. This testing set can prove the robustness of the models. In this dataset, the proposed federated-MobileNet approach performed the best in terms of accuracy (74.77%), precision (77%), and recall (72%). The merged model performed close to it with 74.77% accuracy, 76% precision, and 70% recall. The accuracy of the

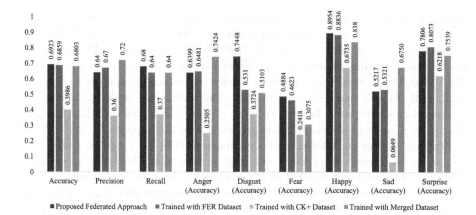

Fig. 7. Performance of the considered models in merged testing set. The proposed method achieved better accuracy, recall, class-wise accuracy of disgust, fear, happy, and surprise class than the other models.

trained model of the FER dataset (60%) and CK+ dataset (53.33%) shows that training in a single dataset could not bring satisfactory robustness. In most of the classes, the proposed model performed better than the other models (from Fig. 8). The proposed model classified 5 fear images as anger images, and 5 anger images as sad images (shown in Fig. 4(d)).

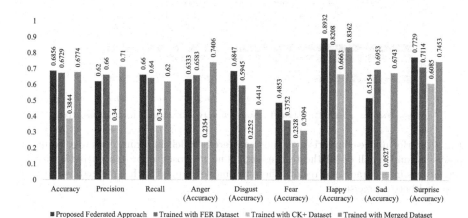

Fig. 8. Comparison of the performance of the models in equal testing set. The proposed approach acquired better accuracy and recall than the other models.

Discussion. The federated approach acquired better accuracy and recall in all the testing sets. In some of the testing sets, the merged dataset achieved better precision. In terms of class-wise accuracy, the proposed approach acquired better accuracy in disgust, fear, happy, and surprise class, where it performed poorly in recognizing anger and sad class in FER and merged dataset. By taking the average of the acquired accuracy, precision, and recall, can be clearly seen in Fig. 9 that, the proposed model acquired much better average accuracy (76.57%), and recall (74.5%) than the other models. The MobileNet model trained in the merged dataset acquired better precision (75%), which was not that far from the achieved average precision of the proposed federated approach (74%). As all the testing set was considered in this comparison (Fig. 9), it can be stated that the proposed federated approach was more robust than the other approaches. The models trained only in FER or CK+ dataset cannot be said as robust at all compared to the performance of the federated approach and classical training approach in the merged dataset. It implies that the models can be trained in the client end with their own dataset, rather than collecting it and training in a central server. The classical approach also hampers data privacy, data access right, and data security. Therefore, the federated approach can be considered a more robust and secure way of training deep learning models from bio-metric information such as a facial image.

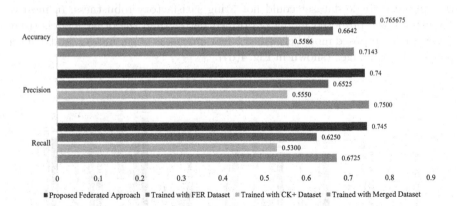

Fig. 9. Performance comparison of the considered models in terms of average accuracy, precision, and recall of all the testing sets. The proposed approach outperformed all the models in accuracy and recall, where the model trained with a merged training set acquired better precision.

5   Conclusions

We proposed a Federated-MobileNet model for privacy-preserving expression recognition from facial images. To the best of our knowledge, we incorporated federated learning and MobileNet in detecting facial expressions. We used two facial expression recognition datasets named FER2013 and CK+. For testing the robustness of the proposed model 4 different testing experiments were done, where the proposed model was tested with only the FER2013 dataset, CK+ dataset, the combination of both, and an equal combination of the two datasets. The result showed that the proposed Federated-MobileNet approach achieved better accuracy and recall in all the testing scenarios. Given that the reported work is an early report of an important research domain, in the future we shall explore ensemble classifiers and compare their performance to the proposed approach. We shall also combine ensemble learning with federated learning possibly using different classifiers on different clients that are more suited to the local data. We shall also aim to automate the model selection process.

Acknowledgements. The authors extend their sincere gratitude to Prof Hongbo Liu from the Dalian University of Technology, China for the useful discussions. Dr Mufti Mahmud is supported by the AI-TOP (2020-1-UK01-KA201-079167) and DIVERSA-SIA (618615-EPP-1-2020-1-UKEPPKA2-CBHEJP) projects funded by the European Commission under the Erasmus+ programme.

Code Availability. The code and datasets are available at https://github.com/tapu1996/AII-2022-Federated-Learning-96104.

References

1. Ahmed, S., Hossain, M.F., Nur, S.B., Shamim Kaiser, M., Mahmud, M.: Toward machine learning-based psychological assessment of autism spectrum disorders in school and community. In: Kaiser, M.S., Bandyopadhyay, A., Ray, K., Singh, R., Nagar, V. (eds.) Proceedings of Trends in Electronics and Health Informatics. LNNS, vol. 376, pp. 139–149. Springer, Singapore (2022). https://doi.org/10.1007/978-981-16-8826-3_13
2. Niamat Ullah Akhund, T.M., Mahi, M.J.N., Hasnat Tanvir, A.N.M., Mahmud, M., Kaiser, M.S.: ADEPTNESS: Alzheimer's disease patient management system using pervasive sensors - early prototype and preliminary results. In: Wang, S., et al. (eds.) BI 2018. LNCS (LNAI), vol. 11309, pp. 413–422. Springer, Cham (2018). https://doi.org/10.1007/978-3-030-05587-5_39
3. Akter, T., Ali, M.H., Satu, M.S., Khan, M.I., Mahmud, M.: Towards autism subtype detection through identification of discriminatory factors using machine learning. In: Mahmud, M., Kaiser, M.S., Vassanelli, S., Dai, Q., Zhong, N. (eds.) BI 2021. LNCS (LNAI), vol. 12960, pp. 401–410. Springer, Cham (2021). https://doi.org/10.1007/978-3-030-86993-9_36
4. Al Banna, M.H., Ghosh, T., Taher, K.A., Kaiser, M.S., Mahmud, M.: A monitoring system for patients of autism spectrum disorder using artificial intelligence. In: Mahmud, M., Vassanelli, S., Kaiser, M.S., Zhong, N. (eds.) BI 2020. LNCS (LNAI), vol. 12241, pp. 251–262. Springer, Cham (2020). https://doi.org/10.1007/978-3-030-59277-6_23
5. Al Mamun, S., Kaiser, M.S., Mahmud, M.: An artificial intelligence based approach towards inclusive healthcare provisioning in society 5.0: a perspective on brain disorder. In: Mahmud, M., Kaiser, M.S., Vassanelli, S., Dai, Q., Zhong, N. (eds.) BI 2021. LNCS (LNAI), vol. 12960, pp. 157–169. Springer, Cham (2021). https://doi.org/10.1007/978-3-030-86993-9_15

6. Biswas, M., Kaiser, M.S., Mahmud, M., Al Mamun, S., Hossain, M.S., Rahman, M.A.: An XAI based autism detection: the context behind the detection. In: Mahmud, M., Kaiser, M.S., Vassanelli, S., Dai, Q., Zhong, N. (eds.) BI 2021. LNCS (LNAI), vol. 12960, pp. 448–459. Springer, Cham (2021). https://doi.org/10.1007/978-3-030-86993-9_40

7. Biswas, M., et al.: Indoor navigation support system for patients with neurodegenerative diseases. In: Mahmud, M., Kaiser, M.S., Vassanelli, S., Dai, Q., Zhong, N. (eds.) BI 2021. LNCS (LNAI), vol. 12960, pp. 411–422. Springer, Cham (2021). https://doi.org/10.1007/978-3-030-86993-9_37

8. Chatterjee, A., Gupta, U., Chinnakotla, M.K., Srikanth, R., Galley, M., Agrawal, P.: Understanding emotions in text using deep learning and big data. Comput. Hum. Behav. **93**, 309–317 (2019)

9. Chen, J., Hu, B., Moore, P., Zhang, X., Ma, X.: Electroencephalogram-based emotion assessment system using ontology and data mining techniques. Appl. Soft Comput. **30**, 663–674 (2015)

10. Chhikara, P., Singh, P., Tekchandani, R., Kumar, N., Guizani, M.: Federated learning meets human emotions: a decentralized framework for human-computer interaction for IoT applications. IEEE Internet Things J. **8**(8), 6949–6962 (2020)

11. Courville, P., Goodfellow, A., Mirza, I., Bengio, Y.: Fer-2013 face database. Universit de Montreal, Montréal (2013)

12. Gharaee, Z., Gärdenfors, P., Johnsson, M.: First and second order dynamics in a hierarchical SOM system for action recognition. Appl. Soft Comput. **59**, 574–585 (2017)

13. Ghosh, T., et al.: An attention-based mood controlling framework for social media users. In: Mahmud, M., Kaiser, M.S., Vassanelli, S., Dai, Q., Zhong, N. (eds.) BI 2021. LNCS (LNAI), vol. 12960, pp. 245–256. Springer, Cham (2021). https://doi.org/10.1007/978-3-030-86993-9_23

14. Ghosh, T., et al.: Artificial intelligence and internet of things in screening and management of autism spectrum disorder. Sustain. Cities Soc. **74**, 103189 (2021)

15. Howard, A.G., et al.: Mobilenets: efficient convolutional neural networks for mobile vision applications. arXiv preprint arXiv:1704.04861 (2017)

16. Huang, K.Y., Wu, C.H., Su, M.H., Kuo, Y.T.: Detecting unipolar and bipolar depressive disorders from elicited speech responses using latent affective structure model. IEEE Trans. Affect. Comput. **11**(3), 393–404 (2018)

17. Huang, Z., Epps, J., Joachim, D.: Speech landmark bigrams for depression detection from naturalistic smartphone speech. In: Proceedings of ICASSP, pp. 5856–5860 (2019)

18. Jain, D.K., Shamsolmoali, P., Sehdev, P.: Extended deep neural network for facial emotion recognition. Pattern Recognit. Lett. **120**, 69–74 (2019)

19. Jesmin, S., Kaiser, M.S., Mahmud, M.: Towards artificial intelligence driven stress monitoring for mental wellbeing tracking during COVID-19. In: Proceedings of WI-IAT, pp. 845–851 (2020)

20. Khaireddin, Y., Chen, Z.: Facial emotion recognition: state of the art performance on fer2013. arXiv preprint arXiv:2105.03588 (2021)

21. Kulkarni, S.S., Reddy, N.P., Hariharan, S.: Facial expression (mood) recognition from facial images using committee neural networks. Biomed. Eng. Online **8**(1), 1–12 (2009)

22. Kwon, S., et al.: Att-Net: enhanced emotion recognition system using lightweight self-attention module. Appl. Soft Comput. **102**, 107101 (2021)

23. Latif, S., Asim, M., Rana, R., Khalifa, S., Jurdak, R., Schuller, B.W.: Augmenting generative adversarial networks for speech emotion recognition. arXiv preprint arXiv:2005.08447 (2020)

24. Lee, H.C., Wu, C.Y., Lin, T.M.: Facial expression recognition using image processing techniques and neural networks. In: Pan, J.S., Yang, C.N., Lin, C.C. (eds.) Advances in Intelligent Systems and Applications. Smart Innovation, Systems and Technologies, vol. 21, pp. 259–267. Springer, Heidelberg (2013). https://doi.org/10.1007/978-3-642-35473-1_26

25. Lucey, P., Cohn, J.F., Kanade, T., Saragih, J., Ambadar, Z., Matthews, I.: The extended cohn-kanade dataset (ck+): a complete dataset for action unit and emotion-specified expression. In: Proceeedings of IEEE CVPR, pp. 94–101 (2010)

26. Mahmud, M., et al.: Towards explainable and privacy-preserving artificial intelligence for personalisation in autism spectrum disorder. In: Antona, M., Stephanidis, C. (eds.) HCII 2022. LNCS, vol. 13309, pp. 356–370. Springer, Cham (2022). https://doi.org/10.1007/978-3-031-05039-8_26

27. McMahan, B., Moore, E., Ramage, D., Hampson, S., y Arcas, B.A.: Communication-efficient learning of deep networks from decentralized data. In: Artificial Intelligence and Statistics , pp. 1273–1282 (2017)

28. Mehendale, N.: Facial emotion recognition using convolutional neural networks (FERC). SN Appl. Sci. **2**(3), 1–8 (2020)

29. Merler, M., et al.: Automatic curation of sports highlights using multimodal excitement features. IEEE Trans. Multimedia **21**(5), 1147–1160 (2018)

30. Al Nahian, M.J., Ghosh, T., Uddin, M.N., Islam, M.M., Mahmud, M., Kaiser, M.S.: Towards artificial intelligence driven emotion aware fall monitoring framework suitable for elderly people with neurological disorder. In: Mahmud, M., Vassanelli, S., Kaiser, M.S., Zhong, N. (eds.) BI 2020. LNCS (LNAI), vol. 12241, pp. 275–286. Springer, Cham (2020). https://doi.org/10.1007/978-3-030-59277-6_25

31. Nan, Y., Ju, J., Hua, Q., Zhang, H., Wang, B.: A-mobilenet: an approach of facial expression recognition. Alex. Eng. J. **61**(6), 4435–4444 (2022)

32. Rana, R., Latif, S., Gururajan, R., Gray, A., Mackenzie, G., Humphris, G., Dunn, J.: Automated screening for distress: a perspective for the future. Eur. J. Cancer Care **28**(4), e13033 (2019)

33. Schoneveld, L., Othmani, A., Abdelkawy, H.: Leveraging recent advances in deep learning for audio-visual emotion recognition. Pattern Recognit. Lett. **146**, 1–7 (2021)

34. Shaffi, N., et al.: Triplet-loss based siamese convolutional neural network for 4-way classification of alzheimerÕs disease. In: Mahmud, M., He, J., Vassanelli, S., van Zundert, A., Zhong, N. (eds.) BI. LNCS, vol. 13406, pp. 277–287. Springer, Cham (2022)

35. Smith, V., Chiang, C.K., Sanjabi, M., Talwalkar, A.S.: Federated multi-task learning. In: Advance in Neural Information Processing System, vol. 30 (2017)

36. Sumi, A.I., Zohora, M.F., Mahjabeen, M., Faria, T.J., Mahmud, M., Kaiser, M.S.: fASSERT: A fuzzy assistive system for children with autism using internet of things. In: Wang, S., et al. (eds.) BI 2018. LNCS (LNAI), vol. 11309, pp. 403–412. Springer, Cham (2018). https://doi.org/10.1007/978-3-030-05587-5_38

37. Tsouvalas, V., Ozcelebi, T., Meratnia, N.: Privacy-preserving speech emotion recognition through semi-supervised federated learning. arXiv preprint arXiv:2202.02611 (2022)

38. Vögel, H.J., et al.: Emotion-awareness for intelligent vehicle assistants: A research agenda. In: Proceedings of SEFAIAS, pp. 11–15 (2018)

39. Wadhera, T., Mahmud, M.: Brain networks in autism spectrum disorder, epilepsy and their relationship: a machine learning approach. In: Chen, T., Carter, J., Mahmud, M., Khuman, A.S. (eds.) Artificial Intelligence in Healthcare. Brain Informatics and Health, pp. 125–142. Springer, Singapore (2022). https://doi.org/10.1007/978-981-19-5272-2_6

40. Wadhera, T., Mahmud, M.: Influences of social learning in individual perception and decision making in people with autism: a computational approach. In: Mahmud, M., He, J., Vassanelli, S., van Zundert, A., Zhong, N. (eds.) BI 2022. LNCS, vol. 13406, pp. 50–61. Springer, Cham (2022). https://doi.org/10.1007/978-3-031-15037-1_5

41. Yang, J., Liu, J., Han, R., Wu, J.: Transferable face image privacy protection based on federated learning and ensemble models. Complex Intell. Syst. **7**(5), 2299–2315 (2021). https://doi.org/10.1007/s40747-021-00399-6

42. Yurochkin, M., et al.: Bayesian nonparametric federated learning of neural networks. In: Proceedings of ICML, pp. 7252–7261 (2019)

43. Zhang, F., Li, Q., Ren, Y., Xu, H., Song, Y., Liu, S.: An expression recognition method on robots based on mobilenet v2-ssd. In: Proceedings of ICSAI, pp. 118–122 (2019)

Television Programs Classification via Deep Learning Approach Using SSMI-CNN

Federico Candela[1]([✉]), Francesco Carlo Morabito[2],
and Carmen Francesca Zagaria[3]

[1] DIIES Department, University Mediterranea of Reggio Calabria,
89124 Reggio Calabria, Italy
federico.candela@unirc.it
[2] DICEAM Department, University Mediterranea of Reggio Calabria,
89124 Reggio Calabria, Italy
morabito@unirc.it
[3] Co.Re.Com. Calabria, 89123 Reggio Calabria, Italy
carmen.zagaria@consrc.it

Abstract. The classification of television programs and their identification is a fundamental point for streaming multimedia services, real-time, social communities, video sharing platforms (Youtube, Twitch, Facebook), and in particular television monitoring systems. The objective of the proposed approach is to use a CNN (Convolutional Neural Network) with an SSIM (Structural Similarity Index Measure) to classify perfectly the start and end of programs and the contents present to detect time overruns during a transmission, easily adaptable for multiple systems. A database of discriminatory images used for the interception Title Sequence of the program is built. The few data of a title sequence and its possible change over time would result in a scarcity of data and new training for a neural network. Presenting the proposed approach, the paper provides an overview of the encouraging experimental results and results obtained from CNN training on five sports classes. 95% accuracy levels and long-lasting video ratings are achieved.

Keywords: SSIM · Deep learning · CNN · Program tv classification · Video classification

1 Introduction

In recent years, AI research has seen tremendous growth involving diverse fields ranging from everyday use cases to domains that analyze high-risk decision-making. One of the fields of this research is Computer Vision (CV), which allows computers to see, observe and understand these processes. Deep learning has made great strides in a variety of computer vision problems such as [1] object detection, [2] motion detection, and [3] semantic segmentation. However, despite

© The Author(s), under exclusive license to Springer Nature Switzerland AG 2022
M. Mahmud et al. (Eds.): AII 2022, CCIS 1724, pp. 293–307, 2022.
https://doi.org/10.1007/978-3-031-24801-6_21

these advances, Došilovic et al. [4] highlight that deep neural networks (DNNs) are criticized because they only serve as approximations of a decision-making process and also require a lot of training data. Among the most important factors contributing to the huge increase in machine vision is the emergence of high quality, publicly available labeled dataset such as ImgageNet and UCF-101 [5] [6], along with the GPU improvement. Parallel computing enabled the transition from CPU-based to GPU-based training, enabling significant acceleration in deep model formation. In this context of computer vision, the following paper pays particular attention to the classification of videos for television monitoring processes by public bodies such as the Co.Re.Com.(Regional Communications Committee). In a video the frames per second (fps) are analyzed [7]; in which the digital image is studied as a rectangular matrix of points called pixels, whose coloring is defined by one or more numerical values, this representation is called raster graphic.

Artificial intelligence techniques allow you to make predictions on fps by discriminating them. The more specific discrimination degree better should be the classification. The leading technologies in this sector are the Deep-CNN Convolutional Neural Networks whose origins date back to the [9] Necrognition, Problems arise when is necessary to make specific discriminations for frames on data that can change continuously, compromising the training dataset, which must be updated. These problems are encountered by storage technologies for large-scale video classification [10]. More sophisticated techniques have reduced the number of training data comparing only small sections between two images of the same video in video surveillance systems [11]. In the classification of long-running television streams, a study was conducted to precisely identify, in television stream, the beginning, end, and title or category of each game, newspaper, magazine, film, documentary, advertisement, trailer, etc., discriminating what is present inside them. This work belongs to the general domain of structuring TV streams. A system has been developed capable of discriminating the significant frames that represent the acronyms of television programs, adaptable to several broadcasters. The fps are considered in a 2D form array, compared with a discriminatory sample image. Using scaling techniques and a variable-sized mask, can perform image segmentation. The following process was applied in support of a pre-trained CNN (on ImageNet with transfer learning and ResNet50) for more general and non-specific discrimination. The framework is effective for categorizing long-form videos. This work is structured as follows. Section 2 presents the related work, Sect. 3 introduces the proposed methodology, Sect. 4 the experiments and results, and Sect. 5 discussions. We conclude with the solution suggested.

2   Related Works

Existing deep learning algorithms are widely used on RGB images or video data. Although RGB video/image classification has been studied for many years, it still is and faces many challenges, such as complicated background, change of illuminance, and occlusion. The emergence of new multimedia broadcasting environments and services, the evolution of internet services (Web Television, VOD, TV Replay), and the enormous growth of television channels have led to an increase in digital video documents. The amount of audiovisual material broadcast has increased enormously every day. Due to the presence of large amounts of content video, effective and quick access to information multimedia has become a difficult undertaking. This difficulty has created a growing demand for suitable methods for allow quick access to unstructured video content that requires segmentation methods and automatic video indexing. Intelligent access to this type of media is continually being studied to motivate researchers to suggest methods that facilitate the segmentation and indexing of video documents. Video segmentation is the first important step in video content analysis. It aims to divide the video stream into a set of meaningful and manageable segments which are used as building blocks for [12] indexing.

An approach followed in [13] made it possible to detect inter-programs, sequences repeated several times in a stream that separates two parts of a single program such as Trailer, commercials, and jingles using a descriptor technique on some frames key.

Dumont and Quénot [14] have developed a sensor that uses multiple modes for systematic segmentation of stories for news videos. This system is based on techniques of classification and methods of machine learning. Combine both audio descriptors (silence segments and words) with visual features such as anchors or logos.

In previous works on the segmentation of television news, for example in [15], the detection of repetitions can be considered a key tool for structuring the flow. After the detection phase, a classification method is applied to separate program repetitions and pauses.

Furthermore, another method by Xavier Naturel et al., [16] was based on detecting segments of silence and monochromatic images. This technique made it possible to detect program changes or the start of advertising. Zlitni presented in [17, 18] a method for identifying programs in two phases: the first phase involves building a reference catalog for the video grammars of visual jingles. In the second phase, the programs are identified by examining the similarity of the video signal with the visual grammar in the catalog. In an advanced stage of the analysis, to structure the TV streams, Hmayda [19] presented an approach for identifying streaming TV programs using deep learning.

Various techniques have been proposed in the literature concerning the segmentation and classification of TV video streams, the following research proposes a new effective methodology.

3   Methodology

The proposed architecture was developed with an SSIM based image comparison system in combination with a Deep-CNN. The key images for identifying a program are called discriminators. A digital image is the numerical representation of a two-dimensional image. The focus and study are placed on the raster type methodology shown in Fig. 1 which the image is composed of a matrix of points, called pixels, whose coloring is defined (encoded) by one or more numerical values (bits). Each pixel has associated a string of bits that contains information such as the position coordinates in the grid and the color code. The set of all information of the virtual pixels of the image, called bit-map (a mapping from some domain) to bits, for example if it indicates only monochrome images, pixmap (refers to a map of pixels, where each one may store more than two colors, thus using more than one bit per pixel) is used as in the case of RGB coding, define a 3D vector:

$$red : \vec{u} = (255, 0, 0) \ green : \vec{v} = (0, 255, 0) \ blue : \vec{w} = (0, 0, 255)$$

the linear combination is vector $\boldsymbol{d}$.

$$\vec{d} = (a\vec{u} + b\vec{v} + c\vec{w})$$

The integer component of $\vec{d}$ are:

$$(255, 255, 255)$$

two datasets were created, the first represents the discriminators to classify the acronyms of a program in a video, second was used to train CNN.

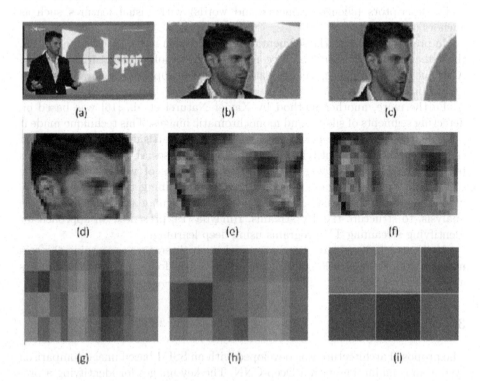

Fig. 1. The figure shows the representation of the RGB digital image

3.1   Structural Similarity Index Measure

The concept of SSIM (Structural Similarity Index Measure) is based on a perceived change in structural information [20]. The model is based on a perceptual metric that quantifies the degradation of image quality as shown in Fig. 2 caused by processing such as data compression or data transmission losses, also incorporating important perceptual phenomena including luminance masking terms where image distortions tend to be less visible in bright areas, and contrast masking, where distortions become less visible where there is significant activity or texture in image. The idea is that pixels have strong interdependencies, especially when spatially close. These dependencies contain important information about the structure of objects in the visual scene.

The system separates the measurement task into three comparisons: luminance, contrast, and structure. The luminance of each signal is compared. Assuming discrete signals, this is estimated as the average intensity:

$$\mu_x = \frac{1}{N} \sum_{i=1}^{N} x_i$$

the luminance comparison function is a function of μ_x and μ_y the standard deviation is calculated as an estimate of the signal contrast. The form is given by:

$$\sigma_x = (\frac{1}{N-1} \sum_{i=1}^{N} (x_i - \mu_x)^2)^{\frac{1}{2}}$$

the contrast comparison $c(x, y)$ is therefore the comparison of σ_x e σ_y. At this point, the signal is divided by its standard deviation to obtain one standard deviation of unity. A comparison of this s (x, y) structure is conducted on these normalized signals:

$$N_x = \frac{x - \mu_x}{\sigma_x} N_y = \frac{y - \mu_y}{\sigma_y}$$

the three components are combined to produce an overall likelihood measure:

$$S(x, y) = f((l(x, y), c(x, y), s(x, y)))$$

we need to define the functions $l(x, y)$, $c(x, y)$, $s(x, y)$ which satisfy the conditions of Simmetry, Boundedness, and Unique maximum. It defines:

$$l(x, y) = \frac{2\mu_x \mu_y + C_1}{\mu_x^2 + \mu_y^2 + C_1}; c(x, y) = \frac{2\sigma_x \sigma_y + C_2}{\sigma_x^2 + \sigma_y^2 + C_2}; l(x, y) = \frac{2\mu_x \mu_y + C_1}{\mu_x^2 + \mu_y^2 + C_1}$$

with:

$$C = (K_i L)^2$$

where the constant C is included to avoid instability. L is the dynamic range of pixel values (255 × 8 bits) and $K_i << 1$ is a constant, thus defining the SSIM index:

$$SSIM(x, y) = [l(x, y)^\alpha \cdot c(x, y)^\beta \cdot s(x, y)^\gamma]$$

$\alpha > 0, \beta > 0, \gamma > 0$ are used to adjust the relative importance of the three componets. In order to simplify the expression. Setting $\alpha = \beta = \gamma = 1$:

$$SSIM\,(x,y) = \frac{(2\mu_x\mu_y + c_1)\,(2\sigma_{xy} + c_2)}{(\mu_x^2 + \mu_y^2 + c_1)\,(\sigma_x^2 + \sigma_y^2 + c_2)}$$

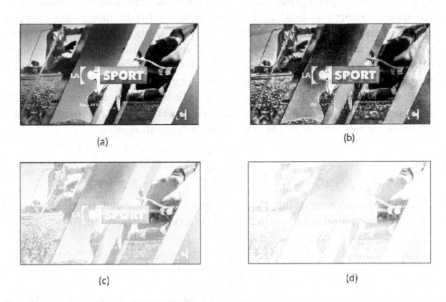

(a)   (b)

(c)   (d)

Fig. 2. The figure show SSIM maps of the compressed images, where brightness indicates the magnitude of the local SSIM index

3.2   CNN (Convolutional Neural Network)

A simple neural network can't learn complex characteristics, unlike a deep learning architecture. A particular type of multilayer perceptron is CNN. The architecture of the Convolutional Neural Network in Fig. 3 was designed by Alex Krizhevsky, Ilya Sutskever, and Geoffrey Hinton at the University of Toronto, winning the ILVSRC challenge in 2012, scoring an error rate of 15.4% in the top 5% with The next best entry got an error of 26% [21]. After many CNN architectures and modifications were proposed that were removed from AlexNet and became household names in the competition, this re-evolution and rebranding of CNN architectures can be linked to the availability of sufficiently large image dataset tagged as

ImageNet [22] which contains over 14 million hand-annotated images, publicly available for research purposes. A CNN is a class of networks applied to analyze visual images trying to reduce the image into a form that is easier to

process, without losing the fundamental functionality for obtaining a good forecast. The idea behind this network is that it can take local functionality from
high-level inputs and transfer them to lower levels for more complex functionality. A CNN includes convolutional, pooled, and fully connected FC levels. The
main level of CNN turns out to be the convolutive one, which contains a good
part of the computational complexity of the network. In this layer, the convolution is performed between a set of filters or kernels [23] learnable from K_j of
size $m \times n$ and the Input map $M_i \in R^{h \times w}$ of the level to determine a tensor of
feature maps:

$$FM = \sum M_i * K_j + B_j$$

where B_j is the bias term and $\sum$ denotes the product of convolution. Kernels
convolve an integer input using "stride" (s) so that the size of an output volume
becomes integer, decreasing the size of an input volume after the convolutional
layer has been used for the striding process [24]. Then each filter rotates with
a local area of l_i and offsets the whole plane with s, sharing the same weight
values, the feature map has dimensions: $o_1 \times o_2$

$$o_1 = \frac{h - K_1 + 2_p}{s} + 1$$

$$o_2 = \frac{h - K_2 + 2_p}{s} + 1$$

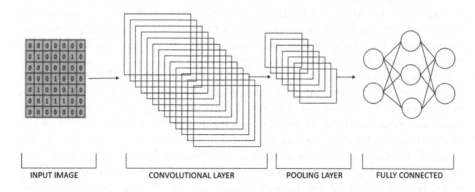

| INPUT IMAGE | CONVOLUTIONAL LAYER | POOLING LAYER | FULLY CONNECTED |

Fig. 3. The figure shows a typical architecture of the convolutional neural network

where p is the zero-padding parameter needed to fill an input volume with zeros
and maintain the size of a low-level function input volume. The level of convolution is usually followed by an activation function, typically the most common is
the Relu "Rectified Linear Unit" ($ReLu, f(z) = max(0, s)$) helping the system in
generalization and improving the learning times [25]. The pooling layer performs
a subsampling of given input size to reduce the number of parameters. Finally,
the characteristics learned are those of a multilayer neural network (MLP) [26]
for the classification task.

3.3   Architecture Proposed

In this study, a method was developed for detecting sports programs and the content contained within them. The structure of this architecture was designed by combining the SSIM system and a pre-trained CNN on ImageNet with Transfer learning and ResNet50 [27].

The SSIM system is supported by CNN for the identification of the specific program, based on comparison metrics between the discriminators and the video fps. All fps are counted on the incoming video, to be segmented. Each fps is processed individually as a 3D RGB vector. The fps and descriptors of interest are shown in grayscale scaling them into 2D vectors. A mask in height and width of dimensions $(h \times l)$ is applied on each fps and discriminator Fig. 4, allowing to eliminate the borders that present info such as date, time, and day of recording, by resizing the image. Once this first phase has been carried out, all the fps and discriminators present will be scrolled to be compared according to the SSIM index, reporting in output a floating-point value $SSIM(d_i) = x_i$. Using a standard parameter threshold $t = x$, it is calculated:

$$SSIM(d_i) > t$$

to identify the frame of interest present in the video. CNN takes the input images by resizing them to (224×224) px. The input data is segmented into training and test subdivisions using 80% of the data for training and the remaining 20% for testing. Two data augmentation objects are initialized, one for training and one for validation. The object is initialized through Data Augmentation techniques for training by performing random rotations, zooms, shifts, cuts, and co-flipping of the data. No augmentation will be conducted for validation data. Following these techniques, the model will be divided into the "base model" in which the ResNet50 will be loaded, leaving the FC layers off, and the "head model" positioned above the "base model". In the "base model" the size pooling parameters (7,7) will be set for the [28] average grouping which, unlike the maximum grouping, takes the average of all the pixel values of the matrix, which limits the operation by pooling the multidimensional matrix becomes a one-dimensional matrix. The dense layer is made up of 512 neurons, where each neuron receives input from all previous state neurons, used to classify the image based on the output of the convolutional layers. Each layer contains neurons that calculate the weighted average of its inputs which will be passed through the activation function ReLu. The Dropout value is set to 0.5 [29], a method used to randomly eliminate nodes. Finally, the "head model" is considered a dense layer for the labels with a soft-max activation function for multiple classes. In Fig. 5 can be observed the network architecture. The "base model" will be frozen so that it is not trained via backpropagation [30]. Finally, the model is compiled with the stochastic descent of the gradient [31] to optimize the parameters $Q(w)$:

$$Q(w) = \frac{1}{N} \sum_{i=1}^{N} Q_i(w)$$

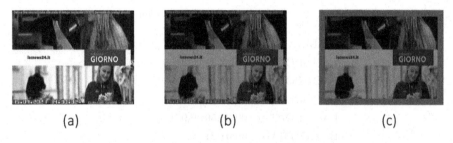

(a)   (b)   (c)

Fig. 4. The figure shows gray-scale scaling and mask application (Color figure online)

where each addendum Q_i represents the cost on the i-th observation in a dataset. The gradient descent method iterates over the form:

$$w := w - \mu \bigtriangledown Q(w)$$

μ is a hyperparameter called learning rate, learning rate decides how much gradient to be back propagated, in this case with learning rate $1\ e - 4$.

Fig. 5. The figure shows an architecture of ResNET50 using Transfer learning

3.4 Post Processing

In this phase, post-processing is done on the outputs obtained. The output obtained is file.csv with the name corresponding to the input video and the date when the processing was launched, showing the following characteristics in Table 1:

Table 1. The table shows a pre-processing output.

LABEL	TIME	$SSMI(d_i) > t$
LAC SPORT	00:00:51	0,9156
LAC SPORT	00:00:52	0,9558
LAC SPORT	00:00:55	0,9821
LAC SPORT	00:00:56	0,9711
BASKETBALL	00:01:21	0
FOOTBALL	00:01:22	0
BASKETBALL	00:01:28	0
.	.	
.	.	
BASKETBALL	00:01:29	0
BASKETBALL	00:10:12	0
BASKETBALL	00:10:13	0
LAC SPORT	00:55:58	0,9238
LAC SPORT	00:55:55	0,9932
LAC SPORT	00:55:55	0,9842
LAC SPORT	00:55:57	0,9632

Table 1 shows the processing output that is cleaned up thanks to a selection script on the highest accuracy index regarding the interception of the frame descriptor given by SSIM. The results obtained by CNN made on individual frames are added to a parameter:

$$D = \sum_{i=1}^{N} F_i \in T : 0 < T < t$$

where F_i represents the i-th frame. If over time T more frames with the same label prevail, the first of these is selected. The Table 1 resized becomes:

Table 2. The table shows a post-processing output.

LABEL	TIME	$SSMI(d_i) > t$
LAC SPORT	00:00:55	0,9821
BASKET	00:01:21	0
LAC SPORT	00:55:55	0,9932

4 Experimental Results

The experiments were carried out on a dedicated system with the following characteristics: Intel (R) Xeon (R) Gold 6126 CPU @ 2.6 64KiB BIOS, 64GiB DIMM DDR4 System Memory, 2 x GV100GL [Tesla V100 PCIe 32GB]. The SSIM and CNN were developed using Python and the Keras package with Tensorflow. For the tests, three programs from three different television broadcasters were taken: LACSPORT, SPORTMEDIASET, and RAISPORT, each having 25fps, identifying the start and end of the program and the sports contents present, to demonstrate the efficency of the system on different broadcasters.

4.1 Dataset Creation

In the experiment two databases are considered, one for SSIM [32] containing discriminators that represent the start and end of television acronyms in width × height (320 × 240) to which a mask is applied, bringing them back to dimensions (300 × 320) to eliminate the borders. The videos show the same format as the discriminators and are also masked for the first phase of SSIM. The second dataset was taken from [33] for CNN and contains 5 classes: basketball (495 images), football (799 images), formula1 (638 images), MotoGP (679 images), tennis (718 images). The latter has been split into 80% and 20%, respectively, for training and validation sets.

4.2 Performance Evaluation and Results Analysis

The following metrics are used to measure the performance of the proposed system by indicating with P a positive condition, with N a negative condition: TP indicates the number of correctly identified sports frames, FP indicates the number of sports frames classified differently, TN non-sporting frames correctly classified, FN denotes not classified sports frames or anomalies.

The performance of the CNN proposal was profound evaluated using standard metrics:

$$Precision = \left(\frac{TP}{TP + FP}\right)$$

$$Recall = \left(\frac{TP}{TP + FN}\right)$$

$$Fscore = 2 * \frac{Precision * Recall}{Precision + Recall}$$

$$Accuracy : \frac{TP + TN}{TP + TN + FP + FN}$$

CNN Accuracy, Recall, and F1_Score are summarized in Table 3.

Table 3. The table shows performance metrics of the model.

Class	Precision(%)	Recall(%)	F1_Score(%)	Support(%)
Basketblall	0.93	0.98	0.95	122
Football	0.94	0.96	0.95	196
Formula1	0.94	0.94	0.94	169
Motogp	0.97	0.92	0.94	167
Tennis	0.95	0.94	0.95	179
Macro avg	0.95	0.95	0.95	833
Weihted avg	0.95	0.95	0.95	833

Graphically in Fig. 6 the performance evaluation of the CNN classifier with accuracy and cross-entropy (loss) in the training and validation phase. The accuracy of training and validation is 95% and 94% at the time 120.

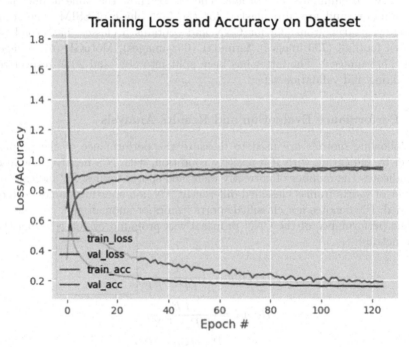

Fig. 6. The figure show evaluation metrics of the survey system based on CNN architecture

5   Discussions

Analyzing the results, it appears that a combination of SSIM and CNN has significant effects on the classification of television programs. CNN scores very well for lower-level discrimination against human actions. Starting from Table 4, it is noted that in some of the proposed systems those that have obtained greater accuracy [34], the architecture is tested in two flows, ConvNet trained on the dense multi-frame optical flow can obtain good performance despite limited training data, as in our case. Also tested on UCF-101 like the other examples reported, obtaining excellent performance on human-object interaction. [38] Performed well on UCF-101 through hybrid representation and the use of local descriptors. We considered a comparison with UCF-101 as our network training is based on human interactions related to sport, which can be found in the UCF-101 [40] dataset. Thanks to the merger of SSIM, with the proposed model, it becomes possible to intercept the specific program, solving the problem of scarcity of training data for television themes only. One could think about creating a dataset done only on the acronyms of different broadcasters but if they were to renew this would lead to problems with the new line-up. Methods such as object detection can be effective in identifying logos and abbreviations, however, this can compromise the classification if the same logo is present in a non-abbreviated program.

Table 4. The table shows a comparison with other technologies

Method	Accuracy(%)
Two-stream model (fusion by SVM) [34]	**88.0**
Two-Stream CNN (Optical Flow + Image Frames, Averaging) [34]	**86.9**
"Slow fusion" spatio-temporal ConvNet [35]	65.4
Improved dense trajectories (IDT) [36,37]	85.9
IDT with higher-dimensional encodings [38]	**87.9**
Res3D [39]	85.8
SSIM CNN	**95.0**

5.1 Conclusion

Since the video classification turns out to be a challenge for the resolution of many problems [41] that may concern social media for the publication of content suitable or not, the television world, for monitoring systems and any reports, we have proposed an effective technique in this area. It allows to perfectly intercept the beginning and end of the programs. We have focused only on sports programs but the developments want a broader horizon. The proposed system has some limitations such as the use of discriminators and therefore the continuous renewal which, however, in the face of new training turns out to be convenient. An intelligent and autonomous mode of acquiring discriminators with adaptation to all dimensions would be part of future development and the dataset will be extended.

References

1. Ouyang, W., Zeng, X., Wang, X., et al.: DeepID-Net: object detection with deformable part based convolutional neural networks. IEEE Trans. Pattern Anal. Mach. Intell. **39**(7), 1320–1334 (2017)
2. Doulamis, N., Athanasios, V.: FAST-MDL: fast adaptive supervised training of multi-layered deep learning models for consistent object tracking and classification. In: 2016 IEEE International Conference on Imaging Systems and Techniques (IST). IEEE (2016)
3. Noh, H., Hong, S., Han, B.: Learning deconvolution network for semantic segmentation. In: Proceedings of the 15th IEEE International Conference on Computer Vision, ICCV 2015, pp. 1520–1528, Santiago, Chile (2015)
4. Došilovic, F.K., Brcic, M., Hlupic, N.: Explainable artificial intelligence: a survey. In: 2018 41st International Convention on Information and Communication Technology, Electronics and Microelectronics (MIPRO), pp. 0210–0215. IEEE (2018)
5. Deng, J., Dong, W., Socher, R., Li, L.-J., Li, K., Li, F.-F.: ImageNet: a large-scale hierarchical image database. In: 2009 IEEE Conference on Computer Vision and Pattern Recognition, pp. 248–255 (2009). https://doi.org/10.1109/CVPR.2009.5206848
6. Soomro, K., Amir, R.Z., Mubarak, S.: UCF101: a dataset of 101 human actions classes from videos in the wild. arXiv preprint. arXiv:1212.0402 (2012)
7. Callway, E.: Variable frame rate technology - change is good!. In: SMPTE 2018, pp. 1–11 (2018). https://doi.org/10.5594/M001823
8. Guibas, L.J., Stolfi, J.: A language for bitmap manipulation. ACM Trans. Graph. (TOG) **1**(3), 191–214 (1982)
9. Fukushima, K., Sei, M.: Neocognitron a self-organizing neural network model for a mechanism of visual pattern recognition. In: Amari, S., Arbib, M.A. (eds.) Competition and Cooperation in Neural Nets. Lecture Notes in Biomathematics, vol. 45, pp. 267–285. Springer, Berlin (1982). https://doi.org/10.1007/978-3-642-46466-9_18
10. Li, F., et al.: Temporal modeling approaches for large-scale Youtube-8m video understanding. https://arxiv.org/abs/1707.04555 (2017)
11. Ramachandra, B., Jones, M., Vatsavai, R.: Learning a distance function with a Siamese network to localize anomalies in videos. In: Proceedings of the IEEE/CVF Winter Conference on Applications of Computer Vision, pp. 2598–2607 (2020)
12. Hu, W.: IEEE transactions on systems, man, and cybernetics-part c: applications and reviews, vol. 41, no. 6 (2011)
13. Ibrahim, Z.A.A., Gros, P.: TV stream structuring. ISRN Signal Processing (2011)
14. Dumont, E., Quénot, G.: Automatic story segmentation for TV news video using multiple modalities. Int. J. Digital Multimedia Broadcast (2012)
15. Manson, G., Naturel, X., Berrani, S.A.: Automatic program extraction from TV streams. In: European Interactive TV Conference, EuroITV'09, Belgique (2009)
16. Naturel, X., et al.: Étiquetage Automatique de Programmes de Télévision, INRIA Rennes Campus de Beaulieu Rennes - France
17. Zlitni, T., Mahdi, W.: A visual grammar approach for TV program identification. Int. J. Comput. Netw. Secur. (IJCNS) **2**(9), 97 (2010)
18. Zlitni, T., Bouaziz, B., Mahdi, W.: Automatic topics segmentation for TV news video using prior knowledge. Multimedia Tools Appl. **75**(10), 5645–5672 (2015). https://doi.org/10.1007/s11042-015-2531-7
19. Hmayda, M., Ejbali, R., Zaied, M.: Program classification in a stream TV using deep learning. In: Proceedings of the 18th International Conference on Parallel and

Distributed Computing, Applications and Technologies, 18–20 December, Taipei, Taiwan (2017). https://doi.org/10.1109/PDCAT.2017.00029

20. Wang, Z., Bovik, A.C., Sheikh, H.R., Simoncelli, E.P.: Image quality assessment: from error visibility to structural similarity. IEEE Trans. Image Process. **13**(4), 600–612 (2004)

21. Krizhevsky, A., Sutskever, I., Hinton, G.E.: Imagenet classification with deep convolutional neural networks. In: NIPS (2012)

22. ImageNet.org, About ImageNet Summary and Statistics (2021). https://www.image-net.org/update-mar-11-2021.php

23. Hasan, A.M., Jalab, H.A., Meziane, F., Kahtan, H., Al-Ahmad, A.S.: Combining deep and handcrafted image features for MRI brain scan classification. IEEE Access **7**, 79959–67 (2019). https://doi.org/10.1109/ACCESS.2019.2922691

24. Gu, J., Wang, Z., Kuen, J., Ma, L., Shahroudy, A., Shuai, B., Liu, T., Wang, X., Wang, G., Cai, J., Chen, T.: Recent advances in convolutional neural networks. Pattern Recogn. **77**, 354–377 (2018). https://doi.org/10.1016/j.patcog.2017.10.013

25. Nair, V., Hinton, G.E.: Rectified linear units improve restricted boltzmann machines. In: Proceedings of the 27th International Conference on Machine Learning (ICML-10), pp. 807–814 272 (2010)

26. Murtagh, F.: Multilayer perceptrons for classification and regression. Neurocomputing **2**(5–6), 183–197 (1991)

27. Krishna, S.T., Kalluri, H.K.: Deep learning and transfer learning approaches for image classification. Int. J. Recent Technol. Eng. (IJRTE) **7**(5S4), 427–432 (2019)

28. Hsiao, T.-Y., et al.: Filter-based deep-compression with global average pooling for convolutional networks. J. Syst. Archit. **95**, 9–18 (2019)

29. Labach, A., Hojjat, S., Shahrokh, V.: Survey of dropout methods for deep neural networks. arXiv preprint. arXiv:1904.13310 (2019)

30. Zhang, Z.: Derivation of Backpropagation in Convolutional Neural Network (CNN). University of Tennessee, Knoxville, TN (2016)

31. Ruder, S.: An overview of gradient descent optimization algorithms. arXiv preprint. arXiv:1609.04747 (2016)

32. https://github.com/itsCandels/SSIM_PROGRAM_CLASSIFICATION

33. https://github.com/jurjsorinliviu/Sports-Type-Classifier

34. Simonyan, K., Andrew, Z.: Two-stream convolutional networks for action recognition in videos. In: Advances in Neural Information Processing Systems **27** (2014)

35. Karpathy, A., Toderici, G., Shetty, S., Leung, T., Sukthankar, R., Fei-Fei, L.: Large-scale video classication with convolutional neural networks. In: Proceedings of the CVPR (2014)

36. Wang, H., Schmid, C.: Action recognition with improved trajectories. In: Proceedings of the ICCV, pp. 3551–3558 (2013)

37. Wang, H., Schmid, C.: Lear-inria submission for the thumos workshop. In: ICCV Workshop on Action Recognition with a Large Number of Classes (2013)

38. Peng, X., Wang, L., Wang, X., Qiao, Y.: Bag of visual words and fusion methods for action recognition: comprehensive study and good practice. CoRR, abs/1405.4506 (2014)

39. Tran, D., Ray, J., Shou, Z., Chang, S.-F., Paluri, M.: Convnet architecture search for spatiotemporal feature learning. arXiv:1708.05038 (2017)

40. https://www.crcv.ucf.edu/data/UCF101.php

41. Ciaparrone, G., Chiariglione, L., Tagliaferri, R.: Un confronto tra modelli di deep learning per il recupero video end-to-end basato su volti in video non vincolati. Neural Comput. Appl. **34**, 7489–7506 (2022). https://doi.org/10.1007/s00521-021-06875-x

A Hybrid Deep Learning System to Detect Face-Mask and Monitor Social Distance

Lutfun Nahar[1], Nanziba Basnin[1], Sirazum Nadia Hoque[1],
Farzana Tasnim[1(✉)], Mohammad Shahadat Hossain[2],
and Karl Andersson[3]

[1] International Islamic University, Chittagong, Bangladesh
farzanatasnim34@gmail.com
[2] University of Chittagong, Chittagong, Bangladesh
[3] Lulea University of Technology, Skelleftea, Sweden

Abstract. Coronavirus Disease 2019 (COVID-19) emerged towards the end of 2019, and it is still causing havoc on the lives and businesses of millions of people in 2022. As the globe recovers from the epidemic and intends to return to normalcy, there is a spike of anxiety among those who expect to resume their everyday routines in person. The biggest difficulty is that no effective therapeutics have yet been reported. According to the World Health Organization (WHO), wearing a face mask and keeping a social distance of at least 2 m can limit viral transmission from person to person. In this paper, a deep learning-based hybrid system for face mask identification and social distance monitoring is developed. In the OpenCV environment, MobileNetV2 is utilized to identify face masks, while YoLoV3 is used for social distance monitoring. The proposed system achieved an accuracy of 0.99.

Keywords: COVID-19 · MobileNetV2 · Convolutional Neural Network (CNN) · YoLoV3 · Deep learning

1 Introduction

SARS-CoV-2 is a highly infectious respiratory illness caused by the virus. COVID-19 was originally identified in China in December 2019 [2]. In China animals exhibitted COVID-19 from where it proliferated globally corresponding to a pandemic [4]. When an infected individual coughs or sneezes, saliva droplets or discharge from the nose are the main ways the virus is disseminated. In those who are afflicted, Covid 19 mainly affects the lungs, and in extreme cases, it can lead to ARDS and pneumonia, which can be fatal. 80% of the time, relatively moderate symptoms will be present, while 14% will develop pneumonia, 5% will experience septic shock and organ failure (most commonly respiratory failure), and 2% will experience fatalities. The main signs of Covid 19 infection include fever, light headedness, dyspnea, headaches, dry coughs that eventually produce

M. Mahmud et al. (Eds.): AII 2022, CCIS 1724, pp. 308–319, 2022.
https://doi.org/10.1007/978-3-031-24801-6_22

phlegm, and in rare cases, loss of taste and smell. Diarrhoea and weariness have also been mentioned in a few occasions. The most important rule for preventing the spread is to maintain social distance and wear a mask when outside. Avoiding crowded places and huge gatherings of people helps to limit the transmission of COVID-19. Furthermore, wearing a mask keeps the coronavirus from spreading. According to the Centers for Disease Control and Prevention (CDC), masks are one of our most useful tactics. However, it is challenging in crowded areas and marginal communities (i.e. among Bangladeshi garment worker communities) to maintain social distancing and facemasks. As a result, technological intervention for controlling the outspread of the infection is necessary [3]. In this research, a deep learning approach is taken into account to detect facemask as well as measure the distance between two people. In order to, build the face-mask detection model model MoblieNet V2 is emplyed in training the dataset collected from Kaggle. This dataset is further testes using testing dataset as well as real-time dataset. To monitor social distancing YOLOV3-tiny is used because of its high speed processing ability of video image datasets. To distinguish the performance of the proposed models, it is compared with CNN, CNN-LSTM and other CNN state-of-the-art modelsutilized in previous studies.

2   Literature Review

In [7] three significant changes has been made to the Viola-Jones (VJ) framework used for object detection. Multi-dimensional (SURF) features, logistic regression and AUC are the changes added to the prior VJ framework. As a result, the convergence rate is faster than that in the previous model. However, this solution cannot beat OpenCV detectors which work in real-time.

In [8] a face mask detection model combining both deep learning methods and classical machine learning is proposed. A CNN pre-trained model ResNet50 is used for feature extraction while decision tree and Support Vector Machine (SVM) are used for the purpose of classification. Inspite of the higher accuracy achieved through machine learning models, the computational speed was slower.

In [5], a deep learning model which uses VGG-16 is proposed for detection of facial emotion and recognition. Using VGG-16 an accuracy of 88% is achieved. However, VGG16 is more than 533MB due to its depth and quantity of completely connected nodes, as a result, deployment of VGG-16 is a challenging task.

[9] uses a SSDMNV2 technique, which is very light and can even be utilized in embedded devices (like the NVIDIA Jetson Nano and Raspberry Pi) to conduct real-time mask detection, employs the Single Shot Multibox Detector as a face detector and MobilenetV2 architecture as a framework for the classifier. The accuracy derived from the method is 0.9264.

In [12] implements the model on a Raspberry Pi 4 to monitor activities and detect violations using camera. When a breach is discovered, the raspberry pi4 notifies the state police control center and the general public of the situation. However, installing the set up can be expensive, moreover the processing power of raspberry pi 4 is much slower.

[10] proposed a system called Covid Vision to assist individuals in relying less on employees while adhering to COVID-19 standards and constraints. Covid Vision is developed using convolutional neural networks (CNNs) for a face mask detector, a social distance tracker, and a face recognition model. The accuracy of the system was found to be 96.49%. The YOLO V3 model performs better than prior models, although good video is crucial.

[11] developed a Face Mask and Social Distancing Detection model as an embedded vision system to help combat the Covid-19 pandemic with the benefits of social distancing and face masks. The pretrained models such as MobileNet, ResNet Classifier, and VGG were employed. Following the implementation and deployment of the models, the chosen one received a confidence score of 100%.

3   Methodology

3.1   System Architecture

Since this research focuses on building a Hybrid Deep Learning system, two different system architectures are used. Figure 1 demonstrates the system architecture for face-mask detection. Initially, the dataset is pre-processed and labeled into categories namely, "no-mask" and "mask". The dataset is then divided into two parts: testing and training. The training set is augmented to expand the size of the image set. This training set is then trained using the Mobile Net V2 in order to develop a learning model. This learning model is then tested to classify whether the images are masked or unmasked against the test dataset. Figure 2 depicts the system architecture which is used to recognize social distancing. To achieve this the input video is trained by applying the YOLOV3 model. The distance between centroids is measured to calculate the distance between two people standing side by side.

3.2   Data Collection

An open-source platform named kaggle is used to acquire the dataset. This dataset [1].

3.3   Data Pre-processing

Grayscale conversion, normalization, resize and data augmentation is performed to pre-process the dataset. Grayscale is merely the conversion of colorful images to black and white. It is commonly used in deep learning techniques to minimize computing complexity. Normalization is the process of projecting image data pixels (intensity) to a preset range (typically (0, 1) or (–1, 1), also known as data re-scaling. This is widely used on many data formats, and you want to normalize them all so that you may apply the same techniques to them. The images are resized into a size of 224 by 224. Afterward, data augmentation is performed in order to make small changes to current data to promote variety

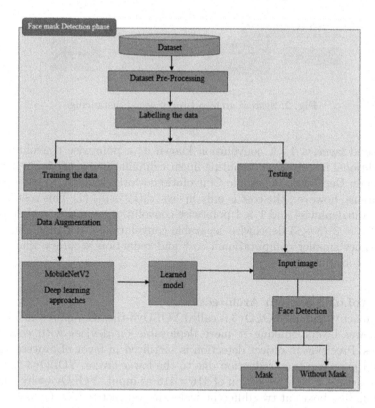

Fig. 1. System architecture of face mask detection

without gathering new data. It is a strategy for increasing the size of a dataset. Horizontal and vertical flipping, rotation, cropping, shearing, and other data augmentation techniques are common which are applied to the dataset.

3.4   System Architecture

3.4.1   MobileNet Architecture for Face-Mask Detection

Depthwise separable convolutions are an essential component of many efficient neural network architecture . An efficient neural network can be developed by using Depthwise Seperable Convolutions as they are an fruitful replacement for standard convolutions. The basic concept is to replace a factorized version of a complete convolutional operator with one that separates convolution into two different layers. In the first layer, a single convolutional filter, known as a depthwise convolution, is applied to each input channel to perform light filtering.

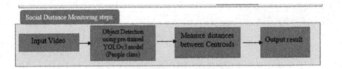

Fig. 2. System architecture of social distancing

The second layer, a 1×1 convolution known as a pointwise convolution, creates additional features by computing linear combinations of the input channels. Empirically Depthwise Seperable Convolutions work similarly to those regular convolutions, however, the cost is only hi · wi · di(k2 + dj) (1) This cost is recognised as the dephwise and 1×1 pointwise convolutions sums. In mobile net the value of k = 3 (3 × 3 depthwise separable convolutions), corresponding to a s 8 to 9 times smaller computational cost and reduction accuracy than that of standard convolutions.

3.4.2 YoLoV3 System Architecture

The compact version of YOLOv3 is called YOLOv3-tiny. Compared to YOLOv3, it has fewer layers, making it more deployable on devices with constrained resources. Precision in object detection is sacrificed in favor of processing overhead and inference time reduction due to the fewer layers. YOLOv3-tiny takes in RGB picture with a resolution of 416 × 416 as input. YOLOv3-tiny only predicts bounding boxes at two different scales, in contrast to YOLOv3. The input image is splited into 13 × 13 grids by the first scale, and 26 × 26 grids by the second scale. In each grid, the framework generates three bounding boxes. The network generates a 3D tensor with class predictions, object class confidence, and bounding box information. The network is made up of five different types of layer categories: convoluted layers, routes, maxpooling, upsamples, and YOLO layer. Up sampling is used in route layers, which are responsible for establishing various flows in the network, to provide a variety of detection scales. The Yolo layer is in charge of generating the output vector.

3.4.3 Measurement of Distance

The Euclidean distance is used to calculate the distance between two centroids (Figs. 3 and 4).

Fig. 3. Sample of images with and without Face mask

$$E(X,Y) = \sqrt{(x_1 - x_2)^2 + (y_1 - y_2)^2}$$
$$d(P,Q) = min(E(p_1,q_1), E(p_1,q_2), E(p_2,q_1), E(p_2,q_2))$$

where, $P = [p_1, p_2]$ and $Q = [q_1, q_2]$ are ground point sets. Every D_{ij} distance matrix D is computed.

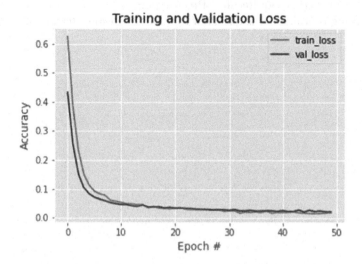

Fig. 4. The flow of data in YOLOV3

3.5   System Implementation

The training module is built using Google Collab. The Goggle drive is used as an external storage device in Collab to retrieve files. This platform enables real-time application execution as well as deep learning libraries (Tensor Processing Unit) by offering access to a powerful GPU and TPU. The darknet GitHub repository is used to clone the whole repository to the root address. Some of the libraries utilized to create models in this work are OpenCV, SKlearn, Tensor Keras, and Matplotlib. The model is ready to train after separating the data into training and testing portions of 80% and 20%, respectively.

4   Result and Desicussion

4.1   Training the Dataset Using MobileNet Model

Figure 5 shows the Training and Validation Accuracy curve of the pre-trained MobileNetV2 model used in the detection of the face-mask. The red line represents the accuracy, while the blue line represents the validation accuracy. There is little to no difference in accuracy between training and testing. Furthermore, it can be deduced that both the line dramatically rises from approximately 5 epochs, after which it remains constant with little change. For evaluation of the performance, there is need some performance metrics.to evaluate the performance for the models MobileNet and YOLOV3, performance matrieces namely, precision, recall, F1-score are used [8].

Accuracy = (TP+TN)/((TP+FP)+(TN+FN))
Precision = TP/((TP+FP))
Recall = TP/((TP+FN))
F1Score = 2 (PrecisionRecall)/(Precision+Recall)

According to Table 1 it is observed that the Precision, Recall and f1-Score is 0.99.

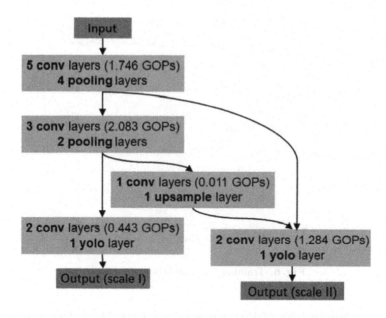

Fig. 5. Training and validation accuracy

Table 1. The proposed model's classification report

	Precision	Recall	F1-score	Support
With mask	0.99	0.99	0.99	383
Without mask	0.99	0.99	0.99	384
Macro avg	0.99	0.99	0.99	767
Weighted avg	0.99	0.99	0.99	767

4.2 Social Monitoring System

The YOLO V3 models are used to detect social distance between objects. Figure 6 illustrates not only pedestrians.

4.3 Face Mask Recognition in Real Time

The dataset is trained using MobileNetV2. The aforementioned model simultaneously detects multiple individuals in real-time. Figure 8 shows the real time detection generated by the model (Fig. 7).

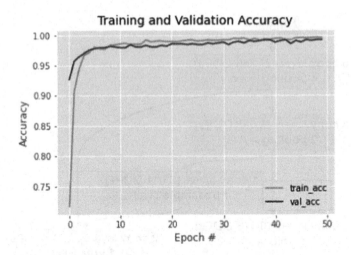

Fig. 6. Training and validation accuracy

4.4 The Comparison of Performance for Face-Mask Detection

As shown in Table 2, the proposed model is compared to other existing work.The proposed model MobileNetV2 outperforms the models used in other research works.CNN has the lowest performance of any of the models.

Table 2. Comparison of performance for face mask detection

Reference	Method	Accuracy
Li et al. 2013 [7]	Yolo Algorithm	93%
Keniya and Mehendale, 2020 [6]	ResNet50, ResNet18, Yolo	92.8%
Hussain amd Al Balushi, 2020 [5]	VGG-16	88%
Prposed method	CNN	20%
Proposed method	MobileNetV2	99%

4.5 The Comparison of Performance for Monitoring Social Distancing

As shown in Table 3, the proposed model outperforms the YOLO-V4 Modelby a difference of 9%.

Table 3. Comparison of performance for monitoring social distance

Method	Accuracy
Yolo-V4 Model	90%
Proposed Model	99%

Fig. 7. Face mask recognition in real time

Fig. 8. Social distance monitoring from real time video

5   Conclusion

This research focuses on providing a cost efficient and computationally cheap deep learning based system which will not only detect face mask but also monitor social distancing among people. Here two systems are developed, the face-mask dataset is trained by using MObileNetV2 model, resulting in an accuracy of

0.99%. Real-Time testing is also carried out, through which the presence of face-mask is detected. Further, YOLOV3-tiny is used to monitor the social distancing among individuals from video footage. The distance among two individuals are measured using the Euclidean distance formula. Further, the Mobilenet is compared with other pre-trained models used in previous studies and CNN models developed solely for the purpose of comparison in this research. It is observed that MobileNet V2 outperforms YOLO algorithm, ResNet 50, ResNet 80, VGG-16 as well as proposed CNN and CNN-LSTM models. In addition, to distinguish the performance of YOLOV3-tiny it is compared to that of YOLOV4. In terms of speed and accuracy YOLOV3-tiny exhibited better performance.

As for future work, this model can be embedded with android application which utilizing mobile cameras. Moreover, we aim to extend our study to include and experiment with people detection by utilizing 3-D dimensions with three parameters (x, y, and z), in which we can feel uniform distribution distance throughout the entire image and do away with the perspective effect.

References

1. https://www.kaggle.com/datasets/prithwirajmitra/covid-face-mask-detection-dataset
2. COVID, C., et al.: Evidence for limited early spread of covid-19 within the united states, january-february 2020. Morbid. Mortal. Weekly Rep. **69**(22), 680 (2020)
3. Dancer, S.J.: Controlling hospital-acquired infection: focus on the role of the environment and new technologies for decontamination. Clin. Microbiol. Rev. **27**(4), 665–690 (2014)
4. Goel, S., Dayal, R.: Novel corona-virus disease 2019 (covid-19): a perilous life-threatening epidemic. Coronaviruses **2**(2), 215–222 (2021)
5. Hussain, S.A., Al Balushi, A.S.A.: A real time face emotion classification and recognition using deep learning model. In: Journal of Physics: Conference Series. vol. 1432, p. 012087. IOP Publishing (2020)
6. Keniya, R., Mehendale, N.: Real-time social distancing detector using socialdistancingnet-19 deep learning network. SSRN 3669311 (2020)
7. Li, J., Zhang, Y.: Learning surf cascade for fast and accurate object detection. In: Proceedings of the IEEE Conference on Computer Vision and Pattern Recognition, pp. 3468–3475 (2013)
8. Loey, M., Manogaran, G., Taha, M.H.N., Khalifa, N.E.M.: A hybrid deep transfer learning model with machine learning methods for face mask detection in the era of the covid-19 pandemic. Measurement **167**, 108288 (2021)
9. Nagrath, P., Jain, R., Madan, A., Arora, R., Kataria, P., Hemanth, J.: Ssdmnv2: a real time dnn-based face mask detection system using single shot multibox detector and mobilenetv2. Sustain. Cities Soc. **66**, 102692 (2021)
10. Prasad, J., Jain, A., Velho, D., Ks, S.K.: Covid vision: an integrated face mask detector and social distancing tracker. Int. J. Cogn. Comput. Eng. **3**, 106–113 (2022)
11. Teboulbi, S., Messaoud, S., Hajjaji, M.A., Mtibaa, A.: Real-time implementation of ai-based face mask detection and social distancing measuring system for covid-19 prevention. Sci. Program. **2021** (2021)
12. Yadav, S.: Deep learning based safe social distancing and face mask detection in public areas for covid-19 safety guidelines adherence. Int. J. Res. Appl. Sci. Eng. Technol. **8**(7), 1368–1375 (2020)

Handwriting and Drawing for Depression Detection: A Preliminary Study

Gennaro Raimo[1]([✉])[iD], Michele Buonanno[1], Massimiliano Conson[1][iD],
Gennaro Cordasco[1][iD], Marcos Faundez-Zanuy[2][iD], Gavin McConvey[3],
Stefano Marrone[4][iD], Fiammetta Marulli[4][iD], Alessandro Vinciarelli[5][iD],
and Anna Esposito[1][iD]

[1] Department of Psychology, University of Campania "Luigi Vanvitelli", Viale
Ellittico 31, 81100 Caserta, Italy
{gennaro.raimo,massimiliano.conoson,gennaro.cordasco,
anna.esposito}@unicampania.it
[2] TecnoCampus Mataro-Maresme Escola Superior Politecnica Mataro, Carrer
d'Ernest Lluch 32, 08302 Mataró, Barcelona, Spain
faundez@tecnocampus.cat
[3] Action Mental Health, 27 Jubilee Road, Newtownards BT23 4YH, UK
gmcconvey@amh.org.uk
[4] Department of Mathematics, University of Campania "Luigi Vanvitelli", Viale
Lincoln 5, 81100 Caserta, Italy
{stefano.marrone,fiammetta.marulli}@unicampania.it
[5] School of Computing Science, University of Glasgow, 18 Lilybank Gardens, G12
8RZ Glasgow, Scotland
alessandro.vinciarelli@glasgow.ac.uk

Abstract. The events of the past 2 years related to the pandemic have shown that it is increasingly important to find new tools to help mental health experts in diagnosing mood disorders. Leaving aside the long-covid cognitive (e.g., difficulty in concentration) and bodily (e.g., loss of smell) effects, the short-term covid effects on mental health were a significant increase in anxiety and depressive symptoms. The aim of this study is to use a new tool, the "online" handwriting and drawing analysis, to discriminate between healthy individuals and depressed patients. To this purpose, patients with clinical depression (n = 14), individuals with high sub-clinical (diagnosed by a test rather than a doctor) depressive traits (n = 15) and healthy individuals (n = 20) were recruited and asked to perform four online drawing/handwriting tasks using a digitizing tablet and a special writing device. From the raw collected online data, seventeen drawing/writing features (categorized into five categories) were extracted, and compared among the three groups of the involved participants, through ANOVA repeated measures analyses. The main results of this study show that Time features are more effective in discriminating between healthy and participants with sub-clinical depressive characteristics. On the other hand, Ductus and Pressure features are more effective in discriminating between clinical depressed and healthy participants.

M. Mahmud et al. (Eds.): AII 2022, CCIS 1724, pp. 320–332, 2022.
https://doi.org/10.1007/978-3-031-24801-6_23

Keywords: Depression · On-line handwriting/drawing features · Emotions · Behavioral and mood disorders

1   Introduction

In recent years, there has been a significant increase of mood disorders: an increase respectively of 18.4% and 14.9% in depression and anxiety cases took place between 2005 and 2015. According to data reported by Mental Health America [17] (https://mhanational.org/), from January to September 2020, there was an increase, compared to 2019, of 62% in the request for depression screening and of 93% in the request for screening to assess anxiety. In addition, the severity of anxiety and depressive symptoms also increased significantly, with about 80% of screened people showing severe anxiety and depression symptoms [17]. This data demonstrates that the extraordinary, stressful pandemic situation had a very strong impact on the emotional life of the worldwide population. Furthermore, this increase in cases shows how much more important is to find new tools to detect the presence (or the absence) of these types of disorders quickly and effectively.

Mood disorders (also called mood affective disorders) are characterized by cognitive (i.e. memory and concentration difficulties, worry/rumination, guilt and self-depreciation), emotional (i.e. low mood, sadness, distress, irritability and hopeless), physical (i.e. loss of energy, fatigue, weight loss or gain, anhedonia and sleep disturbances) and behavioral (i.e. psychomotor retardation, social withdrawal, avoidance, loss of interest in enjoyable activities, suicide thoughts and suicide acts) symptoms [6].

Therefore, the detection of these diseases can be based on the analysis of behavioral signals (e.g. speeches, body motions, physiological data, handwritings, text analysis and drawings; for a review see [8]), which have been proven to be efficient, effective and have no subjective bias.

Specifically, one of these, handwriting, proved useful to identify people's different characteristics: socio-personal data (i.e. age, nationality and gender [1,3]); personality traits [7,9]; neurodegenerative disease [23] and, even more, emotional states [4,12]. Considering previous results and considering that handwriting and drawing skills are common behavioral signals, it is conceivable to think that is possible to identify and discriminate depression patients using these two skills.

Several studies have demonstrated, using a kinematic approach (i.e. motion analysis), that healthy participants are faster [13,14] and more accurate [21] than depressed patients. However, these studies are limited because they analyzes only a specific group or a specific task. Regarding participants, they involved only elderly people [21] or healthy young (students between 18–22 years old) people [13]; instead, for what concerns the tasks, the limits were the use of uncommon and non-naturalistic tasks (i.e. drawing of a circle) [14,21] or a stress load test [13]. Rosenblum [20], still using a kinematic approach, found that pressure analysis could help discriminate between depressed patients and non-clinical participants. Nevertheless, even in this case, the study was focused only on elderly people.

Unlike the previous studies, Gawda [10] found no statistically significant differences in velocity comparing depressed patients, borderline patients, and healthy participants. She found only more tremors and a more descending trait.

As can be seen, results of these studies are heterogeneous, showing that more clarity is needed in this field of study.

Moreover, the use of new tools to discover, discriminate and identify these diseases is also necessary because recent studies [16,24] and even the European community, in last years highlighted the importance of prevention programs for early detection of depression and anxiety. Early diagnosis leads to greater efficacy of therapy and faster improvement in patients' overall health.

At author knowledge, literature shows that no studies have been conducted with comparison between healthy and clinical participants using our approach and our task. The present paper is a pilot study that reports a comparison of these types of participants (clinical and healthy) considering "online" handwriting and drawing skills to evaluate clinical and typical participants' differences.

This paper is organized as follows: in Sect. 2, we describe the characteristics of the handwriting used; in Sect. 3, we describe our approach; Sect. 4 contains the analysis and results of the study; in Sect. 5 we discuss the results, the clinical and research implications and, moreover, we discuss limits and future plans; at last, in Sect. 6 we provide conclusions about this new research approach.

2   Handwriting Analysis for the Detection of Depression and Anxiety

The development of new technologies in handwriting analysis have led to the emergence of a new approach in this field of study, which can analyze "online" writing and drawing skills. This novel approach to handwriting analysis has been possible thanks to the development of pencil and digital tablets, which are able to analyze parameters such as pressure applied on paper, inclination of the pen used, number of strokes used to complete a task, etc.

An INTUOS WACOM series 4 digital tablet was used to collect data. Since the standard pen did not allow writing on a common paper, so participants can't see their stroke in the way they are used to, another pen, which allows to see strokes, named Intuos Inkpen, was paired with the tablet. In this way, it was possible to obtain information both on the strokes (through the sheet of paper), and on other parameters, as time information and in-air movements (through the tablet).

Data was collected for several task and recorded in a comma separated values (.csv) file. The system registered the following data every 8 ms:

- the two-dimensional coordinates of the pen;
- the unix epoch (the number of milliseconds that have elapsed since January 1, 1970;
- the pen status (on paper = 1 or in-air = 0);
- two angles that describes the position of the paper with respect to the tablet;

- the amount of pressure applied by the pen on the paper, expressed using an integer value, from 0 (no pressure) to 255 (maximum pressure). the amount of pressure applied by the pen on the paper, expressed using an integer value, from 0 (no pressure) to 255 (maximum pressure).

3 Methodology

In this section we describe the sample (subsection Participants), the tasks used for data collection and the handwriting features considered in our approach (subsection Tasks and Features).

3.1 Participants

The experiments involved a total of 49 participants (Male = 15; mean age = 28.90; SD = 10.47) partitioned as follows:

- 14 clinical group (depression patients)
- 15 DASS-Severe Group
- 20 DASS-Normal Group.

Description of socio-personal characteristics (group, mean age and standard deviation of age) are reported in the table below (Table 1).

Table 1. Group participants with sample size (N), mean of age (M) and standard deviation of age (SD). CL = Clinical Group, SEV = DASS-Severe Group; NOR = DASS-Normal Group.

Group	N	M	SD
CL	14	39,86	14,40
SEV	15	24,53	2,72
N	20	24,50	2,42

Healthy participants, recruited at Università degli Studi della Campania "L. Vanvitellli", were included only if satisfying the following inclusion criteria: 1. right-handed; 2. no clinical diagnosis of neurological, neuropsychiatric, or psychological disease; 3a. for DASS-Normal group, "normal" score in Depression Anxiety Stress (DASS) questionnaire, in all the three sub-scale (depression, anxiety, stress); 3b. for DASS-Severe group, "severe" or "extremely severe" score in DASS questionnaire in depression sub-scale.

The DASS questionnaire [2] is a self-report measure that estimate affective states of depression, anxiety, and stress. Each scale is composed of seven items (21 total items). Responses are given on a 4-point Likert scale (from 0: Did not apply to me at all; to 4: Applied to me very much or most of the time). The scores obtained for each subscale indicate the severity of the symptoms from normal (healthy individual), to mild, moderate, severe, and extremely severe condition.

The participants of the clinical group are patients with clinical depression, diagnosed by a mental health-care expert (a psychologist or a psychiatrist) with a formal diagnosis. The clinical group participants were also right-handed. All the participants speak Italian as their native language.

3.2   Tasks and Features

The participants in the clinical group and healthy groups completed 2 different protocols (see Fig. 1), which share four drawing or handwriting tasks:

1. drawing of two pentagons;
2. drawing of a house;
3. writing an Italian sentence in cursive letters;
4. drawing of a clock with hours and clock hands.

The "online" data acquisition allows us to obtain detailed information on parameters of the written strokes, such as trajectory, speed, and time features. In addition, this tool also enables us to detect features that have proved useful in this field, such as in-air movements (movements of the pen close to the paper) [19,22].

For this study we separated the traits into three categories, as described in [3] and [4]:

– in-air (but close to the paper), pen status 0;
– on-paper, pen status 1;
– idle (far from the paper), not recorded but recognizable using timestamps.

In particular, we considered 17 features (for a description of these see [3]), divided into five categories:

a) Pressure: a value of the pressure applied by the pen on the paper during a specific task (considering only on-paper traits);
   1. Pmin, the lowest pressure value applied;
   2. Pmax, the highest pressure value applied;
   3. Pavg, the average value of the applied pressure;
   4. Psd, the standard deviation of the applied pressures;
   5. P10, lower 10th percentile of applied pressures;
   6. P90, lower 90th percentile of applied pressures.
b) Ductus: the number of strokes in each pen status;
   7. Nup, amount of in-air traits;
   8. Ndown, amount of on-paper traits;
   9. Nidle, total amount of traits not recognized by the tablet.
c) Time: total time spent, in each pen status, to complete the task;
   10. Tup, time of in-air pen status;

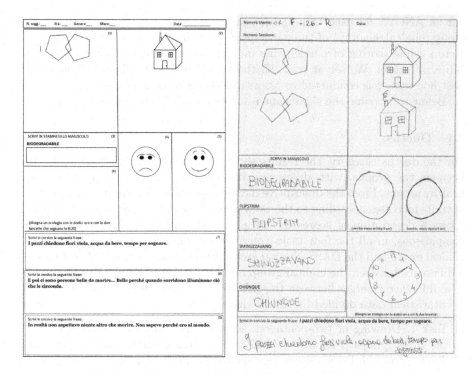

Fig. 1. (left) clinical group protocol; (right) healthy group protocol (filled by one participant). Four tasks are common.

11. Tdown, time of on-paper pen status;
12. Tidle, time of pen status not recognized by the tablet;
13. Ttotal = Tup + Tdown + Tidle, total time used to complete the task.

d) Space: the occupied space by the strokes task (considering exclusively on-paper traits);

14. Sbb, a value obtained computing the smallest axis aligned bounding box containing the stroke and summing its area;
15. Savg, average lengths of empty spaces between consecutive strokes;
16. Stotal, sum of the lengths of empty spaces between consecutive on-paper strokes.

e) Inclination; a value of strokes inclination.

17. Iavg, average inclination of the diagonals of the bounding boxes containing the strokes.

4 Results

Several repeated measures ANOVA analyses were performed to evaluate the efficacy of the considered features in differentiating the groups of writers. We carried out an ANOVA for each task and for each features category. Furthermore, the group (clinical/healthy) of the participants was considered as between subjects' factors while scoring of participants on each feature was considered as within subjects factors. We set at $\alpha < .05$ the significance level; finally, Bonferroni's post hoc tests was conducted to assess differences among means.

Below we provide the significant results for each feature category.

4.1 Ductus

For the ductus category, the results show that emerges a significant difference between the groups, with differences between the clinical patient group and healthy groups. From the descriptive data it is possible to notice how the number of traits increases according to the worsening of the depressive condition. Table 2 shows a description of scores for all groups and all tasks. From the pairwise comparisons, in all the four tasks considered a difference emerges between the clinical group and the DASS-Normal group. Furthermore, in tasks 2–3–4 there is a difference between the clinical group and DASS-Severe group. Finally, in task 1, a difference emerges between the DASS-Severe and DASS-Normal groups.

Statistical data divided by task is shown below:

a) Task 1: Drawing of two-pentagon: a significant difference emerges between the three groups $[F(2; 46) = 13.222; p << .01]$. Clinical group significantly differs from the DASS-Normal group $(p << .01)$. Moreover, DASS-Normal group significantly differs from the DASS-Severe group $(p = .031)$.

b) Task 2: Drawing of a house: a significant difference emerges between the three groups $[F(2; 46) = 19.347; p << .01]$. Clinical group significantly differs from the DASS-Normal group $(p << .01)$. Moreover, Clinical group significantly differs from the DASS-Severe group $(p << .01)$.

c) Task 3: Writing of Italian sentence in cursive letters: a significant difference emerges between the three groups $[F(2; 46) = 18.090; p << .01]$. Clinical group significantly differs from the DASS-Normal group $(p << .01)$. Moreover, Clinical group significantly differs from the DASS-Severe group $(p < .01)$.

d) Task 4: Drawing a clock with hours and hands: a significant difference emerges between the three groups $[F(2; 46) = 18.464; p << .01]$. Clinical group significantly differs from the DASS-Normal group $(p << .01)$. Moreover, Clinical group significantly differs from the DASS-Severe group $(p << .01)$.

Analyzing individually the different parameters of ductus category, the following differences emerge between the groups:

- Nup: Clinical group and DASS-Normal group (all tasks: $p << .01$).
- Nup: Clinical group and DASS-Severe group (task 2–3–4: $p << .01$).
- Ndown: Clinical group and DASS-Normal group (all tasks: $p << .01$).
- Ndown: Clinical group and DASS-Severe group (task 1: $p = .045$; task 2–3–4: $p << .01$).
- Nidle: Clinical group and DASS-Severe group (task 2: $p << .01$).

Table 2. Performance (number of strokes) on the ductus category, separately for group and task. The values are expressed as mean (standard deviations). CL = Clinical Group, SEV = DASS-Severe Group, NOR = DASS-Normal Group

DUCTUS CATEGORY			
TASK	Group		
	CL	SEV	NOR
Task 1	26.286 (3.480)	14.978 (3.362)	3.100 (2.912)
Task 2	49.857 (4.167)	24.600 (4.304)	16.600 (3.494)
Task 3	47.643 (3.665)	25.111 (3.541)	19.733 (3.066)
Task 4	60.214 (3.927)	35.578 (3.794)	30.083 (3.286)

4.2 Time

For the time category, the results show that emerges a significant difference between the groups. Also in this case, observing descriptive data it is possible to notice how time taken to perform a task is conditioned by the depressive situation in progress, with times that increase when the depressive state is worst. Description of scoring separately for tasks and groups are reported in Table 3 (only task with significantly differences is reported). From the pairwise comparisons, in task 1 a significant difference emerges between the DASS-Normal group and the DASS-Severe group; instead, in task 3 a significant difference emerges between the clinical group and DASS-Normal group. No other significant differences emerged in the tasks considered in this research.

Statistical data divided by task is shown below:

a) Task 1: Drawing of two-pentagon: a significant difference emerges between the three groups $[F(2; 46) = 4.068; p = .024]$. DASS-Normal significantly differs from the DASS-Severe group $(p = .045)$.
b) Task 3: Writing of Italian sentence in cursive letters: a significant difference emerges between the three groups $[F(2; 46) = 6,580; p = .003]$. Clinical group significantly differs from the DASS-Normal group $(p = .002)$.

Table 3. Performance (time spent in millisecond) on the time category, separately for group and task. The values are expressed as mean (standard deviations). CL = Clinical Group, SEV = DASS-Severe Group, NOR = DASS-Normal Group.

TIME CATEGORY			
TASK	Group		
	CL	SEV	NOR
Task 1	17675.821 (1556.496	12131.050 (1503.718)	7096.075 (1302.258)
Task 3	23026.286 (2020.529)	18031.850 (1952.016)	13494.300 (1690.496)

Analyzing individually the different parameters of time category, the following differences emerge between the groups:

- Tup: Clinical group and DASS-Normal group (task 1: $p = .002$; task 3: $p = .001$)
- Tup: DASS-Normal group e DASS-Severe group (task 1: $p = .039$)
- Tdown: Clinical group and DASS-Normal group (task 3: $p = .01$)
- Tidle: DASS-Normal group e DASS-Severe group (task 1: $p = .032$)
- Ttotal: Clinical group and DASS-Normal group (task 3: $p = .002$)
- Ttotal: DASS-Normal group e DASS-Severe group (task 1: $p = .045$).

4.3   Pressure

Also for the pressure category, the results show that emerges a significant difference between the groups. Unlike the other two categories, the pressure applied on the paper tends to decrease with the worsening of the depressive state. Looking at the descriptive data it is possible to highlight how in healthy individuals the pressure applied is greater. From the pairwise comparisons, in tasks 1 and 2 a difference emerges between the clinical group and the DASS-Normal group. No significant differences emerged in the other tasks considered in this research. Table 4 described scoring obtained in pressure category separately for groups and tasks (only task with significantly differences is reported).

Statistical data divided by task is shown below:

a) Task 1: Drawing of two-pentagon: a significant difference emerges between the three groups $[F(2; 46) = 9.101; p << .01]$. Clinical group significantly differs from the DASS-Normal group ($p << .01$).
b) Task 2: Drawing of a house: a significant difference emerges between the three groups $[F(2; 46) = 4.555; p = 0.016]$. Clinical group significantly differs from the DASS-Normal group ($p = .020$).

Table 4. Performance (pressure applied by the pen on the paper) on the pressure category, separately for group and task. The values are expressed as mean (standard deviations). CL = Clinical Group; SEV = DASS-Severe Group, NOR = DASS-Normal Group.

PRESSURE CATEGORY			
TASK	Group		
	CL	SEV	NOR
Task 1	369.646 (22.644)	446.241 (21.876)	495.572 (18.945)
Task 2	339.659 (23.303)	417.886 (22.513)	426.029 (19.497)

Analyzing individually the different parameters of Pressure category, the following differences emerge between the groups:

- Pmax: Clinical group and DASS-Normal group (task 1: $p = .015$).
- Pmin: Clinical group and DASS-Normal group (task 2: $p = .003$).
- Pavg: Clinical group and DASS-Normal group (task 1: $p << .01$; task 2: $p = .018$)
- P10: Clinical group and DASS-Normal group (task 1: $p << .01$; task 2: $p = .001$)
- P10: Clinical group and DASS-Severe group (task 1: $p = .021$; task 2: $p = .019$)
- P90: Clinical group and DASS-Normal group (task 1: $p = .002$; task 2: $p = .042$).

5 Discussion

The most recent global burden of disease study [11] estimated that depression, from 1990 to 2017, ranks third among those responsible causes worldwide of years lived with disabilities (YLD). Furthermore, depression also leads the ranking of suicides cause, with estimated 800.000 victims worldwide; moreover, it is the second leading cause of death between 15–29 years [5].

Experiencing adverse life events, like a pandemic or a social isolation lockdown, can increase the likelihood of developing depression, also after many years [15]. Considering that catastrophic events could happen again in the next years, it is essential to develop new tools to recognize and identify depression early and quickly.

Previous studies have shown how it is possible to discriminate between pathological/sub-clinical patients and healthy participants through behavioral analyses [4,8,10]; not only with mood disorders but also with Alzheimer's disease (AD) and of related dementia [18].

In this way, results of this study demonstrates that it is possible to discriminate between depressed clinical patients and non-clinical participants, exploiting online handwriting and drawing features, obtained from specific tasks such as the drawing of: two-pentagons (task 1), a house (task 2), and a clock with the twelve hours and clock hands (task 4), as well as the writing in cursive letters (task 3), focusing on features derived from Ductus, Pressure and Timing measures.

Specifically, the main results show that timing measures are effective in discriminating between healthy individuals and participants with sub-clinical depressive traits. Instead, ductus and pressure measures are well suited for discriminating between healthy and clinical depressed participants.

The limitations of this study are evidently a relatively small number of participants and the greater number of women than men in the sample. For this reason, the present study can only be considered as a preliminary pilot study in the research area of the use of handwriting and drawing for depression detection.

Future studies aim to find more evidence on larger samples of subjects, even better if matched by gender and age. Moreover, machine learning techniques can be used to analyze the data to increase the reliability and validity of this experimental paradigm and to have a classification accuracy. Lastly, future goals can also be considered to arrive at a complete automatic detection of mood disorders and improve in a clinical field all these advances.

6   Conclusion

Considering results of this study, handwriting analysis appears to be a promising tool for speeding the diagnosis of depression, providing quantitative measures about depression signals and decreasing the health care costs associated to long professional interviews.

Furthermore, this approach can offer more reliable and effective results, since it is not linked to subjective evaluation bias, which can be present both in patients and in mental-health experts and could affect the diagnosis.

In conclusion, the aims of this study on handwriting and drawing skills for the detection of depression are: clarify the discordant results present in the literature regarding this topic, to have a specific, effective and quickly and especially standardized methodology for this type of evaluation; rise the interests of scientific community and to all researchers interested in this field of study.

Acknowledgment. The research leading to these results has received funding from the project ANDROIDS funded by the program V:ALERE 2019 Università della Campania "Luigi Vanvitelli", D.R. 906 del 4/10/2019, prot. n. 157264, 17/10/2019, the project SIROBOTICS that received funding from Italian MIUR, PNR 2015–2020, D.D. 1735, 13/07/ 2017, and the EU H2020 research and innovation program under grant agreement N. 769872 (EMPATHIC) and N. 823907 (MENHIR).

Data Availability Statement. Further information on the proposed method, dataset analysed during the current study andd all statistical results are available from the corresponding author (gennaro.raimo@unicampania.it) on reasonable request.

References

1. Al Maadeed, S., Hassaine, A.: Automatic prediction of age, gender, and nationality in offline handwriting. EURASIP J. Image Video Process. **2014**(1), 1–10 (2014). https://doi.org/10.1186/1687-5281-2014-10
2. Bottesi, G., Ghisi, M., Altoè, G., Conforti, E., Melli, G., Sica, C.: The Italian version of the depression anxiety stress scales-21: factor structure and psychometric properties on community and clinical samples. Compr. Psychiatry **60**, 170–181 (2015)
3. Cordasco, G., Buonanno, M., Faundez-Zanuy, M., Riviello, M.T., Likforman-Sulem, L., Esposito, A.: Gender identification through handwriting: an online approach. In: 2020 11th IEEE International Conference on Cognitive Infocommunications (CogInfoCom), pp. 000197–000202. IEEE (2020)
4. Cordasco, G., Scibelli, F., Faundez-Zanuy, M., Likforman-Sulem, L., Esposito, A.: Handwriting and drawing features for detecting negative moods. In: Esposito, A., Faundez-Zanuy, M., Morabito, F.C., Pasero, E. (eds.) WIRN 2017 2017. SIST, vol. 103, pp. 73–86. Springer, Cham (2019). https://doi.org/10.1007/978-3-319-95095-2_7

5. Depression, W.: Other common mental disorders: global health estimates. Geneva: World Health Organization **24** (2017)
6. Edition, F., et al.: Diagnostic and statistical manual of mental disorders. Am. Psychiatric Assoc. **21**, 591–643 (2013)
7. Esposito, A., et al.: Handwriting and drawing features for detecting personality traits. In: 2019 10th IEEE International Conference on Cognitive Infocommunications (CogInfoCom), pp. 79–84. IEEE (2019)
8. Esposito, A., Raimo, G., Maldonato, M., Vogel, C., Conson, M., Cordasco, G.: Behavioral sentiment analysis of depressive states. In: 2020 11th IEEE International Conference on Cognitive Infocommunications (CogInfoCom), pp. 000209–000214. IEEE (2020)
9. Gavrilescu, M., Vizireanu, N.: Predicting the big five personality traits from handwriting. EURASIP J. Image Video Process. **2018**(1), 1–17 (2018)
10. Gawda, B.: Little evidence for the graphical markers of depression. Percept. Mot. Skills **117**(1), 304–318 (2013)
11. GBD, et al.: Global, regional, and national incidence, prevalence, and years lived with disability for 354 diseases and injuries for 195 countries and territories, 1990–2017: a systematic analysis for the global burden of disease study 2017. Collaborators (2018)
12. Likforman-Sulem, L., Esposito, A., Faundez-Zanuy, M., Clémençon, S., Cordasco, G.: EMOTHAW: a novel database for emotional state recognition from handwriting and drawing. IEEE Trans. Hum.-Mach. Syst. **47**(2), 273–284 (2017)
13. Mashio, Y., Kawaguchi, H.: Detecting early symptoms of mental health deterioration using handwriting duration parameters. Neuropsychopharmacol. Rep. **40**(3), 246–253 (2020)
14. Mergl, R., et al.: Kinematical analysis of handwriting movements in depressed patients. Acta Psychiatr. Scand. **109**(5), 383–391 (2004)
15. Phillips, A.C., Carroll, D., Der, G.: Negative life events and symptoms of depression and anxiety: stress causation and/or stress generation. Anxiety Stress Coping **28**(4), 357–371 (2015)
16. Purebl, G., et al.: Joint action on mental health and well-being. Depression, suicide prevention and E-health: situation analysis and recommendations for action (2015)
17. Reinert, M., Fritze, D., Nguyen, T.: The state of mental health in America 2022. Ment. Health Am. (2021)
18. Rentoumi, V., et al.: Automatic detection of linguistic indicators as a means of early detection of Alzheimer's disease and of related dementias: a computational linguistics analysis. In: 2017 8th IEEE International Conference on Cognitive Infocommunications (CogInfoCom), pp. 000033–000038. IEEE (2017)
19. Rosenblum, S., Parush, S., Weiss, P.L.: The in air phenomenon: temporal and spatial correlates of the handwriting process. Percept. Mot. Skills **96**(3), 933–954 (2003)
20. Rosenblum, S., Werner, P., Dekel, T., Gurevitz, I., Heinik, J.: Handwriting process variables among elderly people with mild major depressive disorder: a preliminary study. Aging Clin. Exp. Res. **22**(2), 141–147 (2010)
21. Schröter, A., Mergl, R., Bürger, K., Hampel, H., Möller, H.J., Hegerl, U.: Kinematic analysis of handwriting movements in patients with Alzheimer's disease, mild cognitive impairment, depression and healthy subjects. Dement. Geriatr. Cogn. Disord. **15**(3), 132–142 (2003)
22. Sesa-Nogueras, E., Faundez-Zanuy, M., Mekyska, J.: An information analysis of in-air and on-surface trajectories in online handwriting. Cogn. Comput. **4**(2), 195–205 (2012)

23. Taleb, C., Khachab, M., Mokbel, C., Likforman-Sulem, L.: Feature selection for an improved Parkinson's disease identification based on handwriting. In: 2017 1st International Workshop on Arabic Script Analysis and Recognition (ASAR), pp. 52–56. IEEE (2017)
24. van Zoonen, K., et al.: Preventing the onset of major depressive disorder: a meta-analytic review of psychological interventions. Int. J. Epidemiol. **43**(2), 318–329 (2014)

Identifying Synthetic Voices' Qualities for Conversational Agents

Marialucia Cuciniello[1]([⊠]), Terry Amorese[1], Gennaro Cordasco[1], Stefano Marrone[2], Fiammetta Marulli[2], Filippo Cavallo[3], Olga Gordeeva[4], Zoraida Callejas Carrión[5], and Anna Esposito[1]

[1] Department of Psychology, Università degli Studi della Campania "Luigi Vanvitelli", and IIASS, Caserta and Vietri Sul Mare, Italy
{marialucia.cuciniello,terry.amorese,gennaro.cordasco,
anna.esposito}@unicampania.it

[2] Department of Mathematics and Physics (DMF), Università degli Studi della Campania "Luigi Vanvitelli", Caserta, Italy
{stefano.marrone,fiammetta.marulli}@unicampania.it

[3] Department of Industrial Engineering, BioRobotics Institute, SS Sant'Anna, and Department of Excellence in Robotics & AI, Florence University, Florence, Italy
filippo.cavallo@unifi.it

[4] Acapela Group, Mons, Belgium
olga.gordeeva@acapela-group.com

[5] Universidad de Granada, Granada, Spain
zoraida@ugr.es

Abstract. The present study aims to explore user' acceptance and perceptions toward different quality levels of synthetical voices. To achieve this, four voices have been exploited considering two main factors: the quality of the voices (low vs high) and their gender (male and female). 186 volunteers were recruited and subsequently allocated into four groups of different ages respectively, adolescents, young adults, middle-aged and seniors. After having randomly listened to each voice, participants were asked to fill the Virtual Agent Voice Acceptance Questionnaire (VAVAQ). Outcomes show that the two higher quality voices of Antonio and Giulia were more appreciated than the low-quality voices of Edoardo and Clara by the whole sample in terms of pragmatic, hedonic and attractiveness qualities attributed to the voices. Concerning preferences towards differently aged voices, it clearly appeared that they varied according to participants age' ranges examined. Furthermore, in terms of suitability to perform different tasks, participants considered Antonio and Giulia equally adapt for healthcare and front office jobs. Antonio was also judged to be significantly more qualified to accomplish protection and security tasks, while Edoardo was classified as the absolute least skilled in conducting household chores.

Keywords: Synthetic voice · User' acceptance · Conversational agent

M. Mahmud et al. (Eds.): AII 2022, CCIS 1724, pp. 333–346, 2022.
https://doi.org/10.1007/978-3-031-24801-6_24

1   Introduction

An overriding aim for the scientific research is to face challenges emerged from the increase of life expectancy. The World Health Organization (WHO) has clearly stated that it is a booming event compared to the past [1]. It is necessary to promote an autonomous and independent lifestyle for seniors inside their own homes, offering them sustainable and innovative solutions. The high number of requests, the costs and times foreseen by this type of personal assistance often cannot be satisfied by social and healthcare institutional services. Digital assistants could overcome all these limitations. To implement digital applications devoted to improving personal well-being, the characteristics of the end users have to be taken into account. Seniors are often considered as unaccustomed and inexperienced in the use of technology, and therefore it is essential that these devices are perceived as enthralling and easy to use [2]. Due to their characteristics, mobile and wireless technologies such as smartphones, tablets and wearable devices fall into the category of Mobile Health (mhealth) solutions. These are devices potentially able to provide support and health intervention as they would have the capability to adapt to the context of an individual's daily life [3]. However, seniors' acceptance of mobile health (mhealth) solutions could be undermined by their expectations of performance and effort, social influence, anxiety triggered by the use of technological devices and a proclivity to resist change [4]. It is not possible to better frame the issue of ageing by neglecting the recent health emergency due to the spread of coronavirus disease 2019 (COVID-19), which unfortunately continues to rage all over the world. This emergency has highlighted aspects of profound vulnerability that affect all aged groups of people and different contexts from various points of view. This unexpected change led to an abrupt awareness of the danger and the consequent need to adapt to heavy restrictions imposed by each government, inevitably upsetting people's daily routines. Social isolation and development of mental disorders represent two of the main consequences derived from interruptions in the daily routine [5, 6]. In this context, a viable solution to reduce isolation and facilitate daily interactional exchanges could be the use of technological devices acting as assistants. Widely shared and spread is the burgeoning interest in chatbots, also known as conversational agents or virtual assistants. These digital tools may be suited for simulating conversations with humans. This is made possible thanks to machine learning and artificial intelligence methods used to replicate human-like behaviors and grant an activity-oriented dialogue structure. In terms of mental health research, several studies demonstrate the effectiveness of the therapeutic and preventive intervention provided by chatbots [7]. Noteworthy is Wisa, a chatbot able to elicit positive changes in its user's mood. The Touchkin eServices company has created this free mobile application to help people affected by depression and anxiety in managing their conditions [8]. Other studies have tested the effects of a chatbot focused on cognitive behavioral therapy. Outcomes of one of them report positive psychological interactions in a non-clinical population [9]. Clearly, the use of voice is a fundamental tool to simplify the interaction with these devices. Some successful and commonly used application examples are represented by the hardware-based Amazon Echo running Alexa digital assistant software, the software-based Google Assistant running on Android devices. It appears that the use of synthetic voices helps to increase users' confidence when they are consumers. Due to a lack of data, it is not possible to say with equal confidence that the same occurs with users belonging to healthcare environments. Therefore, further investigation is needed [10]. Studies exploring the role played by voice in agents' acceptance demonstrated that seniors prefer much more to interact with embodied speaking agents [11] and even with speaking not embodied visual interfaces [12], rather than voiceless agents embodied in a visual interface. These studies revealed that seniors strongly preferred to interact with speaking agents or even with agents' voices only rather than with mute agents and, moreover, voice affected seniors' positive assessment of the agents in terms of hedonic and pragmatic qualities. Additionally, female voices were preferred to male voices.

This effect disappeared when both male and female agents were mute, revealing that gender preferences only occurred in the presence of agents' voice. Concerning young adults and adolescents, they did not seem to care whether the agent they were interacting with, was speaking or mute, female, or male. The quality of the synthetic voice has been however neglected; the current research aims to solve this issue. The investigations we are reporting concern the preferences of differently aged users (adolescents, young adults, middle-aged and senior participants) towards two different degrees of quality of synthetic voices (high and low quality) and synthetic voice' gender to draw up useful guidelines for the implementation of talking chatbots.

2   Materials and Method

2.1   Participants

The present study involved 186 volunteers recruited in Campania (a Southern Italy region). Participants were divided in four groups equally balanced by gender. Group 1 was composed by 45 adolescents (24 males, mean age = 15.13; SD = ±0.79); Group 2 by 47 young adults (21 males, mean age = 27.91; SD = ±3.33); Group 3 by 45 middle-aged (22 males, mean age = 48.87; SD = ±4.11) and Group 4 by 49 seniors (23 males, mean age = 75.22; SD = ±8.02). The experiment was dedicated to investigating the degree of acceptance of four Italian synthetic voices represented by two female voices named Giulia and Clara and two male voices named Antonio and Edoardo. The voices differed not only in gender but also in two different levels of synthetic voice quality (low -Edoardo and Clara- vs high – Giulia and Antonio). In addition, participants were also asked to express their preferences regarding the age of the voices (preferred and attributed) and the proposed tasks for which they felt the voices might be more qualified. The whole sample joined the study on a voluntary basis and signed an informed consent formulated according to the current Italian and European laws about privacy and data protection. The research was approved by the ethical committee of the Università degli Studi della Campania "Luigi Vanvitelli," at the Department of Psychology, with the protocol number 25/2017.

Stimuli

Four synthetic voices lasting between 4 and 7 sec., were created for the experiment. Specifically, the low-quality voices (Edoardo and Clara) were created using the Natural Reader synthesizer (www.naturalreaders.com) and subsequently recorded with the free Audacity audio software (www.audacityteam.org). On the other hand, Acapela Group took care of the realization of the high-quality voices (Antonio and Giulia). This group is a European company based in Belgium, with over 30 years of leading experience in the production of high-quality synthetic voices (www.acapela-group.com). The voices were engineered as part of the H2020 funded Empathic project (www.empathic-projec t.eu) aimed at developing an empathic, expressive, and advanced virtual coach to assist seniors in their daily life. The assessment of the two different levels of voice quality was entrusted to Acapela's experts and to the BeCogSys laboratory team at the Università della Campania "Luigi Vanvitelli". Each voice reproduced the Italian sentence "Ciao sono Antonio/ Giulia/ Edoardo/ Clara. Se vuoi posso aiutarti nelle tue attività quotidiane" (Hi, my name is Antonio/ Giulia/ Edoardo/Clara. If you allow me, I can assist you in your daily activities).

Tools

A digitalized version of the Virtual Agent Voice Acceptance Questionnaire (VAVAQ) was exploited to collect data and to assess participants' preferences toward the proposed synthetic voices. The VAVAQ derived from a previous version: the Virtual Agent Acceptance Questionnaire (VAAQ). This questionnaire has been developed inside the Empathic project to assess seniors' preferences toward virtual coach. Further details are reported in previous studies [13].

The digitalized version of VAVAQ was developed using Java scripts and allowed the automatic randomization of the questionnaire's items and sections presented to each participant. The questionnaire was structured as follows: an initial part of six items aimed at collecting socio-demographic information and eight following sections. Section 1 (composed of seven items) aimed at investigating participants' degree of experience and familiarity with technological devices such as smartphones, tablets, and laptops. Section 2 composed by a single item focused on participants' willingness to be involved in a long-lasting interaction with each proposed voice. Sections 3, 4, 5 and 6 (each consisting in ten items) assessed respectively: 1) the Pragmatic Qualities (PQ), i.e., the effectiveness, usefulness, practicality, clarity and controllability perceived by listening the voices; 2) the Hedonic-Identity Qualities (HQI), i.e., the originality, creativity and pleasantness attributed to the voices; 3) the Hedonic-Feeling Qualities (HQF) related to positive or negative arousals elicited by listening to the voices; 4) the Attractiveness (ATT) of the voices, i.e., the ability of the voice to engage listeners. Except for Sect. 1, questionnaire's items required answers on 5-points Likert scale (1 = strongly agree, 2 = agree, 3 = I do not know, 4 = disagree, 5 = strongly disagree). Questionnaire's items included either positive or negative statements, and scores from negative items were corrected in a reverse way. This implies that lower scores summon to more positive and high scores to less positive evaluations of the proposed voices. VAVAQ's Sect. 7, constituted of three items, assessed which age participants were preferring (item 1) and attributing (item 3) to the listened voice along an age range from 1 (between 19–28 years old); 2 (between 29–38 years old); 3 (between 39–48 years old); 4 (between 49–58 years old); to 5 (59+ years old). The item 2 of Sect. 7 explicitly asked participants whether the voice' age would affect their willingness to interact with them. The item contemplated only two possible answers: positive (yes) or a negative (no). In the current study, only participants' answers to item 1 of Sect. 7 are reported. VAVAQ's Sect. 8 consisted of four items exploring the occupations participants would entrust to the listened synthetic voices. Choices were among healthcare, housework, protection/security, and front office. This section required a 5-point Likert scale from 1 = unsuitable, 2 = hardly suitable, 3 = I do not know, 4 = quite suitable, to 5 = very suitable and high scores reflected more positive voices' suitability for the proposed occupation.

Procedures

After being briefed on the study' aims, participants signed an informed consent. Then, they were asked to sit in front of a computer screen and fill the VAVAQ's Sect. 1 for socio-demographic information. Subsequently, they randomly listened the four synthetic voices and after listening they were asked to fill the VAVAQ sections from 2 to 8. This procedure was repeated four times for each participant. No feedback or time limits were given to participants while reporting their answers.

3   Results

3.1   Data Analysis

For the present study, separate ANOVA repeated measures analyses were performed on questionnaire' scores to assess participants' preferences toward voices' quality (high: Antonio and Giulia; low: Edoardo and Clara). To achieve this goal, the scores obtained from VAVAQ' sections were analyzed separately. In the following five initial analyses, participants' gender and their age group (adolescents = Group 1; young adults = Group 2; middle-aged = Group 3 and seniors = Groups 4) were considered as between subjects' factors and VAVAQ' scores derived from sections: 2 (willingness to interact), 3 (PQ), 4 (HQI), 5 (HQF) and 6 (ATT) as within subjects' factors. Due to the reverse correction of negative items, low scores summon to positive voices' assessments whereas high scores to negative ones. An additional ANOVA repeated measures analysis was carried out on the scores obtained from Sect. 7 (item 1, regarding the preferred age range). Also in this case, participants' gender and their age group were considered as between subjects' factors and scores obtained from Sect. 7 as within subjects' factors. Scores from Sect. 7 varied from 1 to 5 and high scores reflected participants' preferences toward more mature voices. Lastly, four separate ANOVA repeated measures analyses were conducted to explore participants' assessments towards the proposed voices' adequacy in performing healthcare, housework, protection and security and front office tasks. Once again, participants' gender and their age group were considered as between subjects' factors and scores obtained from Sect. 8 (concerning entrusted occupations to the synthetic voices) as within subjects' factors. Scores from Sect. 8 also varied from 1 to 5 and high and low scores indicated respectively high and low suitability participants attributed to the four voices in accomplishing the proposed occupations. In all the analyses, the significance level was set at $\alpha < .05$ and differences among means were assessed through Bonferroni's post hoc tests. The full version of the paper including all the data derived from statistical analyses is available at arXiv:2205.04149. The main results of the ten abovementioned analyses are summarized below.

Synthetic Voices Assessment

The following section describes the results of the statistical analyses carried out for the present study (see arXiv:2205.04149 for full experimental details). Specifically, in the following five sections, it will be described the outcomes reflecting the preferences expressed by the four differently aged groups, towards the high- and low-quality male and female voices. To guide the interpretation of the scores shown graphically in Figs. 1 and 2, we invite you to observe that due to the reverse correction of negative items regarding the Willingness to interact, the Pragmatic Qualities (PQ), the Hedonic Qualities- Identity (HQI) and Feeling (HQF) and the Attractiveness (ATT), low scores summon to positive voices' assessments whereas high scores to negative ones.

Willingness to interact

VAVAQ scores related to Sect. 2 (willingness to interact) analyzed through the ANOVA analyses do not reveal significant differences for participants' gender. Significant differences emerged among age groups. In this context, seniors showed a greater willingness to interact with voices than adolescents, young adults, and middle-aged participants. In addition, willingness to interact scores significantly differed among the four proposed voices. Voice quality appeared to have been predominant in determining participants preferences rather than voice gender. High-quality voices of Antonio and Giulia respectively were significantly more appreciated than the low-quality voices corresponding to Edoardo and Clara. Deepening the statistical analysis, differences among the differently aged groups emerged for seniors which were significantly more willing to interact with high-quality male voice and low-quality both male and female voices than adolescents, young adults, and middle-aged participants.

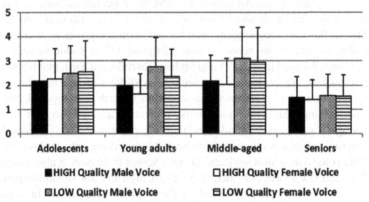

Fig. 1. Adolescents, young, middle-aged, and older adults' willingness to interact respectively with high quality male and female voices and low-quality male and female voices.

Pragmatic Qualities

The statistical analyses revealed that Pragmatic qualities (PQ) were not affected by participants' gender. Significant differences emerged among age groups. Specifically, seniors attributed to the proposed voices significantly higher PQ scores than the other three groups considered. PQ scores significantly differed among the four proposed voices. High- quality both male and female voices were significantly considered as more effective than the low-quality voices. Going into detail, differences among the differently aged groups emerged for seniors that considered high quality both female and male voices significantly more pragmatic than two specific groups (adolescents and middle-aged participants). However, when seniors were asked to evaluate low quality female and male voices, they attributed higher PQ scores to them than adolescents, young and middle-aged participants.

Regarding significant differences in terms of PQ scores attributed to the four voices, within each participants' group, analyses revealed that both young adults and middle-aged participants attributed to high quality male and female voices better PQ scores than those attributed to low-quality female and male voices. Figure 2 illustrates these results.

Hedonic Qualities-Identity (HQI)
Hedonic Qualities- Identity (HQI) were not affected by participants' gender. Significant differences emerged among age groups. Essentially, seniors attributed to the four proposed voices significantly higher HQI scores than adolescents, young and middle-aged participants. HQI scores significantly differed among the four proposed voices. High-quality both male and female voices were significantly considered as more original, creative, and pleasant than the low-quality male and female voices. Significant differences among the differently aged groups emerged for seniors that appreciated the high-quality male voice and both female and male low-quality voices significantly more than adolescents, young and middle-aged participants and they better assessed the high-quality female voice than adolescents and middle-aged participants. Regarding significant differences in terms of HQI scores, within each participants' group, analyses revealed that both young adults and middle-aged participants attributed to high quality male and female voices better HQI scores than those attributed to low-quality female and male voices. Figure 2 illustrates these results.

Hedonic Qualities- Feeling (HQF)
Hedonic Qualities- Feeling (HQF) were not affected by participants' gender. Significant differences emerged among age groups. Seniors attributed to the four proposed voices significantly higher HQF scores than adolescents, young and middle-aged participants. HQF scores significantly differed among the four proposed voices. High-quality both male and female voices elicited significantly more positive arousals than the low-quality male and female voices. Regarding significant differences in terms of HQF scores attributed to the four voices, within each participants' group, analyses revealed that young adults attributed to high quality female voice better HQF scores than those attributed to low-quality female and male voices; they also considered the high-quality male voice more engaging than the low-quality male voice. In addition, middle- aged adults attributed to high quality male and female voices better HQI scores than those attributed to low-quality female and male voices. Figure 2 summarizes these results.

Attractiveness
Attractiveness of voices was not affected by participants' gender. Significant differences emerged among age groups. Seniors attributed significantly more attractiveness to the

four proposed voices rather than adolescents, young and middle-aged participants. High-quality both male and female voices were considered significantly more attractive than the low-quality male and female voices.

Regarding significant differences in terms of ATT scores attributed to the four voices, within each participants' group, analyses revealed that young adults attributed to high quality female voice better ATT scores than those attributed to low- quality female and male voices; they also considered the high- quality male voice more engaging than the low-quality male voice. In addition, middle-aged adults attributed to high quality male and female voices better ATT scores than those attributed to low-quality female and male voices. Figure 2 illustrates these results.

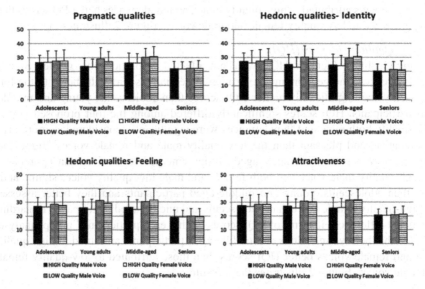

Fig. 2. PQ, HQI, HQF and ATT scores attributed by adolescents, young, middle-aged, and older adults respectively to high quality male and female voices and low-quality male and female voices.

Preferred age range results

This descriptive section summarizes the percentage values of the synthetic voices age preferences computed for adolescents, young adults, middle-aged and older participants as exemplified in Table 1. Supplementary information available (see arXiv:2205.04149).The preferred age was distributed according to the following percentages among the differently aged groups. Data revealed that 53.33% of adolescents (aged between 14–16 years) seemed to prefer the age range between 19–28 years while 36.11% of them selected the age range between 29–38 years suggesting that not having the possibility to select among the different options of choice (1 = 19–28 years; 2 = 29–38 years; 3 = 39–48 years; 4 = 49–58 years and 5 = 59+ years) their own reference age group, they selected the age ranges closest to theirs. Young adults (aged between 22–35 years) mostly showed a stronger preference for the age range between 29–38 years (55.85% of young adults) and then for the two age ranges positioned immediately before and after it, namely those between 19–28 and 39–48 years (23.4% and 18.62% of them, respectively).

Regarding middle-aged participants (aged between 40–55 years), they disclosed their preferences towards synthetic voices that matched their own age range, mainly by choosing the age range between 39–48 years (46.67% of the participants' group). Interestingly, 36.11% of them expressed a clear preference for the age range between 29-38 years by preferring younger voices. Finally, the participants' group of seniors (65+ years old) was the only one who revealed a particularly heterogeneous distribution of preferences. In this context, 26.02% of seniors preferred voices of their same age range (59+), 27.55% of them selected the age range between 29–38 years, 19.9% preferred the age range between 39–48 and 19.9% indicated to prefer the age range between 49–58 years.

Table 1. Preferred age range percentage values attributed to synthetic voices by the four differently aged groups of participants. Scores varied from 1 to 5 and reflected age ranges (1 = 19–28 years old; 2 = 29–38 years old; 3 = 39–48 years old; 4 = 49–58 years old; 5 = +59 years old).

% Age preference	19–28 years	29–38 years	39–48 years	49–58 years	59+
Adolescents	53.33%	36.11%	8.33%	2.22%	0%
Young adults	23.4%	55.85%	18.62%	1.6%	0.53%
Middle-aged	9.44%	36.11%	46.67%	7.78%	0%
Seniors	6.63%	27.55%	19.9%	19.9%	26.02%

Entrusted occupations to the synthetic voices

In the following are reported the suitability scores attributed to the voices to healthcare, housework, protection and security task, and front-office occupations by the four differently aged groups of participants (see arXiv:2205.04149 for supplementary details). However, it must be clear that participants were able to entrust different suitability scores to the voices for the different proposed occupations only by listening to them. To better interpret the scores shown graphically in Fig. 3, we invite you to observe that high and low scores indicated respectively high and low suitability participants attributed to the four voices in accomplishing the proposed occupations.

Healthcare

The statistical analyses revealed that healthcare occupations were not affected by participants' gender. Significant differences emerged among age groups. Seniors considered voices as significantly more suitable than adolescents, young and middle-aged participants to perform healthcare occupations. Suitability scores for healthcare occupations significantly differed among the four proposed voices. High- quality both male and female voices were considered significantly as more appropriate than the low-quality male and female voices for healthcare occupations. Moreover, adolescents better rated low quality both female and male voices than middle-aged participants in performing healthcare occupations. Regarding significant differences in terms of healthcare scores attributed to the four voices, within each participants' group, analyses revealed that young adults attributed to high quality female voice better scores than those attributed to low-quality both female and male voices. In addition, middle-aged adults better assessed high quality both female and male voices in performing healthcare task rather than low-quality female and male voices. Figure 3 illustrates these results.

Housework
Housework tasks were not affected by participants' gender. Significant differences emerged among age groups. Seniors considered voices as significantly more appropriate than adolescents, young and middle-aged participants in performing housework tasks. Additionally, young adults considered the proposed voices more suitable than middle-aged participants to housework occupations. Significant gender differences among the differently aged groups emerged. Specifically, for two groups: male seniors and female middle-aged participants. Male seniors attributed to the voices higher suitability scores than male adolescents, male young adults, and male middle-aged participants in performing housework occupations while female middle-aged participants attributed to the voices lower suitability scores than female young and female older adults. Interestingly, statistical analyses revealed a significant gender difference within seniors' age group. Male seniors considered the voices as more suited than female older adults in performing housework tasks. The four proposed voices differed significantly in their suitability scores to perform housework. Low quality male voice was rated significantly less suited than low quality female voice and high quality both male and female voices for housework occupations. Significant differences among the differently aged groups emerged for seniors that attributed to high quality male voice and low-quality male voice higher suitability scores in performing housework than adolescents, young and middle- aged participants. Furthermore, seniors better assessed high quality female voice and low-quality female voice as more suitable than adolescents and middle-aged participants. Additionally, young adults rated low quality male voice more appropriate than middle-aged adults and young adults attributed higher suitability scores low quality female voice than adolescents and middle-aged participants. Regarding significant differences in terms of housework scores attributed to the four voices, within each participants' group, analyses revealed that middle-aged participants attributed to high quality female voice better scores than those attributed to high quality male voice and low-quality both female and male voices. In addition, middle-aged adults better assessed high quality male voice in performing housework task rather than low-quality male voice. Figure 3 shows these results.

Protection and security tasks

Protection and security tasks were not affected by participants' gender. Significant differences emerged among age groups. Seniors considered the voices significantly more suitable than adolescents, middle-aged participants in performing protection and security tasks. Suitability scores for protection and security tasks differed significantly among the four proposed voices. High quality male voice was considered significantly more qualified than low quality both male and female voices for protection and security tasks. Significant differences among the differently aged groups emerged for seniors that considered high quality male voice significantly more qualified than adolescents in performing these specific tasks. Moreover, seniors also considered low quality male voice as more suited than middle-aged participants and they rated low quality female voice as more suitable than adolescents, young and middle-aged participants. Additionally, middle-aged participants considered low quality female voice significantly less qualified for protection and security tasks than adolescents and young adults.

Regarding significant differences in terms of protection and security tasks scores attributed to the four voices, within each participants' group, analyses revealed that young adults attributed to high quality male voice better scores than those attributed to low-quality female and high-quality female voices. In addition, middle- aged adults better assessed high quality both female and male voices in performing protection and security tasks rather than low-quality female and male voices. Figure 3 illustrates these results.

Front office

Front office tasks were not affected by participants' gender effect and there were not significant differences among age groups. Suitability to front office tasks was rated significantly different among the four proposed voices. High quality both female and male voices were considered significantly more suitable than low quality both female and male voices for front office tasks. Significant differences among the differently aged groups emerged for middle-aged participants that rated high quality female voice as more qualified in performing front office tasks than seniors. Regarding significant differences in terms of front office scores attributed to the four voices, within each participants' group, analyses revealed that young adults attributed to high quality both female and male voices better scores than those attributed to low-quality both female and male voices. In addition, middle-aged adults better assessed high quality both female and male voices in performing front office tasks rather than low-quality both female and male voices. Figure 3 shows these results.

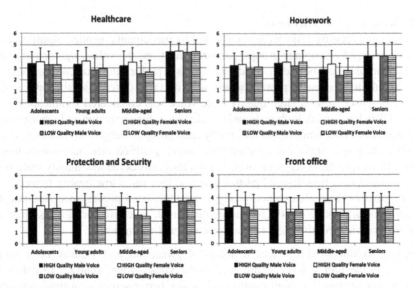

Fig. 3. Suitability scores attributed to the voices in performing healthcare, housework, protection and security and front office tasks.

4 Discussion and Conclusions

The present study explored which synthetic voices' features could influence the way people interact with them. Outcomes revealed that seniors show a greater willingness to be involved in a long-lasting interaction with the four proposed voices regardless of the quality of their synthesis. Seniors' appreciation of voices was also envisaged from the scores they attributed to the voices' pragmatic, hedonic, and attractive qualities. The fact that seniors did not care too much of the voices' quality may reflect their low experience with technology and a low accuracy in detecting the different qualities of the proposed voices. On the other hand, these results certainly show a greater seniors' propensity to potentially receive assistance from automatic devices explicating their human abilities only by voices. This result was not observed for the other differently age groups involved in this experiment. Concerning adolescents, young adults, and middle-aged participants, they seem to be more selective in evaluating the four synthetic voices, suggesting that the new generations are more skillful and accustomed to detecting subtle differences in the voice quality of the proposed devices and call for improved sound's resolution and definition. It was observed, that for all the investigated (PQ, HQI, HQF, and ATT) qualities, high quality voices (respectively, Antonio and Giulia) were significantly more appreciated than low quality voices (Edoardo and Clara). The two high quality voices were judged significantly more practical, controllable, pleasant, original, able to arouse positive feelings and engage users in an effective long-lasting interaction compared to the low-quality synthetic speech of Edoardo and Clara. The lesson learned by these data is that people are more sensible to the voice' quality of their assistive devices rather than to their gender. Antonio and Giulia's voices have both received greater acclaim regardless to their gender. As regard the statistical analyses (widely described in the appendix of the full version of the paper available at arXiv:2205.04149) related to users' preferred age of their assistive devices, it appeared clear that preferences vary with the users' age. Adolescents and young adults feel more pleased to be assisted by peer aged voices, middle-aged participants prefer to be assisted by more mature voices and seniors by even more mature voices than the preferences expressed by middle-aged participants. However, middle-aged and seniors preferred age of their assistive devices is far from their own age. Interestingly, participants' age preferences toward Giulia and Clara's voices, were collocated in the same average age ranges. Focusing on the occupations participants would have entrusted to the proposed synthetic voices, the evaluations took on a more specific connotation. Seniors considered voices significantly more qualified than adolescents, young adults, and middle-aged participants in performing healthcare, housework, and protection/security tasks. Additionally, young adults attributed to the voices higher ability to successfully accomplish housework than middle-aged participants. Antonio and Giulia's high quality synthetic voices were equally perceived as more suited than Edoardo and Clara for healthcare and front office jobs. Besides, Antonio was judged significantly more qualified for protection and security tasks than Edoardo and Clara's voices and surprisingly, Edoardo's voice ranked as the last one in terms of suitability to housework. Future works may include clinical populations. Another objective, related to our investigations, concerns the validation of the shortened version of the VAVAQ' questionnaire that we have recently completed. This shortened version has already been translated into several languages. Therefore, future studies could also concern cross-cultural investigations with the aim of exploring potential cultural differences as well as gender and age groups' differences in assessing the quality of synthetic voices to better understand users' preferences. It is hoped that these findings can be exploited to guide the design and the implementation of chatbots' voices devoted to providing support and intervention in healthcare settings.

Acknowledgments. The research leading to these results has received funding from the European Union Horizon 2020 research and innovation programme under grant agreement N. 769872 (EMPATHIC) and N. 823907 (MENHIR), from the project SIROBOTICS that received funding from Ministero dell'Istruzione, dell 'Università, e della Ricerca (MIUR), PNR 2015–2020, Decreto Direttoriale 1735 July 13 2017, and from the project ANDROIDS that received funding from Università della Campania "Luigi Vanvitelli" inside the programme V:ALERE 2019, funded with D.R. 906 del 4/10/2019, prot. n. 157264, October 17, 2019.

Data Availability. Further information on the proposed method and dataset analysed during the current study are available from the corresponding author (marialucia.cuciniello@unicampania. it) on reasonable request.

References

1. Ageing and Health. https://www.who.int/news-room/fact-sheets/detail/ageing-and-health. Accessed 30 Nov 2020
2. Mannheim, I., et al.: Inclusion of older adults in the research and design of digital technology. Int. J. Environ. Res. Public Health **16**(19), 3718 (2019). https://doi.org/10.3390/ijerph161 93718

3. World Health Organization: "mHealth: new horizons for health through mobile technologies," mHealth: new horizons for health through mobile technologies (2011)
4. Hoque, R., Sorwar, G.: Understanding factors influencing the adoption of mHealth by the elderly: an extension of the UTAUT model. Int. J. Med. Inform. **101**, 75–84 (2017). https://doi.org/10.1016/j.ijmedinf.2017.02.002
5. Liu, J.J., Bao, Y., Huang, X., Shi, J., Lu, L.: Mental health considerations for children quarantined because of COVID-19. Lancet Child Adolesc. Health **4**(5), 347–349 (2020). https://doi.org/10.1016/S2352-4642(20)30096-1
6. Lyall, L.M., et al.: Association of disrupted circadian rhythmicity with mood disorders, subjective wellbeing, and cognitive function: a cross-sectional study of 91 105 participants from the UK Biobank. Lancet Psychiatry **5**(6), 507–514 (2018). https://doi.org/10.1016/S2215-0366(18)30139-1
7. Suganuma, S., Sakamoto, D., Shimoyama, H.: An embodied conversational agent for unguided internet-based cognitive behavior therapy in preventative mental health: feasibility and acceptability pilot trial. JMIR Ment. Health **5**(3), e10454 (2018). https://doi.org/10.2196/10454
8. Inkster, B., Sarda, S., Subramanian, V.: An empathy-driven, conversational artificial intelligence agent (Wysa) for digital mental well-being: real-world data evaluation mixed-methods study. JMIR mHealth Health **6**(11), e12106 (2018). https://doi.org/10.2196/12106
9. Ly, K.H., Ly, A.M., Andersson, G.: A fully automated conversational agent for promoting mental well-being: a pilot RCT using mixed methods. Internet Interv. **10**, 39–46 (2017). https://doi.org/10.1016/j.invent.2017.10.002
10. Qiu, L., Benbasat, I.: Online consumer trust and live help interfaces: the effects of text-to-speech voice and three-dimensional avatars. Int. J. Hum. Comput. Interact. **19**(1), 75–94 (2005). https://doi.org/10.1207/s15327590ijhc1901_6
11. Esposito, A., et al.: Elder user's attitude toward assistive virtual agents: the role of voice and gender. J. Ambient. Intell. Humaniz. Comput. **12**(4), 4429–4436 (2019). https://doi.org/10.1007/s12652-019-01423-x
12. Esposito, A., et al.: The dependability of voice on elders' acceptance of humanoid agents. In: Interspeech, pp. 31–35, September 2019. https://doi.org/10.21437/Interspeech.2019-1734
13. Esposito, A., et al.: Seniors' acceptance of virtual humanoid agents. In: Leone, A., Caroppo, A., Rescio, G., Diraco, G., Siciliano, P. (eds.) ForItAAL 2018. LNEE, vol. 544, pp. 429–443. Springer, Cham (2019). https://doi.org/10.1007/978-3-030-05921-7_35

Identifying Colluding Actors in Social Communities by Reputation Measures

Mariantonia Cotronei[1], Sofia Giuffrè[1], Attilio Marcianò[1(✉)],
Domenico Rosaci[1], and Giuseppe M. L. Sarnè[2]

[1] DIIES - Mediterranea University of Reggio Calabria, via Graziella snc, loc.,
Feo di Vito, 98123 Reggio Calabria, Italy
{mariantonia.cotronei,sofia.giuffre,attilio.marciano,
domenico.rosaci}@unirc.it
[2] Department of Psychology, University of Milan at Bicocca, P.za della Ateneo
Nuovo, 1, 20126 Milan, Italy
giuseppe.sarne@unimib.it

Abstract. In real and virtual communities, complex and sophisticated forms of social interactions and cooperation are increasingly taking place between heterogeneous actors such as people, intelligent objects and virtual entities. At the same time, in such communities the risks of interacting with unreliable partners engaged in malicious activities increase. Therefore, it is important to provide all players with adequate information in order to allow them to choose the most reliable partner to interact with. In this context, we have focused our attention on colluding activities. In particular we propose a reputation method that preliminarily identifies those actors who most likely can be considered colluding players. This method does not introduce side effects to trust scores of honest actors while detecting colluding ones with high accuracy. A simple example supports our results.

1 Introduction

Nowadays, social activities involving people, objects and software entities (like IoT devices and software agents) more and more powerfully emerge in our everyday life. As a consequence, it has become common to operate in environments consisting of a huge number of heterogeneous actors that interact for searching, cooperating, offering and exchanging services in a wide variety of fields (e.g. transport, marketing, information, security, health care, etc.). This implies that data and services are generated, aggregated, and personalized for a multitude of actors that, in turn, generate multidimensional and context-sensitive social infrastructures, potentially rich in interactions [29]. To this aim, suitable social and technological paradigms have been developed to provide support to these emerging necessities.

However, in performing social activities we cannot exclude the presence of untrustworthy players which maliciously act to gain undue advantages, particularly in presence of competitive contexts. For simplicity, in the following we

M. Mahmud et al. (Eds.): AII 2022, CCIS 1724, pp. 347–359, 2022.
https://doi.org/10.1007/978-3-031-24801-6_25

will assume that all considered players exhibit human-like traits (e.g., benevolent, selfish, honest, malicious, etc.) and perform similar roles (e.g., supplier, consumer, prosumer) in their social activities.

In similar scenarios, the list of possible malicious behaviors is wide and includes individual (e.g. selfishness, misjudgment, complaining, alternate, etc.) as well as collective activities (e.g. colluding, etc.). Moreover, not infrequently unreliable players perform more malicious behaviors simultaneously. Therefore, when an actor has to decide to interact with a possible partner whose reliability is still unknown, there exist real risks of deception due to malicious attacks and, obviously, such risks increase as the numerosity of the community increases.

The perpetration of deceptive activities is a destabilizing element for all kinds of communities, but even more in presence of communities operating in virtual environments. To promote safe interactions among members of a virtual community, it is of a primary relevance to create a trusting atmosphere by minimizing deceptive risks. In this respect, it becomes essential to provide each player with appropriate information about the other community members (i.e. potential counterparts) to allow each actor to improve the chances of making the best possible partner choice or, vice versa, to decide not to be engaged with any of them.

To this end, a large number of *Trust and Reputation Systems* (TRS), exploiting different techniques and approaches (e.g. general purpose or dedicated to specific scenarios, centralized or distributed, global or local, etc.) have been proposed in the literature. However, trust is very complex to define and measure because it is driven by both measurable and non-measurable properties (including capability, honesty, reliability, helpfulness, goodness, and many other attributes). Therefore, given the practical impossibility of enclosing the multifaceted nature of "trust" in a unique definition, this has led many authors to provide different definitions, focusing on one or another of its characteristics, over time. The interested reader can find a more complete overview of both trust and TRSs in [14, 19, 24, 39].

TRSs are widely adopted to assess members' trustworthiness in a community, usually represented by a unique numerical score calculated on the basis of direct and/or indirect information provided by the members of the community ("trustors") about another member ("trustee"). More in detail, direct information are those derived by a direct knowledge that the trustor has about the trustee, while indirect information are those that the other members of the community provide to the trustor in the form of ratings or opinions about the trustee. Based on the calculated trust measures, TRSs can play the role of decision support tools to assess the trustworthiness of potential interacting counterparties and help the community in identifying and marginalizing deceitful actors.

In the scenario above introduced, we have focused our attention on colluding activities and, to this end, our contribution consists of a reputation method able to:

- preliminarily identify those actors who are most likely to be candidates for colluding players;

- not introduce side effects relative to honest actors in detecting colluding ones (differently from other well known TRSs, like [25]) with high accuracy.

This reputation method identifies the colluding agents as confirmed in a simple example, reading the information directly from the initial data of the social network.

The rest of the paper is organized as follows. Section 2 describes the related work. The reference scenario and the proposed reputation model are introduced and discussed in Sect. 3, as well as an application to a simple situation. Some conclusions are drawn in Sect. 4.

2   Related Work

A natural process present in any social community, regardless of whether it is real or virtual, is to identify, isolate, and/or send away members whose behaviors are incompatible with the goal of that community. Specifically, with respect to virtual communities that work in areas like communications, agent-based or peer-to-peer activities, and others, the identification of the most unreliable actors (or, conversely, the most reliable ones) independently from their nature of human, software or device is of primary relevance [3,11,15,21,40]. When a community member aims at knowing the trustworthiness of another member (i.e. trustee), a common way to assess it, when there is no information derived from a direct knowledge, is to solicit the opinions of other community members (i.e. trustors), generally referred as indirect experiences [9].

As a preliminary remark, it should be noted that there is no shared concept of trust, since trust is intrinsically multidisciplinary and context sensitive. Therefore, a wide variety of definitions of trust, as well as different approaches (e.g. centralized or distributed, global or local, etc.) have been proposed in the literature [10,24,41].

In particular, direct and/or indirect information is exploited by *Trust and Reputation Systems* (TRSs) to model the behavior of members within a community with respect to a wide variety of deceptive behaviors [13,31,35] that could also be acted upon simultaneously. In this regard, Trust Systems (TSs) can adopt both direct and indirect information as information sources, while Reputation Systems (RSs) exploit only indirect one. Note that, depending on the specific application context, different ways of aggregating information sources can be applied (also varying over time to consider the age of the information [38]) to estimate trustee reliability, generally represented synthetically by a single numerical score, in order to be more resilient as possible to deceptive behaviors [7,19].

In the context outlined above, on the one hand, the percentage of recognized cheaters can be a rough measure of TRS robustness (i.e. effectiveness), and on the other hand, the more robust to malicious attacks the TRS is, the more reliable its trustworthiness measures will be [22]. In the following, we will point out our attention only on the capability of TRSs to recognize malicious actors.

Although it is a hard task to compare TRSs designed for specific contexts and specific malicious behaviors, a significant number of researchers have explored the topic further. For instance, in [19, 23, 42] some early surveys are presented, where the approaches of selected TRSs, with respect to the most common malicious attacks, are described and analyzed. However, these studies are characterized by the absence of a common criterion to provide a clear quantitative approach to identify advantages and disadvantages of each TRS.

Competitions between TRSs, based on simulated scenarios in the presence of honest and malicious actors populations, whose numerosity could also vary over time [27, 43], have been popular. The testbeds proposed for such competitions were intended to place all TRSs in the same conditions without benefiting any one in particular [2, 26, 32]. In reality, it could be complicated to compare TRSs designed for different contexts and, sometimes, some modifications to TRSs were necessary to adapt them to the testbed. ART (Agent Reputation and Trust testbed) [16] is certainly the most well-known testbed that simulates a picture auction house, where the participants (i.e. TRSs) are provided with capital and must generate a profit by making choices driven by their trustworthiness measures. However, because TRSs are generally designed for specific scenarios, adapting them to other contexts may lead to incorrect assessments.

The use of simulations is not however advised in case it is necessary to evidence the worst scenario for a specific TRS; in fact, it cannot be neither realized neither recognized autonomously. For this purpose, mathematical/analytical approaches [6, 17] may alternatively be used to verify the robustness of TRSs, which, although more complex because they require to be specifically designed for each TRS, allow a more precise check.

The RS proposed by eBay [18] is very simple to understand and this has largely contributed to its popularity, although this simplicity exposes it to malicious attacks [8, 18, 37]. To this end, this RS has been subject to several updates that, although they have not changed its basic characteristics, have improved its robustness. The eBay RS estimates a user's reputation based on the number of positive, neutral and negative feedback (i.e. $+1$, 0, -1) received in a given time window (i.e. 1, 6 and 12 months). Each trustor can also leave a textual comment, but it is still the user that evaluates the number of feedbacks received by the potential counterpart on the basis of his/her attitude to risk. The reputation of new entries is set to zero.

An RS considered as resilient to deceptive behaviors is PeerTrust [44]. PeerTrust adopts a distributed architecture on a peer-to-peer overlay network and combines information of different nature, such as the credibility of indirect sources, direct feedback, the number of transactions made by each peer, transaction information and specific context. An overlay network is also used in Hypertrust [33] to connect nodes belonging to large competitive federations of utility computing infrastructures. Hypertrust is a decentralized TRS in which nodes are interconnected via overlay links and form clusters; then a distributed algorithm operates to find and allocate resources associated with trusted nodes. HyperTrust searches for resources in an eligible region and limits its size using both trustworthiness and reputation information. As a result, an efficient search for resources of potential interest is achieved even in the presence of a very large number of nodes.

EigenTrust [25] can be seen as a variation of the PageRank algorithm and is one of the most well-known and studied reputation algorithms. EigenTrust builds a trust matrix with all the (normalized) ratings, called local trusts, that each peer assigns to the trustworthiness of every other peer belonging to its community. These individual ratings are weighted through the trustworthiness of each trustor peer. EigenTrust uses the normalized and weighted local reputation scores to compute the overall reputation of each peer, but assuming reputation transitivity.

FIRE [20] is an example of those TRSs that can operate strictly in the context for which they were designed. In fact, FIRE is a TRS that assumes that all actors are always honest and benevolent, and although its model uses multiple information sources (which also implies a considerable number of parameters that must be correctly configured) in open scenarios, i.e. in the presence of malicious actors, it is not very robust. Therefore, in real contexts, the initial assumption of honesty and benevolence exposes this TRS to a large variety of different attacks.

Recognizing malicious actors in some scenarios is more complex than in others. This is the case, for example, of the Internet of Things (IoT) where a TRS must be designed also considering that IoT devices may have limited computational resources, memory and energy and also may migrate between different environments, even not natively federated. Several TRSs have been designed to address this challenge in distributed, semi-distributed, centralized and/or based on the adoption of the blockchain technology [1, 4, 12, 14].

IoT device communities are frequently dynamic environments where IoT devices can enter and exit (i.e. be online or offline) without any particular constraint. This inherent dynamism of IoT communities poses significant privacy and security issues since deceptive behaviors are facilitated with respect to other scenarios and the use of only authentication techniques may be inadequate to build a trust atmosphere. To this end, the distributed RS presented in [11] is designed to handle the reputation of IoT devices while also counteracting strategies based on alternating behaviors. This RS was verified by simulating vehicular mobility (i.e. IoT devices) on a simple urban transportation network where it proved to be able to quickly identify malicious actors.

Another particularly interesting aspect in agent-based IoT device communities is the formation of groups, fostered by the social attitude of agents. RESIOT [15] is a framework that exploits the well-known concept of social resilience applied to IoT systems to promote the aggregation of agents (i.e. IoT devices) based on their reputation. In RESIOT, an original RS is proposed which proved its resilience in a series of experiments, performed in a simulated environment, where malicious agents carry out different attacks, conducted by simultaneously, implementing different cheating strategies. It is worth noting that the proposed approach is more performing than other RS with which it has been compared.

In [28] a Perceptron-type neural network and a K-means clustering method is adopted to compute trust scores of peers which can implement tamper, drop and replay attacks in both single and multiple modalities. In order to refine the performance of the system over time, a machine learning process is also implemented. Another TS that utilizes machine learning techniques in a SIOT scenario, proving to be resilient to a significant number of attacks and detecting almost all malicious nodes in the network as the number of requested transactions increases, is presented in [30].

To the best of our knowledge, none of the known and effective TRSs presented above, which exploit different approaches to identifying malicious actors in different domains, is explicitly designed to not alter honest measures of trustworthiness in the search for malicious actors as opposed to the RS described in Sect. 3 which also addresses this ethical and formal issue.

3   The Proposed Reputation Model

In the following we describe the proposed reputation model, which has the peculiarity to careful warranty that the reputation scores of honest actors will not be damaged as a result of the dishonest actor search process, differently from other well known RSs, like [25].

To this aim, we will refer to a scenario consisting of a potentially large community of actors which are supported by personal software agents that mutually interact among them, on behalf of their associated actors. Furthermore, we will assume that agents will carry out interactions carried out with other agents in the respect of the following assumptions [36]:

- all agents are long-lived entities, so their past behaviors provide us with information about their expected future ones;
- agents interactions are driven exclusively by the past behaviors held of their potential counterparts;
- agents' reputation scores should be disseminated to the community so that everyone can make an informed choice about potential partners to interact with.

In the above described context, let S be the framework of the personal agents, each one associated with an actor belonging to S, and let n be the number of such agents. For the sake of simplicity, in the following we assume that each agent $a \in S$ is identified by means of an index, e.g. a_i with $i \in [1, \cdots, n]$.

Let a_j be another agent of S and let τ_{ij} be a real number, $0 \leq \tau_{ij} \leq 1$ representing the *trust* perceived by a_j about a_i. Moreover, let $\tau_{ii} = 0$, with $i = 1, \ldots, n$ be the score assigned to the trust that an agent has in itself. Simply, it means that our model does not consider the trust of an agent about itself.

Our reputation model computes the *reputation* ρ of each agent of S as a weighted sum. In particular, let a_i be an agent of S (i.e. trustee); the reputation ρ_i in S of this agent will be computed as:

$$\rho_i = \frac{\sum\limits_{j=1}^{n} \tau_{ij}\, \rho_j}{\sum\limits_{j=1}^{n} \rho_j}, \quad i = 1, \ldots, n \tag{1}$$

where the reputation of a_i is obtained as the ratio between the sum of the trust values τ_{ij} that the trustor agents a_j have about a_i (i.e. the target agent), with $j = 1, \ldots, n$, weighted by means of their own reputation scores and the sum of the reputation scores of all the trustor agents (see also [34]).

Let $\mathbf{T} = [\tau_{ij}]$ be the trust matrix

$$\mathbf{T} = \begin{pmatrix} \tau_{11} & \tau_{12} & \cdots & \tau_{1n} \\ \tau_{21} & \tau_{22} & \cdots & \tau_{2n} \\ \vdots & \vdots & \ddots & \vdots \\ \tau_{n1} & \tau_{n2} & \cdots & \tau_{nn} \end{pmatrix}.$$

The matrix $\mathbf{T}$ can be interpreted as the transpose of the weighted adjacency matrix corresponding to a directed graph, where nodes are associated with the agents and whose arcs (i, j) are associated with a non negative value representing the trust value perceived by a_i about a_j.

The Eq. (1) can be written also as:

$$\mathbf{Tr} = \mathbf{r}, \quad \|\mathbf{r}\|_1 = 1, \tag{2}$$

where the reputation of the agent a_i is represented by the i-th element of the reputation vector $\mathbf{r} = (\rho_1, \ldots, \rho_n)^T$, while the sum of the absolute values of the elements of the vector $\mathbf{r}$ is represented by the 1-$norm$. More specifically, $\|\mathbf{r}\|_1 = 1$ is necessary for the uniqueness of the solution to Eq. 2.

Now, we impose that the sum of the trust value τ_{ij} assigned by each agent a_j to the other agents belonging to $\mathcal{S}$ is 1, i.e.:

$$\sum_{i=1}^{n} \tau_{ij} = 1, \tag{3}$$

which results in the matrix $\mathbf{T}$ being column-stochastic. The solution of the eigensystem problem described in (2) can also be found in terms of the stationary distribution for a Markov chain represented by the transition matrix $\mathbf{T}$. Then, from the Perron Frobenius Theorem, $\lambda = 1$ is the largest eigenvalue[1] of $\mathbf{T}$. Finally, by assuming that $\tau_{ij} > 0$ then there is a unique vector $\mathbf{r} \in \mathbb{R}$, $\|\mathbf{r}\|_1 = 1$, such that:

$$\mathbf{T}\,\mathbf{r} = \mathbf{r}. \tag{4}$$

We observe that the PageRank model [5] is a modified version of the eigensystem (2) that can be formally expressed as:

$$\left(\delta\,\mathbf{T} + (1 - \delta)\,\mathbf{p}\,\mathbf{q}^T\right)\mathbf{r} = \mathbf{r}, \tag{5}$$

---

[1] Note that the other eigenvalues are < 1 in modulus.

where the parameter $\delta \in \mathbb{R}$ ranges in $[0,1]$, $\mathbf{q} = [1,1,\cdots,1]$ and $\mathbf{p}$ (known as *teleportation vector*) is a non-negative vector with unitary 1-norm, i.e. $[1,1,\cdots,1]\mathbf{p} = 1$. If $\delta \neq 0,1$, the solution of (5) exists and it is unique.

Note that in the original PageRank algorithm all the elements of the vector $\mathbf{p}$ are set to $1/n$.

To reduce the reputation of malicious agents, in [25] some agents are considered as *pre-trusted agents* by a priori assuming their opinions to be highly reliable. Let $\mathcal{D}$ be the set of such agents, so that if the i-th agent belongs to $\mathcal{D}$ then $p_i = 1/|\mathcal{D}|$, otherwise p_i is set to 0.

In order to identify colluding agents, our proposal consists of computing the vector $\mathbf{r}$ in a more realistic way on the basis of the information directly available from the matrix $\mathbf{T}$.

Therefore, a pair of agents (a_i, a_j) is assumed to be malicious when they assign each other large values of trust scores while receiving low scores from the other members.

More formally, let $\mathbf{o}$ be a vector storing the out-degree values of the nodes of the graph representing $\mathcal{S}$ and such that $\mathbf{o} = \mathbf{T}\,\mathbf{q}$. and let $\alpha, \beta, \gamma \in \mathbb{R}$ three thresholds ranging in $[0,1]$. Denoting with $\tilde{\mathbf{E}}$ the matrix with elements:

$$\tilde{e}_{ij} = \begin{cases} \tau_{ij}, & |\tau_{ij} - \tau_{ji}| \leq \alpha \text{ and } \tau_{ij} \geq \beta \\ 0 & \text{otherwise} \end{cases} \tag{6}$$

corresponding to the weighted adjacency matrix of the (undirected) sub-graph connecting the potential colluding agents, then, an element (agent) $\tilde{o}_i$ of the vector $\tilde{\mathbf{o}} = \mathbf{o} - \tilde{\mathbf{E}}\,\mathbf{q}$, is classified as malicious if:

$$\tilde{o}_i \leq \gamma.$$

The advantage of knowing a priori which agents are the best candidates to be malicious is obvious. This information can be usefully exploited in a large number of cases to build appropriate reputation vectors.

For example, if $\mathcal{X}$ denotes be the set of pre-identified malicious agents associated with the subgraph connecting all colluding agents. Then the teleportation vector in Eq. 5, can be computed as the vector $\mathbf{v}$ whose elements v_i are set to 0 if i belongs to $\mathcal{X}$ or $1/(n - |\mathcal{X}|)$ otherwise. Thus, all honest agents will receive the same trust score regardless of their initial score, exactly as in EigenTrust, but exploiting the additional information about pre-trusted users.

As an alternative strategy, we propose to construct a new matrix $\tilde{\mathbf{T}}$ in the following way:

- Set a value $\varphi > 0$;
- For each agent pair $a_i, a_j \in \mathcal{X}$, let $\tilde{\tau}_{ij} = \varphi$, otherwise $\tilde{\tau}_{ij} = \tau_{ij}$;
- make all the $\tilde{\mathbf{T}}$ columns stochastic normalized to 1,

and directly solve (4) with such a matrix.

For comparison reasons, as a case study, we consider a community consisting of 6 agents where the malicious agents are identified as a_3 and a_4.

The associated trust matrix is:

$$
T = \begin{pmatrix}
0 & 0.75 & 0.001 & 0.003 & 0.43 & 0.45 \\
0.76 & 0 & 0.002 & 0.001 & 0.46 & 0.45 \\
0.003 & 0.001 & 0 & 0.87 & 0.001 & 0.002 \\
0.002 & 0.003 & 0.88 & 0 & 0.002 & 0.003 \\
0.135 & 0.126 & 0.015 & 0.08 & 0 & 0.095 \\
0.1 & 0.12 & 0.1 & 0.046 & 0.107 & 0
\end{pmatrix}.
$$

Based on our threshold approach in (6), for $\alpha = 0.03$ and $\beta = 0.45$, the weighted adjacency matrix identifying potential colluding agents is:

$$
\tilde{E} = \begin{pmatrix}
0 & 0.75 & 0 & 0 & 0 & 0 \\
0.76 & 0 & 0 & 0 & 0 & 0 \\
0 & 0 & 0 & 0.87 & 0 & 0 \\
0 & 0 & 0.88 & 0 & 0 & 0 \\
0 & 0 & 0 & 0 & 0 & 0 \\
0 & 0 & 0 & 0 & 0 & 0
\end{pmatrix},
$$

from which, by setting $\gamma = 0.45$, we have a confirmation that the only colluding agents are a_3 and a_4.

Let $\mathcal{X} = \{3, 4\}$ and, consequently, let $\mathbf{v} = (0.25, 0.25, 0, 0, 0.25, 0.25)^T$.

As a first approach, we solve (5) with such $\mathbf{v}$ and $\delta = 0.2$. Then the updated trust matrix is computed as:

$$
\tilde{T}_A = \begin{pmatrix}
0.2000 & 0.3500 & 0.2002 & 0.2006 & 0.2860 & 0.2900 \\
0.3520 & 0.2000 & 0.2004 & 0.2002 & 0.2920 & 0.2900 \\
0.0006 & 0.0002 & 0 & 0.1740 & 0.0002 & 0.0004 \\
0.0004 & 0.0006 & 0.1760 & 0 & 0.0004 & 0.0006 \\
0.2270 & 0.2252 & 0.2030 & 0.2160 & 0.2000 & 0.2190 \\
0.2200 & 0.2240 & 0.2200 & 0.2092 & 0.2214 & 0.2000
\end{pmatrix}
$$

On the other hand, by adopting second approach, and setting $\varphi = 0.00033$, the corresponding modified trust matrix is:

$$
\tilde{T}_B = \begin{pmatrix}
0 & 0.7500 & 0.0085 & 0.0230 & 0.4300 & 0.4500 \\
0.7600 & 0 & 0.0169 & 0.0077 & 0.4600 & 0.4500 \\
0.0030 & 0.0010 & 0 & 0.0025 & 0.0010 & 0.0020 \\
0.0020 & 0.0030 & 0.0028 & 0 & 0.0020 & 0.0030 \\
0.1350 & 0.1260 & 0.1268 & 0.6138 & 0 & 0.0950 \\
0.1000 & 0.1200 & 0.8451 & 0.3530 & 0.1070 & 0
\end{pmatrix}
$$

In Fig. 1 we plot the reputation vectors computed in both cases (identified with approach "A" and approach "B"), by employing power method.

It is clear that both approaches penalize bad agents. Nevertheless, while in the first case (approach "A") the trust scores of all non-malicious agents (i.e. a_1, a_2, a_5, a_6) are evenly smoothed out, in the second case (approach "B"), corresponding to our proposed strategy, the "best" honest agents (i.e. a_1, a_2) are paid off.

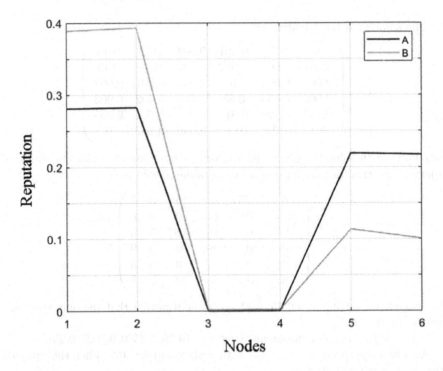

Fig. 1. The reputation vectors obtained applying the approaches A and B.

4   Conclusions and Future Work

Social virtual communities can build multidimensional and context-sensitive smart network infrastructures potentially rich of social interactions. Social interaction can be enacted by associating each community member with a personal software agent. Software agents are able to realize scalable and pervasive cooperation and interactions activities, discovering and/or composition of service by potentially overcoming each form of heterogeneity.

In this context, malicious actors must be considered to avoid the risks of deception. Minimizing these risks is of primary importance to enhance social interaction within the communities. A consolidated solution is to provide each actor with information about the trustworthiness on potential partners. To this purpose, in this paper we have proposed:

- a method to preliminarly identify the best candidates as colluding to use them as pre-untrusted actors;
- a reputation model to identify colluding agents that, differently from other proposals of literature, does not introduce side effects on the reputation scores of honest agents in detecting malicious ones.

For our forthcoming researches, we will pay attention to test our reputation model on:

- real and simulated data in order to confirm the good preliminary results presented here;
- different malicious attacks.

References

1. Abdelghani, W., Zayani, C.A., Amous, I., Sèdes, F.: Trust management in social internet of things: a survey. In: Dwivedi, Y.K., et al. (eds.) I3E 2016. LNCS, vol. 9844, pp. 430–441. Springer, Cham (2016). https://doi.org/10.1007/978-3-319-45234-0_39
2. Adamopoulou, A.A., Symeonidis, A.L.: A simulation testbed for analyzing trust and reputation mechanisms in unreliable online markets. Electron. Commer. Res. Appl. **13**(5), 368–386 (2014)
3. Ahmed, A., Abu Bakar, K., Channa, M.I., Haseeb, K., Khan, A.W.: A survey on trust based detection and isolation of malicious nodes in ad-hoc and sensor networks. Front. Comput. Sci. **9**(2), 280–296 (2015)
4. Altaf, A., Abbas, H., Iqbal, F., Derhab, A.: Trust models of internet of smart things: a survey, open issues, and future directions. J. Netw. Comput. Appl. **137**, 93–111 (2019)
5. Berkhin, P.: A survey on pagerank computing. Internet Math. **2**(1), 73–120 (2005)
6. Bidgoly, A.J., Ladani, B.T.: Modelling and quantitative verification of reputation systems against malicious attackers. Comput. J. **58**(10), 2567–2582 (2015)
7. Bidgoly, A.J., Ladani, B.T.: Benchmarking reputation systems: a quantitative verification approach. Comput. Hum. Behav. **57**, 274–291 (2016)
8. Cabral, L., Hortacsu, A.: The dynamics of seller reputation: evidence from Ebay. J. Ind. Econ. **58**(1), 54–78 (2010)
9. Cho, J.-H., Chan, K., Adali, S.: A survey on trust modeling. ACM Comput. Surv. (CSUR) **48**(2), 1–40 (2015)
10. De Meo, P., Fotia, L., Messina, F., Rosaci, D., Sarné, G.M.L.: Providing recommendations in social networks by integrating local and global reputation. Inf. Syst. **78**, 58–67 (2018)
11. De Meo, P., Messina, F., Postorino, M.N., Rosaci, D., Sarné, G.M.L.: A reputation framework to share resources into IoT-based environments. In: IEEE 14th International Conference on Networking, Sensing and Control, pp. 513–518. IEEE (2017)
12. Din, I.U., Guizani, M., Kim, B.S., Hassan, S., Khan, M.K.: Trust management techniques for the internet of things: a survey. IEEE Access **7**, 29763–29787 (2018)
13. Fang, W., Zhang, W., Chen, W., Pan, T., Ni, Y., Yang, Y.: Trust-based attack and defense in wireless sensor networks: a survey. Wirel. Commun. Mob. Comput. **2020**, 2643546 (2020)
14. Fortino, G., Fotia, L., Messina, F., Rosaci, D., Sarné, G.M.L.: State-of-the-art and research challenges: trust and reputation in the internet of things. IEEE Access **8**, 60117–60125 (2020)
15. Fortino, G., Messina, F., Rosaci, D., Sarné, G.M.L.: ResIoT: an IoT social framework resilient to malicious activities. IEEE/CAA J. Autom. Sinica **7**(5), 1263–1278 (2020)
16. Fullam, K. K.: A specification of the agent reputation and trust (art) testbed: experimentation and competition for trust in agent societies. In: Proceedings of the Fourth International Joint Conference on Autonomous Agents and Multiagent Systems, pp. 512–518 (2005)

17. Ghasempouri, S.A., Ladani, B.T.: Modeling trust and reputation systems in hostile environments. Futur. Gener. Comput. Syst. **99**, 571–592 (2019)
18. Hayne, S.C., Wang, H., Wang, L.: Modeling reputation as a time-series: evaluating the risk of purchase decisions on eBay. Decis. Sci. **46**(6), 1077–1107 (2015)
19. Hoffman, K., Zage, D., Nita-Rotaru, C.: A survey of attack and defense techniques for reputation systems. ACM Comput. Surv. (CSUR) **42**(1), 1–31 (2009)
20. Huynh, T.D., Jennings, N.R., Shadbolt, N.R.: An integrated trust and reputation model for open multi-agent systems. Auton. Agent. Multi-Agent Syst. **13**(2), 119–154 (2006)
21. Jnanamurthy, H.K., Singh, S.: Detection and filtering of collaborative malicious users in reputation system using quality repository approach. In: 2013 International Conference on Advances in Computing, Communications and Informatics (ICACCI), pp. 466–471. IEEE (2013)
22. Jøsang, A.: Robustness of trust and reputation systems: does it matter? In: Dimitrakos, T., Moona, R., Patel, D., McKnight, D.H. (eds.) IFIPTM 2012. IAICT, vol. 374, pp. 253–262. Springer, Heidelberg (2012). https://doi.org/10.1007/978-3-642-29852-3_21
23. Jøsang, A., Golbeck, J.: Challenges for robust trust and reputation systems. In: Proceedings of the 5th International Workshop on Security and Trust Management (SMT 2009), Saint Malo, France, vol. 5. Citeseer (2009)
24. Jøsang, A., Ismail, R., Boyd, C.: A survey of trust and reputation systems for online service provision. Decis. Support Syst. **43**(2), 618–644 (2007)
25. Kamvar, S.D., Schlosser, M.T., Garcia-Molina, H.: The eigentrust algorithm for reputation management in p2p networks. In: Proceedings of the 12th International Conference on World Wide Web, pp. 640–651. ACM (2003)
26. Kerr, R., Cohen, R.: Treet: the trust and reputation experimentation and evaluation testbed. Electron. Commer. Res. **10**(3), 271–290 (2010)
27. Lax, G., Sarné, G.M.L.: Cell Trust: a reputation model for C2C commerce. Electron. Commer. Res. **8**(4), 193–216 (2006)
28. Liu, L., Ma, Z., Meng, W.: Detection of multiple-mix-attack malicious nodes using perceptron-based trust in IoT networks. Futur. Gener. Comput. Syst. **101**, 865–879 (2019)
29. Madakam, S., Lake, V., Lake, V., Lake, V., et al.: Internet of things (IoT): a literature review. J. Comput. Commun. **3**(05), 164 (2015)
30. Marche, C., Nitti, M.: Trust-related attacks and their detection: a trust management model for the social IoT. IEEE Trans. Netw. Serv. Manage. **18**, 3297–3308 (2020)
31. Mármol, F.G., Pérez, G.M.: Security threats scenarios in trust and reputation models for distributed systems. Comput. Secur. **28**(7), 545–556 (2009)
32. Mármol., F.G., Pérez, G.M.: TRMSim-WSN, trust and reputation models simulator for wireless sensor networks. In: 2009 IEEE International Conference on Communications, pp. 1–5. IEEE (2009)
33. Messina, F., Pappalardo, G., Rosaci, D., Santoro, C., Sarné, G.M.L.: A trust-aware, self-organizing system for large-scale federations of utility computing infrastructures. Future Gener. Comput. Syst. **56**, 77–94 (2015)
34. Brin, M.W.P.: The pagerank citation ranking: Bringing order to the web. Stanford Digital Library working paper SIDL-WP (1999)
35. Pourghebleh, B., Wakil, K., Navimipour, N.J.: A comprehensive study on the trust management techniques in the internet of things. IEEE Internet Things J. **6**(6), 9326–9337 (2019)

36. Resnick, P., Kuwabara, K., Zeckhauser, R., Friedman, E.: Reputation systems. Commun. ACM **43**(12), 45–48 (2000)
37. Resnick, P., Zeckhauser, R.: Trust among strangers in internet transactions: empirical analysis of eBay's reputation system. In: The Economics of the Internet and E-commerce. Emerald Group Publishing Limited (2002)
38. Rosaci, D., Sarnè, G.M.L., Garruzzo, S.: Integrating trust measures in multiagent systems. Int. J. Intell. Syst. **27**(1), 1–15 (2012)
39. Sabater, J., Sierra, C.: Review on computational trust and reputation models. Artif. Intell. Rev. **24**(1), 33–60 (2005)
40. Sajjad, S.M., Bouk, S.H., Yousaf, M.: Neighbor node trust based intrusion detection system for WSN. Procedia Comput. Sci. **63**, 183–188 (2015)
41. Sharma, A., Pilli, E.S., Mazumdar, A.P., Gera, P.: Towards trustworthy internet of things: a survey on trust management applications and schemes. Comput. Commun. **160**, 475–493 (2020)
42. Vavilis, S., Petković, M., Zannone, N.: A reference model for reputation systems. Decis. Support Syst. **61**, 147–154 (2014)
43. Wang, Y.-F., Hori, Y., Sakurai, K.: Characterizing economic and social properties of trust and reputation systems in P2P environment. J. Comput. Sci. Technol. **23**(1), 129–140 (2008)
44. Xiong, L., Liu, L.: Peertrust: supporting reputation-based trust for peer-to-peer electronic communities. IEEE Trans. Knowl. Data Eng. **16**(7), 843–857 (2004)

Weakly Supervised Transfer Learning for Multi-label Appliance Classification

Giulia Tanoni[1]([⊠]) [iD], Emanuele Principi[1] [iD], Luigi Mandolini[2],
and Stefano Squartini[1] [iD]

[1] Universitá Politecnica delle Marche, Ancona, Italy
g.tanoni@pm.univpm.it, {e.principi,s.squartini}@univpm.it
[2] MAC Srl, Recanati, MC, Italy
mandolini@mac-italia.com

Abstract. Non-intrusive Load Monitoring refers to the techniques for providing detailed information on appliances' states or their energy consumption by measuring only aggregate electrical parameters. Supervised deep neural networks have reached the state-of-the-art in this task, and to improve the performance when training and test data domains differ, transfer learning techniques have been successfully applied. However, these techniques rely on data labeled sample-by-sample (*strong* labels) to be effective, which can be particularly costly in transfer learning since it requires collecting and annotating data in the target domain. To mitigate this issue, this work proposes a cross-domain transfer learning approach based on weak supervision and Convolutional Recurrent Neural Networks for multi-label appliance classification. The proposed method is based on the concept of *inexact* supervision by modeling NILM as a Multiple Instance Learning problem, exploiting different and less costly annotations called *weak* labels. The learning strategy is able to exploit weak labels both for pre-training and fine-tuning the models.

UK-DALE and REFIT are used in the experiments as source and target domain datasets to train, fine-tune, and evaluate the networks. The results demonstrate the effectiveness of the proposed method compared to the related pre-trained models. In particular, when the model is pre-trained on strongly and weakly labeled data of UK-DALE and then fine-tuned only on REFIT weak labels, the performance improves by 20.3%.

Keywords: Non-intrusive load monitoring · Weak supervision · Transfer learning · Multiple-instance learning · Deep learning

1 Introduction

Non-intrusive Load Monitoring (NILM) refers to the techniques for obtaining appliance power consumption information from the aggregate measurements of a building. This topic has become of great interest in recent years due to the necessity to reduce energy usage and limit carbon dioxide emissions [26].

M. Mahmud et al. (Eds.): AII 2022, CCIS 1724, pp. 360–375, 2022.
https://doi.org/10.1007/978-3-031-24801-6_26

Firstly proposed by Hart in the 1990s [7], NILM has demonstrated to be an effective method for obtaining detailed energy consumption information as it avoids the installation of several meters to monitor individual appliances. NILM can consist in power profile reconstruction, also known as disaggregation, or appliance state detection, also known as multi-label appliance classification. In the literature, Signal processing [35] and Machine Learning (ML) [9,27,34] methods have been proposed for NILM, but recently, the research has been focusing on Deep Neural Networks (DNNs). Indeed, after promising results obtained in several fields and thanks to the availability of public datasets, following the work of Kelly et al. [9], DNNs have been widely applied in NILM and have reached the state-of-the-art [2,8,16,20,23,25,29,30,34,37].

A limit of these techniques is their performance in unseen environments [5] due to significant differences between source and target data domains and the related feature spaces [21]. Transfer learning is an effective strategy for increasing generalization capability in these cases: recent methods operate by pre-training a neural network on a large dataset and then fine-tuning it on data acquired from the target environment [5,15,31]. However, this approach needs an additional acquisition phase in the target environment for fine-tuning and the dataset required for pre-training. Generally, data acquisition and annotation are costly and time-consuming procedures. For NILM, acquiring new data in the target domain requires the installation of electrical sensors for each monitored appliance or the users' involvement in manually annotating appliances' states sample-by-sample.

To reduce the requirement of large amount of labeled data, approaches based on semi-supervised have been proposed recently [17,33]. Differently from supervised learning, these methods exploit unlabeled data and allow to reduce the amount of annotated data for training. However, semi-supervised methods provide no information to the network for a large part of the training dataset. As reported in [14], although it is supposed that unlabeled data will bring a benefit, several empirical works demonstrated that the lack of labels decreased the performance. Reducing the labeling effort while providing data annotations is achievable by training the network with coarser labels, also called *weak* labels [37]. In the multi-label appliance classification task, a single label can be provided for an entire temporal segment of the aggregate signal indicating whether an appliance is ON or OFF within that segment. Differently, *strong* labels used in supervised learning methods are annotations at the sample level, i.e., they indicate whether an appliance is ON or OFF for each sample, thus representing more fine-grained information. In our view, in a target environment, weak labels can be obtained from the users' feedback, asking them if an appliance was active or not during a certain time window.

This work proposes a cross-domain transfer learning approach for multi-label appliance classification that exploits weak labels both for pre-training and fine-tuning a Convolutional Recurrent Neural Network (CRNN). As in [22,28], we model the task as a Multiple-Instance Learning (MIL) [4] problem, and we consider windows of aggregate samples as *bags* and samples inside them as *instances*. In this way, we propose a method able to better generalize to target environments as [5,15,31] but based on coarser annotations that allow to reduce the labeling cost and, at the same time, improve performance. An advantage of the proposed method is that weak annotations can be exploited in the pre-training and the fine-tuning phases, depending on the available annotations.

In the experiments, two public benchmark datasets, UK-DALE [10] and REFIT [18], have been used to evaluate the performance of the proposed method. UK-DALE and REFIT have been used as the *source* and *target* domain datasets to pre-train, fine-tune, and test the neural network. The results showed that weakly labeled data improve the performance when used during fine-tuning, demonstrating that significant benefits can be obtained with a reduced labeling effort.

The outline of this work is the following. Section 2 presents recent approaches for multi-label classification and illustrates the contributions of this paper. Section 3 presents the proposed method. Section 4 describes the experimental settings in detail. Section 5 presents and discusses the obtained results. Finally, Sect. 6 concludes the paper and presents future works.

2   Related Works and Contributions

2.1   Related Works

As highlighted by the number of works published in recent years [8,12,16,20, 23,25,27,29,30,33,36], ML-based multi-label appliance classification has gained great interest in the research community.

ML methods have been developed using different learning approaches, and supervised learning methods that require sample-by-sample annotations, are the most numerous. In Tabatabaei et al. [27], Random k-Label set (RAkEL) and Multi-Label K-Nearest Neighbours (ML-KNN) were trained with both time- and wavelet-domain features. Multi-label Restricted Boltzmann Machine (ML-RBM) was proposed in [29] due to its effectiveness in learning high-level features and correlations. Deep dictionary learning was adopted in [25] to overcome low-frequency sampling-related problems and be more accurate with continuously varying appliances. A Sparse Representation Classification (SRC) approach was adopted in [23] to improve performance while reducing the number of logging data collected for training. Temporal pooling was implemented in [16] to concatenate different time resolution information. A Gated Recurrent Units (GRUs) based approach was proposed in [8], where features from the aggregate signal and spikes are extracted using convolutional layers. In [36], a convolutional-recurrent and random-forest (RF) based architecture has been proposed to address the label correlation and the class-imbalance problems. To deal with the time-varying nature of power signals, Verma et al. [30] proposed an encoder-decoder architecture based on a Long Short-Term Memory network (LSTM) to model their dynamics. In [20], a CNN followed by three different fully connected subnetworks was implemented for multi-label state and event type classification. Deep Blind Compressed Sensing has been proposed by Singh et al. [24], exploiting compressed information to reduce transmission rate to detect devices' states.

To reduce the quantity of annotations required to train the ML algorithms, semi-supervised learning strategies have also been proposed that combine labeled and unlabeled data. In [17], the authors proposed a semi-supervised approach with the Virtual Adversarial Learning strategy. Yang et al. [33] proposed a semi-supervised learning procedure based on teacher-student architecture and a Temporal Convolutional Network.

Both supervised and semi-supervised approaches are effective when deployed in the same data domain but could have low performance when deployed in a target environment. This issue has been mitigated by using transfer learning methods in works that deal with the load disaggregation task. D'Incecco et al. [5] proposed to pre-train a CNN with source domain data and then fine-tune the last dense layer with a smaller dataset from the target domain. Lin et al. [15] proposed the deep domain adaptation strategy to learn an invariant representation across domains using unlabeled target data.

2.2   Contribution

As shown in the examined literature, several works proposed multi-label appliance classification methods based on supervised learning [8,12,16,20,23,25,29, 30,33,36], while few works use semi-supervised learning with unlabeled data [17,33]. Transfer learning methods have been presented to improve the performance on target domains, but they address the load disaggregation task and require data labeled sample-by-sample [5] or unlabeled data [15].

To overcome such limitations, this work proposes a transfer learning method based on weak labels to reduce the cost of labeling data acquired in the target domain and improve performance. The proposed method is based on MIL, and to the best of our knowledge, this is the first work that approaches transfer learning for multi-label appliance classification and with weak supervision.

In summary, the main contributions of this paper are the following:

- we propose a weakly supervised approach to perform cross-domain transfer learning for multi-label appliance classification;
- we present a transfer learning strategy that allows combining strongly and weakly labeled data during pre-training and fine-tuning, demonstrating the effectiveness of weak labels;
- we show that pre-training the network with strongly and weakly labeled data and then fine-tuning it on weakly labeled data only from the target environment significantly improves the performance: this procedure requires a modest effort to label the target dataset while improving the performance compared to the baseline method.

3   Proposed Methodology

Assuming the aggregate active power reading $y(t)$ of a building is known, the individual active power of each appliance is related to it by the following relationship:

$$y(t) = \sum_{j=1}^{J} s_j(t) x_j(t) + n(t), \tag{1}$$

where $n(t)$ is the measurement noise, $x_j(t)$ is the active power of the j-th appliance, and $s_j(t) \in \{0, 1\}$ its state. The state $s_j(t)$ is 0 if the appliance is OFF at the time instant t and 1 otherwise.

Supposing that we are interested in a subset $K \leq J$ of the appliances, the relationship can be rewritten as:

$$y(t) = \sum_{j=1}^{K} s_j(t) x_j(t) + v(t), \tag{2}$$

where the first term is the power of the K appliances of interest and $v(t)$ is the cumulative noise term given by:

$$v(t) = \sum_{j=K+1}^{J} s_j(t) x_j(t) + n(t). \tag{3}$$

The multi-label appliance classification task consists in the estimation of $s_j(t)$ for $j = 1, 2, \ldots, K$ given only $y(t)$.

In this work, appliances' states are estimated using a CRNN, and the task is modeled as a MIL problem to exploit weak labels. Firstly proposed in [4], MIL is a type of learning based on the concept of *instances* and *bags* in which the ground-truth is provided only at the bag level. In our method, instances refer to the raw samples of the aggregate signal $y(t)$, and the corresponding *strong labels* are represented by one-hot vectors $\mathbf{s}(t) = [s_1(t), s_2(t), \ldots, s_K(t)]^T \in \mathbb{R}^{K \times 1}$ composed of the appliances states. Bags refer to segments of $y(t)$ of length L. The i-th bag is represented by the following vector:

$$\mathbf{y}_i = [y(iL), \ldots, y(iL + L - 1)]^T \in \mathbb{R}^{L \times 1}. \tag{4}$$

The related *weak* label is again encoded as a one-hot vector $\mathbf{w}_i$ having the same dimensions of $\mathbf{s}(t)$. Moreover, $\mathbf{S}_i = [\mathbf{s}(iL), \mathbf{s}(iL + 1), \ldots, \mathbf{s}(iL + L - 1)] \in \mathbb{R}^{K \times L}$ represents the set of strong labels of all the appliances related to bag i.

With the above definitions, it is now possible to define more formally the multi-label appliance classification task based on weak labels. Consider a training dataset $\mathcal{D}$ given by

$$\mathcal{D} = \mathcal{D}_{strong-weak} \cup \mathcal{D}_{weak}, \tag{5}$$

where $\mathcal{D}_{strong-weak} = \{(\mathbf{y}_1, \mathbf{w}_1, \mathbf{S}_1), \ldots, (\mathbf{y}_M, \mathbf{w}_M, \mathbf{S}_M)\}$ is a dataset composed of M bags annotated with strong and weak labels, and $\mathcal{D}_{weak} = \{(\mathbf{y}_{M+1}, \mathbf{w}_{M+1}), \ldots, (\mathbf{y}_{M+K}, \mathbf{w}_{M+K})\}$ is a dataset composed of K bags annotated with weak labels only. The objective is to learn a function $\mathbf{f} : \mathbb{R}^L \to \mathbb{R}^{K \times L}$ from $\mathcal{D}$ that provides an estimate $\hat{\mathbf{S}}$ of $\mathbf{S}$ by using only the knowledge of the aggregate power $\mathbf{y}$. The function $\mathbf{f}(\cdot)$ is represented by a CRNN described in the following section.

3.1   Neural Network Architecture

The proposed method is based on a CRNN [3] that comprises a convolutional and a recurrent subpart (Fig. 1). The convolutional one consists of H convolutional blocks composed of a convolutional layer with $F \times H$ filters and kernel size K_e, a batch normalization layer, a ReLu activation layer, and a drop out layer with rate p. The recurrent subpart consists of a bidirectional layer of U GRU units. The output $\hat{\mathbf{S}}$ is provided by a dense layer with sigmoid activation function. This layer will be denoted as *instance layer* in the following. The final layer of the network is the *bag layer* with sigmoid activation function that provides the estimate $\hat{\mathbf{w}}$. The relationship between the instance layer output $\hat{\mathbf{S}}$ and the bag layer output $\hat{\mathbf{w}}$ is defined by a pooling function $\mathbf{p} : \mathbb{R}^{K \times L} \to \mathbb{R}^K$:

$$\hat{\mathbf{w}} = \mathbf{p}(\hat{\mathbf{S}}). \tag{6}$$

Based on the work of Wang et al. [32], we used the linear softmax pooling function defined as follows:

$$\hat{w}_k = \frac{\sum_t \hat{s}_k^2(t)}{\sum_t \hat{s}_k(t)}, \tag{7}$$

where $\hat{w}_k$ is the k-th element of $\hat{\mathbf{w}}$, i.e., the weak label of the k-th appliance. Following the bag layer, instance-level predictions are multiplied to the bag-level output. This learnable procedure is referred to as Clip Smoothing (CS) [6], and it is used to better deal with false activations. This technique is based on the consistency between weak and strong labels. The final predictions are obtained binarizing the instance level output using a threshold.

3.2   Transfer Learning Strategy

Similarly to [5], transfer learning here is performed by pre-training the neural network on a large dataset $\mathcal{D}^{(pt)}$, and then by fine-tuning it on a different dataset $\mathcal{D}^{(ft)}$. Both dataset can be composed as in Eq. (5). $\mathcal{D}^{(pt)}$ can contain data only from the source domain or both from the source and target domains, while $\mathcal{D}^{(ft)}$ contains data only from the target domain.

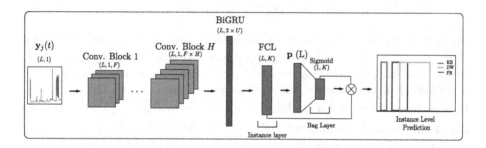

Fig. 1. The employed CRNN architecture.

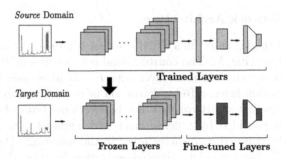

Fig. 2. Transfer learning with weak supervision. The model is trained with *source* domain data. Then the CNN blocks are frozen, and the remaining layers are fine-tuned with *target* domain data.

As shown in Fig. 2, during fine-tuning, all the weights of the convolutional blocks are not updated (frozen) to avoid performance degradation [5]. Fine-tuning is performed only on the recurrent subpart and on the instance layer based on the performance obtained in the validation phase.

Based on the neural network architecture, two loss terms can be defined $\mathcal{L}_s$ and $\mathcal{L}_w$, respectively related to the instance and bag output. Both losses are the binary cross-entropy for the related output and they are calculated as follows:

$$\mathcal{L}_s = -\frac{1}{K}\frac{1}{L}\sum_{k=1}^{K}\sum_{t=1}^{L}[s_k(t)\log(\hat{s}_k(t)) + (1 - s_k(t))\log(1 - \hat{s}_k(t))], \quad (8)$$

$$\mathcal{L}_w = -\frac{1}{K}\sum_{k=1}^{K}[w_k\log(\hat{w}_k) + (1 - w_k)\log(1 - \hat{w}_k)], \quad (9)$$

where the bag index i has been omitted for simplicity of notation.

A significant advantage of the proposed method is that it allows to use strong or weak labels in the pre-training and fine-tuning phases depending on the composition of $\mathcal{D}^{(pt)}$ and $\mathcal{D}^{(ft)}$. Supposing that

$$\mathcal{D}^{(pt)} = \mathcal{D}^{(pt)}_{strong-weak} \cup \mathcal{D}^{(pt)}_{weak}, \quad (10)$$

$$\mathcal{D}^{(ft)} = \mathcal{D}^{(ft)}_{strong-weak} \cup \mathcal{D}^{(ft)}_{weak}, \quad (11)$$

the model can be pre-trained both on strongly and weakly annotated data if $\mathcal{D}^{(pt)}_{strong-weak} \neq \varnothing$, or only on weakly annotated data if $\mathcal{D}^{(pt)}_{strong-weak} = \varnothing$. In the first case, the training loss is $\mathcal{L}_{tr} = \mathcal{L}_s + \lambda\mathcal{L}_w$, where λ balances the contribution of the two losses, while in the second case $\mathcal{L}_{tr} = \mathcal{L}_w$. Moreover, it is possible to combine data from different domains, e.g., $\mathcal{D}^{(pt)}_{strong-weak}$ can contain data from the source domain while $\mathcal{D}^{(pt)}_{weak}$ from the target domain.

Similarly, fine-tuning on the target domain data can be performed differently based on the available annotations: if $\mathcal{D}^{(ft)}_{strong-weak} \neq \varnothing$, fine-tuning is performed

Table 1. Train and Validation sets characteristics of UK-DALE. The number of labels is reported in thousands. SL: Strong Labels. WL: Weak Labels.

Appliance	Train			Validation		
	Houses	Nr. of SL	Nr. of WL	Houses	Nr. of SL	Nr. of WL
KE	1, 3, 5	996.6	43.1	1, 3, 5	196.3	6.9
MW	1, 5	849.7	42.9	1, 5	157.2	7.0
FR	1, 4, 5	1221.9	36	1, 4, 5	709.4	2.9
WM	1, 5	837.7	32.1	1, 5	881.4	1.2
DW	1, 5	554.5	31.9	1, 5	790.1	0.9
Nr. of bags	99.993			10.428		

Table 2. Train, Validation and Test sets characteristics for REFIT. Number of labels is reported in thousands. SL: Strong Labels. WL: Weak Labels.

Appliance	Train			Validation			Test and Fine-tuning		
	Houses	Nr. of SL	Nr. of WL	Houses	Nr. of SL	Nr. of WL	Houses	Nr. of SL	Nr. of WL
KE	3, 5, 6, 7, 19	3217.0	54.1	3, 5, 6, 7, 19	678.6	12.7	2, 4, 8, 9	1182.9	24.4
MW	10, 12, 17, 19	2476.9	59.9	10, 12, 17, 19	606.9	9.9	4	436.6	8.4
FR	5, 9, 12	5433.7	62.0	5, 9, 12	1434.1	2.4	2, 15	1214.6	0.9
WM	5, 7, 15–18	1559.4	57.9	5, 7, 15–18	1788.2	4.1	2, 8, 9	1362.6	2.0
DW	5, 7, 13	520.292	52.7	5, 7, 13	2977.3	3.8	2, 9	2153.8	2.0
Nr. of bags	186.743			21.115			25.452		

using both strongly and weakly labeled data and the related loss is $\mathcal{L}_{ft} = \mathcal{L}_s + \beta\mathcal{L}_w$, with β balancing the two losses. Conversely, if $\mathcal{D}^{(ft)}_{strong-weak} = \varnothing$, fine-tuning is performed only on weakly labeled data and $\mathcal{L}_{ft} = \mathcal{L}_w$.

It is worth noting that the case where $\mathcal{D}^{(pt)}_{strong-weak} \neq \varnothing$, and $\mathcal{D}^{(ft)}_{strong-weak} = \varnothing$ and $\mathcal{D}^{(ft)}_{-weak} \neq \varnothing$ is of particular relevance in a practical scenario since a large number of public datasets with strong annotations is available to pre-train the network, and the model can be fine-tuned by collecting data from the target domain and annotating it only with weak labels, thus reducing the labeling effort.

4 Experimental Setting

4.1 Dataset

UK-DALE and REFIT datasets have been used to evaluate the performance of the proposed method. Kettle (KE), Microwave (MW), Fridge (FR), Washing Machine (WM), and Dishwasher (DW) are the appliances of interest.

UK-DALE contains data from 5 houses, with the aggregate power sampled every 1 s and appliance power sampled every 6 s. The following date intervals were considered: 06/01/2016-31/08/2016 for house 1, 01/06/2013-31/08/2013 for house 2, 16/03/2013-05/04/2013 for house 3 and 4, and 06/29/2014-09/05/2014 for house 5. We downsampled the aggregate active power to 6 s and aligned it with the appliance power using NILMTK [1].

REFIT contains measurements from 21 houses. Data were upsampled uniformly to 6 s. Each house contains a maximum of 4 appliances' power readings, and all the houses except 20 and 21 were considered. As in [31], we considered the following date intervals: 07/12/2013-08/07/2015 for houses 9, 12, 18, 20/11/2013-30/06/2015 for houses 10, 17, 17/09/2013-08/07/2015 for houses 2, 5, 7, 16, 26/09/2013-08/07/2015 for house 13 and 26/09/2013-08/07/2015 for houses 3, 4, 6, 8, 11, 15, 19.

Both datasets have been used to create two sets of bags, one with UK-DALE data and one with REFIT data, using the aggregate power and the individual active power measurements of the selected appliances. The general procedure for creating them consists of four steps:

1. Activations have been extracted using NILMTK [1] with parameters reported in [9] for UK-DALE and in [18,19] for REFIT.
2. Synthetic bags have been created randomly by combining activations. Each bag contains up to 4 appliances.
3. Noise has been extracted aligning the ground truth of $K = 5$ appliances of interest and then subtracting it to the aggregate power signal. The extracted noise is the term $v(t)$ in Eq. (3). This procedure is repeated for each bag, so noise bags are all different.
4. The extracted noise has been added to the synthetic aggregate.

Note that we balanced the occurrence of appliance activations and the number of strong labels associated with each appliance in both sets of bags.

Table 1 and Table 2 report the details about training, validation, and test sets for the two sets of bags created respectively from UK-DALE and REFIT. Data was standardized using mean and standard deviation estimated on the training set.

4.2   Experimental Setup

The experimental setup has been designed to evaluate several possible real-world scenarios that differ in data and annotations availability, based on the formulation in Sect. 3.2. The performance has always been evaluated on 70% of the REFIT "Test and Fine-tuning" set reported in Table 2.

Referring to (10), we defined three pre-training dataset compositions:

1. Only weakly labeled data is available: in this case, $\mathcal{D}_{strong-weak}^{(pt)} = \varnothing$ and $\mathcal{D}_{weak}^{(pt)} \neq \varnothing$ is composed of bags from the UK-DALE dataset. Pre-training and test data in this case are from different domains.
2. Both strongly and weakly labeled data from the same domain is available: in this case, $\mathcal{D}_{strong-weak}^{(pt)} \neq \varnothing$ and $\mathcal{D}_{weak}^{(pt)} \neq \varnothing$, and they are both composed of bags from the UK-DALE dataset. As in the previous condition, pre-training and test data are from different domains.

3. Both strongly and weakly labeled data is available, but in this case they are from different domains: $\mathcal{D}^{(pt)}_{strong-weak} \neq \varnothing$ is composed of bags from the UK-DALE dataset and $\mathcal{D}^{(pt)}_{weak} \neq \varnothing$ from bags of the REFIT dataset. Part of the pre-training and the test data are from the same domain.

Regardless the pre-training condition, the validation set is represented by UK-DALE as reported in Table 1.

Table 3. CRNN hyperparameters after tuning.

Dataset	H	U	K_e	p	CS
S-W UK-DALE	3	64	5	0.1	No
W UK-DALE	4	16	5	0.1	Yes
S-W REFIT	4	64	5	0.1	No

Fine-tuning has been performed on 30% of the bags from each house of the REFIT "Test and Fine-tuning set" reported in Table 2. Referring to equation (11), the fine-tuning dataset can be composed of 1) strongly and weakly annotated data from the target environment ($\mathcal{D}^{(ft)}_{strong-weak} \neq \varnothing$); 2) Only weakly labeled data from the target environment ($\mathcal{D}^{(ft)}_{weak} \neq \varnothing$). The last condition is of particular interest since it considers the case where data from the target environment is annotated only with weak labels. Thus, the labeling effort related to data collected in the target environment is significantly reduced.

Fine-tuned models have been compared to a baseline model (denoted as Baseline) obtained by using REFIT strongly and weakly labeled data both for training and validating the network and without fine-tuning it. The Baseline model, thus, considers the case where data from the same domain of the test set is available for training and represents an ideal case. Moreover, we evaluated also the performance of pre-trained models prior to fine-tuning (denoted as No Fine-Tuning).

For each pre-training condition, the Hyperband algorithm [13] from Keras tuner has been used to select the hyperparameters values that achieve the highest performance on the validation set. Learning is performed by using Adam [11] and the learning rate was fixed to 0.002 and F to 32. The final hyperparameters values are reported in Table 3. When the source dataset is only weakly labeled, fine-tuning the bidirectional and instance layers has proven the best performing method on the validation set. For the other two conditions, only the instance layer has been fine-tuned.

The threshold for binarizing instance level predictions has been determined on the validation set for each pre-training condition.

The code related to this work is available on GitHub[1].

---

[1] https://github.com/GiuTan/WeaklyTransferNILM.

4.3   Evaluation Metrics

Two metrics have been used to evaluate the proposed approach. The first is the F_1-score (F_1) and it is used to evaluate the model prediction ability, balancing between the presence of accurate classification and false activations. F_1-score for the k-th appliance is calculated as:

$$F_1^{(k)} = \frac{2 \cdot TP^{(k)}}{2 \cdot TP^{(k)} + FP^{(k)} + FN^{(k)}}, \tag{12}$$

where $TP^{(k)}$ is the number of True Positive instances correctly assigned to appliance k, $FP^{(k)}$ is the number False Positive instances incorrectly assigned to appliance k, and $FN^{(k)}$ is the number of False Negative instances incorrectly assigned to other appliances. The average performance across appliances is calculated by using the micro-averaged F_1-score:

$$F_1\text{-micro} = \frac{2 \cdot \sum_{k=1}^{K} TP^{(k)}}{\sum_{k=1}^{K} \left(2 \cdot TP^{(k)} + FP^{(k)} + FN^{(k)} \right)}. \tag{13}$$

The second metric is the Average Normalized Error (ANE), introduced in [27] and adopted in several works [24, 25, 33] to evaluate the energy disaggregation error. ANE is defined as:

$$\text{ANE} = \frac{\left| \sum_{c=1}^{C} Average\_power_c - \sum_{c=1}^{C} Actual\_power_c \right|}{\sum_{c=1}^{C} Actual\_power_c}, \tag{14}$$

where $C = L \cdot I$ is the number of samples in the test set.

Table 4. Results related to the Baseline and all the pre-training scenarios. Best results are reported in bold. Kettle: KE, Microwave: MW, Fridge: FR, Washing Machine: WM, Dishwasher: DW.

Method	Labels	Dataset	KE	MW	FR	WM	DW	F_1-micro	ANE
Baseline	Strong & Weak	REFIT	0.82	**0.82**	0.20	0.71	0.77	0.69	0.200
No fine-tuning	Weak	UK-DALE	0.68	0.44	0.01	0.45	0.33	0.41	0.037
Fine-tuning	Strong & Weak	REFIT	**0.87**	0.72	0.22	0.68	0.71	0.68	**0.002**
Fine-tuning	Weak	REFIT	0.66	0.57	0.00	0.49	0.36	0.45	0.241
No fine-tuning	Strong & Weak	UK-DALE	0.82	0.46	0.12	0.74	0.74	0.59	0.105
Fine-tuning	Strong & Weak	REFIT	**0.87**	0.71	0.18	**0.76**	0.74	0.67	0.046
Fine-tuning	Weak	REFIT	0.83	0.74	0.16	**0.76**	**0.78**	**0.71**	0.023
No fine-tuning	Strong & Weak	Mixed	0.78	0.46	0.11	0.42	0.62	0.52	0.037
Fine-tuning	Strong & Weak	REFIT	0.86	0.81	**0.37**	0.62	0.68	0.67	0.081
Fine-tuning	Weak	REFIT	0.85	0.77	0.25	0.44	0.69	0.61	0.078

5   Results and Discussion

Table 4 shows the results obtained with the three pre-training conditions and the related fine-tuning. Observing the results, it is evident that weak supervision and transfer learning play a key role in obtaining performance close to the Baseline while reducing labeling effort. When the network is trained on weakly labeled data, and it is not fine-tuned (second row of Table 4), the performance is significantly lower compared to the Baseline. After fine-tuning with strong and weak labels and weak labels only, the F_1-micro increases by 65.8% and 8.9%, respectively. Compared to the Baseline, the F_1-scores of Kettle and Fridge improve by 6.1% and 9%, respectively, if strong labels are considered in the fine-tuning set. The lowest ANE is obtained after fine-tuning with strong and weak annotations, with an improvement of 99% with respect to the Baseline.

When the CRNN is trained on strong and weak labels from UK-DALE (fifth row of Table 4), both F_1-micro and ANE are lower compared to the Baseline, while the F_1-score of the Washing Machine improves by 4%. Differently, compared to the model pre-trained only on weakly labeled data, all the appliances are better classified. After fine-tuning, the performance increases independently of the type of annotations. Remarkable performance both in terms of F_1-micro and ANE can be observed when the CRNN is fine-tuned with weakly labeled data only (seventh row of Table 4), with an improvement of 20.3% and 78.1%, respectively. Moreover, the result improves by 2.9% for F_1-micro and 88.5% for ANE if compared to the Baseline. This result is particularly significant since it means that pre-training the network with strong and weak labels from the source domain (UK-DALE) and fine-tuning it on weakly labeled data from the target domain (REFIT) results in superior performance compared to training on strongly and weakly labeled data from the target domain (REFIT). Single appliance behavior differs since Kettle and Fridge show the best performance when fine-tuning is performed on strong and weak labels. At the same time, Microwave and Dishwasher are better classified when fine-tuning is performed on weak labels only. For the Washing Machine, in both conditions the performance improves compared to the Baseline by 7% after fine-tuning, meaning that weak labels are useful as well as the strong ones. The F_1-score of the Dishwasher improves by 1.2% with respect to the Baseline.

Without fine-tuning, pre-training the model on strong and weak annotations of the mixed dataset (eighth row of Table 4) obtains better performance compared to pre-training only on weak labels (second row of Table 4), but lower than pre-training on strong and weak annotations (fifth row of Table 4). This is related to the number of strongly annotated bags which are 20% of the entire UK-DALE set. The Mixed pre-trained model has better ANE than Baseline, with an improvement of 81.5%. When fine-tuned with strong annotations, the F_1-micro improves by 30%, while when target data are weakly labeled it improves by 17.3%. After fine-tuning, the ANE is lower than the pre-trained model but better than the Baseline, with 59.5% and 61% improvements. The Dishwasher is classified better when fine-tuning is performed with weak data only. In this condition, the labeling effort is reduced both for the pre-training and the fine-tuning set. Compared to the baseline, Kettle and Fridge F_1-micro improve by 4.8% and 85%, respectively.

In summary, when the model is pre-trained only on weakly annotated data of the same domain, strong labels are required to fine-tune the network and obtain satisfactory performance. Conversely, when the network is pre-trained with strong and weak labels, weak data from the target environment are sufficient to improve performance both in terms of F_1-micro and ANE. For some appliances, by using weak labels for fine-tuning is better than using strong labels to improve performance. In the mixed case, since the quantity of strongly labeled data in the pre-training set is small, strong and weak fine-tuning results better than using only weak data.

Figure 3 shows the predictions produced by each pre-trained model after fine-tuning with weak labels. Since some predictions are overlapped, outputs are re-scaled for better visualization. It is evident that the fine-tuning on weak labels when pre-training is performed on strong and weak labels results in a more accurate prediction compared to the other models. In particular, this is highlighted for the Kettle and the Dishwasher.

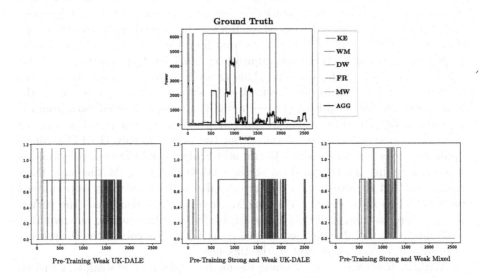

Fig. 3. Classification predictions produced by each pre-trained model after fine-tuning with weakly labeled data. Data is from REFIT house 2. AGG: Aggregate.

6 Conclusion

This work proposed a transfer learning approach based on weak supervision for multi-label appliance classification. The task has been modeled as a MIL problem to exploit the so-called *weak* labels, and classification has been performed by using a CRNN. Transfer learning has been performed by pre-training the network on a large dataset and then fine-tuning it on data belonging to the target domain. In this way, the learning strategy is able to exploit weakly labeled data in both pre-training and fine-tuning phases. The proposed method has been evaluated in different pre-training and fine-tuning conditions using the UK-DALE and REFIT datasets. The results showed that it achieves superior performance compared to models without fine-tuning and compared to the Baseline model trained and validated on data from the same domain of the test set. In particular, when the model is pre-trained with strongly and weakly labeled data and then fine-tuned with only weak data, the performance improves, while the cost of labeling data from the target domain is reduced. This condition is particularly favorable in a practical scenario.

Future works aim to further investigate aspects related to the neural network structure and learning and quantify the improvements in a real-world environment. Moreover, the transfer learning approaches based on weak supervision will be extended to the disaggregation task.

References

1. Batra, N., et al.: Towards reproducible state-of-the-art energy disaggregation. In: Proceedings of BuildSys, pp. 193–202 (2019)
2. Bonfigli, R., et al.: Denoising autoencoders for non-intrusive load monitoring: improvements and comparative evaluation. Energy Build. **158**, 1461–1474 (2018)
3. Cho, K., et al.: Learning phrase representations using RNN encoder-decoder for statistical machine translation. In: Proceedings of EMNL, pp. 1724–1734 (2014)
4. Dietterich, T.G., Lathrop, R.H., Lozano-Pérez, T.: Solving the multiple instance problem with axis-parallel rectangles. Artif. Intell. **89**(1), 31–71 (1997)
5. D'Incecco, M., Squartini, S., Zhong, M.: Transfer learning for non-intrusive load monitoring. IEEE Trans. Smart Grid **11**(2), 1419–1429 (2020)
6. Dinkel, H., et al.: The smallrice submission to the DCASE2021 task 4 challenge: a lightweight approach for semi-supervised sound event detection with unsupervised data augmentation. In: Proceedings of DCASE (2021)
7. Hart, G.: Nonintrusive appliance load monitoring. Proc. IEEE **80**(12), 1870–1891 (1992)
8. Çimen, H., et al.: A dual-input multi-label classification approach for non-intrusive load monitoring via deep learning. In: Proceedings of ZINC, pp. 259–263 (2020)
9. Kelly, J., Knottenbelt, W.: Neural NILM: deep neural networks applied to energy disaggregation. In: Proceedings of the 2nd ACM International Conference on Embedded Systems for Energy-Efficient Built Environment, New York, USA, pp. 55–64 (2015)
10. Kelly, J., Knottenbelt, W.: The UK-DALE dataset, domestic appliance-level electricity demand and whole-house demand from five UK homes. Sci. Data **2**(150007) (2015)
11. Kingma, D., Ba, J.: Adam: a method for stochastic optimization. In: Proceedings of ICLR (2014)
12. Li, D., Sawyer, K., Dick, S.: Disaggregating household loads via semi-supervised multi-label classification. In: Proceedings of NAFIPS, pp. 1–5 (2015)

13. Li, L., et al.: Hyperband: a novel bandit-based approach to hyperparameter optimization. J. Mach. Learn. Res. **18**(1), 6765–6816 (2017)
14. Li, Y.F., Zhou, Z.H.: Towards making unlabeled data never hurt. IEEE Trans. Pattern Anal. Mach. Intell. **37**(1), 175–188 (2015)
15. Lin, J., Ma, J., Zhu, J., Liang, H.: Deep domain adaptation for non-intrusive load monitoring based on a knowledge transfer learning network. IEEE Trans. Smart Grid **13**(1), 280–292 (2022)
16. Massidda, L., et al.: Non-intrusive load disaggregation by convolutional neural network and multilabel classification. Appl. Sci. **10**, 1454 (2020)
17. Miao, N., et al.: Non-intrusive load disaggregation using semi-supervised learning method. In: SPAC, pp. 17–22 (2019)
18. Murray, D., et al.: An electrical load measurements dataset of United Kingdom households from a two-year longitudinal study. Sci. Data **4**(1), 160122 (2017)
19. Murray, D., et al.: Transferability of neural network approaches for low-rate energy disaggregation. In: Proceedings of ICASSP, Brighton, UK, pp. 8330–8334 (2019)
20. Nolasco, L.D.S., Lazzaretti, A.E., Mulinari, B.M.: DeepDFML-NILM: a new CNN-based architecture for detection, feature extraction and multi-label classification in NILM signals. IEEE Sens. J. **22**(1), 501–509 (2022)
21. Panigrahi, S., Nanda, A., Swarnkar, T.: A survey on transfer learning. Smart Innov. Syst. Technol. **194**, 781–789 (2021)
22. Serafini, L., Tanoni, G., Principi, E., Squartini, S.: A multiple instance regression approach to electrical load disaggregation. In: Proceedings of EUSIPCO (2022)
23. Singh, S., et al.: Non-intrusive load monitoring via multi-label sparse representation-based classification. IEEE Trans. Smart Grid **11**(2), 1799–1801 (2020)
24. Singh, S., et al.: Multi-label deep blind compressed sensing for low-frequency non-intrusive load monitoring. IEEE Trans. Smart Grid **13**(1), 4–7 (2022)
25. Singhal, V., et al.: Simultaneous detection of multiple appliances from smart-meter measurements via multi-label consistent deep dictionary learning and deep transform learning. IEEE Trans. Smart Grid **10**(3), 2969–2978 (2019)
26. Sun, M., et al.: Non-intrusive load monitoring system framework and load disaggregation algorithms: a survey. In: Proceedings of ICAMechS, pp. 284–288 (2019)
27. Tabatabaei, S.M., Dick, S., Xu, W.: Toward non-intrusive load monitoring via multi-label classification. IEEE Trans. Smart Grid **8**(1), 26–40 (2017)
28. Tanoni, G., Principi, E., Squartini, S.: Multilabel appliance classification with weakly labeled data for non-intrusive load monitoring. IEEE Trans. Smart Grid **14**(1), 440–452 (2023). https://doi.org/10.1109/TSG.2022.3191908
29. Verma, S., Singh, S., Majumdar, A.: Multi label restricted Boltzmann machine for non-intrusive load monitoring. In: Proceedings of ICASSP, pp. 8345–8349 (2019)
30. Verma, S., Singh, S., Majumdar, A.: Multi-label LSTM autoencoder for non-intrusive appliance load monitoring. Electr. Power Syst. Res. **199**, 107414 (2021)
31. Wang, L., et al.: Pre-trained models for non-intrusive appliance load monitoring. IEEE Trans. Green Commun. and Netw. **2400**, 1 (2021)
32. Wang, Y., et al.: A comparison of five multiple instance learning pooling functions for sound event detection with weak labeling. In: Proceedings of ICASSP, pp. 31–35 (2019)
33. Yang, Y., Zhong, J., Li, W., Gulliver, T.A., Li, S.: Semisupervised multilabel deep learning based nonintrusive load monitoring in smart grids. IEEE Trans. Ind. Inf. **16**(11), 6892–6902 (2020)

34. Zhang, C., et al.: Sequence-to-point learning with neural networks for non-intrusive load monitoring. In: Proceedings of the AAAI Conference on Artificial Intelligence, vol. 32, no. 1 (2018)

35. Zhao, B., et al.: Improving event-based non-intrusive load monitoring using graph signal processing. IEEE Access **6**, 53944–53959 (2018)

36. Zhou, X., et al.: Non-intrusive load monitoring using a CNN-LSTM-RF model considering label correlation and class-imbalance. IEEE Access **9**, 84306–84315 (2021)

37. Zhou, Z.H.: A brief introduction to weakly supervised learning. Natl. Sci. Rev. **5**(1), 44–53 (2018)

Toward an Interoperable Catalogue of Multimodal Depression-Related Data

Terry Amorese[1] , Gennaro Cordasco[1] , Giovanni D'Angelo[2],
Maria Stella de Biase[3] , Michele Di Giovanni[3], Anna Esposito[1] ,
Claudia Greco[1] , Stefano Marrone[3(✉)] , Fiammetta Marulli[3] ,
and Laura Verde[3]

[1] Dipartimento di Psicologia, Universitá della Campania "Luigi Vanvitelli", Viale
Ellittico 31, 81100 Caserta, Italy
{terry.amorese,gennaro.cordasco,anna.esposito,
claudia.greco}@unicampania.it
[2] Centro Clinico D'Angelo, Via Don Bosco 1, 81022 Casagiove, Italy
dott.giovannidangelo@libero.it
[3] Dipartimento di Matematica e Fisica, Universitá della Campania "Luigi
Vanvitelli", Viale Lincoln 5, 81100 Caserta, Italy
{mariastella.debiase,michele.digiovanni,stefano.marrone,
fiammetta.marulli,laura.verde}@unicampania.it

Abstract. The need to establish an intelligent tool for semi-automatic diagnosis of depression on high-quality data, requires trustworthy, interoperable and multimodal data repositories. Such databases should be based on common collection and storage criteria and should enable advanced and open analysis modes without sacrificing data privacy. This paper launches the Depressive Disorder DataBase (D3B) initiative for the definition of a distributed and interoperable network of databases for the collection and the actual usage of depression-related multimodal data. In this database network, multimedia as voice, video, handwriting, and EEG signals could be collected and shared to a considerable community of researchers. This paper focuses on the catalogue schema, on technical-level details and on the mechanisms able to guarantee interoperability and privacy at the same time.

Keywords: Depressive disorders · Artificial intelligence in healthcare · Open data · Data privacy

1 Introduction

Artificial Intelligence (AI) is becoming a concrete and practical tool to build cutting-edge software, based on a considerable body of knowledge spanning from data-driven approach to knowledge representation. To this aim, high quality of data against which Machine Learning (ML) models can be trained and/or validated, are necessary.

The availability of such data sets is of a paramount importance in achieving the general goal of results reproducibility. Reproducibility is *"reproducibility in*

M. Mahmud et al. (Eds.): AII 2022, CCIS 1724, pp. 376–390, 2022.
https://doi.org/10.1007/978-3-031-24801-6_27

empirical AI research is the ability of an independent research team to produce the same results using the same AI method based on the documentation made by the original research team" [16]. According to the author of [15], there are some actions research organizations can carry out to foster this aim: available datasets (and their related structure) are inside the "building infrastructure" and "providing infrastructure" ones.

On the other hand, reproducibility is a cornerstone in the construction of solid and trustworthy ML-based software to which the modern society is delegating more and more critical functions. Let us consider, as examples, transportation planning, smart vehicles controls, energy management and planning, control and planning of smart manufacturing plants and, finally, the usage of AI in the healthcare domain with the construction of Clinical Decision Support System (CDSS).

The healthcare domain, in particular, has received in these years, great attention from both the academic and the industrial communities due to the big challenges that are around this domain and the high potentiality of such a market. From the reproducibility perspective, this domain represents a very hard problem due to the necessity of dealing with a limiting factor for the construction of open and shared datasets: data privacy. Many national and international standards have been defined and enacted in these years to limit the usage of personal data without a proper level of involvement of the data owners. In this context, spreading personal data across borders—even if for scientific reasons—is becoming harder and harder.

This work is framed in the AutoNomous DiscoveRy Of depressIve Disorder Signs (ANDROIDS) research project. This project evaluates the core features of human interactions to model emotional and cognitive processes: a critical brick in building technologies for all-inclusive and sustainable societies. The design and implementation of autonomous algorithms and systems capable of detecting early signs of depression and mood changes by analysing interaction exchanges is the main objective of this project. Additionally, the combination of different sources of information according to the principles of data/decision fusion is investigated [19].

The specific objective of this paper is to provide a framework for the definition of federated database systems for the collection and the analysis of depression-related information. Such database system is named Depressive Disorder DataBase (D3B) and collects not only general information as sex, gender and age, or the results of the main depression-related psychological tests (e.g., Beck Depression Inventor (BDI) [7], Depression Anxiety Stress (DASS) [8]). The D3B contains behavioural data gathered from both from healthy/depressed diagnosed subjects. To this aim, a collection process designs specific scenarios to assess individual emphatic and social competencies: by simple interactions between the subject and some electronic devices, multimodal data are captured and stored in the D3B.

More in the specific, this paper brings the following original contributions:

- **multi-modality:** as in the scientific literature, depression-related datasets are present, they traditionally focus on one specific aspect correlating, as an example, the degree of depression to personal information or to free speech. This initiative, on the other hand, correlates different sources of information of the *same* patient.

- **interoperability:** D3B enables cooperation between different organizations that can share their data, creating larger "virtual datasets";
- **privacy:** as privacy is a primary concern in the healthcare domain, the D3B system is built to create privacy-preserving preprocessing tools, to extract anonymized features from raw data.

Furthermore, this paper does not only bring novel data to this domain (according to the "building infrastructure" action) but also defines a database schema and tools that can be replicable in other contexts, enabling the construction of a federation of databases (according to the "providing infrastructure" action). Such defined federation will enable researchers and practitioners to multiply available data for ML algorithms. In this paper, a sample implementation of the database schema is reported, based on the widespread `MongoDB` technology. Some simple population/querying tools, based on the Python language and on the `pyMongo` library.

This paper is structured as follows: Sect. 2 reports a general description of the ANDROIDS project and review the state-of-art in depression-related databases. Section 3 reports information about the acquisition medical protocol and describes the practical and operative context followed during the acquisition campaign. Section 4 reports the main architecture of the D3B initiative and discusses technical details. Section 5 provides an insight into the privacy-related matters also giving samples of possible data analysis use cases. Section 6 ends the paper and sketches future research activities.

2   Background and Related Works

2.1   The ANDROIDS Project in Brief

ANDROIDS is a project that investigates the core features of human interactions to model cognitive and emotional processes: a critical brick in building technologies for sustainable and all-inclusive societies.

In particular, it must be emphasized that Major Depressive Disorder (MDD) is among the most frequent psychiatric illnesses and is revealed by several impairing symptoms at the cognitive (impairments in speaking or thinking, suicidal ideations, difficulties in pursuing goals), social (loss of interest in relationships and social activities, working failures, suicide tries), emotional (feeling hopeless or sad, anhedonia), and physical (changes in weight or appetite, pain, headaches) functioning [5].

Depression is a widespread and disabling mental disorder. It is the second most prevalent mental illness in the world and a major contributor to years lived with disability [9]. Impaired social functioning constitutes a central disorder generated by the MDD. Scholars have found that a deficit in being able to identify the emotional expressions of others can cause difficulties in social relationships citeTeo2013, as emotional competence is crucial for successful interpersonal relationships [25].

This is because emotional expressions (facial, gestural, and vocal expressions) communicate information on the emotional state of others and enable appropriate social responses to these signals [26]. Studies investigating the ability of depressed subjects to normally interact and decode emotional expressions report contradictory findings. It was both found that depressed subjects are either slow and less accurate [6] or fast and more accurate in decoding negative emotions [31]. In general, depressed subjects may exhibit a global deficit in interacting and decoding emotions and be less accurate than healthy subjects [32].

Based on these considerations, the aim of ANDROIDS is to design and implement autonomous systems and algorithms able to detect early signs of mood changes and depressions through the analyses of interaction exchanges. The idea underlying the project is to combine diverse sources of information, implementing multi-sensor data fusions [19], in addition to data mining techniques focusing on specific domains (text mining, web mining, etc.). This approach should account of both the understanding of the mined data and their internal dynamics implementing an adaptive approach for knowledge management, accounting for run-time changes at both data type and data instance levels [33].

As the goal of ANDROIDS is to set the pillars for a CDSS, patients are not left alone with a machine response: medic personnel are not optional in this vision and their role is intermediating between the ANDROIDS platform and the patient. In both the cases of usage, i.e., by a patient or by a medic, the intelligent system just gives some initial screening information related to depressive signs that can be used inside a medic protocols, possibly but not necessarily supported by automatic applications.

2.2 Related Works

Depression has been study of a long time to investigate about the possibility to build a CDSS for this disturbance. While the first works based their classification on the results of specific tests as BDI and DASS, single-feature behavioural approaches are now widespread in the scientific literature. Various studies demonstrated that behavioural signals such as speech [24], Electroencephalographic (EEG) signals [1], facial expressivity [27], self-touching [30], gross motor activity and gesturing [17], smiling [17], head movements [3], and body expressions [18] can be used to distinguish between depressed and non-depressed subjects.

Here it follows a brief review of the existing datasets and repository for depressive features. Scientific journals are Data In Brief reports more than 60 depression related datasets published in the last 8 years. In [12], a repository containing traces of the motion of depressed and control people is presented. Another database focuses on depression symptoms: significant weight loss/gain, insomnia or hypersomnia, fatigue or loss of energy, are some examples of such symptoms[1]. The dataset reported in [29] focuses on EEG signals. Another work

---

[1] http://data.ctdata.org/dataset/mental-health.

predicts depression on the base of Arabic tweets [22]. Claim data are used in [28]. Some other approaches as [35] use the well-known Audio/Visual Emotion Challenge and Workshop (AVEC) challenge dataset.

Combining two or more features is a growing research trend, as witnessed by some recent papers as [23], combining voice and motion analysis, [4], where verbal and para-verbal analysis is conducted, and [2], where speaking, head poses, and eye gaze behaviours are jointly analysed.

The work in [13] reports a survey of application of ML techniques to the problem of mental health monitoring with multimodal sensing and ML. Even if not focusing on any specific mental disturbance/pathology, this survey remarks the necessity of having multi-modal datasets. As far as we know, an attempt to define an interoperable, multimodal repository of depression-related data does not actually exist.

3   On the Data Collection Procedure

To provide a method of data gathering able to be replicable and to guarantee a clean procedure of acquisition, a clinical acquisition data protocol has been defined in ANDROIDS. Such a protocol has been defined with the collaboration of clinical psychologists and based on the experience of previous research projects as Mental health monitoring through interactive conversations (MEN-HIR)[2] and Empathic, Expressive, Advanced, Virtual Coach to Improve Independent Healthy-Life-Years of the Elderly (EMPHATIC)[3].

The experience exposed in open and publicly available datasets—as the ones reported in Subsect. 2.2 has also been taken into account.

To this aim, several documents have been developed:

- an informed consensus for the patient of the sensitive data processing;
- an acquisition protocol, taking care of ethical issues and dealing with privacy according to current laws and regulations;
- informative summary to explain the aim of the experiment to the patient in a clear and concise way;
- a summary of the clinical history of the patient;
- a cover letter for the patients.

For each subject, the acquisition consists of some tasks to perform, involving writing and speaking tasks. The overall process is depicted in Fig. 1. Data gathering activities have been supported by skilled people who are in charge to psychologically support the subjects as well as technically operate with the acquisition devices and organize collected data.

After presenting the overall process and thanking the subject for his/her time (Introduction), the supporting personnel reads and explain the privacy preserving procedure, informing the subject about the data treatment and procedures (Informed Consensus Acquisition).

After getting the consensus to proceed, four different tasks are conducted:

---

[2] https://menhir-project.eu/.
[3] http://www.empathic-project.eu/.

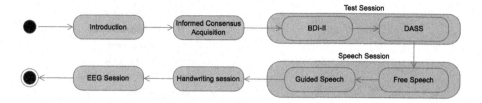

Fig. 1. The acquisition process

- the **Test Session**, where the BDI-II and DASS-21 questionnaires are submitted to the subject;
- the **Speech Session**, where the subject is invited to have both a **Free Speech**—also called *Diary* where he/she talks about his/her day or thoughts—and a **Guided Speech**—also called *Tale*, where the subject is invited to read the "The North Wind and the Sun" tale by Aesop. The tale is a standard phonetically balanced short folk tale (about six sentences all together), frequently used in phoniatric practices;
- the **Handwriting Session**, where the subject is asked to make some writing exercises using an INTUOS WACOM series 4 digital tablet to collect data as pressure, ductus, total time spent, occupied space by the strokes, and strokes inclination. Further details about this points are in [20];
- the **EEG session**, where the subject interacts with a software agent showing him/her some images defined with the intent to provoke emotional reactions and to record EEG signals.

At the end of these phases, the following data are gathered: (1) response to BDI-II and DASS-21 questionnaires—both of 21 questions—, (2) video and audio from of the speech, (3) handwriting traces and (4) EEG signals. It is valuable to remark that subjects can give their consensus to acquire personal information also selectively, i.e., they may decide to allow the usage of audio and handwriting but not video, as usually happened, due to the critical role of taking pictures of the subject's face.

4   The Catalogue Architecture

Figure 2 reports the conceptual model of D3B, expressed in the form of a relational database.

In the schema, four main tables are defined:

- **Patient**, which contains anonymized personal data (age, gender, etc.);
- **Handwritten**, which contains data obtained from the session in which the subject makes various exercises using writing;
- **EEG**, which contains clinical data regarding the subject's electroencephalogram;
- **Speech**, which contains data obtained from the sessions while the subject talks with the psychological specialist;

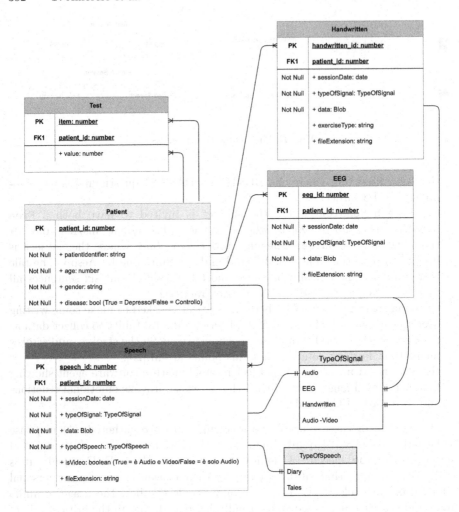

Fig. 2. The D3B schema

- **Test**, which contains the results for each question of both the BDI-II and DASS-21 questionnaires.

For what regards Data Base Management System (DBMS) choice, traditional Relational Data Base Management Systems (RDBMS) have been used since the 1970s and can be considered a mature technology for storing data, storage problems in web-oriented systems have pushed the limits of relational databases, forcing researchers and companies to use non-relational forms of user data storage.

Such limitations start with the increase in the storage capacity of any computational node; this means adding more disk space under the constraints of the underlying hardware. Once a node reaches its storage limit, there is no alternative but to distribute the data among several nodes. Traditionally, RDBMSs have not been designed to be easily deployed, as a result, more and more companies have decided to use Not Only SQL (NoSQL) databases to store such data. Non-relational databases support the handling of structured, unstructured, and semi-structured data to provide greater flexibility. They are characterized by more flexible schemas, which allow the management of heterogeneous data. Additionally, these databases generally avoid data storage-level joins, as these are often expensive, leaving this to each application.

The implementation of D3B is based on the well-known MongoDB, characterized by being: open source, multi-platform, scalable over a network (with the possibility to set automatically synchronized data replicas), supported by a large community of developers (who guaranteed the stability and the advancements of the products), and highly integrable with the most widespread programming languages (for defining an Application Program Interface (API) to support the extension the extensibility and usage of D3B). The storage of large data (files larger than 16 MB) is possible by using `GridFS`.

In the following, both a sample of the JavaScript Object Notation (JSON) file to describe data and a sample of the code needed to upload such data D3B are reported: their full download is possible at https://github.com/stefanomarrone/ d3b. Listing 1.1 reports an excerpt of the JSON file (with dummy data) while Listing 1.2 reports the Python code, interfacing with D3B by means of the `pyMongo` library, and solving a simple query.

Listing 1.1. Exceprt of sample data

```
[
{"patientIdentifier": "P1", "age": "37", "gender": "Female",
    "disease": "False", "handwrittenList": ["P1_hw_a.svc", "
    P1_hw_b.svc"], "speechList": [{"kind":"diary","nature":"
    audio","fname":"P1_diary.wav"}, {"kind":"tale","nature":"
    audio","fname":"P1_tale.wav"}, {"kind":"tale","nature":"
    video","fname":"P1_video.mp4"}], "eegList": ["P1_eeg.edf
    "]}
...
]
```

Listing 1.2. Query for extracting audios of male and healthy patients

```
#!/usr/bin/python3
import pymongo
import gridfs

client=pymongo.MongoClient('mongodb://127.0.0.1:27017/')
db=client.androids
fs=gridfs.GridFS(db)
query = db.patient.find({"disease":"False", "gender":"Male"})
for result in list(query):
    p_id = result["_id"]
```

```
q = db.fs.files.find({"patient_id":p_id, "kind":"diary", "
    nature":"audio"})
for x in q:
  name = x["filename"]
  outputdata = fs.get_last_version(name).read()
  output = open('out_' + name, "wb")
  output.write(outputdata)
  output.close()
```

5   Addressing Privacy and Openness

One of the biggest challenges in setting up D3B is constituted by defining an architecture able to guarantee interoperability and privacy. Since D3B is oriented to the research, openness toward third-party applications is a mandatory requirement. According to this requirement, the architecture must be flexible, becoming in certain points a development framework rather than a simple toolset.

The pillars of this architecture are: the usage of approved code to build privacy-preserving tools; the presence of a federation of D3B instances that can share data for replication purposes; the possibility to use Fully Homomorphic Encryption (FHE) for experimenting applications. Figure 3 depicts a proposal for a privacy/interoperability-oriented architecture. Three participants operate in this architecture:

- *Instance*: that is the D3B instance that is the subject of this analysis.
- *Federation Participants*: that are other D3B instances sharing/replicating data with *instance*.
- *Researcher*: any person/organization that is intended to train/test ML applications on the data present in one or more D3B instances.

Such participants work with tools that are organized by the following layers:

- *Developers' tools*: is the set of tools and APIs that can be used to extend the architecture:
  - *D3B Schema*, that is the MongoDB schema on which instances are built.
  - *Query Builder*: is an API used to define queries on D3B's instances. Query Builder also provides the software primitives for interfacing with the GridFS subsystem of MongoDB to extract multimedia files from D3B;
  - *Feature Extractor*: is an API by which data can be used to first preprocessing tasks;
  - *De-Anonymizer*: is an internal tool used to check privacy preservation;
  - *FHE library*: by which data encryption can be accomplished.
- *Privacy Layer*: used to decouple users from raw data, to ensure data privacy. It consists of:
  - *Concrete Query*, extracting *Raw Data* from the instance(s);
  - *Preprocessing Tool*, whose aim is to extract meaningful features from stored data refining raw data in *Refined Datasets*.

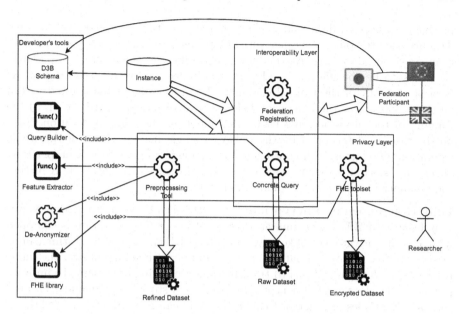

Fig. 3. The D3B privacy/interoperability architecture

- *FHE Toolset*: able to encrypt data according to the FHE library, generating *Encrypted Dataset*.
- *Interoperability Layer*: allowing different instances to work jointly by sharing and replicating data. It is mainly constituted by the Concrete Query and the *Federation Registration* tool. Regarding this last tool, it has the objective to establish replication mechanism parameters and to set up authorization policies among federated partners.

Pre-defined Query Templates: queries may be built in this approach only by using the Query Builder library, which restricts the possibility to read data only to non-sensitive information.

Anonymization: according to the objective to build an open ecosystem of smart tools for the construction of CDSS, preprocessing tools are prime citizens in such a model. In fact, the quality of ML approaches is heavily affected by the choice of the features. Hence, the user must be allowed to share—in a privacy-safe manner—his/her preprocessing and feature extraction tool. To ensure privacy, both a Feature Extractor API, guaranteeing the access to the data, and a De-anonymizer tool are provided in the Developer' toolkit.

The rationale behind the presence of the De-anonmyizer is to validate a preprocessing tool against possible malicious code that steals personal data or code that fails in preserving the proper security level of the data. This step works as follows: 1) the user prepare a preprocessing tool according to the APIs in the Developer's tools; 2) the preprocessing tools is run over (a part of) the dataset producing processed data that are not shared with the researcher, yet; 3) such data are used to train a classifier with the purpose to extract full personal data from processed data [21]. At this point, two different behaviours are possible, according to he specific policy adopred by the federation: a) according to the level of accuracy of the trained classifier, the processing tool is allowed to run on those portions of the federation below a pr-determined security level; b) the running of the pre-processing tool is forbidden in the whole federation. Such possbilities are determined by the policy of single instances and of the whole federation. Of course, such controls are not enough to guarantee a proper level of security, since a malicious code can send data across the Internet. A further code scanner is required as an additional stage.

Fully Homomorphic Encryption: the mechanism to set up to guarantee privacy by using FHE can be summarized as follows. Each federation is equipped with a public/private pair of keys by which the FHE encryption algorithm can be used to encrypt the owned data. Encrypted data can then be sent over the Internet to research organizations to train privacy-preserving classifiers. To improve performances, data can be encrypted once and kept stored in plain and encrypted versions. Examples of usage of FHE in this field can be retrieved at [10,11].

Interoperability: a crucial point is constituted by the fact that the different instances may also have different privacy preserving policies: some instances freely share their data with outer organizations, others don't. Some instances may also adopt a third solution, allowing third-party data usage but not data reading: in this case, external users/applications can process data—e.g., extracting statistical information—and return processed information without revealing original data details. The proposed architecture, hence, guarantees a privacy-preserving shareability of the data, which is the first step toward a full interoperability of instance. Other bricks to the interoperability is consituted by the presence of available common tools that allow an external user to run queries across a federation of instances. A key technology that will be used to enable this crucial feature is the MongoDB Federated Query API.

Use Cases: here, the architecture is presented at the conceptual level. While some attempts have been made in previous research in exploring some specific aspects, the construction of such architecture is ongoing while some preliminary results, made on the base of applicable data, are still present. In the following, an experience on the smart classification of the depression by analysing non-verbal features is described as a valid use case of the presented architecture.

In [34], the certain changes in speech quality that could indicate alterations due to the presence of depressive states were identified, through the analysis of the most relevant acoustic features. These were estimated by speeches of people. In detail, a narrative speech where daily activities of subjects (like a diary) were described. The considered features are:

- Jitter: the cycle-to-cycle changes of fundamental frequency are evaluated from this parameter. Jitter constitutes an estimation of the oscillating pattern of the vocal folds;

- Mel-frequency cepstrum coefficients (MFCC): the functionality of the vocal tract independently of the vocal folds is analysed estimating MFCC.
- Derivatives of cepstral coefficients: the dynamic behaviour of the speech signal is investigated evaluating these coefficients; and
- Spectral Centroid: the alterations of the signal frequency over time are analysed using the spectral centroid.

PRAAT[4], one of the most widespread tools in speech processing, was used to estimate jitter. PRAAT is an open-source software suite, developed at the University of Amsterdam, able to offer the opportunity to record mono and stereo sounds and to edit and analyse sounds with regard to pitch, intensity, formants or duration. MFCC, their derivated and spectral centroid were, instead, estimated by using Matlab, version R2020a through the function *audioFeatureExtractor*.

The accuracy of the approach to discriminate depressed and healthy people was evaluated through an appropriate experimental phase. Waikato Environment for Knowledge Analysis (WEKA) [14], version 3.8.4, was used to perform all tests. This constitutes one of the commonly used tools for ML classification, chosen for its versatility, efficiency and reliability in data mining studies. The accuracy, specificity, sensitivity, F1-score, precision and Receiver Operating Characteristic (ROC) area were calculated to estimate the performance of several ML approaches, applying a 10-fold cross validation. Table 1 shows the different results obtained using different classifiers with respect to the considered metrics.

Table 1. Results analyses to disguish depressed and not depressed subjects achieved by our approach and several ML techniques.

ML classifier	Accuracy (%)	Sensitivity (%)	Specificity (%)	Precision (%)	F1-score (%)	AUC
Our approach	**85.23**	**86.21**	**83.87**	**88.24**	**87.21**	0.850
Random Forest	77.18	85.06	66.13	77.89	81.32	**0.904**
C4.5	73.15	75.86	69.35	77.65	76.74	0.752
BayesNet	75.17	75.86	74.19	80.49	78.11	0.783
Ibk	77.85	75.86	80.65	84.62	80.00	0.782
OneR	64.43	74.71	50.00	67.71	71.04	0.624

6 Conclusion and Future Works

This paper launches the D3B initiatives, matured inside the ANDROIDS project, for the creation of an open collection and sharing system for depressive-related data. The main advantages in adopting the D3B schema and architecture are to guarantee at the same time a good interoperability and openness level, as well as assuring the privacy of data. D3B considers the possibility to federate different repository all across the world to allow research organizations to access to a huge platform of data. Up to this moment, the data base (DB) schema is available on an open repository[5] while at its initial stage: as the architecture will

---

[4] https://www.fon.hum.uva.nl/praat/.
[5] https://github.com/stefanomarrone/d3b..

be further prototyped, this repository aims to become its cornerstone. Future works will investigate on extending the usage of this DB for the construction of a multicultural and multi-language federation to allow complex analyses, able also to learn important lessons on the diagnosis of depression on international data. The role and the building mechanisms of De-anonymizer will also be explored to define a concrete framework for the definition and the sharing of preprocessing experiences. Of course, deep learning techniques will be explored in exploiting the data that will populate D3B instances.

Acknowledgement. The research leading to these results has received funding from the EU H2020 research and innovation program under grant agreement N. 769872 (EMPATHIC) and N. 823907 (MENHIR), the project SIROBOTICS that received funding from Italian MIUR, PNR 2015–2020, D.D. 1735, 13/07/2017, and the project ANDROIDS funded by the program V: ALERE 2019 Universitá della Campania "Luigi Vanvitelli", D.R. 906 del 4/10/2019, prot. n. 157264, 17/10/2019.

The work of Laura Verde is granted by the "Predictive Maintenance Multidominio (Multidomain predictive maintenance)" project, PON "Ricerca e Innovazione" 2014–2020, Asse IV "Istruzione e ricerca per il recupero"-Azione IV.4-"Dottorati e contratti di ricerca su tematiche dell'innovazione" programme CUP: B61B21005470007.

References

1. de Aguiar Neto, F.S., Rosa, J.L.G.: Depression biomarkers using non-invasive EEG: a review. Neurosci. Biobehav. Rev. **105**, 83–93 (2019)
2. Alghowinem, S., et al.: Multimodal depression detection: fusion analysis of paralinguistic, head pose and eye gaze behaviors. IEEE Trans. Affect. Comput. **9**(4), 478–490 (2018). https://doi.org/10.1109/TAFFC.2016.2634527
3. Alghowinem, S., Goecke, R., Wagner, M., Parkerx, G., Breakspear, M.: Head pose and movement analysis as an indicator of depression. In: 2013 Humaine Association Conference on Affective Computing and Intelligent Interaction, pp. 283–288. IEEE (2013)
4. Aloshban, N., Esposito, A., Vinciarelli, A.: Language or paralanguage, this is the problem: comparing depressed and non-depressed speakers through the analysis of gated multimodal units. In: Proceedings of the Annual Conference of the International Speech Communication Association, INTERSPEECH, vol. 2, pp. 751–755 (2021). https://doi.org/10.21437/Interspeech.2021-928
5. American Psychiatric Association: Diagnostic and statistical manual of mental disorders: DSM-5 (2013)
6. Anderson, I., et al.: State-dependent alteration in face emotion recognition in depression. Br. J. Psychiatry **198**(4), 302–308 (2011). https://doi.org/10.1192/bjp.bp.110.078139
7. Beck, A.T., Steer, R.A., Brown, G.K.: Beck Depression Inventory (BDI-II), vol. 10. Pearson (1996)
8. Bottesi, G., Ghisi, M., Altoè, G., Conforti, E., Melli, G., Sica, C.: The Italian version of the depression anxiety stress scales-21: factor structure and psychometric properties on community and clinical samples. Compr. Psychiatry **60**, 170–181 (2015)

9. Collaborators, G.: Global, regional, and national incidence, prevalence, and years lived with disability for 354 diseases and injuries for 195 countries and territories, 1990–2017: a systematic analysis for the global burden of disease study 2017 (2018)

10. Dias, M., Abad, A., Trancoso, I.: Exploring hashing and cryptonet based approaches for privacy-preserving speech emotion recognition, vol. 2018-April, pp. 2057–2061 (2018). https://doi.org/10.1109/ICASSP.2018.8461451

11. Dowlin, N., Gilad-Bachrach, R., Laine, K., Lauter, K., Naehrig, M., Wernsing, J.: CryptoNets: applying neural networks to encrypted data with high throughput and accuracy, vol. 1, pp. 342–351 (2016)

12. Garcia-Ceja, E., et al.: Depresjon: a motor activity database of depression episodes in unipolar and bipolar patients, pp. 472–477 (2018)

13. Garcia-Ceja, E., Riegler, M., Nordgreen, T., Jakobsen, P., Oedegaard, K., Tørresen, J.: Mental health monitoring with multimodal sensing and machine learning: a survey. Pervasive Mob. Comput. **51**, 1–26 (2018). https://doi.org/10.1016/j.pmcj.2018.09.003

14. Garner, S.R., et al.: Weka: the Waikato environment for knowledge analysis. In: Proceedings of the New Zealand Computer Science Research Students Conference, vol. 1995, pp. 57–64 (1995)

15. Gundersen, O.: Standing on the feet of giants - reproducibility in AI. AI Mag. **40**(4), 9–23 (2019). https://doi.org/10.1609/aimag.v40i4.5185

16. Gundersen, O., Kjensmo, S.: State of the art: reproducibility in artificial intelligence, pp. 1644–1651 (2018)

17. Balsters, M.J.H., Krahmer, E.J., Swerts, M.G.J., Vingerhoets, A.J.J.M.: Verbal and nonverbal correlates for depression: a review. Curr. Psychiatry Rev. **8**(3), 227–234 (2012)

18. Joshi, J., Goecke, R., Parker, G., Breakspear, M.: Can body expressions contribute to automatic depression analysis? In: 2013 10th IEEE International Conference on Automatic Face and Gesture Recognition (FG), pp. 1–7. IEEE (2013)

19. Khaleghi, B., Khamis, A., Karray, F., Razavi, S.: Multisensor data fusion: a review of the state-of-the-art. Inf. Fusion **14**(1), 28–44 (2013). https://doi.org/10.1016/j.inffus.2011.08.001

20. Likforman-Sulem, L., Esposito, A., Faundez-Zanuy, M., Clémençon, S., Cordasco, G.: EMOTHAW: a novel database for emotional state recognition from handwriting and drawing. IEEE Trans. Hum.-Mach. Syst. **47**(2), 273–284 (2017)

21. Liu, R.X., Chen, H., Guo, R.Y., Zhao, D., Liang, W.J., Li, C.P.: Survey on privacy attacks and defenses in machine learning. Ruan Jian Xue Bao/J. Softw. **31**(3), 866–892 (2020). https://doi.org/10.13328/j.cnki.jos.005904

22. Maghraby, A., Ali, H.: Modern standard Arabic mood changing and depression dataset. Data Brief **41**, 107999 (2022). https://doi.org/10.1016/j.dib.2022.107999

23. Maxhuni, A., Muñoz Meléndez, A., Osmani, V., Perez, H., Mayora, O., Morales, E.: Classification of bipolar disorder episodes based on analysis of voice and motor activity of patients. Pervasive Mob. Comput. **31**, 50–66 (2016). https://doi.org/10.1016/j.pmcj.2016.01.008

24. Mundt, J.C., Vogel, A.P., Feltner, D.E., Lenderking, W.R.: Vocal acoustic biomarkers of depression severity and treatment response. Biol. Psychiat. **72**(7), 580–587 (2012)

25. Péron, J., et al.: Major depressive disorder skews the recognition of emotional prosody. Prog. Neuro-Psychopharmacol. Biol. Psychiatry **35**(4), 987–996 (2011). https://doi.org/10.1016/j.pnpbp.2011.01.019

26. Phillips, M., Drevets, W., Rauch, S., Lane, R.: Neurobiology of emotion perception I: the neural basis of normal emotion perception. Biol. Psychiat. **54**(5), 504–514 (2003). https://doi.org/10.1016/S0006-3223(03)00168-9

27. Poria, S., Mondal, A., Mukhopadhyay, P.: Evaluation of the intricacies of emotional facial expression of psychiatric patients using computational models. In: Mandal, M.K., Awasthi, A. (eds.) Understanding Facial Expressions in Communication, pp. 199–226. Springer, New Delhi (2015). https://doi.org/10.1007/978-81-322-1934-7_10

28. Qiu, R., Kodali, V., Homer, M., Heath, A., Wu, Z., Jia, Y.: Predictive modeling of depression with a large claim dataset, pp. 1589–1595 (2019). https://doi.org/10.1109/BIBM47256.2019.8982975

29. Savinov, V., Sapunov, V., Shusharina, N., Botman, S., Kamyshov, G., Tynterova, A.: EEG-based depression classification using harmonized datasets, pp. 93–95 (2021). https://doi.org/10.1109/CNN53494.2021.9580293

30. Scherer, S., et al.: Automatic behavior descriptors for psychological disorder analysis. In: 2013 10th IEEE International Conference on Automatic Face and Gesture Recognition (FG), pp. 1–8. IEEE (2013)

31. Schneider, D., et al.: Empathic behavioral and physiological responses to dynamic stimuli in depression. Psychiatry Res. **200**(2–3), 294–305 (2012). https://doi.org/10.1016/j.psychres.2012.03.054

32. Scibelli, F., et al.: Depression speaks: automatic discrimination between depressed and non-depressed speakers based on nonverbal speech features, vol. 2018-April, pp. 6842–6846 (2018). https://doi.org/10.1109/ICASSP.2018.8461858

33. Van Der Aalst, W., Weijters, T., Maruster, L.: Workflow mining: discovering process models from event logs. IEEE Trans. Knowl. Data Eng. **16**(9), 1128–1142 (2004). https://doi.org/10.1109/TKDE.2004.47

34. Verde, L., et al.: A lightweight machine learning approach to detect depression from speech analysis. In: Proceedings of The 33rd IEEE International Conference on Tools with Artificial Intelligence (ICTAI 2021) (2021)

35. Zhang, L., Driscol, J., Chen, X., Ghomi, R.: Evaluating acoustic and linguistic features of detecting depression sub-challenge dataset, pp. 47–53 (2019). https://doi.org/10.1145/3347320.3357693

Explainable Deep Learning Classification of Respiratory Sound for Telemedicine Applications

Michele Lo Giudice[1,2]([⊠]), Nadia Mammone[3], Cosimo Ieracitano[3],
Umberto Aguglia[2,4], Danilo Mandic[5], and Francesco Carlo Morabito[3]

[1] DIIES Department, University "Mediterranea" of Reggio Calabria,
89100 Reggio Calabria, Italy
michele.logiudice@unirc.it

[2] Department of Science Medical and Surgery, University of Catanzaro,
88100 Catanzaro, Italy

[3] DICEAM Department, University "Mediterranea" of Reggio Calabria,
89100 Reggio Calabria, Italy
{nadia.mammone,cosimo.ieracitano,morabito}@unirc.it

[4] Regional Epilepsy Center, Great Metropolitan Hospital
"Bianchi-Melacrino-Morelli" of Reggio Calabria,
Reggio Calabria, Italy
u.aguglia@unicz.it

[5] Department of Electrical and Electronic Engineering, Imperial College London,
SW7 2AZ London, UK
d.mandic@imperial.ac.uk

Abstract. The recent pandemic crisis combined with the explosive growth of Artificial Intelligence (AI) algorithms has highlighted the potential benefits of telemedicine for decentralised, accurate and automated clinical diagnoses. One of the most popular and essential diagnoses is the auscultation; it is non-invasive, real-time and very informative diagnoses for knowing the state of the respiratory system. To implement a possible automated auscultation analysis, the decision-making explanation of complex models (such as Deep Learning models) is crucial for trusted application in the clinical domain. In this context, we will analyse the behaviour of a Convolutional Neural Network (CNN) in classifying the largest publicly available database of respiratory sounds, originally compiled to support the scientific challenge organized at Int. Conf. on Biomedical Health Informatics (ICBHI17). It contains respiratory sounds (recorded with auscultation) of normal respiratory cycles, crackles, wheezes and both. To capture the phonetically important features of breath sounds, the Mel-Frequency Cepstrum (MFC) for short-term power spectrum representation was applied. The MFC allowed us to identify latent features without losing the temporal information so that we could easily identify the correspondence of the features to the starting sound. The MFCs were used as input to the proposed CNN who was able to classify the four above-mentioned respiratory classes with an accuracy of 72.8%. Despite interesting results, the main focus of the present study was to investigate how the CNN achieved this classification. The explainable Artificial Intelligence (xAI) technique of Gradient-weighted Class

M. Mahmud et al. (Eds.): AII 2022, CCIS 1724, pp. 391–403, 2022.
https://doi.org/10.1007/978-3-031-24801-6_28

Activation Mapping (Grad-CAM) was applied. xAI made it possible to visually identify the most relevant areas, especially for the recognition of abnormal sounds, which is crucial for inspecting the correct learning of the CNN.

Keywords: Mel-frequency cepstrum · Deep learning · Convolutional neural network · Explainable artificial intelligence · Grad-CAM · Respiratory sound · Telemedicine

1   Introduction

Auscultation of the lungs by means of the stethoscope is listening to the sound generated by the flow of air inside the lungs [1]; it is one of the most frequent methods applied for diagnosis, to acoustically explore the state of the respiratory system in real-time. It is non-invasive, easy to use and readily available in any clinical setting [2,3]. When the airflow in the lungs is normal, it produces a characteristic sound, which is markedly different when it encounters something that obstructs it, often due to infection or some other problem [3].

Wheezes and crackles are the two lung sound abnormalities that are common during lung infections. Wheeze is caused by airway obstruction that generates a continuous, high-pitched whistling sound [4] and it is usually associated at patients suffering from asthma and chronic obstructive pulmonary disease (i.e. COPD). Crackles, on the other hand, are explosive and discontinuous sounds present during the inspiration and expiration [5] caused by conditions associated to obstructive airways disease and interstitial lung disease.

The automatic detection of pulmonary sound abnormalities has attracted the interest of several researchers who have developed efficient classification pipelines. Acharya et al. [6] developed a hybrid CNN-RNN model to perform a four-class classification of breathing sounds based on the International Conference on Biomedical and Health Informatics (ICBHI17) also used in this article and they obtained score of 66.31% on classification and of 71.81% when the model was re-trained with patient specific data. They also reduced the memory footprint of the networks without significant loss of performance.

Bardou et al. [7] proposed an approach for the classification of lung sounds using CNNs and compared it with three approaches, two handcrafted-features-based and an approach based on the design of CNN. They used MFC statistics extracted from signals and local binary patterns from spectrograms, founding that CNNs outperformed feature-based approaches. They reached an accuracy greater than 90% but using a different dataset from our. Kim et al. [8] developed a CNN for respiratory sound classification by combining the pre-trained image feature extractor. The CNN detected abnormal sounds with an accuracy of 86% on an owner dataset, recorded in a clinical environment.

This paper performs a similar classification but aims to explore the potential of deep learning (DL) applied to the medical environment, encouraging its use by approaching the interpretability of the results. Here we explore the behaviour of a CNN when classifying four types of respiratory sounds (i.e. normals, crackles, wheezes and both) on the ICBHI17 database and then provides a visual explanation of the model by applying explainability techniques, which is useful for understanding the stored features and building reliable diagnostic models for medicine and telemedicine applications. In addition, explainability satisfies the clinicians' requirement for an adequate explanation of the results provided.

The main contribution of this paper can be summarised as follows:

- Classification of normal respiratory cycles, with crackles, wheezes and both by means of four-way classification with a rate of accuracy of 72.8%
- Data-oriented interpretation of EEG signal characteristics for validating classification by visual explanation of CNN performance.

2   Materials and Methods

The largest publicly available database of respiratory sounds, the ICBHI17, was used for our study [9]. The dataset consists of 5.5 h of sound recordings containing 6898 respiratory cycles, of which 1864 contain crackles, 886 contain wheezes, and 506 contain both crackles and wheezes. Whole dataset contain 920 annotated audio samples from 126 subjects [9]. The dataset is very reliable as it reproduces the most common clinical setting, i.e. different recording devices (AKG C417L Microphone, 3M Littmann Classic II SE Stethoscope, 3M Litmmann 3200 Electronic Stethoscope and WelchAllyn Meditron Master Elite Electronic Stethoscope) and background noise that could make the classification more challenging. More details on the dataset and the possibility of downloading it in [9].

2.1   Pre-processing of Pulmonary Sounds

The dataset contains indications of respiratory cycles, lasting from less than one second to more than 10 s. We divided them into fixed windows of 5 s each. The longer breaths were divided into several audio files, instead in the shorter breaths was added padding (silence). To extract the features and use the two-dimensional input data, more manageable by our CNN, we used the Mel Frequency Cepstral (MFC) [10] using the *librosa* [11] Python library. We used 50 MFC Coefficient (MFCC) in order to obtain greater detail, at the cost of greater complexity, which in any case was manageable with the hardware architecture used. To increase the diversity of the training set and allow the network to improve generalization, data augmentation was applied to the dataset by applying random (but realistic) transformations, such as translation and time dilation and reduction of the sounds.

2.2   Convolutional Neural Network

Deep Learning or Deep Neural Networks (DNN) are powerful tools with increasing application due to their capabilities to successfully learn complex patterns from huge amounts of data. CNN is one of the most popular, as it adapts to different data structures with classification results that are often far superior to classical recognition methods and so it will be increasingly used. The advantage of CNNs over ANNs is the possibility to learn directly from raw data (such as biological signals and images), without drastically increasing the number of parameters due to the introduction of affine invariance features with three main properties [12]:

- Local receptive fields
- Shared weights (parameter sharing)
- Spatial subsampling

The local receptive field induces advantages in the recognition of visual patterns in input portions. It is a defined segmented area to which a neuron within a convolutional layer is exposed during the convolution process. Filter dimension defines the size of the receptive field.

Each filter contains a shared weight between all filters used in the same plane. The advantage of this is that we keep the same feature detector used in one part of the input data in other sections of the input data [13].

The CNN is made up of two major building blocks: a feature extractor and an ANN block [14]. The feature extractor block characterises the CNN and leads to the advantages described above as it automatically extracts features from the raw signal in the convolution, activation and pooling layers.

The convolution layer performs the convolution step expressed as:

$$Y_j = \sum X_i * K_j + B_j \tag{1}$$

The output Y_j is a feature map of every K_j filter convolved ($*$) with a local region of X_i (called receptive field) and the bias B_j added.

The dimension of Y_j is derived from padding parameter, size, stride and numer of the filters. Every filter shifts across the input with a specific step size (sharing the same weights), evaluating feature maps C (with C = number of filters). The convolution layer is succeeded by an activation layer, a non-linear transfer function that might be sigmoid, hyperbolic tangent or rectified linear units (ReLu). Recent studies show that ReLu is better in terms of generalisation and learning time for CNN [15, 16]. The pooling level (maximum or average) subsamples the extracted feature maps. The filter scans the feature map of the input and calculates the maximum or average of each sub-region analysed, returning a map of reduced size.

The ANN block is a fully connected neural network widely applied in many classifiers (e.g. MLP). The task of this block is to perform the classification by exploiting previously learnt features. The output of ANN performs the discrimination task.

2.3   Proposed CNN Architecture

We used a customized CNN architecture that includes 5 convolutional layers (+ReLu activation function), 4 max pooling layers, 3 fully connected layers and a softmax layer which performs the classification tasks (four ways: normal, crackles, wheezes or both). The sizing of the network (number of levels, number of filters, size of filters, etc.) was selected empirically after various experimental tests using an iterative approach aimed at optimizing network performance for the right balance of performance and complexity. It is designed to accept the fixed sizes matrix of c × s × f (where c = 50, with c number of MFCC; s = 245, with s number of audio samples; f = 1, with f number of axes added in order to make the matrix presentable as an image. The first convolutional layer (conv2d) has 256 learnable filters, each sized 5 × 5. Each filter involves each input of the MFC representation. It also has "SAME" padding and stride of 2 × 2. Layer outputs generate feature maps of half the size for the first and second axes for each filter (i.e. 25 × 123 × 256). Conv2d is followed firstly by the ReLu, applied to the activations of a prior layer, the Batch Normalization layer (batch_normalization) to standardize the inputs of the next level of the network, and then by the max pooling layer (max_pooling2d) which reduces the features maps size to 13 × 62 × 256 by using 2 × 2 filters with stride s = 1 × 1. The convolutional layer (conv2d_1) has 256 learnable filters sized 5 × 5 with strides 1 × 1. Furthermore, conv2d_1 is followed firstly by the ReLu and then by the max pooling layer (max_pooling2d_1) which reduces the features maps size to 7 × 31 × 256 by using 2 × 2 filters with stride s = 1 × 1. Next, conv2d_2 also has 256 learnable filters sized 5 × 5 with stride 1 × 1, followed firstly by the ReLu and then by the max pooling layer (max_pooling2d_2). Next conv2d_3 with 512 learnable filters sized 3 × 3 with stride 1 × 1 and conv2d_4 with 1024 learnable filters sized 3 × 3 with stride 1 × 1 traced by the ReLu and then by the max pooling layer (max_pooling2d_3). These levels automatically mined the features that were most relevant. Details on the number of parameters used are given in Table 1. The automatically extracted features are flattened by the flatten layer (Flatten) and are used as an input of a densely-connected NN layer (Dense) layer with 2048 hidden neurons. It is beloved by a Dropout layer (of 0.5, to enhance generalization and prevent overfitting) continued by Dense1 containing 1024 hidden neurons this layer is also followed by the dropout layer for the same reasons explained before. The network ends with a softmax layer (Dense3) to estimate the class predictions in four-vay classification. The proposed CNN was made in Python 3.9.7 using Keras 2.8.0 with Tensorflow 2.8.0 backend and trained using the adaptive moment estimation (ADAM) optimizer with lr=0.0001, beta_1=0.9, beta_2=0.999 and decay=0.00 for 10 iterations and with a batch size of 107 until the categorical cross-entropy function converged.

2.4 Classification Metrics

To measure the four-way classification system performance, the following conventional classification metrics have been used:

$$Accuracy = \frac{TP + TN}{TP + TN + FP + FN} \qquad (2)$$

Table 1. Overall number of parameters for the proposed CNN architecture includes 5 convolutional layers (+ReLu), 4 max pooling layers, 3 fully connected layers, 2 dropout layer and a softmax layer. The softmax layer performs the classification tasks.

Layer name	Output Shape	Parameters
Input	$50 \times 245 \times 1$	
conv2d	$25 \times 123 \times 256$	6656
batch_normalization	$25 \times 123 \times 256$	1024
maxpooling2d	$13 \times 62 \times 256$	
conv2d$_1$	$13 \times 62 \times 256$	1638656
maxpooling2d$_1$	$7 \times 31 \times 256$	
conv2d$_2$	$7 \times 31 \times 256$	1638656
maxpooling2d$_2$	$4 \times 16 \times 256$	
conv2d$_3$	$4 \times 16 \times 512$	1180160
conv2d$_4$	$4 \times 16 \times 1024$	4719616
maxpooling2d$_3$	$2 \times 8 \times 1024$	
flatten	16384	
dense	2048	33556480
dropout	2048	
dense$_1$	1024	2098176
dropout$_1$	1024	
dense$_2$	512	524800
dense$_3$	4	2052
Total		*45.366.276*

$$Precision = \frac{TP}{TP + FP} \qquad (3)$$

$$Recall = \frac{TP}{TP + FN} \qquad (4)$$

$$F - measure = 2 \times \frac{PRECISION \times RECALL}{PRECISION + RECALL} \qquad (5)$$

where TP = True Positive, TN = True Negative, FP = False Positive, FN = False Negative. In this application, the k-fold cross validation approach (with k = 5 i.e. 5-fold validation) was applied so as to obtain 20% of the test for each trial. Specifically, CNN was trained iteratively using the entire dataset and omitting 20% of the dataset while balancing the 4-class proportion. Therefore, 5 models were trained. The classification statistics are reported in terms of mean value.

2.5   Grad-CAM for Visual Explanations

Gradient-weighted Class Activation Mapping (Grad-CAM) is a useful data processing technique used mainly in computer vision that employs a position map to detect an interval in a time series or a spatial region of an image that is significant for predictions. It applies complex transformations as gradients back-propagation like weights (grad-weights) [17] but provides intuitive output in order to explain the decisions of the network. Grad-CAM uses gradients from any ground truth, converging in the final convolutional layer to produce an approximated location map that highlights important regions in the image or time series to predict the concept [17]. For obtaining the class discriminative localization map Grad-CAM, given a class c (e.g., normal respiratory cycles, crackles, wheezes or both) let o^c is the score of c before the softmax, we will calculate o^c regarding R^n (with n number of features maps) feature maps of a convolutional layer, i.e. $\frac{\partial o^c}{\partial R^n}$. These back-flowing gradients are global-average-pooled to yield the neuron importance weights $\widehat{w}_n^c$:

$$\widehat{w}_n^c = \frac{1}{z} \sum_i \sum_j \frac{\partial o^c}{\partial R_{i,j}^n} \tag{6}$$

with z as the total amount of pixels in the features map and i, j identifying the pixels. So w_n^c expresses the "relevance" of the feature map R^n for a aim class c. Finally, a weighted map combination of the R^n features is performed followed by a ReLU, which sets all negative values to zero since we are only interested in features that have a positive influence on the class of interest, and we obtain:

$$\widehat{w}_n^c = ReLU(\sum_n \widehat{w}_n^c R^n) \tag{7}$$

where w_n^c are utilised as weights. The output is a rough heat map of the same size as the convolutional feature maps called a Grad-CAM or importance map that can be superimposed on the original input (i.e. the MFC of respiratory sound) to infer information about the relevance of the input regions [18]. In our case it allows us to derive information on how the relevance changes between the temporal regions of the blink (i.e. instant of crackles, wheezes).

3   Results

The ICBHI17 dataset contains 6898 respiratory cycles. It contain 1864 crackles, 886 wheezes, and 506 include both crackles and wheezes. The CNN classified the respiratory cycles with a good classification performance, reporting mean accuracy of 72.8% for the multiclass classification. Encouraging values of recall, precision and F-measure were observed and shown in Table 2. Figure 1 shows an example of the MFC representation of a normal respiratory cycle and the associated Grad-CAM of each convolutional level highlighting the parts of particular interest to the network in order to perform the classification; through visual explanation, instants of special interest can be easily associated.

Table 2. Normal vs crackles vs wheezes vs both respiratory sound mean classification performances (accuracy, precision, recall, F-measure) evaluated with 5-fold cross validation with the proposed CNN.

Normal vs crackles vs wheezes vs both			
Accuracy	Precision	Recall	F-measure
72.8%	72.9%	72.9%	71.9%

In the normal respiratory cycle, the yellow colored region is widespread and no time-limited characteristic is present that determines its classification. In fact, the normal respiratory cycle it has no discernible short-lived feature.

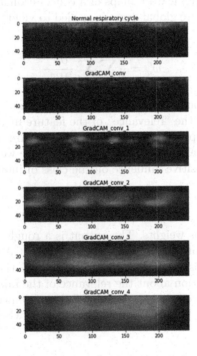

Fig. 1. MFC of a normal respiratory cycle at the top, below the relative Grad-CAM maps of the various levels of the proposed CNN architecture

Figure 2 shows an example of the MFC representation of a respiratory cycle with crackles and the associated Grad-CAM maps of each convolutional level highlighting the parts of particular interest too for the CNN in order to perform the classification;

In this case, the distinctive features are limited to small fractions of the respiratory cycle, in particular, two events were identified.

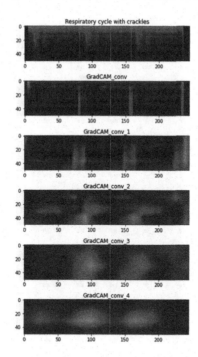

Fig. 2. MFC of a respiratory cycle with crackles at the top, below the relative Grad-CAM maps of the various levels of the proposed CNN architecture

Figure 3 shows an example of the MFC representation of respiratory cycle with wheezes and the associated Grad-CAM maps of each convolutional level;

As in the previous case, the features are time-limited but involve different intervals of MFC. Fig. 4 shows an example of the MFC representation of respiratory cycle with crackles and wheezes on the top and below the associated Grad-CAM of each convolutional level;

4   Discussions

The large amount of data collected was processed and classified until the latest times in the analog format through the listening capabilities of the qualified medical specialist, which allowed accurate classification after so many years of experience [19]. This carries disadvantages and limitations, in that recognition of adventitious lung sounds is possible by a number of physicians disproportionate to the overall population and hinders the rapidity of patient diagnosis.

Traditional auscultation does not allow widespread screening, especially when infections increase as in the Covid-19 pandemic, exposing clinicians to potential infection risks. Traditional diagnoses also suffer from a subjective interpretation gap that cannot be overcome, causing possible dissimilar interpretation of respiratory sounds by different medical professionals.

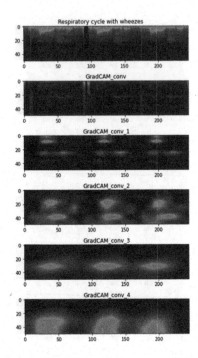

Fig. 3. MFC of a respiratory cycle with wheezes at the top, below the relative Grad-CAM maps of the various levels of the proposed CNN architecture

The development and diffusion of digital stethoscopes [20] can reduce the subjective gap as it is easier to preserve, compare and replay the sound recordered, for later physician comparison, patient follow-up, and for training artificial intelligence (AI) systems. AI systems can emulate narrow complex medical skills such as this one under consideration, until now assigned to the ear's sensitivity and the doctor's acute knowledge and experience.

To correctly classify a signal, a physician takes several years of career and intense work, which current and future studies certainly will not replace, but modelling unique models and reliable classification examples can provide valuable support in choice or difficult diagnoses [8].

In this paper, we developed a DL system capable of discriminating four classes of respiratory cycle sounds with good reliability. In detail, the classification was made possible by a DL algorithm (CNN) that receives as input MFC maps appropriately processed in order to emphasize the sound characteristics of different lung sounds.

The MFC transformation also made it easier to process the data from a CNN, as it converts an audio signal into a matrix of values that is easier for DL systems to understand. Feature extraction was thus data-driven and avoided the time-consuming task of best features for individual classes, which are often latent and therefore increase the difficulty of classification [21].

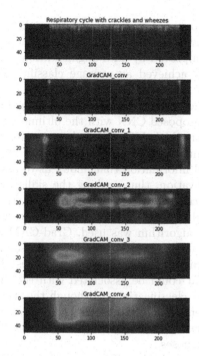

Fig. 4. MFC of a respiratory cycle with crackles at the top, below the relative Grad-CAM maps of the various levels of the proposed CNN architecture

In this work, we classified the four classes examined with good accuracy but the core of our study was to overcome the limitations of DL due to the lack of interpretability. Following the rationality in the choice of nonlinear transformations and the huge number of free parameters to quantify within the network is really very difficult. In the clinical setting, this represents the major limitation in entrusting complex tasks to AI systems, as it already happens in other domains since the validation of the classification would take place without valid tools useful for quantifying the resilience of the generated output, which would increase the confidence in using it compared to a black box.

Transparency in making a choice would generate an appropriate level of trust that will boost the acceptance of these technologies in such critical applications as the challenging classification of respiratory cycles currently relies only on the sensitivity of the human ear, which in recent studies [8], however, has found less sensitivity than complex CNN models. DL explainability would provide a clinician with the tools to detect fault in models and bias in data, validate predictions, improve models and, finally, gain new insights into problems. Solving this difficult problem will open the potential of AI routine visits, telemedicine, and its further evolutions [22].

The chosen dataset made classification as difficult as that of physicians in real-world settings because in adds to the difficulty of classifying respiratory sound alone, the overlapping of background noise makes understanding the correct features more challenging even for AI systems. The generalization ability of the network has been improved by data augmentation.

Our proposed CNN achieved an average classification accuracy of 72.8% which is an interesting result when compared with results in the literature. However, the core of the present study was to investigate the explicability and interpretability of the proposed CNN with the ultimate goal of exploring which portions of the MFC or which MFFC are the most relevant in the process of discriminating the normal respiratory cycle, crackles, wheezes and both, without losing the temporal information that allows us to associate the sound with the level of neural activation, thus probing the skills learned by the network during the training process. To this end, explainable Artificial Intelligence (xAI) techniques were applied. In particular, the Gradient-weighted Class Activation Mapping (Grad-CAM) algorithm was used. Grad-CAM allowed us to visually identify the most relevant MFC areas of respiratory sound that could be associated with the discriminant sound of the four classes. The results allowed us to identify patterns that could be associated with the different sounds and to motivate any borderline classifications. Although the study has limitations and margins for improvement, it aims to highlight how much these techniques can be used to improve decision-making, extract knowledge from past data and for future personalized diagnoses.

The future challenge, indeed, will be to analyze medical choices and make them employable for future prognoses, through the training of AI systems, which would get progressively better over time, overcoming the first limitation we also experienced, that is, the poor amount of data from where to learn. In the specific context early and automated diagnoses would increase prevention and thus people's health conditions, optimizing the work of physicians. The just-past pandemic due to Covid-19 has highlighted the necessity of a resilient health care system, which will become scalable through the emerging development of telemedicine. In fact, telemedicine is increasingly becoming a hot topic due to the horizon of possible development scenarios, which are optimistic when looking at the impressive development of IoT systems that can be used in eHealth. Artificial intelligence will play a major role, however, if it is reliable and transparent to provide a good level of reliability provided by explainability.

Acknowledgments. This work was supported in part by "iCARE" project (CUP J39J14001400007) - action 10.5.12 - funded within POR FESR FSE 2014/2020 of Calabria Region with the participation of European Community Resources of FESR and FSE, of Italy and of Calabria.

References

1. Bohadana, A., Izbicki, G., Kraman, S.S.: Fundamentals of lung auscultation. N. Engl. J. Med. **370**(8), 744–751 (2014)
2. Pasterkamp, H., Kraman, S.S., Wodicka, G.R.: Respiratory sounds: advances beyond the stethoscope. Am. J. Respir. Crit. Care Med. **156**(3), 974–987 (1997)

3. Roguin, A.: Rene theophile hyacinthe laënnec (1781–1826): the man behind the stethoscope. Clin. Med. Res. **4**(3), 230–235 (2006)
4. Meslier, N., Charbonneau, G., Racineux, J.: Wheezes. Eur. Respir. J. **8**(11), 1942–1948 (1995)
5. Piirila, P., Sovijarvi, A.: Crackles: recording, analysis and clinical significance. Eur. Respir. J. **8**(12), 2139–2148 (1995)
6. Acharya, J., Basu, A.: Deep neural network for respiratory sound classification in wearable devices enabled by patient specific model tuning. IEEE Trans. Biomed. Circuits Syst. **14**(3), 535–544 (2020)
7. Bardou, D., Zhang, K., Ahmad, S.M.: Lung sounds classification using convolutional neural networks. Artif. Intell. Med. **88**, 58–69 (2018)
8. Kim, Y., et al.: Respiratory sound classification for crackles, wheezes, and rhonchi in the clinical field using deep learning. Sci. Rep. **11**(1), 1–11 (2021)
9. Rocha, B.M., et al.: A respiratory sound database for the development of automated classification. In: Maglaveras, N., Chouvarda, I., de Carvalho, P. (eds.) Precision Medicine Powered by pHealth and Connected Health. IP, vol. 66, pp. 33–37. Springer, Singapore (2018). https://doi.org/10.1007/978-981-10-7419-6_6
10. Logan, B.: Mel frequency cepstral coefficients for music modeling. In: International Symposium on Music Information Retrieval. Citeseer (2000)
11. McFee, B., et al.: Librosa: audio and music signal analysis in python. In: Proceedings of the 14th Python in Science Conference, vol. 8, pp. 18–25. Citeseer (2015)
12. Alake, R.: Understanding parameter sharing (or weights replication) within convolutional neural networks. https://towardsdatascience.com/understanding-parameter-sharing-or-weights-replication-within-convolutional-neural-networks-cc26db7b645a. Accessed 14 July 2022
13. CS231n: Convolutional neural networks for visual recognition course website tab. https://cs231n.github.io/convolutional-networks/. Accessed 14 July 2022
14. Albawi, S., Mohammed, T.A., Al-Zawi, S.: Understanding of a convolutional neural network. In: 2017 International Conference on Engineering and Technology (ICET), pp. 1–6. IEEE (2017)
15. Zeiler, M.D., et al.: On rectified linear units for speech processing. In: 2013 IEEE International Conference on Acoustics, Speech and Signal Processing, pp. 3517–3521 (2013)
16. Krizhevsky, A., Sutskever, I., Hinton, G.E.: Imagenet classification with deep convolutional neural networks. Adv. Neural Inf. Process. Syst. **25**, 1097–1105 (2012)
17. Selvaraju, R.R., Cogswell, M., Das, A., Vedantam, R., Parikh, D., Batra, D.: Gradcam: visual explanations from deep networks via gradient-based localization. In: Proceedings of the IEEE International Conference on Computer Vision, pp. 618–626 (2017)
18. Morabito, F.C., Ieracitano, C., Mammone, N.: An explainable artificial intelligence approach to study MCI to AD conversion via HD-EEG processing. Clin. EEG Neurosci. 15500594211063662 (2021)
19. Sarkar, M., Madabhavi, I., Niranjan, N., Dogra, M.: Auscultation of the respiratory system. Ann. Thorac. Med. **10**(3), 158 (2015)
20. Swarup, S., Makaryus, A.N.: Digital stethoscope: technology update. Med. Devices (Auckland, NZ) **11**, 29 (2018)
21. LeCun, Y., Bengio, Y., Hinton, G.: Deep learning. Nature **521**(7553), 436–444 (2015)
22. Holzinger, A., Langs, G., Denk, H., Zatloukal, K., Müller, H.: Causability and explainability of artificial intelligence in medicine. Wiley Interdiscip. Rev. Data Min. Knowl. Discov. **9**(4), e1312 (2019)

Nonexclusive Classification of Household Appliances by Fuzzy Deep Neural Networks

Federico Succetti, Antonello Rosato, and Massimo Panella[✉]

Department of Information Engineering, Electronics and Telecommunications, University of Rome "La Sapienza", Via Eudossiana 18, 00184 Rome, Italy
{federico.succetti,antonello.rosato,massimo.panella}@uniroma1.it

Abstract. Fuzzy classification is a very useful tool for managing the uncertainty in a classification problem with non-mutually exclusive classes, whose values can fall into overlapping ranges. This situation is very common in real-life problems, where decisions are often made on the basis of inaccurate or noisy information and a flexible classification is preferred. In this paper, we propose a nonexclusive classification approach based on fuzzy logic to classify household appliances characterized by the time series associated with their power consumption. This issue is crucial for purposes related to user profiling, demand side management and cost optimization in the context of smart grids and green energy communities. To overcome the dependence on an expert for determining the logical rules of inference, we rely on the use of deep neural networks, as they have proved to be an extremely powerful tool in this kind of problems. The advantages and disadvantages present in fuzzy inference systems and deep neural networks almost completely disappear when both models are combined. In this regard, the paper proposes a randomization-based fuzzy deep neural network for the nonexclusive classification of household appliances. Randomization in deep neural networks allows a significant reduction in training times while often maintaining a high level of precision. This enables the adopted model with respect to time constraints causality of the observed time series. The performances obtained from the proposed model compare favorably with those obtained using two benchmark models for time series classification based on the well-known Long Short-Term Memory network.

Keywords: Household appliances · Power consumption · Nonexclusive time series classification · Fuzzy deep neural networks · Randomization-based models

1 Introduction

Classification is an important task in very different application areas as, for instance, sound event recognition [10], fault detection in industrial processes [3].

M. Mahmud et al. (Eds.): AII 2022, CCIS 1724, pp. 404–418, 2022.
https://doi.org/10.1007/978-3-031-24801-6_29

In an ideal classification problem the feature space should be separated well enough to identify the class to which a sample belongs without much effort. However, in many real-life cases some patterns belonging to different classes can have very similar characteristics. In practice, these samples reside in overlapping areas of the feature space, giving rise to the well-known class overlapping problem [18]. In this situation, a standard classifier may not be able to classify the appropriate data into different classes [16] or distinguish among the classes [7].

When dealing with class overlapping problems, most algorithms perform poorly. Typically, such problems are addressed through the use of functions capable of mapping the original data onto a highly dimensional functionality space [2,13]. However, this does not guarantee the elimination of the problem of overlapping among classes. Another approach consists in cleaning up the data in order to simplify the problem [1], but this may also lead to a significant loss of important information. The ability to belong to more classes simultaneously is interesting in the case of overlapping regions. To this end, some popular approaches are based on theories of uncertainty such as possibilities, belief functions, or imprecise probability. All of them inherently define a multilabel approach. Especially in engineering applications, multilabeling of data relies on nonexclusive classification methods based on fuzzy logic and data-driven learning systems, in particular deep neural networks (DNNs), which address the problem of class overlapping by exploiting the advantages of both methodologies and at the same time minimizing their limitations.

In [15], the authors propose a deep neuro-fuzzy classification model to solve the problem of overlapping classes. They use the fuzzy C-means along with fuzzy inference rules to handle the overlapping class problem. This system is subsequently integrated with an approach based on DNNs which carries out the classification for road weight measurement in an intelligent traffic management system. The work in [9] proposed a methodology based on fuzzy Adaptive Resonance Theory clustering to handle the overlapping data without demanding a priori the number of clusters. Thus, it is able to automatically obtain the appropriate number of clusters in an unsupervised way, while dividing the overlapping regions effectively. The authors in [19] use five different classifiers and three overlapping class modeling schemes to perform a comparative study. Another study in [17] faces the problem of class overlapping and imbalance between two classes by introducing a Soft-Hybrid algorithm to improve classification performance. The experimental results show that this methodology can significantly improve the effectiveness in classifying imbalanced data having large overlapping sections.

In the following of this paper, we propose a Randomized Fuzzy Deep Neural Network (RFDNN) to solve the class overlapping problem in a typical real-life application related to the nonexclusive classification of household appliances, which are represented by time series of the related load power consumption. The novelty of the proposed approach lies in the use of the randomized deep neural network and fuzzy logic as a whole, rather than a combination of the two methods, with the gain of automatically determine the logical rules of inference without having to rely on a human expert. The problem of appliances classification is becoming more and more important for several reasons, including demand side management of energy resources and the possibility of profiling the user in order to optimize energy consumptions and costs in a smart grid scenario. The nonexclusive classification of appliances is mandatory because of the physical nature of the time series that describe their operation and, to this end, fuzzy logic can be used to assign the time series a partial degree of membership to each class represented by a suited fuzzy set. Classification of time series is handled efficiently in this context by recurrent DNNs, which make use of data-driven approaches for model selection and identification taking into account the dynamical evolution of the unknown physical system producing the observed time series [4,5].

To overcome the well-known disadvantages of DNNs related to model complexity and slow training algorithms, we rely on the randomization process for maintaining accurate results while reducing the training time. Actually, randomization allows a more flexible use of the model adopted with respect to time constraints, mainly due to the causality of the observed time series; if accuracy is preserved, then the lower (randomized) layers of the DNN still work to extract the most basic patterns from data. Overall, randomization may allow fast re-training and adaptivity in possible applications of the proposed systems in real operation scenarios pertaining to smart grids and energy communities, also limiting the overall cost of investments for a broad penetration to a large social extent. The proposed methodology is compared with two other DNN-based models that represent an acknowledged standard in time series classification tasks; both models are based on the well-known Long Short-Term Memory (LSTM) network.

2   Proposed Methodology

A standard classification problem can be defined as the identification of the category (i.e., a class) to which a given observation belongs with respect to a set of categories. For instance, let us consider a classification problem consisting of C classes with an n-dimensional space Λ. The solution to this classification problem is to divide the space Λ into C disjoint (or mutually exclusive) decision areas, that is:

$$\Lambda = \Lambda_1 \cup \Lambda_2 \cup \cdots \cup \Lambda_C ,$$
$$\Lambda_h \cap \Lambda_k = \emptyset , \quad \forall h \neq k , \tag{1}$$
$$h, k = 1, 2, \ldots, C ,$$

where Λ_k represents the decision area for class k. However, real classification problems can be more complex with data items belonging to several classes at the same time and with different degrees of membership [12]. For a classification problem of this type it is not appropriate to identify crisp boundaries between regions to classify all observations.

The RFDNN model proposed in this paper relies on the synergy between fuzzy logic and deep learning concepts. While DNNs are useful for learning a better representation of data, the fuzzy approach allows to correctly address the problem of class overlapping, as explained in the following. In the specific case of time series classification, this problem is intrinsic given the physical nature of the time series themselves. The latter, representing the load consumption of several appliances, can have similar profiles that in reality may correspond to different operating cycles. For instance, if one wants to classify a washing machine by defining two classes, namely 'motor' and 'non-motor', it is not possible to do it in an exclusive way. This is because a washing machine can rightly be considered an appliance with an engine, but at the same time it has an electronic part, the built-in heater, that makes the washing machine also an appliance using something else than a motor. From the point of view of the energy absorption profile, it is difficult to understand if the washing machine is heating the water or if it is spin-drying. It would be necessary to know the model and make a detailed analysis of the cycles and modes of operation as well as the load size and this is an onerous and expensive task.

Consider a classification problem of M appliances into C classes, where $S_m(t)$, $t > 0$, is the time series associated with the time observation of the mth appliance, $m = 1 \dots M$. In the following, each class will be associated with a fuzzy set with its own membership function $\mu_n(\cdot)$, $n = 1 \dots C$. In order to establish the degree of membership to each fuzzy set, the RFDNN is used to automatically determine the logical rules of inference without having to rely on an expert. From a formal point of view, the neural network implements a mathematical model $\mathbf{f}(S; \boldsymbol{\theta})$, depending on a vector of parameters $\boldsymbol{\theta}$ estimated during the training process, in such a way that, for any input time series $S_m(t)$, the membership functions $\mu_n[S_m(t)]$, $n = 1 \dots C$, are determined:

$$
\begin{bmatrix}
\mu_1 \\
\mu_2 \\
\vdots \\
\mu_C
\end{bmatrix}
= \mathbf{f}\left[S_m(t); \boldsymbol{\theta}\right] .
\tag{2}
$$

The proposed RFDNN model is summarized in Fig. 1; the layers in the architecture are:

- Randomized 1-D Convolutional layer: it applies F sliding 1-D convolutional filters to the input time series $S_m(t)$.
- LSTM layer: it represents the actual recurrent (LSTM) layer with H hidden units.
- Fully connected layer: it is a standard feed-forward layer connecting the H hidden states to C output values.
- Sigmoid layer: it applies a sigmoid function to each neuron of the fully-connected layer, in such a way that each output can be interpreted as a fuzzy membership value in the range $[0, 1]$.

In order to speed up the training process, a randomization process is carried out on the 1-D Convolutional layer. It consists in keeping fixed the weights of the

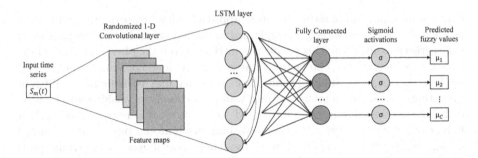

Fig. 1. Proposed RFDNN model for fuzzy time series classification. The final layer after the sigmoid activation functions produces C fuzzy values (each associated with specific class) in the range between 0 and 1: they represent the membership of the input time series to the respective class.

connections among the internal layers of the network, by using a stochastic or heuristic initialization. This way, the learning algorithm operates on a reduced set of weights, losing a possibly negligible part of accuracy to the advantage of a training process that can be orders of magnitude faster than a fully trainable network. The randomization of the 1-D convolutional layer allows us to explain how much the goodness of its performance can be attributed to the architecture or to the training algorithm. In this context, the randomized network can be used as a prior or as a generic feature extractor. As an example, the results reported in [8] demonstrate that random networks are better hand-crafted priors for image restoration tasks, while the research in [14] highlights that, for deep CNNs, it is possible to fix 90% of the parameters and train only the remaining 10% obtaining a negligible drop in accuracy in several scenarios.

3   Data Setup

The proposed approach is developed considering a well-known real case study related to the electricity consumption of individual appliances in private households [11]. Despite devices and appliances having changed a lot since April 2015, which is the last year of dataset collection, this work tends to give a general answer to the related time series classification problem, since it aims at obtaining 'black-box' data-driven models and hence, new types of devices could not greatly affect the overall assessment of the proposed approach.

Before applying the nonexclusive fuzzy classification task, a degree of membership to each fuzzy class is established for every time series. The dataset includes individual measurements (in W) of 20 different appliances, collected continuously at 8-second intervals over a period of two years from 20 houses located near Glasgow, UK. During monitoring, the occupants were conducting their usual domestic activities. Once the data collection period was over, the dataset has been cleaned. This process has involved correcting the time for UK daylight savings and moving sections of Individual Appliance Monitor (IAM) columns to match the appliance they were recording when a reset or householder moved them.

Given the huge amount of available data (tens of millions of samples), the whole dataset would have been quite unbalanced among the classes successively defined. For this reason, we have selected an even number of time series for each appliance considering all houses, referring to the period from June 2014 to April 2015. Future investigations may extend and scale up to a larger extent of data. Accordingly, the training set consists of $20 \times 20 = 400$ time series, while the test set consists of 5 time series per appliance for a total of $5 \times 20 = 100$ data items. We note that the time series do not have the same number of observations since each appliance has a different time of operation. For example, a washing machine cycle can last up to two hours while a blender cycle lasts a few minutes. The time series are taken randomly within the selected period, and time series related to several months are taken in order to have a heterogeneous dataset, which reflects the operation of the appliances at different times of the year. Before applying the learning procedure, a standardization process is carried out on the time series, subtracting the mean and scaling by the standard deviation of the training set.

Subsequently, the dataset has been manually labeled as follows. First of all, two different groups have been created, each consisting of $C = 3$ classes. It is important to underline that these two groups highlight two of the possible characterizations for the different appliances and that the degrees of membership of each time series to each class has been established respecting the structure and functionality of the individual appliances, as reported in Table 1 and Table 2. The two tables also report the original number of time series for each appliance. Note that the 'Kitchen' class in Table 2 specifies whether an appliance is used for cooking, while the 'Other' class reports whether an appliance performs functions other than cooking. Both tables also highlight the need to resort to fuzzy sets to tackle the problem. The class overlapping is well represented by the histograms in Fig. 2 and Fig. 3, where the values reported above the bars represent the number of times a fuzzy label is repeated for each class.

This fuzzy labeling is due to the physical nature of the time series describing the load consumption of the appliances. Let us consider, for instance, the 'Microwave' oven in Table 1; this appliance consists of an electronic part that allows its functioning, which is why it belongs to the 'Electronic devices' class with a degree of membership equal to 0.4. It can also be classified as a 'Motor assisted' appliance, since it is equipped with a mechanical part given by the engine that turns the plate on which food or drink to be heated is arranged; this is highlighted in Table 1 by the degree of membership equal to 0.3. Finally, its main function is to heat food or liquids, which is why it belongs to the 'Non-motor assisted' class with the highest degree of membership, namely 0.9.

The same reasoning has been applied to the fuzzification process carried out on the second group and reported in Table 2. Again, consider the microwave example: it presents a degree of membership of 0.4 to the 'Electronic devices' class for the reasons explained before. It also belongs to the class 'Kitchen' with a membership grade equal to 1, as this class specifies whether the appliance is used for cooking or not. Finally, there is the 'Other' class in which appliances that perform functions other than cooking are classified. In the latter case, the degree of membership of the 'Microwave' oven to this class is obviously zero.

Table 1. Fuzzy membership of appliances to each class (First Group)

Appliances	Original sequences	Class 1 'Electronic devices'	Class 2 'Motor assisted'	Class 3 'Non-motor assisted'
Kettle	17198	0.2	0	1
TV	16668	1	0	0
Food mixer	68	0.1	1	0
Dishwasher	3008	0.4	1	0.4
Washing machine	4267	0.4	1	0.4
Tumble Dryer	1460	0.4	1	0.2
Fridge	125328	0.2	0.8	0
Freezer	87656	0.2	0.8	0
Microwave	13759	0.4	0.3	0.9
Computer	2695	1	0.1	0
Hi-Fi	1175	1	0	0
Game console	268	1	0.1	0
Bread-maker	315	0.1	0.8	0.5
Toaster	3053	0	0	1
Dehumidifier	334	0.2	0.9	0
Electric Heater	4440	0.2	0.4	0.8
Kitchen-mix	192	0.1	1	0
Blender	106	0.1	1	0
Washer Dryer	291	0.4	1	0.4
Overhead Fan	91	0	1	0

4   Experimental Results

The performances of the proposed model are assessed by comparison with three state-of-the-art DNNs. The first one has the same deep neural architecture and number of filters F of the proposed RFDNN with the difference that the 1-D Convolutional Layer is trained; we refer to it as 'Trained Fuzzy Deep Neural Network (TFDNN)'. The other two models are solely based on the well-known LSTM network: the first one is made up of two-stacked LSTM layers (LSTM-2), where the number of LSTM units in each layer is denoted by H and K, respectively; the second one has only one LSTM layer (LSTM-1), where the number of LSTM units in the layer is still denoted by H. As discussed in the following, the latest two LSTM networks do not allow nonexclusive classification as per the main goal of this paper so they are used only for a general assessment, being common DNN benchmarks in the literature, although not directly comparable with the proposed models.

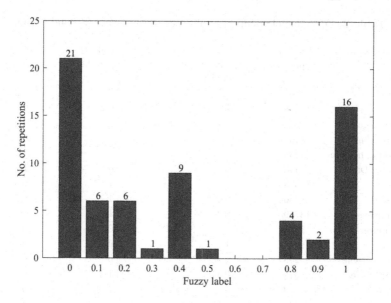

Fig. 2. Histogram representing the number of repetition of each fuzzy label considering all classes of the first group.

All the considered DNNs were trained using the ADAM algorithm [6] with gradient decay factor 0.9 and mini batch size 4. Additional training options and model hyperparameters have been optimized using a grid search procedure for cross-validation on training data. The results of the optimization process are reported in Table 3.

We outline that the problem of identifying the membership degree of a time series to each class is faced as a regression problem since the fuzzy labels are represented by real numbers. Therefore, the training of RFDNN and TFDNN makes use of the standard Half Mean Squared Error loss function, while the final network performance is based on the Root Mean Squared Error (RMSE):

$$\text{RMSE} = \frac{1}{D} \sum_{m=1}^{D} \sqrt{\frac{1}{C} \sum_{n=1}^{C} (t_{n,m} - \mu_{n,m})^2} , \tag{3}$$

where D is the number of samples in the test set (i.e., $D = 100$ in the present case), $t_{n,m}$ represents the target fuzzy membership to the nth class of the time series $S_m(t)$ as per the previous Table 1 or Table 2, whereas $\mu_{n,m} = \mu_n[S_m(t)]$ is the corresponding value estimated by the adopted neural network.

For a further performance analysis, we also report the classification accuracy that is obtained through a defuzzification process for which each pattern is assigned exclusively the class label scoring the largest fuzzy membership value, either from $t_{n,m}$ or $\mu_{n,m}$. Accordingly, the subsequent comparison to obtain the classification accuracy is performed, as usual, by measuring the percentage of correctly classified patterns, that is considering the crisp labels obtained as said.

Table 2. Fuzzy membership of appliances to each class (Second Group)

Appliances	Original sequences	Class 1 'Electronic devices'	Class 2 'Kitchen'	Class 3 'Other'
Kettle	17198	0.2	1	0.2
TV	16668	1	0.2	0
Food mixer	68	0.1	1	0
Dishwasher	3008	0.4	1	0
Washing machine	4267	0.4	0.2	1
Tumble Dryer	1460	0.4	0.2	1
Fridge	125328	0.2	1	0.3
Freezer	87656	0.2	1	0.5
Microwave	13759	0.4	1	0
Computer	2695	1	0	0.1
Hi-Fi	1175	1	0.2	0
Game console	268	1	0	0
Bread-maker	315	0.1	1	0
Toaster	3053	0	1	0
Dehumidifier	334	0.2	0.5	1
Electric Heater	4440	0.2	0.1	1
Kitchen-mix	192	0.1	1	0
Blender	106	0.1	1	0
Washer Dryer	291	0.4	0.2	1
Overhead Fan	91	0	0.5	1

Furthermore, each network is trained considering 10 different runs, each related to a different random initialization of the network's parameters. Namely, we use the same random number generator and the same seeds for all networks to make a fair comparison. The final prediction performance is reported as the average RMSE over these runs.

All the experiments were performed using Matlab® R2021b on a machine equipped with an AMD Ryzen™ 7 5800X 8-core CPU at 3.80 GHz and with 64 GB of RAM, using for training and inference an NVIDIA® GeForce™ RTX 3080 Ti GPU at 1.365 GHz and 12288 MB of GDDR6X RAM. The datasets and the original source code to replicate all of the experiments are stored in a public and persistent repository at https://github.com/NesyaLab/AII-2022/tree/main/AII2022-main.

The performances per appliance obtained by using the proposed RFDNN model are reported in Table 4 for both the first and second group. A low level of RMSE corresponds to a high level of accuracy and vice versa. While the accuracy is good enough for most of the appliances, some of them like the Tumble Dryer in the first group or Dehumidifier in the second group are not classified well; this may be due to the heterogeneity of the time series making the problem harder.

In Table 5, we summarize the RMSE performance of the proposed RFDNN and TFDNN models for all appliances in the first and second group, respectively.

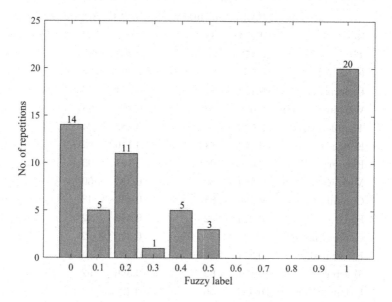

Fig. 3. Histogram representing the number of repetition of each fuzzy label considering all classes of the second group.

Table 3. Structure of DNNs and related hyperparameters

Group	Model	F	H	K	Initial Learn. Rate
First	RFDNN	5	30	–	0.01
	TFDNN	5	30	–	0.01
	LSTM-2	–	10	10	0.01
	LSTM-1	–	20	–	0.01
Second	RFDNN	5	20	–	0.006
	TFDNN	5	20	–	0.006
	LSTM-2	–	10	10	0.006
	LSTM-1	–	20	–	0.006

Table 4. RFDNN performances per appliance

Appliances	First Group		Second Group	
	RMSE	Accuracy (%)	RMSE	Accuracy (%)
Kettle	0.134	84	0.072	100
TV	0.172	80	0.273	36
Food mixer	0.183	100	0.202	100
Dishwasher	0.132	88	0.204	96
Washing machine	0.042	100	0.197	88
Tumble Dryer	0.618	8	0.482	24
Fridge	0.112	84	0.146	92
Freezer	0.082	100	0.181	96
Microwave	0.204	80	0.334	60
Computer	0.208	84	0.485	48
Hi-Fi	0.224	92	0.346	92
Game console	0.249	76	0.425	72
Bread-maker	0.371	60	0.287	84
Toaster	0.201	92	0.346	92
Dehumidifier	0.464	16	0.427	5
Electric Heater	0.162	76	0.083	100
Kitchen-mix	0.129	100	0.215	96
Blender	0.124	100	0.169	96
Washer Dryer	0.051	100	0.251	56
Overhead Fan	0.461	40	0.386	36

Table 5. Performances on all appliances of RFDNN and TFDNN models

Group	Models	RMSE
First	RFDNN	0.216 ± 0.014
	TFDNN	0.217 ± 0.016
Second	RFDNN	0.275 ± 0.020
	TFDNN	0.285 ± 0.018

Both models show comparable performances in terms of RMSE, even if RFDNN performs slightly better with a relative improvement of 0.5% considering the first group and 3.5% considering the second group. The standard deviation is lower for RFDNN in the first group, while in the second group the TFDNN has the lower one.

The average membership grades to each class (i.e., fuzzy labels) obtained by RFDNN are reported for both the first and second group in Table 6 and Table 7, respectively, together with the target values shown in Table 1 and Table 2. It is

Table 6. Average fuzzy labels obtained by RFDNN (First Group)

Appliances	Class 1		Class 2		Class 3	
	'Electronic devices'		'Motor assisted'		'Non-motor assisted'	
	Target	Predicted	Target	Predicted	Target	Predicted
Kettle	0.2	0.2	0	0.2	1	0.9
TV	1	0.5	0	0.8	0	0.3
Food mixer	0.1	0.3	1	0.8	0	0.1
Dishwasher	0.4	0.4	1	0.8	0.4	0.3
Washing machine	0.4	0.4	1	0.9	0.4	0.4
Tumble Dryer	0.4	0.4	1	0.6	0.2	0.3
Fridge	0.2	0.3	0.8	0.7	0	0.1
Freezer	0.2	0.2	0.8	0.8	0	0.1
Microwave	0.4	0.2	0.3	0.3	0.9	0.8
Computer	1	0.7	0.1	0.3	0	0.1
Hi-Fi	1	0.7	0	0.3	0	0.1
Game console	1	0.7	0.1	0.4	0	0.1
Bread-maker	0.1	0.4	0.8	0.6	0.5	0.1
Toaster	0	0.8	0	0.3	1	0.1
Dehumidifier	0.2	0.7	0.9	0.3	0	0.1
Electric Heater	0.2	0.2	0.4	0.4	0.8	0.8
Kitchen-mix	0.1	0.2	1	0.8	0	0.1
Blender	0.1	0.2	1	0.9	0	0.1
Washer Dryer	0.4	0.4	1	0.9	0.4	0.4
Overhead Fan	0	0.6	1	0.5	0	0.1

important to highlight that in Table 6 the 80% of the membership grades are well predicted, while in Table 7 the 70% of the membership grades are well predicted. From a first visual analysis of Table 6 and Table 7, it is clear how the closeness of the predicted values to the target ones varies according to the specific appliance. The functioning of the latter can provide an explanation about the performance. For instance, the TV appliance in Table 6 is erroneously predicted as a 'motor assisted' device, this may depend on the type of available data. Appliances that have very similar consumption profiles are unlikely to be adequately discriminated by the network, with consequent deterioration in performance. Furthermore, although the time series are ordered by length to limit the zero-padding introduced by the software, in some cases this may not be enough and there will always be sequences with a non-negligible number of zeros that affect the prediction.

As a further analysis, the standard classification accuracy is reported after having carried out the defuzzification of both target and predicted labels. In par-

Table 7. Average fuzzy labels obtained by RFDNN (Second Group)

Appliances	Class 1		Class 2		Class 3	
	'Electronic devices'		'Kitchen'		'Other'	
	Target	Predicted	Target	Predicted	Target	Predicted
Kettle	0.2	0.2	1	0.9	0.2	0.2
TV	1	0.5	0.2	0.3	0	0.6
Food mixer	0.1	0.2	1	0.8	0	0.3
Dishwasher	0.4	0.3	1	0.8	0.4	0.3
Washing machine	0.4	0.3	0.2	0.3	1	0.7
Tumble Dryer	0.4	0.4	0.2	0.4	1	0.5
Fridge	0.2	0.2	1	0.8	0.3	0.3
Freezer	0.2	0.2	1	0.8	0.5	0.3
Microwave	0.4	0.2	1	0.7	0	0.4
Computer	1	0.4	0	0.5	0.1	0.4
Hi-Fi	1	0.6	0.2	0.3	0	0.4
Game console	1	0.5	0	0.3	0	0.5
Bread-maker	0.1	0.2	1	0.7	0	0.4
Toaster	0	0.6	1	0.3	0	0.4
Dehumidifier	0.2	0.6	0.5	0.3	1	0.4
Electric Heater	0.2	0.2	0.1	0.1	1	0.9
Kitchen-mix	0.1	0.2	1	0.8	0	0.3
Blender	0.1	0.2	1	0.9	0	0.2
Washer Dryer	0.4	0.4	0.2	0.3	1	0.6
Overhead Fan	0	0.3	0.5	0.6	1	0.5

ticular, each time series is assigned exclusively the class having the highest value of the corresponding fuzzy membership. The classification accuracy is calculated as the number of samples in the test set that are predicted correctly, divided by the whole number of samples in the test set. The average classification accuracy, along with standard deviation and training time, are reported in Table 8 for all models. Considering the first group, the RFDNN performs better than the LSTM-2 in terms of accuracy, with a relative improvement of 3.5%, while it shows comparable results with TFDNN and LSTM-1. The latter presents the highest level of accuracy while the RFDNN has the lowest standard deviation. Considering the second group, the RFDNN performs better than TFDNN in terms of accuracy, with a relative improvement of 4.3%, and it shows comparable results with the two benchmark models. In this case, LSTM-2 reaches the highest accuracy while the lowest standard deviation belongs to TFDNN.

It is worth noting that the RFDNN has a lower standard deviation with respect to LSTM-2 and LSTM-1 and, in this sense, the overall accuracy of

Table 8. Average classification accuracy and training time for all models

Group	Models	Accuracy (%)	Training time
First	RFDNN	78.1 ± 2.4	$15'45''$
	TFDNN	79.3 ± 3.4	$16'44''$
	LSTM-2	75.4 ± 2.7	$25'44''$
	LSTM-1	79.2 ± 4.5	$14'02''$
Second	RFDNN	73.0 ± 4.7	$13'10''$
	TFDNN	70.1 ± 4.1	$13'45''$
	LSTM-2	75.0 ± 6.5	$21'07''$
	LSTM-1	74.4 ± 5.8	$11'40''$

RFDNN may be considered as more robust and better than these benchmarks, probably because of the inherent regularization due to randomization. In any case, this comparison with LSTM networks is borderline, as they are trained in a crisp manner to directly perform the classification in a mutually exclusive way, without using fuzzy labels and therefore out of the scope of the application considered in this paper.

Considering the training times, it is clear that the randomization procedure allows a speed up of the training process. Considering the first group, the RFDNN is faster than TFDNN and LSTM-2 of about 1 and 10 min, respectively; in the second group, RFDNN is faster than TFDNN and LSTM-2 of about 35 s and 8 min, respectively. The LSTM-1 results the fastest one in both cases although with less robust performances.

5   Conclusions

In this paper, we presented a nonexclusive classification approach based on a randomized fuzzy deep neural network to solve the real-life problem of classifying household appliances based on the time series associated with their load power consumption. We relied on both fuzzy logic and deep learning concepts, where the fuzzy logic is used to address the overlapping issues of multiple classes while the DNN is used as the actual classifier. The performances of the proposed approach are compared with the ones of three other models showing comparable, and sometimes better, results. This work can pave the way for future developments regarding energy load management and user level cost minimization in more complex modeling tools based on knowledge granularity and data-driven learning.

References

1. Batista, G., Prati, R., Monard, M.C.: A study of the behavior of several methods for balancing machine learning training data. SIGKDD Explor. **6**, 20–29 (2004)

2. Das, B., Krishnan, N.C., Cook, D.J.: Handling class overlap and imbalance to detect prompt situations in smart homes. In: 2013 IEEE 13th International Conference on Data Mining Workshops, pp. 266–273 (2013)
3. Deng, X., Tian, X., Chen, S., Harris, C.J.: Statistics local fisher discriminant analysis for industrial process fault classification. In: 2016 UKACC 11th International Conference on Control (CONTROL), pp. 1–6 (2016)
4. Faust, O., Hagiwara, Y., Hong, T.J., Lih, O.S., Acharya, U.R.: Deep learning for healthcare applications based on physiological signals: a review. Comput. Methods Programs Biomed. **161**, 1–13 (2018)
5. Hazarika, D., Poria, S., Cambria, E.: Recent trends in deep learning based natural language processing [review article]. IEEE Comput. Intell. Mag. **13**, 55–75 (2018)
6. Kingma, D., Ba, J.: Adam: a method for stochastic optimization. In: International Conference on Learning Representations (2014)
7. Lee, H., Kim, S.: An overlap-sensitive margin classifier for imbalanced and overlapping data. Expert Syst. Appl. **98**, 72–83 (2018)
8. Lempitsky, V., Vedaldi, A., Ulyanov, D.: Deep image prior. In: 2018 IEEE/CVF Conference on Computer Vision and Pattern Recognition, pp. 9446–9454 (2018). https://doi.org/10.1109/CVPR.2018.00984
9. Mak, L.O., Ng, G.W., Lim, G., Mao, K.: A merging fuzzy art clustering algorithm for overlapping data. In: 2011 IEEE Symposium on Foundations of Computational Intelligence (FOCI), pp. 1–6 (2011)
10. McLoughlin, I., Zhang, H., Xie, Z., Song, Y., Xiao, W.: Robust sound event classification using deep neural networks. IEEE/ACM Trans. Audio Speech Lang. Process. **23**(3), 540–552 (2015)
11. Murray, D., et al.: A data management platform for personalised real-time energy feedback. In: Proceedings of the 8th International Conference on Energy Efficiency in Domestic Appliances and Lighting (2015)
12. Rizzi, A., Buccino, N.M., Panella, M., Uncini, A.: Genre classification of compressed audio data. In: 2008 IEEE 10th Workshop on Multimedia Signal Processing, pp. 654–659 (2008)
13. Rosato, A., Altilio, R., Araneo, R., Panella, M.: Embedding of time series for the prediction in photovoltaic power plants. In: 2016 IEEE 16th International Conference on Environment and Electrical Engineering (EEEIC), pp. 1–4 (2016)
14. Rosenfeld, A., Tsotsos, J.K.: Intriguing properties of randomly weighted networks: generalizing while learning next to nothing. In: 2019 16th Conference on Computer and Robot Vision (CRV), pp. 9–16 (2019). https://doi.org/10.1109/CRV.2019.00010
15. Sumit, S., Akhter, S.: C-means clustering and deep-neuro-fuzzy classification for road weight measurement in traffic management system. Soft Comput. **23**, 4329–4340 (2019)
16. Tang, W., Mao, K.Z., Mak, L.O., Ng, G.W.: Classification for overlapping classes using optimized overlapping region detection and soft decision. In: 2010 13th International Conference on Information Fusion, pp. 1–8 (2010)
17. Vorraboot, P., Rasmequan, S., Chinnasarn, K., Lursinsap, C.: Improving classification rate constrained to imbalanced data between overlapped and non-overlapped regions by hybrid algorithms. Neurocomputing **152**, 429–443 (2015)
18. Xiong, H., Li, M., Jiang, T., Zhao, S.: Classification algorithm based on NB for class overlapping problem. Appl. Math. Inf. Sci. **7**, 409–415 (2013)
19. Xiong, H., Wu, J., Liu, L.: Classification with classoverlapping: a systematic study. In: Proceedings of the 1st International Conference on E-Business Intelligence (ICEBI 2010), pp. 303–309. Atlantis Press (2010)

Applied Enhanced Q-NAS for COVID-19 Detection in CT Images

Julia Noce[1]([⊠]), Gianella Chantong[2], Gustavo Jauregui[2], Roberto Mogami[2], Alexandra Monteiro[2], Karla Figueiredo[2], and Marley Vellasco[1]

[1] PUC-Rio, Rio de Janeiro, RJ, Brazil
`noce.julia@gmail.com, marley@ele.puc-rio.br`
[2] UERJ, Rio de Janeiro, RJ, Brazil
`ioga@pobox.com, karlafigueiredo@ime.uerj.br`

Abstract. The Deep Neural Networks are flexible and robust models that have gained attention from the machine learning community over the last decade. During the construction of a neural network, an expert can spend significant time designing a neural architecture with trial and error sessions. Because of the manual process, there is a greater interest in Neural Architecture Search (NAS), which is an automated method of architectural search in neural networks. Quantum-inspired evolutionary algorithms present propitious results regarding faster convergence when compared to other solutions with restricted search space and high computational costs. In this work, we enhance the Q-NAS model: a quantum-inspired algorithm to search for deep networks by assembling substructures. We present a new architecture that was designed automatically by the Q-NAS and applied to a case study for COVID-19 vs. healthy classification. For this classification, the Q-NAS algorithm was able to find a network architecture with only 1.23 M parameters that reached the accuracy of 99.44%, which overcame benchmark networks like Inception (GoogleLeNet), EfficientNet and VGG that were also tested in this work. The algorithm is publicly avaiable at https://github.com/julianoce/qnas.

Keywords: Neural architecture search · Quantum-inspired evolutionary algorithm · Image classification

1 Introduction

In the last decade, Deep Learning methods have become popular for solving a variety of tasks, such as image, speech and automatic translation [15,39]. In most cases, networks built manually by specialists are responsible for the great success of these applications in the literature [17]. For applications in image, Efficient-Net [31], InceptionNet [27] and VGG [25] are examples of successful architectures manually built. However, building a successful network from scratch can be a time-consuming and error-prone process. Because of the cost of the manual process, there is a great interest in Neural Architecture Search, which is an automated method of architectural search in neural networks [15].

Automated Machine Learning (AutoML) has become an important research area with wide applications of machine learning techniques. The goal of AutoML is to make the area of machine learning accessible to other scientists who are interested in applying it to different domains. For that, one of the research areas of AutoML proposes to automate decision making when building and training a neural network [15].

Neural Architecture Search (NAS) is a subarea of AutoML and is an essential step toward automating machine learning methods. It is a technique that aims to automate the construction processes of a neural network architecture [15]. This technique considers the search space aspects of the architectures, search strategy and performance estimation strategy [36]. Several new algorithms have been proposed to solve the Neural Architecture Search problem, but many of them require significant computational resources. The approaches include different techniques such as Bayesian optimization [10], Reinforcement Learning (RL) [3,38,39], Evolutionary Algorithms [2,8,29] or its variation, the quantum-inspired evolutionary algorithms (QIEA), which show promising results when it comes to faster convergence. The first proposal for QIEA used important principles of quantum computing, such as the linear superposition of states, the quantum rotation gate, and the quantum bit. Experimental results show that QIEAs can find better solutions with fewer evaluations when compared to similar algorithms for many optimization problems [5,6]. This characteristic can be crucial in applications like NAS, in which evaluating a possible solution can be very expensive.

The Q-NAS (Quantum Inspired Neural Architecture Search) algorithm was recently developed to address the efficiency issue without relying on the cell search approach. This algorithm was built due to higher computational cost of other methods when compared to QIEAs. Because of this, the authors explored a better balance of trade-offs between the search space, in contrast with the cell strategy that restricts the search space to a great extent [30]. Q-NAS is a QIEA model for searching deep neural architectures and assembling substructures.

This work aims to apply the Q-NAS algorithm to a real chest computed tomography images database to build an architecture that detects COVID-19 in patients. The inclusion of the comparison of such networks in the paper aims to compare and highlight the outperformed accuracy obtained since, to the best of our knowledge, no other works using NAS on 2D CT images for COVID-19 classification have been identified.

However, the following works have been identified that applied NAS in COVID-19 image classification context: [13] proposes an efficient Evolutionary Multi-objective neural ARchitecture Search (EMARS) framework, that automatically searches for 3D neural architectures based on a well-designed search space for COVID-19 chest CT scan classification. Within the framework, they proposed a factorized 3D search space, in which all child architectures use weight sharing among each other to significantly improve the search efficiency and finish the search process in 8 h. In their paper, they use three publicly available datasets, all of which provide 3D chest CT scans. They reached the accuracy of 89.61% in 1.3 GPU days.

In [32], they propose a NAS-based framework that bears the threefold contributions: (a) they focus on the self-supervised scenario, i.e., where no labels are required to determine the architecture,(b) they assume the datasets are imbalanced, (c) they design each component to be able to run on a resource constrained setup, i.e., on a single GPU. The authors also conduct experiments on ChestMNIST [34], which contains 78,468 images of chest X-ray scans [21].

In [24], the authors manually build a network based on SqueezeNet that was capable to classify COVID-19 x Healthy with an accuracy of 99.53%. Moreover, they also classified in COVID-19 x Healthy x Viral Pneumonia with an accuracy of 99.60%. Furthermore, in [22], the authors proposed an inverted bell-curve-based ensemble of deep learning models for the detection of COVID-19 from CXR images. The trained models are combined with the proposed inverted bell curve weighted ensemble method.

As the cited works provide a NAS solution for different types of datasets such as 3D CT images and X-Ray images, it is not possible to compare the execution time and accuracy with these works.

Our goal is to investigate and evaluate enhancements in Q-NAS in order to improve performance in terms of accuracy and processing time. Therefore, we evaluate the algorithm by training the network on CIFAR-10 and CIFAR-100 benchmark databases as a way to mediate and compare with the originally proposed Q-NAS. Moreover, we evaluate the previous Q-NAS version and its evolution strategy and compare it to the proposed Neural Architecture Search strategies. Our focus is to analyze the impact of changing the parameters in CIFAR-10 and CIFAR-100 datasets. As described in the following sections, we observed that changing only the optimizer in the Q-NAS training phase brings positive impacts on the accuracy. The main contributions of this work are highlighted below:

- The results found in the CIFAR-10 database surpass the results obtained in [28] by 1.10%;
- In CIFAR-100 database, the achieved accuracy of this work surpasses by 1.65%, with just 22 GPUs/day (number of GPUs x number of days of execution);
- The Q-NAS algorithm was able to find a network architecture with only 1.23M parameters that reached the accuracy of 99.44%, which overcame benchmark networks like Inception (GoogleLeNet), EfficientNet and VGG;
- As far as the authors are concerned, this is the first QIEA applied to detect COVID-19 in computed tomography chest images.

This paper is organized as follows: Sect. 2 presents an overview of NAS and QIEAs; Sect. 3 briefly describes the Q-NAS algorithm and the proposed enhancements; the experiments and the discussed results are detailed in Sects. 4 and 5; finally, Sect. 6 presents the conclusions.

2   Quantum-Inspired Evolutionary Algorithms

As previously reported, there are different neural architecture search techniques for image classification. The technique that will be covered in this Section is the Quantum Inspired Evolutionary Algorithms, which is based on quantum computing principles.

2.1   Quantum-Inspired Evolutionary Algorithms

The concept of quantum-inspired computing is to take advantage of the basis of quantum physics but with the possibility of executing in classical computers by creating classical algorithms [7,20]. In order to solve optimization problems, the quantum-inspired evolutionary algorithm (QIEA) applies quantum computing fundamentals, such as superposition of states and quantum bits. The authors in [9] presented the first proposal of quantum-inspired evolutionary algorithms where some important principles of quantum computing are used, such as the collapsed quantum bit, the linear superposition of states and the quantum rotation gate.

As well as the evolutionary algorithms the QIEA is defined by an evaluation function, the individual representation and the population dynamics. On the other hand, in QIEA the individual is encoded in a probabilistic fashion, thus representing a superposition of states which are the solutions in the search space [9]. The first practical QIEA used a Q-bit representation, in which a string of Q-bits defines an individual. The state $|\Psi\rangle$ of the Q-bit $\begin{bmatrix} \alpha & \beta \end{bmatrix}^T$ is defined as [9]:

$$|\Psi\rangle = \alpha|0\rangle + \beta|1\rangle$$

where α and β are complex numbers. The Q-bit collapses to the state "0" with probability α^2 and to the state "1" with probability β^2. At the beginning, a Q-bit individual represents all possible states with equal probability, thus better illustrating the population diversity when compared to other types of representations. During evolution, a Q-gate operator can change the probability of each Q-bit, so it progressively converges to a single state – the optimal solution. Since the quantum individuals cannot be directly evaluated, they must first be observed to then generate classical individuals. Particularly, since a quantum individual represents many quantum states, it can only be evaluated when it collapses to a single one.

QIEAs can combine binary and real representation and have been proposed for problems in which both real and categorical parameters need to be evolved, such as the hyperparameters and weights of a neural network [4,23]. In these works, the square pulse scheme represents the numerical variables while the Q-bit scheme represents the categorical parameters. The variation operators (Q-gate, crossover or mutation) are applied correspondingly.

In [37], the authors encode CNNs into quantum chromosomes, which are updated by applying quantum gates and finding the best individual with quantum genetic algorithm. Finally, the algorithm predicts the network performance after a few steps of stochastic gradient descent by means of evaluation estimate strategy, so that the training of networks with poor performance can be interrupted earlier, to speed up the evolutionary process.

Final Remarks. One should note that the motivation of this work involves looking for a more generic architecture in a scalable and fast way, so that it can be applied to computers with less requirements than the ones described before. As mentioned earlier, QIEA can find better solutions with fewer evaluations.

Thus, this work presents Enhanced Q-NAS, an algorithm capable of finding a more complex structure in a larger search space, using only 4 GPUs, and still achieving a competitive accuracy when compared to the related works. In terms of scalability, Enhanced Q-NAS is an improved algorithm that implements a new optimizer and build a network from scratch to apply in CIFAR-100 context. Finally, and most importantly, enhanced Q-NAS is the first QIEA, as far as the authors are concerned, applied to detect COVID-19 in computed tomography chest images.

3   Enhanced Q-NAS

3.1   Q-NAS

In Q-NAS, a quantum individual is encoded in a chromosome that contains two parts: one is responsible for encoding the space for discrete neural architecture, and the other encodes the numerical space of some hyperparameters (such as the weight decay factor). One quantum individual can generate multiples classical individuals, which are then evaluated as solutions containing the architecture and the hyperparameters. However, as stated by the authors in [29], the hyperparameter evolution does not provide better results when compared with the Tensorflow's default hyperparameters values [1] on the same architecture. Thus, this work will not focus on hyperparameters evolution.

Q-NAS Network Representation. In [28], the authors proposed to represent the network structure in a *chain-like* structure with a maximum size L, in which every node has a function associated with it. These functions are basically designed to be a network layer function in a neural network. For example, one node can be one Convolutional layer in the structure. As the task of this work is image classification, the last network layer is fixed to be a classifier (fully connected) layer.

The only restriction specified by the authors is that a node can only be connected in a chain-like structure which means that the use of skip-connections between nodes are not allowed. The user can manually specify a list of predefined possible functions with different kernels, filters and strides that can be selected by the algorithm and be in the search space for every node.In order to represent variable length networks, the authors included the a "no operation" function ($NoOp$) in the function list of possibilities. The quantum gene defines a probability mass function (PMF) for a node in the structure. If there are N individuals, a maximum network size of L layers and M functions in the function list, the quantum population will be an array of shape (N, L, M). If the user does not wish to manually specify the initial probability value of each function, all nodes will start with the same PMF [28].

Figure 1 summarizes generation process for the network part of the chromosome entirely. From the user input parameters to the final decoded network. The Q-NAS' parameters are listed on the left. $Conv(k, s, f)$ stands for a convolution layer with kernel size $k \times k$, stride s and f filters. The observation of the quantum individual is achieved by sampling from the PMF of each node. Moreover, the decoding process is a mapping from integers to function names. As described before, he final architecture includes a fully connected (FC) classifier layer at the end of the structure.

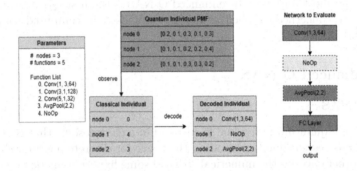

Fig. 1. Q-NAS network quantum individual representation scheme [28]

The quantum individuals can lead to invalid network structures, though. One can assume that there is a pooling operation in the function list that reduces the feature map size in half. Because of this, once we have a given input image size, there is a maximum number of times this pooling function can appear in the network before the feature map reaches unit pixel size. However, since Q-NAS samples each node independently, this cannot be handled directly. Considering these points, the authors [28] decided to penalize invalid architectures. The authors developed a simple method to fix an invalid structure: when building the decoded network for evaluation, they ignore all pooling operations that appear after the allowed number is reached [28].

Q-NAS Algorithm. The Q-NAS algorithm comprises three main operations: (1) population generation; (2) candidate evaluation; (3) ranking and update. The algorithm repeats these steps for T generations, in order to find the best individual [29]. The Algorithm 1 provides the summarized steps of the Q-NAS.

At the beginning of the loop of generations, $Q(t)$ is observed to generate the classical population $C(t)$. As reported before, the user can provide initial probabilities or the program assigns the same probability to all functions, creating a

Algorithm 1. Q-NAS algorithm

1: $t \leftarrow 0$
   Initialize $Q(t)$
2: **while** $t \leq T$ **do**
3:    Generate classical population $C(t)$ observing $Q(t)$
4:    **if** $t = 0$ **then**
5:       Evaluate $C(t)$
6:       $P(t) \leftarrow C(t)$
7:    **else**
8:       $C(t) \leftarrow$ recombination between $C(t)$ and $P(t)$
9:       Evaluate $C(t)$
10:      $P(t) \leftarrow \text{select}(C(t), P(t))$
11:   **end if**
12:   $Q(t+1) \leftarrow$ update $Q(t)$ based on $P(t)$ values
13:   $t \leftarrow t+1$
14: **end while**

---

uniform PMF. Next, once the population is ready, $C(t)$ can be evaluated. The evaluation program involves training the candidate networks for a few epochs - in the previous work it was defined as 50 epochs - with a subset of the training data and using a validation dataset to assign a fitness score to the individual. This work, follows this exact setup. In the first generation, C(t) individuals are ranked and stored in $P(t)$. As it can be observed, the classical recombination is only possible after the first generation. From the second generation, since P(t) exists, a new population C(t) must be evaluated and then select individuals to be stored (line 10). The authors developed Q-NAS to use a steady-state technique, in which they select the best individuals from the old and new populations. This method orders the old and new population and keeps the k best individuals [35].

Finally, quantum individuals are updated based on the best classical individuals. It is important to emphasize that the update increases the probability of the most promising function, based on its fitness, and consequently reduces the other probabilities proportionally so that it continues to add up to 1. This procedure is executed separately for each part of the chromosome, similar to the observation process. Since we want to generate solutions that are closer to the optimal, the quantum population is gradually modified. Thus, the update should reduce the search space and also map promising search areas. The update step is the final step of the algorithm loop and then the same procedure is repeated for T generations [28].

When the evolution is complete, the final architecture is retrained from scratch for 300 epochs with all the available training data. In addition, the network is evaluated every ten epochs using a validation dataset. The periodic evaluations' accuracy is used to save the best model during the retraining phase. After the training step, the best validation model is applied to the test data to obtain the final accuracy value. The test accuracy is used to compare the models among different experiments and with other works [28].

3.2   Enhancements in Q-NAS

In the previous work [28], the authors could not achieve a high accuracy building a network from scratch for CIFAR-100 due to the dataset complexity. Moreover, the authors used 20 GPUs to make all their experiments. The focus of this work is to make Q-NAS more scalable and improve the results without doing huge changes in the algorithm.

For that, we present the experiments related to improving existing individuals found in [28]. Basically, we changed the optimizer RMSProp to the SWATS algorithm proposed by [16]. Furthermore, we conducted an experiment that evolves a CIFAR-100 network from scratch using Q-NAS just changing few parameters of the algorithm and transforming it into a problem to be solved with fewer GPUs. The GPUs used in the following experiments were 4 Nvidia GTX 1080. The resultant network is relatively small (20 layers) compared to other state-of-the-art models and achieved promising accuracy with considerably less computational cost than other NAS algorithms.

Switch ADAM to SGD for CIFAR-10 and CIFAR-100 Improvements
The experiments conducted by [28] showed that it was possible to achieve the accuracy of 93.85% for CIFAR-10 and 74.23% for CIFAR-100 datasets evolving an architecture with Q-NAS using 10000 samples and retraining this same architecture for 300 epochs. In the retraining phase, 60000 samples were used. Additionally, they used RMSProp optimizer in evolution and retraining phase [14] with Tensorflow's default hyper-parameters: *decay = 0.9, learning rate= 1.0e-3, momentum = 0.0, weight decay = 1.0e-4*. Since Tensorflow's default hyperparameters outperforms the hyperparameter evolution in Q-NAS, as described before, it is not the interest of this work to present this evolution. Thus, this work presents a new enhancement for Q-NAS algorithm which is to change RMSProp to SWATS optimizer, proposed by [16].

The interest behind using this optimizer is that RMSprop has been found to generalize poorly compared to Stochastic gradient descent (SGD). These methods tend to perform well in the initial portion of training but are outperformed by SGD at later stages of training [16]. The authors proposed SWATS, a simple strategy that Switches from Adam optimizer to SGD when a triggering condition is satisfied. In the [16] strategy, the switchover point and the SGD learning rate are both learned as a part of the training process.

Since applying SWATS in the Q-NAS evolution phase showed no better performance than using RMSProp, this work proposes to apply SWATS only in the retraining phase. In order to achieve better accuracy, the best architectures found in [28] for CIFAR-10 (which was also applied to CIFAR-100 dataset) were selected. The idea is that Q-NAS should find the set of layers to form an architecture that achieves the best fitness and accuracy. Two evolutions were implemented, with different search spaces: one using functions with convolutional blocks and another using functions with residual blocks in the search space. Finally, the architecture with residual layers was the one with the best accuracy.

When this network was retrained using SWATS optimizer, we achieved an accuracy of 94.95% for CIFAR-10 and 75.88% for CIFAR-100 which surpass the previous work [28] by 1.10% and 1.65%, respectively. The parameters used in the optimizer were chosen using the algorithm's default [16] which were: $\beta_1 = 0.9$, $\beta_2 = 0.990$, $\epsilon = 1.0e-9$ and learning rate $= 1.0e-3$. In this specific case, it was not considered the GPU/days, since it is only changing the retraining phase. Based on these results we can conclude that by changing the optimizer RMSProp to SWATS, we were able to achieve a new higher score for Q-NAS in CIFAR-10 and CIFAR-100 context. The comparative results with other works are described in Table 1 for CIFAR-10.

Table 1. Result models from the literature in comparison with our work. The '*' marks the methods that used other datasets for the search and applied the network on CIFAR-10.

Hand-designed models			
	Accuracy(%)	#params	GPU days
ResNet [11]	93.57	1.7 M	–
VGG [25]	92.06	15.2 M	–
GoogleLeNet [26]	93.64	–	–
NAS			
Meta-QNN [3]	93.08	11.18 M	100
DARTS [19]	97.24	3.3 M	5
NAS-Net [40]	96.86	3.3 M	2000
Block-QNN-S [38]	96.46*	39.8 M	96
Q-NAS [28]	93.85	3.6 M	67
Q-NAS Enhanced	94.95	3.6 M	67

Evolving a Network from Scratch for CIFAR-100 Classification Task
Another experiment was explored in Q-NAS algorithm: to achieve a higher score in CIFAR-100 dataset without using the CIFAR-10 evolved network architecture. In [28], the authors achieved the best accuracy for CIFAR-100 of 74.23% in their single experiment. In the last Q-NAS version, the authors evolved CIFAR-100, from scratch, with 300 generations, 50 epochs per generation, a maximum number of layers of 30, a maximum number of pooling layers of 3 and number of samples to be used in the evolution phase of 10000.

Instead of increasing the maximum number of layers, our approach involves increasing the number of samples to be used in the evolution scheme and also increasing the number of generations. We chose this approach because, differently from [28] that are using 20 GPUs, we are exploring a scenario with only 4 GPUs.

The first step was to increase the number of the dataset samples from 10000 to 20000 and decrease the number of total generations from 300 to 100. Moreover, we decrease the number of maximum layers from 30 to 20 because of the GPU limitation. The first result found with this configuration was an accuracy of 70.74% for 16 GPU/days, which overcame the first value found by [28]. Finally, we decided to increase once more the dataset samples from 20000 to 35000 and decrease the number of total generations to 200. As presented in Table 2, with these settings, we achieved our final accuracy of 76.39% for 18 GPU/day, outperforming by 6.44% the first evolution result from scratch in CIFAR-100 and 2.16% from the retrained network using the best individual CIFAR-10 structure. The best result obtained with model Block-QNN-S [38] has the disadvantage of consuming five times the GPU/days of Q-NAS Enhanced to evolve the results. The results of the hand-modeled networks are included in Tables 1 and 2 just to provide the dimension of the advantages of NAS models with regard to the accuracy.

Table 2. CIFAR-100 results found in the literature. The '*' marks the methods that used other datasets for the search and applied the network on CIFAR-100.

Hand-designed models			
	Accuracy(%)	#params	GPU days
ResNet-1001 [12]	77.30	10.2 M	–
ResNet-164 [12]	75.67	1.7 M	–
Network in Network (NiN) [18]	64.32	–	–
NAS			
Meta-QNN [3]	72.86*	11.18 M	100
Block-QNN-S [38]	81.94	39.8 M	96
Q-NAS [28]	74.23	3.6 M	67
Q-NAS Enhanced	76.39	3.8 M	18

4   Case Study: COVID-19 Detection in Computed Tomography Images

In this section, we present the use of Q-NAS to evolve an architecture for a real case study involving COVID-19 detection in computed tomography images that outperformed benchmark networks.

The computed tomography chest images used in this work were extracted from patients hospitalized, totalling more than 1500 images. Each CT image was evaluated and labeled by three experienced radiologists. It is emphasized that the identification of each patient has been eliminated.

The dataset contains two classes: 827 labeled COVID-19 images and 850 labeled healthy images. During the training phase, the dataset was splitted into 80% training, 10% validation and 10% test.

Figure 2 shows examples of the two types of computed tomography. The first represents the healthy chest CT since there is no presence of changes in the lung parenchyma, which is typical of the presence of the virus. The second image represents the COVID infected chest CT. All the input images were resized to 128-by-128 and each training image was augmented with random cropping, with a scale of 0.5, horizontal flip, random contrast, and random brightness with a factor of 0.2.

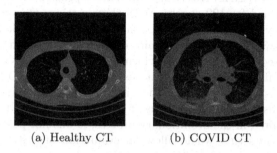

(a) Healthy CT   (b) COVID CT

Fig. 2. Computed tomography examples

Before evolving a Q-NAS architecture, we trained these images in three benchmark networks: VGG, EfficientNet and GoogleLeNet. Furthermore, the dataset was also used to train the most recent network proposed by [33], COVID-Net. Our goal is to compare the accuracy between manually designed networks so that it is possible to prove our motivation that an neural architecture search can find a network that outperform a manually designed one.

VGG [25] is a Convolutional Neural Network architecture proposed in 2014. The original idea is that instead of having a large number of hyper-parameter they focused on having convolution layers of 3×3 filter with a stride 1 and always used the same padding and maxpool layer of 2×2 filter of stride 2. The VGG 16 architecture consists of 13 convolutional layers and 3 pooling layers.

EfficientNet [31] network focus on how to scale Convolutional Neural Networks efficiently. [31] used a compound scaling method: they simply scale each network dimension by a constant ratio to balance all dimensions of network width/depth/resolution.

In the GoogleLeNet network [26], it is proposed a new module called inception. In order to make deep neural networks less computationally expensive, the work presented in [26] limits the number of input channels by adding an extra 1×1 convolution before the 3×3 and 5×5 convolutions. GoogleLeNet has 9 inception modules stacked linearly.

Finally, [33] proposed a deep convolutional neural network based model (COVID-Net) to detect COVID-19 cases using X-ray images.

5   Results

For Q-NAS evolution scheme, we defined the following setting to evolve the CT images: 100 generations, 50 epochs per generation, a maximum number of layers of 20, and a maximum number of pooling layers of 8. For the evolution phase, we used the RMSProp optimizer and, for the retraining phase, we used the SWATS optimizer with the same hyperparameters defined in the other experiments. In the retraining phase it was used a single GPU, thus we did not compare the time because this work is focused on observing the time and performance of the evolution phase of Q-NAS. After the evolutionary process, the best architecture found was retrained for 100 epochs. With these settings we were able to reach the final accuracy of 99.44% for 9 GPU/days. The final network architecture can be seen at Table 3. Our network contains only 15 layers, which is a competitive number compared to GoogleLeNet which contains 22, VGG-16 that contains 16 layers and EfficientNet which contains 237 layers. COVID-Net can not be compared in this context because they introduced a new layer design called projection-expansion-projection-extension (PEPX) [33]. Due to the computational time required in the evolutionary process, it was not possible to generate a number of results that would allow an evaluation of statistical significance among the results in terms of different number of layers.

Table 3. Best Architecture found for COVID Classification Task and the accuracy found for each network

Nodes	Function Names
0	no_op
1	no_op
2	no_op
3	avg_pool_2_2
4	conv_3_1_128
5	conv_3_1_128
6	avg_pool_2_2
7	conv_1_1_32
8	conv_1_1_32
9	conv_1_1_64
10	conv_3_1_64
11	avg_pool_2_2
12	avg_pool_2_2
13	conv_3_1_256
14	conv_3_1_256
15	conv_3_1_32
16	conv_5_1_64
17	conv_5_1_32
18	no_op
19	max_pool_2_2

Network	Accuracy	Number of Layers	Parameters
VGG16	92.86%	16	138M
EfficientNetB0	98.25%	237	11M
GoogleLeNet	96.97%	22	4M
COVID-Net	95.88%	-	-
Q-NAS	**99.44%**	**15**	**1.23M**

The benchmarks networks (VGG-16, EfficientNet, GoogleLeNet and COVID-Net) were trained in the same dataset for 100 epochs using ADAM optimizer.

One of the future investigations is to use a SWATS optimizer in these networks to check if they can achieve a higher accuracy. All these networks were pre-trained with the ImageNet dataset, including COVID-Net. We then trained all these networks in our dataset contemplating all layers. The resulting accuracies can be seen in Table 3 where it can be perceived that Q-NAS outperforms the three benchmarks and COVID-Net networks.

6 Conclusion

In this work, we revisited Q-NAS: a quantum-inspired algorithm to search for deep neural network structures. We were able to enhance the algorithm settings to improve CIFAR-10 and CIFAR-100 results, when compared to [28], using fewer GPUs. The first experiment demonstrated that, by using the SWATS algorithm to retrain the best individual, the original results found in [28] can be improved.

Moreover, this work also evolved and trained a new architecture from scratch for CIFAR-100 image classification. Instead of increasing the number of layers it was decided to increase the number of samples to be used in the evolution phase and decrease the number of generations. We were able to find an architecture that reached an accuracy of 76.39% with only 18 GPU/days.

Finally, the enhanced Q-NAS was applied to a real case study to detect COVID in computed tomography chest images. We were able to find a network that achieved an accuracy of 99.44% for just 9 GPU/days. The network also has 1.23 M parameters.

Future works involve using Q-NAS to evolve a network capable of classifying different types of pulmonary diseases in CT chest images. Furthermore, more complex functions, with skip connections as well as encapsulated functions, can be added to the search space of the evolutionary process, to include some sequence of layers that frequently appear in the structures from the literature. Finally, we plan to extend the parameters analysis, studying their impact when working with other datasets.

References

1. Abadi, M., et al.: TensorFlow: large-scale machine learning on heterogeneous systems (2015). http://tensorflow.org/, software available from tensorflow.org
2. Awad, N., Mallik, N., Hutter, F.: Differential evolution for neural architecture search. arXiv preprint arXiv:2012.06400 (2020)
3. Baker, B., Gupta, O., Naik, N., Raskar, R.: Designing neural network architectures using reinforcement learning. arXiv preprint arXiv:1611.02167 (2016)
4. Cardoso, M.C., Silva, M., Vellasco, M.M., Cataldo, E.: Quantum-inspired features and parameter optimization of spiking neural networks for a case study from atmospheric. Procedia Comput. Sci. **53**, 74–81 (2015)
5. da Cruz, A.V.A., Vellasco, M.M., Pacheco, M.A.C.: Quantum-inspired evolutionary algorithms applied to numerical optimization problems. In: IEEE Congress on Evolutionary Computation, pp. 1–6. IEEE (2010)

6. da Cruz, A.V.A., Vellasco, M.M.B.R., Pacheco, M.A.C.: Quantum-inspired evolutionary algorithm for numerical optimization. In: Abraham, A., Grosan, C., Ishibuchi, H. (eds.) Hybrid Evolutionary Algorithms. Studies in Computational Intelligence, vol. 75, pp. 19–37. Springer, Berlin, Heidelberg (2007). https://doi.org/10.1007/978-3-540-73297-6_2

7. Cruz, A.: Quantum-inspired evolutionary algorithms for problems based on numerical representation. PhD Thesis (2007)

8. Den Ottelander, T., Dushatskiy, A., Virgolin, M., Bosman, P.A.N.: Local search is a remarkably strong baseline for neural architecture search. In: Ishibuchi, H., et al. (eds.) EMO 2021. LNCS, vol. 12654, pp. 465–479. Springer, Cham (2021). https://doi.org/10.1007/978-3-030-72062-9_37

9. Han, K.H., Kim, J.H.: Quantum-inspired evolutionary algorithm for a class of combinatorial optimization. IEEE Trans. Evol. Comput. 6(6), 580–593 (2002)

10. Han, S., Eom, H., Kim, J., Park, C.: Optimal DNN architecture search using Bayesian optimization hyperband for arrhythmia detection. In: 2020 IEEE Wireless Power Transfer Conference (WPTC), pp. 357–360. IEEE (2020)

11. He, K., Zhang, X., Ren, S., Sun, J.: Deep residual learning for image recognition. In: Proceedings of the IEEE Conference on Computer Vision and Pattern Recognition, pp. 770–778 (2016)

12. He, K., Zhang, X., Ren, S., Sun, J.: Identity mappings in deep residual networks. In: Leibe, B., Matas, J., Sebe, N., Welling, M. (eds.) ECCV 2016. LNCS, vol. 9908, pp. 630–645. Springer, Cham (2016). https://doi.org/10.1007/978-3-319-46493-0_38

13. He, X., Wang, S., Ying, G., Zhang, J., Chu, X.: Efficient multi-objective evolutionary 3D neural architecture search for COVID-19 detection with chest CT scans. arXiv preprint arXiv:2101.10667 (2021)

14. Hinton, G., Srivastava, N., Swersky, K.: Neural networks for machine learning lecture 6a overview of mini-batch gradient descent. Cited 14(8), 2 (2012)

15. Hutter, F., Kotthoff, L., Vanschoren, J. (eds.): Automated Machine Learning. TSSCML, Springer, Cham (2019). https://doi.org/10.1007/978-3-030-05318-5

16. Keskar, N.S., Socher, R.: Improving generalization performance by switching from adam to sgd. arXiv preprint arXiv:1712.07628 (2017)

17. LeCun, Y., Bengio, Y., Hinton, G.: Deep learning. Nature 521(7553), 436–444 (2015)

18. Lin, M., Chen, Q., Yan, S.: Network in network. arXiv preprint arXiv:1312.4400 (2013)

19. Liu, H., Simonyan, K., Yang, Y.: Darts: differentiable architecture search. arXiv preprint arXiv:1806.09055 (2018)

20. Moore, M., Narayanan, A.: Quantum-inspired computing. Dept. Comput. Sci., Univ. Exeter, Exeter, UK (1995)

21. Ozturk, T., Talo, M., Yildirim, E.A., Baloglu, U.B., Yildirim, O., Acharya, U.R.: Automated detection of COVID-19 cases using deep neural networks with x-ray images. Comput. Biol. Med. 121, 103792 (2020)

22. Paul, A., Basu, A., Mahmud, M., et al.: Inverted bell-curve-based ensemble of deep learning models for detection of COVID-19 from chest X-rays. Neural Comput. Appl. (2022). https://doi.org/10.1007/s00521-021-06737-6

23. de Pinho, A.G., Vellasco, M., da Cruz, A.V.A.: A new model for credit approval problems: a quantum-inspired neuro-evolutionary algorithm with binary-real representation. In: 2009 World Congress on Nature & Biologically Inspired Computing (NaBIC), pp. 445–450. IEEE (2009)

24. Prakash, N., Murugappan, M., Hemalakshmi, G., Jayalakshmi, M., Mahmud, M.: Deep transfer learning for COVID-19 detection and infection localization with superpixel based segmentation. Sustain. Urban Areas **75**, 103252 (2021)
25. Simonyan, K., Zisserman, A.: Very deep convolutional networks for large-scale image recognition. arXiv preprint arXiv:1409.1556 (2014)
26. Szegedy, C., et al.: Going deeper with convolutions. In: Proceedings of the IEEE Conference on Computer Vision and Pattern Recognition, pp. 1–9 (2015)
27. Szegedy, C., Vanhoucke, V., Ioffe, S., Shlens, J., Wojna, Z.: Rethinking the inception architecture for computer vision. In: Proceedings of the IEEE Conference on Computer Vision and Pattern Recognition, pp. 2818–2826 (2016)
28. Szwarcman, D.: Quantum-inspired Neural Architecture Search. Ph.D. thesis, PUC-Rio (2020)
29. Szwarcman, D., Civitarese, D., Vellasco, M.: Quantum-inspired neural architecture search. In: 2019 International Joint Conference on Neural Networks (IJCNN), pp. 1–8. IEEE (2019)
30. Szwarcman, D., Civitarese, D., Vellasco, M.: Quantum-inspired evolutionary algorithm applied to neural architecture search. Appl. Soft Comput. **120**, 108674 (2022)
31. Tan, M., Le, Q.: Efficientnet: rethinking model scaling for convolutional neural networks. In: International Conference on Machine Learning, pp. 6105–6114. PMLR (2019)
32. Timofeev, A., Chrysos, G.G., Cevher, V.: Self-supervised neural architecture search for imbalanced datasets. arXiv preprint arXiv:2109.08580 (2021)
33. Wang, L., Lin, Z.Q., Wong, A.: Covid-net: a tailored deep convolutional neural network design for detection of COVID-19 cases from chest x-ray images. Sci. Rep. **10**(1), 1–12 (2020)
34. Wang, X., Peng, Y., Lu, L., Lu, Z., Bagheri, M., Summers, R.: Hospital-scale chest x-ray database and benchmarks on weakly-supervised classification and localization of common thorax diseases. In: IEEE CVPR, vol. 7 (2017)
35. Whitley, L.D., et al.: The GENITOR algorithm and selection pressure: why rank-based allocation of reproductive trials is best. Citeseer (1989)
36. Wistuba, M., Rawat, A., Pedapati, T.: A survey on neural architecture search. arXiv preprint arXiv:1905.01392 (2019)
37. Ye, W., Liu, R., Li, Y., Jiao, L.: Quantum-inspired evolutionary algorithm for convolutional neural networks architecture search. In: 2020 IEEE Congress on Evolutionary Computation (CEC), pp. 1–8. IEEE (2020)
38. Zhong, Z., Yan, J., Wu, W., Shao, J., Liu, C.L.: Practical block-wise neural network architecture generation. In: Proceedings of the IEEE Conference on Computer Vision and Pattern Recognition, pp. 2423–2432 (2018)
39. Zoph, B., Le, Q.V.: Neural architecture search with reinforcement learning. arXiv preprint arXiv:1611.01578 (2016)
40. Zoph, B., Vasudevan, V., Shlens, J., Le, Q.V.: Learning transferable architectures for scalable image recognition. In: Proceedings of the IEEE Conference on Computer Vision and Pattern Recognition, pp. 8697–8710 (2018)

Application of AI and Informatics in Network, Security, and Analytics

Beware the Sirens: Prototyping an Emergency Vehicle Detection System for Smart Cars

Michela Cantarini⊙, Leonardo Gabrielli[✉]⊙, Lucia Migliorelli⊙,
Adriano Mancini⊙, and Stefano Squartini⊙

Dipartimento di Ingegneria dell'Informazione, Università Politecnica delle Marche,
via Brecce Bianche 12, 60131 Ancona, Italy
`michela.cantarini@pm.univpm.it`, `l.gabrielli@staff.univpm.it`

Abstract. Vehicle drivers should be able to react coherently in anomalous circumstances, such as the quick arrival of an emergency vehicle with sirens wailing. This situation requires all regular vehicles to give way or slow down, depending on the road and traffic conditions. In this paper, we address an automatic system that assists the driver in reacting to the arrival of an emergency vehicle by employing audio and video algorithms based on Deep Learning. More specifically, by leveraging sound recognition algorithms, the vehicle is able to detect the arrival of the emergency vehicle by its siren sound. In such an event, by making use of computer vision algorithms, the vehicle intelligence can monitor the driver's gaze and awareness towards the emergency vehicle and assess his/her awareness. The paper describes the process of integrating these technologies into a commercial car, the creation of new datasets and the challenges encountered.

Keywords: Emergency vehicle detection system · Audio classification · Computer vision

1 Introduction

Current vehicles show increasing degrees of safety devices that encompass many aspects related to accidents and driver distraction. They include lane control, obstacle detection, speed limit sign recognition and more. The complexity of these systems has evolved: while the first prototypes could only measure physical quantities such as speed or the distance from the next car, recent devices include image sensors or a fusion of several sensors and provide data to artificial intelligence algorithms that must be robust to issues such as noise, darkness/extreme brightness, obstacles, and adverse weather conditions.

While the innovations in this field will eventually take to fully autonomous driving vehicles, at the moment, vehicle safety systems are auxiliary services that help the driver to reduce the chances of error or distraction. Most of them are based on RADARs and LiDARS [7,14,16,27,36], but acoustic sensors are being

M. Mahmud et al. (Eds.): AII 2022, CCIS 1724, pp. 437–451, 2022.
https://doi.org/10.1007/978-3-031-24801-6_31

considered for a few tasks such as pavement dry/wet and smooth/rough detection [1,12,24]. Image sensors play a fundamental role both inside and outside the car cabin: they are used, e.g., to detect and classify road signs [29] or to monitor the state of the driver and, in particular, drowsiness [2,26].

Among the safety services that are yet to be found on commercially-available cars, we can find those that require a tight interaction with the driver or those that are not based on the measure of a physical quantity but rather on understanding the surrounding context. In this scenario surely falls the detection of approaching emergency vehicles, such as an ambulance or a firefighters truck. Recognizing the presence of these vehicles is crucial when they arrive at high speed due to an emergency situation. In these occurrences, the driver must be aware of the approaching vehicle well before it is close, understand what actions might be suitable based on the traffic and road conditions and act then safely considering surrounding vehicles, pedestrians, and generic obstacles.

In those situations, the emergency vehicle has powered sirens. Despite some regulatory differences in the sound emission parameters among different countries, the role of the high-intensity acoustic alarm is considered paramount to alert citizens and drivers and let them safely get out of the way. Unlike other visual signals, sound can immediately reach receivers and capture their attention even if the emergency vehicle is around a corner or surrounded by other vehicles. It is natural, therefore, to build emergency vehicle detection devices based on its acoustic signal. The detection of siren signals in city traffic has been object of several works in the past, as we will discuss later, and may be considered quite mature.

In this paper, instead, we aim at building a complete prototype of a car fitted with an emergency vehicle detection system that, monitors and understands the behavior of the driver, thus improving the safety of the car and the other vehicles surrounding it. We will, thus, describe how the work has been conducted, what engineering choices have been done and what challenges such a system will be facing in the real-world. We will also describe how audio and video datasets have been created and describe preliminary results from the analysis of human behavior in response to siren stimuli. This will help in guiding the video detection phase and focus on the most salient features.

The outline of the paper follows. In Sect. 2 we describe the state of the art in detecting sirens acoustic signals, and in monitoring the driver attention by computer vision techniques. Then, we move on to describing our prototype in Sect. 3. In Sect. 4 we describe some of the present and future challenges. Finally, Sect. 5 outlines the conclusions.

2   State of the Art

2.1   Audio-Based Emergency Vehicle Detection

Emergency Siren Detection (ESD) is the research area included in the broader field of sound event detection [20] dealing with the identification of emergency vehicle alarms. Among generic sound event classification tasks that can find multiple real-world applications, ESD is typically employed in automotive. Despite different algorithms and detection strategies, the common goal is the implementation of embedded in-car devices called Emergency Vehicle Detection Systems. Several works in the literature tackled this issue, and in the years they reached remarkable results. Some research has focused on developing low computational cost digital signal processing techniques such as Module Difference Function and Peak Searching [21], the Least Mean Squared [10], and the Longest Common Subsequence [17] methods, which can also be implemented into microcontrollers [22]. Some of these algorithms may require the whole siren sound pattern (alternation of the two tones) to be completed in order to provide a classification outcome, resulting in detection times between 3.6 and 4.2 s [8] even if short processing audio frames are used (e.g. 0.1 s).

More challenging scenarios, such as siren sound recognition in noisy contexts, have been addressed with machine learning [6,9,31] and deep learning techniques [3,4,19,23]. Even if those works employ different datasets, it seems that currently, one among the best results has been achieved with a two-branch convolutional neural network that simultaneously learns the characteristics of raw audio and its time-frequency representation [33], achieving an accuracy of 98.24% with 1.5 s frames. In [34] the audio frames have been shortened to 0.25 s, to reduce the classification latency, and a residual network has been employed, yielding comparable results.

2.2 Driver Monitoring

Modern Advanced driver-assistance systems (ADASs) have been developed to support (actively or passively) the driver. In recent years the loss of attention is one of the main causes of road accidents (e.g., smartphones). In this context it is clear how ADASs play a key-role to identify anomalous behaviors. Loss of attentions and/or drowsiness could be monitored using different technologies as pattern analysis (i.e., road lines, steering wheel pressure), eye analysis and facial expression, and physiological signals analysis (i.e., EEG, heart rate,...) [30]. Vision sensors are optimal candidates considering that this kind of technology is contact-less and could be used to monitor drivers and if needed passengers. Potential tasks that could be supported by artificial vision range from face detection, to pose estimation of driver's head and gaze. Different challenges involve the use of artificial vision as the real-time processing, robustness to light changes, cost, privacy. The use of edge processors as edge Tensor Processing Units (eTPU) supports the use of neural networks on embedded devices. Modern approaches to the above-mentioned tasks relies on deep learning that sets complex computing requirements. New generation of devices are also emerging in the automotive area as the Dynamic Vision Systems (DVSs) or event cameras. These devices are suitable in scenes where the dynamic range is a key factor to manage in a proper way critical light conditions (e.g., direct sun light, abrupt change due to entrance/exit into/from a tunnel) [13,18]. The processing of data from event cameras is different from classical frame ones. Recently, approaches have been developed to simultaneously detect and track faces and eyes [28] also estimating the gaze [11] of a driver. As reported by [25], high frame rate (30fps+) is required to identify in a proper way events as eye-blinking that is a key factor to monitor the driver. In this scenario the use of new generation of devices as event cameras opens a new perspective to acquire high temporal resolution that is a key factor to properly monitor the driver. Finally, pre-processing of images to enhance contrast using a geometrical fuzzy approach could improve the quality of output from the processing pipeline [35].

3   Architecture of the Prototype

The proposed emergency siren detection system is designed with the goal of interacting with the driver in the case of an emergency vehicle approaching. These are the main objectives we expect from such a system:

- constantly monitor for the presence of emergency vehicles;
- in case of an emergency vehicle approaching verify that the driver is aware of the approaching vehicle;
- in case the driver seems not to be aware, raise his/her attention with an audio or visual cue.

The driver awareness can be verified using computer vision algorithms to extract several key insights from the eyes activity. Of particular interest are those quick movements directed towards the mirrors (i.e., left, rear and right mirrors). These are sign of the driver searching for the source of the sound and are an important index of awareness in this context. As we shall discuss later, from a preliminary experimental phase, the driver will often direct the gaze towards the mirror when hearing a siren coming from behind the car with small movements of the head that are really complex to detect in a robust way.

Of course, we are not addressing the case of a high or full driving automation (levels 4 and 5 of the standard [32]), where the human is not required to be in the loop and the car can take action by pulling the car out of the lane or slowing down. These scenarios lay outside of the scope of the paper. Here we are interested in the siren detection and the subsequent analysis of the driver behavior. Figure 1 shows the flow diagram of the system.

In the rest of the section we describe the prototype from both hardware and software perspective highlighting the main software components to reach the goals.

3.1   HW Architecture

Given the objectives outlined in the previous section, the prototype requires imaging and acoustic sensors, the former pointing towards the driver, the latter monitoring the outside acoustic scene. Their data must be processed by a device with sufficient computational power to run classification algorithms in real-time and some glue logic software to implement the flow diagram in Fig. 1. A heads

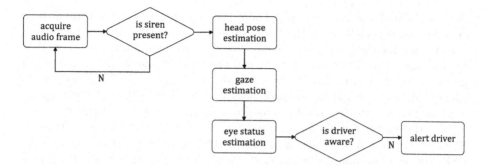

Fig. 1. Flow diagram of the expected behavior of the system: the audio acquisition system detects the sound of the siren in real-time, after which the camera is activated to monitor the driver's awareness, focusing on the pose of the head, the gaze orientation and the state of the eyes. In case the driver is unaware of the emergency vehicle, an alarm warns of its arrival.

up display (HUD) is also necessary to alert the driver if needed. All these devices are fitted in a prototype car, a Mercedes Class A, provided by a partner in the project that supports this research work. The car has been also employed to collect the datasets required to train and test the algorithms.

As for the software, all the functionalities have been factored in one single computing device for the sake of simplicity, and to fit the reduced space and power supply of the car. The device must be sufficiently powerful to allow the real-time execution of audio and video detection algorithms. To get a working prototype with low effort and short time, off-the-shelf components are better suited. For this reason, we decided to opt for a x86 machine with the ability of hosting a graphics processing unit (GPU) to obtain a speedup with Deep Learning and image processing algorithms and a power-efficient execution of the algorithms. In principle, any x86 personal computer would suit, however at the moment the smallest footprint x86 computer form factor is Intel NUC, providing reduced size and power, and in some of its versions is capable of hosting an external GPU, in our case a GTX 1650 GPU, a small GPU designed to fit the NUC. The maximum power of the system is 60W (worst case), which in this prototyping stage will be provided by a power inverter that converts the 12V DC outlet of the car to a 230V AC source for the equipment. The NUC also has USB and HDMI connectors and drivers to connect the HUD and can run any GNU/Linux distribution, allowing for an effortless software development.

For the acoustic sensors we opted for omnidirectional ECM8000 measurement condenser microphones, to allow detecting sound in all directions. The placement and number of microphones follows previous studies [24], where we observed the advantages and disadvantages of various positions. To analyze the acoustic scene outside of the vehicle, microphones inside the car cabin are not adequate since the outside sounds are damped and inside the cabin the conversations or the radio can interfere with the task. The microphone can be placed near the back of the car, e.g. behind the license plate. There the exposure to sounds coming from outside (and especially from the back, where an incoming emergency vehicle is hard to spot for the driver) is optimal. However, the microphone is also exposed to wind and rain. The trunk of the car represents a trade-off between weather protection and exposure to external sounds. A maximum of 8 microphones is enough to record sound in all these position, therefore a Roland Octacapture 8-channel audio interface has been used to capture sound with the NUC.

For the vision sensors we evaluated two different technologies. Standard RGB camera and in particular we used the IDS UI-3160CP-C-HQ camera. This USB3.0 camera is equipped with a 2/3" global shutter CMOS sensor PYTHON 2000 from onsemi providing a full resolution of 2.3 MP (1920 × 1200 pixels) with up to 165 fps. We also evaluated the use of Dynamic Vision System (DVS) also known as event cameras. In particular we adopted the DAVIS346[1] camera that is able to provide at the same time both frames (grayscale) and events (location, polarity and timestamp). Both cameras are synchronized with the Pulse per second signal generated from an external GPS receiver based on u-blox NEO-M8 GNSS device with an external antenna. Figure 2 shows the position of camera and GNSS.

1 DVS Camera **2** GNSS Receiver and sync cable (from receiver to camera and audio interface)

Fig. 2. The dashboard of the prototype car fitted with the DVS camera and the GNSS receiver.

3.2   SW Architecture

The software architecture to implement the prototype requires several tasks to be executed in parallel. For this reason we have built a system based on parallel threads distinct in their functionality. An overview is provided in Fig. 4. The chosen programming language for the implementation is Python, since it allows

---

[1] DAVIS346 Datasheet available at the following URL: https://inivation.com/wp-content/uploads/2019/08/DAVIS346.pdf.

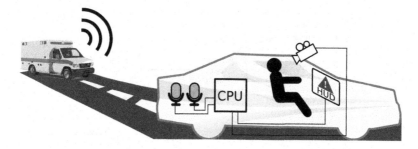

Fig. 3. An overview of the hardware components involved with the prototype.

for multi-threading, it can implement flexible graphic user interface (GUI), it can be ported to all common operating systems, and it has bindings for the most common deep learning, audio processing and image processing libraries.

As can be seen, the main process spawns the GUI, the audio processing task and the video task. The main application is realized using the Kivy library[2]. The GUI simulates a car dash (see Fig. 5 and, besides some service buttons, once started, shows the status of the detection. Whenever a siren is detected it shows an alert to provide a visual cue. In this case. The audio thread employs the `sounddevice` python library. This relies on the widely adopted cross-platform PortAudio C library[3]. Sounddevice allows to register a callback function which can process the audio frame by frame. Our callback, in turn, calls the forward method of a `torch`[4] neural model that has been previously trained to detect the presence of sirens in traffic and noisy signals according to the methods described in Sect. 2.1. At the detection of the siren a signal is passed to the video thread to indicate the presence of a siren through the business logic thread that manages the whole system. The video processing pipeline evaluates if the gaze of user is pointing to a mirrors when the siren is active (i.e., left, right, and rear view mirrors). A similar signal is sent when the siren has disappeared. By receiving the signal, the video process knows when the user should be looking for signs of an emergency vehicle and starts monitoring his/her eyes.

3.3   Siren Detection

The emergency siren detection algorithms have been developed by taking into consideration the objective and installation requirements. We opted for the following approaches:

- a binary *siren vs. noise* classification task, since the purpose of the system is to detect only one target event among all possible sounds surrounding the vehicle;

---

[2] https://kivy.org/.

[3] http://www.portaudio.com/.

[4] https://pytorch.org/.

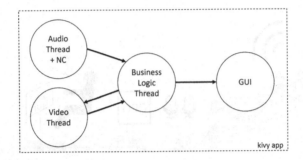

Fig. 4. An overview of the software nodes involved with the prototype (NC stands for neural classification.

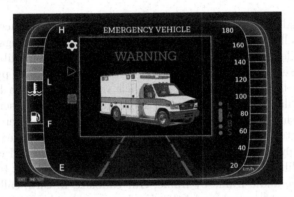

Fig. 5. The HUD GUI showing a car dashboard with a siren alert in the middle.

- convolutional neural networks 2D that simultaneously exploit the convolutional layers for feature learning of time-frequency signal representations and perform the classification task in the final fully-connected layers;
- the investigation of acoustic features with reduced dimensionality and the deployment of architecture with a limited number of layers to minimize the computational cost of the algorithm.

For this purpose, we employ a convolutional neural network that, in previous work [4,5], has demonstrated its robustness in the ESD task. In order to avoid excessive reduction of the input size, the first part has been implemented with 3 convolutional blocks, each including 2 convolutional layers and a max-pooling layer. In all convolutional layers, we employ a 3×3 kernel with strides equal to 1×1 to accurately capture the details of the input spectrogram. Then, in the max-pooling layer, the stride step is set to 2×2 to obtain a representation with accentuated features at halved dimensionality. In the first, second, and third blocks, the number of convolutional filters is 4, 8, and 16, respectively. The second part of the network consists of a fully connected layer composed of 10 neurons and the final output classifier. Such an algorithm proved lightweight: on the chosen hardware platform it only requires 19% of one of the 16 CPU cores, therefore we do not resort to the available GPU and leave it to the video processing tasks.

In addition to the previously used synthetic dataset [4], a new dataset has been gathered on the prototype car, traveling in real traffic conditions. The car has been fitted with 8 microphones placed inside the cockpit and outside the vehicle. The recordings have been done on roads where ambulances are expected to be found more frequently (e.g. close to hospital or urban areas). Notwithstanding this, the siren recordings amount to 200 s over 10.5 h of total recordings, making the dataset strongly unbalanced.

Training of the described architecture and evaluations of the computed models were conducted in several configurations, based on different datasets, acoustic features, and filtering techniques or dimensionality reduction applications. We investigated the effectiveness of the gammatone, the log-Mel and the STFT spectrograms as time-frequency representations of audio data.

3.4   Vision System to Monitor the Driver

Visual data could support the monitoring of driver's action when an emergency vehicle with powered siren is approaching. We conducted experiments in a static condition inside a semianechoic chamber to monitor the actions of drivers (inside a vehicle) when hearing the tone of a siren incoming and passing by simulated using virtual acoustic techniques. The main objective of this test that involved 14 people (age range from 25 to 39 years old) was to evaluate the reaction of drivers. The siren stimuli occurred randomly and the drivers were not aware of the objective of the test. The analysis revealed that most of the people are not rotating the head but they change their gaze pointing the attention to left/rearview mirror. Our initial assumption was that the reaction of drivers would be to change the orientation/pose of head, but this is not always true, and we recorded that most of the involved drivers just changed their gaze without changing the main orientation of the head. If we want to understand if the driver is aware of incoming emergency vehicle then we need to focus the monitoring on the following main features: pose of head (in terms of roll, pitch, yaw), gaze orientation and status of eyes (opened/closed). These main features are then used to evaluate if there is some reaction to an active siren.

Head Pose Estimation. The estimation of head pose was performed by extracting 3D facial landmarks from RGB or gray-scale images (IR images could be also used for this purpose). We rely on MediaPipe Face Mesh [15] that estimates 468 3D face landmarks from a single camera without requiring deep data. Starting from a sub-set of landmarks we estimate the pose of the head to derive the main angles in terms of roll, pitch, and yaw. To reduce the computational load, we exclude from the computation the area that includes the passenger, and, in this way, it is possible to exclude multiple faces in a single frame. Figure 6 shows an example of landmark detection inside the test vehicle using MediaPipe Face Mesh [15]. Landmarks related to eyes and lips are then used to generate

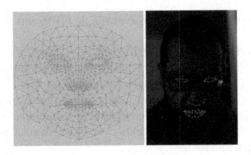

Fig. 6. Left: mesh map for facial landmarks. Right: extracted landmarks. Red and blue landmarks are linked to eyes. (Color figure online)

regions of interest (bounding box with external offset) that could be used to estimate the status (opened/closed) as discussed in the following sections.

Gaze Estimation. The estimation of gaze was necessary to evaluate if driver's gaze is pointing to a region of interest when events occur (e.g., approaching emergency vehicle). Gaze estimation is performed using both deep and RGB or IR images from Intel RealSense D455. We defined different areas (screens) of interest: the front windscreen, the left mirror and rear-view one. Starting from the Eyeware toolchain [5] we integrated the data from Intel RealSense D455 to estimate the head pose and track the gaze of driver. The developed module outputs the head pose (used to cross-check the data with the pose estimated using MediaPipe), the direction of user's gaze and the screen that is "hit" by the drivers. All the data are in a global reference system that is centered on the camera. Figure 7 shows an example of gaze estimation using RGB frames. Data are then shared with other applications to correlate the head pose and gaze with the siren detection application.

Fig. 7. Gaze Estimation from vision system using a RealSense D455.

Eye Status Estimation. Starting from the extracted landmarks we extract three main sub-images. Two images are related to left and right eye while the third one is related to lips (mouth). We decided to estimate the status of eyes

---

[5] Eyeware toolchain (public) https://github.com/eyeware.

and mouth (opened/closed). A dataset was created by looking for images of faces of male and female for different ranges of ages and races. A first pool of images have been extracted using the SerpApi web-scraper to retrieve images from the Google Images API[6] Images have been filtered by a manual check to include only useful images. We included 10,000 images with opened and closed eyes (balanced). We finally executed the Facemesh to extract facial landmarks and selecting the eyes by using a bounding box on the landmarks that belong to left and right eyes. We also apply an offset of 20 pixels to the bounding box (external) to include more data. Figure 8 shows an example of images extracted from our dataset.

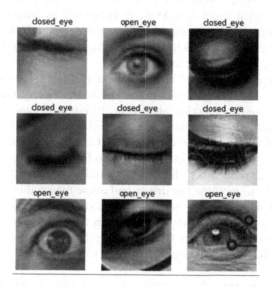

Fig. 8. Example of images of opened/closed eyes from our dataset.

We apply data augmentation by applying flipping and small rotations ($\pm10°$). We decided to use a MobileNet V2 using 80% of sample for training and 20% for validation. We have two classes (opened eye and closed eyes) and we use binary cross entropy as loss. We adopt a pre-trained set of weight from imagenet performing transfer learning to adapt that model to our task. We also perform fine-tuning to improve the overall performance of our model. Training and validation accuracy are over the 97.5%.

The developed model could be also optimized to make it lighter. This task has been accomplished using TF lite converter. From preliminary results the accuracy is reduced of a small factor (0.97) with a 3.5× performance gain in terms of time required to predict a single frame.

---

[6] SerpApi - Google Image API https://serpapi.com/.

4   Challenges

Building such a prototype allowed us to investigate on the feasibility of an ESD system in a real car environment. Several challenges are ahead to engineer such a system on a commercial car, but overall the results seems promising. In this section we shall highlight some of the issues and challenges that we observed from the work conducted so far.

The engineering of the system as a whole does not seem to pose any particular issue: miniature acoustic and imaging sensors are already integrated in commercial cars. The main issue seems related to the processing unit and its algorithms. However, the computational cost of the algorithms described thus far is compatible with small computing devices such as fanless x86 processors, or even better, with modern embedded Tensor Processing Units (TPU) such as the Edge TPU by Google, which provides sufficient processing power for deep learning at a very small energy footprint.

For the system to be useful in a real scenario, latencies must be reduced. The main source of latency in our prototype is the size of the audio window employed by the audio detection algorithm. In our previous and current algorithms, to maximize detection accuracy, the audio frame provided to the detection algorithms is usually of the order of 0.5 s. Considering that the arrival of an emergency vehicle may take seconds, this audio frame size may seem sufficiently small. However, to reduce the chances of troubles, the shorter the frame size, the more the time to monitor the driver and allow reasonable reaction times by the automatic system. Finally, for a real-world system to be acceptable it needs to generalize to any siren sounds considered in the regulations of all the countries where the car will be driven. Currently, our dataset only contains ambulance sounds from the Italian regulation. Other siren tones should be added to increase the dataset.

From the perspective of vision sensors there are several challenges in the scenario of this paper. The capability to generalize the developed models to wide set of faces is one challenge that of course will be mitigate by integrating other data-set. In some case, if the driver wears sunglasses the detection of eyes fails and then the gaze estimation could be affected considering that we can detect only the pose of head without having data on the pose of eyes. Another challenge related to vision systems is related to the cost considering the system requires one camera and a computing unit with a proper computing power to process frames in real time. The processing is safe from the point of view of privacy considering that frame are not stored and shared on the cloud. Another challenge we identified is also related to the robustness of detection in case of changes of light conditions. In some case sun-light or absence of it could affect the detection. The use of event cameras is interesting and from preliminary tests that we performed represent a good solution considering the ultra high value of dynamic range (>120 dB); the issue is related to the resolution of sensors (typically <0.3 MP).

Finally, human factors must be considered to deploy such a system: the driver should be aware of the presence of an ESD system in the car, and the alert information provided should be clear and not distracting.

5   Conclusions

In this work we have described a prototype of an emergency vehicle detection system, implemented in a real car and capable of detecting the presence of incoming sirens, monitoring the driver attention and potentially providing an alert in case the system has not spotted any sign of awareness from the driver. The audio system is based on deep learning algorithms and has been trained on datasets created with a commercial car in road traffic conditions. Experiments on human reactions have been conducted in a semianechoic room with virtual acoustic simulation of a siren. Finally, eyes and face datasets have been collected from several sources including a web-scraper.

The integration of the devices in the car poses no particular issues, however other challenges in the algorithms and in the interaction with the human can be envisioned and have been summarized.

The system has not been yet tested on the road. Assessing its validity in a real environment will require a substantial effort in enrolling participants and make them run into emergency vehicles on the street.

Acknowledgement. This work is supported by Marche Region in implementation of the financial programme POR MARCHE FESR 2014-2020, project "Miracle" (Marche Innovation and Research fAcilities for Connected and sustainable Living Environments), CUP B28I19000330007.

References

1. Abdić, I., et al.: Detecting road surface wetness from audio: a deep learning approach. In: 2016 23rd International Conference on Pattern Recognition (ICPR), pp. 3458–3463. IEEE (2016)
2. Ahmed, M., Masood, S., Ahmad, M., Abd El-Latif, A.A.: Intelligent driver drowsiness detection for traffic safety based on multi CNN deep model and facial subsampling. IEEE Trans. Intell. Transp. Syst. (2021)
3. Beritelli, F., Casale, S., Russo, A., Serrano, S.: An automatic emergency signal recognition system for the hearing impaired. In: 2006 IEEE 12th Digital Signal Processing Workshop & 4th IEEE Signal Processing Education Workshop, pp. 179–182. IEEE (2006)
4. Cantarini, M., Brocanelli, A., Gabrielli, L., Squartini, S.: Acoustic features for deep learning-based models for emergency siren detection: an evaluation study. In: 2021 12th International Symposium on Image and Signal Processing and Analysis (ISPA), pp. 47–53. IEEE (2021)
5. Cantarini, M., Serafini, L., Gabrielli, L., Principi, E., Squartini, S.: Emergency siren recognition in urban scenarios: synthetic dataset and deep learning models. In: Huang, D.-S., Bevilacqua, V., Hussain, A. (eds.) ICIC 2020. LNCS, vol. 12463, pp. 207–220. Springer, Cham (2020). https://doi.org/10.1007/978-3-030-60799-9_18

6. Carmel, D., Yeshurun, A., Moshe, Y.: Detection of alarm sounds in noisy environments. In: 2017 25th European Signal Processing Conference (EUSIPCO), pp. 1839–1843. IEEE (2017)

7. Cho, H., Seo, Y.W., Kumar, B.V., Rajkumar, R.R.: A multi-sensor fusion system for moving object detection and tracking in urban driving environments. In: Robotics and Automation (ICRA), 2014 IEEE International Conference on, pp. 1836–1843. IEEE (2014)

8. Ebizuka, Y., Kato, S., Itami, M.: Detecting approach of emergency vehicles using siren sound processing. In: 2019 IEEE Intelligent Transportation Systems Conference (ITSC), pp. 4431–4436. IEEE (2019)

9. Fatimah, B., Preethi, A., Hrushikesh, V., Singh, A., Kotion, H.R.: An automatic siren detection algorithm using fourier decomposition method and MFCC. In: 2020 11th International Conference on Computing, Communication and Networking Technologies (ICCCNT), pp. 1–6. IEEE (2020)

10. Fazenda, B., Atmoko, H., Gu, F., Guan, L., Ball, A.: Acoustic based safety emergency vehicle detection for intelligent transport systems. In: 2009 ICCAS-SICE, pp. 4250–4255. IEEE (2009)

11. Feng, Y., Goulding-Hotta, N., Khan, A., Reyserhove, H., Zhu, Y.: Real-time gaze tracking with event-driven eye segmentation (2022). https://doi.org/10.48550/ARXIV.2201.07367

12. Gabrielli, L., Ambrosini, L., Vesperini, F., Bruschi, V., Squartini, S., Cattani, L.: Processing acoustic data with siamese neural networks for enhanced road roughness classification. In: 2019 International Joint Conference on Neural Networks (IJCNN), pp. 1–7. IEEE (2019)

13. Gallego, G., et al.: Event-based vision: a survey. IEEE Trans. Pattern Anal. Mach. Intell. **44**(1), 154–180 (2022). https://doi.org/10.1109/TPAMI.2020.3008413

14. Hakobyan, G., Yang, B.: High-performance automotive radar: a review of signal processing algorithms and modulation schemes. IEEE Signal Process. Mag. **36**(5), 32–44 (2019)

15. Kartynnik, Y., Ablavatski, A., Grishchenko, I., Grundmann, M.: Real-time facial surface geometry from monocular video on mobile GPUs. arXiv preprint arXiv:1907.06724 (2019)

16. Li, Y., Ibanez-Guzman, J.: Lidar for autonomous driving: the principles, challenges, and trends for automotive lidar and perception systems. IEEE Signal Process. Mag. **37**(4), 50–61 (2020)

17. Liaw, J.J., Wang, W.S., Chu, H.C., Huang, M.S., Lu, C.P.: Recognition of the ambulance siren sound in Taiwan by the longest common subsequence. In: 2013 IEEE International Conference on Systems, Man, and Cybernetics, pp. 3825–3828. IEEE (2013)

18. Maqueda, A.I., Loquercio, A., Gallego, G., García, N., Scaramuzza, D.: Event-based vision meets deep learning on steering prediction for self-driving cars. In: 2018 IEEE/CVF Conference on Computer Vision and Pattern Recognition, pp. 5419–5427 (2018). https://doi.org/10.1109/CVPR.2018.00568

19. Marchegiani, L., Newman, P.: Listening for sirens: locating and classifying acoustic alarms in city scenes. IEEE Trans. Intell. Transp. Syst. (2022)

20. Mesaros, A., Heittola, T., Virtanen, T., Plumbley, M.D.: Sound event detection: a tutorial. IEEE Signal Process. Mag. **38**(5), 67–83 (2021)

21. Meucci, F., Pierucci, L., Del Re, E., Lastrucci, L., Desii, P.: A real-time siren detector to improve safety of guide in traffic environment. In: 2008 16th European Signal Processing Conference, pp. 1–5. IEEE (2008)

22. Miyazakia, T., Kitazonoa, Y., Shimakawab, M.: Ambulance siren detector using FFT on dsPIC. In: Proceedings of the 1st IEEE/IIAE International Conference on Intelligent Systems and Image Processing, pp. 266–269 (2013)

23. Padhy, S., Tiwari, J., Rathore, S., Kumar, N.: Emergency signal classification for the hearing impaired using multi-channel convolutional neural network architecture. In: 2019 IEEE Conference on Information and Communication Technology, pp. 1–6. IEEE (2019)

24. Pepe, G., Gabrielli, L., Ambrosini, L., Squartini, S., Cattani, L.: Detecting road surface wetness using microphones and convolutional neural networks. In: Audio Engineering Society Convention, no. 146. Audio Engineering Society (2019)

25. Picot, A., Caplier, A., Charbonnier, S.: Comparison between EOG and high frame rate camera for drowsiness detection. In: 2009 Workshop on Applications of Computer Vision (WACV), pp. 1–6 (2009). https://doi.org/10.1109/WACV.2009.5403120

26. Ramzan, M., Khan, H.U., Awan, S.M., Ismail, A., Ilyas, M., Mahmood, A.: A survey on state-of-the-art drowsiness detection techniques. IEEE Access 7, 61904–61919 (2019)

27. Roriz, R., Cabral, J., Gomes, T.: Automotive lidar technology: a survey. IEEE Trans. Intell. Transp. Syst. (2021)

28. Ryan, C., et al.: Real-time face & eye tracking and blink detection using event cameras. Neural Netw. 141, 87–97 (2021)

29. Saadna, Y., Behloul, A.: An overview of traffic sign detection and classification methods. Int. J. Multimedia Inf. Retr. 6(3), 193–210 (2017). https://doi.org/10.1007/s13735-017-0129-8

30. Sahayadhas, A., Sundaraj, K., Murugappan, M.: Detecting driver drowsiness based on sensors: a review. Sensors 12(12), 16937–16953 (2012)

31. Schröder, J., Goetze, S., Grützmacher, V., Anemüller, J.: Automatic acoustic siren detection in traffic noise by part-based models. In: 2013 IEEE International Conference on Acoustics, Speech and Signal Processing, pp. 493–497. IEEE (2013)

32. Society of Automotive Engineers: SAE j3016 standard: Taxonomy and definitions for terms related to driving automation systems for on-road motor vehicles (2021)

33. Tran, V.T., Tsai, W.H.: Acoustic-based emergency vehicle detection using convolutional neural networks. IEEE Access 8, 75702–75713 (2020)

34. Tran, V.T., Tsai, W.H.: Audio-vision emergency vehicle detection. IEEE Sens. J. 21(24), 27905–27917 (2021)

35. Versaci, M., Calcagno, S., Morabito, F.C.: Image contrast enhancement by distances among points in fuzzy hyper-cubes. In: Azzopardi, G., Petkov, N. (eds.) CAIP 2015. LNCS, vol. 9257, pp. 494–505. Springer, Cham (2015). https://doi.org/10.1007/978-3-319-23117-4_43

36. Waldschmidt, C., Hasch, J., Menzel, W.: Automotive radar-from first efforts to future systems. IEEE J. Microw. 1(1), 135–148 (2021)

Indoor Positioning and Navigation Using Bluetooth Low Energy and Cloud Service in Healthcare Perspective

K. Shayekh Ebne Mizan[1]([✉])[ID], M. Shamim Kaiser[1,2][ID],
Shamim Al Mamun[1,2][ID], Milon Biswas[3][ID], Nusrat Zerin Zenia[1,4][ID],
Mufti Mahmud[5][ID], and Abzetdin Adamov[6][ID]

[1] Institute of Information Technology Jahangirnagar University,
Savar, Dhaka 1342, Bangladesh
shayekhebnemizan@gmail.com, {mskaiser,shamim}@juniv.edu
[2] Applied Intelligence and Informatics (AII) Lab, Wazed Miah Science Research
Centre, Jahangirnagar University, Savar, Dhaka 1342, Bangladesh
[3] Department of Computer Science and Engineering, Bangladesh University,
of Business and Technology, Mirpur-02, Dhaka 1216, Bangladesh
milon@ieee.org
[4] Department of Electrical and Software Engineering, University of Calgary,
Calgary, Canada
nusratzerin.zenia@ucalgary.ca
[5] Medical Technologies Innovation Facility, Nottingham Trent University,
Nottingham, Clifton NG11 8NS, UK
mufti.mahmud@ntu.ac.uk
[6] ADA University, Baku, Azerbaijan
aadamov@ada.edu.az

Abstract. People are able to explore unfamiliar surroundings with more
ease due to navigation devices. Users can now incorporate these systems
into handheld devices as a result of recent technological advancements
that have increased the popularity and number of people using navigation systems. Due to poor reception of Global Positioning System (GPS)
signals and a non-line of sight with orbiting satellites, it is more difficult to navigate within a building using GPS signals. Tracking and
navigation within a structure can be accomplished by a handheld device
(such as a smartphone or wearable) through the use of a wireless interface such as Bluetooth Low Energy (BLE). This type of technology can
be used to monitor and guide patients with neurological illnesses, such
as Alzheimer's disease (AD), within the hospital premises. This study
describes a system for indoor navigation based on wireless sensors, a
mobile health application (mHealth app), and Bluetooth beacons. The
study goes into great detail about how the mHealth app interacts with
the cloud-based architecture.

Keywords: Alzheimer's disease · IoT · IPS · LBS · RSSI · Cloud
service · Smart care

1   Introduction

Indoor positioning is a technology that assists in locating objects or people within a building. Because satellite-based global positioning systems (GPS) lose significant power owing to attenuation and reflection indoors, indoor positioning is a widely utilized technique in shopping malls, clinics, airports, and other indoor locations where mapping and other location-based services (LBS) are essential [1]. Inside Positioning System (IPS) technology uses the built-in sensors in mobile phones to calculate the device's indoor positioning by employing strong mathematical methods. By ingeniously merging the incoming data from several sensors, a very perfect positioning may be established with little to no latency, resulting in a trouble-free consumer interaction. The three distinct elements that IPS typically relies on for the perfect user interaction that is both exact and swift, are the underlying dynamic positioning method framework, the transmitted beacon signals that are picked up by the smartphone and, after that, fed to the positioning system, and apps built on top of the positioning system that annex value and make the process alluring to consumers [2].

Bluetooth Low Energy (BLE) is a low-power wireless communication technology that facilitates short-distance communication between smart devices. The Bluetooth Special Interest Group (SIG) has deployed a new Bluetooth standard known as BLE that focuses on low energy. It enables device manufacturers to incorporate a low-power communications interface into their existing products. BLE beacons are low-cost, energy-efficient components that can operate on button batteries for up to five years. Furthermore, Bluetooth beacons do not interact with medical or industrial devices, and they do not interfere with other radio networks. It has also been used to create innovative low-power devices like beacons that may operate for months or even years on a single coin cell battery. Indoor positioning systems, health and fitness, security, home automation, home entertainment, smart industries, and the Internet of Things are just a few of the uses for Bluetooth Low Energy [3]. It's also readily available on our cellphones and laptop computers, which we use every day [4]. Cloud services refer to a variety of internet-based facilities. The services are intended to offer simple, low-cost access to applications and resources without the demand for internal infrastructure or hardware. All components of cloud services are monitored via cloud computing. Moreover, these services are overseen by cloud computing vendors and service providers. Consumers can access them utilizing the providers' servers. Therefore, a firm does not need to host the applications on its own servers [5,6]. A mobile phone that is portable can have a mobile application as well as a large number of sensors for healthcare, wellness, and navigation. In this context, Wi-Fi or beacons are usually employed to develop an indoor positioning and navigation system. They additionally enable a smartphone user to detect the actual level of the floor, unlike GPS. In most cases, an "inside addressing" component is necessary, which guides people through buildings and dynamically calculates their location using an inside navigation system [7–10].

The primary goal of this research is to create an indoor positioning and navigation system using BLE and cloud services to support patients and caregivers in healthcare facilities. The study's contributions are as follows:

- To build a framework for indoor positioning and navigation with BLE tags and cloud service;
- To implement indoor positioning and navigation system using mobile application and cloud based framework;
- To evaluate the performance of the proposed system based on a case study; and
- To compare the proposed indoor positioning system with the state-of-the-art techniques.

Rest of the report is structured as follows: Sect. 2 discusses the related works; Sect. 3 introduces about the proposed model; Sect. 4 explains about the implementations; Sect. 5 discusses about the algorithm analysis; Sect. 6 depicts the performance analysis; finally, Sect. 7 is conclusion and Sect. 8 is about the acknowledgements.

2   Related Work

Many different methods and strategies as well as modern technologies [11–16] have been offered in the literature for healthcare industry specially in indoor positioning and navigation, and many of them are still being developed. Using received signal strength to estimate the real location, Lin and Lin [17] investigated the performance of several indoor positioning algorithms, including the probabilistic method, k-nearest-neighbor, and neural networks, for determining the actual location. The accuracy, precision, complexity, resilience, and scalability of the system were all considered when evaluating its performance.

For patients with neurological illnesses, Biswas et al. [18] developed an indoor navigation system based on the integration of wireless sensor nodes, a mobile application, and WiFi/Bluetooth beacons to link and lead them. Gallagher et al. [19] showed a simple method for configuring a positioning system both indoors and outdoors. For indoor positioning, the system used WIFI fingerprinting, while GPS was used for outdoor positioning. Faragher and Harle [20] presented the use of BLE beacons over WiFi for the fingerprinting of indoor positioning. Bai et al. [21] demonstrated a low-cost method of indoor positioning using BLE sensing infrastructure. In this system, the tracking object was a BLE beacon, and the BLE sensing-based approach pinpointed the location of the target object using two different algorithms. The trilateration algorithm was employed in one system, while the fingerprinting-based process was used in the other. Park et al. [22] represented a distance-based filtering algorithm using trilateration method for indoor positioning. The proposed system was evaluated by several experiments and the result minimized the error of location tracking. Bisio et al. [23] illustrated the architecture of an asset tracking system that favors the use of Android devices equipped with BLE and RFID over the conventional tracking method. The performance of the design was evaluated based on estimated distance accuracy, tag-finding probability, and smartphone battery discharge time. Chen et al. [24] proposed a new FLIPS (fuzzy logic indoor positioning system) to point out the location of an object at a distorted measured distance. The proposed system shows that FLIPS are more stable and action-better than the triangulation process. The raised approach is simple enough to use as hardware or in an embedded system. Yang and Shao [25] introduced WiFi-based indoor positioning systems that improve Time of Arrival (ToA) over the super-resolution approach and Angle of Arrival (AoA) to reduce the need for numerous antennae. The demonstrated method required no hardware configuration changes. Yim et al. [26] proposed a new decision tree-based fingerprinting approach over probabilistic method, K-NN, and Neural networks for indoor positioning. In the offline phase, the system generated a decision tree and displayed indoor location based on the tree. The performance was evaluated based on examination of time complexity and precision. A number of information modeling and processing issues concerning a human-centered navigation service were described by the authors [27]. This service is primarily aimed for persons who have difficulty navigating and follows to the goal of smart position solutions for ubiquitous computing systems. The total service is divided into many services (geometric path computation, semantic path filtering, reactive route assisting solution) and employs a layout of user account. The primary purpose is to combine the knowledge of semantic engineering tools in novel ways with traditional location-based applications. Such integration, is a critical enabler of omnipresent solutions that prioritize user experience. Terán et al. [28] describes the design, implementation, and assessment of an IoT-based indoor positioning system based on BLE technology. A data collection system was in charge of recognizing and sending sensed data to a central server for further computation over WiFi TCP connections in the proposed general architecture. A central server is in charge of integrating the data transferred by the first system over UNIX sockets into a SQL database and offering historical data and location results to be queried via a web interface. Finally, a dashboard was created using Ubidots cloud services to allow access to data results from any Internet-connected device. In another work [29], researchers looked at the performance and usability of two computer-vision-based systems and a Bluetooth Low Energy-based system. The first system, CamNav, was a computer vision-based system that employs a deep learning model that has been trained to recognize places, while the second system, QRNav, uses visual markers (QR codes) to determine locations. A field test with ten blinded users utilizing the three navigation systems was carried out.

To summarize, while most systems consider the geographical coordinates of the indoor positioning using BLE, wifi and other technologies, they do not consider the users' physical and perceptual abilities, while also their preferences for routing; they specifically employ weights to compute the indoor positioning in the geographical - topological layer, depending on the unique properties of the accessible positioning technology. On the contrary, comparing with the state-of-the-art techniques, this proposed system simultaneously represents the indoor positioning and navigation by using BLE beacons and considers the user with neurological disorder to assist them for decorous navigation and guidance.

3   Model Proposal

3.1   Context

Globally, the number of elderly people is increasing, and mean lifespans are greater than they have ever been. And the bulk of these circumstances had neurological issues alike Alzheimer's disease. The tendency of a patient with a neurological condition to forget crucial things is one of the most common symptoms. During their stay at home, patients frequently receive assistance from family members or personal caregivers, but it is challenging for hospital administration to provide one-on-one support in hospitals, and it is costly. This system proposed a Bluetooth system to let patients route the hospital based on this. When a patient enters the hospital perimeter (Fig. 1), the mobile application establishes a link between the hospital network and the patient. The patient can then select the desired destination to navigate within the hospital.

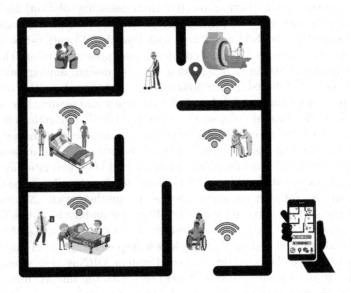

Fig. 1. Scenario of indoor navigation for Alzheimer's patients (AD). A smartphone software may build internal routing maps of a health centre employing augmented reality (AR) and bluetooth beacons, which can assist Alzheimer's patients.

3.2   Indoor Positioning Paradigm

The indoor positioning process is a cutting-edge technology that is being utilized to solve difficult problems in shopping malls, hospitals, and retail stores, among other places. Indoor positioning across the hospital benefits patients and visitors by reducing interruptions from medical workers seeking instructions. The optimal route to their goal will always be given to patients, visitors, and staff.

Initial interior positioning starts by catching the BLE node signals. The BLE node is shown to receive the RSSI from other BLE access nodes that are located in different places in Fig. 2. The BLE node then chooses the RSSI that is considered to be the strongest. After that, the system or the app sends the beacon_id and the corresponding RSSI value to server side. The server then analysis with the signal and RSSI value and sends the indoor coordinates to the app as well as the location report system.

For example, based on the RSSI value the user is located at Cell_b.

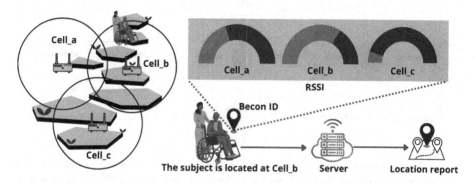

Fig. 2. Indoor positioning paradigm. The app user received the RSSIs were delivered to the app user by the BLE access nodes. As the user's location information, the location of the BLE access node with the highest RSSI is being selected.

4   Deployment

4.1   Indoor Positioning and Navigation

Initially, the user registers their user equipment via their mobile number. Then he selects the desired place. Here the user selected place is uploaded with a unique user id to the cloud database. This enhances the security and user monitoring. The admin panel can track which user is looking for which destination. The user then turns on the device's Bluetooth via the app. In the selected indoor premises, there are BLE tags, which are placed at different points and generate and spread signals where each corresponding signal depicts each point range. The app scans to catch the nearby BLE signals. To overcome the overlapping signal issues; the app sorts among the received signals by RSSI values and only receives the greatest RSSI value, which means the strongest tag signal.

Different signals at different positions point the indoor positioning of a user at the corresponding positions. The user then taps for direction button. An algorithm that works with the target location and the received signal determines the navigation or next move direction. Thus, the user reaches his desired destination. In this environment, voice command and notification messages are displayed to provide navigation to the user. For example, commanding to go north. A simulated compass is used, which refers to the direction. The magnetometer sensor is used for the implementation of the compass in the Android operating system. Alongside, a line map represents indoor premises and shows the user's current position with a dot, which makes it more user-friendly and transparent (Fig. 3).

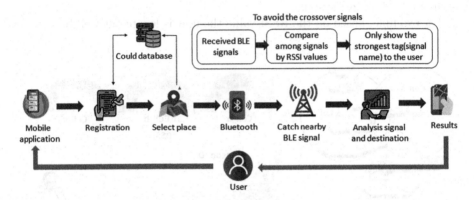

Fig. 3. Indoor positioning and navigation schematic: the way consumers interact with the mobile app is demonstrated, from the registration procedure to the navigation map as a consequence, as well as how to prevent the crossover signal.

Android Studio (Arctic Fox—2020.3.1 Version) IDE is used here for deployment of this app and the development language is Java. The minimum SDK version is 19 and the target SDK version is 28. Bluetooth, location and background location permissions are needed to act this application properly.[1]

4.2   Registration

The user provides the mobile number into the app. The app system then requests for OTP from firebase. After that, the firbase sends OTP to the app. The app again requests for credential from firebase. The firebase auth system then sends the credential to the app. At the end, the firebase sends the user info to the app server (Fig. 4).

Firebase is a NoSQL real-time cloud database which provides the service of user authentication,

---

[1] https://github.com/shayekh/Alzheimer-master.

User
App
Firebase
App Server
Use add a mobile number to the app interface
App sends a request for OTP
App receives OTP
Request for credential
Send credential
Send user info

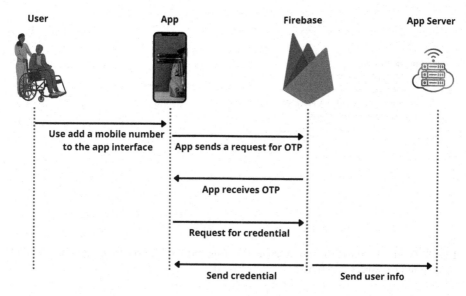

Fig. 4. Sequence diagram of various operations within the proposed registration process via the mobile number, OTP verification and authentication credential.

4.3 Cloud Database

As a cloud database, Firebase is used in this project. Firebase is a NoSQL database, and a real time DB is deployed in this perspective. Figure 5 represents the unique user id. Alongside, it depicts the user's mobile number, creation and signed in time period.

Search by email address, phone number, or user UID
Add user
Identifier
Providers
Created
Signed In
User UID
+8801952613365
Jul 25, 2020
Jul 25, 2020
DBnc0Ti7AEU112gnb0rBU2um2N...
+8801552465681
Jul 25, 2020
Jul 25, 2020
yBk6SPJLjhdBBuESegJhMEO5Rnx2
+8801717807462
Jul 24, 2020
Oct 19, 2021
sSGyHtrDv7ZZWtOlhXn0MLc75Wr2
Rows per page: 50
1 – 3 of 3

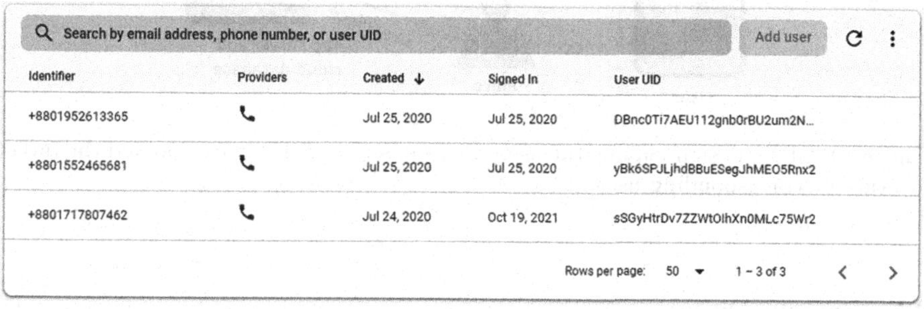

Fig. 5. Cloud database. It preserves user mobile number, unique UID, creation and signed in time period.

The database tracks the user by unique user id with their selected destination place. It keeps the record of the user in the indoor premises and ameliorate the security (Fig 6).

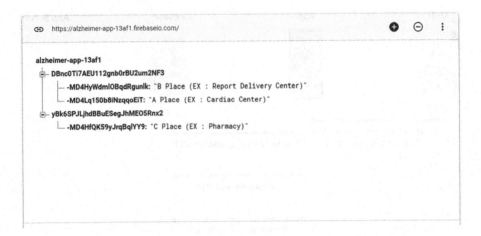

Fig. 6. Cloud database for monitoring. Pointing individual user by unique user id and corresponding target locations.

4.4 Database Design

The synopsis of database design is to save the user id in the cloud DB after successful registration. Furthermore, for security reasons, the chosen location is saved with corresponding user id at cloud DB (Fig 7).

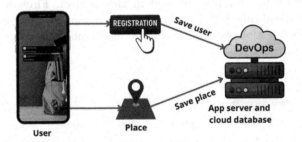

Fig. 7. Database design. Saving the user info after successful registration and the target location by corresponding user id.

4.5 System Design

Figure 8 defines the system design of the proposed model. The user registers via mobile number with the help of Firebase OTP and authentication process. After that consumer picks the target location which is saved in the cloud database.

The system BLE access node then receives the BLE tag signals and sort the signals order by the highest RSSI values. Only the strongest signal is pushed in the algorithm analysis process. As a result, the system provides the direction to the user.

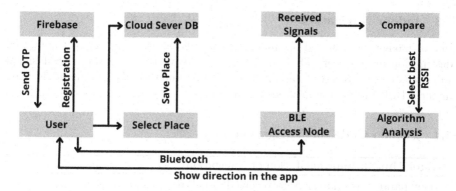

Fig. 8. System design.

5 Algorithm Analysis

Indoor positioning and navigation algorithm architecture in this context relies on detecting the user and navigating to the desired destination.

5.1 Indoor Positioning

Catching the nearest BLE tag signal defines the user's position, which indicates that the user's location is inside a circle range from the received tag. The Android device catches the signal emitted by the BLE tag. To avoid crossover signals, only the highest RSSI value signal is selected. The system sorts all the received signals according to maximum RSSI.

5.2 Pseudo Code for Avoiding Crossover Signals

During navigation and positioning, the app must detect the strongest signals among numerous. Crossover signals occur as a result of this scenario. Figure 3 represents the procedure to avoid the crossover signals as well as during implementation our application follows this process (Algorithm 1) to avoid crossover signals.

Algorithm 1: Implementation of Avoiding Crossover Signals

---

1 **Call** avoidCrossOver(signals [ ]);
2 **Call** compare(signals);
3 **Set** result = highestRSSI;
4 **Return** result;

The avoiding crossover signals (Algorithm 1) ensures the elimination of the signals which have less RSSI values and selects only the strongest RSSI signal. Here the received signals are sorted according to RSSI values and only the highest RSSI tag is picked and the rest of the signals are knocked out.

5.3   Indoor Navigation

Indoor navigation is based on under which BLE tag the user is and the desired destination of the user. The current tag is always the maximum RSSI signal value among the received tag signals. In this scenario, the command is fixed under a BLE tag for the desired destination.

5.4   Pseudo Code for Navigation

Algorithm 2: Implementation of Navigation

---

1 **Set** params as analysisAlgo(receivedSignal, desiredLocation):;
2 **if** *desiredLocation ='A' and receivedSignal ='T'* **then**
3 | **Set** result=Move Right;
4 **else if** *desiredLocation ='B' and receivedSignal ='K'* **then**
5 | **Set** result=Move Left;
6 **else if** *desiredLocation ='C' and receivedSignal ='M'* **then**
7 | **Set** result=Move Forward;
8 **else if** *desiredLocation ='D' and receivedSignal ='N'* **then**
9 | **Set** result=Move Back;
10 **else**
11 | **Set** result = destination;
12 | **Return** result;
13 **end**

The navigation algorithm (Algorithm 2) makes decision with the help of received signal and the desired location. As a result, the app shows the direction to the user. This process goes on until the user reaches his/her destination. For instance, if a user selects the desired place A and the current received BLE tag is T, then the app commands the movement to the right. Here, T is the currently received highest RSSI tag signal. On the other hand, if the selected place is B and the received signal is K, then the app commands it to move to the left. The process goes on until the app commands the success result of reaching the destination.

5.5   Complete Pseudo Algorithm

The pseudo algorithm (Algorithm 3) depicts the complete process of the proposed system design (Fig. 8).

Algorithm 3: Implementation of Complete Algorithm

---

1 **Call** registration();
2 **Call** selectPlace();
3 **Call** uploadDesiredPlace();
4 **Call** onBluetooth();
5 **Call** catchNearbyBleSignal();
6 **Call** analysisAlgo(receivedSignal, desiredLocation);
7 **if** *(result == destination)* **then**
8 | **Return** result;
9 **else**
10 | **Call** analysisAlgo(receivedSignal, desiredLocation);
11 **end**

---

6   Performance Analysis

6.1   Assessment

This concept was developed into an Android app, and the user interface will look like (Fig. 9). BLE technology collects data for contact tracking, which is subsequently recorded in a cloud server and utilized to notify doctors and family members if necessary. Along with this interior navigation model, the user can reach his intended destination.

The system was evaluated at indoor premises where 4 BLE tags were used for transmitting the beacon signals and each signals represents a unique destination id. The system app worked in a very decorous way for utter positioning and navigation.

(A)   (B)   (C)   (D)

Fig. 9. User Interface for Indoor Navigation: (A) Represents the landing page (B) Shows the app registration with a mobile phone number, (C) reflects the selection of a location using voice command or drop down menu selection, and (D) shows the Indoor Routing Map and placement. The app's compass guides the user to the exact location.

7   Conclusion

This article describes the design, implementation, and assessment of an app-based indoor locating system based on BLE technology. Handheld devices can use wireless interfaces to track and deliver indoor navigation whenever conventional navigation systems (such as GPS) fail. This study describes a system of internal navigation that can be used to monitor and track individuals with neurodegenerative disorders such as Alzheimer's. The device enables real-time remote monitoring for primary medical care for the family and clinicians of Alzheimer's patients. Alzheimer's patients will benefit from the planned interior navigation system, which will assist them in navigating the building.

Acknowledgements. This research is a part of ICT (Information and Communication Technology) Fellowship and supported by ICT Division, Bangladesh. The authors would like to thank the Ministry of Posts, Telecommunications and Information Technology, Government of the People's Republic of Bangladesh. The authors would also like to acknowledge the cooperation of the IIT (Institute of Information Technology), Jahangirnagar University.

References

1. Namiot, D.: On indoor positioning. Int. J. Open Inf. Technol. **3**(3), 23–26 (2015)
2. Kaluža, M., Beg, K., Vukelić, B.: Analysis of an indoor positioning systems. Zbornik Veleučilišta u Rijeci **5**(1), 13–32 (2017)
3. Kaiser, M.S., et al.: iWorkSafe: towards healthy workplaces during COVID-19 with an intelligent pHealth app for industrial settings. IEEE Access **9**, 13814–13828 (2021)
4. Kalbandhe, A.A., Patil, S.C.: Indoor positioning system using bluetooth low energy. In: 2016 International Conference on Computing, Analytics and Security Trends (CAST), pp. 451–455. IEEE (2016)
5. Terán, M., Carrillo, H., Parra, C.: Wlan-ble based indoor positioning system using machine learning cloud services. In: 2018 IEEE 2nd Colombian Conference on Robotics and Automation (CCRA), pp. 1–6. IEEE (2018)
6. Afsana, F., Asif-Ur-Rahman, M., Ahmed, M.R., Mahmud, M., Kaiser, M.S.: An energy conserving routing scheme for wireless body sensor nanonetwork communication. IEEE Access **6**, 9186–9200 (2018)
7. Asif-Ur-Rahman, M., et al.: Toward a heterogeneous mist, fog, and cloud-based framework for the internet of healthcare things. IEEE Int. Things J. **6**(3), 4049–4062 (2018)
8. Kaiser, M.S., et al.: 6G access network for intelligent internet of healthcare things: opportunity, challenges, and research directions. In: Kaiser, M.S., Bandyopadhyay, A., Mahmud, M., Ray, K. (eds.) Proceedings of International Conference on Trends in Computational and Cognitive Engineering. AISC, vol. 1309, pp. 317–328. Springer, Singapore (2021). https://doi.org/10.1007/978-981-33-4673-4_25
9. Mahmud, M., et al.: A brain-inspired trust management model to assure security in a cloud based IoT framework for neuroscience applications. Cogn. Comput. **10**(5), 864–873 (2018)

10. Kaiser, M.S., et al.: Advances in crowd analysis for urban applications through urban event detection. IEEE Trans. Intel. Transp. Syst. **19**(10), 3092–3112 (2017)

11. Mahmud, M., Kaiser, M.S., McGinnity, T.M., Hussain, A.: Deep learning in mining biological data. Cogn. Comput. **13**(1), 1–33 (2021)

12. Jesmin, S., Kaiser, M.S., Mahmud, M.: Artificial and internet of healthcare things based Alzheimer care during COVID 19. In: Mahmud, M., Vassanelli, S., Kaiser, M.S., Zhong, N. (eds.) BI 2020. LNCS (LNAI), vol. 12241, pp. 263–274. Springer, Cham (2020). https://doi.org/10.1007/978-3-030-59277-6_24

13. Biswas, M., et al.: Prototype development of an assistive smart-stick for the visually challenged persons. In: 2022 2nd International Conference on Innovative Practices in Technology and Management (ICIPTM), vol. 2, pp. 477–482. IEEE (2022)

14. Chaki, S., Ahmed, S., Biswas, M., Tamanna, I.: A framework of an obstacle avoidance robot for the visually impaired people. In: Kaiser, M.S., Bandyopadhyay, A., Ray, K., Singh, R., Nagar, V. (eds.) Proceedings of Trends in Electronics and Health Informatics. LNNS, vol. 376, pp. 269–280. Springer, Singapore (2022). https://doi.org/10.1007/978-981-16-8826-3_24

15. Biswas, M., Kaiser, M.S., Mahmud, M., Al Mamun, S., Hossain, M.S., Rahman, M.A.: An XAI based autism detection: the context behind the detection. In: Mahmud, M., Kaiser, M.S., Vassanelli, S., Dai, Q., Zhong, N. (eds.) BI 2021. LNCS (LNAI), vol. 12960, pp. 448–459. Springer, Cham (2021). https://doi.org/10.1007/978-3-030-86993-9_40

16. Noor, M.B.T., Zenia, N.Z., Kaiser, M.S., Mamun, S.A., Mahmud, M.: Application of deep learning in detecting neurological disorders from magnetic resonance images: a survey on the detection of Alzheimer's disease, Parkinson's disease and schizophrenia. Brain Informat. **7**(1), 1–21 (2020). https://doi.org/10.1186/s40708-020-00112-2

17. Lin, T.N., Lin, P.C.: Performance comparison of indoor positioning techniques based on location fingerprinting in wireless networks. In: 2005 International Conference on Wireless Networks, Communications and Mobile Computing, vol. 2, pp. 1569–1574. IEEE (2005)

18. Biswas, M., et al.: Indoor navigation support system for patients with neurodegenerative diseases. In: Mahmud, M., Kaiser, M.S., Vassanelli, S., Dai, Q., Zhong, N. (eds.) BI 2021. LNCS (LNAI), vol. 12960, pp. 411–422. Springer, Cham (2021). https://doi.org/10.1007/978-3-030-86993-9_37

19. Gallagher, T.J., Li, B., Dempster, A.G., Rizos, C.: A sector-based campus-wide indoor positioning system. In: 2010 International Conference on Indoor Positioning and Indoor Navigation, pp. 1–8. IEEE (2010)

20. Faragher, R., Harle, R.: Location fingerprinting with bluetooth low energy beacons. IEEE J. Sel. Areas Commun. **33**(11), 2418–2428 (2015)

21. Bai, L., Ciravegna, F., Bond, R., Mulvenna, M.: A low cost indoor positioning system using bluetooth low energy. IEEE Access **8**, 136858–136871 (2020)

22. Park, J., Kim, J., Kang, S., et al.: Ble-based accurate indoor location tracking for home and office. Comput. Sci. Inf. Technol. (CS & IT) CSCP, 173–181 (2015)

23. Bisio, I., Sciarrone, A., Zappatore, S.: Asset tracking architecture with bluetooth low energy tags and ad hoc smartphone applications. In: 2015 European Conference on Networks and Communications (EuCNC), pp. 460–464. IEEE (2015)

24. Chen, C.Y., Yang, J.P., Tseng, G.J., Wu, Y.H., et al. An indoor positioning technique based on fuzzy logic. In: MultiConference of Engineers and Computer Scientists, pp. 854–857. Citeseer (2010)

25. Yang, C., Shao, H.-R.: WiFi-based indoor positioning. IEEE Commun. Mag. **53**(3), 150–157 (2015)

26. Yim, J.: Introducing a decision tree-based indoor positioning technique. Expert Syst. Appl. **34**(2), 1296–1302 (2008)
27. Tsetsos, V., Anagnostopoulos, C., Kikiras, P., Hasiotis, P., Hadjiefthymiades, S.: A human-centered semantic navigation system for indoor environments. In: 2005 Proceedings of the International Conference on Pervasive Services (ICPS), pp. 146–155. IEEE (2005)
28. Terán, M., Aranda, J., Carrillo, H., Mendez, D., Parra, C.: Iot-based system for indoor location using bluetooth low energy. In: 2017 IEEE Colombian Conference on Communications and Computing (COLCOM), pp. 1–6. IEEE (2017)
29. Kunhoth, J., Karkar, A.G., Al-Maadeed, S., Al-Attiyah, A.: Comparative analysis of computer-vision and BLE technology based indoor navigation systems for people with visual impairments. Int. J. Health Geogr. **18**(1), 1–18 (2019). https://doi.org/10.1186/s12942-019-0193-9

Science Parks Externalities on Financial Performance of Small Firms Through Business Intelligence Tools

Valentina Mallamaci[1]([✉]) [iD] and Massimiliano Ferrara[1,2] [iD]

[1] Department of Law, Economics and Human Sciences and Decisions Lab, Mediterranea University, 89124 Reggio Calabria, Italy
{valentina.mallamaci,massimiliano.ferrara}@unirc.it
[2] Department of Management and Technology, ICRIOS – The Invernizzi Centre for Reasearch in Innovation, Organization, Strategy and Entrepreneurship, Bocconi University, 20136 Milano, Italy

Abstract. Many firms' success hinges on their ability to use data effectively to make quicker and more informed choices. Companies may leverage Business Intelligence (BI) and other powerful and efficient technologies as catalysts to help them automate analysis, decision making, strategy creation, and forecasting.

Accordingly, the study's primary goal is to reveal whether or not integrating Business Intelligence, Organizational Learning (OL), and Innovation into operational procedures improves businesses' bottom lines. This study is an example of applied research since it applies theoretical frameworks to a real-world setting—the Shanghai Zizhu Science-based Industrial Park—in order to show the sort of externality it creates for the enterprises involved.

The introduction of business intelligence systems within a firm is directly associated with technological advancement since it allows the organization to make full use of all accessible data. In reality, BI approaches transform unstructured data sets into information to assist decision-making processes, maximize knowledge, and speed up and improve processes via the use of a wide range of coordinated operational just as chosen help apps and databases.

The last factor to think about is organizational learning, which is founded on the system of organizational characteristics, practices, and problems that make possible the organization's capacity to learn.

In conclusion, studies show that Business Intelligence and innovation have a major impact on how businesses function. However, we found no statistically significant correlation between Organizational Learning and the financial success of these same businesses.

Keywords: Science Park · Business Intelligence · Artificial intelligence

M. Mahmud et al. (Eds.): AII 2022, CCIS 1724, pp. 467–477, 2022.
https://doi.org/10.1007/978-3-031-24801-6_33

1   Introduction

1.1   Framing of the Research

The contemporary business context is significantly influenced by an interdisciplinary approach for which the impact of Business Intelligence, especially with respect to performance evaluation, is decisive for the integration and practical implementation of all the tools and decision-making variables considered.

Studying a business context in terms of Business Intelligence allows to accelerate business innovation by supporting decision-making processes by converting raw data sets into optimized information and knowledge.

The study presented, in fact, aims to identify the most efficient Business Intelligence tools in terms of their impact on the improvement of company performance. In particular, the represented research aims to provide effective criteria for evaluating the financial results of a company inserted in an incentive context such as a Science Park. This allows to test the strength of the connection between the scientific pole, the company and performances and how each element affects the relationship. The variables considered, in addition to Business Intelligence, for the analysis of this relationship are: financial performance, Innovation and Organizational Learning.

The Business Intelligence methodology allows to accelerate business innovation by supporting decision-making processes by converting raw data sets into optimized information and knowledge.

To foster the growth of creative companies and regional clusters, science parks are intricate entities used as policy instruments.

They do a great job of facilitating the transfer of information across businesses, government agencies, and academic institutions. Since there are only so many resources and pieces of information that can be used to improve communication between businesses and Science Parks, it is crucial to analyze the variables that affect a company's bottom line [1, 4].

International Association of Science Parks published the following description of a Science Park in the literature: a Science Park is a business support and technology transfer project that fosters and supports the beginning and incubation of innovation-led, high-growth knowledge-based firms; it creates an environment where bigger and international businesses may build specific and close relationships with a particular center of knowledge production for their advantage [5].

Though it is a pioneering approach, Ferrara and Mavilia's (2014) findings on the effects of TP/SP on regional economic growth and the revenue growth of connected (or fostered) enterprises are rather intriguing. In particular, they discovered that the effects of TP/SP vary depending on the place under consideration and that these differences persist even when considering the model as a whole. There appears to be a favorable correlation between the number of TP/SP in an area and the continued economic growth of that region. Patent applications and the establishment of research facilities also have a multiplier effect on the expansion of related businesses, which in turn influences macroeconomic indicators at the regional level.

Contrarily, the distance between the TP/SP and associated enterprises dampens the expansion potential of the latter. Newer structures are more likely to encourage patenting activity and high-level growth, and enterprises inside a TP/SP outperform (mostly) the area average. High dispersion rates are also a feature of newly built buildings [3].

1.2 Originality

Because experiments in this area are so rare in the literature, the novelty of the analysis proposed in this study stands out. The study's authors hope to determine the effect that three key factors—business intelligence, organizational learning, and innovation—have on the financial success of startups that are members of a Science Park.

The purpose of this article is to examine how factors such as business intelligence, organizational learning, and innovation affect the financial performance of Science Park start-ups. The primary goals are the same for all three of these studies: to investigate the impact of business intelligence, organizational learning, and innovation on the financial effectiveness of startups. The study's secondary goals are to verify BI's relevance to op-ed learning, investigate BI's effect on innovation, and analyze op-ed learning's effect on innovation.

Because innovation is actively working to enhance company capacity and build a culture of value-added goods, organizations with greater innovation rates are more likely to be profitable. It's essential to have higher quality than rivals to obtain and retain a performance advantage.

Finally, the research makes it possible to evaluate the financial performances of start-ups in an innovative way thanks to the relationships with the above-mentioned variables which previously, in the current literature, had not been considered as a whole.

In this way, the added value made by the inclusion in a Science Park is measured as well as how this value is expressed in terms of financial improvements. This provides an original assessment tool for nascent companies with respect to the decision-making process of choosing on joining a Science Park or, having joined, on which particular Business Intelligence, Organizational Learning and Innovation tools to invest to optimize their results avoiding the waste of resources in the sensitive start-up phase [2, 4].

2 Artificial Intelligence vs Business Intelligence: Some Complementarities

A startup is a firm, partnership, or temporary organization created with the intention of finding a repeatable and scalable business model, according to Steve Blank's well-known definition [7]. It is important to emphasize the words "temporary" and "search", as a startup's future depends on whether it will succeed and join a large company or fail and move on to another opportunity.

Scholars have recently emphasized a variety of success factors, including new financial and technological tools as well as structures to promote startup growth through organizations like seed accelerators and their supporting tools. In this arena, technology is amazing since it allows us to "do more with less".

Artificial Intelligence may have an impact on "firms' decision-making and interactions with their external stakeholders (such as workers and consumers)" [8]. AI-based systems may do cognitive and routine duties, while human employees may concentrate more on the "feeling side" of the company [9]. This should result in an improvement of the current methods used by businesses to achieve their goals, but new opportunities may also arise in place of incremental improvements (Magistretti et al. 2019). AI may have an impact on managerial procedures, assisting businesses in finding fresh avenues for growth and integration.

The current discussion demonstrates AI as a multipurpose technology with fresh chances to come since decision-making efficiency increases tremendously. According to Huang et al. [9], the adoption of AI is seen as the next source of competitive advantage as well as a lever to encourage new investments and promote an entrepreneurial mindset. AI companies should be viewed as business labs that base their trials on recent algorithmic research. Therefore, the emphasis should not be on a quick return on investment and on R&D outcomes. Indeed, it should be important to provide larger incentives in terms of risk and return, with a concomitant improvement in the likelihood of acquiring businesses, making exits more profitable.

Artificial intelligence may be viewed as a supporting component that encourages the introduction of new goods, services, and ways of doing things. As a result, it dramatically accelerates innovation in enterprises.

With the introduction of artificial intelligence, this initial idea complements and broadens the research on the relationship between entrepreneurship and innovation. In fact, it serves as a catalyst for innovation for businesses to alter not only how markets are constructed but also how operations are carried out and services are provided [10].

However, it also emphasizes manufacturing, service design, and service provision as three processes that are primarily affected by artificial intelligence, which may alter how markets, marketing, and services are approached through new technologies.

Furthermore, innovation has shown to be both a property of artificial intelligence itself and a way a business may use to enter markets and create new proposals. Artificial intelligence does, in fact, have an influence on how firms approach the market, both generally and through marketing efforts.

Therefore, the beneficial effects of new technologies should promote micro- and macro-level measures. In fact, at the micro level, artificial intelligence may work in tandem with fresh investments in startups as a carrier of fresh chances to be infused in fresh businesses and generating the potential to revolutionize markets and organizations' operations. The positive effects of artificial intelligence on innovation, employment, and competitiveness should be encouraged at the macro-level by national and international agencies.

All in all, the opportunity to pursue rapidity and scalability, two essential characteristics of startups, was mirrored by the development of artificial intelligence. This is because the diffusion of innovation through artificial intelligence-driven processes is quicker and can easily operate on a wider scale because frequently large amounts of data are needed and a variety of applications - both in B2B and B2C markets - are feasible [6].

It stands to reason that the business intelligence procedures used inside an organization in order to turn any and all accessible data into useful information would have some sort of relationship to technological advancement. In reality, BI approaches transform unstructured data sets into information to assist decision-making processes, maximize knowledge, and speed up and improve processes via the use of a wide range of coordinated operational just as chosen help apps and databases. Therefore, the growth of BI is crucial to a company's innovative capabilities and the success of the business as a whole [11].

3 Methodology

3.1 Data Collection and Research Method

The study's goal is to improve the economic viability of new businesses, so it falls under the category of "applied research." The study's methodology involves an examination of theoretical structures in scientific and real-world contexts and situations. Because a questionnaire was employed to investigate all of the criteria and variables, this study also falls under the category of survey research for methods of acquiring scientific data.

The study's descriptive-correlational nature stems from its focus on establishing and quantifying links between variables. New businesses in the Science Park area are included in the study's sample population (Shanghai Zizhu Science-based Industrial Park, located in the southeast of Minhang District, Shanghai). In this study, participants were selected at random. Table 1 shows the results of using a Morgan table to display the sample size.

It was determined that there are 400 CEOs working for start-ups in the Science Park; as a result, 196 samples were sought; 280 questionnaires were given to account for potential sampling error [1].

Table 1. Krejcie and Morgan Table (1970) for determining sample size of a known population[1]

N	S	N	S	N	S	N	S	N	S
10	10	100	80	280	162	800	260	2800	338
15	14	110	86	290	165	850	265	3000	341
20	19	120	92	300	169	900	269	3500	346
25	24	130	97	320	175	950	274	4000	351
30	28	140	103	340	181	1000	278	4500	354
35	32	150	108	360	186	1100	285	5000	357
40	36	160	113	380	191	1200	291	6000	361
45	40	170	118	**400**	**196**	1300	297	7000	364
50	44	180	123	420	201	1400	302	8000	367
55	48	190	127	440	205	1500	306	9000	368

(continued)

[1] N is the population size; S is the sample size.

Table 1. (*continued*)

N	S	N	S	N	S	N	S	N	S
60	52	200	132	460	210	1600	310	10000	370
65	56	210	136	480	214	1700	313	15000	375
70	59	220	140	500	217	1800	317	20000	377
75	63	230	144	550	226	1900	320	30000	379
80	66	240	148	600	234	2000	322	40000	380
85	70	250	152	650	242	2200	327	50000	381
90	73	260	155	700	248	2400	331	75000	382
95	76	270	159	750	254	2600	335	1000000	384

The research process relies heavily on the acquisition of data, a stage that calls for the employment of efficient methods. Inaccurate information precludes relying on the resulting conclusions as reliable. It is crucial to consider the instrument's psychometric quality during the design or selection process, since failing to do so might affect the reliability of the data gathered and, in turn, the validity of the research.

There are 47 items of research variables and demographic information (such as age, gender, education, and job experience) in the present study's questionnaire (financial performance – 12 questions; business intelligence – 12 questions; innovation – 12 questions; organizational learning – 11 questions). The survey was given out in person and online (according to the Corona pandemic). Careful data collection and analysis were done in an effort to verify the study's hypotheses.

The theoretical framework for this study is depicted in Fig. 1.

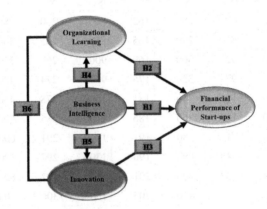

Fig. 1. Conceptual model of research.

3.2 Questionnaire Validity and Reliability

We have thoroughly checked the validity and reliability of the online survey.

In this situation, the instrument's reliability is satisfactory; Cronbach's alpha was used to calculate this, and the results showed that all variables had alphas more than 0.7 (0.913 for the entire questionnaire).

Demographic information was analyzed using SPSS and presented using descriptive statistics, frequency tables, and pie charts.

Two major challenges exist in accurately assessing concepts in the social and cognitive sciences. A. Quantitative evaluations, and B. Causal links between factors. The two components of a structural equation model are the measurement model (or external model) and the structural function model (internal model).

Types of Structural Equation Models Many issues and challenges associated with measuring latent variables and inferring causal links between these variables are resolved by combining the two models of confirmatory factor analysis and structural function analysis.

Multivariate analysis, which involves looking at how several factors are related to one another theoretically, is a powerful and useful approach of study. The kind of measurement variable distribution is irrelevant to the default partial least squares approach. As a result, it is applicable and useful for data with an irregular distribution or uncertain distribution [1].

4   Main Results

Examining hypotheses was made easier with the help of the internal model. By examining and verifying the original model, the research pattern hypotheses have been confirmed; if a predetermined rate of the t-statistic is less than 1.96, the null hypothesis is settled; if the predetermined rate of the t-statistic is greater than 1.96, the null hypothesis is rejected.

The hypothesis might be tested by comparing the calculated value of "t" for each path's coefficient. Therefore, significance at the 95% confidence level is shown if a given rate of the "t" statistic is greater than 1.96. All analysis routes, excluding the one connecting organizational learning to financial performance, have a "t" statistics value greater than 1.96, making the analysis significant at the 95% confidence level.

The calculated perception coefficient for the financial performance variable is 0.62, which indicates that the OL, BI, and Innovation variables might jointly explain 62% of the variations in financial performance. Based on the values of the standard coefficient and t-statistic, the variables of Innovation (0.568) and BI (0.233) had the greatest influence on the financial performance variable, whereas the OL variable did not have a significant effect.

A similar 0.66 explanatory power is provided by the OL and BI variables for the variations in Innovation. As shown by the standard coefficient and t statistic value, the OL variable is more influential on the innovation variable than the BI variable. Coefficients of determination suggest that the BI variable accounts for 27% of the variation in OL.

Thus, it can be concluded that business intelligence plays an essential and beneficial role in the development of knowledge inside a company. To be more specific, boosting business intelligence can enhance institutional knowledge.

Innovation is greatly aided by organizational learning. Innovation may be boosted in particular through organizational learning.

Intelligence in the workplace has a significant and beneficial effect on creative thinking. In particular, BI may boost creative thinking in the workplace.

Despite prior research suggesting a connection between organizational learning and creative firms' financial performance, this study's data disproved the idea that such a relationship exists. The difference between the organizational maturity of start-ups and that of major corporations is one possible explanation.

Financial effectiveness is significantly impacted for the better by the application of business intelligence. The financial aspects of a business are one area where BI may make a difference. At the 0.05 significance level, this route coefficient is notable.

The effectiveness of a company's finances is positively and critically impacted by innovations. Financial results are one area where innovation may make a difference [1].

5   Managerial Implications

The Italian economic companies have stood out for their binomial character: large private or public enterprises, on the other a myriad of small and medium-sized enterprises. The latter, when locally close to each other and belonging to the same sector, have often given rise to forms of collaboration whose evolution can be favored by participation in a Science Park.

As anticipated, the Science Park operates as an innovation incubator and a priority vehicle of knowledge distributing added value to the participating start-ups. This is made possible above all thanks to the formal and operational interactions with knowledge creation poles such as universities, higher education institutions and research organizations with which outside the Park it would be more complex to interact.

In the future, these innovative systems of cooperation and coordination between the scientific and research apparatus and the company will probably continue to develop more and more, becoming one of the pillars of Italian economic development. In fact, the Scientific-technological Park operates as a geographic aggregator of innovative realities, based precisely on the correlation between physical proximity and exchange of knowledge.

So, the first positive implication for every company and especially for start-ups is determined precisely by the improvement effects obtained by being part of a Science Park. It is a complex institution designed to foster the development of start-ups thanks to the smooth flow of knowledge between universities, research and development institutes and companies. They have the role of stimulating innovation and attracting greater investments for research to be allocated to participating start-ups, providing for specific selection criteria (for example patent applications) to identify the most virtuous, also considering the expenses incurred by each for research and development.

Moreover, the advantages of this research for management are mainly related to Business Intelligence applications. Through the results that emerged from the survey to which the start-ups included in the Science Park were subjected, it is possible to obtain performance evaluation indicators applicable to public and private companies to measure the quality of management, the potential for improvement and the trend of some distinctive parameters such as financial, innovation and strategic organization.

Furthermore, these measurements can allow to measure two other aspects: from the internal point of view of the company, the convenience for a start-up to join a science park, evaluating its impact quantitatively and qualitatively; from the external point of view of the company, the positive effects of a high-profile managerial management and, therefore, the implications of the presence of a Science Park in the area in which they operate.

It should also be added that the push to increase the innovativeness of the Italian entrepreneurial fabric seems to emerge as a direct consequence of the following consideration: where there is "agglomeration", there is a "force" (centripetal to change) and where there is "sharing of knowledge" everyone benefits, especially in those specific areas characterized by what is called sticky knowledge. Hence the need to organize catching up paths, to enhance human capital and disseminate absorption capacities, to promote endogenous innovation generation skills. This also means seeking a fair and difficult mix between opening up to the global market for the acquisition of codified knowledge and stimulating competition as an incentive for innovation, and public intervention to promote the construction of regional innovation systems based on the various drivers of innovation. The recipe foresees to combine spillover dynamics, in order to favor important induced effects and progressive advancement of local companies in global value chains, in terms of contamination and diffusion of innovation, even more if accompanied by the internationalization of other drivers such as research centers and service centers.

6 Conclusion and Future Research Improvements

This is an experimental and pioneering work which, therefore, involves significant results compared to the management of startups but at the same time has limits due to the absence of other contributions in the literature to compare these results.

Due to the experimental character of this work, the businesses taken into account are some of the most successful, but a larger sample size might result in more thorough and pertinent analysis. The research was also completed as a desk analysis using a variety of sources, thus using other approaches could yield fresh findings. In fact, we think that more study on these issues can broaden the data presented in this work by shifting the emphasis to other nations as well, in order to determine whether or not entrepreneur preparedness is influenced by the environment.

Such research should be extended to other Science Parks with the same internal characteristics but belonging to other territorial contexts and therefore subjected to different regulations, policies, training, management and decision-making processes.

Moreover, the difficulty of this research lies in the unions of scientific intersections that characterize it: business intelligence, artificial intelligence, machine learning, data science, business analytics, innovation management, corporate finance.

Another limitation is related to Science Parks which are one of the elements that characterize this research. Despite the growing diffusion of these Parks around the world, the experiments and tests of their impacts on the effective support to the business performance of companies within the Science Park are still limited and characterized by conflicting opinions. The same problem also concerns the measurement of the overall positive impact on the surrounding region.

Furthermore, regarding relations between Science Parks and member companies, the positive implications in terms of support for innovative performance and research and development functions are demonstrable, but the implications in terms of sales growth and increased profits are not yet clearly demonstrable.

Another variable not yet considered in the existing studies is time: the time necessary for the Science Park to generate positive consequences for the member companies has not been assessed and whether this time, therefore, is sufficient to guarantee their survival and adequate profitability.

This limitation is also due to the heterogeneous framework currently existing in Science Parks and the relative approaches of the member companies. This is typical of a phenomenon caught in its pioneering phase. The use of these tools to aggregate innovative forces and to catalyze innovative activity took place in these first years not in a univocal and centrally planned way, but following different choices and paths, through a model that we could define empirical: that is, in a continuous succession of trial and error.

It is therefore necessary to identify shared and ratified performance measures and indicators, which form the basis of a truthful assessment of the effective activity of Science Parks, as well as the efficient and transparent use of the funds intended for them. A correct evaluation of the performance of these knowledge intermediaries is a useful tool in the hands of all the protagonists but also of possible external stakeholders.

The former, in fact, self-assessing themselves within what have been commonly recognized as the crucial dimensions for success, will be able to recognize any shortcomings in the internal management during construction, avoiding those correctable problems create an unsustainability of the project in the long period.

The latter, on the other hand, will have an objective tool on which to base their evaluations and choices of proactive interactions and collaborations.

Finally, in order to identify differences in economic success, customer perceptions, and business model quality, future study may compare startups in the same industry, with a focus on those utilizing AI and those not using it. Analysis of user feedback on their satisfaction, loyalty, and overall experience as B2B and B2C customers might further strengthen the case for AI's role in propelling businesses forward. More research is needed in the future, and it will take a while to complete.

References

1. Yang, M., Sulieman, R., Yin, Y., Mallamaci, V., Alrabaiah, H.: The effect of business intelligence, organizational learning and innovation on the financial performance of innovative companies located in Science Park. Inf. Process. Manage. **59**(2), 102852 (2021)
2. Hailekiros, G.S., Renyong, H.: The effect of organizational learning capability on firm performance: mediated by technological innovation capability. Eur. J. Bus. Manage. **8**(30), 87–95 (2016)

3. Ferrara, M., Mavilia, R.: The effects of technopoles and science parks on regional economies in Italy. WSEAS Trans. Bus. Econ. **11**(1), 537–549 (2014)
4. Ferrara, M., Lamperti, F., Mavilia, R.: Looking for best performers: a pilot study towards the evaluation of science parks. Scientometrics **106**(2), 717–750 (2015). https://doi.org/10.1007/s11192-015-1804-2
5. Lamperti, F., Mavilia, R., Castellini, S.: The role of Science Parks: a puzzle of growth, innovation and R&D investments. J. Technol. Transf. **42**(1), 158–183 (2017)
6. Di Bernardo, I., Tregua, M., Fabio, G., Andrea, R.: AI as a boost for startups companies: evidence from Italy. Univ. South Florida M3 Center Publ. **5**(2021), 53 (2021)
7. Blank, S.: Why the lean start-up changes everything. Harvard Bus. Rev. **91**(5), 63–72 (2013)
8. Haenlein, M., Kaplan, A.: A brief history of artificial intelligence: on the past, present, and future of artificial intelligence. Calif. Manage. Rev. **61**(4), 5–14 (2019)
9. Huang, M.H., Rust, R., Maksimovic, V.: The feeling economy: managing in the next generation of artificial intelligence (AI). Calif. Manage. Rev. **61**(4), 43–65 (2019)
10. Nenonen, S., Storbacka, K.: Smash: Using Market Shaping to Design New Strategies for Innovation, Value Creation, and Growth. Emerald Publishing, Bingley, UK (2018)
11. Nithya, N., Kiruthika, R.: Impact of business intelligence adoption on performance of banks: a conceptual framework. J. Ambient Intell. Humaniz. Comput. **12**(2), 3139–3150 (2021)

A Novel Approach to Identifying DDoS Traffic in the Smart Home Network via Exploratory Data Analysis

Asmau Wali[(⊠)], Oluwasegun Apejoye, Thejavathy Raja, Jun He[iD], and Xiaoqi Ma[iD]

Department of Computer Science, Nottingham Trent University, Nottingham, UK
{asmau.kazaure2018,Oluwasegun.apejoye2020,
thejavathy.vengapparaja2018}@my.ntu.ac.uk, {jun.he,
xiaoqi.ma}@ntu.ac.uk

Abstract. Smart homes are gaining more popularity by the day due to the ease they provide in terms of running our homes. However, the energy and resource constrained nature of these devices make security integration challenging, thus making them prone to cyber-attacks. DDoS remains one of the most threatening attacks to this network and IoT in general. In order to curb this issue, there is a need to study the behavioral pattern of this attack and smart home devices at a low level. This will aid in designing a timely and more effective DDoS detection and mitigation framework and policy. DDoS visualization tools can also be improved using this approach. This paper collects DDoS and benign traffic in a real smart home environment and performs an Exploratory Data Analysis (EDA), visualizing the behavioral pattern of 3 types of DDoS flooding attacks when targeted at smart home networks in comparison to the benign smart home traffic pattern. The attacks covered are TCP SYN, ICMP and UDP flooding attacks. For each of the covered attacks, specific smart home traffic properties were selected, correlated and visualized showing their reversed behavior during an attack compared to their normal benign nature. To further validate the findings, public IoT datasets were analyzed in the same manner and the same results were achieved. Finally, this paper proposes a novel approach on how the EDA findings can be applied to better detect DDoS traffic in the smart home network.

Keywords: Exploratory data analysis · Smart home network · DDoS detection · DDoS attack patterns · Smart home security · Smart home traffic properties

1 Introduction

IoT devices are becoming more popular in our daily lives due to the advantageous services they render to users. These devices cover a broad surface in terms of connectivity ranging from but not limited to, healthcare, home automation, weather forecast, transport, agriculture, security and a variety of other dimensions. IoT further gives us the ability to have more control over our IoT ecosystem. By tailoring these devices to run exactly when we need them, this improves our energy conservation plans. We also get to monitor devices' usage in real time, which paves way for accountability when the need arises. It is estimated that 150,000 IoT devices join the global network every minute [1].

However, the energy and resource constrained nature of these devices make them prone to cyber-attacks [2–6]. This, in addition to their heterogeneous nature, makes security implementation challenging [7, 8]. The device vendors are not helping matters too as their focus is more aligned to device functionality and features rather than security [9]. This poses risks in terms of security as the lives of individuals are directly affected [10]. DDoS flooding attacks remain a big threat to the IoT network. During the first quarter of 2020 there has been a significant rise in DDoS attacks witnessing an 80 percent increase from 2019 [11]. This attack tends to flood a targeted server with voluminous unnecessary traffic, in the process over saturating its capacity causing service to be denied or halted to legitimate devices. Several of the server's resources get negatively affected like processing power and memory capabilities as it is preoccupied in dealing with more traffic than it is designed to handle.

For this persistent attack to be detected and mitigated, there is a prerequisite need to study the individual attack traffic properties in relation to the benign corresponding properties of the smart network. This will help in identifying the affected traffic properties and what to look out for during a DDoS flooding attack. The best way to do this is by using data visualization techniques, as the network traffic is vast and multidimensional. This visualization method will also be beneficial to network security operators as the human brain tends to better process images than text [12]. It can also give network operators the advance notice needed in case of a sensed attack. Although there have been immense contributions in DDoS visualization, detection and mitigation areas, there are still open challenges on the best way to identify and visualize DDoS attack patterns which will pave way for better detection and mitigation approaches [13, 14].

In order to bridge the afore-mentioned gap, this paper collects both attack (DDoS flooding) and benign smart home traffic and performs an Exploratory Data Analysis (EDA) comparing corresponding traffic properties. EDA is a method, used to analyze datasets summarizing their main characteristics using data visualization techniques. The paper addresses the lack of low-level analysis and comparison of specific attack and benign IoT traffic properties. It further proposes a novel method on how the EDA findings can be applied in DDoS traffic detection in the smart home network. This paper serves as an extension to our previous paper on benign smart home traffic EDA [15]. To the best of our knowledge this is the first paper carrying out a detailed low-level analysis and visually comparing attack and benign smart home traffic properties side by side.

The contribution of this paper is 2 folds:

- First, it collects benign and DDoS (TCP, UDP, ICMP) traffic in a real smart home environment and performs EDA on each of the attacks stating and visualizing how each attack affects some selected smart home benign traffic properties (protocol, packet length, sequence number, TCP flags, encryption). Recent literature has not analyzed and visualized these network properties independently, thus creating a gap in the low-level analysis and understanding of both attack and benign traffic behavior in the smart home network. It further validates the findings by subjecting public datasets (normal and attack) to the same EDA method and attaining the same results.

- Secondly, it presents a DDoS detection approach by combining 3 smart home network characteristics derived from the EDA which are feature variance, absent features and feature range of the considered smart home traffic properties. This tends to be a more universal and practical approach as compared to current literature which employs methods like user sequential behavior, single packet inspection and user centric parameters (port numbers, IP addresses, timings) which are either highly biased or impractical in real life situations. Furthermore, it changes the narrative from only focusing on present or visible statistics in attack detection as seen in the literature, to using the prolonged absence of certain network features (encryption, sequence numbers, TCP flags) that are normally present in the smart home traffic flow.

This paper is organized as follows: Sect. 1 introduces the paper. Section 2 covers the related works. Section 3 presents the methodology followed. Section 4 delves into data collection. Section 5 is about the EDA processes and visualized results. Section 6 proposes a novel approach for DDoS detection in smart home networks while Sect. 7 concludes the paper.

2 Related Work

Several works have addressed DDoS detection in the smart home network, however, there remain open challenges in this avenue [13, 14, 16, 17]. For the attack to be efficiently and effectively detected and mitigated, analysis of the smart home network characteristics in relation to the attack patterns remain crucial.

Wang et al. [18] proposed the use of Device Usage Description (DUD) model for device behavior and flow rules extraction to detect DDoS attacks in a smart home network. Nevertheless, this method tends to be device specific and may be problematic in large-scale networks as extracting each device DUD may not be feasible and bring about significant overheads. The paper also states traffic properties considered in generating flow rules for DDoS detection but without any visual representation or comparison. User behavioral pattern was also used by Yamauchi et al. [19] to develop anomaly detection model in IoT device operations. The sequence of activities performed by the user is learned and any deviation from this sequence is classified as an anomaly. However, this could be problematic as any change in user behavior can raise a false positive alarm.

CPU utilization rate of SDN controller was used as a basis for TCP SYN attack detection by Swami et al. [20]. Nonetheless, this was implemented and tested on a traditional network. Mon et al. [21] also carried out a simulated analysis of TCP SYN attack in IoT network. Their main metric of detection was limited to TCP flags. An algorithm was proposed by Saxena et al. [22] for DDoS detection in IoT. Some of the features used in the detection are packet length, data rate and time between responses. The downside to this research was lack of proper analysis on malicious and benign behaviors coupled with a low accuracy rate of 78%. The proposed algorithm was not presented as well as the type of attacks covered in the paper which makes it difficult to reconstruct and validate.

An ML based IoT botnet detection model was proposed by Pokhrel et al. [23]. The paper first analyzes the behavioral pattern of the benign and malicious data based on raw statistics. However, this analysis lacked visualization and the metrics used were limited to packet count over time, which might hinder the accuracy of detection. Similarly, Vinayakumar et al. [24] proposed a botnet detection model on a two-layered ML architecture to differentiate bot related DNS service from legitimate ones. This work tends to be centric on DNS related attacks and can't be applied to detect other attacks. An ML based DDoS detection mechanism in IoT through network traffic analysis is presented by Costa et al. [25]. The selected network features used were not analyzed in depth and no visual comparison was made to IoT benign behavior. The types of DDoS attacks covered were not also identified. Another ML based DDoS detection model was developed by Doshi et al. [26]. A very limited number of network features were used like packet inter-arrival time and number of terminals, which might limit detection rate.

Supervised based IDS for anomaly detection in smart home IoT is proposed by Anthi et al. [27]. Another SDN based IDS is presented by Niyaz et al. [28]. Both [27] and [28] follow a similar approach of single packet inspection or computation to determine whether it is malicious or not. This approach appears to be time and resource consuming as having to deal with each packet for feature extraction and classification takes up significant time and processing power. Another SDN based framework for DDoS detection in IoT is proposed by Bhayo et al. [29]. Various metrics like number of flow entries, similar payload packet count, number of sent and received packets on each node, power ratio of each node, in/out traffic load and session IP counter among others. Due to the intricacy of processing these metrics, it results in high detection time and consumes a lot of processing power, thus the need to investigate on a light weight and intelligent method to detect attacks.

Galeano et al. [30] presented an entropy-based DoS/DDoS detection and mitigation system In IoT. The detection metrics are source/destination IP addresses coupled with their respective port numbers and protocols. This experiment was simulated and when the window size is increased, the switches stop responding. Another downside to this approach was the fact that the entropy is calculated in real time at the beginning of the set window or threshold. If an attack starts at the very beginning of this window, then no entropy is calculated as no prior variation to compare with is present, thus the failure to detect the attack. Similarly, Li et al. [31] brought forward another entropy-based DDoS detection mechanism with the same detection metrics and downsides as [30].

From reviewed literature, there have been numerous contributions in terms of DDoS detection in smart home networks and IoT at large. Nevertheless, there are still gaps in the approach relating to better and improved methods of DDoS traffic identification. There is lack of detailed analysis and visual comparison of attack and benign traffic patterns. Some solutions make use of outdated or simulated data, which might hinder the accuracy when deployed in real life scenarios. In addition, some of the approaches used are not very practical or feasible in some scenarios. For example, using the single packet inspection method to determine if it's malicious or benign. This not only is time and resource consuming, but a less effective way of identifying DDoS patterns. This is due to DDoS flooding attacks being volume based, thus will need a volume based or cumulative approach to determine an attack pattern as opposed to the single packet approach. The approach of employing sequential user behavior or DUD model is not very practical as the former will raise false positives when there is slight change in user pattern while the latter is not practical in large scale scenarios as it's a device centric solution and not a generalized one.

To design an efficient and effective DDoS detection system, there is a need to have an in-depth understanding with regards to the attack pattern and network changes that occur during the attack and in the process monitoring the most affected network properties. These can be used as a baseline for attack identification. To bridge the gaps, this paper does an EDA on the normal and attack network characteristics in a real smart home environment and proposes a better way to identify a DDoS pattern based on the analyzed network features. This paper presents the use of network properties that can be applied to detect several kinds of DDoS flooding attacks in any smart home environment, thus making the approach more generalized and not device, user or attack specific.

3   Methodology

The various processes and sub processes followed in this research are broken down and explained in this section as shown in Fig. 1. It has three phases, which are data collection, exploratory data analysis and proposed novel method of DDoS detection based on the EDA results.

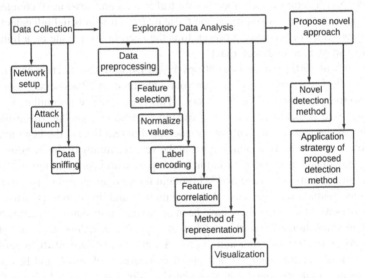

Fig. 1. Methodology

3.1   Data Collection

Setup: Network topology for data generation and collection was designed and tested.

Benign Data: Normal smart home traffic was collected here, which was generated from using the smart home devices and public datasets.

Attack Data: Three types of DDoS flooding attacks were launched on the smart home network and the traffic from this attack was collected. Each attack was collected separately. Public datasets for attack data were also sourced.

3.2 Exploratory Data Analysis (EDA)

Data Preprocessing: Each dataset was filtered to have only the relevant traffic flows from the target devices needed for analysis. This involves eliminating background traffic generated by other devices on the network.

Feature Selection: The corresponding attack and benign network traffic properties to be analyzed were selected and extracted. The most affected benign traffic properties during an attack were chosen and filtered out. This was done for each attack. These properties include protocol, packet length, sequence number and TCP flags bearing in mind the time stamps and packet ID or frame number for each packet.

Data Normalization: Among the selected network features (packet length and packet sequence), those with a wide range of numeric values were normalized using the min-max scalar to have a more befitting range during visual representation.

Label Encoding: Non numerical values like the protocols were encoded using a numerical value. This means each protocol corresponds to a number on the plotted figures.

Feature Correlation: The selected benign features were analyzed side by side to find out if they get affected simultaneously during each attack.

Method of Representation: Various methods of visual representation were used like bar charts, pie charts, frequency polygons and scatter plots. The most befitting method of representation was chosen based on the network feature(s) being visualized.

Visualization: Python programing was used on Google Colab to plot the charts and graphs. Corresponding network features for each attack and benign scenario were compared. Each of the analyzed network feature (protocol, packet length, sequence number, TCP flag) was plotted against the respective frame number of the corresponding packet.

3.3 Proposed Novel Approach

Propose Novel Detection Method: A novel DDoS identification approach is proposed based on the derived EDA results.

Novel Method Application Strategies: Ways by which the proposed novel method can be incorporated into the smart home network for better DDoS detection are outlined.

4 Data Collection

The smart home devices used in this study include a smart hub (to integrate the smart devices), a motion sensor, a smart plug and a smart bulb. The network communication that takes place when these devices are being flooded with DDoS packets is the main point of interest, thus a setup to collect this network data for further analysis was carried out.

Three types of DDoS flooding attacks were launched on the smart devices with the smart hub serving as the main gateway. These are TCPSYN, UDP and ICMP attacks. LOIC is the software used in attack generation as it supports the three covered attacks. For each attack, the target IP address and desired flooding rate of packets was specified and then launched. Each attack was directed to the target device using 3 different machines on the same private network to make it a distributed attack. Traffic generated from/to the target smart home device (hub) was captured separately for each propagated attack in order to know the network changes that relate to each attack. In order to get very detailed network traffic, the capture setup was made to collect traffic at layer 2 (datalink). This was done by connecting the hub to port 1 of the switch. Port 8 of the switch was then connected to the router (for internet connection). In order to capture all that flowed in and out of the hub and all devices paired to it, port 1 was mirrored on port 4. Port 4 was connected to the laptop using a Local Area Network (LAN) cable and Wireshark was used to capture this traffic. This connection is shown in Fig. 2.

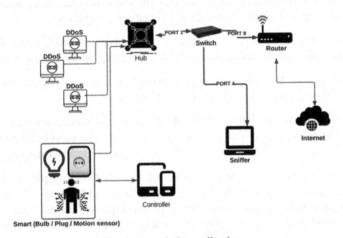

Fig. 2. Attack data collection

The benign data used in this research is from our previous paper [15] which addresses EDA on benign smart home traffic. This consists of the same network devices and topology as mentioned in the attack data collection above just excluding the DDoS attacking points.

The IoT-23 dataset [32] is the public dataset used for validation of the EDA on benign smart home traffic. This dataset consists of IoT network traffic from real devices. It has 20 malware captures executed in IoT devices, and 3 captures for benign IoT devices traffic. These traffic flows were captured in the Stratosphere Laboratory, AIC group, FEL, CTU University, Czech Republic. The benign traffic flows were extracted from this dataset and used in this research.

The BoT-IoT dataset [33] is one of the public attack datasets used for the EDA validation. It was created at Cyber Range Lab of UNSW Canberra by designing a realistic network environment. The network environment incorporated a combination of normal and botnet traffic. The dataset includes DDoS, DoS, OS and service scan, keylogging and data exfiltration attacks, with the DDoS and DoS attacks further organized, based on the protocol used. TCPSYN and UDP DDoS attack flows were extracted from the dataset and used in this research. Lastly, public ICMP DDoS attack flow was extracted from the BUET-DDoS2020 dataset [34]. It consists of several DDoS flooding attack flows including TCPSYN, DNS, HTTP and UDP.

5 Exploratory Data Analysis (EDA)

Exploratory Data Analysis is a statistical method of analyzing data to summarize the main characteristics of the dataset by using data visualization tools and techniques to represent the derived results for ease of understanding. Google Colab has been used for this purpose in this research. As outlined in the methodology, the EDA process has several sub processes of data pre-processing, feature selection, data normalization, label encoding, feature correlation, method representation and lastly visualization.

After collecting the data, it was filtered to have only the relevant flows relating to the smart home devices. Certain network features were found to be greatly affected during a DDoS flood. These features were filtered out and focused on for further analysis. They are as follows:

Protocol: These are the various communication entities necessary for different types of data transmission between devices. They include TCP, UDP, NTP, ICMP, DNS, MDNS, TLS, SSH. Each transmitted data packet is associated with a protocol.

Sequence Number: This is a counter based mechanism attributed to packets to keep track of transmitted and received packets. Packets in the same flow carry an incremental value of sequence numbers, thus you can identify what packet comes after which by computing these numbers.

Packet Length: This is the payload size carried by each packet.

TCP Flags: These are the labels carried by each TCP packet to indicate the state of connection. These are also present during the 3-way TCP handshake. For a complete TCP handshake to take place, these flags must be present in their sequential manner depending on the type of communication. These include SYN, ACK, SYN+ACK, ACK, FIN+ACK.

Encryption: A secure communication channel is bound by encryption protocols. These include TLS and SSH.

As each packet is attached to some or all the above listed network properties, they were observed to be simultaneously affected during an attack, thus the reason they were correlated as a baseline for attack detection.

5.1 Benign Flow

The benign smart home traffic was analyzed based on the listed features. One minute traffic was filtered out and visualized to show how these properties behave.

The protocols in a benign flow are dynamic. They tend to change from one packet to the next or every few packets. These varying protocols can include DNS, TCP, MDNS, TLS, NTP, DHCP, ICMP, SSDP and the like. This is shown in Figs. 3 and 4 for both the private and public benign traffic flows respectively.

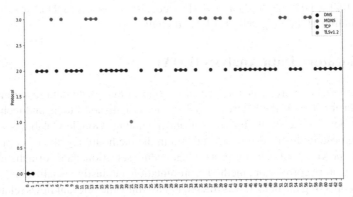

Fig. 3. Varying protocol (private data)

Both figures show the alternating pattern of the protocols having various combinations. Encryption protocols (TLS.v2, SSH) also tend to be predominant in a flow as most exchanged packets are securely encrypted. This results in encryption protocols being one of the frequent ones among the pool of protocols utilized by the devices.

The packet length of the benign flow had the same varying property as the protocol. Figures 5 and 6 show the private and public packet length dynamic nature. We can see that the lengths fall in different ranges from one packet to the next.

Sequence numbers also had the same varying nature. This is shown in Figs. 7 and 8. However, not all protocols carry sequence numbers like DNS, NTP, ICMP and the like. Nonetheless sequence numbers were found to be persistent as majority of the packets in a traffic flow are sequence number carriers like TCP, TLS or HTTP. This makes the appearance of sequence numbers frequent as the predominant protocols are attached to sequence numbers. In addition to that, the sequence numbers were observed to be incremental from one packet to the next in a flow. This starts from a 0, 1 and shoots up to very high values as shown in Figs. 7 and 8. This shows that apart from being dynamic in nature, the sequence numbers have a wide range that they fall within.

Due to the 3-way handshake that takes place for TCP flows, varying TCP flags were observed to be present in a flow. Figure 9 shows the various proportions of these flags contained in a one-minute window for both private and public datasets respectively. This observation also validates TCP flags having several combinations in a flow, thus also having a dynamic pattern like the previous features.

5.2 Attack Flow

The results from the attack flow EDA for the 3 considered attacks (TCP, UDP and ICMP) are visualized and discussed here.

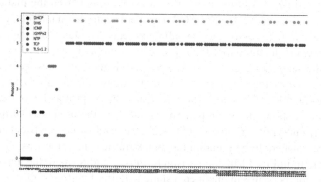

Fig. 4. Varying protocol (public data)

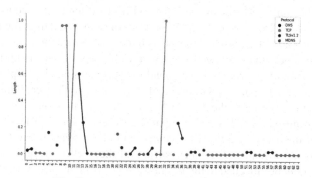

Fig. 5. Varying packet length (private data)

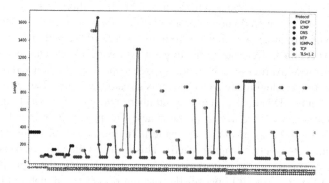

Fig. 6. Varying packet length (public data)

1. TCPSYN: This attack takes advantage of the 3-way TCP handshake, initiating the process without completing it. It floods the target server with SYN requests which arrive faster than the target server can process them, thus leaving it saturated. This results in the connection being half open as it is never acknowledged or ended. After some time of waiting without acknowledgement from the malicious source, the target server sends a bulk of TCP reset packets to the malicious source with the aim to wake it up to respond to the half open requests. During this flooding process, certain network features lose their dynamic nature and get stalled at a single state making the network pattern static. The protocol in the traffic flow gets stalled at TCP for however long the attack runs. Figure 10 shows the 1st 50 packets of both the private and public TCP attack traffic focusing on the protocol. Comparing these to Figs. 3 and 4 shows the static pattern exhibited by the protocols during the attack. Moreover, encryption protocols (TLsv.2) that tend to be persistent in the benign traffic are nowhere to be found in the attack traffic. The same was observed for the packet length in Fig. 11 in comparison to Figs. 5 and 6 where the lengths vary. The sequence numbers also maintained a static pattern of getting stalled at 0 or 1 for all the attack packets. These are shown in Figs. 12 as compared to Figs. 7 and 8 where they exhibit a wide range of varying values. The TCP flags were also affected as the SYN flag became predominant as shown in Fig. 13 when compared to Fig. 9 where the flags vary. In Fig. 13 we can see a proportion of the TCP flags are RST because of the target server trying to reconnect with the malicious source.

2. UDP: This attack floods a target server with UDP packets. This in turn overwhelms the server's ability to process and respond to the packets and in the process denying service to legitimate packets. The protocol and packet lengths were found to lose their varying nature as seen in the TCPSYN attack. Figure 14 shows the static protocol pattern during this attack when compared to Figs. 3 and 4. The same is seen in Fig. 15 for the packet lengths when compared to Figs. 5 and 6. Furthermore as this protocol is not a sequence number carrier, all the packets were found to have no sequence numbers attached to them. This deviates from the normal traffic pattern of having sequence numbers frequently as observed in Figs. 7 and 8 in a 1 min window. Another unusual pattern observed during this attack was the absence of encryption protocols (TLsv.2) as compared to the normal traffic pattern in Figs. 3 and 4 where TLsv.2 is one of the predominant protocols. TCP flags also tend to be absent for the duration of this attack, which is not so in the benign traffic pattern.

3. ICMP: This attack overwhelms the target server with ICMP echo requests (pings). The server tries to process each incoming packet and responds to it and in the process failing to process legitimate packets as it is already saturated. This attack pattern is very similar to UDP attack as sequence numbers, encryption protocols and TCP flags are also absent for the duration of the attack. The protocols in Fig. 16 and packet lengths in Fig. 17 also exhibit a static pattern. In Fig. 17 we can see the packet length alternating between two lengths strictly. This is due to the reply packets directed to each ping. The incoming pings have the same length while the reply packets have the same length. This still opposes the varying packet length nature of the normal traffic flow from Figs. 5 and 6.

Even with the flash and spikes of benign traffic amid the attack flow as observed in Figs. 11 and 12, this still does not affect the predominant static effect the attack causes to the network pattern. The EDA has clearly shown the difference in pattern between a benign and attack traffic flow regardless of the dataset being analyzed.

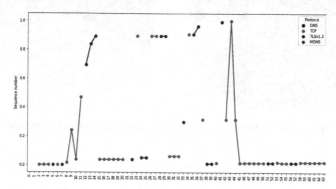

Fig. 7. Varying sequence number (private data)

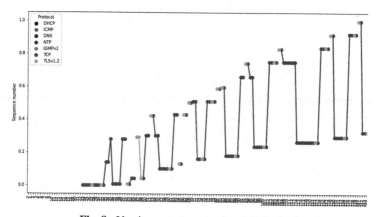

Fig. 8. Varying sequence number (public data)

6 Proposed Novel Detection Method

The proposed detection mechanism takes into consideration four characteristics of IoT traffic as a benchmark for DDoS traffic identification as derived from the EDA. These characteristics are often neglected when it comes to DDoS detection. They are:

Feature Randomness: From the EDA we can observe that certain network features like protocol, packet length and sequence numbers have a dynamic property. They tend to be randomized as opposed to the static nature they exhibit during a DDoS attack. For instance, when you take a window of 20 packets, you sometimes find the protocols

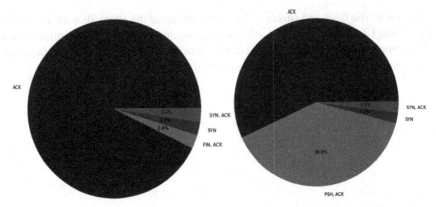

Fig. 9. Varying TCP flags (private data on left and public data on right)

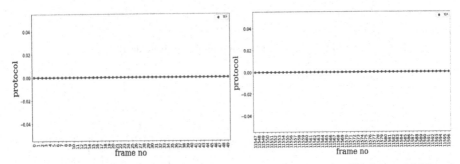

Fig. 10. Protocol pattern, 1st 50 packets, private dataset (left) and public dataset (right)

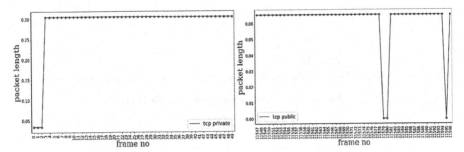

Fig. 11. Packet length pattern, 1st 50 packets, private dataset (left) and public dataset (right)

changing after every three to four packets. The sequence number also varies in most cases for each packet having an incremental value. The packet length exhibits the same property of varying lengths every few packets. TCP flags also fall in this category as a normal TCP flow contains varying flags (SYN, SYN+ACK, ACK, FIN+ACK) as opposed to the single flag exhibited during attacks like TCPSYN flood. Lack of this alternating or dynamic characteristic in the smart home traffic flow should raise flags.

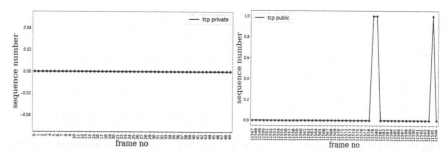

Fig. 12. Sequence number pattern, 1st 50 packets, private dataset (left), public dataset (right)

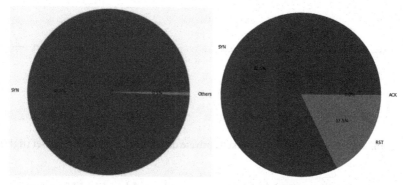

Fig. 13. TCP flags proportion (private data on left and public data on right)

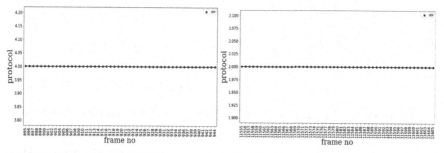

Fig. 14. Protocol pattern, 1st 50 packets, private dataset (left) and public dataset (right)

Absent Features: To identify or detect an attack, we should change the narrative from only focusing on the statistics or behavior of present network features. Rather, features that are normally meant to be present but for some reason are absent for a prolonged period or certain threshold of packets should be a point of concern. For example, the normal network flow we have observed in the EDA tends to have a continuous flow of sequence numbers, as they are required for majority of the packets. However, during a UDP or ICMP attack, the sequence numbers are absent as these two protocols are not sequence number carriers naturally. A prolonged exhibition of this absence should raise a flag.

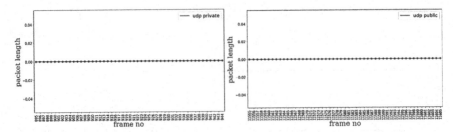

Fig. 15. Packet length pattern, 1st 50 packets, private dataset (left) and public dataset (right)

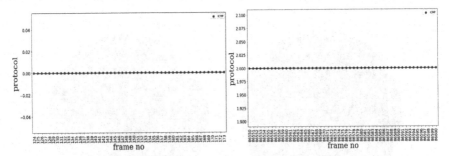

Fig. 16. Protocol pattern, 1st 50 packets, private dataset (left) and public dataset (right)

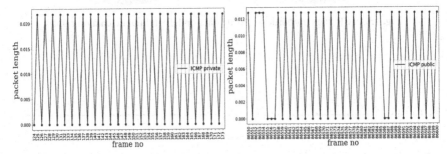

Fig. 17. Packet length pattern, 1st 50 packets, private dataset (left) and public dataset (right)

The same rule applies to missing encryption protocols in the traffic flow. For smart home devices that make use of encryption protocols like the TLSv.2 from the benign EDA, this protocol is persistent whenever a TCP connection is established. However, during any of the flooding attacks in this paper, this encryption protocol appears to be absent as attacks of this sort do not carry encryption protocols normally. As mentioned earlier, a complete established TCP flow carries several TCP flags. Having completely absent or some missing flags in a flow should raise concern as this is a common characteristic of flooding attacks. This shows that focusing on the missing features can also aid in identifying a malicious traffic flow. This should be an important avenue to consider for a more effective approach of attack detection.

Feature Range: Another important neglected point in DDoS identification is the range in which some features normally fall into. If we look at the sequence number range for the benign smart home traffic, we see the values are mostly double, triple or quadruple digits with a few single digits of 0's and 1's at the beginning of a flow. This pattern contrasts with an attack flow which carries only single digits of sequence numbers of just 0's or1's for all the packets.

After considering the points above, a DDoS traffic detection approach is designed, shown in Fig. 18. The network features considered in this proposed approach were found to be simultaneously affected during an attack. This means the packet lengths, sequence numbers, protocols and TCP flags all lost their variance at the very onset of an attack by exhibiting a static pattern as well as missing encryption protocols or sequence numbers in some cases. This novel approach is composed of the following processes and sub processes:

Define Target Address: The target IP/MAC address of the device is set here.

Specify Flow Direction: The desired flow direction of packets is specified. For instance, incoming/outgoing or bidirectional. However, for a lighter weight detection module with clearer variance and less redundancy during the flow, a single direction of flow is advised being incoming traffic to the specified device.

Set Threshold/Time Window: A cumulative sum of packets on which the subsequent checks will be carried out is set. This can be capped at every 20 packets or what best suits the type of network. Alternatively, a time window of some seconds or minutes can be used here for instance the n number of packets after every 60 s.

Network Feature Checks: This is where feature presence, absence and variance are inspected, after which a decision is made of the pattern being malicious or not. This is done for the following network components:

Protocol & Packet Length: The protocol and packet length variance for the specified number of packets are checked. If the ratio of the various protocols and lengths present are balanced, then this is passed. However, if the ratio is found to be imbalanced like one protocol being present thorough out or the same value of length for all packets or majority of the packets, then is also logged.

Sequence Number: The sequence number is first checked for presence or absence. If absent, this is logged. If present, variance and range are checked. If the variance ratio is imbalanced or majority of packets have the same value of sequence number, this is logged. The range is also checked. If the values are all single digits of either 0's or 1's or both, this is also logged. Alternatively, if the range of values is incremental or maintains values with multiple digits, then this is passed.

Encryption & TCP Flags: The presence or absence of encryption protocols and TCP flags are checked. If found absent for all packets, this is logged. On the other hand, if found present, this goes through a balance check. If found to be evenly distributed, this is passed. On the contrary if it is found to be highly uneven, this is logged. For example, with the SYN flag being predominant or completely dominant.

For a malicious pattern to be declared and passed for mitigation, a minimum of 3 logged features must take place to avoid false positives. Moreover, the fact that these listed components get affected simultaneously during an attack makes it more likely for all components to be logged during an attack. For instance, a TCPSYN attack will log absence of encryption, imbalanced sequence number, imbalanced packet length, imbalanced protocol and imbalanced TCP flags with the SYN flag predominant. On the other hand, a UDP or ICMP attack will log an absence of sequence numbers, absence of TCP flags, absence of encryption, imbalanced protocol and an imbalanced packet length.

6.1 Benefits of the Proposed Approach

The network features used as a basis for detection gives this approach a generalized edge in terms of not being device, user or attack centric as seen in related works. This is due to all detection metrics being derived from general network characteristics shared by IoT devices. The various checks incorporated in this approach gives it the robust edge when dealing with the detection of several kinds of attacks. This is not only limited to the attacks covered in this paper but other attacks with similar propagation pattern to the ones covered here like NTP, ARP and DNS flooding attacks. The entropy or variance of the detection metrics is not calculated in real time based on the network statistics. Rather, a set of rules and conditions are used to identify an attack traffic. This will handle the failure in detection experienced by some approaches as seen in the related works when an attack starts at the very beginning of a set window. This is because no prior variance or entropy statistics are available to compare the current attacks entropy to. As a result, this approach does not rely on prior real time network statistics. This approach is also light weight in terms of time and resource consumption as the flexibility to monitor a single flow direction (incoming traffic to target device) is possible. This results in clearer and less redundant variance statistics as opposed to a bidirectional flow (incoming/outgoing) which might hinder the clarity of the variance and carry redundant statistics like protocols, lengths, Flags, and sequence numbers.

This approach also eliminated the use of certain network features that can result in higher rates of false positives/negatives. For instance, the use of incoming/outgoing distribution will raise a false negative for attacks like ICMP flooding. This is due to the nature of the attack traffic whereby majority of the echo requests have a paired reply packet from the target, thus making the incoming/outgoing ratio evenly distributed. Same applies to the use of source IP addresses and port numbers in highly distributed attack scenarios where the source IP's and ports are spoofed. Moreover, IP addresses and ports tend to bring about biases especially in Machine Learning domains as they are specific to each scenario.

This approach can be incorporated into areas like *Data visualization tools, Intrusion Detection System (IDS), Software Defined Network (SDN) & Machine Learning* for better DDoS detection. The proposed network features used as detection metrics can be integrated into data visualisation tools and IDS. This will provide clearer low-level statistics as to how the network is deviating from its normal pattern during an attack. These features can also be defined as flow rules and conditions at the SDN gateway coupled with the appropriate mitigation measure in the case of a detected attack. The visualised EDA images can also be trained on a Convolutional Neural Network (CNN)

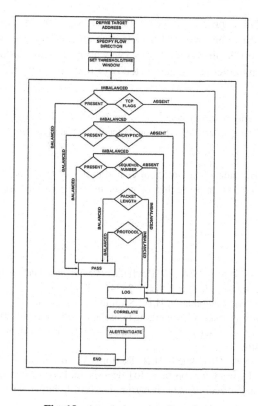

Fig. 18. Attack detection flow chart

using ResNet, as deep learning models especially CNN achieved high significance due to their outstanding performance in the image processing field.

7   Conclusion

This paper has carried out an EDA on collected smart home data, comparing the behavioral pattern of certain network features in a benign and DDoS attack flow. The same results have been derived for both privately collected data and public datasets. Based on the EDA results, a novel DDoS detection approach has been proposed which is neither user, attack nor device centric as it is applicable to IoT devices in general and a variety of DDoS flooding attacks. The detection model is based on the observed general network behavior of the smart home devices. These include feature variance, absent features and feature range which tend to be neglected in attack detection as observed from related works. The narrative needs to be changed from only focusing on present network feature statistics to detect attacks, rather features that are normally present but tend to be absent for a prolonged period also contribute to rapid attack detection as seen in this paper. However, this proposed approach relies heavily on the static nature of DDoS attack traffic and as such, low stealth DDoS attacks that exhibit a dynamic nature are not detected by this approach. The approach also detects a DDoS pattern at a certain threshold of packets which if not reached will fail to detect an attack. However, the overwhelming nature of the attack traffic always tends to go way above the threshold. As this detection method has not been implemented and tested over real time traffic, future work aims to implement this.

Acknowledgement. This research was funded by Petroleum Technology Development Fund (PTDF) Nigeria, with support and expertise guidance by Nottingham Trent University (NTU).

Availability of Source Code. The results presented in this work has been generated using the code which can be found at: https://github.com/asegun-cod/smart-home-device-cyberattack-detection.

References

1. Kostas, K., Just, M., Lones, M.A.: IoTDevID: a behavior-based device identification method for the IoT. IEEE Internet Things J. **9**(23), 23741–23749 (2022)
2. Notra, S., Siddiqi, M., Gharakheili, H.H., Sivaraman, V., Boreli, R.: An experimental study of security and privacy risks with emerging household appliances. In: 2014 IEEE Conference on Communications and Network Security, pp. 79–84. IEEE (2014). https://doi.org/10.1109/CNS.2014.6997469
3. Loi, F., Sivanathan, A., Gharakheili, H.H., Radford, A., Sivaraman, V.: Systematically evaluating security and privacy for consumer IoT devices. In: Proceedings of the 2017 Workshop on Internet of Things Security and Privacy, pp. 1–6 (2017). https://doi.org/10.1145/3139937.3139938
4. Andrea, I., Chrysostomou, C., Hadjichristofi, G.: Internet of Things: security vulnerabilities and challenges. In: IEEE Symposium on Computers and Communication (ISCC), Larnaca, Cyprus, pp. 180–187. IEEE (2015). https://doi.org/10.1109/ISCC.2015.7405513
5. Moskvitch, K.: Securing IoT: your smart home and your connected enterprise. Eng. Technol. **12**(3), 40–42 (2017). https://doi.org/10.1049/et.2017.0303
6. Dhanjani, N.: Abusing the Internet of Things: Blackouts, Freakouts, and Stakeouts. O'Reilly Media Inc., Sebastopol (2015)
7. Fernandes, E., Jung, J., Prakash, A.: Security analysis of emerging smart home applications. In: IEEE Symposium on Security and Privacy (SP), San Jose, CA, USA, pp 636–654. IEEE (2016). https://doi.org/10.1109/SP.2016.44
8. Chaabouni, N., Mosbah, M., Zemmari, A., Sauvignac, C., Faruki, P.: Network intrusion detection for IoT security based on learning techniques. IEEE Commun. Surv. Tutor. **21**(3), 2671–2701 (2019). https://doi.org/10.1109/COMST.2019.2896380
9. Hussain, F., Hussain, R., Hassan, S.A., Hossain, E.: Machine learning in IoT security: current solutions and future challenges. IEEE Commun. Surv. Tutor. **22**(3), 1686–1721 (2020). https://doi.org/10.1109/COMST.2020.2986444
10. Bezawada, B., Bachani, M., Peterson, J., Shirazi, H., Ray, I., Ray, I.: Behavioral fingerprinting of Internet-of-Things devices. In: Conference on Computer and Communications Security, Toronto, Canada (2018). Association for Computing Machinery, New York, pp. 41–50 (2018). https://doi.org/10.1145/3266444.3266452
11. Kupreev, O., Badovskaya, E., Gutnikov, A.: DDoS attacks in Q1 2020. Kaspersky DDoS Reports (2020). https://securelist.com/ddos-attacks-in-q1-2020/96837/. Accessed 1 Jan 2022
12. Marty, R.: Applied Security Visualization. Pearson Education, Crawfordsville (2008)

13. Huang, H., Chu, J., Cheng, X.: Trend analysis and countermeasure research of DDoS attack under 5G network. In: IEEE 5th International Conference on Cryptography, Security and Privacy (CSP). Zhuhai, China, pp. 153–160. IEEE (2021). https://doi.org/10.1109/CSP51677. 2021.9357499

14. Wu, C., Sheng, S., Dong, X.: Research on visualization systems for DDoS attack detection. In: IEEE International Conference on Systems, Man, and Cybernetics (SMC), Miyazaki, Japan, pp. 2986–2991. IEEE (2018). https://doi.org/10.1109/SMC.2018.00507

15. Wali, A., Apejoye, O., He, J., Ma, X.: An exploratory data analysis of the network behavior of hive home devices. In: 8th International Conference on Internet of Things: Systems, Management and Security (IOTSMS), Gandia, Spain, pp. 1–8. IEEE (2021). https://doi.org/10. 1109/IOTSMS53705.2021.9704944

16. Cinque, M., Cotroneo, D., Pecchia, A.: Challenges and directions in security information and event management (SIEM). In: IEEE International Symposium on Software Reliability Engineering Workshops (ISSREW), Memphis, TN, USA, pp 95–99. IEEE (2018). https:// doi.org/10.1109/ISSREW.2018.00-24

17. Miranda-Calle, J.D., Reddy, V., Dhawan, P., Churi, P.: Exploratory data analysis for cybersecurity. World J. Eng. (2021). https://doi.org/10.1108/WJE-11-2020-0560

18. Wang, J., et al.: IoT-praetor: undesired behaviors detection for IoT devices. IEEE Internet Things J. 8(2), 927–940 (2020). https://doi.org/10.1109/JIOT.2020.3010023

19. Yamauchi, M., Ohsita, Y., Murata, M., Ueda, K., Kato, Y.: Anomaly detection in smart home operation from user behaviors and home conditions. IEEE Trans. Consum. Electron. 66(2), 183–192 (2020). https://doi.org/10.1109/TCE.2020.2981636

20. Swami, R., Dave, M., Ranga, V.: Detection and analysis of TCP-SYN DDoS attack in software-defined networking. Wireless Pers. Commun. 118(4), 2295–2317 (2021). https:// doi.org/10.1007/s11277-021-08127-6

21. Thant, Y.M.: IoT security: simulation and analysis of TCP SYN flooded DDOS attack using WireShark. Trans. Netw. Commun. 8, 16–25 (2020). https://doi.org/10.14738/tnc.83.8389

22. Saxena, U., Sodhi, J.S., Singh, Y.: An analysis of DDoS attacks in a smart home networks. In: 10th International Conference on Cloud Computing, Data Science & Engineering (Confluence) (2020), Noida, India, pp. 272–276. IEEE (2020). https://doi.org/10.1109/Confluenc e47617.2020.9058087

23. Pokhrel, S., Abbas, R., Aryal, B.: IoT security: botnet detection in IoT using machine learning. arXiv preprint arXiv:2104.02231 (2021)

24. Vinayakumar, R., Alazab, M., Srinivasan, S., Pham, Q., Padannayil, S.K., Simran, K.: A visualized botnet detection system based deep learning for the internet of things networks of smart cities. IEEE Trans. Ind. Appl. 56(4), 4436–4456 (2020). https://doi.org/10.1109/TIA. 2020.2971952

25. Costa, W.L., Silveira, M.M., de Araujo, T., Gomes, R.L.: Improving DDoS detection in IoT networks through analysis of network traffic characteristics. In: IEEE Latin-American Conference on Communications (LATINCOM), Santo Domingo, Dominican Republic, pp. 1– 6. IEEE (2020). https://doi.org/10.1109/LATINCOM50620.2020.9282265

26. Doshi, R., Apthorpe, N., Feamster, N.: Machine learning DDoS detection for consumer internet of things devices. In: IEEE Security and Privacy Workshops (SPW), San Francisco, CA, pp. 29–35. IEEE (2018). https://doi.org/10.1109/SPW.2018.00013

27. Anthi, E., Williams, L., Słowińska, M., Theodorakopoulos, G., Burnap, P.: A supervised intrusion detection system for smart home IoT devices. IEEE Internet Things J. 6(5), 9042– 9053 (2019). https://doi.org/10.1109/JIOT.2019.2926365

28. Niyaz, Q., Sun, W., Javaid, A.Y.: A deep learning based DDoS detection system in software-defined networking (SDN). arXiv preprint arXiv:1611.07400 (2016)

29. Bhayo, J., Hameed, S., Shah, S.A.: An efficient counter-based DDoS attack detection framework leveraging software defined IoT (SD-IoT). IEEE Access **8**, 221612–221631 (2020). https://doi.org/10.1109/ACCESS.2020.3043082
30. Galeano-Brajones, J., Carmona-Murillo, J., Valenzuela-Valdés, J.F., Luna-Valero, F.: Detection and mitigation of DoS and DDoS attacks in IoT-based Stateful SDN: an experimental approach. Sensors **20**(3), 816 (2020). https://doi.org/10.3390/s20030816
31. Li, J., Liu, M., Xue, Z., Fan, X., He, X.: RTVD: a real-time volumetric detection scheme for DDoS in the internet of things. IEEE Access **8**, 36191–36201 (2020). https://doi.org/10.1109/ACCESS.2020.2974293
32. Garcia, S., Parmisano, A., Erquiaga, M.J.: IoT-23: a labeled dataset with malicious and benign IoT network traffic. Zenodo **20**, 15 (2020). https://doi.org/10.5281/zenodo.4743746
33. Koroniotis, N., Moustafa, N., Sitnikova, E., Turnbull, B.: Towards the development of realistic Botnet dataset in the internet of things for network forensic analytics: Bot-IoT dataset. Future Gener. Comput. Syst. **100**, 779–796 (2018). https://doi.org/10.1016/J.FUTURE.2019.05.041
34. Hasan, M., Islam, S.: BUET-DDoS2020. Mendeley Data (2021). https://doi.org/10.17632/bzgf9r36kp.2. Accessed 3 Mar 2022

A Novel Framework to Detect Anomalous Nodes to Secure Wireless Sensor Networks

Muhammad R. Ahmed[1](✉), Thirein Myo[1], Badar Al Baroomi[1], M. H. Marhaban[2], M. Shamim Kaiser[3], and Mufti Mahmud[4]

[1] Military Technological College, Muscat, Oman
muhammad.ahmed@mtc.edu.om
[2] Faculty of Engineering, University Putra Malaysia, Seri Kembangan, Selangor, Malaysia
[3] Institute of Information Technology, Jahangirnagar University, Savar, Bangladesh
[4] Department of Computer Science, Nottingham Trent University, Nottingham, UK

Abstract. The application driven technology wireless sensor networks (WSNs) are developed substantially in the last decades. The technology has drawn the attention for application in the scientific as well as in industrial domains. The networks use multifunctional and cheap sensor nodes. The application of the networks ranges from military to the civilian application such as battlefield monitoring, environment monitoring and patient monitoring. The network goal is to collect the data from different environmental phenomenon in an unsupervised manner from unknown and hash environment using the resource constrained sensor nodes. The construction of the sensor nodes used in the network and the distributed nature of the network infrastructure is susceptible to various types of attacks. In order to assure the functional operation of WSNs and collecting the meaningful data from the network, detecting the anomalous node and mechanisms to secure the networks are vital. In this research paper, we have used machine learning based decision tree algorithm to determine the anomalous sensor node to provide security to the WSNs. The decision tree has the capability to deal with categorical and numerical data. The simulation work was carried out in python and the result shows the accurate detection of the anomalous node. In future, the hybrid approach combining two algorithms will be employed to further performance improvement of the model.

Keywords: Security · Decision Tree · Machine learning · Wireless Sensor networks

1 Introduction

The recent innovation and improvement in material sciences, semiconductor technologies allow the electronic devices becoming smaller and smarter. The development of networking technology makes it possible to build a wireless network that is self-configuring and infrastructure-free. It is known as Wireless Sensor Networks (WSNs) [1]. Typically, WSNs comprise of hundreds of thousands of low-cost resources constrained autonomous

M. Mahmud et al. (Eds.): AII 2022, CCIS 1724, pp. 499–510, 2022.
https://doi.org/10.1007/978-3-031-24801-6_35

sensor nodes deployed in an area. The sensor nodes monitor the environmental and physical phenomenon and send the data over the network to the sink [2]. The sink has a higher
resource in which the data are observed and analyzed. The technology was first inspired
by the military application such as battlefield monitoring and surveillance. Recently, the
application driven WSNs technology is using in a range of civilian application which
includes monitoring the environment, agriculture field, infrastructure, transportation,
and health sector [3]. There are few challenges in WSNs such as efficient deployment,
energy management and security. The deployment strategy for an application is usually
determined by the different scenarios and the environment of the application, including harsh fields, disasters, or toxic surroundings [4]. In order to have efficient energy
management, the design of the hardware and software needs to consider minimizing
the energy usage. Radio transmission energy consumption can be reduced if we use the
data compression technology. Energy consumption is depending on the application as
well. In some application, the node may not be active continuously [5]. A WSNs and
the construction of the sensor node is shown in the Fig. 1.

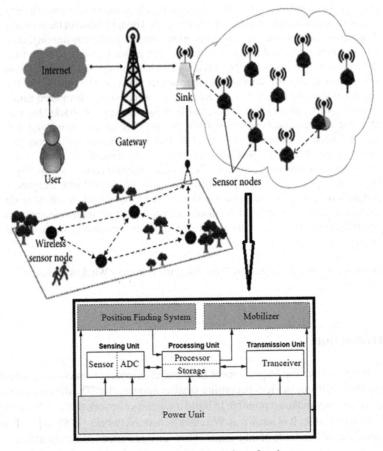

Fig. 1. WSN and construction of node

In this information and communication technological age, all the network is interconnected utilizing different communication media. The provision of security is a mandatory requirement both for wired and wireless communication [6]. WSNs use wireless communication media to construct the network. Moreover, the characteristics of WSNs includes open nature of wireless media, unattended operation and resource constrained nodes with short communication range and low processing unit, limited energy, memory, communication bandwidth as well as computation power. This makes the network vulnerable to faults and different kinds of attacks. Considering the nature and characteristics of the WSNs, security is a challenging and critical task [7]. In order to have an efficient functionality and collect the meaningful data from the deployed WSNs, securing the network is essential. One of the major and important tasks is to find the anomalous node in the network so that the node can be fixed or isolate if required to secure the network.

Numerous algorithms have been developed by researchers to secure the Wireless Sensor Networks and collect the meaningful data from a functional WSNs. Most of the works focus on the attack defense, authentication process as well as pair wise key establishment. Currently available works rely mostly on cryptographic data and authentication of the sensor data to establish sensor relationships and trust.

But the non-reliable communication using the wireless communication media make it easy for the adversary to compromise the sensor nodes [8]. If any anomalous node or compromised exists in the network, it is almost impossible to have a secure functional WSNs and to extract the meaningful data for the specific application scenario. In the case of deploying WSNs in a sensitive application such as battlefield monitoring, nuclear plant monitoring, detecting of all the adversary is necessary as the anomalous node act like a legitimate node. Whenever the node is compromised by the adversary, the anomalous node will behave abnormally and the node will temper the original message, will drop, or send the excessive packet.

Detection of anomalous node is a significant task to have a secure and accurate significant information from the network. In this research, a machine learning based supervised learning technique called decision tree is applied. The algorithm has the capability of mimic human thinking while making the decision and the logic behind the decision is easily understood as it follows the tree structure. Moreover, the algorithm has benefit of running from different initial points, and this can better approximate the near optimal classifier [9]. This method begins with the root tree and then compares the root and recorded attributes to predict a class level. After comparing the value with the branch, it moves on to the next value [10]. The algorithm can work with the resource constrained nodes and for any sample data.

The rest of the paper is organized as follows: the overview of some recent existing works is discussed in Sect. 2 followed by the assumptions and architecture of the network is in Sect. 3. The detailed methodology of decision tree and implementation is explained in Sect. 4. The result and evaluations are presented in Sect. 5. The last section is the summary of the work in conclusion.

2 Related Works

The sensor nodes are dispersed over an area generally labeled as sensor field in WSNs to collect the specific data for a dedicated application. Securing the communication network is an obligatory task both for wired and wireless medium. WSNs use radio communication link of wireless media within the network. The construction of nodes, features, and operating nature of WSNs make the network more vulnerable. Therefore, securing the WSNs is critical and important for their efficient functioning. Hence, it has attracted the attention of the researchers. Several researchers have developed different algorithms to secure the network. Some of the recent works are discussed in this section.

To develop the detection algorithm for anomalous node the researchers mainly focus on high cost of communications, network topology, resource constrained nodes, distributed streaming data as well as high dimensional data. The existing data driven developed technique can be categorized by the detection's approaches named: (a) statistical based, (b) classification based, (c) artificial intelligence based, (d) distance based, and (e) cluster based.

The statistical based model uses the representation-based process. Normally, anomaly or outlier is detected based on the irregular data points in these techniques. In this method, if the data instance occurrence probability is low, it will be considered as the node is compromised. The compromised node act as legitimate node. The nonparametric methodology of statistical was analysed and studied by Smarpathi et al. in [11], their research the researchers considered the streaming data that collected from the sensor node and calculated the data density. A certain degenerated data density value is considered, and the network outlier is decided. The kernel density estimators are used by the researchers to compute and analyse the data from the streaming sensors. Normally, only the univariate data can be analysed using the method. Wu et al. In [12], designed a parametric-based method which can do the classification of the abnormal sensor nodes in the networks as well as the events that is associated with the sensor networks. The method has good computation accuracy and less false alarm, but in this approach the time-based association was not given attention.

The classification-based approach utilizes the training data as well as compare the freshly received data with training data set to come up with a decision about the anomalous node in WSNs. In [13], Poornima et al. has presented a classification based method using Online Locally Weighted Projection Regression (OLWPR) to detect anomalous node of WSNs. The principal component analysis (PCA) is used for reduction of the unrelated and unwanted data at the level of input. This establishes the estimated value considering the PCA outcome. Mario et al. worked on the wearable sensor networks and formulated the deep recurrent combined method in order to find the outliers in the sensor network, in [14]. In their research, it was considered human activities and used two data set. This method produces good results, but it is computational cost is high and works with multivariate data. The approach using classification depends on the good training sets, which is difficult to obtain. the high dimensional and mixed structured data was not well studied.

Numerous researchers have studied the artificial intelligence (AI)-based methods to secure the network. This methods in WSNs use prediction to detect the anomalous node with the decision-making theory. A fuzzy rule-based methodology was introduced in [15] by Thangaramya et al. The approach detects the outliers or anomalous node on basis of the routing decision. To do that, the method utilises the key and trust management technique. In this approach, assigning the degree of trust for every member in the sensor network is difficult. Nauman et al. has presented an extended support vector machine (SVM) known as Quarter-Sphere formulation of One-Class SVM in [16]. In his work, a new One-Class Quarter-Sphere SVM formulation was developed to classify the data online and find the outliers in the wireless sensor networks. The method is online approached. The method did not consider the data which is infected with noise and faults. The AI-based method needs training and it is hard to train. To train the network well, the high dimensional data set is necessary. Moreover, the learning algorithm requires good learning rate.

A distance-based method is the most common approach used in detection of anomalous node in the wireless sensor networks. The approach works with the nearest neighbour distance measurement. Amel et al. formulated a method that uses the nearest neighbour based techniques with game theory to deal with the outliers, in [17]. The method has a complex computation. Tianwei et al. has come up with an approach to detect the outlier which has low computation and uses less memory in [18]. It detects or eliminates the forge measurement of the sensors with the weighted average distance factor. The method is good as it runs on the independent nodes of the networks. The challenge is to get the finest results. Asmaa et al. presented a method in [19]. This method uses the in-network knowledge discovery which then detected the outlier and do the clustering of the data simultaneously based on the nearest neighbour. In this method, the computational complexity is high. In the distance-based approach, the selection of the suitable distance for the real time application is difficult. So, the selecting the correct and appropriate neighbour is a problem in this type of method.

In data mining research community, the cluster-based approach is considered to be the most modern approach. Xiang et al. [20] have worked on the cluster-based methodology to identify the outliers in the network. To detect the outlier, their investigation of the work developed an unsupervised contextual model. In their research work, the researchers found that the method was able to detect anomalies as well as abnormalities in the network. There are some drawbacks to this type of method, including the fact that the same set of data may show higher density in one specific area of the collection field. Nikos et al. presented a method by dividing the multidimensional and unidirectional outlier in [21]. In their method, the researchers utilize the in-network proposal that deals with the both dimensions of data (unidentical and multidimensional). The researchers assume that the error data is generated from the elements of the individual sensors. The method uses hashing technique, so the computational cost and high memory is needed. The clustering-based approach uses the distance metrics (Euclidian as well as Mahalanobis). Both metrics used are not well studied for the hi-dimensional data as well as the mixed type of structure.

The mechanisms presented in the literature by the researchers have some limitations. Most of the proposed mechanisms use the fixed threshold value, need sensitive parameter selection and many have a complex computation as well as high energy consumption. Moreover, the algorithm implemented distributed structure did not taken into account the appropriate data transmission reference model among the nodes. They do not have the capability distinguishing the events and errors. Studying the facts and the characteristics of the WSNs node, we have established the facts that new method is needed that can deal with the small data set and can make the network sustainable based on the network developed with resource constrained sensor nodes. In this research paper, a decision tree-based techniques is presented to find the anomalous node and secure the network.

3 Assumptions and Architecture of the Network

The sensor network is assumed to be deployed in an area intended to measure the environmental phenomenon. Parameters to be measured or detected are provided by users in the deployed area. The network grid of the area of attention is Ω of $N_x \times N_y$ points scenario. Whenever the network deployment is done completely and it is in operation, the channels of communication and nodes are static. The static sensor nodes have the task to observe the data and send the observed data to the sinker utilizing wireless media. During the operation of the network, some sensor nodes may be compromised by the adversary, and it is anomalous node. This node compromises the security of the overall network and does not let the network to function properly. To reflect the scenario, we have simulated our network for the environmental monitoring. To do that, we have hypothetically deployed the network in sunshine cost, Australia and simulated for January to March weather data for temperature and humidity. According to the weather and climate information in sunshine coast during the mentioned period, the temperature stays between 20 to 30°C, and the humidity is about 66%. We accept temperature data that lies within the 2 sigma range (the standard deviation of the Gaussian distribution) based on the Gaussian distribution standard deviation method. In accordance with the research conducted by Holder et al. [22], a good collection of data found in 2 sigma choice. Hence, we will have 95.46% of sensor data in our implementation.

4 Method

Decision three is the machine learning algorithm, which is the type of supervised learning technique, to come up with a strategy to accomplish a specific goal. The algorithm can be used to solve both regression problems and classification problems. In which, the information data is constantly separated corresponding to a specific parameter. The algorithm is using tree like decision making formation where each leaf nodes correspond to the class labels, and internal nodes correspond to the attributes. The network consists of internal nodes representing tests on attributes, branches representing test outcomes, and leaves (terminal nodes) storing class labels. Among the most important Decision Tree terms are [23]:

a) Root Node: In general, the root node represents the entire sample, which can be subdivided into several homogenous clusters. The root node represents the decision tree at its very top.
b) Splitting: A process that divides a node into two or more sub-nodes.
c) Decision Node: This is a node that divides data into further sub nodes.
d) Leave Node: These are nodes that do not split; they provide the final output of the decision tree. it known as leaf
e) A pruning is an opposite action to splitting. The process of pruning involves removing a sub-node from a decision node

f) Sub-tree: A branch or sub-tree is the sub-division of an entire tree.
g) Parent Node: Nodes that are divided into sub-nodes constitute the parent node
h) Child Node: Sub-nodes that make up the parent node

The method starts with the root node of the tree in response to the dataset for class prediction. A comparison is made between the values of the root attribute and the values of the recorded attribute, based on the comparison, follows the branch, and moves to the next node. In the next step, the method evaluates the value of attributes against the values of the other sub-nodes and moves to the next node. In order to reach the leaf node of the tree, the process must be repeated (Fig. 2).

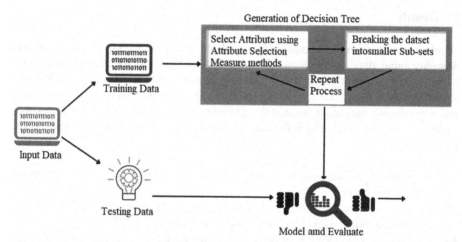

Fig. 2. The decision tree method

In order to select the Attribute, the attribute selection measure (ASM) methods is used. A dataset's entropy refers to the uncertainty in it or the measure of disorders in it. An individual node's entropy value reflects its randomness. In such a situation, the margin of difference for a result is thin, and the model has little confidence in the accuracy of the forecast. In general, the higher the entropy, the more random the dataset will be [24, 25]. When using a Decision Tree algorithm, low entropy is preferred. Entropy is calculated as shown in the following Eq. (1):

$$Entropy(S) = \sum_{n=1}^{n} P_i * log\ P_i \qquad (1)$$

In the Eq. (1), P_i represent the probability of the data class. Using information gain, we can decide what attributes belong in which nodes of a decision tree and whether a specific feature should be used to split the node or not. An information gain is simply the change in entropy after a dataset has been segmented based on an attribute. The feature provides us with the amount of information that a class provides us. Creating a decision tree involves dividing each node by the value of the information acquired. A decision tree method splits the node or attribute with the highest information gain first, which maximizing the information gain. The information gain is calculated in Eq. (2) as:

$$Information\ Gain,\ I = S - [(\overline{w}) * S_i] \tag{2}$$

where, S is the total sample space entropy, $\overline{w}$ is the average weight) and S_i is the entropy of each feature Information.

The method is effective for anomaly detection in WSNs as it is not necessary to normalize or standardize the collected measure data by node. Moreover, the missing values of the data do not need to be credited. In a decision tree making model, preprocessing steps require less coding and analysis.

5 Result

Wireless sensor network hypothetically simulated in Python with the temperature and humidity input data. In the simulation, we have considered the temperature varies between 20 to 30° centigrade and the humidity between 60% to 70% based on the sunshine coast data. The packet forwarding should be 5 to 8 packets in a minute. Considering this scenario, we have implemented the decision tree algorithm to find the anomalous node to secure the node. The following assumptions are made while constructing the Decision Tree:

I.   In the beginning, we consider the whole dataset as a Root Node and start the process of the decision tree.
II. Decision trees are best constructed using categorical feature values. In order to construct a model with continuous values, they must be discretized
III. Recursively, records are distributed based on attribute values. The attribute values are impotent to make the decision.
IV. Statistics are used to determine which attributes should be placed as root nodes or internal nodes of the tree. One attribute is not chosen at random.

In the hypothetical wireless sensor networks, which comprises of 300 sensor nodes to measure the temperature and humidity. In the simulation in python, we determined that 75% of the original data would be used for training and 25% for testing. The extracted sample from the dataset is shown in the Table 1. In the table, the predicted possible scenarios are labeled as No Fault (NF), Fault Temperature (FT), Fault Humidity (FH), Fault Packet (FP), Fault Temperature and Humidity (FTH), Fault Temperature and Packet (FTP), Fault Humidity and packet (FHP), Fault in all (FTHP).

Table 1. Sample of extracted from dataset

Node	Temperature (°C)	Humidity (%)	Packets	Label
1	22	66	5	NF
2	35	67	7	FT
3	28	67	6	NF
4	23	58	5	FH
5	20	66	6	NF
9	29	65	9	FP
19	19	71	7	FTH
23	22	73	4	FHP
50	18	72	4	FTHP
202	35	67	7	FT

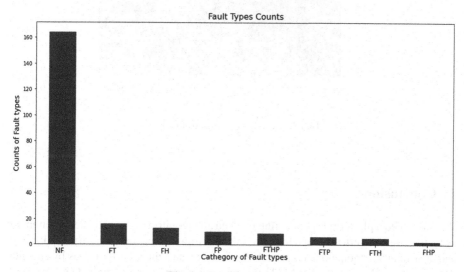

Fig. 3. The fault data count

Figure 3 shows the count of the types of fault data in the dataset. The confusion matrix shown in Fig. 4 for test dataset consisting of 75 nodes. In order to solve classification problems, confusion matrixes are very popular measures. In addition to binary classification, it also works with multiclass classification problems. In the carried-out simulation, only 6 nodes are showing in wrong category. Though they are showing in wrong category of faults type, they are still lies in Faults groups. There is no single error appear in "No Fault" category. So, the error of 6 nodes will not affect in isolating the anomalous nodes as they will be considered as Fault nodes. In multi-class classification, hamming Loss is a good measure of model performance. The smaller hamming loss will give better model performance. Hamming loss is calculated as dividing wrong labels by the total number of labels. In this case study, the hamming loss was calculated as 0.080. It shows that the performance of the proposed algorithm is more than satisfactory. The simulation is uploaded in https://github.com/trmyo/Aii2022.git.

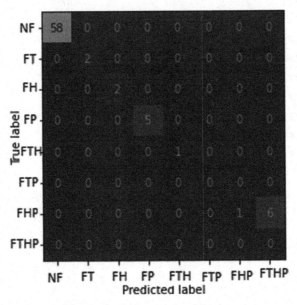

Fig. 4. Confusion matrix of the data

6 Conclusion

WSNs created a platform for collecting the data and monitoring desired phenomenon. In order to extract the effective and meaningful data from the network, security is a difficult and critical task. Anomalous node in the network creates the security issues by causing the integrity problem in the WSNs. In this research paper, we have studied and done the investigation for the detection of anomalous nodes to secure the networks. To do that we have used the machine learning algorithm-based decision tree mechanism which use the supervised learning technique. The model is consuming less energy and it needs less computation power. Moreover, it is using minimum memory as decision tree does not need to scale the data and it takes less time to make the decision in the preprocessing steps. The simulation result shows that the humming loss is only 0.08 which proves that the accuracy of the proposed approach gives promising result. In future, we would like to combine it with another algorithm to create the hybrid method for better performance.

References

1. Ahmed, M., Huang, X., Sharma, D.: A novel framework for abnormal behaviour identification and detection for wireless sensor networks. Int. J. Comput. Commun. Eng. **6**(2), 148–151 (2012)
2. Gurewitz, O., Shifrin, M., Dvir, E.: Data gathering techniques in WSN: a cross-layer view. Sensors **22**(7), Art. no. 7 (2022). https://doi.org/10.3390/s22072650
3. Kandris, D., Nakas, C., Vomvas, D., Koulouras, G.: Applications of wireless sensor networks: an Up-to-Date survey. Appl. Syst. Innov. **3**(1), Art. no. 1 (2020). https://doi.org/10.3390/asi 3010014
4. Ahmed, M., Huang, X., Cui, H.: Smart decision making for internal attacks in wireless sensor network. Int. J. Comput. Sci. Netw. Secur. **12**(12), 15–23 (2012)
5. Abdul-Qawy, A.S.H., Almurisi, N.M.S., Tadisetty, S.: Classification of energy saving techniques for IoT-based heterogeneous wireless nodes. Procedia Comput. Sci. **171**, 2590–2599 (2020). https://doi.org/10.1016/j.procs.2020.04.281
6. Ray, P.P.: A survey on Internet of Things architectures. J. King Saud Univ. Comput. Inf. Sci. **30**(3), 291–319 (2018). https://doi.org/10.1016/j.jksuci.2016.10.003
7. Ahmed, M.R., Huang, X., Sharma, D., Cui, H.: Protecing WSN from internal attack with multi-criteria evaluation using dempester-shafer Theory. In: Proceedings of International Conference on Information Systems, 2012, Penang, Malaysia, vol. 62, December 2012
8. Gautam, A.K., Kumar, R.: A comprehensive study on key management, authentication and trust management techniques in wireless sensor networks. SN Appl. Sci. **3**(1), 1–27 (2021). https://doi.org/10.1007/s42452-020-04089-9
9. Brijain, M., Patel, R., Kushik, M., Rana, K.: A survey on decision tree algorithm for classification.
10. Jin, C., De-lin, L., Fen-xiang, M.: An improved ID3 decision tree algorithm. In: 2009 4th International Conference on Computer Science & Education, pp. 127–130, July 2009. https://doi.org/10.1109/ICCSE.2009.5228509
11. Samparthi, V.S.K., Verma, H.K.: Outlier detection of data in wireless sensor networks using kernel density estimation. Int. J. Comput. Appl. IJCA **5**(7), 28–32 (2010)
12. Wu, W., Cheng, X., Ding, M., Xing, K., Liu, F., Deng, P.: Localized outlying and boundary data detection in sensor networks. IEEE Trans. Knowl. Data Eng. **19**(8), 1145–1157 (2007). https://doi.org/10.1109/TKDE.2007.1067
13. Poornima, I.G.A., Paramasivan, B.: Anomaly detection in wireless sensor network using machine learning algorithm. Comput. Commun. **151**, 331–337 (2020). https://doi.org/10.1016/j.comcom.2020.01.005
14. Munoz-Organero, M.: Outlier detection in wearable sensor data for human activity recognition (HAR) based on DRNNs. IEEE Access **7**, 74422–74436 (2019). https://doi.org/10.1109/ACCESS.2019.2921096
15. Thangaramya, K., et al.: Intelligent fuzzy rule-based approach with outlier detection for secured routing in WSN. Soft. Comput. **24**(21), 16483–16497 (2020).https://doi.org/10.1007/s00500-020-04955-z
16. Shahid, N., Naqvi, I.H., Qaisar, S.B.: Quarter-Sphere SVM: attribute and spatio-temporal correlations based outlier & event detection in wireless sensor networks. In: 2012 IEEE Wireless Communications and Networking Conference (WCNC), pp. 2048–2053, April 2012. https://doi.org/10.1109/WCNC.2012.6214127
17. Arfaoui, A., Kribeche, A., Senouci, S.M., Hamdi, M.: Game-based adaptive anomaly detection in wireless body area networks. Comput. Netw. **163**, 106870 (2019). https://doi.org/10.1016/j.comnet.2019.106870

18. Dai, T., Ding, Z.: Online distributed distance-based outlier clearance approaches for wireless sensor networks. Pervasive Mob. Comput. **63**, 101130 (2020). https://doi.org/10.1016/j.pmcj.2020.101130

19. Fawzy, A., Mokhtar, H.M.O., Hegazy, O.: Outliers detection and classification in wireless sensor networks. Egypt. Inform. J. **14**(2), 157–164 (2013). https://doi.org/10.1016/j.eij.2013.06.001

20. Yu, X., et al.: An adaptive method based on contextual anomaly detection in Internet of Things through wireless sensor networks. Int. J. Distrib. Sens. Netw. **16**(5), 1550147720920478 (2020). https://doi.org/10.1177/1550147720920478

21. Giatrakos, N., Deligiannakis, A., Garofalakis, M., Kotidis, Y.: Omnibus outlier detection in sensor networks using windowed locality sensitive hashing. Future Gener. Comput. Syst. **110**, 587–609 (2020). https://doi.org/10.1016/j.future.2018.04.046

22. Holder, C., Boyles, R., Robinson, P., Raman, S., Fishel, G.: Calculating a daily normal temperature range that reflects daily temperature variability. Bull. Am. Meteorol. Soc. **87**(6), 769–774 (2006). https://doi.org/10.1175/BAMS-87-6-769

23. Kretowski, M.: Evolutionary Decision Trees in Large-Scale Data Mining. Springer, Heidelberg (2019). https://doi.org/10.1007/978-3-030-21851-5

24. Molnar, C.: Interpretable machine learning. Lulu.com (2020)

25. Rokach, L.: Data mining with decision trees: theory and applications. World Scientific (2008)

A Graph-Based Approach to Detect Anomalies Based on Shared Attribute Values

Steffen Brauer[1], Marco Fisichella[2], Gianluca Lax[3(✉)], Carlo Romeo[3], and Antonia Russo[3]

[1] Project Holi, Hamburg, Germany
`steffen.brauer@posteo.de`
[2] L3S Research Center, Leibniz University of Hannover, Hannover, Germany
`mfisichella@L3S.de`
[3] University Mediterranea of Reggio Calabria, Reggio Calabria, Italy
{`lax,carlo.romeo,antonia.russo`}`@unirc.it`

Abstract. Anomaly detection is an important task in many fields such as eHealth and online fraud. In this paper, we propose a new technique for anomaly detection based on a graph that connects transactions with the same attribute values and searches for dense clusters indicative of an anomalous pattern. The experimental evaluation shows that the graph-based approach outperforms two other approaches in the considered dataset. The extension of this approach to the eHealth domain is reserved as future work.

Keywords: Outlier detection · Anomaly detection · Fraud detection

1 Introduction

Anomaly detection in eHealth is a new challenge for Smart Hospital Systems, where an intelligent environment allows the medical team to monitor patient vital signs and receive alerts when anomalous readings are detected [4]. Such readings are collected by sensors and processed by *smart* algorithms. The large amount of sensitive data that is collected should be protected to enable accurate event detection and efficient decision making [18]. Many e-health applications are based on IoT sensors to collect data. Since such sensors are often constrained devices, they are exposed to several attacks that aim to badly affect patients' care and the monitoring infrastructure.

This is one of the issues addressed by the iCARE project, and in this paper, we show the first results of a technique to detect anomalies in collected data. Since real data from the eHealth are not yet available, we present our technique in another area, which is fraud detection, that has similar characteristics and is also timely.

Online fraud is one of the results of the new development of information technology, which has increased the number of electronic payments. According to

M. Mahmud et al. (Eds.): AII 2022, CCIS 1724, pp. 511–522, 2022.
https://doi.org/10.1007/978-3-031-24801-6_36

J.P. Morgan's 2021 Payment Trends report [6], there are more and more ways to pay, and this trend will continue as payments become more seamless, embedded and contextual. The increase in online transactions has not only created new types of customers, but also a growing interest from cybercriminals who have found new illegal ways to get money. The increase in financial transactions leads financial institutes to face an arduous challenge, that of limiting the risk of fraud.

Research in this area has produced many techniques to contrast fraud. Machine learning algorithms are used to detect fraud in credit card records: some studies report that Random Forest and Decision Tree methods have the highest accuracy with a reasonable F-score [11], while others find that KNN and Logistic Regression are better at detecting fraudulent transactions [3].

One promising approach is based on temporal anomaly detection. This involves examining the trend of data over time and exploiting the fact that user actions (such as web browsing, product views, and product purchases) have a specific temporal and geographic characterization. A user behavior that deviates from the expected values calculated by one or more predictive models is an *anomaly*. The reasons for such deviations are many: multiple attempts to log in; multiple attempts to purchase goods (with stolen credit cards); purchase of goods to overcome automatic system locks.

In this paper, we evaluate three different methods for detecting outliers using a dataset of labeled transactions (fraudulent and non-fraudulent). The first method we apply uses the moving average over the time series of transactions in specific geographic areas to model normal behavior. It triggers an alert when a new value shows a high deviation from the average. The second method calculates changes in the distribution of available attributes using the Kullback-Leibler (KL) divergence from one day to the next one. These values are then fed into a classifier that detects the anomalies based on the labeled data. We also introduce a new technique based on a graph that connects the transactions of a given day. Here we connect transactions with the same attribute values, where dense clusters indicate an anomalous pattern that triggers an alert. The evaluation shows that the graph-based approach outperforms the previous two approaches on the given dataset. The graph-based technique could be extended to the smart hospital domain by exploiting the fact that the data collected from patients may have similar spatial or temporal dimensions: the experimental evaluation remains as future work.

The structure of the paper is as follows. In the next section, we give an overview of the current state of the art on this topic. The outlier detection methods used in this work are presented in Sect. 3. The description of the experimental setup and the obtained results can be found in Sect. 4 and Sect. 5. Finally, we draw our conclusions and outline future work in Sect. 6.

2   Related Work

The research literature in the field of fraud detection has been extensively explored over the years. Many solutions and studies have been proposed to solve the problem of unbalanced data. Indeed, fraud detection datasets suffer from a low number of "positive" labels with respect to the number of "genuine" entries in the dataset.

To detect fraud, [17] has proposed the use of standard and hybrid methods such as AdaBoost and majority voting. To assess the robustness of these algorithms, some noise was added to the input data. The majority voting technique leads to robust performance in the presence of noisy data.

The authors of [16] compare the performance of ten standard machine learning methods divided into two groups: Classification and Ensemble algorithms. Results are measured with and without the use of the time feature, which can improve performance depending on the algorithm. The Logistic Regression, Random Forest and Gradient Boosted Regression Trees algorithms performed best in both cases. A further comparison was conducted in [15], in which the authors compared different machine learning algorithms to evaluate performance in finding pattern anomalies.

A Deep Learning approach was explored in [9] to transfer knowledge between different fraud detection application domains. Also, an adaptation of [5] is proposed to learn domain invariant features. The latter technique achieves better results than the former.

In [2], the authors present a simple, scalable, easy-to-program algorithm called SpotLight that outlines a graph to enable fast and reliable anomaly identification, where an anomaly is the sudden appearance (or disappearance) of a large, dense, directed subgraph. The use of a graph can be useful to establish connections between transactions.

In [1], the authors integrate unsupervised techniques with a supervised classifier and introduce different levels of granularity that can be used to compute outlier scores. The main inspiration comes from the work of Michenkova et al. [12], who developed the best-of-both-worlds approach. Therefore, three levels of granularity are described and analyzed to assess which one is the best. The Balanced Random Forest algorithm is used as a supervised classifier to maintain the balance between the training data. The results show that the cluster granularity level is the most promising.

The authors of [10] examine machine learning solutions and their weaknesses using an imbalanced dataset and find that imbalanced classification approaches are not able to handle highly imbalanced data.

The authors of [19] aim to develop fraud detection models that can satisfy the main characteristics of the VAT subdomain. The contribution of this work is to solve some methodological problems by proposing four unsupervised methods. To solve the problem of unbalanced anomaly records, [7] implements the Multiple Classifier System. As the authors explain, their approach has set a new milestone in anomaly detection.

In [21], the authors present a feature engineering framework based on a homogeneity-oriented analysis of behavior capable of generating feature variables to represent behavior information in fraud detection models.

To emphasize the great impact of unsupervised versus supervised learning techniques in fraud detection, the authors of [14] analyze special case studies where supervised learning cannot be applied. In addition, the authors build a Deep-Auto-encoder and Restricted-Bolzmann-Machine model that is able to reconstruct normal transactions to identify anomalies within them.

3   Methods

From the wide variety of work on temporal anomaly detection with its different problem definitions, we select two approaches that fit the retail domain. In this section, we also introduce a novel technique that aims to detect anomalies based on shared attribute values in the same temporal and spatial dimensions.

3.1   Moving Average Approach

A well-known algorithm applied to time series is the Moving Average Approach [13]. In general, let T be a series of values from a continuous variable and W be a set of subsets of those with a fixed length l. The moving average is obtained by computing the average of the initial subset w_0 from the beginning of the series in time (i.e., W represents a window over the series). Then w_0 is shifted in time and becomes w_1, which excludes the first number and includes the next one following the initial subset w_0. Thus, we have a new averaged subset. This process is repeated until the entire data series is covered. In summary, a moving average is a set of numbers representing the averages of successive subsets w_i over T.

In our scenario, this approach models the number of transactions that occur in a given geographic area (identified by zip codes) as an average over a given time window (1 day). When the value of a given combination of day and zip code exceeds a certain threshold above the calculated average, an alert is triggered. Using this approach, it is possible to detect an anomaly corresponding to a specific day within a specific spatial area. To evaluate the approach, each pair of day and zip code is assigned a label depending on whether an alert was triggered or not.

3.2   Entropy-Based Approach

Relative entropy, also called Kullback-Leibler divergence (KL), is a non-symmetric and non-negative difference between two discrete probability distributions P and Q and represents the loss of information that occurs when P is approximated by Q. In the context of machine learning, P characterizes the *real* data distribution, while Q represents a model that approximates the real data. The KL divergence is defined in [8] as follows:

$$D(P||Q)_{KL} = \sum_{i \in A} P(i) \log_{10} \frac{P(i)}{Q(i)}$$

where $P(i)$ and $Q(i)$ are the probability of the discrete value i in the respective probability distribution given by

$$P(i) = \frac{m_i}{\displaystyle\sum_{i \in A} m_a}$$

where A is the set of all possible values i in the probability distributions, and m_i and m_a are the cardinality of element i and element a in the current distribution P, respectively.

In our scenario, we consider 5 global attributes: article type, total order value, zip code, city, and street. These attributes are tied to a specific time period (e.g., a day of a specific geographic area). Let P be the distribution of an attribute for a given time period t (e.g., a given day). Let Q be the distribution of an attribute for the next time period $t+1$, then we can calculate the relative entropy $D(P\|Q)_{KL}$ per attribute of each time period. Finally, we can calculate 5 relative entropies with respect to the previous day t per area for each day. Using the pair of day and geographic area as an identifier, we can assign labels to the relative entropy values. Finally, all relative entropy values are passed to classifiers (Logistic Regression, Naive Bayes, and Random Forest) with a label *burst* or *no burst* to identify the anomalous bursts based on the entropy values.

Low relative entropy indicates regularity in the sense that the two distributions P and Q are similar. Anomalies are detected in cases where the value $D(P\|Q)_{KL}$ increases.

3.3 Graph-Based Approach

The previous two approaches attempt to detect anomalies based on measurements of single attributes without considering the correlation of values between attributes. In contrast, the graph-based approach is able to detect anomalies by finding unusual patterns in the common attribute values of transactions.

From the transaction dataset, we create several graphs. Each graph $G = (V, E)$ consists of a time window of 1 day containing transactions as vertices: two vertices are connected by an edge if there is a common attribute value between two transactions.

Thus, an edge is added to the graph if a pair of transactions has at least one of the following properties:

- Same customer number;
- Same delivery address (street, house number, zip code, city);
- Similar delivery address (based on 2-gram distance);
- Same article type;

In the case of multiple common properties (e.g., when two transactions have the same customer number and address), we add a unique edge to the graph with a weight w indicating how many common properties there are (2 in this example).

Intuitively, a graph consisting of transactions from one day without anomalies should contain mostly isolated vertices (i.e., transactions) and few vertices with a small number of connections based on the same article type or the same/similar address.

In contrast, an anomaly in such a graph would correspond to a dense cluster that can be detected and reported by a human inspector. With the identification of the transactions responsible for the burst, the presented approach is not only able to trigger an alert for a day and geographic area pair, as the above mentioned approaches, but it is also able to identify the anomalous transactions.

To select the fraudulent bursts from the daily graphs, we compute the features for each component with more than 2 transactions. A component is a set of vertices in G that is only internally connected, but not connected to vertices that are not included in the set. For each component in each daily graph, we compute the following features:

- number of edges in the component;
- number of triangles (i.e., fully connected subgraph with cardinality 3);
- density (i.e., the ratio of existing edges over all possible edges);
- average edge weight;
- variance of edge weight;
- number of frauds in the component.

Because of the identification of the transactions in the burst and not just the day and area, new labels have to be assigned to each component. A component is labeled *anomalous* if it contains more than half of the transactions tagged as fraudulent, otherwise it is labeled *non-anomalous*.

This labeling focuses more on the fraudulent behavior and less on the sudden increase in transactions with a common pattern. By using the zip code and date information of each component, it is also possible to match the components with the results of the previous approaches. Then, the created dataset is used to train a Random Forest classifier.

4   Experiments

In this section, we describe the experimental setup consisting of the features of the dataset used to evaluate the approaches introduced above and provide a definition of anomalies in the context of the retail sector. We also present the results of the evaluation on this basis.

4.1   Experimental Setup

We evaluate the approaches using a transaction dataset[1] which spans 16 months and contains 6.5 million commerce transactions. These transactions were partially labeled by human investigators: Table 1 contains a detailed description of a transaction's attributes.

---

[1] For privacy reasons, we cannot share the dataset.

Table 1. Attribute description.

Name	Description
created	Timestamp of transaction creation
customer_number	Primary key of customer account
street_name	Address information
house_number	
city	
zip_code	
total_price	Total price of the transaction
article_types	List of article types in shopping cart

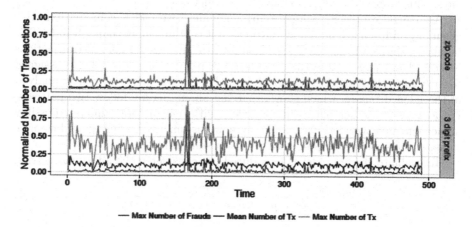

Fig. 1. Comparison of normalized number of transactions over time by zip code and larger 3-digit zip code prefix.

In summary, each transaction considered as a unique instance of a particular time series has two particular dimensions: the temporal dimension and the spatial dimension. While the temporal dimension is given by the attribute created, the spatial dimension can have different granularities ranging from the full postal address (i.e., the concatenation of *street_name*, *house_number*, *zip_code* and *city*) to only the *zip_code*.

The data follow the distribution shown in Fig. 1, which shows the maximum, average, and number of fraudulent transactions in each 1-day time interval and for each zip code and larger areas identified by the first 3 digits of the zip codes. The data are normalized.

We can define an anomaly as an event that occurs outside of normal behavior. An intuitive definition of normal behavior could refer to the assumption that there is a near-continuous number of transactions from any geographic area, including seasonal changes (e.g., Christmas sales) or trends. In addition, the number of transactions could depend on the population density in the area. In this scenario, an anomaly could be characterized by a high deviation from the average value of transactions in the region in question.

The above definition of normal behavior is not confirmed by the figure. While the average number is almost stable over time, the maximum number of transactions per area shows higher dynamics and reaches peak values in both graphs. More precisely, the difference between the average and maximum number of transactions per area is more dynamic on the larger scale (the first 3 digits of the zip codes) than on the zip code scale. On the other hand, if we look at the maximum number of frauds per day, on the zip code scale it exceeds the average quite often and the peaks are usually visible. On the larger scale, the fraud cases are masked by the average number of transactions. An important point is that the most notable outbreak occurs around time 180 and extends over several days. This large outbreak is followed by smaller outbreaks.

As a first approach to identifying anomalies, we call a combination on a given day and in a given area an outbreak if it contains more than 7 frauds. This number is derived from the observation that the average number of transactions is 6.67 when there is more than one fraud. Finally, a breakout label is assigned to each burst that matches the above logic. For clarity, we performed an analysis of the labeled bursts, which shows that the bursts mainly follow two patterns: i) the same customer places many orders with a high total amount, possibly an account takeover; ii) there are many new customers ordering many low-price items in the same geographic area or at the same address.

To evaluate the approaches introduced, we considered the following metrics:

$$TPR = \frac{true\_positives}{true\_positives + false\_negatives} \tag{1}$$

$$FPR = \frac{false\_positives}{false\_positives + true\_negatives} \tag{2}$$

$$BurstRatio = \frac{num\_burst\_components}{num\_burst\_components + num\_normal\_components} \tag{3}$$

As an example, for the graph-based approach, the dataset contained 42 *anomalous* and 4,660 *not-anomalous* components, resulting in an anomalous ratio of 0.009.

Finally, we calculated the *AUC-ROC* curve. The Receiver Operator Characteristic (ROC) curve is an evaluation metric for binary classification problems. It is a probability curve that plots the TPR against the FPR at various thresholds. The (AUC) is the measure of a classifier's ability to discriminate between classes and is used as a summary of the ROC curve. It has values between 0 and 1. The higher the AUC value, the better the performance of the model in discriminating between the positive and negative classes.

Table 2. Evaluation results for the 3 approaches at different scales and with different labels.

Approach	Label	Scale	Burst ratio	AUC	TPR	FPR
Moving Avg.	Burst	Day/Zip Code	0.00001	0.63	0.27	0.00002
	Burst	Day/Region	0.0001	0.64	0.31	0.025
Entropy-based	Burst	Day/Region	0.0001	0.46	0	0
	Moving Avg.	Day/Region	0.0003	0.53	0	0
Graph-based	Component	Day	0.009	0.60	0.66	0.56

5   Results

The results of the evaluation can be found in Table 2. It contains different combinations of the approaches presented in Sect. 3 with two geographic scales and burst labels.

5.1   Moving Average Approach

We evaluated the moving average approach in a 1-day time window on both the zip code scale and the scale of the first 3 digits of the zip code. At the zip code scale, we were able to achieve an area under the ROC curve (AUC) of 0.63 with a True Positive Rate (TPR) of 0.27 in correctly identifying flagged bursts. A grid search was performed to determine the threshold above the calculated average at which an alarm would be triggered. This threshold was set to a factor of 3.8 above the moving average. Different results were obtained on the scale of the first 3 digits of the zip code scale: while the AUC is similar on the smaller scale, the false positive rate (FPR) is higher by a factor of 10, 000.

5.2   Entropy-Based Approach

Unlike the previous approach, the evaluation of the entropy-based approach was performed on the scale of the first 3 digits of the zip codes, because there are a large number of entries on the scale of the zip codes that have no or only 1 transaction per day per zip code; this leads to a relative entropy value with a very low significance. Confirming a natural intuition, all spatial attributes (zip code, city, street, and house number) are highly correlated. Finally, all relative entropy values per day are passed to classifiers (i.e., Logistic Regression, Naive Bayes, and Random Forest). The highest AUC values were obtained with the Random Forest algorithm, although it has poor performance. The small burst ratio worsens the performances with TPR and FPR equal to 0.

5.3   Graph-Based Approach

We tested the graph-based approach on a temporally sliding window of 1 day. The dataset contained 42 *anomalous* and 4, 660 *not-anomalous* components, resulting in an anomalous ratio of 0.009. We trained a Random Forest classifier with 10-fold cross-validation. The evaluation of the classifier shows an AUC of 0.60 with a TPR of 0.66 in correctly identifying the labeled components. While the reported FPR is the highest of the three approaches, the corresponding total is the lowest.

6 Discussion and Conclusion

In this paper, we presented a scientific study aimed at addressing the research on anomaly detection, and we proposed three different methods: (i) moving average; (ii) entropy-based approach using KL divergence of multiple individual features from one day to the next one; and (iii) our novel technique based on a graph connecting daily transactions. All approaches were experimentally evaluated in the domain of fraud detection.

Specifically, the moving average approach was studied with different trigger levels. Different results were obtained on the scale of the first 3 digits of the zip code scale: While the AUC is similar on the fine-grained geographic scale, the FPR is 4 order of magnitude higher.

The entropy-based approach was performed exclusively on the scale of the first 3 digits of the zip codes to increase the relative entropy value. However, the small burst ratio degrades performance with TPR and FPR equal to 0.

Finally, we tested the graph-based approach with a time-sliding window of 1 day. Evaluation of the classifier resulted in the highest FPR of the three approaches.

The next step is to extend the graph-based approach to the smart hospital domain by exploiting the fact that the data collected from patients may have similar spatial or temporal dimensions. This will be done thanks to the results of the iCARE project, which will allow the collection of real-life sensors' data from a real hospital. However, these data typically contain sensitive information, leading to the need for privacy-preserving distributed machine learning solutions, such as federated learning, where a model is trained locally on the edge device, and only the trained model weights are shared with a central server [20]. This task and the subsequent experimental evaluation remain as future work.

Acknowledgements. This work was partially supported by "iCARE" project (CUP J39J14001400007) - action 10.5.12 - funded within POR FESR FSE 2014/2020 of Calabria Region with the participation of European Community Resources of FESR and FSE, of Italy and of Calabria.

References

1. Carcillo, F., Le Borgne, Y.A., Caelen, O., Kessaci, Y., Oblé, F., Bontempi, G.: Combining unsupervised and supervised learning in credit card fraud detection. Inf. Sci. **557**, 317–331 (2019). https://doi.org/10.1016/j.ins.2019.05.042

2. Eswaran, D., Faloutsos, C., Guha, S., Mishra, N.: Spotlight: detecting anomalies in streaming graphs. In: Proceedings of the 24th ACM SIGKDD International Conference on Knowledge Discovery and Data Mining (KDD 2018), pp. 1378–1386. Association for Computing Machinery, New York, NY, USA (2018). https://doi.org/10.1145/3219819.3220040

3. Faraji, Z.: A review of machine learning applications for credit card fraud detection with a case study. SEISENSE J. Manag. **5**(1), 49–59 (2022)

4. Fisichella, M.: Unified approach to retrospective event detection for event- based epidemic intelligence. Int. J. Digit. Libr. **22**(4), 339–364 (2021). https://doi.org/10.1007/s00799-021-00308-9

5. Ganin, Y., et al.: Domain-adversarial training of neural networks. J. Mach. Learn. Res. **17**(1), 2030–2096 (2016)

6. J.P. Morgan Merchant Services: Key Trends to Drive Your Payments Strategy (2021). https://www.jpmorgan.com/content/dam/jpm/merchant-services/insights/e-commerce/key-trends-to-drive-your-payments-strategy.pdf. Accessed 18 Apr 2022

7. Kalid, S.N., Ng, K.H., Tong, G.K., Khor, K.C.: A multiple classifiers system for anomaly detection in credit card data with unbalanced and overlapped classes. IEEE Access **8**, 28210–28221 (2020). https://doi.org/10.1109/ACCESS.2020.2972009

8. Kullback, S., Leibler, R.A.: On information and sufficiency. Ann. Math. Stat. **22**(1), 79–86 (1951)

9. Lebichot, B., Le Borgne, Y.-A., He-Guelton, L., Oblé, F., Bontempi, G.: Deep-learning domain adaptation techniques for credit cards fraud detection. In: Oneto, L., Navarin, N., Sperduti, A., Anguita, D. (eds.) INNSBDDL 2019. PINNS, vol. 1, pp. 78–88. Springer, Cham (2020). https://doi.org/10.1007/978-3-030-16841-4_8

10. Makki, S., Assaghir, Z., Taher, Y., Haque, R., Hacid, M.S., Zeineddine, H.: An experimental study with imbalanced classification approaches for credit card fraud detection. IEEE Access **7**, 93010–93022 (2019). https://doi.org/10.1109/ACCESS.2019.2927266

11. Mathew, J.C., Nithya, B., Vishwanatha, C., Shetty, P., Priya, H., Kavya, G.: An analysis on fraud detection in credit card transactions using machine learning techniques. In: 2022 Second International Conference on Artificial Intelligence and Smart Energy (ICAIS), pp. 265–272. IEEE (2022)

12. Micenková, B., McWilliams, B., Assent, I.: Learning outlier ensembles: the best of both worlds-supervised and unsupervised. In: Proceedings of the ACM SIGKDD 2014 Workshop on Outlier Detection and Description under Data Diversity (ODD2), pp. 51–54. Citeseer, New York, USA (2014)

13. Politis, D.N.: Moving average processes and maximum entropy. IEEE Trans. Inf. Theory **38**(3), 1174–1177 (1992)

14. Pumsirirat, A., Yan, L.: Credit card fraud detection using deep learning based on auto-encoder and restricted Boltzmann machine. Int. J. Adv. Comput. Sci. Appl. **9**, 1–8 (2018)

15. Raghavan, P., Gayar, N.E.: Fraud detection using machine learning and deep learning. In: 2019 International Conference on Computational Intelligence and Knowledge Economy (ICCIKE), pp. 334–339 (2019). https://doi.org/10.1109/ICCIKE47802.2019.9004231

16. Rajora, S., et al.: A comparative study of machine learning techniques for credit card fraud detection based on time variance. In: 2018 IEEE Symposium Series on Computational Intelligence (SSCI), pp. 1958–1963 (2018). https://doi.org/10.1109/SSCI.2018.8628930

17. Randhawa, K., Loo, C.K., Seera, M., Lim, C.P., Nandi, A.K.: Credit card fraud detection using AdaBoost and majority voting. IEEE Access **6**, 14277–14284 (2018). https://doi.org/10.1109/ACCESS.2018.2806420
18. Said, A.M., Yahyaoui, A., Abdellatif, T.: Efficient anomaly detection for smart hospital IoT systems. Sensors **21**(4), 1026 (2021)
19. Vanhoeyveld, J., Martens, D., Peeters, B.: Value-added tax fraud detection with scalable anomaly detection techniques. Appl. Soft Comput. **86**, 105895 (2019). https://doi.org/10.1016/j.asoc.2019.105895
20. Younis, R., Fisichella, M.: FLY-SMOTE: re-balancing the non-IID IoT edge devices data in federated learning system. IEEE Access **10**, 65092–65102 (2022). https://doi.org/10.1109/ACCESS.2022.3184309
21. Zhang, X., Han, Y., Xu, W., Wang, Q.: HOBA: a novel feature engineering methodology for credit card fraud detection with a deep learning architecture. Inf. Sci. **557**, 305–316 (2019). https://doi.org/10.1016/j.ins.2019.05.023

Impact of Emotional State on Food Preference by Students: A Machine Learning Approach

Nadia Nasrin[1], Biraj Saha Aronya[1(✉)], Nusrat Jahan[1,2], Imran Mahmud[1],
Afsana Begum[1,2], and Zahereel Ishwar Abdul Khalib[2]

[1] Daffodil International University, Dhaka, Bangladesh
`aronya.taf@diu.edu.bd`
[2] Universiti Malaysia Perlis, Arau, Malaysia

Abstract. Everyone has a problem in this contemporary, progressive world. Many people get lost in a maze and miss the solution to their problems. Small things cause them stress or depression. Students typically cope well with their mood swings. Everyone wants something to comfort them at this crucial time. When people are not in a comfortable emotional state, they prefer to do many things like eating, playing video games, and watching movies. There is a strong link between emotions and food. We examine the comfort foods that students turn to in their various emotional states because these two things are connected. The first study is based on questionnaires and surveys of psychological nature. In this study, we use four data-driven machine learning models to predict students' comfort food preferences based on their emotional state. The dataset was gathered from a source that is openly accessible. Mercyhurst University conducted a survey to gather the information. Over 60 questions and a total of 400 data points were asked of the 526 students who responded to the survey. In this study, we sought to identify the comfort foods that students enjoy eating in various mental states. We use four machine learning models including Linear Regression Model, Support Vector Machine, Random Forest and Naïve Bayes. We found there is a consensual relationship between food selection and emotional state. Moreover, Naïve Bayes works better having an accuracy of 96.66%, which is acceptable.

Keywords: Emotion · Comfort food · Machine learning · Linear regression

1 Introduction

Every person in this developed world fights for his or her life. Depression shatters you. When under stress, people tend to want to flee from life and make poor choices. Among students, the propensity for depression has risen. Teenagers today risk their lives for pointless things. They attempt to effortlessly get rid of everything because they believe this to be a workable solution. However, those with self-control make an effort to remain composed and defend themselves. When their mental health is poor, people participate in a variety of activities like watching movies, traveling, reading books, and more.

Since the beginning of time, there has been a link between food and emotions. Food choices can be strongly influenced by emotions and feelings. We eat not only to satiate our

---

The original version of this chapter was revised: In the originally published version of the proceedings volume this chapter was erroneously omitted. It has been added as chapter 37. The correction to this chapter is available at https://doi.org/10.1007/978-3-031-24801-6_39

M. Mahmud et al. (Eds.): AII 2022, CCIS 1724, pp. 523–538, 2022.
https://doi.org/10.1007/978-3-031-24801-6_37

physical needs but also to satiate our spiritual needs. The process of food selection can involve both physiological (i.e. hunger) and psychological (i.e. emotional) influences [1] and once eaten, these foods can affect our mood [2]. There is no comparison for how food affects people. For instance, by being aware of a person's go-to comfort food during stressful times, we can help them relax and avoid negative outcomes like suicide. Therefore, understanding how to respond in these circumstances is crucial. Researchers frequently use survey data to identify comfort foods. In order to get accurate results and determine which model performs best, we used machine learning models, linear regression, and SVM to identify comfort foods based on subject's mood, age, and weight. Food can alter someone's mood, as we are aware of the connection between food and emotions. When upset, people occasionally overeat, which has a negative impact on their health. For instance, if we are aware that someone regularly consumes fast food while under stress and weighs 180 kg. His doctor can quickly determine what is causing his obesity. In this context, this research is also beneficial. College students who do not have an eating disorder, such as B. food preferences, have reported experiencing stress. Higher levels of stress have been associated with greater preference for sweet foods (e.g., candy, ice cream), mixed meals (e.g., pizza, fast food) [3], increased consumption of snacks, and decreases in meal consumption brought. Foods like fruits, vegetables, meat and fish.

Researchers have been working on different aspects of this topic like how eating food can change a person's mood, etc. [4]. However, research to date relies on survey and physiological terms [1–3]. But this is a very important question for this modern era where many people are depressed and stressed. So, you have to know how to go about it. All previous work is theoretical and the result is not yet exact. It is quite difficult to understand the results because they are not visualized in tables or graphs. That's why we wanted to address the topic and use machine learning models for the implementation. I found a recording on a public platform called Kaggle [5]. 400 students completed the survey and answered all questions.

There is no comparison for how food affects people. When people are upset, they occasionally overeat, which leads to numerous health issues. Loneliness is one of the emotional states which has also has a potential impact on food selection [6–9]. Loneliness, both social and emotional, influences food preferences, more specifically unhealthy food [10]. It undermines people's ability to maintain appropriate eating routines and makes them more susceptible to developing different eating disorders including anorexia nervosa and bulimia nervosa [11]. This is due to the fact that unhealthy foods like pizza, chocolate, and buttered popcorn provide more immediate, emotional satisfaction and hedonic benefits [9]. Previous work has used different types of questionnaires such as the Trier-Social Stress Test, the Dutch Eating Behavior Questionnaire [12] to learn the result. We cannot expect reasonable accuracy from these results as they have not been tested with any algorithm. We can therefore not predict the results of the surveys. We must use specialized terms, such as machine learning models, when we plan. Machine learning can assist in demonstrating the right response and demonstrating correctness.

There are important questions that we are trying to clarify. The first is what are the ingredients that define comfort food? Can machine learning accurately determine comfort foods based on emotional state? Another important fact is: which machine learning model says the best about comfort food?

- The main goal of this study is to identify the students' comfort foods based on their emotional states.
- The next goal is to pre-process the data using various methods and make the dataset usable.
- The final goal is to test various machine learning models and determine which is most effective for this investigation.

Currently, this topic has a huge field of research. Researchers are working on this subject, but most studies are based on physiological questionnaires. Since no work has been done with the dataset to date, there are plenty of opportunities to go further. We tested four machine learning models (Linear Regression, SVM, Random Forest, Naïve Bayes) to see which worked best. But there are also other models. The main objective of this research is to implement different machine learning models to predict student comfort food and also to determine which model works best. Additionally, there is an association between food choices and weight in this data set. Therefore, we can also predict that he has the possibility of suffering from diabetes or heart disease by analyzing his eating habits.

2 Literature Review

Is ease food really comfort food for emotive eaters? A (moderate) mediation analysis [12] in this article shows that highly emotional people eat more when they are stressed and that comfort food can reduce their stress where less emotional people eat less. For the survey, they used the DEBQ, and to observe behavior, they used the Trier social stress test. The Universities of Valencia and Barcelona conducted this survey (Spain). The participants in this study were instructed not to eat anything for at least two hours prior to their visit as part of the protocol. Another study claimed that while women prefer snacks like chocolate or ice cream, men prefer to eat hot foods as comfort foods when their mental states are unstable. The idea of the comfort food preferences of men and women being different from one another was intended to be clarified. They surveyed 1000 people, with the supposition being that respondents had to be 18 or older. The main finding of this study is that comfort food preferences vary depending on both age and gender [8]. In a study on "chocolate addiction" that took into account age and gender, it was discovered that roughly 97.2% of women, or 70 out of 72, are addicted to chocolate [13]. In the work titled "A sad mood increases awareness of unhealthy food images in women with binge eating" [14], 86 students were enrolled through a web-based research participation system. They utilized the YFAS survey, which has 27 questions. In the paper, they theorized that the result is hazy because of the disparity in the data, and that the YFAS measure of binge eating is another backtrack. The lack of technical terms is to blame for these flaws. Although maintaining a balance between the psychological value of food and the need for food to satisfy hunger is challenging, it is occasionally possible to do so without interoceptive awareness, which results in a habit of overeating [15]. Higher perceived stress would be associated with higher consumption of unhealthy foods and beverages, and lower consumption of healthy foods was partially supported in another study, "Perceived stress and dietary choices: The moderating role of stress management" [16].

3 Research Methodology

The model suggested for this study involves a number of data collection steps to ensure an accurate model. After gathering the data, we had to pre-process it in order to use it in our model. But the pre-processing part has some techniques that we must follow. Then we select which functions we need for this study. This is a very essential element of research. The success rate of the study depends heavily on it. We then extract features from the dataset, code the labels so we can use them fluently, and use them in a machine learning model. In this study, we ran four machine learning models (one regression model, three classification models). For the correct implementation of all tasks, we need a workflow. The workflow of the proposed task is shown in Fig. 1.

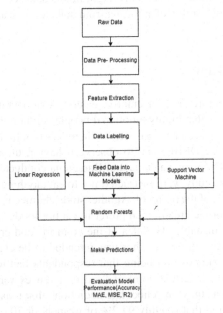

Fig. 1. Workflow of the model.

3.1 Dataset

The dataset used for this study was taken from a public source "Kaggle" [5]. The survey data used in this dataset was gathered at Mercyhurst University. 126 students consented to take the poll. 400 different data points were gathered from the survey. The purpose of gathering this information was to learn more about how different emotional states affect people's food preferences. This dataset contains details about the students' dietary preferences, gender, a childhood favorite, and a lot more. The students themselves provided the knowledge. The dataset was impure and ambiguous. This information is organized into 5 rows, including gender, calories, comfort foods, comfort food-related reasons, and weight. The reason for the comfort food craving tells us what emotional state the individual is in. We have converted some data into digits in order to arrange the data set neatly. We must pre-process the data in order to make the data set useful.

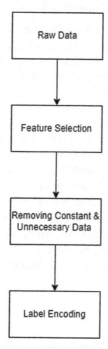

Fig. 2. Steps of Data Pre-processing.

3.2 Dataset Pre-processing

The data set was taken from the section Food Choices and Cooking Preferences of College Students: Food Choices of a publicly accessible source. On this data set, nothing was done [4]. As a result, we eliminated a lot of cluttered and unnecessary data during pre-processing. The most important step when using machine learning models is data pre-processing. A real-world data set contains some noise and missing values by default. Pre-processing data improves model productivity and accuracy. The data set contains 5 columns and 6 justifications for comfort food. We had to prepare the dataset because it had not been sanitized before pre-processing. We must adhere to a number of steps in the pre-processing of the data. The steps of pre-processing the dataset are given below in Fig. 2.

3.2.1 Feature Selection

One of the fundamental components of machine learning is feature selection. The main goal of feature selection is to purge the model of redundant or uninformative predictors [17]. This is the procedure of removing the outrageous features from the data set and choosing a subset of pertinent features/attributes, such as a column in tabular data that is most episodic to model. The following are some advantages of feature selection: B. Increasing precision and cutting training time.

3.2.2 Removing Constant and Unnecessary Data

While not improving the outcome, a machine learning constant can cause errors in the prediction. Additionally, it does not aid in data set training. We removed the columns from the dataset because the first column in our study had some constant characteristics (such as grade point average, nutrition stream, and vitamins).

3.2.3 Label Encoding

Any variable with two or more categories is considered to be categorical. Usually, string values are used to reposition these variables. As an illustration, consider traveling, reading, and hiking. The categorical variables in our situation are gender and comfort food-related factors. When dealing with categorical variables, there are several options. In this study, categorical variables were interacted with using label coding. For example, there are two genders.: male and female which we converted into female $\rightarrow$ 1, male $\rightarrow$ 2. Another feature is comfort food reasons, where we have 6 different values: stressed, boredom, sadness, anger, happiness, and depression. After applying label encoding, values will encode into digits like stressed $\rightarrow$ 1, boredom $\rightarrow$ 2, sadness $\rightarrow$ 3, anger $\rightarrow$ 4, happiness $\rightarrow$ 5, depressed $\rightarrow$ 6.

3.3 Model

There are several models like ANN, Naïve Bayes, logistic regression, SVM in machine learning. In this research, we used linear regression, which is LR in the short run, and we will also perform SVM to predict students' feel-good eating.

3.3.1 Linear Regression

Modeling a target value using independent predictors is called regression [13]. Finding the cause-and-effect relationship between variables is the main use of this method. Regression comes in two flavors: multivariate regression and univariate regression (Fig. 3).

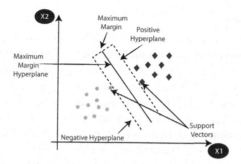

Fig. 3. SVM Hyperplane.

When the number of feature variables is one, it is called univariate regression. We also know it as simple regression. However, if there is more than one trait variable, it is a multivariate regression. The simple linear regression equation is shown below

$$\hat{Y} = \beta_0 + \beta_1 x + \epsilon 1 \tag{1}$$

where,

$\hat{Y}$ = Predicted Output
β = Coefficient
x = Input
ϵ = Error

3.3.2 SVM (Support Vector Machine)

The SVM model can be applied to datasets for classification and regression. For binary classification, Cortes & Vapnik (1995) created Support Vector Machines (SVM) [19]. It is based on the idea of a hyperline that establishes the boundaries of the decision. Robustness is increased by hyper line segregation. SVMs treat the classification task as a task involving two classes, with labeled training examples represented using feature vectors. Formally, two classes **yi (−1, 1)** are to be identified using **N** labelled training samples represented by **x1, y1, ... (xN, yN)**, where **xi** the feature vector is representing individual training samples [15]. If **yi**'s are linearly separable then SVM find the optimal weight vector w such that:

$$|w| \text{ 2 is minimum and yi} * (\mathbf{w} * \mathbf{xi} - \mathbf{b}) \geq 1$$

Hyperplanes that define the decision boundaries divide the data points in this model, but the kernel determines the type of hyperplane used. The data points that are close to the hyperplane and have an effect on the orientation and position of the hyperplane are known as support vectors. A decision line called a hyperplane is used to classify information from two or more data points. The distance between two or more points is known as distance. We calculate the margin using the spacing between the support vectors.

3.3.3   Random Forest

Random Forest (RF) is an ensemble learning method for solving classification, regression, and other machine learning problems by building a variety of decision trees at training time and returning the class, which is the class's mode (classification) or medium Prediction (regression) of each tree. The first random decision forest algorithm was introduced by Tin Kam Ho [21]. Random forests are a combination of tree predictors such that each tree depends on the values of a random vector sampled independently and with the same distribution for all trees in the forest [22]. It uses two powerful machine learning techniques: bagging [23] and random feature selection. In bagging, each tree is trained with a bootstrap sample of the training data, and predictions are made by majority voting of the trees. RF randomly chooses a subset of features to split at each node as a tree grows, rather than using all features. In order to assess the prediction performance of the random forest algorithm, RF performs a kind of cross-validation parallel to the training step by using the so-called out-of-bag (OOB) samples.

3.3.4   Naïve Bayes

A Naïve Bayes classifier is a probabilistic machine learning model that is used for classification prob-lems. The crux of the classifier is based on the Bayes theorem [24] (Table 1).

Table 1.   Result of Linear Regression.

Evaluation of Metrics	Linear Regression
Coefficient	[−0.41282793, 0.00075782, −0.71960378, −0.00320168]
Intercept	9.4982
MAE	2.2623
MSE	7.0659
RMSE	2.6581
R2	0.0588
Accuracy	0.0588

Bayes Theorem:

$$P(A/B) = \frac{P(B/A)P(A)}{P(B)} \tag{2}$$

Here, the probability of **A** take place, given that **B** has occurred. Here, **B** is the evidence and **A** is the hypothesis. The assumption made here is that the predictors are independent.

3.4 Performance Evaluation Metrics

After gathering data, pre-processing it, and applying various models, we obtain some outputs in the form of probabilities. The next step is to determine the model's viability based on a few metrics using test datasets. To assess the effectiveness of machine learning models, many different performance metrics are used. We only used Regression evaluation metrics in this study. We have chosen Coefficients, MAE, MSE, RMSE, and Accuracy for evaluating our models.

The results of multiplying the predictor values are called coefficients (Frost, coefficient).

- MAE is a simple regression error metric. It is the sum of absolute differences between our target and predicted variables.
- MSE is the average of the square of the errors.
- RMSE is the derivation of the root-square of the MSE.
- RES is an average deviation between the actual outcome and the true regression line.

3.5 Accuracy

Using an accuracy score is the quickest way to assess a set of predictions made regarding a classification issue. This matrix is used to assess classification models. The percentage of accurate predictions to total predictions is known as the classification accuracy score. In binary format, the precision calculation formula Issue with classification is listed below:

$$Accuracy = \frac{TruePositives + TrueNegatives}{Total\ Number\ of\ Examples} \tag{3}$$

4 Results and Discussion

In this study, we experiment with 2 machine learning models. We will go into great detail about the outcomes of these two models in this section. The LR model was tested first, followed by the SVM model.

4.1 Experiment 1

The linear regression model forms the basis of Experiment 1. Following the creation of those models, we evaluate the performance using various evaluation metrics. From this article [25] we now know how regression coefficients can make more definable our research (Fig. 4 and Table 2).

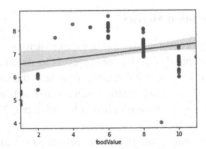

Fig. 4. Reg Plot of Linear Regression.

Table 2. Result of Support Vector Machine

Evaluation of Metrics	Support Vector Machine
MAE	0.0666
MSE	0.1333
RMSE	0.3651
R2	0.9822
Accuracy	0.9583

In this experiment, we divided our dataset into a training dataset and a test dataset, storing 70% of the data in the training dataset and 30% in the test dataset. We gave LR the data set and asked it to estimate the accuracy. But LR doesn't perform well with our data set. As a result, both the training set and the test set have low accuracy. The train set has a 12% accuracy rate while the test set has a 5% accuracy rate. The final accuracy is unacceptably low at 5.884%. The Reg chart is shown in Fig. 5 below

We saw in the reg plot that the majority of food names stray from the main line, which is why they Don't provide the precise information.

4.2 Experiment 2

Experiment 2 is based on the SVM model. We use the same "food choice" dataset to run the SVM model. So that we can compare the results of these two models. The result we see from this model is shown below:

In SVM we saw that on the reg plot most of the food names are around the hyperplane. We also ran confusion metrics where the value of G is the highest number of iterations.

4.3 Experiment 3

This experiment is based on the random forest algorithm. We used the same data set. But we have different accuracy. We know that in RF a large number of individual decision trees operate as an ensemble. Each individual tree in the random forest spits out a class prediction, and the class that gets the most votes becomes the output.

The values of MAE, R2 and others are given below (Figs. 6, 7, 8, 9 and Tables 3, 4):

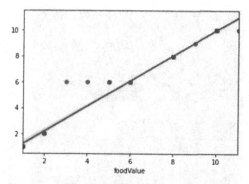

Fig. 5. Reg Plot of SVM.

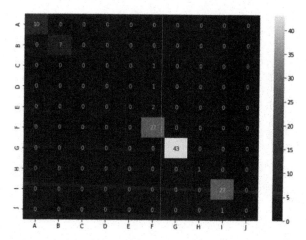

Fig. 6. Confusion Matrix of SVM.

Table 3. Result of Random Forest.

Evaluation of Metrics	Random Forest
MAE	0.2333
MSE	1.5
RMSE	1.2247
R2	0.8002
Accuracy	0.925

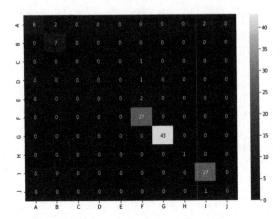

Fig. 7. Reg Plot of Random Forest.

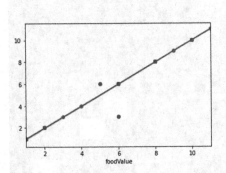

Fig. 8. Confusion Matrix of Random Forest.

Table 4. Result of Naïve Bayes.

Evaluation of Metrics	Naïve Bayes
MAE	0.0666
MSE	0.1666
RMSE	0.4082
R2	0.9778
Accuracy	0.9667

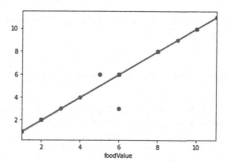

Fig. 9. Reg Plot of Naïve Bayes.

4.4 Experiment 4

In our experiment 4, we have performed The Naïve Bayes classifier algorithm. This algorithm works based on the bayes theorem. We get the accuracy by determine the four combinations. The values of MAE, R2 and others are given below:

We can see that the line is touching almost all the dots. That means there are less errors in this model and we can expect a good accuracy from this [26]. We can also assure this from the confusion matrix shown below:

4.5 Comparison Between Experiments

We used four different machine learning models. 1. Linear Regression 2. Support Vector Machine 3. Random Forest and 4. Naïve Bayes algorithm to predict a student's comfort food preferences based on their emotional state. From the accuracy we get from all four algorithms shown in Table 5, we concluded that Nave Bayes (96.67% accuracy) works best for this dataset than the other three models. We have an SVM model in second place with 95.83%. Even from the plots, it is clear that in SVM, the data points are closer to

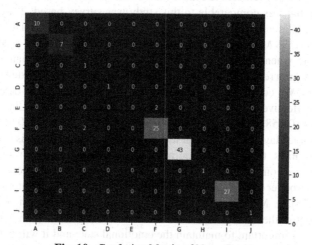

Fig. 10. Confusion Matrix of Naïve Bayes.

the hyperplane than in linear regression, where the data (comfort foods) are outside the main line's boundary (Fig. 10).

Table 5. Comparison Between the Four Algorithms

Evaluation of Metrics	Linear Regression	Support Vector Machine	Random Forest	Naïve Bayes
MAE	2.2623	0.0666	0.2333	0.0666
MSE	7.0659	0.1333	1.5	0.1666
RMSE	2.6581	0.3651	1.2247	0.4082
R2	0.0588	0.9822	0.8002	0.9778
Accuracy	0.0588	0.9583	0.925	0.9667

And we are aware that there are errors and the model is not performing well if the data points are not closer to the main line. Regression models are better suited for problems where we get results like (1/2) because, as we also know, they provide us with numerical results. However, because our results are categorical, classification models work much better. Because of this, Naïve Bayes accuracy is 96.67%, SVM also gives us 95.833% accuracy, Random Forest accuracy is 92.5%, with LR giving us the lowest accuracy of 5.884%.

5   Conclusions

In this study, we begin with an unclean set of raw data. To make the dataset clean, ideal, and well-ordered, we used 4 different data pre-processing techniques. For this study, we will focus on 5 key features. Because the dataset has never been used before and all prior research that was comparable to this study was survey-based. They didn't use a machine learning model in any studies. In this study, we combined data analysis with linear regression, SVM, random forest, and naive bayes modeling to predict students' feel-good eating when they are depressed, anxious, happy, etc. Humans and food are related. Our research revealed that a student's preferred food corresponded to a particular emotional state. We compared the results of the four experiments to determine which model is more effective. We have different accuracy from the models, Linear Regression (0.0588), SVM (0.0588), Random Forest (0.925), and Naïve Bayes (0.9667). Here the accuracy of Naïve Bayes is better than the other models. One reason is, the outputs are categorical variables, the classification models work better than the regression model because the regression model provides numeric outputs. So, we can conclude that the Naïve Bayes is a better option for finding out students' comfort food preferences based on their emotional state. Moreover, there are some students who are facing eating disorder and want to control their food habit. So, in this case, from our research outcome we can say that it is very important to maintain the emotional state and it will control the food preference. In future we can work with other impact factors on food behavior.

References

1. Desmet, P.M., Schifferstein, H.N.: Sources of positive and negative emotions in food experience. Appetite **50**(2–3), 290–301 (2008)
2. King, S.C., Meiselman, H.L., Carr, B.T.: Measuring emotions associated with foods in consumer testing. Food Qual. Prefer. **21**(8), 1114–1116 (2010)
3. Kandiah, J., Yake, M., Jones, J., Meyer, M.: Stress influences appetite and comfort food preferences in college women. Nutr. Res. **26**(3), 118–123 (2006)
4. Hsu, T.A., Forestell, C.A.: Mindfulness, mood, and food: the mediating role of positive affect. Appetite **158**, 105001 (2021)
5. BoraPajo: Food choices. Kaggle, 23 April 2017. https://www.kaggle.com/borapajo/food-choices. Accessed 20 Dec 2021
6. Andrade, E.B., Cohen, J.B.: On the consumption of negative feelings. J. Consum. Res. **34**(October), 283–300 (2007)
7. Edwards, J., Hartwell, H., Brown, L.: The relationship between emotions, food consumption and meal acceptability when eating out of the home. Food Qual. Prefer. **30**, 22–32 (2013)
8. Garg, N., Lerner, J.S.: Sadness and consumption. J. Consum. Psychol. **23**(1), 106–113 (2013)
9. Garg, N., Wansink, B., Inman, J.J.: The influence of incidental affect on consumers' food intake. J. Mark. **71**(1), 194–206 (2007)
10. Saine, R., Matos, G., Zhao, M.: An empirical exploration of digital media strategies and connectedness level. Academy of Marketing Science full paper (2020)
11. Levine, M.P.: Loneliness and eating disorders. J. Psychol. **146**(1/2), 243–257 (2012)
12. Strien, T.V., Gibson, E.L., Baños, R., Cebolla, A., Winkens, L.H.: Is comfort food actually comforting for emotional eaters? A (moderated) mediation analysis. Physiol. Behav. **211**, 112671 (2019)
13. Wansink, B., Cheney, M., Chan, N.: Exploring comfort food preferences across age and gender. Physiol. Behav. **79**(4–5), 739–747 (2003)
14. Tuomisto, T.M., Hetherington, M.T., Morris, M.-F., Tuomisto, M., Turjanmaa, V., Lappalainen, R.: Psychological and physiological characteristics of sweet food? Addiction? Int. J. Eat. Disord. **25**(2), 169–175 (1999)
15. Frayn, M., Sears, C.R., Ranson, K.M.V.: A sad mood increases attention to unhealthy food images in women with food addiction. Appetite **100**, 55–63 (2016)
16. Ouwens, M.V., Strien, T.V., Leeuwe, J.V.D., Staak, C.: The dual pathway model of overeating. Replication and extension with actual food consumption. Appetite **52**(1), 234–237 (2009)
17. Kuhn, M., Johnson, K.: Applied Predictive Modeling, p.488. Springer, New York (2016)
18. Gandhi, R.: Introduction to machine learning algorithms: linear regression. Medium, 28 May 2018. https://towardsdatascience.com/introduction-to-machine-learning-algorithms-linear-regression-14c4e325882a. Accessed 20 Dec 2021
19. Cortes, C., Vapnik, V.: Support-vector networks. Mach. Learn. **20**(3), 273–297 (1995)
20. Ding, L., Kolari, P., Ganjugunte, S., Finin, T., Joshi, A.: SVMs for the blogosphere: blog identification and splog detection. In: AAAI spring symposium on computational approaches to analysing weblogs (2006)
21. Ho, T.K.: Random decision forests. In: Proceedings of 3rd International Conference on Document Analysis and Recognition, vol. 1, pp. 278–282 (1995)
22. Breiman, L.: Bagging predictors. Mach. Learn. **24**(2), 123–140 (1996)
23. Gandhi, R.: Naive bayes classifier. Medium, 17 May 2018. https://towardsdatascience.com/naive-bayes-classifier-81d512f50a7c. Accessed 20 Dec 2021
24. Frost, J.: Regression coefficients. Statistics By Jim, 05 May 2017. https://statisticsbyjim.com/glossary/regression-coefficient/. Accessed 20 Dec 2021

25. Pascual, C.: Tutorial: understanding regression error metrics in Python. Dataquest, 26 September 2018. https://www.dataquest.io/blog/understanding-regression-error-metrics/. Accessed 20 Dec 2021
26. Ouwens, M.V., Strien, T.V., Leeuwe, J.V.D., Staak, C.: The dual pathway model of overeating. Replication and extension with actual food consumption. Appetite **52**(1), 234 (2009)

Detection of Autism Spectrum Disorder by a Fast Deep Neural Network

Francesco Di Luzio, Federica Colonnese, Antonello Rosato,
and Massimo Panella[✉]

Department of Information Engineering, Electronics and Telecommunications,
University of Rome "La Sapienza", Via Eudossiana 18, 00184 Rome, Italy
{francesco.diluzio,antonello.rosato,massimo.panella}@uniroma1.it

Abstract. Autism spectrum disorder is a psychiatric illness that refers to a wide range of conditions caused by a biologically determined developmental disorder with onset of symptoms within the first three years of life. Autism can be diagnosed at any stage of life with problems beginning in childhood and continuing into adolescence and adulthood. Given the immense attraction gained by deep learning as one of the most successful paradigms for a plethora of real-world medical applications, in this paper we explore the possibility of using fast deep learning models for the detection of autism in children. To this end, random deep neural networks are one of the most important alternatives, in particular because they strike a good balance in the trade-off between accuracy and efficiency. We propose a deep neural architecture that employs the randomization of some parameters in a complex structure for the detection of autism spectrum disorder. The proposed approach is validated by using a three-dimensional dataset consisting of body joint positions taken from videos of both suffering and sane children. To evaluate the classification performance of the proposed network, the latter is compared with a fully trainable, non-randomized version of the same model and with state-of-the-art binary classifiers applied to the same data. Numerical results show that the proposed method outperforms reference benchmarks in terms of accuracy and speed, demonstrating the inherent capabilities of the implemented system that makes use of such specific features.

Keywords: Deep Learning · Autism Spectrum Disorder · Randomization-based Neural Network · Behavior Analysis

1 Introduction

Artificial Intelligence is now recognized as a reliable tool for supporting clinical and biomedical decision making [15]. In particular, Deep Learning (DL) received an increasing hype in the last decade for biomedical and healthcare applications, driven by the growing computational power available and by the employment of massive datasets, which are relevant to improved medical devices and biomedical

The original version of this chapter was revised: In the originally published version of the proceedings volume this chapter was erroneously omitted. It has been added as chapter 38. The correction to this chapter is available at
https://doi.org/10.1007/978-3-031-24801-6_39

M. Mahmud et al. (Eds.): AII 2022, CCIS 1724, pp. 539–553, 2022.
https://doi.org/10.1007/978-3-031-24801-6_38

sensors [10]. It is expected that neural architectures will assist doctors in examining patients in the near future, revolutionizing medical research from both the theoretical and practical sides [28,33]. Actually, several exciting and promising applications of DL models have emerged in the biomedical and clinical fields during the last years, which achieved interesting results, even outperforming human-level performance, in some domains such as radiology [30], ophthalmology [13], pathology [4], dermatology [9], and so forth.

The autism spectrum disorder (ASD) is a psychiatric disease that refers to a broad range of conditions that can be caused by a biologically determined developmental disorder with an onset of symptoms within the first three years of life [27]. There is not a single type of autism, and each sub-type is characterized by a set of traits with a high irritability rate [32]. In particular, children with autism show very serious qualitative impairments of language up to a total absence of the same and are affected by several behavioral characteristics including abnormal responses to different sensations such as sights, sounds, touch and smell. The main ways of measuring ASD are based on different criteria, which are divided into social communication criteria and non social criteria. The social communication criteria are three: lack of socio-emotional reciprocity, deficits in non-verbal communication and impairment in developing and maintaining relationships. The non social criteria are four: stereotypical behaviors, restricted interest, cognitive inflexibility and sensory aberrations [21]. This mental and physical conditions give the subject some characteristics that are permanent. Current research on ASD is mainly focused on genetic factors and on the study of the brain through new neuroimaging techniques [3]. Given the prominence of such disorders and independently of the adopted criteria, a fast, reliable and cheap way of automatically diagnosing ASD in children would be greatly beneficial from the medical point of view.

In this paper, we present an application of DL to ASD detection, therefore extending the DL application in the biomedical context also to mental and physical disorders. Namely, we will focus on the so-called 'stimmings', which are self-stimulatory behaviors such as physical movements and sound repetitions, or patterns related to the gait analysis. Stimmings can be represented by simple movements or more complex motions, from shaking hands to jumping and marching in place [18]. These motions are considered as a self-regulatory mechanism that can help the subjects alleviate the exaggerated feelings of these uncontrolled emotions such as anxiety, fear, anger and also excitement [23]. Stimmings are almost always present in children with ASD and one possibility to observe and catch them is in an environment, where children daily activities can be visually captured for further analysis, possibly leading to early intervention and diagnosis. In this regard, gait analysis provides detailed quantitative measurements about locomotion, by measuring body posture and muscle activity together with their deviations. Gait analysis of ASD children is becoming a source of interest as highlighted by recent research studies, since motor development does not have a relationship with social and linguistic skills, it can be with high probability a marker for ASD [2]. The main motivation of our research work, whose results are illustrated in the paper, is the possibility to detect ASD from visual data using DL to analyze postural and muscle activities.

When dealing with visual data, DL techniques have established themselves as a robust and reliable tool for obtaining the inherent visual information carried by images and videos [14]. To this end, Convolutional Neural Networks (CNNs) have established themselves to be an incredibly powerful tool for the feature extraction process for visual data [8]. The increasing hype on multi-layered deep neural networks (DNNs), underlined the need for a mechanism of weights randomization for an essential speeding up of the optimization algorithms. In particular, randomization of one or more layer in the network can significantly reduce the complexity of the learning procedures typical of deep architectures. In this paper, we propose a randomized CNN that aims at identifying traits of ASD based on gait analysis and stimming detection in videos of walking children.

With a more general analysis, several DL approaches have been presented in order to investigate the ASD detection problem. In particular, a large brain imaging dataset is employed in [16] to develop a DL algorithm for identifying ASD, achieving a 70% accuracy in the disorder identification. In [19], 3D-CNNs and recurrent neural networks are implemented for investigating the structural and strategic bases of ASD using for the experiments Magnetic Resonance Imaging (MRI) datasets. In [29], a CNN-based architecture is used for developing an automatic stereotypical motor movements detection system from multi-sensors accelerometer signals. Another interesting work is presented in [26], where a deep CNN model is built to detect ASD from electroencephalogram (EEG) data, with promising results.

The approach presented herein differs from the ones in the previously cited papers from a two-fold perspective of novelty: on the one hand, the input pattern to the CNN embeds several numerical features extracted from all of the frames of a video sequence, so as to catch simultaneously the spatial and temporal correlation within pathology-related data; on the other hand, the randomization of the convolutional layer allows the trade-off between accuracy and training time, thus enabling a large-scale application of the proposed approach in the social context with optimized costs for ASD diagnosis and therapy follow-ups. The proposed approach will be explained in detail, with an accurate description of the adopted dataset and of the training procedure exploiting the randomized nature of the CNN layer.

The rest of the paper is organized as follows. In Sect. 2, the preprocessing steps are described together with the feature extraction process. In Sect. 3, the implemented deep neural model is illustrated, while in Sect. 4 there is reported the evaluation of the model performance by using a well-known dataset. Finally, in Sect. 5 the conclusive remarks are drawn.

2   Data Preprocessing and Feature Extraction

We consider in this paper a specific case study based on several videos of walking children aged from 4 to 12 years old, pertaining to the dataset proposed in [1]; the videos are recorded using two different devices:

- Microsoft Kinect V2® that is composed of two cameras: one with a Full HD resolution (1920 × 1080 pixels) for capturing the motion in the RGB visible spectrum without the employment of any wearable sensor, and a depth camera with resolution 512 × 424 with time-of-flight depth sensors, which give a depth map of the field of view [22]. The depth map, along with the RGB information is also used to track 25 skeletal joints. The maximum capture frame rate for both streams is 30 fps.
- Samsung Note 9® Rear Camera with a digital 0.45X professional wide-angle lens (58 MM) employed for recording Full HD videos at 60 fps, using a wide-angle lens for a wider view. Videos recorded by this device are not used in the following of this work.

The dataset employed in this study consists therefore of the videos recorded by Microsoft Kinect V2 only, specifically 708 samples relevant to 372 children with ASD and 336 children belonging to the control group, each walking in the camera direction at a normal speed. The videos, each of different length, are saved in the .avi format. The Kinect has a fixed position for all the recordings.

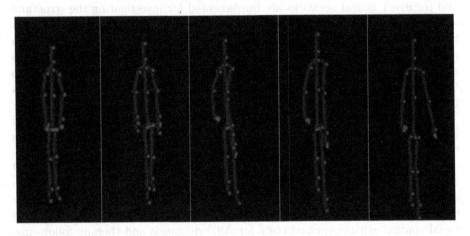

Fig. 1. Graphical representation of the joint landmarks (highlighted) for five video frames of a child walking.

Instead of using, as usual, each video frame as the basic input to the convolutional layer of the CNN, in this paper we use the numerical features associated with the spatial coordinates of L postural landmarks extracted from every frame of the video. Each joint landmark in the video frame is represented by a generic 3-uple $\{x, y, z\}$, where each coordinate is measured in meters:

- $x \in [-6, 6]$ is the lateral distance from the camera, being -6, the maximum distance from the right side of the camera and $+6$ the maximum distance from the left side of it;
- $y \in [-5, 5]$ is the vertical distance from the camera, where -5 is the maximum distance from the bottom and $+5$ is the maximum distance from the top;

– $z \in [0, 8]$ is the depth measuring the distance from the camera along an axis perpendicular to the camera plane, where 0 represents the camera's surface, whilst 8 represents the maximum distance (in depth) from the camera.

In this study, we will employ the $L = 25$ joint landmarks detected by the Microsoft Kinect V2, as illustrated in [1] and listed in Table 1.

Table 1. Joint Landmarks of the Considered Dataset

Skeletal joint(s)	Landmark code(s)
head	1
neck	2
spine shoulder	3
shoulders	4, 5
elbows	6, 7
wrists	8, 9
thumbs	10, 11
hands	12, 13
hands tips	14, 15
spine mid	16
spine base	17
hips	18, 19
knees	20, 21
ankles	22, 23
feet	24, 25

The joint landmarks are obtained using the algorithm presented in [34] consisting in training a randomized decision forest algorithm with a subset of depth scans of a variety of movements including dancing, driving, running, kicking, etc. For a complete description of the methodology refer to the aforementioned work [34]. Overall, we will have 3×25 or $3L$ numerical values (i.e., spatial coordinates) per video frame. An example of five video frames of a typical child walking in video, with joint landmarks highlighted, is shown in Fig. 1.

In general, when the data can be represented by sequences, as for videos streams, recurrent neural networks are considered as the state-of-the-art solution because they are able to catch the temporal correlation between different samples. On the other hand, these architectures and their learning procedures are notably resource-consuming and this aspect is even more obvious when dealing with deep structures. In order to avoid this problem, we added a further novelty on the proposed approach in which the network is fed by a unique input pattern that represents the video at a whole. By this approach, it is the convolutional layer that extracts both spatial and temporal features from the video without using a subsequent recurrent layer. This way, we reinforce the goal of having a light training task, by using a feed-forward network stack that is even randomized in its (most complex) convolutional layer.

Let F be the number of frames in each video; V the total number of videos in the dataset (i.e., $V = 708$ in the present case); $\left\{ x_{i,j}^{(h)}, y_{i,j}^{(h)}, z_{i,j}^{(h)} \right\}$ the 3-uple representing the jth landmark, $j = 1 \ldots L$, of the ith frame, $i = 1 \ldots F$, for the hth recorded video, $h = 1 \ldots V$. Each video will be associated to a single matrix $\mathbf{X}[h] \in \mathbb{R}^{F \times 3L}$, which will be the input pattern to the adopted CNN:

$$
\mathbf{X}[h] = \begin{bmatrix} x_{1,1}^{(h)} & y_{1,1}^{(h)} & z_{1,1}^{(h)} & \cdots & x_{1,L}^{(h)} & y_{1,L}^{(h)} & z_{1,L}^{(h)} \\ x_{2,1}^{(h)} & y_{2,1}^{(h)} & z_{2,1}^{(h)} & \cdots & x_{2,L}^{(h)} & y_{2,L}^{(h)} & z_{2,L}^{(h)} \\ & & & \cdots & & & \\ x_{F,1}^{(h)} & y_{F,1}^{(h)} & z_{F,1}^{(h)} & \cdots & x_{F,L}^{(h)} & y_{F,L}^{(h)} & z_{F,L}^{(h)} \end{bmatrix} \tag{1}
$$

An idea of the whole information embedded in input patterns like $\mathbf{X}[h]$ can be given by the graphic representation of the landmarks trajectories along the different frames of a single video, as illustrated in Fig. 2.

The videos composing the dataset are, as already stated, of different lengths. To change this aspect and obtain the same number of frames for all the samples, we employed the padding and cutting procedure described in the following:

1. F is selected as the average value over the lengths F_h, $h = 1 \ldots V$, of each video in the dataset;
2. if $F_h > F$, then the hth video is cut removing the latest $F_h - F$ frames;
3. if $F_h < F$, then the hth video is padded by inserting in the latest $F - F_h$ frames the 0 value for all the landmarks coordinates;
4. if $F_h = F$, then no further operations are needed.

We outline that, by adjusting the padding, the stride, and the number of convolutional kernels, we can control the output size of the randomized 2-D convolutional layer at the beginning of the CNN network stack. This is also a way to control, by a proper model selection, the embedding of the spatial coordinates associated with the postural landmarks in order to recognize the spatial correlation among the different frames of each video. This is a brand new approach that puts stress on the portion of the body motion that brings more quantity of information in terms of presence of ASD.

3   Deep Neural Architecture

In this work, the CNN backbone is used for classifying the data obtained as illustrated in Sect. 2, viz. for a binary classification problem to distinguish patients

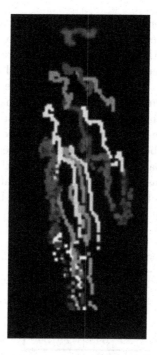

Fig. 2. Trajectories of joint landmarks for the entire duration of the video. Each line of a different color represents a single landmark three-dimensional trajectory over the different frames.

with ASD from typical children. The potentialities of convolutional layers in image and video related classification problems are widely assessed in the literature [24]. In the proposed approach, the convolutional layer is randomized: the connections with the other hidden layers are fixed after a random initialization and never trained. This implies that the learning algorithm has to operate on a smaller set of weights, resulting in a considerable reduction in computational power and training time needed.

Employing randomization may turn out to be an interesting crossroad for the real-world ASD detection problem. In fact, speeding up the learning procedure can result in the possibility of retraining the model, being able to use always new data with children with different intensity of ASD and from different age groups. In other words, reducing the computational cost of the optimization procedure gives the opportunity to train the network with basic hardware equipment, aiming therefore at obtaining a final system that may be used as an home-based healthcare appliance, with reduced economical investments but with the possibility to customize the neural model by re-training it using local and personal video sequences.

The implementation and study of deep neural architectures with random weights is not new in itself, but it is attracting more and more interest at present time mainly on the balancing between the computational cost of the optimization procedure and the final performance of the model [11]. In particular, numerous studies are showing how, even if one or more randomized layers are employed in DNN implementation, the reduction of the accuracy can be acceptable and it is balanced by the lightening of the computational power needed for learning and optimization [6,31,36]. By the way, in [35] there is shown that a randomly initialized CNN contains enough architectural information to be employed as an effective prior in several image processing problems and applications. These considerations determined the choice of such an architecture based on randomized CNN. This way, we could benefit from the ability to extract features from structured data of convolutional networks by speeding the optimization procedure and hence, resulting in a fast and precise network that does not use heavy structures and complex models for the final classification but is fed by an embedded representation of the input data to convolve.

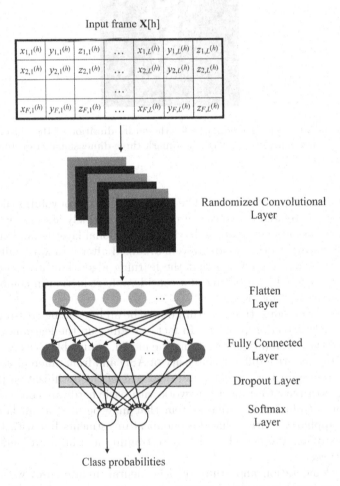

Fig. 3. Architecture of the randomized CNN used for binary classification.

As previously explained, the input to the 2-D convolutional layer is a one-channel $F \times 3L \times 1$ tensor $\mathbf{X}[h]$, which is associated with the subject walking in the hth video and it is matched with one and only one binary label corresponding to either *ASD affected* or *sane*. The proposed network architecture, which will be referred to in the following as 'Randomized CNN (R-CNN)', is illustrated in Fig. 3 as per the following layer-by-layer description:

- Randomized 2-D convolutional layer: it applies Q sliding 2-D convolutional kernels with $K \times K$ dimension. The stride of the convolutional filters is set to $1, 1$ for all the experiments and the padding of the layer is set to "same";
- Flatten layer: it is employed for serializing the data filtered by the convolutional kernel, to be used as input of the subsequent fully-connected layer;
- Fully connected layer: it is a standard feed-forward layer with H hidden neurons, each using as nonlinear activation function the sigmoid function;
- Dropout layer: it is employed for empowering the generalization capabilities of the proposed model by removing some neurons of the previous layer along with all its connections; P is the dropout factor, the probability of each unit in the layer to be removed;
- Softmax layer: it is another standard feed-forward layer with two hidden neurons receiving the output coming from the H neurons of the fully connected layer, possibly dropped out, and produces two values (one for each neuron in the layer) in output which can be interpreted as probabilities of each class for the final classification.

4   Experimental Results

In order to assess the overall performance of the proposed ASD classification and detection approach, the R-CNN is compared with a fully trained version of the same network, denoted as 'Trained CNN (T-CNN)', where also the filter weights of the convolutional layer are learned. Apart from hyperparameters that were optimized by cross-validation, as explained successively, both R-CNNs and T-CNNs were trained using the ADAM algorithm [20] for 300 epochs, with learning rate equal to 10^{-4}, mini-batch size equal to 8, and binary cross-entropy loss function.

As we are dealing with relatively fast feed-forward architectures, two other reference classifiers were also adopted: K-Nearest Neighbors (K-NN) [7] and Support Vector Machine (SVM) [5]. More precisely, we considered both 3-NN and 5-NN classifiers working with the same input patterns as obtained in Sect. 2, where the relative distance among them is measured by the Frobenius norm $\| \mathbf{X}[h] - \mathbf{X}[k] \|_F$ [12]. The latter is adopted as a metric to measure the difference between two matrices, right as an extension of the usual Euclidean distance, which is applied to common vector-shaped patterns in the dataset in order to evaluate the distance between two patterns and take the consequent decision according to the NN classification algorithm. Regarding SVM, we considered a version working with the inputs proposed herein as for R-CNN, T-CNN and K-NN classifiers, using a Radial Basis Function (RBF) kernel with the hinge loss function and the training algorithm presented in [17]. In addition, we report also the results obtained in [1], where a Multilayer Perceptron (MLP) neural network is used for on the same dataset; in that case, different inputs were used, consisting of 11 features obtained by Principal Component Analysis (PCA) on the statistical measures (mean, variance, standard deviation) of the landmarks coordinates. The MLP proposed in that paper has a single hidden layer with 6 neurons and 2 output nodes for distinguish children with ASD from typical. No further descriptions of model selection were provided by the Authors.

As previously said, the adopted dataset is composed of 708 samples and it is balanced between 372 children with ASD and 336 sane children belonging to the control group. The 80% of the available data was used for training the classifiers, while the remaining 20% was employed for testing the final performance. The tuning of model hyperparameters for R-CNNs and T-CNNs was carried out by the grid search procedure discussed successively, using 10% of the training samples for cross-validation. All of these sets are kept balanced against the two classes. Experiments were conducted launching 10 runs, each using a different random initialization of model parameters and a different random partition among training, validation and test sets. Independently of the adopted loss function for each model, the final performance is measured on both validation or test sets by the standard classification accuracy (%):

$$A = \frac{100}{S} \sum_{i=1}^{S} |t_i - y_i|, \tag{2}$$

where S is the number of video sequences to be tested or validated (143 or 57, respectively); $t_i \in \{0,1\}$ is the target binary label of the ith sample, being $t_i = 0$ the label of a sane child and $t_i = 1$ the one of a child with ASD; $y_i \in \{0,1\}$ is the binary label estimated by the classifier on the same sample, which in case of R-CNNs and T-CNNs corresponds to the class with highest softmax output or probability. The following accuracy results refer to the average obtained over the different 10 runs carried out in similar test conditions.

All the experiments were performed using Python and Keras® backend on a machine equipped with an AMD Ryzen™ 7 5800X 8-core CPU at 3.80 GHz, 64 GB of RAM, and an NVIDIA® GeForce™ RTX 3080 Ti GPU at 1.365 GHz and 12288 MB of GDDR6X RAM. The datasets and the original source code to replicate all of the experiments are stored in a public and persistent repository at https://github.com/NesyaLab/AII-2022/tree/main/AII2022-2-c-main.

In order to avoid overfitting and to obtain a good generalization capability of the proposed models, a grid search procedure was applied on the training set only for tuning the remaining hyperparameters of the convolutional networks, namely the number of convolutional filters Q, their size K, and the number of hidden neurons H in the fully connected layer. Given a specific set of the hyperparameters' values in the grid, the average classification accuracy over the 10 different runs was evaluated on the validation set for T-CNN only. The configuration of hyperparameters associated with the best accuracy obtained by cross-validation of T-CNN during the grid search was selected. By using such optimal hyperparameters, both R-CNN and T-CNN were trained using the whole training set (i.e., 80% of samples with no distinction between training and validation set) for other 10 different runs and the average accuracy on the test set was computed. The optimal configuration of hyperparameters obtained by this procedure is listed in Table 2 along with the details about the initial set of values within which the optimal one was searched.

Table 2. Network Hyperparameters CNNs and SVM Models after Cross-Validation

Model	Parameter	Searching set	Optimal
R-CNN T-CNN	Conv. filters (Q)	$Q = 2q, \ q \in \{1, 2, 3, \ldots, 38, 39, 40\}$	58
	Filter size (K)	$K \in \{1, 2, 3, \ldots, 8, 9, 10\}$	3
	Hidden neurons (H)	$H = 2^h, \ h \in \{1, 2, 3, \ldots, 8, 9, 10\}$	64
SVM	Regularization (C)	$C \in \{0.01, 0.02, 0.05, 0.1, 0.2, 0.5, 1, 2, 5, 10\}$	5
	Influence (γ)	$\gamma = 10^n, \ n \in \{-6, -5, -4, -3, -2, -1\}$	0.001

A similar grid search procedure was implemented for tuning the SVM hyperparameters, in particular the regularization parameter C determining the margin size and the influence coefficient γ of RBF kernel (the γ parameter can be seen as the inverse of the radius of influence of samples selected by the model as support vectors). The optimal values are reported in Table 2 as well.

The numerical results in terms of prediction accuracy for both training and test sets are reported in Table 3; regarding the MLP, we remark that no details about training performance were reported in [1]. The numerical results show that the proposed T-CNN method for feature extraction and data embedding, processed then by feed-forward classification models, assures up to 97.9% of classification accuracy, which reflects the excellence of the proposed method in terms of very high absolute performance. Our convolutional models outperform the other architectures considered herein, while the accuracy of the randomized R-CNN model is slightly smaller than the one obtained by the fully trained version with a relative drop of only 1.26% on the test set. These results prove the effectiveness of the convolutional layer that, even when randomized, represents an extremely powerful tool for automatic feature extraction.

In Table 3, we also reported the standard deviation for the accuracies of the CNN-based networks, while NN and SVM models use deterministic algorithms with no randomness in the obtained results. Once more, the standard deviation for the MLP network was not reported in [1]. It can be therefore noted that for the fully trained T-CNN the standard deviation over the different runs is slightly smaller in training set, as expected, but during inference the R-CNN has a smaller volatility that proves a higher robustness of the randomized approach.

An example of confusion matrix obtained in one run of the R-CNN test is reported in Fig. 4. This behavior is typical in every test of the convolutional networks and it proves that the number of false positive and false negative samples

Table 3. Classification Accuracy (%) of Adopted Models

Classifier	Training Set	Test set
R-CNN	99.22 ± 0.64	96.64 ± 0.64
T-CNN	99.40 ± 0.55	97.90 ± 0.94
3-NN	96.10	94.40
5-NN	95.39	90.90
SVM	95.93	95.11
MLP	N/A	95.00

is very limited, giving a further confirmation of the robustness of the proposed approach from a medical point of view.

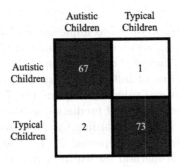

Fig. 4. Typical confusion matrix obtained by R-CNN on the test set. Each row of the matrix represents the instances in an actual class while each column represents the instances in a predicted class.

Regarding the average training times, which are reported in Table 4, we first note that 3-NN and 5-NN classifiers are non-parametric models requiring costly procedures for memory storage and inference time that do not have a real training time and hence, they do not cope with the application goals considered in the present research. So they have been used only as reference models for comparing the accuracy. What is meaningful is the average training time of R-CNN of 70.49 s, whilst the one necessary to train completely T-CNN is 79.96 s. As expected, the randomization of the convolutional layer reduces the training time by 11.84% and thus, it is effective to speed up the training procedure without a substantial loss in the accuracy. The training time needed for training the parameters of the SVM model is notably smaller, about 1.51 s with a drop in the accuracy performance of more than 2% with respect to the proposed convolutional networks. In this sense, even the SVM model might be a suitable solution whenever we aim at reducing mainly the time of the optimization procedure and the whole complexity of the model, paying in this case the price of a reduced detection accuracy. For sake of completeness, we also trained the MLP model proposed in [1] by using our own HW/SW environment. In this case, the R-CNN architecture outperforms the MLP both in terms of accuracy and training-speed, resulting in a more effective and efficient model.

In order to further appreciate the importance of even small improvements in the classification accuracy, it is fundamental to underline that in the United States of America, for instance, there are more than 60 million people aging between 3 and 17 years and the 2.5% suffers from ASD, resulting in a total of 1.5 million sick children [25]. In other words, each point in the accuracy percentage represent more than 15 thousand children for whom the ASD detection can be appropriately done in a fast and automatic way, such as to be reliable and easily deployable.

Table 4. Average Training Time (s) of Adopted Models

Architecture	Training Time
R-CNN	70.49
T-CNN	79.96
SVM	1.51
MLP	76.63

5 Conclusion

Given the push for exploring and discovering novel and useful applications of DL techniques in the medical context, it is of great interest to find new solutions that are tailored to real-world problems where the trade-off between accuracy and computational cost is strategic for the consequent diffusion of the obtained system to a broad social extent.

In this paper, we proposed a CNN solution employing randomization for gaining a speed advantage on classically trained architecture, focusing on the challenging and crucial problem of ASD detection on children given its intrinsic social importance. By the experimental analysis, the positive edge of the random-ized model is confirmed, confidently reporting advantages in both accuracy and training time when compared with the state-of-the-art shallow and deep neural models, with a classification improvement even with respect to SVM although it results much faster than everything else.

Considering the many possible deep neural models employing randomization-based layers, and given the recent expansion of this practical field, we believe that this work can pave the way for studying even more complex and deeper solutions for ASD detection and other medical applications in general in which the balance between accuracy and efficiency can be further investigated.

References

1. Al-Jubouri, A.A., Ali, I.H., Rajihy, Y.: Generating 3D dataset of gait and full body movement of children with autism spectrum disorders collected by kinect v2 camera. COMPUSOFT **9**, 3791–3797 (2020)
2. American Psychiatric Association, A., et al.: Diagnostic and Statistical Manual of Mental Disorders, vol. 3. American Psychiatric Association Washington, DC (1980)
3. Anagnostou, E., Taylor, M.J.: Review of neuroimaging in autism spectrum disorders: what have we learned and where we go from here. Mol. Autism **2**(1), 1–9 (2011)
4. Bejnordi, B.E., et al.: Diagnostic assessment of deep learning algorithms for detection of lymph node metastases in women with breast cancer. JAMA **318**(22), 2199–2210 (2017)
5. Cristianini, N., Shawe-Taylor, J., et al.: An Introduction to Support Vector Machines and Other Kernel-Based Learning Methods. Cambridge University Press, Cambridge (2000)
6. Di Luzio, F., Rosato, A., Succetti, F., Panella, M.: A blockwise embedding for multi-day-ahead prediction of energy time series by randomized deep neural networks. In: 2021 International Joint Conference on Neural Networks (IJCNN), pp. 1–7 (2021)
7. Dudani, S.A.: The distance-weighted k-nearest-neighbor rule. IEEE Trans. Syst. Man Cybern. **SMC-6**(4), 325–327 (1976)
8. Egmont-Petersen, M., de Ridder, D., Handels, H.: Image processing with neural networks-a review. Pattern Recogn. **35**(10), 2279–2301 (2002)
9. Esteva, A., et al.: Dermatologist-level classification of skin cancer with deep neural networks. Nature **542**(7639), 115–118 (2017)
10. Esteva, A., et al.: A guide to deep learning in healthcare. Nat. Med. **25**(1), 24–29 (2019)
11. Gallicchio, C., Scardapane, S.: Deep randomized neural networks. Recent Trends in Learning From Data, pp. 43–68 (2020)
12. Golub, G., Loan, C.V.: Matrix Computations, 3rd edn. Johns Hopkins, Baltimore (1996)
13. Gulshan, V., et al.: Development and validation of a deep learning algorithm for detection of diabetic retinopathy in retinal fundus photographs. JAMA **316**(22), 2402–2410 (2016)
14. Guo, Y., Liu, Y., Oerlemans, A., Lao, S., Wu, S., Lew, M.S.: Deep learning for visual understanding: a review. Neurocomputing **187**, 27–48 (2016)
15. Hamet, P., Tremblay, J.: Artificial intelligence in medicine. Metabolism **69**, S36–S40 (2017)
16. Heinsfeld, A.S., Franco, A.R., Craddock, R.C., Buchweitz, A., Meneguzzi, F.: Identification of autism spectrum disorder using deep learning and the abide dataset. NeuroImage: Clin. **17**, 16–23 (2018)
17. Hsu, C.W., Chang, C.C., Lin, C.J., et al.: A practical guide to support vector classification (2003)
18. Kapp, S.K., et al.: 'people should be allowed to do what they like': autistic adults' views and experiences of stimming. Autism **23**(7), 1782–1792 (2019)
19. Ke, F., Choi, S., Kang, Y.H., Cheon, K.A., Lee, S.W.: Exploring the structural and strategic bases of autism spectrum disorders with deep learning. IEEE Access **8**, 153341–153352 (2020)

20. Kingma, D.P., Ba, J.: Adam: a method for stochastic optimization. arXiv preprint arXiv:1412.6980 (2014)
21. Leyden, J., Fung, L., Frick, S.: Autism and toe-walking: are they related? Trends and treatment patterns between 2005 and 2016. J. Child. Orthop. **13**(4), 340–345 (2019)
22. Maisto, M., Panella, M., Liparulo, L., Proietti, A.: An accurate algorithm for the identification of fingertips using an RGB-D camera. IEEE J. Emerg. Sel. Top. Circ. Syst. **3**(2), 272–283 (2013)
23. Masiran, R.: Stimming behaviour in a 4-year-old girl with autism spectrum disorder. Case Rep. **2018**, bcr-2017 (2018)
24. Nebauer, C.: Evaluation of convolutional neural networks for visual recognition. IEEE Trans. Neural Netw. **9**(4), 685–696 (1998)
25. Ning, M., et al.: Identification and quantification of gaps in access to autism resources in the united states: an infodemiological study. J. Med. Internet Res. **21**(7), e13094 (2019)
26. Nur, A.A.: Autism spectrum disorder classification on electroencephalogram signal using deep learning algorithm. IAES Int. J. Artif. Intell. **9**(1), 91 (2020)
27. Park, H.R., et al.: A short review on the current understanding of autism spectrum disorders. Exp. Neurobiol. **25**(1), 1 (2016)
28. Qayyum, A., Qadir, J., Bilal, M., Al-Fuqaha, A.: Secure and robust machine learning for healthcare: a survey. IEEE Rev. Biomed. Eng. **14**, 156–180 (2020)
29. Rad, N.M., Furlanello, C.: Applying deep learning to stereotypical motor movement detection in autism spectrum disorders. In: 2016 IEEE 16th International Conference on Data Mining Workshops (ICDMW), pp. 1235–1242. IEEE (2016)
30. Rajpurkar, P., et al.: CheXNet: radiologist-level pneumonia detection on chest X-rays with deep learning. arXiv preprint arXiv:1711.05225 (2017)
31. Rosenfeld, A., Tsotsos, J.K.: Intriguing properties of randomly weighted networks: Generalizing while learning next to nothing. In: 2019 16th Conference on Computer and Robot Vision (CRV), pp. 9–16. IEEE (2019)
32. Sandin, S., Lichtenstein, P., Kuja-Halkola, R., Larsson, H., Hultman, C.M., Reichenberg, A.: The familial risk of autism. Jama **311**(17), 1770–1777 (2014)
33. Shailaja, K., Seetharamulu, B., Jabbar, M.: Machine learning in healthcare: a review. In: 2018 Second international conference on electronics, communication and aerospace technology (ICECA), pp. 910–914. IEEE (2018)
34. Shotton, J., et al.: Real-time human pose recognition in parts from single depth images. Commun. ACM **56**(1), 116–124 (2013)
35. Ulyanov, D., Vedaldi, A., Lempitsky, V.: Deep image prior. In: Proceedings of the IEEE Conference on Computer Vision and Pattern Recognition, pp. 9446–9454 (2018)
36. Zhang, X., He, K., Bao, Y.: Error-feedback stochastic configuration strategy on convolutional neural networks for time series forecasting. arXiv preprint arXiv:2002.00717 (2020)

Correction to: Applied Intelligence and Informatics

Mufti Mahmud ⓘ, Cosimo Ieracitano ⓘ, M. Shamim Kaiser ⓘ,
Nadia Mammone ⓘ, and Francesco Carlo Morabito ⓘ

Correction to:
M. Mahmud et al. (Eds.): in: *Applied Intelligence*
***and Informatics*, CCIS 1724,**
https://doi.org/10.1007/978-3-031-24801-6

In the originally published version of chapter 2 the author affiliation references were incorrect. The author affiliations have been rearranged in the correct way.

In the originally published version of this volume the chapter "Impact Of Emotional State On Food Preference By Students: A Machine Learning Approach" was erroneously omitted. It has been added as chapter 37.

In the originally published version of this volume the chapter "Detection of Autism Spectrum Disorder by a Fast Deep Neural Network" was erroneously omitted. It has been added as chapter 38.

The updated original version of these chapters can be found at
https://doi.org/10.1007/978-3-031-24801-6_2
https://doi.org/10.1007/978-3-031-24801-6_37
https://doi.org/10.1007/978-3-031-24801-6_38

Correction to: Applied Intelligence and Informatics

M. Ahmed, Sheikh Mohammed Shariful Islam, Al-Sakib Khan Pathan, and Paul Haskell-Dowland

Correction to:
M. Ahmed et al. (Eds.): Applied Intelligence and Informatics, CCIS 1724,
https://doi.org/10.1007/978-3-031-24801-5

Author Index

Printed in the United States
by Baker & Taylor Publisher Services

Printed in the United States
by Baker & Taylor Publisher Services